THE PUBLICATIONS OF
THE CHAMPLAIN
SOCIETY

ONTARIO SERIES

XV

ONTARIO SERIES EDITOR:
BRIAN STUART OSBORNE

THE

PUBLICATIONS OF THE CHAMPLAIN SOCIETY

THE ELDON HOUSE DIARIES: FIVE WOMEN'S VIEWS OF THE 19TH CENTURY

TORONTO

THE CHAMPLAIN SOCIETY

ELDON HOUSE – THE FLATS AND THE THAMES RIVER, Oil painting by James Hamilton (1810–1896)

THE
ELDON HOUSE
DIARIES:

FIVE WOMEN'S VIEWS OF THE 19TH CENTURY

Edited with an Introduction by
Robin S. Harris and Terry G. Harris

TORONTO
THE CHAMPLAIN SOCIETY
IN CO-OPERATION WITH
THE GOVERNMENT OF ONTARIO
1994

Reprinted in paperback 2015
ISBN 978-0-9693-4253-3 (cloth)
ISBN 978-1-4426-3141-0 (paper)

Typeset in Canada by
University of Toronto Press Incorporated

The Champlain Society gratefully acknowledges the support and financial assistance of Queen's University, Kingston, Ontario and the Ontario Government Ministry of Culture, Tourism and Recreation.

FOREWORD

ELDON House is a distinctive element in the historical townscape of London, Ontario. By the mid-nineteenth century, its original owners, John and Amelia Harris, were prominent members of society in that dynamic community. Their children grew up in the affluent and cultured setting of a family whose increasing prosperity advanced with that of London and western Ontario. If London had an elite, the Harris family was part of it, and Eldon House was an important focal point of the social regimen of the day.

But there were many such families and houses throughout Ontario. Like the Harrises, other Loyalist families experienced the rites of passage from dislocation and adjustment to prosperity and prominence. To be sure, this was not the lot of all Loyalists. For many, however, a combination of toil, rewards for past services, and the wit and ability to recognize the opportunities afforded by an expanding economy ensured material affluence and social prestige. The symbols of their success were the architectural gems that – like Eldon House – may be found in so many Ontario communities. There are good reasons, however, why Eldon House is distinctive.

First, many of these former homes of the elite have been much modified by subsequent development, and seldom do they survive in their original context. Thanks to the bequest of the Harris family, Eldon House is preserved largely as it was in its late nineteenth century form, and is surrounded by the open lands of the Harris Park that retains the essence of the park-like setting.

Secondly, the existence of a considerable corpus of family papers has meant that personalities, activities, and voices are added to the bricks and mortar to re-create the household regimen of the Harrises of London. Prominent among these papers is a collection of diaries that are excerpted in this volume. These diaries are valuable because of the details of the warp and woof of daily life in the nineteenth century. But, more importantly, they are women's diaries. As such, they speak to us of the verities of personal, domestic, and societal life in the neglected voice of women. Together, they provide a fascinating perspective of these women's lives in, around, and beyond Eldon House.

Founded in 1905, The Champlain Society's mission is the "editing and publication of works pertaining to Canada . . . in such a style as to make the volumes a pleasure to book-lovers." In 1957, the appearance of E.C. Guillet's *The Valley of the Trent* marked the commencement of a new initiative whereby the Society, in co-operation with the Government of Ontario, published volumes concerned with the province's distinctive heritage. Subsequent volumes have concerned themselves with individuals, institutions, communities, and regions that have been prominent in Ontario's history. The present volume is the fifteenth in the Ontario Series. It advances that declared mission and future plans call for volumes concerned with such themes as the French in the "Upper Country," the Welland Canal, the development of Ontario's hospitals, native treaties, and the Sudbury region.

The editor of the present volume, Robin S. Harris, formerly served the University of Toronto as a professor in the departments of English and Higher Education, Principal of Innis College, and University Historian. Apart from his several scholarly studies in the field of Higher Education, Robin Harris, as a descendant of John and Amelia Harris, has long nurtured a personal and scholarly interest in his family. Indeed, he has previously published accounts of John Harris' role in the Owen-Bayfield survey of the Great Lakes and St. Lawrence, as well as a biographical study of the matriarch of Eldon House, Amelia Harris. His co-editor, Terry Gonçalves Harris, brings to the volume a scholarly expertise from the field of literary studies, as well as a sensitive appreciation of the women's voices.

Together, Robin Harris and Terry Gonçalves have assembled a selection of materials that will be of interest to the scholar and general reader alike. Further, they have added a valuable item to the growing collection of historical studies of London, Ontario, women's history, and the history of the province.

Queen's Park
Toronto
November 1993

BOB RAE
Premier of Ontario

PREFACE

ELDON House, together with its eleven acre lot, was donated to the city of London on 1 January 1960 by the great grandchildren of John and Amelia Harris – George Harris, Lucy Harris Little, and Robin Sutton Harris. The house is presently a public museum, while the estate lands are known as Harris Park. Much of the original parkland has now gone or been much altered, but there has been little change to Eldon House itself. It remains essentially as it was in 1882 when Amelia Ryerse Harris died. Eldon House has always had a museum-like quality – certainly to a child growing up there in the 1920s and 1930s.

The L-shaped hallway running from the front door was, as it still is, adorned with the horns of wild game and with cabinets of African artifacts. These trophies had been acquired by my father at the turn of the century when he was employed by one of Cecil Rhodes' companies as a mining engineer in Angola, Portuguese West Africa, Kenya, and Uganda. There is also a collection of guns, shells, helmets, and other World War I memorabilia assembled by his brother Edward, and a six-foot tarpon caught by his sister, Amelia Archange (Aunt Milly) Harris, in the Caribbean in the 1920s. In the library, in addition to leather-bound volumes of historical, literary and theological works, there is a specially designed cabinet containing twelve volumes of botanical specimens representing one quarter of the flora of England in 1817.

The dining room is a small art gallery with oil portraits and miniatures of most of the members of my grandmother Ronald's ancestors. The walls of the drawing room feature watercolour portraits of John and Amelia Harris and nine of their children by the nineteenth century Canadian artist, J.W. Wandesforde. Both the drawing room and the adjacent Blue Room are full of china and objects d'art acquired by the George Becher Harris and his family on their world-tour in 1897 and 1898. This is where the Harris ladies received morning visitors. The upstairs hall is lined by framed engravings of scenes from Shakespeare's plays and of Piraneso views of the Roman Forum and leads to the bedrooms with their four-poster beds.

Then there is the attic – the "garret," as Amelia Harris called it – a seemingly inexhaustible treasure trove extending the full breadth and length of the house, with bookshelves, huge linen cupboards, and oddly shaped compartments for such items as toys, sporting equipment, and trunks. One of these trunks contained the Eldon House diaries, while hundreds of letters in their original envelopes were stored in others. There were also fifty-year runs of the *London Illustrated News* and *Punch*, several stamp albums, and two busts – one of Amelia Harris and one of her son, John. A dressmaker's mannequin stood next to them.

As a child, I did not read any of the diaries or letters. I was more fascinated by the envelopes, which came from all over the world. One winter, I carefully cut out the postmarks, which I then arranged country by country and pasted in alphabetical order on blank sheets in a three-ring binder. In recent years, as I have systematically worked on the Harris family's correspondence, I have had good cause to regret my misdirected enthusiasm as it has deprived us of the date and place of origin of many of the letters. Would that I had instead read some of the hundred minor novels that were on a bookshelf a few yards away.

During the 1920s, Fred Landon, the Librarian of the University of Western Ontario, learned of the existence of the Eldon House diaries and asked the family to permit him to publish excerpts from those of Charlotte Owen Harris and of Amelia Ryerse Harris in the *London Free Press*. He also suggested, in the interests of long-range preservation, that certain of the letters, notably the correspondence in the late 1830s and early 1840s between Amelia Ryerse Harris and Julius Airey, a nephew of Colonel Thomas Talbot, be deposited in the University Library on permanent loan. In the late 1940s the family also agreed to the request of James Talman, Landon's successor, to reprint the "Historical Memorandum on the founding of Port Ryerse," which Amelia Harris had originally prepared in 1859 at the request of her first cousin, Egerton Ryerson, for inclusion in his *The Loyalists of America*.

In the summer of 1953, while visiting my mother and Aunt Milly at Eldon House, I spent a morning rummaging in the stable. I opened several sealed bags and discovered that they contained letters. The first letter I glanced at was from Egerton Ryerson to his daughter Sophia, the wife of my uncle Edward Harris. I subsequently found that in these bags and in the attic of Eldon House there were 373 of Ryerson's letters to Sophia and about as many of Sophia's to her father, her mother, her brother Charley, and her husband Edward Harris. After placing these in order, I showed a sample to Professor Charles B. Sissons, a colleague of mine at the University of Toronto and author of the two-volume *Egerton Ryerson: His Life and Times*. The result was the publication of *My Dearest Sophie: Letters from Egerton Ryerson to His Daughter*, edited by Sissons in 1955.

My enthusiasm for asking Professor Sissons to undertake this task was based in part on his known competence and unrivalled knowledge of one of Canada's most important figures. But it also reflected my realization that other material contained in what are known as the Harris Papers was also worthy of publication and that the sooner I settled down to examine all the material the better it would be for all concerned. I began to do so late that summer on a part-time basis – weekends, spare evenings, summer vacations. I continued to do this until my retirement from the staff of the University of Toronto in June, 1985, by which time I had read most of the material, arranged for the typing and indexing of the diaries and the more interesting letters, and developed a plan for their publication.

However, when my work on this fascinating project was interrupted by ill-health in 1991, I invited my wife, Terry Gonçalves Harris to share with me the responsibility of publishing the diaries in a volume in The Champlain Society's "Ontario Series." I am fortunate that she agreed to do so and put aside her own book, a family history to be published in Brazil. Terry drew up a new outline and undertook further transcriptions, considerable rewriting of the "Introduction," and prepared vignettes of each of the diarists. I am grateful to her for deferring her own project to ensure that mine was brought to completion.

ROBIN S. HARRIS

We thank the staff of the Regional Collection of the University of Western Ontario, where the Harris Papers are now deposited, and our friend, Fred Armstrong, emeritus professor of History, for continual support and encouragement over many years.

We have been very fortunate in having a skilled and devoted editor in the person of Brian Osborne of Queen's University at Kingston. We wish to publicly express our gratitude to him.

TERRY G. HARRIS

CONTENTS

FOREWORD TO THE ONTARIO SERIES BY THE HONOURABLE BOB RAE, PREMIER OF ONTARIO . . . vii

Preface . . . ix

Introduction
- The Eldon House Diaries . . . xix
  - The Nature of the Diaries . . . xix
  - The Diarists . . . xxiii
- Beginnings . . . xxxi
  - Who was John Harris? . . . xxxi
  - Who was Amelia Ryerse? . . . xxxiii
  - The Kingston Years . . . xxxv
  - Life at Port Ryerse . . . xxxvi
  - A New Life in London . . . xl
- The Matriarch of Eldon House . . . xlvii
  - Early Trials and Challenges . . . xlvii
  - A Troubled Household . . . l
  - The Declining Powers of the Matriarch . . . lv
- The View from Eldon House . . . lxii
  - Life at Eldon House . . . lxii
  - Social Life and Entertainment . . . lxv
  - Courtship, Betrothal, and Marriage . . . lxxi
  - Religion and Politics . . . lxxx
  - Health and Healing . . . lxxxvi
  - The World Beyond Eldon . . . xci
- The End of a Matriarchy . . . xcvii

The Eldon House Diaries
- The Diary of Charlotte Owen Harris . . . 3
- The Diary of Amelia Ryerse Harris . . . 40
- The Diary of Sophia Ryerson Harris . . . 373
- The Diary of Lucy Ronalds Harris . . . 417
- The Diary of Amelia Archange Harris . . . 475

Appendices
1. The Harris Family Tree 481
2. John and Amelia Harris' Wedding Certificate, 28 June 1815 482
3. Extracts from Amelia Harris, "Historical Memorandum," 1859, 1879 483
4. Last Will & Testament of John Harris, 1837 . . . 486
5. Maurice Portman, Address to the Electors of the the East Riding of Middlesex, 11 June 1861 . . . 491
6. Last Will & Testament of Amelia Ryerse Harris, 1871, with 1878 and 1882 codicils 494
7. Amelia Harris, "A Memorandum for my Children," 22 January 1881 497

Bibliography 499

Index 509

ILLUSTRATIONS AND MAPS

Frontispiece
Eldon House – The Flats and the Thames River,
Oil painting by James Hamilton (1810–1896).

Maps
The Harris' Ontario, facing page lxii
The Harris' London, facing page lxiii

Illustrations
The following illustrations will be found between pages xciv and xcv
Amelia Harris and John Harris
Sarah and Robert Dalzell
Amelia and Gilbert Griffin
Mary and Shuldham Peard
Eliza and General Crutchley
Charlotte and Edward Knight
John and Elizabeth Harris
Edward and Sophia Harris
Helen and Maurice Portman
George and Lucy Harris
Teresa and William Scott
Amelia, Edward and Chasse Harris
Three generations of Ronalds
The Hydrographer's House in Kingston
Eldon House at mid-19th century
A gathering at Niagara
A family visit to the Falls

The following illustrations will be found between pages 280 and 281
The front of Eldon House
The golfers
A leisurely day at Eldon
Raleigh House
The grounds of Eldon House
Family and friends at Eldon
"Col. Talbot's Den" (1850)

Lady Alexander's "Steeplechase" (1843)
"Go it Chasse" (c. 1846)
"Moving Day" (c. 1848)
The library at Eldon House
The Ryerse clock at Eldon
Tea party at Eldon House
The new generation at Eldon

Portraits of the diarists
Charlotte Owen Harris, facing page 4
Amelia Ryerse Harris, facing page 42
Sophia Ryerson Harris, facing page 374
Lucy Ronalds Harris, facing page 418
Amelia Archange Harris, facing page 476

THE ELDON HOUSE DIARIES:

FIVE WOMEN'S VIEWS
OF THE 19TH CENTURY

INTRODUCTION

THE ELDON HOUSE DIARIES

The Nature of Diaries

THE ELDON HOUSE diaries document the life of a large upper middle-class Canadian family living in London, Ontario, during the nineteenth century. Amelia Ryerse Harris, John Harris, and their then eight children moved into Eldon House on 10 September 1834 and members of the family occupied it thereafter for the next 125 years. This house and the lives of its occupants and their families dominate the pages of the Eldon House diaries selected for the years between 1848 and 1882.

The genre of journal and diary writing in the English speaking world changed considerably between the sixteenth and nineteenth centuries. Starting as objective records of public events, personal interactions, and family memorabilia, personal journals came to be transformed into more reflexive and introspective evaluations of self, others, and society.[1] Several formative influences may be noted: the impact of the new literary mode of the novel; the assertion of a secular self associated with Romanticism; industrialization's segmenting of life into public and private realms; and latterly, the influence of psychoanalysis.[2] Whatever the reason, diaries came to accommodate commentary not only on the public domain, but also on the semi-public world of family life, and the inner intimate world of the individual's emotions, consciousness, and psyche.

By the nineteenth century, the array of diary forms constituted a "healthily eclectic genre."[3] It included log-books, journals of travels, lists of activities, as well as writers' reactions to particular events, peoples, and places. One scholar of the genre has argued provocatively that "the best diaries are written by bores,"

[1]Harriet Blodgett, *Centuries of Female Days: Englishwomen's Private Diaries*, New Brunswick, N.J.: Rutgers University Press, 1988, p. 23, cited in Helen M. Buss, *Mapping Our Selves: Canadian Women's Autobiography*, Montreal and Kingston: McGill-Queen's University Press, 1993, p. 36. See also Kate O'Brien, *English Diaries and Journals*, London: Collins, 1944; William Matthews, *Canadian Diaries and Autobiographies*, Berkeley: University of California Press, 1950.

[2]Margo Culley (ed.), *A Day at a Time: The Diary Literature of American Women from 1764 to the Present*, 1985, pp. 3–28, cited in Buss, 1993, p. 18.

[3]Buss, 1993, p. 37.

that is, "persons who mention everything."[4] Another has claimed that it is the comprehensiveness and inclusivity of diaries that renders them important sources arguing that they are,

> . . . a unique kind of writing; all other forms of writing envisage readers, and so are adapted to readers, by interpretation, order, simplification, rationalization, omission, addition, and the endless devices of exposition. Although many diaries, too, are written with readers in mind, they are in general the most immediate, truthful, and revealing documents available to the historian.[5]

Often, it is the repetitive multitude of details about daily thoughts, emotions and actions which would normally be pruned out in the careful topiary of biographical writing. Pepys gives details of his sex life and his bowel movements, other diarists comment critically on the social and political realms. Some diarists regularly report on the weather, while others concern themselves with more existential problems of life.

Diaries, therefore, have great utility for discovering personal insights into the lived-worlds of the past. Taken together, the Eldon House diaries comprise the full range of modes of diary-journal writing. Lists of visitors, records of letters written and received, and notes on the weather are accompanied by critical commentary on contemporary society and the innermost hopes and fears of the diarist. But if this is the essential rationale for studying the Eldon House diaries, the fact that they are women's diaries is particularly important.[6] One of the central premises of writing women's history is that women's experience can only be comprehended properly when recorded in women's language and

[4]O'Brien, 1944, p. 7.

[5]William Matthews, *American Diaries*, Boston: J.S. Canner, 1959, pp. ix–x.

[6]That the need for, and importance of, women's history has been accepted by the Canadian academy is due to the efforts of several scholars: Susan Mann Trofimenkoff and Alison Prentice (eds.), *Essays in Canadian Women's History: The Neglected Majority*, Toronto: McClelland and Stewart, 1977; Alison Prentice and Susan Mann Trofimenkoff (eds.), *Essays in Canadian Women's History: The Neglected Majority* (Vol. 2), Toronto: McClelland and Stewart, 1985; Veronica Strong Boag and Anita Clair Fellman, *Rethinking Canada: The Promise of Women's History*, Toronto: Copp Clark Pitman, 1986; Linda Kealey, "Special Issue on Women's History," *Can. Hist. Rev.* LXXII, 1991; Franca Iacovetta and Mariana Valverde, *Gender Conflicts: New Essays in Women's History*, Toronto: University of Toronto Press, 1992.

voices.[7] Women's diaries contribute to the collective consciousness and "social memory" of their distinctive experience of life by retelling their life-histories.

Taken as a group, women's diaries do exhibit certain commonalities.[8] Generally, they make less reference to "public" history than do men: they are usually less involved in it; and if they do comment on it, they do so from the perspective of the family, partner, or outside observer. In particular, the remembrance of war differs from the often nostalgic and romanticized view of men. What women's diaries do stress, however, is the commemoration of home-life, especially the themes of emotion, birth, child-rearing, and the day-to-day organization of the domestic scene. After all, this is the one realm in which women had some autonomy and in which they were the principal actors in the "key moments" of romantic love, birth, nurturing, and death. Conversely, this is often an area of silences and even mystery in male chronicles of their worlds.

While it may be argued that the Eldon House diaries reinforce an existing bias in the literature towards "articulate, white, middle-class women,"[9] the particulars of their life-paths contribute to a gendered experience of contemporary society. What emerges is a distinctive women's historical consciousness. They present women's perspectives of the stages in women's life-cycles in women's voices: birth; adolescence and education; courtship, marriage, and domesticity; pregnancy; aging and death.

Particularly prominent in the Eldon House diaries are accounts of domains that need to be better understood: the responsibility of managing complex households; the carnivalesque rituals of courtship, betrothal, and marriage; the all-pervasive fear of pregnancy and the loss of young ones; and the details of mother-daughter and sister-sister bonding so crucial to "gender difference and female specificity."[10] It is in these more private

[7]Alison Prentice, Paula Bourne, Gail Cuthbert Brandt, Beth Light, Wendy Mitchinson, Naomi Black, *Canadian Women: A History*, Toronto: Harcourt Brace Jovanovich, 1988, p. 12.

[8]James Fentress and Chris Wickham, *Social Memory*, Oxford: Blackwell, 1992, pp. 140–3.

[9]Iacovetta and Valverde, 1992, p. xiv.

[10]Marianne Hirsch, *The Mother/Daughter Plot: Narrative, Psychoanalysis, Feminism*, Bloomington and Indianapolis: Indiana University Press, 1989, p. 15, quoted in Buss, 1993, p. 34. See also Simone de Beauvoir, *The Second Sex*, New York: Alfred A. Knopf, 1952, pp. 577–81.

realms that women's voices are privileged and allow empowered insights into their lived experiences.

This being said, women's diaries should not be considered solely as ethnographic records of the lives of a category of others. They are more powerful than mere documents of events, places, and people. Thus, starting with the premise that diaries are a mode of autobiographical expression, Buss has recently challenged the metaphor of text as mirror of reality in her exploration of women's experience. They are not mere reflections of lived realities.[11] They are nuanced, and even coded, commentaries on the cultural context in which women were required to function.

For Potter-MacKinnon, the predominant constraint was that of patriarchy and paternalism: women functioned in a world in which men dominated personal, familial, economic, social, and political relationships.[12] She defers to Parr's assertion that language is "culturally constructed" and itself serves as evidence of past realities rather than merely communicating impressions of them.[13] The essential problem in determining the distinctive female view of the past is that women's very language is shadowed by, even patterned by, male hegemony. Most women had little autonomy outside their domestic worlds of family and friends and their life-narratives consequently focussed on a society syncopated by male dominated activities. Often, therefore, women rendered male perspectives and their own discourses were muted. It has even been argued that traditionally, most written genres are constructed by men, even when the texts are composed by women, and that they require "close reading to pick out any authentic female discourses."[14]

But there are strategies that need to be identified. Several recent studies have suggested that the customary usages, accepted rhetoric, and nuanced expressions of women's words often belie or camouflage actual beliefs and practices.[15] Male lan-

[11]Buss, 1993, p. 8.

[12]Janice Potter-MacKinnon, *While the Women Only Wept: Loyalist Refugee Women in Eastern Ontario*, Montreal and Kingston: McGill-Queen's University Press, 1993, p. 7.

[13]Joy Parr, "Nature and Hierarchy: Reflections on Writing the History of Women and Children," *Atlantis* II, 1985, p. 43, quoted in Potter-MacKinnon, 1993, p. 8.

[14]*op. cit.*, Fentress and Wickham, 1992, p. 138.

[15]See Potter-MacKinnon, 1993, pp. 104–5, and her references to the following: Cheris Kramarae, *Women and Men Speaking*, Rowley, Mass.: Newbury House Publishers, 1981; Joyce Penfield (ed.), *Women and Language in Transition*, Albany, N.Y.: State University of New York Press, 1987; David Graddol and Joan Swann, *Gender*

guage is rendered in the voice of action, decision, and authority; the female voice reflects submission, dependency, nurturing, and suffering. Whereas men's records are of individual involvement, women's chronicles often privilege relationships with dependent others. The degree to which these are sustained as stylized forms rather than reflections of reality needs to be unpacked. Further, Buss has assembled arguments that suggest that another one of women's strategies for self-expression in a patriarchal world is to mythologize their roles and lives.[16] Glamorous myths of womanliness, motherhood, virtue, and romance should be considered as strategies of empowerment as much as reflections of cultural norms. Finally, the communications may also contain disguises, rhetoric, and even falsehoods to camouflage reality and appear to conform to the established order.[17]

Rich in social content and personal insights, therefore, diaries such as those of the ladies of Eldon House should be read critically for insights into women's personal, public, and psychological realities. Indeed, Culley concludes that they should be appreciated as much for their "surprises, mysteries and silences" as for the accessible narrative and facts.[18]

The Diarists

The crucial element in any diary is the personality, imagination, and range of interests of the writer. This is demonstrated clearly in the Eldon House diaries. Five women, between the ages of thirteen and eighty-four, lived in the same atmosphere and recorded their observations of this fascinating world, each in her own unique and interesting way.[19]

Voices, Oxford: Basil Blackwell, 1989; Alette Olin Hill, *Mother Tongue, Father Time*, Bloomington and Indianapolis: Indiana University Press, 1986; Bryan Palmer, *Descent into Discourse: The Reification of Language and the Writing of Social History*, Philadelphia: Temple University Press, 1990.

[16]Buss, 1993, p. 19 quotes Patricia Meyer Spacks, "Reflecting Women," *Yale Review* 8, 1973, pp. 26–42.

[17]Buss, 1993, refers to Patricia Meyer Spacks, "Female Rhetorics," in Shari Benstock (ed.), *The Private Self: Theory and Practice of Women's Autobiography*, Chapel Hill and London: University of North Carolina Press, 1988, pp. 177–91, and Timothy Drew Adams, *Telling Lies in Modern American Autobiography*, Chapel Hill and London: University of North Carolina Press, 1990, p. ix.

[18]Culley, 1985, p. 21, quoted in Buss, 1993, p. 19.

[19]Amelia Ryerse Harris willed her "journals" to her son George; Sophia Ryerson Harris speaks of "writing her journal"; Lucy Ronalds Harris wrote a "Daily Journal";

The lengthiest diary was written by Amelia Ryerse Harris, who began keeping a daily journal on 10 September 1857 as a series of notes for the weekly letters she was writing to her oldest son, John Fitzjohn, and continued it until within three weeks of her death in 1882. The earliest of the diaries (1848–51) was written by Charlotte (Chasse), the fifth daughter of John and Amelia Harris. Two of the other diarists were Amelia Harris' daughters-in-law: Sophia Ryerson and Lucy Ronalds provide accounts of the family story and of their lives at Eldon House as they adjusted to the values, practices, and traditions of a large, long-established, and widely dispersed family. The shortest selection is from the diary of Amelia Archange Harris (Milly), a thirteen-year-old schoolgirl.

Of these five diarists, Amelia Harris emerges as the most fully developed character we encounter in any of the Eldon diaries. Her commentary reveals a remarkably wide range of interests: local, provincial and national politics, international affairs, religion, history, and literature, as well as the mundane, the curious, the bizarre, and even the macabre. Underlying all these was a fascination with the variety of human experience and the nature of the human condition. The two topics that preoccupied her most were the welfare of her extended family and the state of her soul. But she was interested in everything. Like Pepys, she was an acute observer of life.

This is well reflected in the topics selected for comment in the entries for the first year, 1857, and they are typical of the next twenty-five years of commentary. None proves to be an event of universal and timeless significance, but most would have been of interest at the time to her fellow citizens: the sinking of a transatlantic steamer with the loss of several hundred lives; the installation of the first Bishop of Huron; the election of a Member of Parliament for London; the murder in a local brothel of the son of the town's leading lawyer; and the attempt of some "body snatchers" to steal the corpse of a recent suicide victim. Conversely, references to the return of her oldest son, John, from a visit to England, and the need for the Eldon House cook to return to her home because she had cut her fingers, would have

---

Amelia Archange firmly printed "Diary for 1882" before her first entry; Charlotte Harris did not specify what her record was. Despite these various usages, the personal records of their lives and times kept by the Harris ladies have always been referred to as diaries.

been of interest only to the Harris family. Always clear, often witty, Amelia's diary frequently juxtaposes the significant and the trivial, the routine and the unusual.

While Amelia Harris' diary is not a play or a novel, it often reads like one. This is because the diarist is continuously engrossed in the welfare of the individual members of her family, one or more of whom seem at any given time to be involved in a personal crisis. This was the case when the diary began: the oldest son in ill health; one son-in-law in financial trouble; another unemployed in England. But, as it happened, none of these difficulties posed major challenges for the family as a whole. Other family problems became more immediate and serious, however, and the diary, while continuing to be a collection of daily observations, presents a series of domestic dramas centred on one or another of the members of the family. The first of these dramas, described in the sequence of entries between 27 November 1858 and 18 August 1859, could be classified as a comedy of manners and entitled "The Courtship of Teresa Harris."

Two things are worthy of remark about Amelia's detailed description of this courtship, and equally of the other domestic dramas which she subsequently chronicled. First, because the events are described in detail, the reader has the sense of participating personally in an evolving drama rather than simply reading about it and experiencing it vicariously. The second characteristic is the candidness with which the events are described. Amelia's diary was kept on a table in the drawing room at Eldon House and any member of the family was at liberty to consult it. What, one wonders, were her children's reactions when reading of their mother's almost daily assessment of their relations with their fianceés, husbands, and wives?

But Amelia Harris' diary was more than a personal record of events and private thoughts. Rather than an internal document, it played a didactic role and was intended to instruct, sensitize, and even direct family members according to Amelia's wishes. Even when her journal "came under discussion" and was criticized by Edward, Amelia could not resist the opportunity to turn her desire for humility into an instruction for the others.[20] Similarly, family members were sermonized on the need for "strong

[20]Amelia's diary, 4 June 1859.

family affection and a loving bearing" in another entry intended to be for the general good rather than for private contemplation.[21] If patriarchy is defined in terms of male dominance and control of public and private affairs, it appears that after the death of John Harris, it stopped at the gates of Eldon House. There, for many years, Amelia Harris was the dominant figure and her diary played an important part in her strategy of matriarchal control.

Whatever the motives, one of Amelia Harris' great literary strengths is her ability to establish the character of the persons with whom she was in almost daily contact. Her diary produces an invaluable gallery of portraits of immediate family, closest friends and associates as they appear in a succession of domestic events and crises. The secret of Amelia's skill in characterization is that she is able to show her "characters" in interaction with others: conflict is the essence of drama. In this way, every member of the family is rendered in the pages of the diary as a distinct personality.

The characterization is remarkably vivid. The portraits of Maurice Portman and Gilbert Griffin, for example, are far from flattering, though in both cases their redeeming characteristics are noted. Portman's womanizing is plainly stated, but so is his enthusiasm and imagination. Griffin's short-comings in financial matters are abundantly documented, but so are his good works and thoughtfulness. While all the portraits of the members of the family are tinged with affection, they are often judgmental. Amelia appreciated idiosyncracy and she found a good deal of it in her children and their spouses. She found a good deal of it, too, in her brothers, George and Edward Ryerse, in her cousin Egerton Ryerson, and in her life-long friends, Henry Becher, and John Wilson. The portraits of the latter three can be assembled in some detail as they were among the *dramatis personae* in many of the dramas.

Dozens of other persons emerge from Amelia's diary as living human beings but they are sketched rather than portrayed: casual visitors to Eldon House like Lord Althorpe; Jane Steers, the children's former governess; the succession of Curates at St. Paul's Church; a half dozen Eldon servants; long-time friends of John and Amelia Harris such as the Cronyns, the Askins, the

[21]Amelia's diary, 16 August 1859.

Goodhues, and the Lawrasons. But, the most fully drawn portrait is of the diarist herself. Her personality dominates the diary and in large measure explains why it is so readable.

Amelia's diary prose is characterized by clarity and grace and many of the entries contain jewel-like vignettes such as the following:

> After the child was buried yesterday, Mr Griffin asked the man who has charge of the cemetery to rake off the little plot of ground which had been disturbed by digging the grave & make it look tidy as he should bring Mrs Griffin up before dark to see the grave. When Amelia went there she was so surprised to see the little grave all surrounded with pretty flowers. The man had brought from his green house many pots in bloom & foliage plants & sank the pots in the earth & every thing looked so pretty & bright. A perfect little flower garden, & it was the poor man's own kind heart that prompted the delicate act. Amelia feels that she can never forget it while she lives.[22]

It does not matter that the gardener is unnamed and the reader's knowledge of the Griffins relatively slight. The poignancy of the incident does not depend upon knowing that the child's name was Teresa, that she died of scarlet fever, that the adjoining graves included that of a sister who had also died of scarlet fever, or even that the Amelia mentioned was the diarist's daughter. Our lives are enriched simply by knowing of this "delicate act." The passage is a good example of Amelia Harris' ability to sketch in a very few words an incident, a "character," a scene.

Another remarkable characteristic of Amelia's diary is her crisply stated wit: "I have always advised my sons to look at the mother before they made love to the daughters";[23] "They are two unfortunate women. The husband of the one is conceited, coarse and vulgar and the husband of the other is debauched, dissipated and worthless";[24] "Our cook is a very good woman but a very poor cook";[25] "It is strange what stupid sons a clever father will have . . . or is the other theory correct that it requires

[22]Amelia's diary, 21 October 1874.
[23]Amelia's diary, 19 August 1859.
[24]Amelia's diary, 28 November 1858.
[25]Amelia's diary, 23 November 1860.

a clever mother to make clever children."[26] Acerbic, perceptive, and economical in her commentary, Amelia must have been as sharp a conversationalist as she was a diarist.

Three of Amelia's qualities as an excellent diarist are also to be found in the diaries of Charlotte, Sophia and Lucy: a competent prose style; an ability to describe a scene briefly but accurately and to bring characters to life; and the capacity to recognize the dramatic possibilities inherent in a developing situation. However, these three diaries are found wanting in some areas: they lack the wit that enlivens Amelia's recording of her daily experiences; they give a sense that some matters are not being treated; and that not all of the writer's experience is being drawn upon. It is not that the diarist is falsifying the record, rather that some of the realities of life are being ignored.

This is the case with Chasse and Sophie, both of whose diaries end abruptly. Charlotte's description of the social life of the Harris daughters is a detailed and amusing one but she has little to say about major problems confronting her family at the time. In particular, she fails to comment on her father's declining health and the difficulties he was experiencing as District Treasurer. Similarly, her treatment of her engagement to Frank Campbell is less than realistic, and reads more like the romanticized accounts in one of the contemporary novels of which she was so fond.[27]

Sophie's interpretation of the early months of her own marriage is also a romanticized one, and it is significant that she ceases to write when her relationship with her husband, Edward Harris, becomes strained and their marriage breaks down. Sophie's record and perception of the events of those years would have been of great interest, especially as she was given to self-analysis and was remarkably honest in describing her own role in the crises that periodically confronted her family and her close associates. She was also an adept wordsmith, able to capture the essence of a situation. Consider her snide, if perceptive, comments on the militaristic posturing when rumours of war and invasion excited the menfolk of London:

> The townspeople are all excitement in anticipation of war & people who have hitherto been looked upon as candidates for any

[26]Amelia's diary, 13 December 1858.
[27]Campbell first appears in Charlotte's diary on 23 June 1850.

> peace Society or congregation of Quakers have undertaken to form & command Rifle companies & are to be manufactured into soldiers as fast as fear of the Yankees, love of their country, & the drill sergeant can make them.[28]

Furthermore, of all of the Eldon diarists, Sophie's "view of the duties of a married woman"[29] did most to challenge the contemporary standards of propriety, domesticity, and womanliness. Certainly, her actions provoked critical commentary from others; her own reflections and assessments on this would have been revealing.

One cannot accuse Lucy of ignoring the trials and vicissitudes in her relations with her husband throughout her marriage. Her limitation as a diarist is in her treatment of these matters. It is not that she fails to emerge as a distinct personality, but that she does not appear a more interesting person. Nevertheless, her allusions to her pregnancies, fears for her children, and reflections on her marriage are tantalizing probes into the domestic realities of nineteenth century women. It is Lucy who ponders that "a husband and lover are quite different people,"[30] makes preparations during her pregnancy "if I should die,"[31] and complains of a life that is "a pretty lonely one, with looking after the children and sewing."[32] In all, she provides the richest testimony of women's domestic challenges in that particular social setting.

The youngest of the Eldon diarists, Amelia Archange Harris, is represented only by a few entries from her diary of 1882 when she was a young girl of thirteen. It is not until the 1890s that her diaries begin to reveal her full and interesting personality. One hardly expects thirteen year olds to produce great diaries, but she does render the perspective of a granddaughter on the dramatic events surrounding her in 1882.

However, taken together, these diverse, and sometimes discordant, voices are heard as a single chorus concerned with the fortunes and misfortunes of the family. They present their personal views of people and of situations involving domestic and

[28]Sophia's diary, 16 December 1861.
[29]Amelia's diary, 8 July 1862.
[30]Lucy's diary, 3 February 1871.
[31]Lucy's diary, 9/10/11 May 1870.
[32]Lucy's diary, 17/18 January 1875.

social life, courtship, marriage, and death. The basic subject matter is the story of the family, but they also present commentary on such matters as economics and politics, religion and mores, and the social regimen of the everyday life around them. In conjunction with other material that has been preserved in the Harris Papers, the diaries provide the basis for a detailed history of a particular Canadian family for three-quarters of the nineteenth century. From them, we are able to arrive at our own conclusions about the diarists and about life in the community which eventually developed into the city of London.

The death of the family matriarch, Amelia Harris, in the year 1882 has been selected to conclude this volume as it marks a natural turning point in the history of Eldon House and the Harris family. To appreciate the diaries one must understand the Harris family, who they were, how they came to live in London, Canada West, and what role they played in the development of that community.

BEGINNINGS

Late in April 1815, a large canoe manned by half-a-dozen paddlers and carrying naval personnel engaged in a naval survey arrived at Port Ryerse.[33] Located on the north shore of Lake Erie near Long Point, the settlement there had been founded in 1795 by Colonel Samuel Ryerse, a United Empire Loyalist.[34] When their boat approached the Port Ryerse dock, the whole community of perhaps twenty people turned out to greet them. One of these was Samuel Ryerse's daughter, Amelia.

According to the Harris family lore, on seeing John Harris standing in the boat, she said to her girl friend, "There's the man I shall marry." Whatever the truth to this story, the fact is that John Harris and Amelia Ryerse were married at Port Ryerse a little over a month later. On 28 June 1815, Amelia's uncle, John Ryerson, a justice of the peace, conducted the ceremony before an assembly of some 25 persons. The marriage certificate stated that "because John Harris of His Majesty's *Prince Regent* on the Lakes and Amelia Ryerse of Woodhouse were desirous of intermarrying with each other and there being no parson or minister of the Church of England within eighteen miles of them they had applied to him in his capacity of justice of the peace."[35]

Who was John Harris?

John Harris was born on 21 June 1782, at Dartington in Devon, "the son and base child of Mary." His father, also John Harris, was a local curate.[36] Twelve years later, he ran away to sea as a cabin boy.

According to the Admiralty records, in 1797 John Harris was apprenticed in the merchant marine, and in 1803, the year of Trafalgar, he was impressed into the Royal Navy.[37] He served

[33]See Robin Harris, "The Beginning of the Hydrographic Survey of the Great Lakes and the St. Lawrence River," *Historic Kingston* 14, 1966, pp. 24–39.

[34]See Daniel J. Brock, "Samuel Ryerse (Ryerson)," *Dic. Can. Biog.* V, pp. 732–735; also L.H. Tasker, *The United Empire Loyalist Settlement at Long Point, Lake Erie*, Toronto: W. Briggs, 1900.

[35]The marriage certificate is deposited in the Harris Papers.

[36]Records of St. Mary the Virgin, Dartington, Devonshire, England.

[37]John Harris' certificates of naval service are in the Harris Papers.

initially on *H.M.S. Explosion Bomb* under Captain James Prevost,[38] and when Prevost was transferred to *H.M.S. Saracen* in September 1804, he took Harris with him. Promotion from midshipman to able bodied seaman soon followed and, on 9 June 1809, Harris appeared before a Board of Inquiry at Malta and was certified as a fully qualified Master in the Royal Navy. Subsequently he served as Assistant Master of *H.M.S. Ocean* and as Master of *H.M.S. Porcupine*.

Harris' initial service with the Royal Navy was in the Mediterranean but early in 1810 the *Porcupine* returned to England and was despatched to South American waters. On his return to England, he was appointed Master of *H.M.S. Zephyr*, and in March 1813 he was ordered to report to Spithead prior to "particular service in North America." The "particular service" was in connection with the War of 1812 and John Harris was among the navy personnel who transported the British and Canadian troops from Kingston to Crysler's Farm in November 1813. On 4 October 1814, he was appointed Master of *H.M.S. Prince Regent* based at Kingston where, after some twenty years of active naval duty, he was transformed into a hydrographer.

Following the War of 1812, the British Admiralty assigned overall naval command of the Great Lakes to Commodore Edward C.R. Owen, with specific instructions to undertake a thorough examination of the factors affecting the naval defence of the frontier. Precise information was needed about navigation on the lakes, the routes to, and the sites of, naval stations, and the availability of timber for shipbuilding. With few charts available, Owen needed the services of an experienced hydrographer, and he requested the assistance of his brother, Captain William Fitz William Owen.[39] The latter received his instructions from Commodore Owen on 5 November 1815 and a full-scale hydrographic survey of the Great Lakes and the St. Lawrence River was initiated, a task that was finally completed in 1856 under Captain Owen's successor, Captain Henry W. Bayfield.[40]

[38]Captain John Prevost, the younger brother of Sir George Prevost, Governor General of Canada (1812–15), died in 1816.

[39]See Paul Cornell, "William Fitz William Owen," *Dic. Can. Biog.* VIII, pp. 668–673.

[40]NAC, RG8, I, C Series, Vol. 370, pp. 64–70, E.C.R. Owen, "Instructions for the Conduct of the Surveying Department of the Lakes of Canada to Captain W. Owen, 5 November 1815."

Captain Owen's first task was to catch up with Harris whom Commodore Owen had instructed would henceforth work under him. On 10 April 1815, John Harris and John Aldersley, Foreman of the Kingston Shipyard, had been ordered by Commodore Owen to report on the most appropriate site for a harbour and ship-building plant on the north shore of Lake Erie.[41] Travelling in a large canoe manned by a half-dozen paddlers, they had proceeded immediately from Kingston to Niagara, then by way of the Chippewa and Grand Rivers to Lake Erie, then continued westward along the Lake to Long Point. It was here that John Harris met Amelia Ryerse, his future wife.

Who Was Amelia Ryerse?

Amelia Ryerse, was the eldest daughter of Colonel Samuel Ryerse, U.E.L., and his second wife, Sarah Underhill, the widow of another Loyalist, Captain John Davenport.[42] The Ryerses constituted a large and influential clan, some of whom anglicized their name to Ryerson from its original Dutch form.[43] Amelia was born into this clan on 19 February 1798 and she left a record of the circumstances:

> One bitter cold night in February, the household was alarmed by the announcement of my mother's illness. No assistance was to be had nearer than three miles; no horses and no roads – only a track through the woods. Mr Powel . . . volunteered to go in search of Granny McCall. . . . After some weary hours . . . Mrs McCall soon stood beside my mother, and very soon after the birth of a daughter was announced. That daughter is now making this record of the past.[44]

This description is extracted from an "Historical Memorandum" written by Amelia in 1859 in which she recounts the

[41]*NAC, RG8, I, C Series, Vol. 370,* "E.C.R. Owen, Instruction for Mr. John Harris . . . and Mr. Aldersley . . . dated 10 April 1815," pp. 24–6.

[42]Captain John Davenport, like Samuel Ryerse, had taken land in New Brunswick in 1783 where he married Sarah. He had emigrated to the United States, and then re-emigrated to Canada in 1795. After Samuel's death, Sarah lived with her daughter and John Harris on their farm at Port Ryerse.

[43]For Amelia (1798–1882), see Robin S. Harris, "Amelia (Harris) Ryerse," *Dic. Can. Biog.* XI, pp. 782–783.

[44]Egerton Ryerson, *The Loyalists of America and Their Times from 1620–1816*, Toronto: Briggs, 1880, Vol. II, p. 238.

founding of Port Ryerse in 1795 by her father, Colonel Samuel Ryerse. This document originally concluded with the death of her father in 1812, but in 1879, again at Ryerson's request, she extended it to 1814, the year when the Ryerse farm was burned by American invaders.[45] But while the "Memorandum" is an admirably organized and charmingly written chronicle of the early days of Port Ryerse, it is not an autobiography. She makes no reference to the fact that she declined an offer of marriage when she was fifteen from an army officer named Bela Brewster Brigham of the Oxford Militia. Nor does she make any reference to her schooling. In his "Key to the Diary of Charlotte Harris," her son Edward stated, "My mother was born in a log house which had been built from felled trees. Her education and training was home instruction from father and mother assisted by some educated ladies who had immigrated during the troublous times of the French Revolution and Napoleonic wars."[46] Later, Edward Harris expanded on this in a letter to his niece, Helen Peard:

> [When Amelia married] she was under 17 years of age. She had never been away from home. There was no other place to go to. She had never been at school; there were neither teachers nor schools. Her mother happily was well educated, and would now be called a society woman. In my mother's case it was wholly home instruction. Her education must have been something like that of Miranda on the desolate island described in Shakespeare's masterpiece, "The Tempest." Prior to her marriage she had read "Plutarch's Lives" many times, and Fielding's works, and could all her life repeat the best passages from "Paradise Lost." The Bible was read every day. The books were few in number and almost committed to memory. In fact, the mental training must have resolved itself into cultivation of the memory and habits of thought, an education which might make a woman very companionable; nor was it of that dull kind to check further advancement.[47]

[45]The "Memorandum" is reprinted in its entirety in J.J. Talman, *Loyalist Narratives of Upper Canada*, Toronto: The Champlain Society, 1937. The original is in the Harris papers.

[46]Edward Harris' "Key" was written in 1912 and is in the Harris Papers.

[47]Harris Papers, Edward Harris to Helen Peard, 4 June 1919.

Amelia did in fact briefly attend a school, as an entry in her diary for 26 July 1864 refers to the days "when I was a child at school in Niagara."[48]

This is all we know of the young woman who married John Harris on 28 June 1815.

The Kingston Years

John Harris' marriage to Amelia must have afforded a very brief respite from his survey duties. Captain Owen had retraced Harris' route from Kingston to Long Point and by August he and his survey party – which by this time included Harris and two Royal Navy lieutenants, Alexander Vidal and Henry Bayfield – sailed west along the Lake Erie shore as far as Point Pelée, up the Detroit River and into Lake St. Clair.

Returning to Kingston in the fall of 1815, Owen announced that the scope of the enterprise had been greatly enlarged. It was now decided that there would be a thorough hydrographic survey of Lakes Ontario, Erie and Huron and the St. Lawrence River from Kingston to Montreal. During the winter of 1815–16, Owen's party completed the required work on Lake Ontario and the St. Lawrence River.

It is at this point that Amelia joins her husband at Kingston, the headquarters of the survey, and sets up household in a building called the Hydrographer's House. Here, not only did Amelia serve as domestic chatelaine but also as amanuensis to Harris and the other surveyors. That her duties were not restricted to domestic matters only is evidenced in 1816 by a letter from John Harris addressed to her as "Deputy Assistant Mariner Surveyor and Housekeeper to the Establishment":

> My Dear Ame:
> As you are one of the assistants, we send . . . [to] you for a trace on oil paper for that part of the charts of the Thousand Islands. . . . You must be very particular in placing those points on the chart . . . We depend on you sending it as soon as possible. Lose no time. . . . I shall be at home soon. I should not wish you to go [to Port Ryerse] until I see you. . . . I wish we could always be together.[49]

[48]The "Niagara" referred to here is Niagara-on-the-Lake.
[49]Harris Papers, letter from John Harris to Amelia Ryerse Harris, 23 June 1816.

One of the simpler tasks Captain Owen's party had to deal with was the naming of as yet unidentified geographical features. One group of islands in the St. Lawrence River was named after the individual ships which Captain Owen had commanded before he was sent to Canada and was known collectively as "The Old Friends." Another group became "The Hydrographers," with individual islands named Owen, Fitzwilliam, Bayfield, Becher, Harris, Vidal, and Amelia. Unfortunately, these islands fell on the American side of the international boundary when it was redrawn in 1825, and all were renamed. "Amelia" became "Sport."

However ephemeral their place in cartography, the "Hydrographers Group" remained close friends. For the next quarter century, both Bayfield and Owen corresponded regularly with the Harrises, and there were occasional letters and visits from Vidal and Becher. It was to the latter that Amelia wrote within days of John Harris' death in 1850 to see what could be done about a naval pension. All these letters resonate with an affection and a sense of mutual respect that is as charming as it is unmistakable.

John and Amelia's first child, William Edward, was born at the Hydrographer's Office on 18 August 1817. They did not settle in Kingston, however, as Owen received orders to return to England and on 1 September 1817 Harris retired from the Navy with the rank of Master, half-pay. The Harrises then left Kingston for Port Ryerse.

Life at Port Ryerse

As the daughter of a United Empire Loyalist, Amelia was entitled to a land grant and she selected a homestead close to her father's at Port Ryerse. On moving there, the Harrises faced several initial set-backs. Apart from the problem of meeting the capital expenses related to the farmhouse and the property on a Master's half-pay, their first child died from injuries caused by a fall from a horse-drawn carriage and their second, Amelia Helen, born in 1819, died of croup in 1821. Other children soon followed, however, including Sarah in 1821, and Amelia Andrina in 1823. Six more children were born at Port Ryerse: the twins, Mary and Eliza (1825), Charlotte (1828), John Fitzjohn (1830), Edward (1832), and Helen (1834). Subsequently, two more children – George (1836) and Teresa (1839) – would be born following the Harris' move to London.

One of these children, Edward, left a chronicle of these early years and commented in particular on the education of his sisters and brothers:

> Six daughters were born before a son. The education of those daughters was Greek, Latin & Mathematics, from educated settlers and home instruction from father and mother. I was taught my early Greek by an older sister [Sarah], . . . [then] I was turned over to a clerical expert.[50]

The schooling and education of their large family was a priority for the Harrises and is a matter of concern in correspondence with William Owen and Henry Bayfield during the Port Ryerse years. In one epistle, Amelia reviews their situation after nine years at Port Ryerse:

> My little family are growing rapidly. In a few years I shall be surrounded with young women. They are all blessed with good dispositions and with very fair natural talents which I hope we may have the means of cultivating. Amelia and Eliza bid fair to be clever.
>
> There is a great difference in the twins. Eliza is very industrious and has a most retentive memory. Mary is a good natured laughing girl and takes the world easy. . . . Sarah goes to the district school, but the others are taught by a governess in the house. . . . The [geographical] globes arrived safe for which we return you many thanks. Sarah is learning the use of them.[51] . . .

That Bayfield had his own ideas on the subject of education, especially on what was appropriate education for girls, can be seen from his advice to Amelia on the matter:

> I think you are quite right in keeping your daughters under your own eye . . . if Harris had leisure . . . there would be no occasion for you to part with them for he is well able to educate them in the essential points. But I suppose you want to teach them French.[52]

[50]Edward William Harris, "The Early Women of the Country," Address to the Norfolk Historical Society, 1903, in Harris Papers.

[51]Harris Papers, Amelia Harris to Lieutenant Henry Bayfield, R.N., 14 February 1830.

[52]Harris Papers, Bayfield to Amelia Harris, 22 November 1828.

On another occasion, he commented,

> I am delighted to hear, that all your little ones are well, and approve much of Harris' ideas with respect to their education, and the qualities of their hearts as the first object of attention, he will not, I am sure, forget that external accomplishments have a certain, although a much lower value. Latin is of importance to a Lady in so far as it facilitates acquisition of modern languages but in no other respect as far as I am aware of. Your daughters will certainly have greater advantages than you had, at the commencement of life, with respect to education, but you had also great advantages. Nature has been kind to you & made a present of some of her highest gifts – a good virtuous heart – a sound understanding & had not forgotten to make the external appearances correspond with what lies within – the casket fit to contain the contents.[53] . . .

Apart from providing the Harrises with globes, advice, and pretty compliments, Bayfield also sent books to add to their library of volumes dealing with geology, theology, mythology, algebra, animal economy, vegetable physiology, and the English constitution.[54]

The expenses associated with providing for their growing family must have pressed hard upon John Harris during these years. Like many other settlers, he had little experience, and possibly even less interest, in farming. Fortunately, Amelia Harris had grown up on a farm and her brother, George Ryerse, held an adjoining property. By 1830, therefore, Amelia could report that "[n]ine years has made a very great alteration in the appearance of our farm (as well as in the proprietors of it). We are now in possession of every comfort and many luxuries."[55]

Harris' initiatives elsewhere were to prove to be less than promising. In 1818, his ambitions to captain a steamboat based at Kingston fell through when another was appointed to the position.[56] Fortune did smile on him in 1821 when, due to the efforts of Captain William Owen, he recieved £200 in prize-

[53]Harris Papers, Bayfield to Amelia Harris, 5 May 1829.
[54]Harris Papers, Bayfield to Harris, 15 May 1830.
[55]Harris Papers, Amelia Harris to Lieutenant Henry Bayfield, 14 February 1830.
[56]Harris Papers, Michael Spratt to John Harris, 13 February 1818.

money from his years in naval service, although his subsequent claims for additional compensation proved to be fruitless.[57]

John Harris had, however, "married well" and he was fortunate in having the support of the Ryersons and Ryerses, several of whom occupied important political positions in the London District. Certainly, such contacts were not a disadvantage in his winning such appointments as Coroner (1819), Treasurer (1821–50), and School Trustee (1822–50). After a few months, he found it necessary to resign the coronership because of a conflict of interest. The school trusteeship was an unpaid position but a prestigious one. The treasurership, however, while also prestigious, was well paid and effectively solved Harris' financial problems for the balance of his life.

Furthermore, despite the perquisites of office, John Harris did not neglect the development of a professional career as "marine engineer," with particular reference to the building of canals. In 1819, he applied successfully for certification as a provincial land surveyor. His talents were put to good use when, in 1822, he was appointed as a surveyor on the Commission for the Improvement of Inland Navigation. Assigned to the survey of a canal route from Burlington Bay to the Niagara River above the Falls, he worked full-time on this project in 1822 and continued to work on a part-time basis until 1827 and is described in its final report as "Superintending Engineer."[58] Other projects included the 1825 construction of a harbour at the mouth of Kettle Creek to the west of Port Stanley, and in 1839 he conducted a resurvey of Long Point at the request of Henry Bayfield. A proposal to mount a further survey of Lakes Erie and Huron was not acted upon and, after 1840, Harris turned his full attentions to his municipal position.

These extracurricular activities did serve to cultivate John Harris' interest in things scientific and he became an early advocate of the promotion of science in Canada. As member of Canada's earliest learned society, the Literary and Historical

[57]Harris Papers, W.F.W. Owen to John Harris, 31 July 1818, 18 December 1820; Thomas Clark to John Harris, 30 June 1830.

[58]See references to these appointments in correspondence in Harris Papers, dated 2 February 1822 and 20 September 1827. See also *Journal of the Upper Canada Assembly*, 1826–7 (2), "Report N of the Select Committee, ...John Ralph, Chairman, John Harris, Master R.N. [Superintending Engineer], Survey and Estimates, Burlington Bay Canal, 1825–7.

Society of Quebec, for some years Harris provided them with systematically arranged metereological readings. For this and other contributions, he was made an honorary member. However, his most significant contribution to the advancement of science in Canada, resulted from his 1833 petition to the Upper Canada Assembly that an astronomical observatory be established in the province. The petition was referred to the Education Committee, which endorsed the proposal with remarkable enthusiasm:

> It is not out of place for your Committee to express their high respect for the scientific attainments of that gentleman, Mr Harris, and his incessant exertions, since his first coming into the Province, . . . that means may be afforded to the youth of Upper Canada to acquire that instruction in literature and science, which is not denied the youth of any enlightened community whose population is not one-sixth of that of this Colony.
>
> The Committee recommends that King's College be put immediately into operation, with such alterations in the Charter as may be deemed fit and expedient; and that it be recommended that an Observatory, and Practical Professorship of Astronomy, be among the very first arrangements made.[59]

As John Harris' participation in the affairs of the district increased, and as London was the principal focus of his activities, residence at Port Ryerse came to be inconvenient. Accordingly, the Harrises moved to London in 1834 and established their new household there.

A New Life in London

John Harris, Amelia, and their eight children occupied Eldon House upon their arrival in London, and in 1836 Amelia gave birth to another son, George. Two years later Amelia experienced the trauma of losing her mother, Sarah Underhill. She was still in mourning for her mother when another daughter, Teresa, was born in 1839.

[59]Upper Canada, House of Assembly Journals, 1833–34, p. 42. See also Suzanne Zeller, *Inventing Canada: Early Victorian Science and the Idea of a Transcontinental Nation*, Toronto: University of Toronto Press, 1987, p. 120. The University of King's College, already chartered (1827), was subsequently reconstituted as the University of Toronto (1850). A Toronto observatory was established on the university grounds in 1839.

On their arrival in London, six of the children were enrolled in the District Grammar School. John, aged four, studied Reading and Spelling, while the five older girls took English Grammar, Arithmetic, and Writing. Both Sarah and Amelia were enrolled in Latin and Sarah in Greek and French. In 1835 all six children attended a private school taught by Mary Proudfoot, daughter of the Reverend William Proudfoot, the Presbyterian minister. The combined tuition fee for the six Harris children was £10 with an additional charge of £1 1s. 3d. for two pencils and other extras, including a *Shorter Catechism* and four copies of *Murray's Grammar*.[60]

In 1838, a Miss Atkinson addressed the following letter to Amelia Harris from Toronto:

> Miss Atkinson's comp[liments] to Mrs Harris, and is informed by Mr Bryanston that she requests to treat with her on the subject of the Education of her Daughters. Miss A begs to say she has been engaged as governess for the last six months in a family in the Country, . . . She is qualified to instruct her daughters in all the necessary branches of Education including music, pencil drawing and painting . . . Miss A is a member of the Episcopal Church and is respectably connected. Miss A will feel obliged by Mrs Harris' informing her by letter what she requires of her. Terms £50 including washing considering there is a large family.[61] . . .

Miss Atkinson was not hired but Jane Steers, an American, was and she lived at Eldon House as the governess of the Harris children for the next six or seven years. A charming and gifted woman, she was a friend and confidant of Amelia Harris as well as an employee and she returned as a visitor to Eldon House several times in the 1860s and 1870s.[62]

It is quite apparent that the primary objective in educating the girls was to prepare them for marriage. The boys, however, were directed to a suitable profession which, as it turned out for all three of them, was to be the practice of law. In 1843, John, the eldest, was sent to Upper Canada College but he remained there

[60]For details on the education of the Harris children see Edward William Harris, 1903, *op. cit.*

[61]Harris Papers, letter from Atkinson to Amelia Harris, 7 April 1838.

[62]Eleven of her letters are in the Harris Papers.

for only one year. As Amelia Harris explained to her daughter Eliza,

> we are not going to send John back to college for a year or two. Edward is far ahead of him in everything at an expense of £5 a year while John is costing us £100 and learning nothing.[63]

Ultimately, all three sons completed their education at the District Grammar School before moving on to the Upper Canada Law Society's law school at Osgoode Hall. Nevertheless, John's single year at Upper Canada College was to prove to be a consequential one. While there, his friends included Edward Blake, Lukin Robinson, W.H. Boulton, and Christopher Hagerman, all sons of leading figures in Toronto's business and political worlds. They were to remain his friends for the rest of his life. As his sister Helen observed, "I believe John went to school with every man in Toronto. Wherever I am introduced to a gentleman he begins the conversation by saying he went to school with my brother."[64]

While the Harrises may have been preoccupied with such domestic matters, this did not prevent John Harris senior from making his mark in the affairs of the community. As District Treasurer, he was already a well known figure in London before he established residence there. He soon became an active participant in local society, particularly at St. Paul's Church, where he was one of the first churchwardens. In 1838, he was one of the six leading citizens who petitioned the Bishop of Montreal to establish the church in London.[65]

John Harris was also the principal founder of the London Mechanics' Institute. He presided at its first meeting on 26 January 1835 and delivered a presidential address a week later in which he proposed that,

[63]Harris Papers, Amelia Harris to Eliza Harris, 18 November 1843. While John was at Upper Canada College, Edward was attending the District Grammar School in London.

[64]Harris Papers, Helen Harris to Amelia Harris, 17 September 1854.

[65]Orlo Miller, *Gargoyles and Gentlemen: A History of St. Paul's Cathedral, London, Ontario, 1834–1964*, Toronto: Ryerson Press, 1966, p. 161. The other petitioners were James Givens, a lawyer; George Moore, a doctor; two business men, Lawrence Lawrason and George Goodhue; and James Hamilton, a banker, to be distinguished from James Hamilton, Sheriff of the London District. See also F.H. Armstrong, *The Forest City: An Illustrated History of London, Canada*, Northridge, California: Windsor Publications, 1986, pp. 82–3.

> the object of the institution is to promote the intellectual cultivation of an important and numerous class of individuals in this town and its neighbourhood . . . For assuredly all the knowledge that is commonly known has a tendency to make men sober and reflective, it will direct them to church on a Sunday evening instead of a tavern, and to the library in the evening instead of a gambling table . . . or dozing the evening away over a jug of whisky.[66] . . .

Unfortunately, the organization collapsed within a year, but it was revived by Harris and others in February 1836, a library had been established by 1838, and by 1841 it was on firm footing. Harris was one of nine persons who were made honorary members of what was to become an important community institution.

The years 1837–38 were to be important for John Harris. When on 1 January 1819, he had applied to reside in Canada for twelve months as a half-pay Royal Navy Master, permission was granted on the condition that "in the event of an armament he offer his services to the Senior Officer in Canada."[67] Clearly, this moral, if not legal, commitment still motivated him twenty years later at the time of the threat of armed rebellion in the province. On 18 October, in company with Colonel J.B. Askin, John Burwell, and Lawrence Lawrason, all members of the London elite, he wrote an open letter to Colonel James Hamilton, Sheriff of the London District, calling for a "public meeting to adopt measures to prevent the assembling of great numbers of misguided individuals bearing firearms and other dangerous weapons." Askin subsequently led a party of Londoners, including Harris, to St. Thomas where they joined the forces of Allan MacNab. These had been sent to the London District to deal with the Duncombe uprising after the collapse of William Lyon Mackenzie's forces at Montgomery's Tavern, Toronto, on 12 December 1838.[68]

While Harris was not involved in the skirmish near Oakland that defeated Duncombe's followers, Harris accompanied MacNab to Niagara where his naval eye recognized the threat posed

[66]The untitled address is in the Harris Papers.

[67]Harris Papers, E. Nelson, Navy Office to John Harris, Master in the British Navy, Woodhouse, London District, 19 April 1819.

[68]Fred Landon, "The Duncombe Uprising of 1837 and Some of its Consequences," *Proceedings and Transactions of the Royal Society of Canada* XXV, 1931, pp. 83–98.

by the *Caroline*, an American sailboat hired by Mackenzie to supply his forces situated on Navy Island in the Niagara River. His plans to launch an invasion of Canada were thwarted by the effective destruction of the *Caroline*. As Navy Island was in American territory, and as the *Caroline* was an American vessel, the incident was downplayed at the time in fear of exacerbating the already tense relations between Great Britain and the United States. Nor were the British and Canadian authorities anxious to draw attention to the involvement of the Royal Navy in the affair. At a more personal level, however, John Harris' involvement in the "cutting out" of the *Caroline* added to his local reputation and prestige.[69]

By the 1840s, Harris had withdrawn from canal work and restricted his activities to local politics and the duties of the treasureship. As London grew and prospered, his responsibilities as treasurer increased. Apart from the collection of taxes, he also distributed revenue from provincial sources, and managed the funds designated for road-building, education, and salaries. Further, in 1845, he was given an additional responsibility. In recognition of his integrity, prominence, and no doubt, proven loyalty, he was one of two commissioners appointed by the Government to adjudicate the claims of persons who had suffered losses during the 1837 troubles.

Towards the close of his career, the stress of these routine responsibilities was compounded by having to face competition for the lucrative position of Treasurer he had occupied for nearly thirty years. Shortly prior to the District Council meeting at which his reappointment as Treasurer for 1846 was to be decided, John Buchanan, a Radical and warden of the London District, began campaigning actively for Harris' position.[70]

When the vote was taken, Harris and Buchanan each received the same number of votes. As chairman, Buchanan had a casting vote, and he voted in favour of himself. However, Harris continued to maintain the District accounts, to pay and receive monies,

[69]For more on the "Caroline incident" see E.A. Cruikshank, "The Invasion of Navy Island in 1837–38," *Ont. Hist. Soc., Papers and Records* XXXII, 1937, pp. 7–84; Andrew Drew and R.S. Woods, *The Burning of the Caroline and other Reminiscences of 1837–38*, Chatham: Banner Printing, 1896; John S. Island, "Andrew Drew, the Man who Burned the Caroline," *Ont. Hist.* LIX, 1967, pp. 137–156; Howard Jones, "The Caroline Affair," *The Historian* 38, 1976, pp. 485–502.

[70]This acrimonious and somewhat carnivalesque election is given much coverage in the pages of the *London Free Press* in 1846.

and to perform all the normal duties of the office. Not surprisingly, the local citizens, tax collectors, and government officials looked upon this unusual situation with some incredulity, especially when both Harris and Buchanan inserted notices in the *London Free Press* – published side by side on the same page – advising tax payers to make their payments to them. Council members were divided on the issue: politically, Harris was a Conservative (some would say an arch-Conservative) while Buchanan was a Radical; regionally, the town and northern townships supported Harris while the southern townships supported Buchanan. No advice was forthcoming from Government – at least officially.

Such an imaginative, if somewhat incongruous, resolution of a democratic stalemate could not be allowed to continue, however. Accordingly, John Wilson, the local member of parliament and a long-time friend of John and Amelia, offered the rather self-evident advice: government could not recognize two treasurers. He also observed that Harris had been ill, expressed the hope that it was not the result of "fretting about anything that the Council or government can do or has done," and urged him to put his trust in a "higher power."[71] Wilson wrote to Amelia a month later, expressing hope that "spring will cheer Mr Harris and renew his strength" and suggesting that the entire issue be left to "the guidance of God."[72] Henry Becher was also worried about Harris and communicated his concerns to Col Talbot.[73] Despite his despondancy and illness, Harris was able to retain his position until his death on 25 August 1850. Six days later, Henry Becher wrote to Col Talbot:

> I am commissioned to give you the sorrowful intelligence that our poor old Friend Mr Harris is no more. He died last Sunday after great suffering from disease of the heart, & as you may suppose those he leaves behind him have been most sadly plunged into grief – & the more from the knowledge that the late [District] Council matters connected with the Treasurer's books preyed terribly upon his mind & indeed hurried him to the grave.[74]

[71]Harris Papers, John Wilson to John Harris, 14 February 1849.
[72]Harris Papers, John Wilson to Amelia Harris, 13 March 1849.
[73]Harris Papers, H. Becher to Colonel Talbot, 14 August 1850.
[74]Harris Papers, H. Becher to Colonel Talbot, 29 August 1850.

John Harris had made a minor mark in Canadian history as a member – arguably, the original member – of the Owen-Bayfield Hydrographic Survey. Throughout western Ontario, he was well known because of his early years as surveyor, his service as Treasurer of the London District for thirty years (1821–50), his active role in the affairs of St. Paul's Church, and as founder of the London Mechanics' Institute. His part in the "*Caroline* Incident" had also brought him acclaim. For the Harris family, however, the chief impact of his life upon the lives of widow and daughters was that of patriarch to a large household. With his death, the family was obliged to seek new arrangements.

THE MATRIARCH OF ELDON HOUSE

A new life began for Amelia Ryerse Harris with the death of her husband. She was now the acknowledged head of the family – a "matriarch." It was a role she had sometimes played before, particularly with respect to the education of the children, but it was always a shared role. Following the death of her husband, she moved to centre stage and, as matriarch, the responsibility for running and administering family affairs and ensuring the integrity of the Harris household fell upon her shoulders. For the thirty-two years of her widowhood, she applied all her strength, energy, and imagination to holding the family together. Clearly, she perceived that it was her responsibility to ensure that the Harris household did not disintegrate. Indeed, Amelia's efforts at pursuing this self-appointed mission constitutes the dominant theme of the several diaries.

Early Trials and Challenges

When John Harris died, Amelia's family at Eldon House comprised eight children ranging in age from twenty-seven to eleven. Two of them had married: Sarah, the eldest, had married Captain Robert Dalzell [81st Reg] in 1846 and, after living a year in Toronto, had accompanied him when his regiment returned to England in 1847. Two days before the death of her father, Mary had also married an army officer, Lieutenant Shuldham Peard [20th Reg]. She only heard of her father's death after she and her husband returned from their honeymoon.

Apart from grief at the loss of her husband, Amelia's most pressing concern was her financial situation. Within days of John Harris' death, Henry Becher had written to Thomas Talbot advising him of the passing of his old friend. Becher also took it upon himself to express his apprehension over Amelia's economic difficulties and broached the subject of a possible pension for the youngest children:

> . . . They will be much straitened . . . as his death will take away £150 a year from them and leave them only about £260 a year to live on – little enough indeed for so large a family. I have written to my brother Captain Becher that he may endeavor to

get the three youngest children Helen, George, & Theresa in the Compassionate List . . . Can you do anything to further the application?[75] . . .

In a subsequent letter Becher refers to the closure of outstanding financial obligations regarding John Harris' former position as treasurer:

You will be gratified to hear that I effected a capital arrangement with the [District] Council about their claim against Mr Harris. The whole sum is £2,000 in round numbers and for this they have agreed to take the brick house at 9 Dundas St, the balance in promissory notes which he held in payment for Wild Lands. . . . Mrs Harris will not have to advance a shilling. . . . I hope to see them . . . out of debt. I think George & Teresa (the youngest children) will get the pension.[76]

Amelia's application for a Royal Navy pension was approved in due course, but John Harris' salary as a half-pay master ceased on his death, as did his salary as Treasurer of the London District. Given her several familial obligations and commitments, Amelia's financial situation was, to say the least, precarious. In the early 1850s, her main source of income was the rental of her property and what she received as John Harris' beneficiary. When his will was eventually probated, it was certified that "eight orphans" were dependent upon Amelia, "none at schools supported by government funds," and that Amelia's income exclusive of pension was not in excess of £100.[77] Eldon House was not encumbered with mortgages, but there were still the expenses of the household, the funds needed to support the sons until they established themselves, and to maintain the five girls in a style likely to lead to suitable marriages.

In 1851, a degree of financial relief was afforded by the marriage of two eligible daughters, Chasse and Eliza, to officers in the London garrison. And by 1856, two of the remaining daughters, Amelia and Helen, had also married: Amelia to Gilbert Griffin, the London Postal Inspector, and Helen to Maurice

[75] *Ibid.*
[76] Harris Papers, H. Becher to Thomas Talbot, n.d., 1850.
[77] Harris Papers, Probate of John Harris's will, 14 May 1851.

Portman, the son of an English peer. By this date, only Teresa and the three sons remained at home.

The Harris' financial fortunes were further advanced when, in 1854, the oldest son, John, completed his legal studies and established a law practice at London. By 1855, he was making £2,300 a year and had become the major contributor to Eldon House. His brother Edward also became a lawyer and established a law practice in St. Thomas. Much of their income resulted from administering the investments of their six English-based brothers-in-law.[78] In 1857, John and Edward became partners in a London based practice and subsequently, their youngest brother, George, joined the family firm of Harris Brothers. Discussions over the operation of the firm, the managing of family affairs, and the proper division of profits between the brothers were to exercise Amelia and her sons on several occasions.

However, just as Amelia's financial circumstances appeared to be improving, she had to face her worst trial since the death of her husband: the tragic death of her daughter, Chasse and her young family. In April 1854, a newspaper report of a shipwreck in the Mediterranean off Nice referred to the loss of fifteen passengers, including a "Mrs Knight and family." The Harris family's worse fears were confirmed a week later by a letter from Knight's sister, Helen. Knight himself sent a full account of the tragedy to Henry Becher:

> Will you break to Mrs Harris as gently as you can the dreadful calamity which has happened to me. We left Genoa [for] Marseilles in the *Ercolano* steamer at 2 o'clock in the afternoon. They went to bed early before dark and I went to see them several times. The last time was about half past nine o'clock. . . . I was awakened by a tremendous shock and jumping up, ran to their cabin. I could not get there, the deck being crushed down before the door. I broke into the adjoining cabin, but found I could not get through to theirs. I then got a partition from the gentlemen's cabin and climbed up on deck where I found the maids, one jammed up to the knees, among the ruins on the deck. I put her out and asked where was her mistress. She could not answer but the other maid pointed down into the cabin but only said, you can't save them, save yourself. I then began tear-

[78]Harris Papers, Amelia to Eliza Crutchley, 12 April 1855.

> ing up the ruins of the deck to get down into the cabin, but the lantern went out and the next moment as I was moving a piece of timber fell from above and took off my left thumb at the first joint. I tied my neck handkerchief around it and then finding that the ship was all broken up amid and the remains of the deck w[h]ere I was being only just above water and seeing no more of the maids I went toward the quarter deck. As I got there all the remaining persons at that end of the ship jumped overboard, except one.[79] . . .

This dramatic account closes abruptly, and the sentence, "Wife, children and servants are all lost" was added at the end in someone else's hand. Knight returned to England and remarried two years later.

As well as enduring the tragic loss of a daughter and two grandchildren, Amelia became increasingly concerned about the health of her son, John. He had never been strong, and by 1857 his condition had so deteriorated that he decided to seek medical advice in England. During his three-month absence, Amelia sent him a weekly letter describing the activities at Eldon. John brought all his letters back with him to Canada. One of them included this passage, "We . . . mind what we say at home, . . . Mamma [is] taking down items of news for a grand letter which she has undertaken to write you today."[80] Thus began the twenty-five year diary of Amelia Ryerse Harris.

A Troubled Household

When Lord Althorpe arrived at Eldon House on 12 September 1857 for a two-day visit, he found himself in a crowded household. Two married daughters were living temporarily at Eldon House: Helen and Maurice Portman, their five-month old son, Berkeley, and their servant would soon leave for the American south where they planned to purchase a cotton plantation;[81]

[79]Harris Papers, Edward Knight to H. Becher, 27 April 1854.

[80]Harris Papers, Edward Harris to John Harris, 24 May 1857.

[81]Portman's decision to invest in "the sin of owning slaves" much disturbed Amelia (12 and 14 January 1858). For more on Canadian anti-slavery sentiments and refuge-settlements in Ontario see William Pease, *Black Utopia: Negro Communal Experiments in America,* Madison: State Historical Society of Wisconsin, 1963; Jason H. Silverman, *Unwelcome Guests: Canada West's Response to American Fugitive Slaves, 1800–1865*, Millwood, New York: Associated Faculty Press, 1985.

Amelia and her husband, Gilbert Griffin, would soon be moving to their own home near Eldon House. But even after their departure, Amelia still had four unmarried children. Preparing Teresa for her Toronto debut in 1858 was a pleasurable preoccupation, and her youngest son, George, presented her with few problems other than worrying about his enthusiasm for cricket and other sports. However, Edward's deafness was cause for concern, as was the health of her oldest son, John.

Family finances continued to be a perennial problem during this period. Close to home, Amelia's son-in-law, Gilbert Griffin, consistently demonstrated his inability to live within his means as Postal Inspector, and his genius for not paying his debts on time. But economic hardships were also occasioned by the failure of several businesses in London, Toronto and Hamilton. These affected many people, including some of the Harris' close friends. Apart from expressing her concern and sympathy, Amelia was not above intervening on their behalf. Thus, when her cousin, Egerton Ryerson, got involved in some difficulties in connection with the Bank of Upper Canada, Amelia took the opportunity to bring up Ryerson's problem with Sir Edmund Head, the Governor General of Canada, when he was a guest at Eldon House.[82] On the following day she wrote to her cousin to communicate Sir Edmund's advice on the matter.

Amelia's own trials had been considerable. The year 1860 had seen the death of her daughter, Helen, soon after giving birth to her third child. Amelia's account of Helen's death is very moving as she communicates the family's suffering at the loss of a loved one.[83] The event was to change the course of the life of Helen's husband, Portman, and constituted a tragic drama that attracted considerable attention throughout the community. Soon after her death, Helen's two older sons were taken to England but the baby, Maurice, remained with the grandmother.

For the next few months, the widowed Portman was to occupy much of Amelia's attention. Interest in his election campaign and public life was exceeded only by her concern over his emotional problems and private life.[84] Soon after Portman was elected to Parliament and moved to Quebec City, Amelia was

[82]Amelia's diary, 6 July 1858.
[83]Amelia's diary, 15 April 1860.
[84]Amelia's diary, 22 to 27 July 1862.

disturbed to hear gossip concerning his liaison with a young woman there. In Amelia's eyes, his behaviour was insensitive and irresponsible as it could endanger his political career. Clearly, Portman had another view on the matter, but the diary records only the opinions and judgments of the matriarch of the Harris family. She did acknowledge that both Lord and Lady Portman had written urging their son to remarry, but Amelia had her own idea of the kind of wife that suited him. She was accustomed to having her children follow her advice and asserting her matriarchal authority. She was used to being in control of such situations. But this was not to be the case with Portman. He had an independent mind. Predictably, such interference in his affairs occasioned conflict and friction between he and Amelia, followed by an emotional reconciliation. The last blow fell, however, when her grandson, little Maurice Portman, left for England with the Dalzells to join his father and brothers.

Throughout these years, Amelia's energies were absorbed to some extent by the ongoing sagas of courtship and marriage – not all of which were uneventful. Thus, 1859, Teresa's relationship with William John Scott was marked by a series of dramatic turns of events and was the cause of much anxiety, but it did eventually culminate in matrimony in August of that year. In November of the same year, Eldon House celebrated the marriage of the eldest son, John, and Elizabeth Loring. But if Amelia accepted John's wife, she was determined to protect her position at Eldon: "She cannot come here and be head as long as I am equal to managing my own household, however willing I might be to resign in her favor."[85]

The union of Edward Harris and Sophie Ryerson in 1860 would also have been an occasion for great celebration if the circumstances had been different. However, as only four months had elapsed since the death of Helen, they were pronounced man and wife in an unostentatious ceremony at the Ryerson's home in Toronto.[86] Initially, the marriage was a very happy one as is evident from the comments in both Amelia's and Sophia's diaries throughout 1861. Sophia's description of the final hours they spent together in a hotel at Niagara Falls, immediately prior to Edward's departure for England to seek relief for his deafness,

[85]Amelia's diary, 26 August 1859.
[86]Amelia's diary, 7 July 1860.

is arguably the most passionate entry in any of the Eldon House diaries. Upon Edward's return they continued to live a happy life for some months.

June 1861 found the Harrises in mourning once again with the death of the oldest son, John, whose health had been a continuing source of anxiety for Amelia. Following his death in England, his young wife, Elizabeth, returned to Eldon House where her presence caused some considerable family conflict. Disagreements over possessions and property added further stress to that occasioned by the loss of a loved one.[87]

Commencing in 1862, a major concern to the Harris family, and a matter of comment in the local society, were the tensions within Edward and Sophie's marriage. This new crisis served not only to challenge Amelia's domestic world but also offended her sense of propriety. Edward had, at the request of her parents, chaperoned a Miss Meredith on his return from England; however, his scrupulous attention to this duty was such that it disturbed Sophie. But it was the appearance in the Eldon household of Captain Edward Osborne Hewitt that was to provoke the most stress.[88] Sophie's friendship with Hewitt and their mutual interest in riding aroused Edward's wrath and prompted gossip in town. What had initially been nothing more than an innocent friendship developed into a serious issue threatening the survival of the marriage, and Amelia's diary records a mother's concern: "What the end will be who can tell, but I fear happiness is gone from both of them."[89] The Harrises and the Ryersons intervened as the estrangement intensified, but things deteriorated and a separation ensued. While Sophie's diary is closed by the end of 1861, her earlier comments, together with those of Amelia, provide sensitive insights into the personal and public mores of the day.

Somewhat predictably, both families, the Harrises and the Ryersons, blamed each other for the separation, and thus a relationship of long standing turned sour. Not until August, 1864 did a reconciliation seem possible and Amelia chronicles the steps that were taken on both sides. Edward went to Toronto to meet with Sophie and her father to negotiate a new marriage

[87]Amelia's diary, 1 November–16 December 1861.
[88]Amelia's diary, 17 April 1862.
[89]Amelia's diary, 4 July 1862.

settlement. Talks continued over the fall and, in November, Edward and Sophie returned to Eldon House. With the reconciliation, relations between the respective families were restored, but it was not until February, 1869, following a three day stay at Eldon, that Amelia's diary refers to Egerton Ryerson in friendly terms again.

Amelia's concerns about the wisdom of her childrens' choice of partners was not restricted to Edward. In October 1866, her diary turns its attention to her youngest son, George, who was beginning to show an interest in Lucy Ronalds, a lady from an established family in Sandwich, near Windsor. The worried mother had some reservations about this match and warned George of the history of insanity in the Ronalds family.[90] He paid no attention to this and continued seeing Lucy. George was the last of Amelia's children to leave the nest and expressions of depression in her diary increased in frequency as the wedding day approached. George and Lucy married in September 1867 and left for a three month honeymoon. On their return, the young couple were gratified that Lucy's allowance from the Ronalds Estate had been increased from £60 to £200 a year, although Amelia complained that "not one of [Lucy's] relatives in England" had sent her a wedding present.[91] Amelia was not to know, however, that Lucy's eventual present from her English connections would come later in 1892, and would be quite considerable.[92] Whatever Amelia's initial reservations about this match, she grew very fond of Lucy, especially after the birth of a daughter. Named Amelia after her grandmother, she came to be known to the family as "Milly," and occupied a special place in her grandmother's affections.[93]

Amelia had entered her seventieth year in 1867 and she commented frequently on her loneliness, loss of vitality, and all the consequences of growing old. As she put it, "It is the natural result of old age. We all have to journey the same road. It would not be called the *dark valley* of the shadow of death if the ap-

[90]Lucy Ronalds was the granddaughter of Elizabeth Robertson Ronalds (1798–1892) who had been in a lunatic asylum in England since 1849.

[91]Amelia's diary, 18 December 1867.

[92]In that year, as the sole survivor of seventeen grandchildren, Lucy came into a substantial fortune on the death of her grandmother, Elizabeth Robertson Ronalds.

[93]Eventually, at the age of thirteen, Milly was to emulate her grandmother, commence her own diary, and thus become one of the five Eldon House diarists.

proach to it were not gloomy."[94] Despite her preoccupation with her own frailties, the frequent domestic crises, and the personal failings of others, Amelia continued to observe and report on contemporary events: the visit by the Prince of Wales,[95] the discovery of oil nearby,[96] the fear of invasion by the Fenians,[97] a well-attended public hanging,[98] and the whole calendar of balls, commemorative days, and croquet games.

The Declining Powers of the Matriarch

Amelia Harris' two decades of widowhood had been witness to her emergence as the central strength and dominant figure in the Harris family. She was the unquestioned matriarchal figure. But the role had taken its toll on her health, emotions, and enthusiasm for life. She had endured a series of trials and tribulations. The tragic deaths of Charlotte in 1854, Helen in 1860, and John in 1861 had caused her much anguish. Moreover, with the departure of Teresa and Scott for England, four of her daughters were living overseas. To be sure, she still had family living in London, but their presence was a mixed blessing. The troubled marriages of the Griffins and of Edward and Sophie must have been a great disappointment, as was the squabbling between Edward and George because of their personal incompatibility and business differences. There were also signs of tensions between some of the English members of the Harris clan and the firm of Harris Brothers regarding the management of their investments. By 1865, the relationship between Edward and George had deteriorated to the point that George was threatening to dissolve the partnership and establish his own business. Naturally, the conflict between the two brothers affected Amelia,

[94]Amelia's diary, 7 September 1865.

[95]Amelia's diary, 5–21 September 1860. See *The Tour of H.R.H. The Prince of Wales through British America and the United States*, Montreal: John Lovell, 1860.

[96]Amelia's diary, 11 February 1862. See Hugh M. Grant, "The 'Mysterious' Jacob L. Englehart and the Early Ontario Petroleum Industry." *Ont. Hist.* LXXXV, 1993, pp. 65–76; Dianne Newell, *Technology on the Frontier: Mining in Old Ontario*, Vancouver: University of British Columbia Press, 1986; Edward Phelps, "Foundations of the Canadian Oil Industry," in Edith G. Firth (ed.), *Profiles of a Province: Studies in the History of Ontario*, Toronto: Ontario Historical Society, 1967, pp. 156–65.

[97]Amelia's diary, 8 March 1866. See also Hereward Senior, *The Last Invasion of Canada: The Fenian Raids, 1866–1879*, Toronto: Dundurn Press, 1991.

[98]Amelia's diary, 29 December 1868.

prompting the comment, "My trials are not to end this side of the grave."[99]

All these problems received Amelia's attention and commentary. While she could derive some comfort from her growing extended family and the increased security of the family's financial position, the loss of control and responsibility was irksome. She complained to her diary, "I had so many leaning and depending upon me, now all are gone & I am old and helpless & have to lean upon others."[100] The circumstances of Amelia's life at Eldon House had changed. No longer the matriarch of a large and bustling family, she now occupied a house that was empty, apart from Edward and Sophie. By 1870, their relationship had settled into a solid, if cool, partnership; they pursued their individual interests, but continued to share an active social life. Amelia comments on the several dances, dinner parties, and musicales hosted at Eldon House, and was gratified that the close relationship with Sophie's parents, the Ryersons, had been restored.

However, Amelia was far from happy with this life as part of the household of others. Edward's business commitments kept him out late and Sophie waited to dine with him. Consequently, Amelia often dined early and alone. She resented this new arrangement, regretted her lack of independence, and complained of the misfortune of parents living with married children.[101] And what she resented most was the loneliness of eating alone after years of life in a household dominated by a dining table surrounded by her large family.

Not surprisingly, Amelia could not reconcile herself to these changed circumstances and she became subject to increasingly frequent bouts of depression as she entered her seventies. In particular, her diary demonstrates a marked preoccupation with death, especially in the context of her frequent dreams. Dreams and their interpretation are a prominent feature of Amelia's diaries and her interpretations of them constitute another insight into her psyche.[102] Frequently, these dreams were connected

[99]Amelia's diary, 4 December 1865.

[100]Amelia's diary, 7 September 1865.

[101]Amelia's diary, 5 November 1870.

[102]For Amelia's dreams and visions see the following entries in her diary: 27 September 1859; 3 March, 9 May 1860; 3 July 1862; 31 January 1864; 6 May 1865; 19 August, 4 September, 22 October 1868; 16 May, 26 July, 13 August, 9 October, 11 December 1870; 8 January 1871; 29 March 1880.

with the deaths of her husband, son, and daughter and they had a profound spiritual significance for her. That they appeared to be so real led her to reflect upon her own mortality, and did much to depress her.

For example, in 1859, when her son, John, was very ill, she dreamt that she was travelling with him, "in the same carriage," that he got out first, and that she continued for "a short distance and, then got out also." In her analysis, she concluded that John's life was "near an end" and that she herself would die shortly after him.[103] Her prediction was correct to the extent that John did die less than two years later, but she herself lived for another twenty years.

In the 1870's, Amelia's dreams tended to be preceded by physical complaints or by mental "indisposition" caused by dwelling on incidents in her past, current domestic crises, or her loss of authority and independence in the constrained Eldon household. Intellectually, she understood that her circumstances had changed with the passage of time, but the loss of both her health and domestic power led her to deep periods of depression.

Amelia had a recurrent "going home dream," which she claimed to have had for some fifty years.[104] In the "many hundred" of these dreams,[105] Amelia never succeeded in reaching her dream-destination, her old home at Port Ryerse. However, one entry in 1871 records that she had actually got home for the second time in all her dreams, and prompted her to predict that perhaps her third dream-visit would mark her return to where "I may be home in earnest."[106] Clearly, "home" had a dual meaning for Amelia: in one sense, it was a return to a past happiness with lost loved ones; in another it was a future when she would be "at rest" with her loved ones who had gone before. Her reminiscences of Port Ryerse were of a mythic past made up of memories of her childhood, early married years, and her young family.

However much time Amelia may have spent in these reveries

[103]Amelia's diary, 27 September 1859.

[104]Amelia's diary, 16 May 1870. For more on the significance of dreams and their meaning see Sigmund Freud, *The Interpretation of Dreams*, James Strachey (ed.), New York: Avon Books, 1965. Also, Carl G. Jung, *Man and his Symbols*, London: Aldus Books, 1964.

[105]Amelia's diary, 8 January 1871.

[106]*Ibid.*

in her later years, she never ceased to be pragmatic in matters affecting the material well-being of her family. This can be seen in the will she drew up in 1871 to secure the future of Eldon House after her death. That there would be no confusion, she elaborated further on her wishes in a letter to her son, Edward:

> My Dear Edward,
> I have in accordance with the wishes of yourself & George altered my will and have left Eldon House and grounds to you free from all encumbrances . . . it is my wish, should you die without children, either Male or Female, that you should leave Eldon House and grounds to George, should he survive you, if not to one of his children. I should wish Sophie to have possession of the House during her life should she survive you, and should she wish to live here. Should she wish to leave here I should wish her to transfer the place to George or the next heir at a reasonable rental if they chose to take it, in preference to letting any one else have it. I trust to your affection and sense of right to act in this as I wish.
>
> Your affectionate Mother.[107]

Edward replied promptly:

> My dear Mother,
> I think the property – Eldon House – is far better unentailed but the wishes expressed in your letter of the 29th March 1871 will be carried out by me if I have the power to do so.
>
> Your affect. son Ed. W. Harris.[108]

More specifically, Amelia's will left Eldon House and its eleven acres to Edward Harris, ninety-six acres at Port Ryerse to George, twenty-five acres on the outskirts of London to each of her daughters, Sarah, Eliza, Mary and Teresa, and twenty-five acres jointly to the three sons of Helen Portman. Ultimately, by way of a codicil, she left the London property other than Eldon House to Amelia Griffin. Her will also provided for the distribution of her personal belongings.[109]

[107]Harris Papers, Amelia Harris to Edward Harris, 29 March 1871.
[108]Harris Papers, Edward Harris to Amelia Harris, 29 March 1871.
[109]Harris Papers, Amelia Harris' will.

These letters and the will are more indicative of the essential family ties and relationships than are the diary record of the various family disagreements and misunderstandings that marked the stresses of everyday life. This was certainly the case with Edward and Sophie with whom she shared her home in her later years, although her resentment of Sophie's challenge to authority was also accompanied by memories of the traumatic separation a decade earlier. On the other hand, Amelia's relationship with her son George, his wife, Lucy, and their daughter, Milly, had always been harmonious, and it was to their home that she went in May 1877 while Eldon was undergoing renovations. As for her daughter, Amelia Griffin, Amelia felt it necessary to be protective and authoritative in response to the fecklessness of Gilbert Griffin, her unsuccessful son-in-law.

But if we know a great deal about Amelia's relationship with her family in London because of the daily chronicling of events of immediate interest, we know less about her relations with her "English" daughters. There are some diary comments on the receipt of the "English mail" and on their occasional visits to Eldon House. Letters could not substitute for their presence and Amelia frequently commented on how she missed the presence of a daughter in her declining years.[110] Indeed, each of her "English" daughters visited their mother at least once, and Teresa actually returned to Canada five times.[111] But however fond Amelia may have been of her English daughters, she spent little time with them, sustaining a relationship vicariously through their accounts of their lives and travels abroad.

Reality for Amelia was Eldon House where she was surrounded by those who were there when she needed them. In 1873, Amelia recorded her joy at the birth of another Harris baby, George and Lucy's son, George Henry Ronalds. Increasingly, however, she remarked on age and tiredness and began to value dearly her time alone, her happiest evenings being spent by herself with her books and memories. Nevertheless, as late as January 1875, she entertained the thought of travelling to the Peards in England for "summer & remain there" for the rest of

[110]Amelia's diary, 28 August 1859.

[111]The Scotts visited for the last time in 1874 from 16 May to 24 August, William Scott dying a year later on 18 August 1875 while crossing the Red Sea. Teresa remarried in 1877 and returned to visit her mother with her new husband, St. George Littledale, en route to a hunting trip in the Rockies.

her life.[112] Her decision not to act on this impulse had less to do with Edward's approval and George's disapproval than with her own confession that the thought of leaving her home "made me nervous & almost ill."[113]

As we read Amelia's entries year after year, it would appear that the elderly matriarch's ailments were partly caused by anxiety derived from the divisions within the family, which to a mother of Amelia's personality, were hard to accept. Her increasingly frequent bouts of depression were intensified by the discomforts of old age and her confinement to the house and grounds at Eldon. On 19 February 1878, her eightieth birthday, she described the day as a happy one with many visitors, but it was "a great effort to keep up." Nonetheless, receiving visitors, writing letters and making entries in her diary was not all Amelia did in the 1870s. Occasional trips delighted her. An expedition to Niagara Falls with the Griffins, a visit to the Ryersons in Toronto, and one with George to see her brother, Edward, at Port Ryerse were a tonic. The most pleasant of all was a five-week vacation with George and his whole family in the summer of 1879 when they travelled to New York and the seaside at New London, Connecticut. It was an experience, she claimed, that she would never forget.

Throughout the 1870s, Amelia did strive to maintain contacts with those of her friends who had survived, though not with the same frequency as in previous years. The Harris circle had narrowed. Many family members were gone, so were many of her old friends. Her diary tells us how their lives and deaths had affected her. She continued seeing some of those who were close to her, such as Egerton Ryerson, who would visit and often spend Christmas at Eldon House. She still kept herself busy. Indeed, as late as 1879, Ryerson was able to persuade her to extend her "Historical Memorandum" from 1812 to 1814.

The absence of those who had died and of those who had left the nest was particularly noticeable at the Christmas table. At this time of year in particular, Amelia recalled earlier years "when the table was surrounded by bright little faces,"[114] and she commented that "looking back upon past years & the

[112]Amelia's diary, 8 February 1875.
[113]Amelia's diary, 18 March 1875.
[114]Amelia's diary, 25 December 1867.

changes that have taken place brings painful recollections."[115] The occasion had lost its significance for her because the family gathering focussed attention on the absence of the loved ones and many old friends. Reading her diary, we feel that the tone has lost its vitality. In 1879 Lucy organized Christmas dinner at her own home but Amelia declared she was too ill to attend. True or not, it does serve to underscore her withdrawal from all that had once been so important to her.

In the solitude of her last years, Amelia devoted much of her time to recollecting her past. She had been the mother of twelve children. Of her four sons and eight daughters, two sons and three daughters had died, most in tragic circumstances, and they were often in her thoughts. But one of Amelia's greatest regrets in the final years of her life was that she lacked the presence and attention of her surviving daughters. Ironically, she had been partly responsible for this. She had always been ambitious about the future of her seven daughters, and her very success in helping them establish their independence had made her daughterless. Of her five living daughters, four lived abroad. Only Amelia Griffin had stayed in London for much of her life and, in 1880, she too left, moving to Kingston to join her husband who had been transferred to a new position in the Post Office there. Teresa could always be relied upon for excitement with her frequent, albeit brief and unpredictable, visits.

Amelia's latter years were closely interwoven with the lives of her sons' families in London: Edward and Sophie at Eldon House, and George and Lucy at Raleigh House. Indeed, when Edward and Sophie left on a two-month trip to England, Amelia moved into Raleigh House where she enjoyed the vibrant atmosphere of a family with children. Towards the end of Amelia's life, however, Sophie was obliged to spend more time in Toronto with her father, Egerton Ryerson, whose health was also failing. Accordingly, Amelia came to rely more upon George and Lucy for comfort and support and on the 22 December 1881, with Sophie still absent, Amelia returned to Lucy and George at Raleigh House where she was to remain until her death, returning to Eldon House only for her funeral.

[115]Amelia's diary, 25 December 1880.

THE VIEW FROM ELDON HOUSE

Eldon House is a substantial two-storey building, set in an eleven acre lot overlooking the Thames River, located close to what has become downtown London. For much of the nineteenth century, it was the home of the Harris family and, as such, the focal point of the lives of the diarists. The windows of Eldon House were a prism through which they looked out upon the wider world about them. In the diaries, that wider world was often reported upon objectively, but it was more often evaluated in relation to the affairs and interests of the Harris family.

Beyond the bounds of the Eldon property lay the community of London, the broader region of western Ontario, the rest of Ontario and Canada, and the greater world. They exist as a nested set of realities, all centred on the immediate world of Eldon House, and all connected together by the flows of people, correspondence, and news. Taken together, they constitute the action space, the lived-in-world, of the growing urban elite that was emerging throughout Canada in the nineteenth century.

Life at Eldon House

The five diarists provide a detailed chronicle of the domestic and social routine of a relatively well-to-do family living in a small Ontario town in the mid-nineteenth century. Personal activities, family practices, and social customs are placed in a living context centred on one household, Eldon House.[116]

The rooms, verandah, garden and grounds made up the domestic realm of the Harris household and the setting of the daily regimen. Adjacent to the house, stood a building that served originally as a combination barn and hay loft, greenhouse, carriage shed (later a garage), work shop and root cellar. At the

[116]The name of Eldon House is interesting. Family-lore has it that John Harris named his home in honour of Lord Eldon, Lord Chancellor in Lord Liverpool's administration from 1801 to 1827. He continued to be prominent in British political life and Harris was impressed by a speech given by the arch-conservative Eldon at the time of the debates concerning the Reform Bill. For more on Lord Eldon see Anthony L.J. Lincoln and Robert L. McEwen, *Lord Eldon's Anecdote Book*, London: Stevens & Sons, 1960.

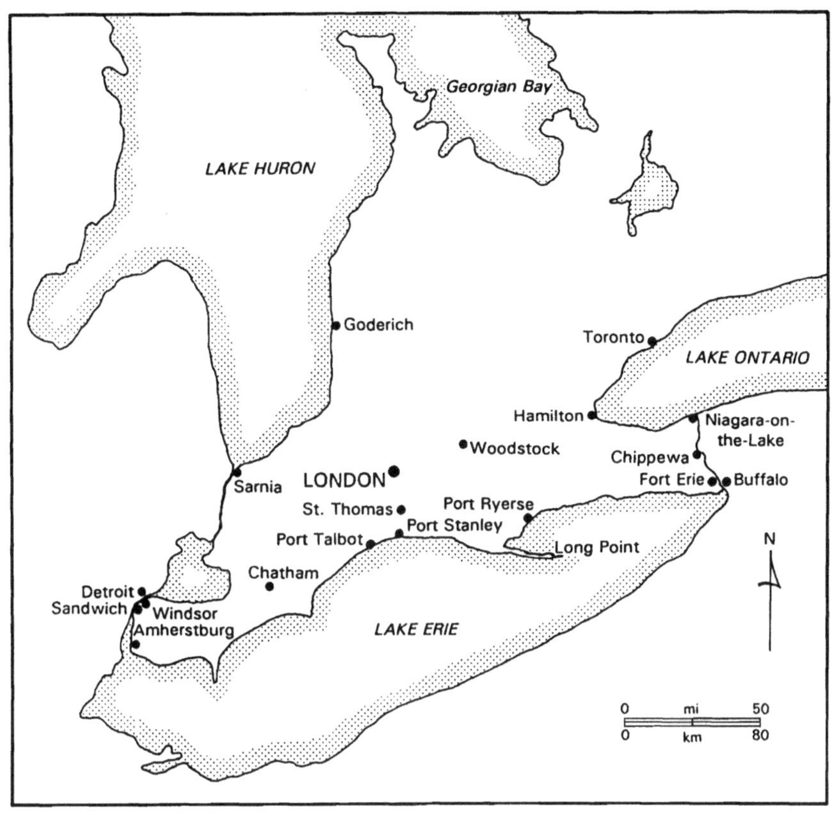

The Harris' Ontario

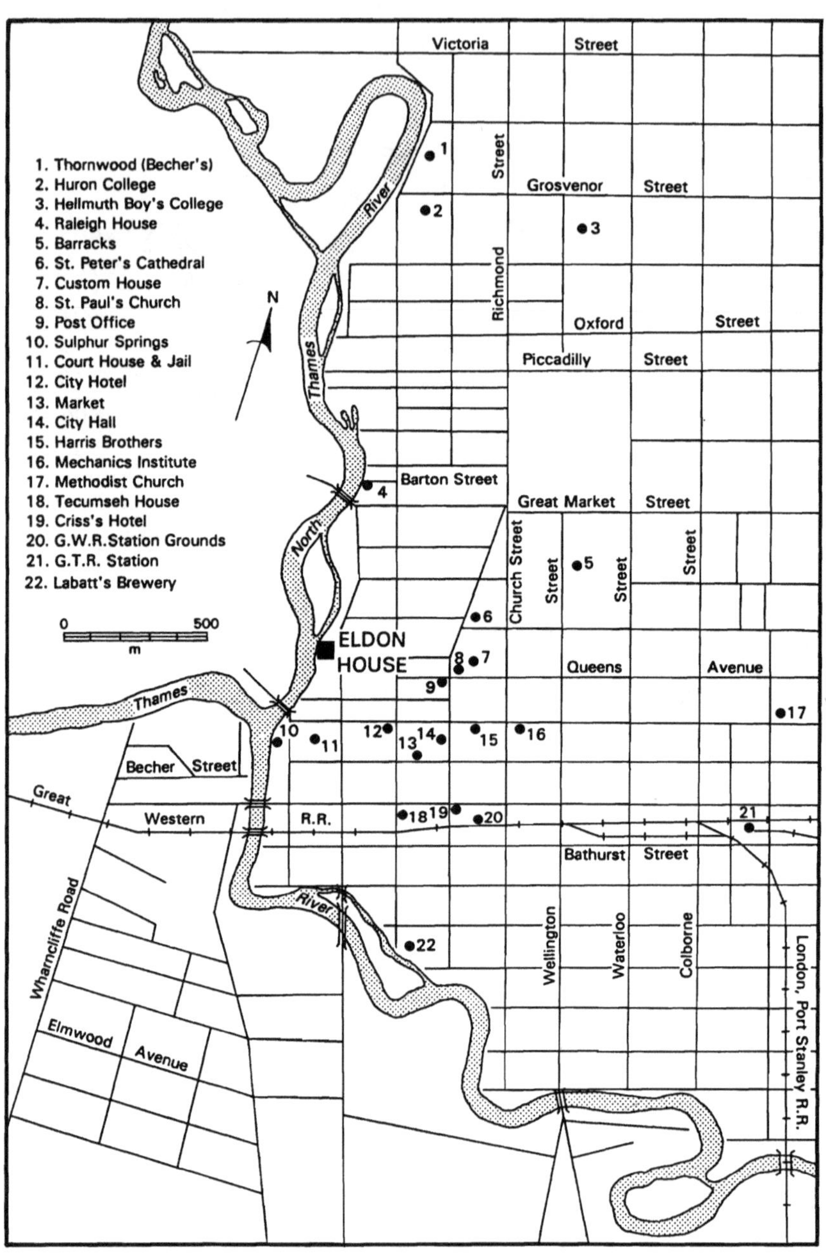

The Harris' London

rear of it, adjacent to the hay loft, was a winter stable for the cows that grazed on the parklands adjoining the river Thames from April to November.[117] These parklands, known for over a century as "The Flats," were crossed by a creek beyond which there was a very large vegetable garden. There was also plenty of space there for the children of the neighbourhood to play baseball and, in the winter, the creek was their ice hockey rink.[118]

The Eldon household, consisting initially of John and Amelia Harris and their ten children, depended normally on the services of four servants: a cook, two housemaids, and a manservant who did the outside work in the garden and stable, and also doubled as coachman. In addition, young boys were sometimes hired for outdoor work. When the family was younger, the Harrises had also retained a governess, Jane Steers. She was not regarded as a servant, however, and returned to stay at Eldon House on several occasions in the 1860s and 1870s. In 1881, Sophie and Edward brought back a cook and butler from England, although Amelia thought the latter to be an unnecessary affectation, commenting that the "butler is a mistake & does not suit our establishment."[119]

During her years as matriarch of Eldon House, Amelia was consistently concerned with the servants' welfare and advised the family that too much entertainment at Eldon was not fair to the staff. By the same token, she was critical of some and praised others. A maid, Nancy Cameron, who had lived with the Harrises for twelve years and whom Amelia considered a friend,[120] died at Eldon House on Christmas Day after being tended by the family.[121] Lucy was also considerate of her servants' needs, letting them attend church on Sundays, and sending her maid, Raquel, to the same "evening school of

[117]This pattern continued until 1937 when high water delayed the annual moving of the cows from the winter stable at street level to the summer pasture on the "Flats." The cows protested in the only way they could, and their irate lowing disturbed the slumber of the neighbours, including those of the incumbent mayor. The result was that the City Council enacted a by-law prohibiting cows from the precincts of London. Needless to say, the Harris family did not support his worship at the next election!

[118]A croquet lawn, grass tennis court, swimming pool, and pitch-and-putt golf course were later additions.

[119]Amelia's diary, 4 June 1881.

[120]Amelia's diary, 23 February 1859.

[121]Amelia's diary, 25 December 1860.

cookery" that she herself, Sophie, and other ladies in town attended. Two of the maidservants married menservants at Eldon House, one of the couples staying at Eldon on their wedding night. It should be noted, however, that Amelia insisted that they not sleep in the same room.

But there is another side to the domestic management of Eldon House. The troubles of hiring and maintaining servants is a frequent theme in Lucy's diary, as are the petty jealousies and disagreements between the members of the house staff. Amelia, more experienced at managing troublesome help, advised Elizabeth to be "very cautious how she listened to reports of Roman Catholic servants against Protestant ones."[122] However, some of the incidents are quite amusing: a wedding where the tipsy servants "pelted them [gentlemen] with bread & potatoes";[123] and a consistently ill-tempered cook, Mrs MacKenzie, who terrorized the household and threatened to quit in the middle of the preparations for Christmas Day.[124] A blacker side of these "disagreeables" is seen when a discharged servant was thought to have "last night cut our cow in a most brutal manner."[125]

Little reference is made of the cost of maintaining and running a household such as that of Eldon House although Henry Becher complained to Amelia that his domestic expenses were between £1,500 and £1,800 a year.[126] None of the Eldon diaries are as specific for their own operation although details of household expenditures at Eldon for the years 1844–49 are listed in one surviving account book.[127] It records quantities and prices of wheat and oats, wages for the servants, pin money for the daughters, and the prices of suits and shoes for the sons. Some sense of the cost of running a contemporary household may be gained from Lucy's diaries which itemize monthly expenditures for Raleigh House. For example, she records that she hired a governess for her children for $30 for three months, her hours being 9.00 a.m. to 1.00 p.m. daily.[128] Lucy also engaged a

[122]Amelia's diary, 12 June 1860.
[123]Amelia's diary, 20 January 1864.
[124]Amelia's diary, 25 December 1878.
[125]Amelia's diary, 11 September 1859.
[126]Amelia's diary, 7 July 1858.
[127]This account book is to be found in the Harris Papers.
[128]Lucy's diary, 26 August 1880.

nurse at $200 a year,[129] and we also learn she gave each of the servants a Christmas box of $2.00 each.[130] Other costs of contemporary domestic operations were listed at the back of several of Lucy's diairies.

Social Life and Entertainment

Together, the five Eldon House diaries present an extended record of social life in a nineteenth century town whose well-to-do inhabitants were conscious of what they considered to be appropriate and proper. Eldon House and the Harrises were very much part of this emerging society. As Treasurer of the London District since 1821, John Harris, together with Colonel J.B. Askin (Clerk of the Peace) and James Hamilton (District Sheriff), was one of the small group of men who constituted what has been called "The London Elite," the local version of the Upper Canadian "Family Compact." The other members of this unofficial but powerful group were Benjamin Cronyn, the resident Church of England minister, the two leading London merchants, George Goodhue and Lawrence Lawrason, and two non-residents, Mahlon Burwell and Colonel Thomas Talbot, both of Port Talbot. John Harris remained one of London's leading citizens throughout his life and the Harris family was prominent in London society during the 1840s and subsequent years.

Much of the social ritual and calendar focussed on homes such as Eldon House. "Visiting" was a required formality to maintain a presence in the social life of the town. On New Year's Day, Eldon House could expect as many as fifty callers.[131] Chasse's comment that "I had to undergo the misery of shaking hands 105 times today" suggests that social prominence and popularity could be a mixed blessing.[132] Others would visit after the evening service at St. Paul's Church, or else make social visits throughout the week. In the early years covered by the diaries when the seven daughters of Eldon House were still not spoken for, admirers and potential suitors were frequent callers.

[129]Lucy's diary, 7 February 1880.

[130]Lucy's diary, 26 December 1877.

[131]Charlotte's diaries record fifty callers in 1849, fifty-two in 1850, but none in 1851 when the Harrises were still in mourning for John Harris.

[132]Charlotte's diary, 1 January 1850.

Members of the military were frequent and prominent callers at homes such as Eldon House. One of the consequences of Mackenzie's uprising in 1837 had been the decision of the British government to station a succession of British regiments at London. They were to be a visible and vital part of the town's society from 1838 until their withdrawal in 1852.[133] Thus, when in 1848, Edward Stanley, the son of a British peer, Lord Stanley, arrived at Eldon House for what proved to be a lengthy stay, six young British officers called.[134] But they did not call to see Stanley, whom they had never met. Three of them called again on the following day: Shuldham Peard, was unofficially engaged to Mary Harris; Arundell Neave was a suitor of her twin sister, Eliza; and Edward Lutyens, a close friend of both Peard and Neave, was to call at Eldon at least fifty times in the following three years. No wonder Amelia and others regretted the prospect of the withdrawal of the British garrison. In 1862, George and some of the departing officers prevailed upon her to host a party at Eldon House following a grand military review that attracted some 30,000 spectators.[135] Clearly, many Londoners shared in Amelia's lament that "London will be very dull without the red coats."[136]

Visitors were offered tea and refreshments, occasionally wine or spirits, and there was piano music, singing, and impromptu dancing – but not on Sundays. And, however disagreeable or traumatic the domestic events throughout the 1850s, the day usually closed with the entry, "We played euchre." Actually, a remarkable number of card games were played including whist, euchre, loo, monte, and bezique, as well as backgammon, and chess. Amelia Harris appears to have enjoyed a reputation of being proficient in chess and Julius Airey refers to her prowess in a letter in 1841:

> I hope that since I left, you have all been well, and the baby less troublesome . . . and that you have beaten poor Haddon constantly at chess. Do try your hand against Dr Dartnell, who is held up as a *scarecrow* and give him one thorough defeat, so

[133]See Fred Landon, "British Regiments in London," *Western Ontario Historical Notes*, Vol. 13, No. 3, 1955, pp. 5–9.

[134]Charlotte's diary, 22 October 1848.

[135]Amelia's diary, 6 September 1864.

[136]Amelia's diary, 12 September 1864.

as to prove your preeminence over all your foes. I should be very glad to hear of your beating him![137]

There were also formal dances, and Charlotte describes one given by the George Goodhues.[138] It was the subject of a scathing sermon in St. Paul's the next day, the Reverend Benjamin Cronyn likening it to Belshazzar's Feast.[139]

After Sophie joined the household at Eldon House, there was a great deal more music. She played the piano well and frequently performed after dinner. In the 1870s, she organized a number of musicales. The first of these was described by Amelia as "entertainment of the meekest kind," but some other adjective would have to be used to describe the one held in 1877 when she had over a hundred acceptances.[140] Sophie and Edward were fond of dinner parties but Amelia rarely joined them on such occasions. Sophie once organized a small dance at Eldon House for thirty-five guests, and she, Edward, and George occasionally attended the "Bachelors Ball," dances organized by one of the regiments, and the Government House Balls in Toronto. Amelia Harris attended her last ball on 10 February 1859, when she agreed to be patroness at one held at the Tecumseh House. However, Amelia continued to make comments on the changes in the social scene, and her opinion of them. Of a dance given by one of the regiments she observed, "very few gentlemen & still fewer ladies, though there were plenty of people."[141] And of a Masonic Ball attended by Lucy and George Harris three months before her death, "it is a new generation that now fills the ball room."[142]

But if the members of the self-defined elite were anxious to ensure that London society conformed to the social practices and decorum that befitted their rank, there were occasional short-

[137]Julius Airey to Amelia Harris, 11 September 1840. Quoted in Honor de Pencier, *Posted to Canada: The Watercolours of George Russell Dartnell, 1835–1844*, Toronto: Dundurn Press, 1987, p. 61.

[138]Charlotte's diary, 9 December 1848.

[139]The most notable dance at Eldon House occurred in 1843. At approximately 8.00 p.m., the ghost of one of Sarah's suitors arrived; he had been drowned after falling off his horse at 6.00 p.m. the same evening. See W.T. Stead, (ed.) *Real Ghost Stories*, Christmas Number of the *Review of Reviews*, November 1891, p. 67.

[140]Amelia's diary, 29 December 1877.

[141]Amelia's diary, 31 October 1862.

[142]Amelia's diary, 30 December 1881.

comings. It was a society that celebrated petty slights, imagined or real. Frequent rounds of visiting ensured rapid flows of information, and gossip nurtured byzantine intrigues and scandals. Redress was sought by a variety of strategies ranging from "cutting" and ostracization, to black-eyes, horse-whipping, and even duelling.[143] At various times throughout her diaries Amelia condoned such actions to defend the family honour. She did, however, draw the line where matters of the heart were concerned commenting, "Any man is a fool that fights a duel for a false or frivolous woman."[144]

More public, albeit less exciting, entertainments in London in the late 1840s took the form of lectures given at the Mechanics' Institute, and frequently the lecturer stayed overnight at Eldon House.[145] In the early 1840s officers of the First Royals were responsible for establishing a theatre in London, but the diaries do not disclose how successful it was. Things improved in the 1860s: more public lectures; regularly scheduled band concerts; in 1859 Edward and George attended the first opera presentation in London;[146] amateur and professional theatre; theatrical readings by the likes of Mrs. Sarah Siddons; visiting circuses, vaudeville, Japanese jugglers, and Christie's Minstrels. The city now had a skating rink where professionals periodically performed and an annual carnival was held there. There were also steamboat excursions on the Thames River, although its pleasures turned to tragedy in 1881 with the sinking of the *Victoria* in ten feet of water with the loss of over 200 lives.[147]

When not entertaining or socializing elsewhere, the members of the Harris family turned their attentions to other activities. Two merit particular attention. First, the arrival of the mail, and especially the "English" mail, was an important event. The maintenance of family links across the Atlantic was sustained by much letter writing as is evidenced in the considerable collection in the Harris Papers. The second important activity was reading contemporary British novels, current British magazines, and the

[143] Amelia's diary refers to the threatened horse-whipping of Edward Ermatinger (7 October 1859), Dr. Anderson (16 April 1860), and Captain Hewitt (6 January 1863). Duelling, or "calling out," was suggested as an option too (Charlotte's diary, 7 November 1848 and 18 January 1849; Amelia's diary, 6 January 1863).

[144] Amelia's diary, 19 November 1862.

[145] Ralph Waldo Emerson stayed at Eldon House on such a visit in 1854.

[146] Amelia's diary, 2 July 1859.

[147] Amelia's diary, 25 May 1881.

local newspaper. Many of the British novels mentioned by Charlotte – Dickens', *David Copperfield*, Thackeray's *Pendennis*, Bronte's *Wildfell Hall*, Scott's *Waverley*, (some of them borrowed from officer friends) – were read in monthly paperback installments. The diaries do not refer to any newspaper other than the *Times* of London but after the establishment of the *London Free Press* in December 1851 they had access to a local journal.[148]

Much of the social activity was conducted in the outdoors. Several diary entries report that the men of the family indulged in bass or trout fishing at Dorchester, five miles east of London, and in spear fishing on the Thames River, as well as hunting farther afield. "Pic-nics" were always mixed parties and usually involved musical entertainment or dancing. Sketching parties, again usually mixed, were to scenic places in London or its immediate vicinity and James Hamilton, a local bank manager, and Captain J.H. Caddy, both assisted the Harris children with technical advice on painting and criticism of their work.[149]

A grass tennis court was laid out below the Eldon House hill in the 1870s but was not heavily utilized. The most popular sport for the Harris family was croquet and from the 1860s on was a prominent feature of summertime at Eldon. It was also hotly pursued at Thornwood, Henry Becher's home further north on the river, and there was much rivalry – resulting in some "disagreeables" – between the two families.[150] A charming, if ponderous, piece of doggerel composed by Gilbert Griffin, reflects the enthusiasm for the game, and affords an opportunity to identify some of the characters in the Eldon House circle:[151]

Now, from the small room's window,
Could the dear Mother spy
The lines of combat all drawn out,
Whereof the least was I

[148]On 2 January 1849, William Sutherland published the first issue of the *Canadian Free Press* which was sold to Josiah Blackburn in 1852 to become the *London Free Press*. See Armstrong, 1986, *op. cit.* p. 80.

[149]James Hamilton (1810–96) was General Manager of the London branch of the Bank of Upper Canada; Captain John Herbert Caddy (1801–83), an officer in the Royal Engineers, settled in London and became the first City Engineer.

[150]Amelia's diary, 17–27 June 1865.

[151]Harris Papers, "Croquet, A Macaulay Flower, (Which can't be beet), Cabbaged by G. [Griffin], London, Canada West, 1863."

The Mother wise of Eldon,
She sat there still and smiled,
And tea and cakes distributed,
And thus the time beguiled.

Then outspake Georgius Harris
A Horseman bold was he!
"And keep the goal with thee;
For ne'er yet, in lady's quarrel,
Spared I either land or gold;
Not having wife, I reck not life,
As in the brave days of old!"

Then Galloway croque'd Boyoh
Up to the Tree of Pears,
Went to Plummer for repairs;
Then Griffin miss'd a croquet,
And loud the shouts arose
Of "Deary me! how stupid!"
From all the "dear man's" foes.

When Grandma is mending a stocking,
And George is reading Punch;
When Ned is quietly rocking,
And G. comes into lunch;
With joking and with laughter,
Still is the story told,
How the fair Leslie won the game
In the brave days of old.

Two team sports became popular in London in the 1860s. Cricket (said to have been introduced by Henry Becher shortly after his arrival from England in 1835) was played initially on the Eldon House Flats. George Harris was an avid cricketer, playing against several visiting sides, including "England's Eleven."[152] It was not to be the game of the future, however, and by 1878 Londoners were celebrating Queen Victoria's birthday with baseball games, the local "Tecumseh Club" being beaten by visitors from Buffalo.[153] But curling would continue,

[152]Amelia's diary, 17 October 1859.
[153]Amelia's diary, 24 May 1878.

early venues being coves along the Thames River and George Harris added this sport to his athletic portfolio.

Courtship, Betrothal, and Marriage

The social prominence of the Harrises and the central location and size of Eldon House do much to explain the social activity there. Another factor was that at the time of John Harris' death, eight of his ten children were still living at home. The search for appropriate partners for these seven girls and three boys was to be one of Amelia Harris' life-projects. Indeed, courtship, betrothal, and marriage are a major preoccupation of most of the Eldon House diarists.[154] Amelia must have experienced a combination of relief, pride, and satisfaction when she declared of Teresa in 1859, "I went to chaperone the last Miss Harris for the last time."[155]

Viewed from the perspective of love and happiness, they are private and personal matters. In nineteenth-century Ontario society, however, it was a matter not left to the young people alone; it was regarded as a significant event in which the parents had their duties to perform. One of these self-appointed duties was to assist young lovers in looking to the future to consider the social, economic, and personal implications of possible matches. It was assumed that their own judgement would be clouded by inexperience and the flame of passion. The advice of parents and other elders was thought to be a parental prerogative in dealing with the perplexities of this emotional period. Certainly, Amelia exercised her prerogative without stint in the Harris household.

Being judged "eligible" was a matter of some importance and social standing, intelligence, "prospects," and good looks were not unimportant prerequisites for approval. Amelia was as

[154]The diaries of Chasse, Amelia, Sophie, and Lucy all provide much information on courtship, marriage, and the trials of adapting to a new life, pregnancy, and of raising children. Apart from the Harris family, they also comment on the marriages of several friends and associates, while Amelia's diary refers to the amatory problems faced by young women and men who continually sought her advice. Also, the letters in the Harris Papers contain a wealth of material on courtship and marriage in the nineteenth century. For more on this subject see Peter Ward, *Courtship, Love, and Marriage in Nineteenth Century English Canada*, Montreal and Kingston: McGill-Queen's University Press, 1990.

[155]Amelia's diary, 4 August 1859.

gratified that Helen was beautiful as she was concerned that Teresa was thought to be homely. Indeed, her brother Edward's somewhat unkind comment on Teresa was that his mother would be "clever" if she could "marry her off."[156] As ever, Amelia had firm views on the matter: a "good wife" should be industrious, prudent, and economical; the preferred male qualities were "a good profession, health, youth and energy."[157]

While waiting for their future matches, trips to towns in the vicinity of London gave young people opportunities to meet friends, as did various private and public events in their own community. There was also a domestic regimen: the young ladies of the household entertained themselves by playing the piano, singing, dancing, telling stories; they sewed and made "jelly"; they nursed those who were ill. Horseback riding, sleighing and other outdoor entertainments consumed their physical energy, reading and writing letters enhanced their social skills and honed their wit. Chasse amused herself by keeping a diary, while Eliza and John enjoyed painting.[158] Strolling, visiting and gossiping were also ways of passing the time. As the diaries reveal, London was still very much a small town in which little went unnoticed and where everyone's problems were everyone else's.

Being the home of ten young people, there were always enough family members to improvise entertainment, but a shortage of visitors was never a concern. With its array of young people of marriageable age, Eldon House was a popular location for social gatherings and entertainment – provided one respected the social proprieties of visitation and invitation. It was not difficult for the young women at Eldon House to get acquainted with the British officers of "Garrison London." These single, lonely, and eligible men in barracks were prominent members of the London social scene and frequent visitors at Eldon House. Indeed, four of the Harris girls met their partners among those officers while the civilians who found Harris partners had been introduced as friends of visiting officers.

Matchmaking was a common procedure, young men and women meeting their partners through friends or members of the

[156] Harris Papers, Edward's "Key to the Diary of Charlotte Harris."

[157] Amelia's diary, 1 June 1863.

[158] A good example of Eliza's accomplishments as an artist is demonstrated by one of her works, "Moving Day."

family. An organized riding party or an invitation for tea or dinner could be an excuse to introduce two people to each other. But there was a danger of being thought to be overzealous in these matters. Thus, Mrs. Loring, Elizabeth's mother, expressed the view that the Harrises were "all incorrigible matchmakers" and she cautioned her daughter against her suitor, John Harris, who was said to be looking "for a wife with money."[159] The parents of such girls who were possessed of property and income were naturally suspicious of the motives of intending suitors. In Mrs. Loring's case, her anxiety was appeased by John's sincere demonstrations of affection for Elizabeth. For their part, the Harris family could not have been indifferent to Sophie's intelligence that her friend from Toronto was "a very nice girl with £1,000 a year."[160]

In upper class families, although not required by law, parental approval of a match was essential. Given propitious signs during courtship, and following informal enquiries through family and friends, the prospective suitor approached the woman's family for permission to marry. In some cases, the progress from courtship to proposal to betrothal was remarkably speedy: John Harris proposed for Elizabeth only one month after meeting her,[161] while George Harris escorted Lucy to a band concert on 29 September, and proposed seven days later.[162] However, no matter how receptive a woman might have been to her admirer's advances, the nineteenth century ritual of matchmaking required the formality whereby the man approached the woman's parents or guardian to make his official proposal, and await their decision.

While often deferring to their daughter's wishes, in many instances the parents exercised a great influence on the final decision.[163] But it would be a mistake to think that these nineteenth century women only married a man chosen and approved by their parents, or that men made the choice and that a woman's initiative was restricted to acceptance or rejection. Men were encouraged or discouraged in their approaches; they

[159]Amelia's diary, 19 May 1859.

[160]Amelia's diary, 22 February 1859, refers to the communication from Sophie to Teresa.

[161]Amelia's diary, 27 May and 27 June 1859.

[162]Amelia's diary, 30 September–8 October 1866.

[163]See Amelia's diary, 30 May 1859.

were given indications of their possible acceptance or not; and women could, and did, reject suitors.[164] Indeed, young women were not always passive subjects in this choreography of emotion and economics. In the case of Elizabeth Loring, when wooed by two suitors, a Mr. Jackson and John Harris, she took steps to encourage John. The spurned lover "rode off in a fury and went through the streets like a madman."[165] Even Amelia Harris appears to have respected her daughters' wishes in those affairs that she suspected were more of the heart than of the brain. She confided her fears to her diary – and, thus, to other family members as well as Teresa:

> I am very much afraid that Teresa will make a mistake and refuse him [Scott] without any good reason, and if she does I can read her future but too plainly. She will by and by form an attachment to some young fellow that will take her fancy and marry as she will think to please herself and place herself in a position in which she will never be happy.[166]

That Sophie was not passive in pursuing relationships was all too evident to the Harris family, as well as to contemporary society in London and Toronto.

However, while flirting and courting were socially acceptable tactics to attract suitors, any woman who had more than one suitor at any one time would be chastised for having "too many strings to her bow."[167] However innocent it may have been thought to have been, inappropriate actions could destroy reputations, and families and the community were much concerned about the conduct of young people – especially that of "young ladies." As for married women, Amelia's diary chronicles the misfortunes that befell Sophie because of her relationship with Hewitt, and admonished her: "Young married women cannot be too cautious in avoiding remark."[168] The conduct of another married women prompted Amelia to conclude

[164]See Amelia's diary for further details, especially 22 February, 17 March, 25 April, 8 May 1859.

[165]Amelia's diary, 12 May 1859. Jackson was a civilian friend of the officers as were Maurice Portman and William Scott.

[166]Amelia's diary, 8 March 1859.

[167]Amelia's diary, 22 January 1859.

[168]Amelia's diary, 21 June 1862.

that "she has walked so near the precipice that it is difficult to believe that she has not made a step over it."[169]

In some cases, however, a proposal could be made over the head of the young woman concerned and come as a complete surprise to her. This was the case with Teresa Harris when William Scott asked for her hand in marriage in a letter addressed to her brother, John, in his capacity as male head of the family.[170] While the whole Harris family – on both sides of the Atlantic – pondered the matter, Teresa continued to meet with Scott under carefully chaperoned circumstances, and it was clearly understood that both parties were free to withdraw from the proposed match.

The final decision was based on a careful evaluation of the suitor's personal integrity, social standing, financial status, and even his health, personality, and attractiveness. Age does not seem to have figured much in the decision. At a time when, much more than is the case today, the man was expected to be the older partner, three of the Harris women were senior to their suitors; Eliza was three years older than Crutchley, Mary four years older than Peard, and Teresa twelve years older than her second husband.[171]

Whatever the concern with such personal qualities, the principal criteria were financial status and social standing. Amelia was the first to accept that the approval and, hopefully blessing, of the suitor's family were important to the success of a match. She did recognize, however, that blessings alone would not bring happiness and commented frequently on the importance of the financial position of potential suitors, if tempered by other considerations. Thus, Amelia had had serious doubts about her feelings towards William Scott, Teresa's suitor. Though rich and well-mannered, she found him to be ugly, or at least "the reverse of handsome."[172] Amelia did not consider "beauty an essential feature"; her paramount concern was that "money alone will not make people happy. But money excludes a great deal of unhappiness."[173] No wonder some anxious

[169]Amelia's diary, 6 August 1865.

[170]Amelia's diary, 27 February 1859.

[171]It is worth commenting that the Harris sons married relatively late for this period at between twenty-eight and thirty-two years. The reasons may have been financial, establishing their sisters, or at least in George's case, an enthusiasm for sports.

[172]Amelia's diary, 27 February 1859.

[173]Amelia's diary, 18 March 1859.

suitors resorted to offering appropriate gifts to the woman and members of the family to gain their good will. But this could back-fire – even on St. Valentine's Day.[174]

Not content with their own assessments, families turned to friends and associates in their investigations of the character and background of the suitor. If there were doubts, further enquiries would be made by letters to members of family and friends, and even by recourse to private detectives.[175] That all of Amelia's sons-in-law were British, had posed a particular problem for the matriarch in her long-distance investigations into their background and eligibility. In the case of Teresa's suitor, Scott, the subject was put on hold until information arrived from England to enable the family to make a judgement.

Similarly, the consent and blessing from the suitor's family was often obtained by prolonged transatlantic correspondence. Thus, while Amelia Harris authorized Helen's engagement to Maurice Portman, it was subject to the approval of his parents, Lord and Lady Portman, who subsequently wrote to John, Helen's oldest brother:

> My son Maurice has discussed with me his projected marriage with your sister Miss Helen Harris and as I trust the alliance is fully approved by your family . . . you will kindly notify me what are your wishes as to any Marriage Settlement being made . . . Maurice has about £4,000 of his own which is invested in Canada . . . and I am able to place £6,000 min[imum] at his disposal on his Marriage. . . . I hope, if I live, to be able to add to Maurice's fortune.[176] . . .

Clearly, this had all the makings of an acceptable arrangement.

Even after such rigorous scrutiny, once accepted, the anxious suitor often had to endure the parents' expression of happiness, apprehensions about the match, and their advice on the uncertainties of life.[177] However, with parental consent and blessing, the wedding date was set, the couple was officially recognized

[174]Amelia's diary, 14 February 1859.

[175]Amelia's diary, 27 March 1859, 1, 12, 19, 30 April, 14 June 1859.

[176]Harris Papers, Lord Portman to John Harris, 7 March 1856.

[177]In Edward Harris' case, he was required to endure Egerton Ryerson's commentary on the affect his deafness would have on a career in politics, and on the wisdom of staying out of politics altogether. See Amelia's diary, 8 November 1859.

as "affianced," and the preparations commenced for the wedding. But during the engagement family and friends continued imposing their demands and restrictions on the couple's attitude and actions. Not only did the parents exercise their influence on a young woman's decision about her future husband, social conventions also had to be taken into consideration. Amelia Harris reports on the humiliation of Henry Becher, a close friend of the family, when his daughter married during his absence.[178] In the case of another unfortunate woman, the weight of social convention and public opprobium was even more dramatic as it resulted in her suicide.[179] Society expected its young people to follow its customs and traditions and could be cruel when they failed to do so.

Being engaged to an officer could be particularly trying as postings to another city or country could result in lengthy, or even broken, engagements. For example, four days after his proposal to Charlotte, Captain Frank Campbell departed for England, promising to return to marry her and take her home with him to New Zealand. During their long separation, Charlotte prayed that God would "bless & prosper" her lover: he may have been blessed and prospered, but he never returned.[180]

Another cause of a broken engagement could be an unsatisfactory "wedding settlement." Just as the financial resources of a prospective suitor were crucial to the betrothal, so were the terms of the disposition of property and allowances. Details of the settlement were established before the wedding took place and a disagreement over the terms could jeopordize the marriage. Thus, Lucy and George's engagement nearly foundered. Eventually, Amelia was able to record with some satisfaction that the engagement was on again as "Lucy shall have her money settled upon herself" and that in the event of Lucy's death, George was "to have the income during his life."[181]

But the fact that Helen married without a settlement did not bother the mother since Maurice himself had "promised that she should be suitably provided for as his wife either by his father's

[178]Amelia's diary, 17 January 1872.
[179]Amelia's diary, 17, 18, 25 December 1857.
[180]Charlotte's diary, 1 August 1850, and subsequent entries.
[181]Amelia's diary, 21–22 May, 15 June 1867.

will or his own."[182] Maurice's father, Lord Portman, had also given his own assurances: "The absence of Marriage Settlements is no evil in my view; the laws of England and Canada effectively provide for a Widow and Children when the estate is personal, and we hope that Life is before them and that Death is the more remote event."[183] . . . Ironically, Helen died four years later.[184]

With all the preliminaries taken care of, preparations for the wedding began. Overwhelmed by her daughter's happiness and her own, Amelia expressed her feelings on the forthcoming marriage of her oldest daughter in a letter to her brother Edward Ryerse: "We are all in a state of the greatest excitement. Sarah is to be married . . . he is going to take her to England, Ireland, Scotland and all over the Continent. . . . You can easily imagine what a state of confusion we are in with all her things to get ready."[185] She was to exhibit less enthusiasm for her sons' weddings, however. The explanation is suggested on the occasion of George's marriage: "I felt very sorry to see George married. . . . They are now all off and no longer mine in the same sense that they were."[186]

The wedding ceremony, the climax of all plans and preliminaries, was normally performed at the bride's home. The diaries record subtle differences. Amelia Harris described Helen and Maurice Portman's wedding ceremony at Eldon House in a letter to Lady Portman:

> My dear Lady Portman.
>
> The day was beautiful, and everything went off well. As all my daughters had been married at home, I wished Helen to be married here also. Very few people in this country are married in church. We had not a very large party, about thirty guests, Mr Portman's friends and our own. Mr Portman was in a great state of excitement. He got up at 4 AM to be in a readiness at 12 – Helen looked very subdued. . . . At half past twelve the Rev'd Dr [Benjamin] Cronyn arrived – a few minutes after his arrival my son led Helen into the Drawing Room accompanied by her four

182 Harris Papers, Amelia Harris to Lady Portman, 7 June 1856.
183 Harris Papers, letter from Lord Portman to Amelia Harris, 27 March 1856.
184 Amelia's diary, 15 April 1860.
185 Harris Papers, Amelia Harris to Edward Ryerse, 9 August 1846.
186 Amelia's diary, 5 September 1867.

brides maids – Mr Portman was awaiting her there, . . . soon [they] were pronounced man and wife.[187]

The letter continues with a description of Helen's dress and flowers, Portman's speech which was greatly applauded, and reports how much he was loved by all at Eldon House. It also gives a vivid picture of the newly married couple's prospects for the future and encloses a copy of the marriage certificate.

The account of Lucy's wedding at Windsor was reported on with less approval by the matriarch. She looked with some disdain upon the event: "The guests were not very distinguished looking. They looked like a good sort of countryside people . . . "; the bride and the bridesmaids dresses were subjected to her scrutiny; she implied displeasure at wedding breakfast served in "Yankee fashion." However, she did express admiration, and even a touch of envy, at a valuable piece of inherited jewelry worn by the bride, "a set of pearls that had descended to her from her grand mother, they were worth over £200."[188]

Elizabeth's Toronto wedding was attended by a hundred guests and the bride made her mark in Amelia's eyes with a dress that cost £70.[189] Amelia reports that the wedding was elaborate and well organized, and everything done with good taste – but she was critical of the practice of displaying the wedding presents.

Niagara Falls and the eastern seaboard were favourite locations for honeymooning couples in the nineteenth century, but the United States, Europe, and even more exotic destinations figured in the plans of the more affluent. Teresa and Littledale went to Kashmir for their long honeymoon,[190] while Lucy and George went on an extended trip to England and France.[191]

Upon returning from their honeymoon, husband and wife began life afresh, bringing their dreams and hopes for the future into their new home.[192] It was the time to face the realities of

[187]Harris Papers, Amelia Harris to Lady Portman, 7 June 1856.

[188]Amelia's diary, 5 September 1867.

[189]Amelia's diary, 9 November 1859.

[190]Amelia's diary, 17 February 1877.

[191]Amelia's diary, 5 September 1867.

[192]Eldon House was large enough to accommodate more than one family at once and several of the Harris children commenced their married life there. Edward and Sophie lived there permanently until George, Lucy and their family took possession of the house after Amelia Harris' death.

life. That not all of the matches at Eldon House were happy ones prompted the remark, "[t]here are but too many unsuitable marriages."[193]

Religion and Politics

A good precept for polite social intercourse is to avoid the discussion of two potentially inflamatory topics: religion and politics. Luckily, the diarists did not follow this principle too closely.

Indeed, it is symbolic that the first four words in the first of the Eldon diaries should be "[w]e went to Church," we being the entire Harris family.[194] Religion occupied a central position in the lives of both John and Amelia Harris. During his service in the Royal Navy, John had a religious experience which converted him from sceptic to convinced Christian. Amelia's parents were Episcopalian United Empire Loyalists, and though there was no Church of England parish in the Long Point Settlement until the 1820s, she was an Anglican all her life.

In 1838, four years after moving to London, John Harris was one of six local worthies who petitioned the Bishop of Quebec for the consecration of an Anglican church in London, St. Paul's, situated a quarter mile from Eldon House. For her part, Amelia was active in providing her home community, Port Ryerse, with a suitable place of worship. One of her life-long wishes was fulfilled when the present Anglican Church at Port Ryerse, constructed on land donated for that purpose by her father in 1795, was consecrated in 1870.[195] A year earlier she had successfully solicited donations for the construction of the church from such local worthies as Donald McInnes, George Goodhue, Edward Blake, Casimir Gzowski, and Thomas Street, none of whom had any connection with Port Ryerse, although they were all well acquainted with Amelia and the Eldon household.[196]

As committed Christians, Amelia and John Harris ensured that all their children were baptized as members of the Church of

[193]Amelia's diary, 29 September 1864.
[194]Charlotte's diary, 22 October 1848.
[195]Amelia's diary, 5 July 1870.
[196]Amelia's diary, 17 July 1869.

England. Thus, some or all of the Harrises were in the Harris pew at the morning service for each of first ten Sundays recorded in Charlotte's diary for 1848. On eight of these, two or more of the daughters, accompanied by two or more young officers, were also at the evening service, following which the officers escorted the girls back to Eldon House and spent the evening "with us." While the Harris attendance record was rarely as regular as this, this general pattern continued for the next three years: the whole family except those who were ill went to the morning service, two or three of the older girls and as many officers to the evening service, followed by supper for all at Eldon House.

Clearly, during these years, church attendance was as much an aspect of social life of the Harris family as it was of their spiritual well-being. However, the later period referred to in Amelia's diary reveals a different pattern. The household was now smaller and Amelia and Teresa, the one unmarried daughter remaining at Eldon House, were the only regular church-goers. Even they were only present at morning service, which they attended about half the time. The rest of the family were even more lax in their devotions prompting Amelia to comment "with sorrow" that "[a]t one time all of my family that were old enough used to attend the Sacrament table, now only Amelia, Teresa & myself, and occasionally John."[197]

The importance of the sacrament to Amelia Harris is apparent in her own diary, from 1857 through to 1882. Amelia was genuinely devout. Her children though regular church-goers could not be so described. On the other hand, her three daughters-in-law, Elizabeth Loring (on the evidence of her letters), and Sophie Ryerson and Lucy Ronalds (on the evidence of their journals) were strong believers. The sons were, at best, only nominal Christians, although all three of them were active participants in the affairs of St. Paul's Church and the Diocese of Huron.[198]

While the religious dedication of the Harris family may have varied between members, their social connection with leading church figures in the community was strong. Benjamin Cronyn,

[197]Amelia's diary, 5 June 1859.

[198]The diocese of Toronto was subdivided in 1857, thus establishing the new diocese of Huron.

the first rector of St. Paul's Church, was a close friend of the Harrises since at least 1834, and performed the marriage service for six of the seven Harris daughters. Amelia's diary records with pride his consecration as Bishop of Huron at Lambeth Palace in London, England in 1857.[199] Cronyn's successor in 1872 was Isaac Hellmuth and he and his wife also became members of the Harris family circle.

As Amelia grew older she found it increasingly difficult to attend St. Paul's. Nevertheless, her faith and interest in spiritual matters continued to be strong to the end. On virtually every Sunday in the 1860s and 1870s, her diary records her devotions by entries such as, "I read the service in my own room," or "I read Dr. [Isaac] Watts' sermons."

Despite – or because of – her husband's long career as a public servant and active role in municipal and provincial affairs, politics do not seem to have interested Amelia. "I dislike elections and have a good reason to do so," she asserted during Maurice Portman's campaign.[200] In fact she and the other diarists only comment on candidates and elections in detail when they relate to their family and friends. Fortunately, there were several instances of this as many notables and leading political figures of the day were passing acquaintances, if not confidantes, and Amelia's diary refers to many of them.[201] Most of the word pictures produced by Amelia are miniatures rather than full portrait studies but they often capture the essentials. Thus, while she consistently misspelled John A. Macdonald's name, she did provide lively vignettes of him: "He is a clever man whose moral character I despise."[202] Or again:

> This is the conversation of J.A. Macdonald *sober*. He condemns and despises what in drunkeness and debauchery he gives himself

[199]Amelia's diary, 15 November 1857. Sophie and Egerton Ryerson were present at this ceremony.

[200]Amelia's diary, 9 March 1860.

[201]The following is a sample of politicians referred to in Amelia's diary: George Brown (31 May 1879); John Hillyard Cameron (15 November 1876); Malcolm Cameron (1 June 1876); Francis Hincks (6 July 1858, 21 April 1859, 16 July 1872); Allan MacNab (9 August 1862); John A. Macdonald (14 July 1860, 16 July 1872); John Sandfield Macdonald (31 June 1863, 18 January, 17 February, 19 December 1871). The diary also refers to two Governor Generals: Lord Elgin (29 December 1863) and Sir Edmund Head (2, 5–7 July 1858).

[202]Amelia's diary, 16 August 1862.

up to. How melancholy that men of sense and talent, who know the right, will yet choose the wrong.[203] . . .

However, two public figures are the subject of Amelia's close and illuminating scrutiny: Egerton Ryerson and John Wilson.

Egerton Ryerson was Amelia's life-long friend, who apart from being a cousin and former schoolmate, was the father-in-law of her son, Edward. As such, he was heavily involved in the problems which faced the couple during their courtship, and for the first twenty years of their marriage. Ryerson's posthumous autobiography portrays an austere and rather humourless man, and attention was directed more to his public role and image than to his private life.[204] The publication of his letters to his daughter, Sophie, revealed a more complex human being as well as a gifted educational administrator and a devoted churchman.[205] The portrait that emerges from Amelia's accounts of his interaction with the Harris household adds another dimension. In her eyes, at least, he was an opinionated, often bad-tempered, troubled man, if also loving and warm-hearted. This suggests that still another re-assessment of Ryerson may be in order.

John Wilson was another friend of the Harris household for over thirty years, and was largely responsible for Sophie and Edward's reconciliation. He is a relatively unknown figure in Canadian history despite being a three-term Member of Parliament, a commissioner on the inquiry into the cost of the Government Buildings at Ottawa (1863–64), and the presiding judge at the trial of the sixteen Fenians who were charged with sedition in 1867. Indeed, he very nearly became Premier of Canada West in 1854.[206] His close relationship with Amelia Harris is evident throughout her diary but particularly in her description of their last meeting.[207]

The most detailed commentary about matters political in the Eldon diaries are Amelia's and Sophie's accounts of Maurice

[203]Amelia's diary, 18 August 1862.

[204]Egerton Ryerson, *The Story of My Life*, 1883, edited by his life-long assistant J. George Hodgins.

[205]See C.B. Sissons, *My Dearest Sophie: Letters from Egerton Ryerson to his Daughter*, Toronto: Ryerson Press, 1955.

[206]See Colin Read, "John Wilson," *Dic. Can. Biog.* IX, pp. 843–844.

[207]Amelia's diary, 17 April 1869.

Portman's brief political career. Portman had been invited to stand as Conservative candidate for the East Riding of the County of Middlesex when the incumbent, Marcus Talbot, was rumoured to have perished while crossing the Atlantic.[208] Portman was reluctant to do so on two accounts: his interest in investing in a plantation in South Carolina; and the declared candidacy of a close family friend of the Harrises, Henry Becher. For Amelia, however, family loyalties came before friendship and she encouraged Portman to run: "Mr Becher is [the] one who ought to go . . . he stands well with the Government. . . . but he does not stand well with the general class of voters. Mr Portman, though a stranger, stands very much better."[209] While Portman was ambivalent, his mind was made up for him by the death of his wife, Helen, and he withdrew his candidacy. In July 1860, Portman left for England, returning almost a year later in time for the election called for July 1861.[210]

Faced with the prospect of competition from two other candidates – Henry Becher and Frank Cornish, mayor of London – Portman refused to run unless the party was united behind him. A convention was held on 11 June and Portman presented to the voters his views on such current issues as "Representation by Population," "Confederation," "The British Connection," and "Immigration from the United States." He won the nomination and subsequent election, and was formally declared the member for East Middlesex on 13 July.

Portman was sworn in as a Member of Parliament at Quebec City on 20 March 1862.[211] His career as a politician began promisingly when he was selected by Prime Minister John A. Macdonald as the seconder to the Speech from the Throne. At this time it was rumoured that Macdonald wanted him to join the Cabinet. Portman was not offered the appointment, however, which was perhaps a good thing: the Conservative administration was riddled with dissension and within two months Macdonald's

[208]Amelia's diary, 27 February 1860.

[209]Amelia's diary, 3 March 1860.

[210]Amelia Harris became ill on 11 February 1861 and made no entries in her diary (except for 4 May) until 2 June. However, Sophie was living at Eldon House at this time and her diary covers Portman's campaign between 10 May and 9 July 1861.

[211]Technically, he served until the 7th Parliament was dissolved on 12 May 1863. However, he did not attend the House after it recessed on 9 June 1862.

government was defeated and John Sandfield Macdonald and Louis Victor Sicotte were invited to form a government.[212]

For Portman, however, the consequences of the defeat of Macdonald's administration were most unfortunate. He had always been a backbencher, but now he was an opposition backbencher with little to do but amuse himself. On receiving a letter from him in May 1862, Amelia was not surprised to find that, while he was enjoying himself, he was hating political life, "for the Government nor House of Assembly stand high either for gentlemanlike manners, honesty or morality."[213] Amelia received this letter on the day John A. Macdonald's government was defeated. It took Portman almost a month to make his way from Quebec City to Eldon House, where Amelia's displeasure awaited him. Rumours of his dalliances while at Quebec troubled her and she also subjected Portman to her jaundiced views on Quebec and political life: she had a "horror of Quebec society"; she believed that very few who went to the House of Assembly, which she called a "large brothel," escaped "its contaminating influence"; she referred disparagingly to the "ladies" in Quebec.[214] John A. Macdonald confirmed that he too shared some of Amelia's concerns about Portman in a conversation with Amelia Griffin:

> He said Mr Portman worked hard and was steady in the House until after his Ministry went out, that after that he had not much to do, and he gave himself up to Quebec society, which, from the free and easy manner of the Quebecans he supposed had a charm for Mr Portman, but if he was not led into matrimony that he would get over his liking for it after a short time.[215] . . .

It was Macdonald's hope that Portman, who had gone to England to visit his children, would get married there.

On 8 May 1863, the Macdonald-Sicotte government was in its turn defeated, the House was dissolved, and a general election

[212]The difficult situation John A. Macdonald faced in the 7th Union Parliament is concisely described in Donald Creighton, *John A. Macdonald: the Young Politician*, Toronto: Macmillan, 1952, pp. 315–41; see also Bruce W. Hodgins, "John Sandfield Macdonald," in J.M.S. Careless, *The Pre-Confederation Premiers: Ontario Government Leaders, 1841–67*, Toronto: University of Toronto Press, 1980, pp. 264–82.

[213]Amelia's diary, 21 May 1862.

[214]Amelia's diary, 1 July 1862.

[215]Amelia's diary, 18 August 1862.

called. Earlier that year, however, Portman had a serious fall while hunting, announced that he would be unable to return for the session, and resigned his seat.[216] This proved to be the end of Portman's parliamentary career, and of the political aspirations of the Harris family.

Municipal politics, while a less significant arena, are also recorded in the diaries, if not in great detail. Lucy, however, loyally followed the fortunes of her husband, George, in the 1873 election, reporting tersely, "George defeated as Alderman having 230 votes."[217]

In general, however, the diarists reveal an antipathy to contemporary politicking. For Amelia, "nothing perverts the mind like politics,"[218] and she complained "[e]lections, elections, I hear nothing but elections."[219] Amelia could never be charged with being a populist and she despised political meetings for being "low and vulgar" and politicians for having to "court the mob."[220] Her assessment was that contemporary politics was a melange of drunken debauchery, bribery, and corruption.[221] Certainly, she did not encourage members of the Harris family to participate in it.

Health and Healing

The various medical crises that afflicted men, women, and children in nineteenth century Ontario are reported at the personal level in the Harris diaries. It was an age of pre-scientific medical practice, when society resorted to an amalgam of traditional healing and proto-scientific diagnosis and treatment.[222] But however much the need for improved professionalism in the medical field, all were appalled by the incident of "body snatchers," presumably prompted by the

[216]Amelia's diary, 3, 4, and 7 February 1863.

[217]Lucy's diary, 6 January 1873.

[218]Amelia's diary, 10 September 1858.

[219]Amelia's diary, 13 January 1874.

[220]Amelia's diary, 15 November 1860.

[221]Amelia's diary, 26 November 1860.

[222]See Edwin Seaborn, *The March of Medicine in Western Ontario*, Toronto: Ryerson, 1944; H.E. MacDermot, *One Hundred Years of Medicine in Canada*, Toronto: McClelland and Stewart, 1967; S.E.D. Shortt (ed.), *Medicine in Canadian Society: Historical Perspectives*, Montreal and Kingston: McGill-Queen's University Press, 1981.

demands of the medical schools in Toronto or Detroit, that shocked London in 1857.[223]

Amelia, Sophie and Lucy each comment regularly on the state of their own health, and that of any one else in the family who was sick. They record the medical diagnoses and ministrations of the several doctors called upon by the Harris family which, because of the emotional trauma of so many of these domestic medical crises, are reported upon vividly. Taken together, these entries provide a rich commentary on personal fear and frailty in the face of disease, inadequate medical treatment, and the frequent loss of loved ones.

Not all the medical tragedies that beset the Harris family occurred in London. In 1875, Teresa's husband, Scott, died of typhoid. Though themselves familiar with the ravages of this disease that was endemic throughout nineteenth century Ontario, the Harrises were advised by a friend of the circumstances of his death in dramatic detail:

> . . . Mr Scott died this morning of typhoid fever. Two or three days after leaving Bombay the ship's baker died of heat apoplexy & [Scott] seemed to be in low spirits from that time dreading the Red Sea very much. Two or three days afterwards he complained of not being able to eat anything & he spent most of the time lying down. When we got to Aden Mrs Scott & I went ashore and got a quantity of Triby's extract of meat the only thing he seemed to care for. We also got 150 lbs. of ice . . . which melted in two or three days. He seemed to be better & worse alternate days. On one day particularly we thought he was quite well only a little weak but the next days he was worse. I think the Doctor was in a great measure to blame as he only found out it was typhoid after he had been ill 8 or 10 days & then she pointed out the symptoms to him. For the last three or four days he has been delirious half the time, . . . A day or two before he died the Doctor said the case was hopeless. The last night he was conscious for a few minutes & said Teresa three times & tried to say wife, but could not. When he died I took her down to her cabin & the Doctor brought her a sleeping draught but it was some time before she went off. She was much more composed when she awoke & she went to say the last goodbye & cut off

[223]Amelia's diary, 19 December 1857.

some of his hair, afterwards she gave me a lock of her hair & asked me for a photo she had given me, & at her request I had them placed on his heart.[224] . . .

Closer to home, during the 1840's and 1850's, the Harris family physician, Dr. Alexander Anderson, was their next-door neighbour. Anderson, a graduate of Aberdeen, had opened a practice in London in 1835; he was an old fashioned doctor, who was an avid advocate of the application of leeches. Edward Harris described him as "the last of the Bleeders," and recorded how on one occasion he had "bled him in the arm for toothache."[225] It was Anderson who was nominally in charge of the care of John Harris in the last years of his life. However, Harris, refused Anderson's bleedings, and in his final months John Harris was attended principally by two British military surgeons from the garrison: Edward Howard, 23rd Regiment, a great favourite at Eldon House; and, a Mr. Fisher, Royal Artillery, who combined visits on John Harris with dancing lessons from one of his daughters. The cause of John Harris' death is not mentioned in Henry Becher's letter to Colonel Talbot reporting the death of their friend.[226] However, when he was examined by Mr. Howard with a "stethescope" his lungs were said to be "affected."[227]

The death of John Harris' son, John Fitzjohn, is described in detail in 1861. The cause of death was disputed and, since there was no autopsy, never officially determined. John consulted specialists in New York and in England, and at least three doctors in London, Upper Canada. They variously diagnosed cancer, enlarged spleen, and kidney malfunction. Indeed, the record of his symptoms over the last five years of his life provides a rich commentary on contemporary medicine, if not a precise diagnosis of John's complaints.[228]

The most emotional and traumatic events in all of the Harris diaries is the death, following child-birth, of Amelia's daughter, Helen Portman. At first attended upon by Dr. Anderson, two other doctors, Dr. V.A. Brown and Dr. W. Woodruff, were also

[224]Harris Papers, St. Littledale to Eliza Crutchley, 16 June 1875.

[225]Harris Papers, Edward Harris' "Key to the Diary of Charlotte Harris."

[226]Harris Papers, Henry Becher to Thomas Talbot, 29 August 1850.

[227]Charlotte's diary, 5 February 1849.

[228]Sophie's diary, 19 April, 17 May, and 28 June 1861.

consulted. Dr. Brown replaced Dr. Anderson, and he in turn called in a Toronto doctor, Dr. Hodder. The ultimate diagnosis of puerperal fever was followed by a series of medical ministrations: opium, leeches to the abdomen, hot fomentations, and stimulants such as port, tea, and brandy. Helen died on the evening of 28 March 1860. She was laid out "in her robe of white" by Amelia Griffin, Mrs. William Lawrason, and her nurse, and was buried two days later.

Amelia recapitulates "these weeks of sorrow and despair" lasting from 27 March to 14 April in an omnibus entry for 15 April which she writes "from memory" in a sustained, admirably written and organized, 5,000 word narrative. In addition, she transcribed ten letters that discussed the case and which had been published in the *London Free Press* between 13–23 April. That puerperal fever caused Helen's death had never been in dispute; the issue was incompetence and culpability.[229]

Such mistakes were not uncommon. When Lucy's second daughter, eight-year-old Charlotte, "had a convultion" [sic], Dr. Woodruff diagnosed worms.[230] A few weeks later, the same doctor diagnosed epilepsy, and she subsequently died at the age of sixteen.[231] Other more common killers at the time, especially of children, were scarlet fever, typhoid, and croup. One of the Griffin's twins died of scarlet fever,[232] and Lucy's diary for the winter of 1874–5 is a veritable litany of childrens' deaths, including one poor family that lost five children in one month.[233]

Lucy also makes several references to a fear that many women of her day shared: pregnancy and child-birth were major hazards in their lives. She confided her innermost dread to her diary: "I half fear that July will be the end for me at times. I think I shall not recover";[234] "I hope my life may be spared";[235] "When I think of what is before me, I feel afraid."[236] With other

[229]Amelia's diary, 3/4/5 May 1860 also records the subsequent drama involving the confrontation between George and Dr. Anderson that transported the domestic tragedy into the streets and courts of London.

[230]Lucy's diary, 3/4 January 1879.

[231]Lucy's diary, 23 January 1879.

[232]Amelia's diary, 3 January 1869.

[233]Lucy's diary, 5 January 1876.

[234]Lucy's diary, 28 February 1868.

[235]Lucy's diary, 22 March 1880.

[236]Lucy's diary, 24 March 1880.

women's experience constantly before, and especially that in her immediate family circle, her concerns were justified.

Fear of such killers, fatality, and scepticism are palpable throughout the diaries, Amelia concluding on one occasion that "hope will do more for him [John] than medicine."[237] This is not surprising given their knowledge of some of the current treatments and "prescription" favoured by physicians of the day. Amelia had learned to be realistic about the limitations of certain treatments, concluding that "I have never known the knife save a life from cancer."[238] Port wine, whisky, and brandy were prescribed for colds, flues, headache, heart problems, and to women after giving birth. "Face ache," probably tooth-ache, prompted a successsion of doses of brandy, cayenne pepper, and hot vinegar; not unexpectedly the patient reported "I felt most stupid & miserable all day."[239] A simple treatment for frozen extremities was rubbing with snow, or the application of a "poultice of raw potatoes grated."[240]

Amelia Harris reports regularly on the general state of her own health from 1857 to within three weeks of her death. She describes the symptoms and treatment prescribed in three of her half dozen "serious" illnesses, each of which resulted in her putting her diary aside temporarily.[241] In 1882, she commented that Dr. Woodruff had prescribed the same "old medicine" and that it was the only one he had given to her "for the last five years."[242] Over the years, she was treated by Dr. V.A. Brown, Dr. Henry Landor,[243] and in 1862 she had consulted a Toronto homeopath named Adams who had prescribed "diet & fresh air and infinitissimal globules."[244] Amelia obviously had a heart condition and suffered from rheumatism, though the more meaningful cause of her death may be said to have been "old age."

[237]Amelia's diary, 16 May 1860.

[238]Amelia's diary, 19 March 1859. See also reference to cancer of the breast, 14 September 1858.

[239]Sophie's diary, 22 September 1860.

[240]Amelia's diary, 1 February 1880.

[241]Amelia's diary, February–June 1861, January–June 1862, May–December 1863.

[242]Amelia's diary, 14 January 1882.

[243]Landor was eventually appointed Superintendent of the London Asylum. He was succeeded in this position by Dr. R.M. Bucke, the friend and literary executor of Walt Whitman. Bucke visited Eldon House on at least one occasion, but his relationship with Amelia Harris was casual rather than close. Given her literary propensities, this is unfortunate, although her taste does not seem to have extended to Whitman's work.

[244]Amelia's diary, 27 May 1862.

The World Beyond Eldon

When the Harris family made their entry into London society in 1834, the community was a rapidly expanding settlement with much optimism for the future.[245] Governor Maitland had officially recognized the site at the "Forks" as capital of the London District on 30 January 1826, and no one was recorded as living in the area designated as the "town lot" at that time. A year later, 133 persons were listed as residents of London Township, which included the town. Harris family tradition has it that when the construction of Eldon House was completed in September 1834, approximately 400 people, almost all the local inhabitants, lent a hand in raising the roof. By 1840, when London was incorporated as a town with an elected Board of Police, its population was just under 2,000, a figure that had risen to 5,000 when it was re-incorporated in 1848. No longer a "police town," it was served by all the trappings of municipal governent of mayor and aldermen, and when it was incorporated as a city in 1854 it had a population of over 10,000 people. Nevertheless, it was still a community where the countryside was never far from the town centre, rural life was still part of many town-dwellers' experience, and where "Cows are allowed to pasture [the cemetery] and of course eat off all the shrubs planted about the graves."[246]

Throughout the period covered by Amelia Harris' diary, the city continued to progress in both regional importance and economic diversity. The key event in the early development of London, the coming of the Great Western Railway in 1853, is not described in the Eldon diaries because no one at that time was keeping a journal. The advent of rail prompted a real estate boom and inflated real estate prices. However, in the 1860s, with the completion of railway construction, the end of the Crimean War, and the decreased demand for Canadian agricultural products in Europe, London found itself in a serious depression, marked by the failure of three-quarters of its small businesses. Nevertheless, it continued to grow in the 1870s, and Amelia lived to see the city expand as the grounds of former estates

[245]On the development of London from village, through garrison town, to city and metropolis, see F.H. Armstrong, 1986, *op. cit.*, and O. Miller, 1988, *op. cit.*

[246]Amelia's diary, 30 July 1858.

were "laid out into lots & sold & a good many very nice houses have been built."[247] By the time of her death in 1882, the population had doubled to over 20,000.

From 1848 to 1882, the Harris diaries make reference to most of the more important events in the development of London and district, and comment on a diverse range of human activities. However, the world with which the Harris family first interacted and observed was, of necessity, very constrained by the tyranny of poor transport. Thus, the mid-century London of Charlotte's diary is a small relatively isolated town, connected to the surrounding district by rather primitive roads that were still "muddy & tedious" a decade later.[248] It was very much a pedestrian town, a place where everyone walked to church, to market, to the shops, and to and from friends' houses. The Harris household was served by two or three carriages and a sleigh and the diaries refer to outings for picnics, sketching parties, visits to Port Talbot, or trips to Port Stanley to take the steamboat across Lake Erie to Cleveland, Ohio.[249] Longer expeditions to Port Ryerse, Toronto, Hamilton, or Niagara Falls were taken by public stage coach. Visits to more distant places such as Kingston, Montreal, or New York required travel by lake steamers and canal boats.

When Amelia commenced her diary, London's connections with the outside world were developing rapidly. Rail had entered the city in 1853 and by 1858 the "English letters" now only took two weeks.[250] In that same year, bells were rung and salutes fired to celebrate the completion of the telegraphic line between England and the United States.[251] With such enhanced connections with the outside world, it had become much easier for the Harrises and other Londoners to transact legal business in Toronto, to court a young lady in Chatham or Windsor, to buy a carpet or a dress in Hamilton, or to spend a week at Niagara Falls. Not surprisingly, the diaries reveal that as the period progressed, there was a significant increase in the frequency of trips and the distances travelled. Diaries refer to hunting and fishing trips to Long Point, Sarnia, the "Prairies,"

[247]Amelia's diary, 29 August 1876.
[248]Sophie's diary, 7 October 1860.
[249]Charlotte's diary, 22 June 1849.
[250]Amelia's diary, 1 April 1858.
[251]Amelia's diary, 5 and 6 August 1858.

Lake Superior, and the Gaspé, summer family vacations on the eastern seaboard of the United States, and several European excursions. In the more immediate vicinity of London, however, the diaries refer to two particular communities that were closely connected to the life of the Harris family: Port Ryerse and Port Talbot.

Frequent reference is made to the former family-home at Port Ryerse, seventy miles to the south-east of London. In her later life, Amelia Harris returned to the community in 1875 and found that little had changed since 1834, her nostalgic report being essentially a commentary on Port Ryerse and the Long Point area as it was when she was a child and a young bride.[252] She also records the activities of her brothers, George and Edward Ryerse, who had lived there all their lives, and those of her son, Edward, who was involved in the development of the harbour and in several small businesses in the village. Edward was also founder and president of the Long Point Company, a fishing and duck-hunting club that was patronized by the Harris sons and sons-in-law and by Egerton Ryerson. But having seen it and remembered how it had once been, she sadly commented that "I have taken my last look at my old home & have no wish ever to go there again."[253]

Port Talbot, thirty miles to the south, was the home of Colonel Thomas Talbot, a close friend of the Harrises.[254] Between 1848 and 1851, Charlotte's diary records ten visits to Port Talbot by members of the Harris Family. The relationship between the Harrises and Talbot was a close one. Talbot and Richard Airey, his nephew and designated heir, who also lived on the Talbot Estate, visited Eldon House on a number of occasions. One particularly dramatic arrival, and equally dramatic departure, together with commentary on the tangled relationship of Talbot and Airey, are graphically described in Charlotte's diary.[255] Amelia only refers to one visit to Port

[252]Amelia's diary, 30 August and 1 September 1875.

[253]Amelia's diary, 31 August 1875.

[254]For more on Talbot see, F.C. Hamil, *Lake Erie Baron: The Story of Colonel Thomas Talbot*, Toronto: Macmillan, 1955. Also, see Alan G. Brunger, "Thomas Talbot," *Dic. Can. Biog.* VIII, pp. 857–862.

[255]Charlotte's diary, 28 March to 24 June 1850. Talbot had been taken ill on the first stage of a journey to England and had to stay at Eldon House for almost three months. He died in 1853. Airey was recalled to England in 1852. His subsequent career included writing the order for the Charge of the Light Brigade during the Crimean War.

Talbot in her diary. After an eighteen year absence, she returned on a visit by train and carriage arranged by Henry Becher. Her only comment was, "Col Talbot used to give an interest to the place by the eccentricity of his life."[256]

The diaries contain periodic snapshots of other communities in Ontario, particularly of Toronto, Windsor, Woodstock, and Niagara Falls. Even distant Kingston was recalled as a former home, although reports from the British military stationed there were that "it was exceedingly dull & stupid."[257] The focus of several of the Toronto visits was on the home and social context of Sophie's family, the Ryersons. Other visits were for particular events such as Elizabeth Loring's wedding to John Fitzjohn Harris,[258] and that of Sophie to Edward Harris,[259] and at least a dozen balls at Government House. None of these is of more than passing interest, but cumulatively they provide a picture of Toronto high society in the 1860s. Certainly, the scandalous behaviour of some of the ladies in the "upper ten" there caused Amelia to have a somewhat jaundiced view of the "immorality of the City of Toronto."[260]

Lucy's diary provides a comparable portrait of social life in Windsor from 1867 into the 1880s. The Ronalds maintained numerous connections with society across the river in Detroit, but they were not as socially prominent as the Ryersons were in Toronto. The Harrises often stopped at Woodstock en route to Port Ryerse, and they were occasionally invited to dances there. Amelia's diaries make frequent reference to visits of a week or more by members of the Harris family to the homes of two prominent Niagara families, the J.H. Plumbs and the Thomas Streets, or at one of its several popular hotels. The most memorable of these was a trip taken by Amelia in 1864 which included a visit to Niagara-on-the-Lake, which she had not seen since she attended a school there in 1810.[261]

Excepting Amelia Harris who seldom left Eldon House, all of the Harrises were remarkable for their frequent and extensive travels abroad. As much as Amelia was sedentary, each of the

256 Amelia's diary, 4 July 1867.
257 Sophie's diary, 1 January 1861.
258 Amelia's diary, 9 November 1859.
259 Amelia's diary, 6 July 1860.
260 Amelia's diary, 15 December 1858.
261 Amelia's diary, 26 July 1864.

Amelia Ryerse Harris

John Harris

Sarah (Harris) Dalzell

Robert Dalzell

Amelia (Harris) Griffin

Gilbert Griffin

Mary (Harris) Peard

Shuldham Peard

Eliza (Harris) Crutchley

General Crutchley

Charlotte (Harris) and Edward Knight

John Fitzjohn Harris

Elizabeth (Loring) Harris

Edward Harris

Sophia Ryerson Harris

Helen (Harris) Portman

Maurice Portman

George Becher Harris

Lucy Ronalds Harris

Teresa (Harris) Scott

William John Scott

Harris children
Amelia, Edward, and Chasse

Three generations: Grandmother Mrs. Ronalds (c. 1870), her daughter Lucy (1876), and grandaughter Milly also in 1876.

The Hydrographer's House in Kingston in the late 19th century. John and Amelia Ryerse Harris lived there during their Kingston years.

Eldon House and surroundings at mid-19th century.

The Scotts and the Griffins with their friends, the Leslies and others from the 16th Regiment in Niagara Falls. (c. 1865)

Another family visit to the Falls.

other four diarists travelled a great deal within Canada and beyond its limits.

Charlotte, like her other sisters who married army officers, went to Europe with her husband and children. She was returning from Italy to England when she died in the accident on the *Ercolano*.[262] Sophie had accompanied her father on a six-month tour of Europe and went back several times after marrying. Her husband, Edward Harris, would often travel to England on business. In fact, he crossed the ocean several times between 1859 and 1880, and Sophie accompanied him on three of those trips. Lucy made her first trip to England with her parents at the age of sixteen. After marrying George Harris, She spent her honeymoon in England and France and, later, together with her husband and children she visited England regularly. Their frequent travels throughout North America and Europe were motivated by the Ronalds' business interests and by the search for treatment for their epileptic daughter, Charlotte.

Amelia Archange, or Milly, was sent to England in 1882 when she was thirteen. She studied there for two years. Later, with her parents she visited Italy on three occasions as well as France, Germany, Norway, Syria, Jerusalem, and Japan. Except for Teresa, Milly was probably the most travelled person in the Harris family, and her many journeys abroad are described in enchanting detail in her long run of diaries.[263]

Amelia's son, John, lived in England with his wife Elizabeth for almost a year and died there in 1861. The two daughters who remained in Canada also travelled. Helen lived in the United States after marrying Maurice Portman; he continued to travel back and forth between Canada and England for a few years after the death of his wife until he finally settled in England with his three sons. Amelia Griffin travelled within Canada and was in England for a few months visiting her sisters in 1861.

The three other daughters, Sarah, Mary, and Eliza, left Canada with their husbands for England shortly after their marriages and lived there. They travelled within Europe and each of them returned once to Canada to visit their mother. The fourth daughter, Teresa, and her first husband, William Scott, being childless and wealthy, devoted much of their time to travelling:

[262]See Harris Papers, letter from Knight to H. Becher, 27 April 1854.
[263]For the purposes of this volume, only the year 1882 is reproduced here.

in 1868 they visited Spain and Gilbraltar; in 1873, they made a tour of the Middle East, visiting Cairo, Constantinople, and Jerusalem; in 1875 the Scotts travelled to Eldon House and returned to England by way of the Pacific Ocean, Japan, and India. It was during this trip that Scott died, while crossing the Red Sea. Teresa remarried, and together with her second husband, St. George Littledale, she continued her travels, including visits to her mother, Amelia, in 1879 and 1881. Typically, their 1881 visit to Eldon House was part of a more extensive expedition to the Rocky Mountains and Yellowstone Park. For the next twenty years, the Littledales continued to divide their time between their home at Bracknell and travelling.

Increasingly through the years, therefore, the diarists transcend the original constraints of transport and they add to their diaries their views of peoples and places in the wider world beyond the London District. For Amelia, however, the focus seldom shifts from her home community, and in particular, her own household.

THE END OF A MATRIARCHY

During her last months at Raleigh House, Lucy did much to make Amelia feel at home. The daily routine of receiving local callers and writing letters to distant family continued and Lucy organized a party for her eighty-third birthday. Nor did Amelia neglect her journal. Amelia continued to give an account of her activities, and those of others, and although her entries become more terse with time, they record her daily routine with perceptive wit. However, a particularly vivid premonition of her death in a dream convinced her of her imminent end and the curate at St. Paul's called to administer the sacrament to her on 15 January 1882.

On 19 February 1882, Amelia's eighty-fourth birthday, a telegram from Edward announced the death of her good friend, Egerton Ryerson, "surrounded by his family." Six days later, the last entry of her diary refers to a biographical sketch of Ryerson which she was sending to her daughters in England.

Amelia did not neglect arrangements for her own family after her death. She prepared a "Memorandum" for her sons, Edward and George, with copies for her daughters. Amelia Griffin's copy has survived. In it, Amelia Harris directs that each of her children should have "a little remembrance of their old home," and went on to stipulate her wishes with respect to the portraits. On 27 February 1882, Amelia dictated another "Memorandum," this time to Lucy, about the distribution of some cash. On 9 March she dictated a final directive:

> Tell them all in England how loving dear Edward has been. Tell Mr Becher and his family that I thought of him on my death bed [also] Mr Portman and Captain Knight and that I prayed God to bless all my dear children and grandchildren, Major and Mary Leith and their little ones. Give your Amelia [Milly] twenty dollars to put with her hoard to buy something in memory of me and give more to the servants than I first said as I have been longer ill than I thought. I will change my will. It is not marked in my memo that as George paid for the fence on the pasture he is to have the use of it for five years by paying taxes. Should it be sold George is to be paid for the fences. If Scott Griffin should die I wish Amelia Griffin, his mother, to give the twenty-

five acres to either Mary or Sarah which one will seem to need it most. Teresa knew and I talked with her about it.[264]

On 22 March, Lucy wrote, "I must give up my journal." The reason was quite evident: Amelia's end was close. On the 24th, she noted that the family doctor, Dr. William Woodruff, could offer no hope of her recovery. Later the same day, Lucy recorded Amelia's death at 8.25 p.m. and observed later, "a peaceful and painless end. A life well spent brings its own reward."[265] Milly, the young granddaughter, profoundly impressed by death, wrote "[a] most distressing day. I saw Grandma. I was not afraid and kissed her. Grandma is to be moved to Eldon tonight. She wished to be buried from there. . . . She looks beautiful, . . . all the wrinkles have gone."[266]

Amelia's body was returned to Eldon House which she left for the last time on 27 March in a "small but respectable funeral."[267] Following a service at St. Paul's officiated at by the Very Reverend Boomer, Dean of Huron, and two of the St. Paul's clergy, she was buried at Woodlands Cemetery. There were eight pall bearers: Henry Becher, James Hamilton, and Lawrence Lawrason were long-standing friends from the 1830s, while a fourth, Verschoyle Cronyn, was the son of the late Benjamin Cronyn. The principal mourners were equally representative of Amelia's eventful and long life: Edward, George and Gilbert Griffin; Dr. Woodruff; Dr. George Sterling Ryerson; Edward's law partner, James Magee; and Ephraim and John Plummer, long-time neighbours of the Harrises on Ridout Street.

As it happened, Egerton Ryerson had died on Amelia's birthday, 19 February. Amelia and Ryerson had been closely associated for almost eighty years and she is reported to have declared that since Ryerson had died on her birthday, she would reciprocate the honour and die on his, 24 March. She kept her promise.

[264]Harris Papers, Memorandum from Amelia Harris to Lucy Ronalds Harris, 9 March 1882.

[265]Lucy's diary, 24 March 1882.

[266]Milly's diary, 25 March 1882.

[267]Lucy's diary, 27 March 1882.

THE ELDON HOUSE DIARIES

The Diary of Charlotte Owen Harris (1828–1854)

Although neither the longest nor the richest of the Eldon House diaries, Charlotte's (Chasse) diary was the first to be written. She began making daily entries on 22 October 1848 when she was 20 years old and, apart from a three month interruption between 7 August and 16 November 1850, she continued to write until 24 January 1851. Her complete diary consists of two bound notebooks of a hundred pages each.

Chasse's diary serves as a good introduction to the other diaries as it introduces all the members of the Harris family. It also provides a lively picture of town life in Ontario West at mid nineteenth century. She records the teas, dinner parties, visits by friends and associates, and the comings and goings of members of the family. While the depictions of the people themselves are somewhat blurred in her diary, she does render a vivid picture of the contemporary social round.

Some of Chasse's entries suggest that the purpose of her diary was to entertain herself and her sisters. Indeed, the subjects of special interest to her appear to be those related to their active social life in general, and their courtships in particular. There is much detailed commentary on courtship, engagements, marriages, illusions and disillusions. Some of the romantic developments in her own life are described, including her engagement to Captain Frank Campbell, his precipitate departure, and failure to return.

Other entries refer to the lives of her parents, but the three month interruption in 1850 produces a significant gap in her monitoring of domestic events: the marriage at Eldon House of her sister, Mary, the deterioration of her father's health, and the trauma of his sudden death. When she resumed her commentary, she appears to have lost some of her former zest for life, and the tone of her diary has changed. She registered her father's death in a somewhat laconic note and continued her observations on the daily routine at Eldon House.

Chasse married Captain Edward Knight on 12 June 1851. Later that year, she committed her innermost thoughts to her journal: "how little we know what is in store for us."[1] . . . Three years later, Charlotte and her children were drowned in the Mediterranean.[2]

[1]Charlotte's diary, 16 November 1850.
[2]Harris Papers, E. Knight to H. Becher, 27 April 1854.

Charlotte Owen Harris (Knight) 1828–1854

Sunday. October 22nd 1848.
We went to church, on our return we found Mr Stanley a son of Lord Stanley's, here. He brought letters of introduction to Papa. Mamma asked him to stay with us, which he of course was delighted to do. Mr Simson called to bid us adieu, he only stayed five minutes as Lord Mark Kerr was waiting for him. We were very sorry to say good bye to him. Mr Pearce & Mr Lutyens called with him. Mr Beatty called for a minute we asked him to come back and spend the evening with us. Captain Knight came to say good bye. We were exceedingly sorry to see him leave & shall miss him very much. Mr & Mrs Becher called. Papa & Mr Stanley went out driving. Eliza, Amelia & I went to the evening service Mr Gray. Mr Ward & Mr James walked home with Eliza & Amelia. Edward & I walked quickly on before them. Mr Beatty, Mr Ward, & Mr Pearce came in the evening. Was the

Chasse commences her diary

Charlotte Owen Harris' Diary

1848

Oct 22 We went to church, on our return we found Mr Stanley, a son of Lord Stanley's here.[3] He brought letters of introduction to Papa. Mamma asked him to stay with us, which he of course was delighted to do. Mr Tomson called to bid us adieu, he only stayed five minutes as Lord Mark Kerr[4] was waiting for him. We were very sorry to say good bye to him. Mr Neave[5] & Mr Lutyens[6] called with him. Mr Beatty called for a minute. We asked him to come back and spend the evening with us. Capt Knight[7] came to say good bye. We were exceedingly sorry to see him leave & shall miss him very much. Mr & Mrs Becher[8] called. Papa & Mr Stanley went out driving. Eliza,[9] Amelia[10] & I went to the evening service. . . . Mr Beatty, Mr Peard[11] & Mr Neave came in the evening. It was the last night Mr Beatty was to spend with us. Mama talked a short time to him & I sat with him all the evening. Amelia talked to Mr Stanley all the evening. He is an exceedingly nice person & very clever. Mama asked Mr Beatty to breakfast. I gave him a purse. . . . They left at ten & we retired an hour afterwards.

Oct 23 Mr Beatty could not come to breakfast but came in for a minute afterwards. Mama asked Mr Wilson,[12] Mr Askin,[13] Mr Good-

[3]Edward Stanley (1826–93), the son of Lord Stanley, 15th Earl of Derby, Prime Minister of England in 1852.

[4]All the officers mentioned in this entry, including Knight and Peard, were members of the 20th Regiment (Royal Welch Fusiliers), stationed in London since September 1847.

[5]Arundell Neave (1829–77) was attached to the Commissariat at Toronto. He was the son of Sir Digby Neave, who had arranged this posting to prepare his son to manage the family estate in England. He succeeded as 4th Baronet in 1868.

[6]Charles Henry Lutyens (1829–1915), a close friend of Neave and a favourite of the Harrises, was a talented amateur painter. He was the father of the well-known British architect Charles Lutyens.

[7]Edward Lewis Knight (died 1882) was to marry Charlotte in 1851.

[8]Henry Corry Rowley Becher (1817–85) had lived with the Harrises from 1835 to 1842 while qualifying as a lawyer under John Wilson, 1835–41. He married Sarah Leonard, sister of Elijah Leonard, in 1842. There are several references to his home, "Thornwood."

[9]Charlotte's sister, who was to marry Charles Crutchley in 1851.

[10]Charlotte's sister, who was to marry Gilbert Griffin in 1855.

[11]Lieut. George Shuldham Peard (1829–1918) was to marry Mary Harris in 1850.

[12]John Wilson (1807–69), London's leading lawyer and M.P. for London 1847–51, 1854–57, was a close friend of the Harrises.

hue,[14] Mr Hamilton, Mr Becher & Mr Lawrason to dinner. Mr Wilson declined the honor. Mr Beatty came again at one o'clock to say good bye. . . . Amelia, Mary,[15] Mr Becher, Mr Stanley & Mr Peard went out riding. Mr Lutyens called, he only saw Papa, I did not want to see him, & did not come down. Mr Neave called & saw me making jelly in the kitchen the cook being ill. We dined at six, the party went off better than we expected. Mr Goodhue opened his conversation with Mr Stanley by asking him "Was you ever in South Carolina?" Mr Neave, Mr Peard & Mr Lutyens came in the evening. The dinner party left at ten, the others at eleven. Mary sent me to talk to Mr Lutyens but I could not, my thoughts were of the last evening & the morning [i.e. on Lt. Beattie]. I went to my room as soon as I could get away. It was the longest and most miserable day I ever spent.

Oct 24 Very wet. Mr Stanley & Jack[16] have put off their visit to Port Talbot[17] until tomorrow. Mr Allen[18] & Mr Hamilton called on Mr Stanley. Amelia & Eliza tried to get up a riding party but it was too wet. Mr Peard called to tell us he was going to see Mrs Becher. Mr Stanley went out to pay some visits. Mary tried to induce me to go out riding but I did not feel inclined to do any thing. Mr Peard & Mr Neave called. Mama asked them to come in the evening. We dined at six. I thought the day would never end, & went to my room at half past nine.

Oct 25 Mr Stanley & Jack left for Port Talbot. . . . Mr Stanley could scarcely tear himself away, he has fallen desperately in love with Amelia. We did not breakfast until ten and afterwards the four of us retired to Amelia's room where we worked, read & talked. Becher came to dinner. Mrs Caddy[19] called to read us Minnie's letter, which she had just received. Mrs Wilson called & was in hopes of seeing Mr Stanley but the bird had flown. She says the reason Mr Wilson does not call on him is because "he admires the good not the great." He did

[13]John B. Askin (1788–1869), Clerk of the Peace for the London District since 1819.

[14]George J. Goodhue (1799–1870), merchant, landowner, and politician, was President of London's first Council in 1840. See F.A. Armstrong, "George Jervis Goodhue," *Dic. Can. Biog.* IX, pp. 323–324.

[15]Charlotte's sister Mary, who was to marry Shuldham Peard in 1850.

[16]Charlotte's brother, John, often referred to as Jack.

[17]The home of Col Thomas Talbot (1771–1853). See A. Brunger, "Thomas Talbot," *Dic. Can. Biog.* VIII, pp. 857–861.

[18]Henry Allen, a County Court judge.

[19]Wife of J.H. Caddy (1801–83), a Royal Engineers officer stationed in London (1842–44). He retired in 1844 and was appointed City Engineer for London. He was also an excellent painter. Minnie was their daughter.

not get the good when he got her. Mary, Amelia & I went out walking but each took a different road. I did some shopping, met Mr Lutyens riding. The town looked more gloomy than ever. . . . Amelia & Eliza wrote to Mr Peard & Mr Neave asking them to dine with us tomorrow & to join the riding party. We named Mr Neave's house "Bow Wow Cottage."

Oct 26 Mr Stanley & Jack returned from Port Talbot at twelve. We waited breakfast for them until eleven. Amelia & Mary lost two pairs of gloves each to Becher by their not returning at eleven. Amelia, Eliza, Mr Stanley & Mr Neave went out riding. Mamma & I called on Mrs Gordon[20] & unfortunately met them going out. Mrs Gordon looks very untidy & judging from appearances does not know the use of a toothbrush. Coming home we met Mary. I joined her, did some shopping, then went out for a walk. We met Mrs Gordon & followed her up Dundas Street that Mary might see her. . . . Mr Stanley proposed for Amelia. She nearly fainted & retired for some time. We are not supposed to know it, but imagine a secret among us. Mr Neave & I had a waltz round the table. He suspects Mr Stanley has proposed. We sent them away as soon as possible, & did not retire until one o'clock. . . .

Oct 27 We heard from Sarah[21] & Capt Hale [82nd]. Mr Goodhue called to offer Mr Stanley & us his carriage & horses if we wished to get up riding or driving parties, & also asked Mr Stanley, Papa & Jack to breakfast tomorrow morning & to drive Mr Stanley every where if he wished. Mr Stanley was obliged to accept the invitation to breakfast but we came to the rescue & asked if he was not engaged for the rest of the day. He was delighted to get any excuse, & said he was. . . . Mrs Becher called to ask us to ride & found we had arranged a party without her chaperonage. Amelia asked her to join it but she thought she was not wanted & declined. I amused myself at Mrs Hamilton's for an hour nursing the baby. Amelia, Eliza, Mary, Mr Stanley, Mr Peard & Mr Neave went out riding. Mr Neave did his best to persuade me to go but I did not feel inclined & resisted all his persuasions. . . . Mr Peard & Mr Neave dined with us. Mr Neave & I had a full explanation of every thing that had happened since our first quarrel, and have taken a fresh start. He tried to persuade me to ride with him tomorrow. I half consented but doubt my going. They left at ten.

[20]Wife of a major in the 20th Regiment.

[21]Charlotte's sister, Mrs. Robert Dalzell, who had been living in the United Kingdom since 1848.

When they were going I put on Mr Peard's cloak & did a little [imitation] of Captain Knight for the amusement of Mary & Eliza.

Oct 28 Papa, Mr Stanley & Jack breakfasted with Mr Goodhue, half the town were there. Mrs Montserrat[22] called to ask for flowers to put on poor Thompson Wilson's[23] body. He died yesterday evening . . . it was the most melancholy thing I ever saw. Capt & Mrs Dacres [R.A.] were very kind to them during his illness. Mr Stanley & Amelia went out driving. . . . Mr Stanley paid some visits. Mary & Eliza went in the town. I went walking with Jack. Mr Peard & Mr Neave called. Dr Anderson[24] & Mr Hamilton dined with us. I was not well & went to my room at nine.

Oct 29 I was not well enough to go to church. Our old nurse, Mrs Perry[25], arrived from Simcoe. We were delighted to see the dear old creature again. She intends spending a week with us. Mr Neave called for a minute, he saw me in my dressing gown getting dessert. I gave him cake & left him. Mr Becher & Mr Lutyens called, I did not see them. Amelia & Eliza went to the evening service. Jack, Edward & George[26] went to Thompson Wilson's funeral. Jack was one of the pall bearers. Mr Peard & Mr Neave came in the evening. We sent them away at ten o'clock. Mamma & Mr Stanley are supposed to have sat up all night. . . .

Oct 30 Mr Stanley called at Mr Cronyn's.[27] Amelia, Eliza, Mary, Mr Stanley, Mr Peard & Mr Neave went out riding. I spent my afternoon in my room finishing Mrs Becher's work for her. We were supposed to dine at six & as usual no one was ready until seven. Mr Peard & Mr Neave honored us in the evening. I sat on the footstool at Mary's feet nearly all the evening talking to her & Mr Peard played backgammon with Mr Neave. We sent them away at half past ten as it was pouring with rain before. It is but one long week since Mr Beatty left. He will never see us all together again.

Oct 31 We all dressed quickly that we might be down to breakfast one morning before Mr Stanley & have the gratification of sending for

[22]Wife of Charles Montserrat, a bank-manager. Their son, Nicholas, later became a partner in the Harris Brothers' law firm.

[23]Son of John Wilson.

[24]Alexander Anderson (1808–73), a Scottish-trained doctor and land speculator. He was a next door neighbour of the Harrises on Ridout Street.

[25]Mrs. Perry, the retired nurse, had attended all eight Harris children, including Charlotte.

[26]George Becher Harris (1836–1923) was Charlotte's youngest brother.

[27]The Reverend Benjamin Cronyn (1802–71) arrived in London in 1832 and was rector of St. Paul's Church.

him. A most unfortunate accident happened to an indispensible part of his wardrobe. Eliza saw some wax on them & told Philip[28] to take it out with French chalk & a warm iron, but he like a true Irishman must take a hot iron & burn out the piece. He brought them to us with a very long face, we of course laughed at him. Eliza made him promise not to tell that she had anything to do with it. But Mamma could not keep it, & told Mr Stanley, & consequently Eliza has no peace as Mr Stanley alludes to it in every possible way. Mr & Mrs Becher called, we told them Amelia was engaged to Mr Stanley. They were in a frantic state of delight. Amelia, Mr Stanley & Jack went out driving. Mr Peard & Mr Neave called, we asked them in the evening. Mr Neave gave me a Prayer Book. . . . He & I played backgammon. Eliza borrowed Captain Caddy's portfolio to show Mr Stanley. Mrs Airey[29] wrote to Mamma to ask some of us to go over there [Port Talbot] next week for an unlimited time but as Mr Stanley will still be with us, Mamma intends to decline until a later period. Mr Howard[30] is to be invited when we go. Dear old Perry is as fond of us as ever & tries to do everything for us. She dreads the idea of leaving on Monday.

Nov 1 Mr Peard lunched with us. . . . Mr Tomson sent Eliza some music by Capt Crespigny [23rd]. We all appreciated the attention, it showed we were not yet forgotten. I did some shopping for Perry & myself. Mr Peard & Mr Neave dined with us. Mr Neave & I sat together at dinner and made a great noise, our end of the table certainly was the merriest. After coffee I tried to leave them but Eliza & Jack came for me & I was obliged to return & play backgammon with Jack while Eliza tried to take my profile, but she did not succeed, she always fails.[31] Mary & I waltzed & galoped[32] in turn with Mr Neave around the table. We sent them away at ten.

Nov 2 We heard from Mr Tighe & Mr Chichester [32nd]. The latter correspondence I intend dropping. . . . We met Mr Peard & Mr Neave, they said they had called but found no one at home. Coming home Mary & I saw two gentlemen across the street, whom we thought we knew & bowed to them; they returned it in a most condescending way

[28]The Harris' man servant.

[29]Wife of Sir Richard Airey (1803–81), a nephew of Colonel Thomas Talbot and his recently named heir, had been living on Talbot's estate since 1846.

[30]Edward Howard, a surgeon attached to the 23rd Regiment, was a great favourite at Eldon House where he often attended professionally on John Harris.

[31]Profiles were pencil sketches of visitors and were taken by various of the daughters. None of those mentioned here has survived but there are other examples in the Harris Papers.

[32]Galop, a lively dance in duple measure.

& crossed over, when to our horror we found they were strangers. We went to Miss Lynch's [shop], they followed us & when we came out, they went in & asked who we were. They again followed us & we went into a shop & avoided them. When we returned home Mr Peard & Mr Neave told us they were Captain Crespigny & Mr Meshurst [23rd]. Mamma asked Captain Crespigny & Mr Howard to dinner tomorrow. Mrs Becher invited us all to a Christening party tomorrow.
Nov 3 Papa is not at all well. . . .
Nov 4 It poured with rain all day. Mrs Becher wrote to me to beg we would not disappoint her. We promised to go through anything. Mr Peard, Mr Neave & Mr Lutyens called to see if we were going. Mr Peard was stupid & would not go. I read the news, . . . Mr Peard & Mr Neave called. Mr Neave & I made friends but quarrelled immediately afterwards as he was annoyed that Eliza did not come in the room. Mamma asked them to come in the evening. . . . Mr Peard came in the evening but Mr Neave sent a note to Mamma saying he had a headache & "that I ought to think myself lucky that for to night I had escaped with my iniquities (all imaginary) towards him unpunished." I wrote to him asking "if his headache was not in consequence of the absence of a certain person & a little Black Dog he had on his back" but thought better of it & did not send it.[33] Jack however went up to see him. Mr Stanley teased Mary & Mr Peard all evening & would scarcely let them speak to each other & would not let them sit together. He is the merriest person possible & delights in playing tricks & teasing. When he was going to his room he sent a large plum cake to Eliza who was in bed & looked through the crack of the door to see how she received it. Jack returned at twelve having spent a very pleasant evening. When he went to Mr Neave's he could not find him in the house & after searching everywhere at last found him in nothing but a dressing gown & a pair of slippers looking in Mrs [J.W.B.] River's window. They returned to the Cottage & Mr Neave tried to make coffee. He brought in the coffee pot & began pouring it out & found he had forgotten the coffee. Jack was at last obliged to make it. Mr Neave walked home with him in the same costume & looked in every window but we had fortunately drawn every curtain.
Nov 5 We went to church in the morning. Mary, Eliza, Helen,[34] Mrs Perry & I went also in the evening. Amelia was not well & staid at

[33]According to Edward Harris' Key, "to have a black dog on one's back" was to be bad tempered.

[34]Charlotte's sister Helen (1834–60), considered the prettiest among the sisters, married Maurice Berkeley Portman (1833–88).

home. Jack dined with Mr Neave. Mr Peard & Mr Neave came in the evening. Mr Neave & I had another quarrel because I wrote "From Dear Little Arry" in the Prayer Book he gave me, & it hurt his vanity being called little.

Nov 6 Mrs Perry left us this morning for Sarnia. It has been snowing & blowing all day. Mrs Wilson asked us all to spend tomorrow evening with her, but as she has not asked Mr Stanley, we are only too delighted to decline. . . . Mary went to Mrs Caddy who is ill. I went to Becher's office to get *Blackwood's Magazine* & found Mary & Miss Leonard there reading the *London [Illustrated] News*. . . .

Nov 7 This has been the merriest day since Mr Stanley has been here. Mr Peard wrote to Mary complaining of Mr Stanley & Eliza's conduct last night. He said "I hope your sister Eliza & Mr Stanley spent a pleasant evening. It is a pity they did not endeavor to amuse *all* their friends, instead of keeping the amusement *entirely* to themselves. I think the only way to avoid it another time will be for me to go with Mr Neave. I can promise them *I* won't be the source of amusement for another *whole* evening at all events." Amelia stole the note & showed it to Mr Stanley, he was delighted with it & immediately asked Jack to be his friend if Mr Peard called him out. Mr Stanley & Amelia went out driving. Mr Peard & Mr Neave called. Mr Stanley would not let Mr Neave speak to Eliza & sat by her all the time. I talked to Mr Neave to assist Mr Stanley. . . . Mr Stanley proposed that we should write an advertisement & send it to the *Times* about the Black Dogs, we accordingly wrote one – "Found, on the premises of Mr A--N----- of B--W-- Cottage, on the evening of Monday, November 6th, two Black Dogs, supposed to have strayed. Any person claiming them is requested to call & take them away as they have already given considerable annoyance to the advertiser & his friends."[35]

Nov 9 Mr Stanley was frantic to go out sleighing so we made up a party & went out. Jack drove Amelia, Mr Stanley & me, & Mr Peard drove Eliza, Mary & Mr Neave. The sleighing of course was stretched but we had a delightful drive. . . .

Nov 10 I was not well enough to go out. Mr Neave sent me *Wildfell Hall* & Mr Peard brought me *Waverley*.[36] Amelia & Mr Stanley went out driving. We heard from Sarah. . . . When Mr Stanley was going to his room last night he sent Amelia to take our combs, hairpins, we having retired early, that we might not be able to dress our hair in the

[35]Such an advertisement was actually published.

[36]Novels written respectively by Ann Bronte and Sir Walter Scott.

morning, but put it up in some fancy costume. He got up early & went down to see us make our appearance, but as soon as he had left his room we sent Theresa[37] in & she brought us our combs, etc and we came down dressed & turned the laugh against him.

Nov 11 . . . Mr Peard called, he brought me some smelling salts for my head ache. . . . Eliza proposed that we should have a pic nic on Thursday & sent to Colonel Airey to meet us at Talbotville Royal,[38] it was decided that if there was sleighing it should come off. I hope if it does come off they will let me stay at home. . . .

Nov 12 Eliza, Mary & I did not go to church, our colds being worse. Mr Peard came before breakfast to enquire after our precious healths. We asked him to stay but he was obliged to return to the Roman Catholic Chapel to march the men back to the Barracks. . . . Mr Stanley goes on Wednesday. How much we will miss him.

Nov 13 Capt Herbert [23rd] has at last arrived, we had almost given up all idea of ever seeing him here again. There has been no end to the talking. He met Mr Tomson & Mr Beatty in Montreal. He dislikes Mr Tomson & thinks him the most conceited, self opinionated wretch he ever met. . . .

Nov 15 Mr Neave breakfasted with us & left at twelve for Toronto. Mr Stanley also left – he could scarcely tear himself away. Amelia wanders about like a lost spirit. He is to return in the Spring. Eliza, Captain Herbert, Mr Peard & I went out driving. . . .

Nov 16 We asked Mrs Becher to give Captain Herbert a party. She very obligingly said she would & drove in for me to go with her to ask the people. Eliza & Captain Herbert went to Captain Caddy's. Mr Peard called & told us that Mr Law [20th] & Mr Lutyens had gone out shooting & Mr Law's gun had gone off accidentally & shot Mr Lutyens. He was very badly hurt & Mr Howard went out and brought him in. Eliza, Jack, Captain Herbert & I went to the Bechers. It was a small party & rather stupid. We asked everyone to spend tomorrow evening with us. . . .

Nov 17 I wrote the invitations for our party & invited nearly every one in the town. Capt Herbert went out hunting. . . . Captain Herbert returned within two hours after he had left, having in a most unaccountable way lost the hunting party in the woods. He & Eliza drew in the afternoon & then went out walking. Our party was excessively

[37]Charlotte's youngest sister, Teresa Julia, became Mrs. William John Scott (1859–75), and Mrs. St. George Littledale (1875–1928). She is sometimes referred to as Theresa and in one entry as Julia.

[38]Located near Port Talbot.

stupid, nearly all the ladies having come & very few gentlemen. Mr Peard, Mr Howard & Mr Hay being the only military people who made their appearance. The only part of the evening I enjoyed was when I was playing for them to dance which I managed to do a great deal. I missed Mr Beatty so very much. He made every party pleasant. The people left at one o'clock. Amelia & Mary not being well went to bed at half past eleven. Jack found it stupid & also went to bed. Mama, Eliza & Capt Herbert & I sat up talking until half past two. Mama & I then went to bed but Eliza & Capt Herbert talked until nearly four o'clock. We decided it was one evening lost.

Nov 18 . . . We spent a delightful evening, no one but ourselves.

Nov 19 Mamma was not well & could not go to church. Capt Herbert tried to go to the Roman Catholic but it was so full he could not get in & returned & went out walking with Mary. The rest of us went to church. Mr Peard dined with us. . . .

Nov 20 Capt Herbert & Eliza were drawing all the morning. . . . Eliza & Capt Herbert, Mr Peard & I went out riding, . . . We had a delightful ride. Mamma asked Mr Peard & Capt Neave to come in the evening. Mr Neave gave Eliza & Helen each a ring.

Nov 21 Capt Herbert left at two o'clock, we were exceedingly sorry to see him go. We have talked incessantly since he came & have not said half that we wished. Mary gave him a drawing, Eliza & I promised to do one for him. Mr Becher & Mr Wilson lunched with us. Mr Wilson told Amelia he heard she was engaged to Mr Stanley. She did not tell him she was. . . . I was obliged to go out riding with Mrs Becher, Miss Leonard, Mr Hay & Mr Dowling. Nothing shall ever induce me to go out with such a party again, but I was obliged to this time or for ever offend Mrs Becher. . . . Mr Peard gave Helen a velvet Bible & Prayer Book & me some music his sister sent him from England. He proposed for Mary but she will not engage herself to him as he cannot marry for some time.

Nov 22 . . . Mrs Ermatinger[39] came over from St Thomas & spent the day with us. Mr Law rode in to the Kitchen Door & sent in his card, a gentlemanlike way of returning Papa's call. . . . I finished *Guy Mannering*[40] & I gave it to Mr Peard to take home.

Nov 23 . . . Mr Peard called to speak to Mamma about Mary. She will not allow an engagement, but leaves it so that if they like each other

[39]Wife of Edward Ermatinger (1797–1876) who settled at St. Thomas, Upper Canada. In 1830 he became a banker, and from 1844–47 he represented Middlesex in the Legislative Assembly of Upper Canada.

[40]*Guy Mannering, or The Astrologer*, novel by Sir Walter Scott (1815).

as well at the end of two years they may marry, but if they meet others they like better they are not to consider themselves engaged. . . .

Nov 24 A rainy day. Captain Caddy came up to stretch some drawing paper for Mary & me, he dined with us. . . . Mr Neave wrote to me to ask if he might come & draw & sent two books, which if I answered his note, George was to give me, but if not he was to take them back again, but I answered it & gave him leave to come, & got the books. . . . Amelia heard from Mr Stanley. . . .

Nov 25 Snowing heavily. Mrs Becher brought Amelia some jelly. I commenced a watercolored drawing. . . . Papa had a letter from Capt Lefroy[41] in which he, in the most flattering way asked Jack to take observations on the Aurora Borealis.

Nov 26 . . . We spent a very pleasant evening. Mr Lutyens was excessively amusing. He told us an anecdote about Capt Berdmore. When he was ill some one went to see him & finding all the curtains closely drawn, was going to open them when Capt Berdmore called out "Don't open them, I am not shaved, I'm a beast, a beast, a be--a-st, be-a-st," his voice gradually dying away.

Nov 27 . . . Miss Brough called to ask us when we should like Mrs Goodhue to give her ball. We said we were quite ready for it. On Wednesday we are to have a quiet party at Bow Wow Cottage. Mr Lutyens brought Amelia a drawing he did while he was ill. . . .

Nov 29 We received our invitation to Mrs Goodhue's Ball on Friday the 8th December at Waverly Hall. . . . Mr Peard & Mr Neave called to ask if we were going to Bow Wow Cottage this evening, but as it is pouring with rain we have put off the party until Friday & asked them all to come here. . . .

Dec 1 Mr Neave called to see if we were going to spend the evening with him. He sent a covered carriage for us at half past six. Helen went there at six to assist him in arranging the tea table. He received us with a frantic scream. . . . Mr Lutyens, Mr Howard, Mr Peard arrived about a half an hour after we did. We had a most sumptuous tea. Mr Neave placed me at the top of the table. After tea Mamma, Mary, Mr Howard & Mr Peard played whist. Eliza, Mr Neave & Jack & Mr Lutyens & I played backgammon. At eleven we had supper. I then played backgammon with Mr Neave. We did not leave until half past twelve. It was a delightful party.

[41]Sir John Henry LeFroy (1817–90) was in charge of the magnetic observatory at Toronto from 1844 to 1853.

Dec 5 Amelia heard from Mr Stanley. We heard from Col Airey. They are not coming over to the Waverly Ball. Mrs Becher called. Mr Dowling told her he did not intend waltzing much at the Ball. She begged him not to say so publicly as perhaps it might prevent many people going or perhaps . . . put off the Ball. The wretch did not like the answer & looked rather taken aback. Mr Peard called & Mr Neave came to take Helen out sleighing. He gave me a drive while she was getting ready. Mrs Wilson called. . . . Mr Howard, Mr Lutyens, Mr Peard & Mr Neave came at seven to spend the evening. We had a delightful evening.

Dec 8 Amelia, Mary & I went in the town. Mr Peard & Mr Neave called. We asked for an invitation to the Ball for Mr Campbell & got one.

Dec 9 Everyone was charmed with the Ball, it was decidedly the best private one that has ever been given in London. We did not leave until half past three. . . . there was the greatest collection of plain people I ever had the misfortune to meet. I danced very little. . . . Capt Crespigny & Mr Lutyens paid me devoted attention. Mr Campbell was an invaluable addition in the dancing way. Mr Pipon came out in a new character, waltzed & danced the Polka beautifully. I missed Mr Beatty, . . . Mr Hay & Miss Leonard are carrying on a desperate flirtation tho' every-one say Mrs Becher is the fair object. . . .

Dec 10 We all went to church. Mr Campbell sat in our pew. Mr Cronyn preached against the Ball & compared it to Belshazzar's Feast. . . .

Dec 11 . . . [Mr Neave] is ordered to go to Toronto immediately . . . We are very sorry he is going & he is enraged. Theresa is very ill. . . .

Dec 14 Mary & Eliza went to Port Talbot. Amelia would not go because she did not hear from Mr Stanley. . . .

Dec 22 Colonel Airey & Mr Howard breakfasted with us . . . & left at eleven. Col Airey left his wagon & went home in our sleigh. Becher came in to talk. Mrs Becher & Miss Leonard came in their large sleigh & took Amelia, Mr Peard who came to call & [take] me out driving. We had a very pleasant drive, she asked us all out to Thornwood tomorrow evening. . . .

Dec 23 Mr Peard called to ask us to go out driving with him & Mr Lutyens . . . we drove to the Gordons & found they had started & we were to join them on the Plank Road. When we arrived there we met Mrs Gordon walking home & Major Gordon a few yards on standing over the wreck of what was once a beautiful sleigh. They had had a smack! Edward gave up his seat in Mr Peard's sleigh & they took Mrs Gordon in, & we proceeded, leaving Major Gordon to take his wreck home. We then met Dr Combe pulling his horse out of the ditch, &

asked him what was the matter. "Oh! nothing, the horse only went into the Ditch, it is no matter. Never mind!" So we left him. Driving through the town Mr Lutyens drove over a small boy – but, fortunately for him, he was not . . . hurt. . . .

Dec 24 . . . Yesterday we heard from Mary. Louisa Airey is dying, . . .

Dec 25 Xmas Day. We all went to church. Amelia, Eliza, Teresa, George & I went walking. . . . Mr Butler called. Mr Peard & Mr Lutyens dined with us. We played whist, cronoco, etc, etc, etc – they left at eleven o'clock, rather a pleasant evening. Mr Peard gave me a letter to enclose to Mary, which I told him to write as I thought it might relieve his anxious heart a little. I heard from Mr Neave. Our Xmas party was quite broken up, Mary & Mr Howard being at Port Talbot & Mr Neave at Toronto and not able to get leave.

Dec 26 . . . Amelia & I went out walking. I met Mr Peard, he said Mamma was going out driving with him & asked me to go also, which I did. Mr Lutyens asked me to go with him, but I declined. Becher & Mr Wilson called. . . .

Dec 29 Becher dined with us. Jack returned & brought us a letter from Mary. She does not know when she will return. Louisa Airey still lingers on. They expect her to die every hour tho' . . . Mr Neave returned, he & Mr Peard came down in the evening. He brought Eliza a beautiful ring. They want us to drive to St Thomas tomorrow.

Dec 30 Mamma did not want to go to St Thomas so we went out driving instead . . . Coming home we met Edward at the Junction, he had just upset. We stopped & picked them up & took Teresa with us. He stopped at the Inn until Edward & George had again started. . . . Mr Butler is trying to get up a pic nic . . . with the Woodstock people on the third. We promised to support it. . . .

1849

Jan 1 New Year's Day. Mamma, Amelia & Eliza went to church. Jack went to the election in the Township of London. We had about fifty visitors. Mr Hay & Mr Butler had too much wine. This is the first time anyone has called here in that state. Mr Butler had an answer from Woodstock, he brought it to us – we are to have the pic nic on Thursday. Mr Neave & Mr Peard dined with us. Mr Wilson came in after dinner to talk over the election.

Jan 3 . . . Capt Crespigny came to ask me to drive to the pic nic with him. I declined as Mamma does not wish us to drive alone with gentlemen. . . . Mamma . . . & I should go in one coach & Mary, Eliza, Mr Howard, Mr Neave & Mr Peard in the other.

Jan 4 Mr Peard came down before breakfast to know if the arrangements of yesterday are final & he was to hire the coach. He told us that last night at Mess Captain Crespigny was describing his visit here & said that one young lady came in evidently "got up" for the occasion & *tried to be a Lady but could not succeed.* We do not know which one it was as Amelia, Mary & I were the three who appeared. We were enraged with him & determined he should not go with us. . . . The pic nic was rather slow, tho' I enjoyed myself very much having had very good partners to dance with. . . .

Jan 16 . . . At 12 o'clock last night we were awakened by the cry of Fire. Nearly one block has burnt in the centre of Dundas Street.

Jan 18 Mr Becher called on his way to St Thomas. He said the Ball was delightful. We heard that Mr Dowling had insulted Miss Hall & Mr Staunton (from St Thomas) had given him two black eyes in the Ball room. He had taken too much wine. It happened at five o'clock in the morning . . . Mr Howard & Mr Peard told us Mr Dowling's affair was nearly ending in a duel but Mr Staunton apologized. We congratulated ourselves we had not been there. . . .

Jan 19 Mary wrote an invitation to Mr Stevens & a request that he would bring his flute. . . . Our party went off very well, not very brilliant. We danced. I played [the piano] nearly all the evening, sometimes with Mr Stevens and sometimes by myself. . . .

Jan 22 . . . Mamma & Jack returned from Port Talbot. Mamma enjoyed her visit but John was very glad to come home. Amelia remained there. The Aireys want her to stay until after Easter but she declined. . . . Mr Becher, Mr Hay, Capt Crespigny, Mr Lutyens, Mr Howard, Mr Peard & Edward went out driving on the ice, which broke & Becher's sleigh with himself, Capt Crespigny, & Mr Hay went in. The horses were nearly drowned & they were very wet. . . .

Feb 5 . . . Mr Howard called to see Papa. He examined him with a stethescope & thinks his lungs are affected. He is very unwell. . . .

Feb 6 Papa very ill. We sent for Mr Howard before breakfast. . . . Mr Becher called to see Papa. . . . Mr Webb called to see Papa. . . . Dr Anderson came in to see Papa & took tea with us. . . .

Feb 9 We received a most amusing letter from Edward. He has passed as a law student. . . .

Feb 11 . . . Uncle Edward [Ryerse] is very ill again. Mamma & I are going to Long Point tomorrow to see him. None of us shall go to the pic nic. . . . The Bechers are annoyed at our not going . . . as it was put off last Friday because Papa was not well enough for us to go [with] them & now it is impossible as our uncle is dangerously ill.

Feb 12 . . . We left at eleven & took two children down with us, a

boy for Uncle Edward & a girl to stay with an old woman who is living alone. It was very cold. My hands were so cold driving that we stopped at Ingersol to warm ourselves, . . . staid an hour at Woodstock, . . . I[t] was quite dark when we reached Dormans[42] where we remained all night. . . . I made Joe, who is a musical genius, play on the violin for our edification until we thought we should [have] every one who was in the inn in our rooms to dance a jig or Highland fling, or something equally enlivening. I did not sleep more than an hour during the night. . . .
Feb 13 We left again at a quarter to nine. . . . We arrived at Port Ryerse at half past one. They did not expect us . . . there was not a man to be had for love or money, so I had to unharness the horses, put their clothing on & feed them. . . .
Feb 14 I went to the stable to see the horses, then took my sketch book, & tried to take a sketch of Uncle George's house but it was so very cold I was obliged to give it up.[43]
Feb 28 Becher called. Mrs Becher came in to say she could not ride. I persuaded her to & gave her a bouquet. We asked Mr Lutyens, Mr Howard, Mr Law & Mr Peard to ride. . . . We had a very pleasant ride tho' . . .
Mar 8 . . . Papa went out for the first time for seven weeks. . . .
Mar 14 . . . Mr Peard called. He had written a note to Mary in the morning complaining of her conduct last night, which was rather an extraordinary proceeding & unauthorized, but he is so frightfully in love & jealous. He repented having written it & apologized. I drew all the afternoon. . . .
Mar 22 . . . The *on dit* is that Mary is to be married to Mr Peard tomorrow, nearly everyone believes it.
Mar 26 . . . Mr Neave wrote to Mr Peard & told him that the report of his engagement had reached England. . . . The *good* people of the town now say that Mary's marriage with Mr Peard is put off until the third of April. . . .
Mar 28 I called today my birthday. I told Mamma I wanted a party, she said I might have one. So we asked Mr Pipon, Mr Lutyens, Mr Howard, Mr Hay, Mr Peard & Mr Law. Mr Peard declined because Mr Law was coming. . . .
Apr 6 Good Friday. Jack came home last night at half past eleven. The party at Mess was excessively noisy, he left at ten & went to Mr

[42]An inn near Burford.

[43]On a later visit to Port Ryerse, Charlotte completed a watercolour of Edward Ryerse's house which is now in the Harris Papers. The house is still standing.

Howard's room. We went to church. Becher called, he told us they had a very scientific argument at the Mess table last night & that Jack had taken an active part in it & shone brilliantly. Becher wanted me to ride with him & Mrs Becher but Sally [horse] was not well enough & Edward had got up at four o'clock & gone to Dorchester to fish, & taken Charlie [horse]. Col Airey & George left at ten o'clock.[44] . . . Edward returned at seven o'clock, having caught two dozen trouts. Jack went out spear-fishing.

Apr 16 . . . Mr Peard called & told us there was a plot against us at the Givins' party to prevent our dancing. Mr Hay & Capt Crespigny were at the head of it. I suppose I was excepted as Mr Hay danced three times with me. . . .

Apr 18 We heard from . . . Sarah. Her boy[45] is very ill again, she fears she will lose him.

Apr 26 . . . Papa sent us to the Wilsons to hear what news Mrs Wilson had from Montreal, as the loyal people of Canada hissed & pelted Lord Elgin as he was going to the House to give his assent to the Bill for paying the Rebels.[46] They burnt Parliament House & every thing was lost. Mrs Wilson was not at home. We had a very nice party. . . .

Apr 27 . . . Amelia [heard] from Mr Stanley. He has spoken to his father who had heard of their engagement before he went home. His father will not allow him to marry so that is over. Poor Amelia feels it deeply, how unfortunate it was he ever came here. . . .

Apr 29 Col Talbot came to the Aireys to breakfast. Col Airey & Jack went out walking. . . . Col Airey read prayers as there was no service in the church. We lunched at one o'clock. Col & Mrs Airey, Jack & I went out walking in the garden. We dined at six. We all called to see Col Talbot. He was dressed in his Sunday's best writing to Lady Wharncliff & Lady Frances Hope. . . .

Apr 30 Col Talbot came over after breakfast. Jack took our parcels from him which he had brought out for us from Sarah & Mr Tighe & which we immediately opened much to the horror & surprise of the Aireys. Sarah sent each of us a broach, Papa a dressing gown & some Arrow Root.[47] . . .

May 2 . . . Peard, George & I went to the pasture for the cow. . . . Mr

[44]They were going to Port Talbot.

[45]Sarah Dalzell's two year old son, Robert.

[46]This is a reference to Governor General Elgin's decision to sign the Rebellion Losses Bill, the signing of which confirmed the establishment of responsible government, and prompted the burning of the Parliament buildings by the infuriated Montreal Tories.

[47]Medicinal plant.

Peard came down after Mess & brought Amelia the *Spectator*. . . . Mrs Dixon brought Amelia Miss Austin's works.
May 13 . . . Amelia, Eliza, Papa, Mr Neave & I went to church. . . .
May 16 . . . Mrs Wilson called to ask Julia & George to a children's party tomorrow. . . .
May 22 . . . Mr Neave received a telegraph message & was obliged to leave. . . . When the Stage drove up & we were saying Good Bye! he came to me & put his arms round me & said – "Good Bye Miss Chasse, my own Love!" We heard a voice at the door say "Are your things ready, we are in a hurry." We turned round & it was the Stage driver. Mr Neave gave one of his screams & burst out laughing. I laughed & ran away. Fortunately Mamma, Mr Peard & all were there so he cannot think it was a tender scene going on between us. . . .
May 24 . . . Papa went to the Barracks to read the news. . . . Coming home we met a procession with torches, the town band playing, fireworks, etc in honour of the Queen's birthday. We drove about the town (it being night) to see them, with the true spirit of loyalty. . . .
May 28 . . . Mr Lutyens brought us his drawing of the "Deer Stalkers" & Capt Hallowell's drawings. He has also given us "The Evening Gun."[48] . . .
Jun 8 . . . Papa, Eliza, . . . & Jack called at Becher's & went out driving. . . .
Jun 22 We left at half past four in the morning for Port Stanley. Mr Peard drove Mamma, Mary & Papa in our carriage. . . . At eight we went on board the boat. . . . There were three hundred people on board, a band from Buffalo which played all day & the rabble danced. . . . It was half past four when we arrived at Cleveland. We went in all the shops. . . . We had tea at seven & went on board again at eight, having had great fun. . . . The band played all night & the rabble danced again. We took our dresses off & put on our dressing gowns. . . . we had the ladies saloon to ourselves, Papa & Mamma went to bed, Mr Peard & I & Eliza & Mr Howard talked. We went to our berths at eleven. The gentlemen could not get berths so [we] took the sofas out of the ladies cabin for them & gave them our blankets & pillows & they slept outside our cabins. We got up at two o'clock in the morning as the boat arrived at Port Stanley at four. It was nine o'clock when we reached home. The gentlemen went to the Barracks to dress [and] came down again to breakfast at eleven. . . .

[48]Both paintings are at Eldon House.

Jun 27 We heard from Becher. He tells us Mr Street has proposed to Amelia & she refused him. . . .
Jul 4 Mr Neave received a telegraphic message & was obliged to leave at one o'clock. He told Amelia he had written to his father for leave to marry Eliza. His father had no objection but said he had better wait two or three years as he was not well enough off to allow him to marry on.
Jul 11 . . . Mamma wrote to Mr Stanley.
Jul 22 . . . All went to church except Papa & Mamma who are not very well. . . . Mr Howard told us that Captain Knight was kept a Prisoner of War at Rome & is to get three months more leave. I am very sorry for it as I long to see him. . . .
Jul 25 . . . Col Cunnyngham advised Mr Peard privately to take care of himself as he heard he was going to marry one of the Misses Harris, & not marry rashly as he would more than likely repent it, & if he did fall in love not to go too far. Mr Peard is furious. It is all that viper Col Airey's doing. . . .
Jul 28 . . . Mr Wilson called. Mamma told him all about our troubles & Mary's engagement. He & Becher will exert themselves to get us out of our difficulties. What invaluable friends. How much we have to be thankful to them for. . . .
Aug 4 . . . I went out sketching & took my sketch to Mr Hamilton for him to point out the faults & tell me how to correct them. . . .
Aug 8 . . . Mr Neave sent Mary her trace patterns & a short cool note, he is enraged that Eliza did not answer his letter. He wrote to Mr Peard & told him. Mr Peard immediately brought the letter to us to read. Eliza wrote to him.
Aug 18 . . . Four companies of the 20th have orders to hold themselves in readiness to go to Kingston at a moment's notice as there are riots expected in Montreal.
Aug 21 . . . Mr Lutyens, Edward & I went out walking. I took my sketch book with me. Mr Lutyens & I made a sketch. . . .
Sep 11 I had to go with Mamma, Amelia, Eliza & Mr Howard in a carriage to hold four. I wanted to stay home but Mamma would not let me. We reached Delaron at half past ten o'clock. The Gordons, Cunnynghams, Askins [etc.] were there. Mr Lutyens went with the Cunnynghams, Capt Crespigny drove four in hand & took Miss Askin & Col Askin. Mr Dowling took Cynthia [Askin], Mr Hay went alone, he was so angry he would not speak to us. I envyed them so much when I saw them ride off, & had to follow in the carriage. There were not

many Indians at Munsee Town,[49] [sic] the Oneidas had not come. We went to the . . . Mr Mills' house, . . . We saw the Indians run a race. They also played ball[50] but we did not wait to see the game. We dine[d] at Delaron on our return. Mr Hay forgave me & talked to me before I left. It was eight o'clock when we reached home. We found Mr Law & Mr Peard here, we were very tired.

Oct 1 Papa received an invitation from the Goodhues to dine with them on Wednesday, & we [are] to spend the evening.[51] . . .

Oct 3 . . . Mamma, Amelia, Mary & I went to the Goodhues. It was a delightful party. . . .

Oct 4 . . . Lord Elgin & Capt Bruce, Mr Goodhue, & Mr Wilson called. . . .

Oct 9 . . . Papa has lost the Treasurer's office.[52]

Oct 31 I went out riding with Mrs Becher. While I was dressing Mr Wilson ran in & said there was a bear on the Flats[53] & told John & Edward to get the guns & shoot him, which they immediately did. Half the town was after him, we rushed to the bank to see the hunt. John shot him five times & Edward & Mr Carr when he took to the river got in to the canoe & went after him & killed him with the oar & an axe. The excitement was intense. They landed the bear & some detestable Yankees claimed him as they were hunting him in the morning. It was most unjust, John & Edward killed him & did not get any part of him. . . .

Nov 2 . . . We asked Mrs Becher to go to the concert with us. . . . The concert went off very successfully. The room[54] was crowded, the children played very well, but there was too much of it . . . Helen played well. . . .

Nov 13 . . . Jack received a letter from Mr Neave telling him how Col Airey abused us to all his visitors in a most shameful way. Mr Peard read the letter & was as much enraged as we are. Jack is to write to Col Airey & tell him what we hear, it will rather astonish him. Mamma & Papa went to the Goodhues. Mr Goodhue sent his carriage for them, . . . [they] returned at eleven having had a very pleasant party.

Nov 17 . . . Mr Tomson came down in the morning to consult Papa about some maps he is to draw. . . .

[49]Muncey is an Indian Reservation twenty miles south of London.

[50]Probably lacrosse.

[51]The dinner was in honour of Lord Elgin, Governor General, who was a guest of the Goodhues.

[52]This was a false report.

[53]The flood land below Eldon House.

[54]The concert was held in the Mechanics' Institute.

Nov 19 . . . Mamma wrote the letter to Col Airey.
Nov 21 . . . Mr Tomson was here all the morning drawing maps. . . .
Nov 24 Shuldham came down in the morning to drink some champagne he gave us. We received an answer from Col Airey. He denies all. . . .
Nov 27 Mrs Airey wrote Amelia another most impertinent letter. I hope we have done with them now. . . .
Dec 4 . . . The dance was delightful.[55] Mr Beatty had descended from his high horse & was very agreeable, he is improved. The finale spoiled our pleasurable feeling. Mamma was not taken to supper which enraged us all, it was Col Cunnyngham's bad management as when supper was announced Mr Wilson, Becher, Lawrason were playing whist, & either of them ought to have taken Mamma, but that was no excuse for the others. We left at one o'clock to people's disgust as it broke up the party. . . .
Dec 16 . . . Jack went to the Barracks for Dr Fisher[56] to come & see Papa as Mr Howard told us to send for him while he is away. He came down after Mess. He laughs at the 20th Invitations[57] as much as everyone else do. . . . Mr Beatty heard from Capt Knight. He asks about us & hopes I have not pined away for Mr Beatty & have recovered my spirits now that he has returned. He will find that I have recovered my imaginary lost spirits & not to talk to him. He also says he heard that Mr Stanley has had a flirtation with one of the "Democrats," which coming with the other I suppose means one of us. What wretches men are! . . .
Dec 20 . . . Mary is ill. Shuldham came down in the morning to ask after her. . . . [and] was here all the afternoon. He went up at eight o'clock to dress to take Mamma into the Ball room. Mamma, Eliza, Edward & I went to the Ball. It went off very well, nearly all the Londoners were there. . . . It was three o'clock when we came home. Mr Goodhue brought us home in his carriage. Mr Fisher came to see Papa. Mamma asked him to dine with us on Xmas day. He said he would come & was evidently much pleased.
Dec 25 Xmas Day. Edward & I went to church. There was so heavy a snow storm the others were afraid to venture. Mr Becher called & proposed that his party should come in & spend the evening with us, which we decidedly advocated. Edward dined with them. . . . Mr Peard

[55]The 20th Regiment dance was held at the home of the Cunnynghams.
[56]A doctor attached to the 20th Regiment.
[57]A reference to the 20th Regiment's dance.

& Mr Fisher dined with us. The Bechers, Mr Hay & Mr Stoneham came in the evening. We had a very merry evening. Mr & Mrs Becher, Mamma & Eliza played whist. Mamma left the table soon & Mr Fisher took her place. She then played with Helen, Edward & Mr Stoneham. Mr Fisher & I played backgammon in the beginning of the evening. Mr Hay & I played chess the remainder of the evening. Becher was in great force. They left at half past eleven.
Dec 30 All went to church. . . . Eliza, Miss Watson, Helen, Edward & I went to the evening service. The evening was rather dull. Shuldham heard from Mr Neave. . . .
Dec 31 Mr Becher & Mr Fisher called. Mamma & Mrs Watson spent the evening at the Cronyns, it was rather a large party. We received invitation to the Lawrasons' for Friday evening, it is to be a grand Ball & Shuldham was here in the evening. He, Jack & all of us danced as usual. I played.

1850

Jan 1 New Year's Day. . . . Papa, John, Edward & George went out visiting. We received fifty two visitors & were very tired when it was all over. . . . I had to undergo the misery of shaking hands 105 times today.
Jan 10 . . . George Macbeth called.[58] He abused the Aireys to his heart's content. They are in town. Thank heaven we are done with them . . .
Jan 13 . . . Shuldham came down to drive Mary. She did not go. Papa did not like her going on Sunday. . . .
Jan 17 Papa went down to vote for Mr Wilson, & Becher with great delight told him he could not vote as he is a receiver of Public Money. . . . Mr Wilson won the Election. . . . Mr Wilson is very bitter about the Election & still denies being a radical. Col Airey is in town, John met him & had the pleasure of cutting him.
Jan 25 Shuldham was here in the evening, he was writing the letter to his mother telling her of his approaching marriage. Mamma & I wrote to Sarah.
Jan 26 . . . [Amelia] enclosed a letter from Mr Neave in which he says

[58]The Macbeth family settled in the Talbot Settlement in 1838 when George was 12, but in 1839 the father left. George remained and became servant, friend, companion, advisor, and finally heir to Colonel Talbot and on the death of the latter, received about £50,000 from Talbot's estate. Macbeth's son, Talbot, a lawyer and later a judge, lived next door to Eldon House for many years.

he fears he never shall be able to marry Eliza. His family have been writing to him about his marrying & threaten never to see him if he marries, tho' they can keep him out of nothing except reducing his allowance during his father's life. . . .
Feb 12 We had a delightful letter from Amelia who is the acknowledged Belle of Albany & is enjoying herself very much. . . .
Feb 16 . . . Minnie Street brought back *Pendennis* & took the 7th number of *David Copperfield* for Mrs Leonard. . . .
Feb 22 Captain Caddy came up in the morning to sketch in the background of Eliza's picture . . . Shuldham brought me [Scott's] *Woodstock.*
Mar 8 . . . Mr Widder came in the evening & made himself very agreeable. He told us the 20th were to remain here another year, we were shocked beyond measure at the intelligence, but fortunately it is not true. . . .
Mar 12 . . . Becher came in & told us Col Talbot was very unwell & if possible would be here next week. . . .
Mar 15 . . . I took the "Bear Hunt" & the "Three Horse's Heads"[59] to Mr Hamilton to see if they must be varnished. He varnished them for me. . . .
Mar 17 . . . Mr Fisher had no idea Eldon was so pretty & so large a place, he was charmed with it. Mr Becher returned from Port Talbot. Col Talbot is better, he & George [Macbeth] are going to leave for England next week never to return. He stays a few days with us on his way. Poor old man is not at all happy. Fanny Becher came in to play with Teresa. . . .
Mar 19 . . . There is a report that we are to have the Canadian Rifles here instead of the 20th. What a dreadful falling off that will be.
Mar 20 We heard from . . . Mrs Peard, she is in a dreadful state about Mr Peard [and] says it is impossible for him to marry before two or three years as he has nothing. Shuldham heard from his mother, sister, uncle [General Ellacombe] & Mr Kekewich.[60] His mother spoke very strongly to him & wants him to get leave & go home – which he will not do – his sister's letter is ridiculous, she speaks very angrily &

[59]Both of these works hang at Eldon House.

[60]Edward Kekewich was a brother of the husband of Peard's sister and a close personal friend. They were fellow officers in the 20th Regiment, but at this time Kekewich was stationed in England. They served together throughout the Crimean campaign, in which Kekewich was wounded and subsequently died of cholera. G.S. Peard's *Narrative of a Campaign in the Crimea*, London: R. Bentley, 1855 describes their relationship.

abusively & not at all a good letter. Mr Kekewich's is the best letter of all. They seem more annoyed that he had not told them before that he wished to marry, only giving them two months notice does not please them. They speak very well of us & do not disapprove of the match after he is twenty three but think it ridiculous his marrying before he is twenty one. He will have to wait a year. They are both miserable. But the course of true love never did run smooth. It is a most unfortunate thing but what we might have expected. Becher came in. Mamma gave him Mrs Peard's & his uncle's letters to read. He does not know what to say about it & feels as unhappy as we do about it. General Ellacombe wrote to Col Cunnyngham [20th] about it & Col C sent for Mr Peard & spoke to him & was excessively kind & instead of preventing it & sending Shuldham away, Shuldham thinks [he] will do as much as he can for him. . . .

Mar 22 . . . She [Amelia] brought a great many things for Mary, her wedding dress is beautiful. . . .

Mar 27 . . . Becher went to Port Talbot. Mamma sent Col Talbot some oranges & Eliza sent him her picture of the "Den" which she painted for him.[61] . . .

Mar 28 . . . Mary & I went out walking. Coming home the Palestons drove up to us & asked us if we had heard of Col Talbot. We said we had heard he was much worse & dying. He then told us he had met Mr Becher driving to our house with two gentlemen in his carriage, one very much wrapped up. We could not imagine who it was, & could scarcely think it was Col Talbot as we heard he was so ill. We hurried home & to our great delight found Col Talbot there. He is very ill. Becher & George [Macbeth] carried him to his room & Becher sent for Dr Anderson who says he had erysipelas[62] in his leg, which is swollen immensely. He says he feels very happy here, he kissed us all & cried. He said to Mamma "Oh! Mrs Harris you have no idea what I have suffered, it is mind." He alluded to the Aireys. He look[s] very miserable. When Becher arrived at Port Talbot, Col Talbot said "I am going with you tomorrow if I die on the road." He came over on a bed. Becher drove furiously for fear he would die before he arrived here. His parting with Col Airey was very cold. Col Airey told him the Robinson Hall[63] was very comfortable, exceedingly comfortable! So George told me [that] the last time he was in London . . . Col Talbot

[61]"The Den" was one of the buildings of the Talbot Estate.

[62]An acute infectious skin disease characterized by deep-red inflamation of the skin.

[63]A hotel in London.

[said], "But I intend to stay with Mrs Harris, for if all the world quarrel with them that is no reason I should." Col Airey had been trying, ever since our quarrel, to find out if Col Talbot knew it, & could not, & Col Talbot's parting speech was rather startling. Shuldham came down in the evening & when we told him Col Talbot was here he was as delighted as we were. . . .

Mar 29 Good Friday. Capt Paleston sent to enquire after Col Talbot. We went to church. Becher came in to breakfast. Dr Anderson came to see Col Talbot. He was too ill to get up. Mrs Becher came home from church with us. . . . Amelia, Eliza, John, Edward & I went to the Lawrasons . . . & came home at eleven o'clock. We found Mamma, Mary & George Macbeth having a long talk, George was telling them about Col Airey. He is a greater villain. . . . We went in to see Col Talbot before he went to bed, he looked so ill that we were very anxious & Eliza & I went over to Dr Anderson to tell him but he said there was no danger & if he got worse to come & tell him but he did not. . . .

Mar 31 All went to church. Mr Cronyn came in the morning to enquire after Col Talbot & Col Cunnyngham sent to enquire. He is a little better. Becher came in to sit with him to let George [Macbeth] go out, he went riding with Jack. Capt Crespigny & Mr Butler called, we were at dinner & did not let them in. They told Mr Peard we would not receive visitors while Col Talbot was so ill. . . . Dr Anderson came twice to see him. . . . Col Talbot is in very low spirits to night, he thinks he will never recover. George is very anxious, he & John sit up with Col Talbot at night. . . . George gave Amelia a beautiful seal that Col Talbot had given him, it had been in his family for more than two hundred years. It is very large & has a thin old crest on it.

Apr 1 Col Talbot is better. Amelia, Mary, Eliza & I sat with him for a short time. Becher came twice to see him. He said he would go on to Toronto tomorrow & Becher was obliged to tell Dr Anderson to forbid it positively so Dr Anderson came & told him he should not go as he would not answer for the consequences, that it would be sure to kill him & said he should not think of it for six or seven days at the least. So he gave it up. . . .

Apr 3 Col Talbot is better but not able to sit up. . . . Dr Anderson & Mr Becher were here in the morning & evening to see Col Talbot. He says he will leave on Friday but we shall try to persuade him to remain at least until Monday. He says he is very unhappy & wishes to be out of Middlesex as quickly as possible & be far away from Col Airey. Poor old man his heart is breaking. . . .

Apr 4 Mr Goodhue, Mr Birrell[64] & Col Cunnyngham called to enquire after Col Talbot, he saw them. Becher came three times to see him. He adores Becher. He has given up all idea of leaving tomorrow & says he will remain ten days or a fortnight. He says he is not quite as obstinate as we think as he yielded to our entreaties. . . .
Apr 5 Col Talbot passed a very bad night & is worse today. Dr Anderson came twice to see him. Yesterday he would not take any medicine & today he is afraid he will die & does anything he is told to. Becher is so kind to him. Col T asked him to come every fourth hour & give him his medicine which he did & at two o'clock he fed him, & it was the first he had eaten for three months. He sent several times for Mamma & asked her if she thought he would die & spoke to her of a future state. Poor old man, he is very miserable. . . .
Apr 6 Col Talbot passed a very good night but was very ill the first part of the day. His eyes are very sore. Amelia & Mary bathed them very often. . . . Col Airey came over he wrote a note to Mamma asking if she would allow him to call & see Col Talbot. Mamma read the note to Col T & he dictated the answer. Col Airey came & saw no one but Col Talbot. I met him in the town & cut him dead. Mr Hay [20th] rode up to me & said something about the cool way I cut Col A & asked if he was going to dine with the Bechers & if Col A was he would not. I said I thought not. George [Macbeth] is ill. Shuldham was here the afternoon & evening. Mr Wilson called twice. Col Talbot asked to see him & made friends, there was a mutual apology. Mr W was very much pleased.
Apr 7 Col T is not any better & in very low spirits. Dr Anderson came in the morning & evening to see him. He seems doubtful about his recovery but says nothing. Becher came in & sat with him from eleven until four. All went to church except Mamma, Papa & Mary. Eliza heard from Mr Neave. Mr Askin came to see Col Talbot, & Mrs & Mr Ermatinger, he saw Mr A & Mr E but declined seeing Mrs E. While we were at church Col Airey came, he walked upstairs to Col T's room & met Mary coming out, there was a sort of half bow & nothing more. He stayed for an hour & bored Col T who told him three times to go away before he did. . . .
Apr 9 Col Airey came to say good bye to Col Talbot, he has returned to Port Talbot. . . .
Apr 30 Col T is the same. Becher came three times. . . . Col Airey &

[64]John Birrell (1815–75) was trained in business in Glasgow, emigrated to Canada in 1840, and settled in London. He was a successful merchant for about thirty-five years and was also President of the London, Huron and Bruce Railway.

Mrs A came to see Col T who did not receive them at all graciously. . . .

May 1 Papa was taken ill in the night. Eliza & I were up with him. We were going to send for Mr Fisher but he got a little better. Mamma sent for Mr F at six in the morning, she asked him to stay & breakfast with us but he declined as he had not completed his toilette. Becher came in twice. Col T is not quite so well. The Aireys came twice, Col T received them still more ungraciously. Mr Fisher came again, I asked him to come in the evening. Shuldham was here in the evening. Mr F came, I had the entertaining of him as no one else appeared. Papa is better. . . .

May 24 . . . Dr A came. Col T sat up in an arm chair & was carried to the hall window. He looked wretched & only staid up a very short time. . . .

May 26 . . . George carried Col Talbot out in the garden where he sat in an arm chair for an hour. When they all came from church they were surprised & delighted to see him. He was charmed with his feat & thinks if it was not for his leg he would be quite well. Becher came to see him & Dr Anderson. We sat in his room all afternoon. He was very merry. Papa came in, Col Talbot asked where he had been wandering & commenced singing "Goosey Goosey Gander" much to our amusement. He thinks of nothing but going to England & returning in two or three years to see us & stay some time in Canada. He thinks he will live for ever. . . .

May 27 We got up at six o'clock to see Papa off.[65] Mr & Mrs Wilson breakfasted with us. Mrs Wilson came to see the last of her husband as he goes to Toronto to attend the Session [Legislative Assembly]. . . . Col & Mrs Airey came at ten o'clock to see Col Talbot, & again to say good bye to him, he was sitting in the garden looking much better. . . .

Jun 1 . . . Papa returned from Long Point. He met with an accident, the shafts broke, he was thrown out & very much hurt. John went up for Mr Fisher, he was not at home. Major Chester[66] sent his servant to look for him & Captain Bell[67] left a note in his room for him. Capt Bell came to tea, he talked some time to Col Talbot. Becher came two or three times.

[65]He was going to Long Point with John Wilson.

[66]Henry Chester, who became commanding officer of the Royal Welch Fusiliers, was killed in action in the Crimean War.

[67]Edward Bell, Royal Welch Fusiliers, was awarded the Victoria Cross in 1857 for gallantry in the Crimean War.

Jun 2 Mr Fisher came down early in the morning, he breakfasted with us. We heard from Sarah. Eliza, Helen & I went to church. Amelia & Mary have the mumps. Mr Fisher came again after church, he saw Col Talbot. Becher came for him. . . .

Jun 13 . . . Col Talbot is the same & says he will go on Monday.

Jun 15 . . . Mamma went with Papa to Mr Strathy's office to assist them with Papa's accounts.[68] . . . Col T has consented to stay another week with us. . . .

Jun 18 . . . Col Talbot is not so well. Dr Anderson saw him & thinks he had better go as going or staying will make no difference with him. . . .

Jun 22 Amelia heard from Mr Townsend[69] he wrote from Buffalo & expected to be here today, he did not come. . . .

Jun 23 Mr Townsend arrived at three o'clock in the morning. John went to the Hotel for him & brought him up to breakfast. He appeared a very nice person. He would never be mistaken for anything but an American. . . . We took him to see Col Talbot. Mr Barwell called to see Col Talbot. Mr Townsend & all of us went to the evening service. Captain Campbell.[70] . . . Becher came in, he was very much pleased with Mr Townsend. Col Airey arrived, he came to see Col Talbot. . . .

Jun 24 Col Talbot dressed & was carried to the drawing room at half past eight in the morning. Col Airey came to see him, we were all in [the] room & gave him a distant bow, he only stayed a minute & returned a short time before Col T left to see him off. Dr Anderson called to say good bye to him. Becher came at half past ten. Mamma went to Woodstock with Col T. They left at eleven. We were very very sorry to say goodbye. They were equally sorry to pack, George looked very sad. Col Airey was out at the carriage with us all the time, after they drove off he took off his hat & said good morning, we bowed low. . . . Becher & Eliza left for Woodstock at nine o'clock in the evening. Becher goes to Toronto with Col Talbot. . . .

Jun 25 . . . Mamma & Eliza returned at one o'clock. Col Talbot was improving every hour. . . . Mrs Anderson sent Annie Caddy to beg us to go & bring Mr Townsend with us. I went & spent a delightful evening, talking first to Mr Wilkerson then to Col Crutchley,[71] Capt

[68]James Strathy, District Clerk and later County Clerk, was consulted by John and Amelia Harris with regard to the muddled state of the Treasurer's book-keeping.

[69]John Jacob Townsend, an Albany lawyer, whom Amelia had met while visiting the J.H. Plumbs, had homes in both Albany and Niagara.

[70]The first reference in the diary to Captain Frank Campbell, 23rd Regiment, who later proposed to Charlotte.

[71]The first reference in the diary to Charles Crutchley, 23rd Regiment, who married Eliza Harris in 1851.

Bell, Capt Campbell, Capt Anderson, Captain Phillott & John Fraser.[72] Edward came for me at half past ten. Sat up & talked to my sisters & Mr Townsend for half an [hour] telling all I heard, said & did. . . .

Jun 27 . . . We sent a note to Capt Campbell by Capt Phillott . . . & Eliza put a thorn through the envelope & sent it to him that way. . . . I talked to Capt Campbell the greater part of the evening. Col Crutchley admires Eliza very much. . . .

Jun 28 . . . Mr Townsend left at twelve o'clock at night, he was very sorry to go & we were very sorry to say good bye. Eliza taught him to dance the deux temps valse. . . .

Jul 3 Mary heard from Shuldham, he finds it very difficult to get his leave & almost doubts being able to. Amelia heard from Mr Townsend. . . .

Jul 4 . . . Captain Campbell came to tea. I talked to Capt Campbell. . . . Col Crutchley goes to Port Talbot next Monday, which is a very great pity as Col Airey will stuff him with all kinds of falsehoods.

Jul 6 Mary heard from Shuldham, he is almost sure of getting his leave, if he does he will be here in less than a fortnight. . . . This is the first evening we have been by ourselves since the 28th of March, the day Col Talbot came to us. . . .

Jul 8 Mamma went to Mr Strathy's office again. Colonel Fraser called, only Papa & Mamma saw him. Becher came here three or four times. . . .

Jul 9 . . . Becher was here as usual. . . . Mamma & I went to the Hotel to call on Mrs Gourley. She is not at all a nice person, dresses like a witch. If I had known who she was before I went I would have seen her further before I had called on her. . . .

Jul 11 . . . Capt Campbell brought me a book to read, *The Ogilvies.*[73] . . .

Jul 13 Mamma & Papa went to Strathy's Office. . . .

Jul 15 Mary heard from Shuldham. . . . Colonel Crutchley called. We are all invited to the Hamiltons. Eliza, Mary, John, Edward, Helen & I went. We had a little dancing, talking etc & spent a very pleasant evening, a few people there. Mamma went to Strathy's office.

Jul 16 Mamma went to S's office. Amelia, Eliza, Mamma, Helen, Teresa & Ellen went up to see the cricket match. When we went all the gentlemen were at luncheon, so we went over to the Shake-

[72]Anderson, Phillott, Fraser and Wilkerson were other 23rd Regiment officers.

[73]A novel by Dinah Maria Milock, published in London in 1849.

speares[74] until we were sent for. The gentlemen were afraid we were offended because none of them were there to receive us, but we were not. They had refreshments, jelly, ices, etc for us. We stayed there until six o'clock & talked to every one & had "quite a pleasant time." . . .

Jul 17 Mamma went to Strathy's office. Becher came. Captain Campbell called, he brought me *Woman's Friendship*[75] to read at Long Point. We asked him to tea. We went to the Barracks & returned at seven. He & I played backgammon all the evening & talked. . . .

Jul 18 Mary heard from Shuldham. She is very anxious to leave for Long Point today but we could not get ready early enough. . . . Amelia, Mary & I went out to Thornwood to see Mrs Becher, she asked us to stay to tea, we declined. . . . Capt Bell came to tea. Capt Campbell promised to call & did not, I cannot conceive why. Mr Hammond brought us some books. Mamma & Papa went to S's office again. . . .

Jul 19 Mary & I left at half past ten for Long Point, we arrived at Woodstock at four o'clock, left Charlie [her horse] at the hotel to be fed, . . . called at Mrs Barwick's,[76] she gave us tea & was very kind to us & asked us to stay with her on our return. We left Woodstock at six, called at the Vansittarts'[77] en passant, saw Van & Mrs East, they tried to persuade us to stay all night with them, but we declined as we were in a hurry to go on, but promised to stay on our return. It was eight o'clock when we arrived at Dorman's where we remained all night. Mary was very ill, fatigue & other ailments, I sat up nearly all night with her.

Jul 20 Mary had quite recovered in the morning. We left at eight, arrived at Simcoe at one o'clock. The Salmons[78] would not allow us to go to the Lake, we were very tired & were very glad to stay. Tom Jones[79] spent the evening with us.

Jul 21 We all went to church. Tom Jones walked home with us. Mr George Salmon called. Tom Jones came to tea. He is as much attached as ever to Amelia. The Salmons were very kind.

Jul 22 We went on to the Lake. . . . Uncle Edward [Ryerse] was at Dover but came home soon after we arrived. They were very glad to

[74]Officer in the Royal Artillery.

[75]Grace Aquilar, *Woman's Friendship: a Story of Domestic Life*, London, 1850.

[76]Née Hughes, a sister of Mrs. John Wilson.

[77]Henry Vansittart (1799–1844) retired from the Royal Navy as Vice-Admiral. He settled near Woodstock in 1834.

[78]William Thomas Salmon (1802–65), a judge at Norfolk county, resident of Woodhouse Township since 1812.

[79]Tom Jones, son of Judge John Jones of Simcoe.

see us & had given us up as we were to have been there on Saturday. I wrote home, Mary wrote to Shuldham. We caught a humming bird which we killed & packed up & wrote a note & sent it to Mr Fisher. We drove to Vittoria in the evening & called at Mrs Fraser's . . . & took our letters to the post office. . . .

Jul 23 Uncle George [Ryerse] came to see us. . . . We went to see Uncle George's family – William & Mary & James & his wife. Went to Vittoria again in the evening. Uncle Edward, Tom, Mary & I went out walking. We sent to Vittoria for our letters, got one from Amelia & one from Shuldham. . . .

Jul 26 We went to say good bye at Uncle George's . . . went to the Lake just before we left, William joined us & Uncle Edward came to meet us. We went to the mill & were weighed. We left at five o'clock, went to Simcoe & stayed with Mrs Salmon. Called to see Maria & Perry. . . .

Jul 28 Mr Salmon, Willie & I went to church. . . . I intended writing home but was very ill all the afternoon. Mary went over & drank tea with Perry, she came over to see me & asked why I had not sent for her to come & nurse me. . . .

Jul 29 We left for Woodstock, bought an umbrella. . . . When we were about four miles from Simcoe it began to rain & poured until we reached Scotland where we rested & dried our cloaks. We stopped two hours at Burford, then went on to Woodstock, . . . at the last Toll gate we talked to the woman who had been out raspberrying, she gave us some raspberries. I was very tired & hungry & threw myself back & said "Oh! I am so hungry. I have tasted nothing since eight o'clock this morning." "Oh dear" said she running into the house & bringing out a raspberry tart, which she immediately broke in two & gave one piece to Mary & one to me, saying "there eat it, my hands are clean." I was so surprised I broke out laughing. "Now don't be laughing" said she, "but drive on, there is a buggy coming." So away we went with our tart. We arrived at the Vansittarts at seven o'clock, there was not a soul at home, not even the groom. Mr Harry Graham came over & took our horse as we were going to put him in the stable, the maid took us to our room. We ordered tea & the cold mutton & had dressed & refreshed ourselves with something substantial. When Mrs East returned, the dear old lady was very much grieved that there should have been no one at home when we arrived & was delighted that we had ordered all we wanted. They had expected us last Saturday & did not expect us again until tomorrow. Mrs Van returned at nine o'clock & was very glad we had come. Mrs East sat up an hour longer than usual to talk to us.

Jul 30 We heard from Amelia, & Mary from Shuldham. We helped Mrs Van stone cherries. . . . We talked to Mrs Van & Mrs East all day. I wrote home. . . .
Jul 31 We had serious thoughts of going home, Mrs Van was very anxious we should stay, she was in hopes we were going to remain until the end of the week. It began to rain so we put it off until tomorrow morning. . . . Mary drove Mrs East into Woodstock & Mrs Van drove me, we saw all the beauty & fashion.
Aug 1 We left the Vans at eight o'clock & were home at half past one & very glad to get there. Found all well, & talked an immense quantity. Amelia told us that Captain Campbell is to leave for England on Monday. Oh, how sorry I was to hear it, he is to be here this evening. Amelia wrote up to ask Major Chester & Capt Bell. Becher came to see us. Major Chester, Capt Bell & Capt Campbell came in the evening. We had a little dancing. About the middle of the evening Capt Campbell asked me to go out & sit at the door. We went & he asked me if I remembered a promise we made of making confidantes of each other & that now he wished to make me his. He told me the reason he sells out is because his father is in difficulty, & he sells his commission to relieve him & enable him to accept an appointment in New Zealand where he is to go immediately & that Lord Lyttleton has promised him an appointment there also, he then told me that he liked me better than any of us & in fact proposed. I scarcely know what we said. I was too happy & too bewildered to know anything, he begged me not to say a word to anyone & that he would come tomorrow & speak to me again about it. Capt Bell & Major Chester coming out to go home then we were obliged to part. When I went in Eliza & Amelia saw tears in my eyes & took me in the dining room & asked what had happened. I was obliged to tell them, they were delighted & hope it may all turn out well. Heaven grant it may.
Aug 2 . . . Capt Campbell came in the afternoon, we sat on the terrace, he told me all he knew of his father's affairs & his own, he does not know when we can marry, he wishes very much that he could take me to New Zealand with him but cannot tell if it will be possible until he goes to England & knows how much he will have. I told him I had told Amelia & Eliza. He left at half past eleven to go up & dine & asked me for some of my hair. I said he should have it & I would . . . give it to him when he came down to tea. He came early, I was not dressed & did not come down until some time after he had been there. I was trying to put the hair in & could not. He was in a state of mind because I did not come until I appeared & told the reason. Col Crutchley came. Capt C & I sat out at the door nearly all the evening, we

then went in & played écarte on the sofa. Amelia came & talked a short time, they left at one o'clock.

Aug 3 Becher, Capt & Mrs Anderson called. Captain Campbell came down after Mess. We walked in the garden after tea, then sat at the door until ten o'clock when he left.

Aug 4 We went to church. Frank [Campbell] came in the afternoon, we sat in the bower. He walked to the church with us in the evening & dined at the Mess for the last time by particular request. He & Capt Bell came down afterwards. I told him to talk to Amelia all about his plans which he did. We then walked in the garden. He will do his best to return from England for me & take me to New Zealand with him. We sat at the door afterwards until eleven when Capt Bell came out to go, it was the happiest day I ever spent. He is to leave from [here] tomorrow & lunches with us. We asked him to breakfast but he cannot come as he has so much to do.

Aug 5 Frank came down at twelve, lunched with us. Capt Bell came for him at half past one & drove him to Woodstock where he took the stage. Frank is to write to me as soon as he arrives in London. Oh how sorry I was to part with him. Heaven knows when we shall meet again. John & Edward went to Woodstock to play in the match against the Woodstock Cricketers. Amelia, Eliza & I went out walking. I took my ring to Gammets to have dear Frank's hair set in it. Papa is not at all well.

Aug 6 Mary heard from Shuldham, he cannot get his leave. Colonel Crutchley called. I am sure Frank has told Col C everything for he wiped his eyes when I came in the room & said he did not like to call yesterday as he thought my eyes would be red, but thought they looked a little better today. . . . Papa is not at all well. How much I miss dear Frank, the days are so long without him.

Nov 16 More than three long months have passed since I have written & Oh! how much has happened, how little we know what is in store for us. Dear Mary was married on the 22nd of August & our dear beloved father died on the 23rd.[80] He did not see Mary married.[81] How dreadful it was & how changed everything is.

This is our first day of winter. We were not able to go out as usual. We heard from Uncle Edward, he is not at all well & will try & come & stay with us in January. Mamma & I had a long talk about dear dear Frank. She says I shall never see him again, that it will be years

[80]Actually, John Harris died on the 25th. See Amelia Harris' diary 25 August 1858.

[81]John Harris was very ill when Mary married on 22 August and, although in the House, he did not attend the ceremony.

before he can leave New Zealand & marry. I cannot give him up he will return to me, God will bless & prosper him. It will be months & months before I can hear from him.

Nov 17 Went to church. Colonel Crutchley called. Helen asked him to spend tomorrow evening with us. Mr Jervoise [23rd] was also asked. It was too wet & stormy to go to the evening service. Amelia, Mamma, & I walked up & down the Hall & talked of dear Frank. I told Mamma I wished very much to write to him, she said I might. I cannot wait till I hear from him which will be the end of next summer. She says we shall never be married, that it will be years before he can leave New Zealand. Dear, dear Frank would that I could go to you.

Nov 20 Mrs Becher came in . . . she dined with us. . . . I sent my letter to dear Frank. Amelia wrote a short note to him. . . .

Nov 22 . . . Dear, dear Frank, how I have longed to see you today.

Nov 23 . . . How I wish I could hear from dear, dear Frank.

Nov 25 . . . Frank my own Love, how I long for you, May God ever bless you dearest.

Nov 29 . . . My own Frank how I long to see you. The months seem years to me.

Dec 2 I went out walking. Met Col Crutchley, he walked with me & asked if he might come down in the evening. Capt Bell called & stayed to tea, he told me he is going to write to dearest Frank by the next mail & if we wanted to write anything he would enclose it. I am so glad to write to you again my own Love. . . .

Dec 3 . . . I shall not if I can by any means stay home. Amelia, Eliza & I went out walking. All the children[82] spent the evening at the Wilsons. Mr Radcliffe lent me a number of *David Copperfield*, we had all but that one. Amelia wrote to Mary, Eliza to Mr Neave. It is two months today since dear Frank sailed from England, God grant that he is safe. How I wish I could be with him.

Dec 5 . . . Amelia [heard] from Mr Townsend. Becher called. We were surprised & delighted by seeing Mr Townsend walk in this afternoon, he said nothing about it in his letter. . . . Eliza & I went out walking, met Col Crutchley, he walked with us. This day four months dearest Frank left. How I wish he [were] back again, I long to hear his loved voice again.

Dec 6 Becher came in the morning to see Mr Townsend, he was surprised to hear he was here & is sure he is come to see Amelia. . . . Mr Townsend proposed for Amelia. She accepted him, but it is not at

[82]Presumably a reference to Helen (16), George (14), and Teresa (11).

all settled as Mamma wishes to find out a little more about him. Amelia, Mr Townsend & John went out walking. Col Crutchley came in the evening. John spent the evening with the Bechers. Col C enjoys the Townsend affair & watches with intense interest. Dear dear Frank it made me think so of you & wish you were here again. Oh! how happy I was with you.

Dec 7 We heard from Mary, they have been very ill again, she enclosed a letter from Sarah. Becher called, he asked us all to go to Thornwood this evening & sent his sleigh for us. . . . Mamma will not allow me to write to dearest Frank. How I wish I could it is so great a pleasure.

Dec 8 . . . [Capt Bell] asked me if I had the note for dear Frank ready. I told him Mamma would not let me write it, but sent a little message to him. I should so like to have written, I had so much to say to you dear dear Frank. . . .

Dec 9 Mr Townsend left at nine o'clock in the morning. He wants Amelia to marry him in July, but it is not at all settled . . .

Dec 10 Mamma wrote to Mr Plumb[83] to ask about Mr Townsend, what he is & what he is likely to be, as we know nothing about him. . . .

Dec 16 . . . Col Crutchley came down in the evening & is here now talking to Eliza on the sofa – where we so often sat dearest Frank. The Bechers give a large Ball on Thursday evening, they have invited every one here & at St Thomas, thank heaven we are not going.

Dec 17 . . . Becher called, we laughed at his Ball & told him it was an election Ball, to court popularity. He was rather taken aback & wanted to know who said so, we made him believe everyone said so.

Dec 18 Mr Wilson called, he was charmed to hear about Amelia & Mr Townsend, . . .

Dec 19 . . . Mr Wilson called, he had a long talk to Amelia, he asked where Mr Townsend lives & all we knew about him & will write to a secret agent in New York & find out everything public & private about him. He is very anxious the marriage should come off. . . .

Xmas Day We went to church. Spoke to Col Crutchley, Captain Phillott & Capt Bell asked Col Crutchley to come down in the evening & bring Mr Jervoise & Mr Radcliffe & he said he would. We asked Capt Bell, he was engaged to the Bechers. Capt B called & stayed until it was time to go to the Bechers, . . . Mrs Goodhue asked us to spend tomorrow evening with them, it is to be a large party, . . . Amelia read Shakespeare to us until it was time to dress. . . . Col C, Eliza, Helen &

[83]Josiah B. Plumb (1816–88), an Albany banker who also had substantial property at Niagara Falls, settled at Niagara after the American Civil War.

John played whist, Amelia & Mr Jervoise played backgammon & écarte, Mamma & Edward chess & Mr R & I chess & écarte, . . . My own Frank how often I wished for you. I do love you so truly my dearest.

Dec 27 . . . Mamma heard from Mr Plumb, he wrote a most satisfactory letter & said every thing that was good of Mr Townsend. . . . Col Crutchley called & was charmed by Mr Plumb's letter. . . .

Dec 31 I called at the Andersons, not at home, then went to the Caddys to get the pattern of a baby's shirt. Saw Mrs A there. The Caddys wanted me to stay to tea & I drove in with Minnie who had to do some shopping & Eliza returned with us. We spent a very pleasant evening, looked through Capt Caddy's portfolio & Mrs Caddy & I looked through her trunk of baby things. . . . Capt Bell called. Amelia asked him here for Wednesday evening & with Mr W. Jervoise visiting him & Mr Redcliffe.

1851

New Year's Day . . . Col Crutchley sent Helen a pair of fur cuffs & Theresa a book. We went to church . . . We did not receive visitors. A good many left their cards. We admitted Mr Brough.[84] Eliza went on with Amelia's likeness. Amelia read Shakespeare to us in the evening before we dressed for our visitors. . . . My own Frank how very very often I wished for you. May this New Year bring you every happiness & prosperity.

Jan 13 We heard from Sarah. Becher came in, he was not well, . . . Amelia went out to the Bechers in the morning. She invited us all to spend Wednesday evening with them. I went out walking, Capt Bell came for Eliza to go to Capt Caddy's room to look at the drawings, they afterwards went to the Hamiltons & looked through Mr H's portfolio. Amelia & Helen spent the evening at the Goodhues. Dr Anderson came over in the evening to see us. . . . Mr Wilson received an answer from the secret agent in New York & brought it up to show us, he said every thing that was satisfactory of Mr Townsend. . . .

Jan 20 Mrs Wilson came in the morning to ask what she should wear at the Odd Fellows Ball, she is to be one of the Lady Patronesses. . . . Amelia & I went for a long walk. Eliza heard from Mr Neave. Mamma sent her letter to Mrs Newcomen. Mr Jervoise returned from Port Talbot & John went up to see him. He is full of Col Airey & has been terribly humbugged.

[84]The Reverend Brough (1794–1883) presided at John Harris' funeral.

Jan 21 Eliza wrote to Mr Neave. I was drawing all the morning. Mr & Mrs Cronyn, Miss Watson, Mr & Mrs Goodhue, Becher, Capt Phillott & Mr Jervoise called. I went to the Wilkinsons. . . . My own Frank, I do so long for you, it is nearly six long months since I heard your dear voice. God grant that you may prosper & come back to me.
Jan 22 Mr Wilson called & told us Mrs Wilson & Edward were coming to spend the day. Mrs W came but not Edward. . . . Mrs Wilson brought flowers for us to make a wreath for her to wear at the Odd Fellows Ball. Mr & Mrs Becher called, they had been riding. Mrs B tried to be very civil to Mrs W but it would not do. Mrs W took it for what it was worth, & treated Mrs B as she ought to be treated, the bridge is wider than ever. Mrs B borrowed *David Copperfield.* Capt Campbell called. Amelia asked him to stay to tea. He took his dogs to the Barracks & came back. Amelia told me to play chess with him, I won, it was a hard fought game. He is such a wise owl. He should not stay anywhere to tea, it lets people find out there is nothing in him & he is by way of being a philosopher & knows nothing. This was my birthday, dear, dear Frank, how I wish I could be with you before my next. God only knows when we shall meet again. May he watch over you & prosper you Dearest.
Jan 24 Had a long letter from Mary & Shuldham.[85] Shuldham sent for their Marriage certificate, we sent it by return of post. Mr Wilson came in while we were reading the letters. . . .

[There are no further entries in Charlotte's Diary]

[85]Shuldham had married and moved to Montreal.

The Diary of Amelia Ryerse Harris (1798–1882)

Amelia Ryerse Harris kept a diary from 12 September 1857 to 25 February 1882.[1] The following entries have been selected out of the total 8,907 entries over this twenty-five year period and amount to approximately a fifth of the total. This judicious pruning was necessary to make the diaries accessible to the reader, care being taken not to sacrifice the integrity and authenticity of the text. Editorial intervention has been kept to a minimum and while the more exotic features of her idiosyncratic and inconsistent modes of expression have been adjusted, care has been taken to retain the essential flair of her literary style. Those interested in Amelia's flexible lexicon of spellings, punctuation, and capitalizations should consult the originals.

The diary was written in five, identical, 8 by 5 inch, hardback books. The twenty-five year coverage of events is thorough, and over 100 missing dates (1861–63) when she was seriously ill, and some other omissions (1871–72 and 1877), were summarized when she resumed her diary. On some occasions (for example, 24 October 1857, 7 September 1863, and 6 June 1865) there are two entries on a single date and the same information is recorded twice on 4 January 1866. She herself removed an entry (1 October 1872), which read, "I wrote last night in bitterness. Why should I have a record of what pains me." On 1 August 1877 she was "not well enough to write." Also removed from the diary, are five lines in May 1869, a page in 1870 covering the dates 11 August and 16–20 August, and the entries of 18 September and 20–22 September. The second volume includes fifty pages of newspaper clippings, most of them reporting the visit of the Prince of Wales to London in September 1860. The fourth volume includes 9½ double pages of material bearing on the office of the Treasurer of the London District. The fifth volume includes twelve pages of household accounts for 1854–1856. The entries in this volume (19 July–24 August 1879) when she made a trip to New York and New London, Connecti-

[1]Selections from Amelia Harris' diary, edited by Fred Landon, Chief Librarian, University of Western Ontario, were published in the *London Free Press* in the fall of 1928.

cut were written on separate sheets and subsequently pasted into the diary.

Amelia commenced her diary at the age of fifty-nine, identifying her enterprise by the comment on the inside cover of the first of her five manuscript books: "Mrs Harris' Journals, commencing with Lord Althorp's arrival and ending with – her death." While failing to keep to the latter commitment, she did manage to sustain a remarkable dedication to commenting on the affairs of Eldon House. Her diary was both a private journal and public document – at least, to the family – as it was always kept on a table in the drawing room where it was sure to attract the family's attention.

Amelia's daughter Mary Peard once wrote to her about the diary, asking Amelia "leave it to me in your will. Put in a codicil to that effect – *At Once*."[2] However, Amelia wrote on the front cover of the second volume, "I give to my son George my journal . . . this 12th day of May 1880," presumably, because she wanted it to be available to the family at Eldon House.

Through her diary, Amelia introduces numerous unfamiliar people who soon become familiar to the reader. Each of these is analysed in terms of their attitudes toward each other, and she also expresses her own opinion of them, and their relationship to her life and her various domestic dramas. Seen through her eyes, people appear to be revolving around Amelia. In this way, the large family and circle of friends, assume their own positions in the various dramatic events of the Eldon household and Harris family. Amelia shares with us their and her concerns and, in so doing, the reader is allowed to participate in them.

Her diary contains over two hundred characters, but only those of the immediate family and closest friends play a significant role, the others are assigned walk-on parts. Whether Amelia places herself in the centre of the family as a genuine matriarch-type, or whether circumstances dictate that she becomes a matriarch, is left to the reader to decide. Whatever the reason, she plays her role with confidence. Ultimately, in her anxiety to help, Amelia focuses her attention on the core of each of the individual problems. Sometimes impartial, she can also be vulnerable and prejudiced, as in the case of her son Edward when she assesses his marriage with Sophie.

[2]Harris Papers, Mary Peard to Amelia Harris, 15 June 1874.

One dimension of Amelia Harris' diary is different from that of the other four diaries: while the other diarists revolve around her, she herself occupies a privileged position from which she can observe what is happening in her surroundings and can carefully select the material that is appropriate for her diary. Without ever losing her perspective, she turns her attention from members of the family to friends, from Eldon House to the town of London, or from event to event without losing her perspective.

With the marriage of the last of her children in 1867, Amelia began to feel her solitude. Although three of them lived at Eldon House or nearby, they had their own families. The weight of the past becomes heavier as time passes, and her ability to move declines. The same was happening with her former wide circle of friends. Her isolation increased as mutual visits diminished and Church service was substituted by prayers in the quietness of her own room. Amelia Harris continues recording her diary with the compulsiveness of a twenty-five year habit, but her perspective becomes increasingly restricted and self-focussed as circumstances beyond her control came to limit her world.

Amelia Ryerse Harris

12th Sept 1857 Lord Althorpe arrived here He brought a letter
of introduction to Mr Portman from his Father (Lord Portman)
Mr Portman dined with the Kings, did not come home until late
Sunday the 13th Helen Teresa Lord Althorpe & George went to Church
arrangements were made to go to Camp Meeting after dinner—
Lord Althorpe, Mr Portman Edward and Mr Parke drove five miles
to the Camp Ground the assemblage of people were estimated at
from 6 to 10 thousand, the Gentlemen made very few remarks
about the Meeting, all their arrangements seemed to have been
made with great order, and there were none of the excesses so usual
in former days— we like Lord Althorpe He appears not only moral
but religiously disposed He is a great Anti Slavery Man and is
going to Chatham to visit the Negro settlement where Lord
Harvey is to join him. It is insinuated that Lord Althorpe knows
the value of a penny

An example of one of Amelia's personal vignettes

Amelia Ryerse Harris' Diary

1857

Sep 12 Lord Althorpe[3] arrived here. He brought a letter of introduction to Mr Portman from his father (Lord Portman). Mr Portman[4] dined with the Kings.[5] Did not come home until late.
Sep 13 Helen, Teresa, Lord Althorpe & George went to Church. Arrangements were made to go to [the] Camp Meeting after dinner. Lord Althorpe, Mr Portman, Edward and Mr Parke[6] drove five miles to the Camp Ground.[7] The assemblage of people were estimated at from 6 to 10 thousand. The gentlemen made very few remarks about the Meeting. All their arrangements seemed to have been made with great order, and there were none of the excesses so usual in former days. We like Lord Althorpe. He appears not only moral but religiously disposed. He is a great Anti Slavery man and is going to Chatham to visit the Negro Settlement where Lord Harvey is to join him.[8] It is insinuated that Lord Althorpe knows the value of a penny.
Sep 14 Lord Althorpe left after luncheon. I promised to send him some grafts of the early red apple. Mr Portman and Helen are to meet him at Dwight [Missouri] & at St Louis. Mr Portman had arranged to go to St Louis today to purchase a farm and then return for Helen, but has altered the arrangement and they are all to leave on Monday next in search of a home in a more genial climate.
Sep 16 News from India[9] continues bad. More troops to be sent out.

[3]Frederick Spencer, Tenth Lord Althorpe, an ancestor of Diana, the present Princess of Wales.

[4]Three of Amelia Harris' six daughters were in residence at Eldon House in September 1857: the unmarried Teresa (aged 18), Amelia who had married Gilbert Griffin in 1855, and Helen who had married Maurice Portman in 1856, together with her year-old son. As well as Mr. Griffin and Mr. Portman, two of the three unmarried sons, Edward (23) and George (21) also lived at home. The remaining son, John (27), normally at Eldon House, was visiting his three sisters who were living with their families in England: Sarah Dalzell, Mary Peard and Eliza Crutchley.

[5]Edwin H. King (1828–96) was General Manager of the London branch of the Bank of Montreal.

[6]Either Thomas Parke (1793–1864), who designed and built the London courthouse in 1826 and who represented the London area in the Legislative Assembly and Union Parliament (1834–1840), or, more probably, his son, E. Jones Parke, who began to practice law in 1852.

[7]The meeting was held at the Provincial Exhibition Building in London.

[8]This is a reference to one of the several settlements of escaped slaves throughout southwestern Ontario, such as Elgin, Dresden, North Buxton and Chatham.

[9]Reference to the Indian Mutiny, or Sepoy Rebellion, that shocked the British Empire in 1857.

The cruelties committed by the Sepoys does away with even feeling of mercy. The wish of almost every christian is that not a Sepoy may be spared as no one for a moment doubts the success of the British arms in the end. Commercial distress in the States is very great. Every paper is full of failures of the first Houses of New York, Baltimore, Boston, Philadelphia, I might say of every city in the Union.

Sep 18 Mr Portman and Helen have paid their bills, paid their visits and finished their packing. All ready to leave on the Monday.

Sep 19 Teresa, George and myself went to Church. Versy Cronyn[10] came to tea.

Sep 20 The Portmans are gone. I felt very sad at parting with Helen and the baby. He is a dear little fellow. Tom [servant] remains here until Mr Portman sends for him. Mr Portman gave his horse to Teresa.

Sep 21 The loss of the steamer *Central America* on the 12th is causing great excitement. She had 500 passengers on board and a crew of 160. More than half are lost. Many of the women and children are saved as Capt Horndon unlike the Capt of the *Arctic* endevourd to save the weakest and most helpless first and he, poor fellow, went down with the Ship. The *Central America* was on the line between California and Charleston and had treasures on board to the amount of two millions one hundred and fifty thousand dollars. One million and sixty thousand dollars was covered by insurance, the greater part of it in offices in England.

Sep 22 Mr Gzowski[11] came in to tea. He has just returned from England where he has left his daughters Helen & Charlotte at school. He saw John and thought him looking much better. Mr Griffin has taken a house from Mr Garrett.[12] They intend moving somewhere about the 12th of October.

Sep 24 Amelia and Mr Griffin have gone to Toronto to purchase carpets. On Tuesday George came in and told us that Mr Lucas, the teller of the Gore Bank had absconded with 22 thousand dollars but it appears that he has given property in security that will more than cover all his liabilities. Not so Mr Street,[13] the Bank Agent and Dis-

[10]Verschoyle Cronyn (1833–1920), a young lawyer and oldest son of Reverend Benjamin Cronyn, rector of St. Paul's Church.

[11]Casimir Stanislaus Gzowski (1813–98) met the Harrises in the early 1840s while in practice as an engineer in and near London. Amelia Harris often spelled his name Gzowskie.

[12]Edward Garrett, a London alderman. He is not the Garrett mentioned in the entry of 17 December 1857.

[13]William Warren Street (1814–79) was an associate of John Harris in the Treasurer's Office in the late 1840s. He and Henry Becher married sisters. See J.K.

trict Treasurer. He is a defaulter to a large amount. Mr Becher[14] came in today. He is the solicitor and says that things are so bad that he cannot see how Mr Street could *live* or stay to face the expose.[15]
Sep 25 Mr Street's defalcations is the only subject spoken of. Every day brings things to light that are more and more iniquitous.
Sep 26 Heard from Mary [Peard], Eliza [Crutchley] & John today. John has taken his passage in a Cunard steamer on the 10th of October. Eliza gives many directions from Doctor O'Grady to John about diet and exercise and says he must not expect good health in less than a year. I wrote to Sarah [Dalzell] and Mary. Mr Street has made his escape. Three warrants were out against him. If he had remained he would have gone to the penitentiary. He escaped through our garden. Mr Maclen was waiting for him with a carriage near Blackfriars Bridge and drove him to Sarnia – his frauds are great and numerous. Poor people that came to put money in the Savings Bank of which he was actuary he would persuade them to let him have the money at 10 per cent interest and take his note which is now worth nothing.
Sep 27 Amelia, George, Teresa and myself went to Church. Mr Becher and Mr Hammond[16] followed Mr Street last night to Port Huron[17] to get him to sign some papers. Mrs Street & family are at Stamford.[18] Mr Street has an agreeable manner and people have a liking for him notwithstanding his villanies, and every one seems glad that he has made his escape. I never thought him honest nor honorable and firmly believe that he was the cause of all Mr Harris' difficulties in the Treasurer's office. From the time Mr Street compounded with his creditors about 12 years ago poor Mr Harris employed him to keep his accounts, first from a feeling of charity and then from necessity as Mr Harris was in bad health and no one could understand his accounts but Mr Street, who had all to do with them and mystified [them] so that no one could understand them. Mr Street was the worst enemy Mr Harris ever had. He wanted the Treasurer's office and worked in all

---

Johnson, "The Business Man as Hero: The Case of William Warren Street," *Ont. Hist.* LXV, 1973, 125–32.

[14]Henry Corry Rowley Becher (1817–85), a lawyer, was virtually a daily visitor to Eldon House throughout both Charlotte and Amelia Harris' diaries. See Chasse's diary, footnote 8.

[15]Street and Becher were respectively the Agent and Solicitor of the Gore Bank.

[16]A.C. Hammond, a young lawyer and a land agent in partnership with Charles Hutchinson (1826–92). Together they were associated with W. Street in his land speculations. Hutchinson was engaged to Street's daughter, Frances. He later became a partner of H. Becher.

[17]Port Huron is across the river from Sarnia and in the United States.

[18]Stamford is close to Niagara Falls.

under handed ways to get Mr Harris out of it. He succeeded and got it himself. The *accusation* of dishonorable conduct killed Mr Harris. The actual commission of the basest crimes will never kill Mr Street. I have looked forward to this finale to Mr Street's career with as much confidence as I look for the sun's rising and setting.

Sep 28 There begins to be a reaction in peoples' feelings about Mr Street and complaints are made that he was allowed to escape when any poor man that steals a turkey is sent to the penitentiary. Mr Street's property it is supposed will cover his securities as he has made an assignment in their favour. Mr Lawrason,[19] Mr Goodhue[20] and Mr Becher are securities to the Bank for £1,000 each. Mr Lawrason and Dr Anderson[21] are securities to the district for £1,000 each. His defalcations it is said will amount to £40,000 to the District, the Bank and private individuals.

Sep 29 Mr Griffin came home last night. He heard yesterday that Mr De Blacquiére and Mr Farmer had been arrested at Woodstock for having made use of money belonging to the Woodstock and Port Dover Rail Road. They were both directors and there is a deficiency of 50 or £60,000. Mr Barwick, the cashier of the Montreal Bank in Toronto, was supposed to give evidence but refused to come. The examination is postponed until Monday next when measures will be taken to bring Mr Barwick. Mr Leponetion is subpoened also and is requested to bring a letter which Mr Barwick sent to him in mistake. The letter was intended for Mr Barwick's brother but put in the wrong envelope. In this letter the whole proceedings of the rail road directors is detailed. Mr Barwick who is one of them declares his intention to withdraw as death or the penitentiary will be the reward of their proceedings.

Oct 1 Mr McInnes[22] called this morning. He anticipates great commercial distress next winter. Mr Griffin gave George a pass to the Provincial [Agricultural] Show at Brantford.

Oct 2 George had a fatiguing day at the Show. The day was excessively wet, and there was great delay with the trains. The general arrange-

[19]Lawrence Lawrason (1803–82), a merchant and M.L.A. for London (1843–45), and Alderman for London in 1850.

[20]George J. Goodhue (1799–1870), London's leading merchant. See Charlotte's diary, 23 October 1848.

[21]Harris' next door neighbour on Ridout Street.

[22]Donald McInnes (1824–1900), a Hamilton businessman, railway investor, senator, and friend of the Harris family. In 1863 he married Mary Amelia Robinson, daughter of Sir John Beverley Robinson (1791–1863). He purchased Dundurn Castle from the Allan MacNab estate in the 1870s. See Ben Forster, "Donald McInnes (MacInnes)," *Dic. Can. Biog.* XII, pp. 631–634.

ments for the fair were defective, the dinner cold and attendance bad. The guests found it difficult to get a glass of wine. Sir William Eyre[23] the Hon J.H. Cameron,[24] Van Kounet [sic][25] & several Americans of distinction were among the guests. The provincial Show for 1858 is to be held in Toronto. George returned at one in the morning wet, hungry and tired.

Oct 3 Received a letter from Mary. Through Sir George Wetherall's[26] recommendation, Ld Downshire[27] has offered Shuldham [Peard] a Company in his Regiment of Militia. Shuldham accepts of course. We are all very glad as he is too young to be without employment. John left London on the 15th Sept for Paris with Dr Ryerson[28] and Sophia.

Oct 4 Went to Church. Amelia, Teresa & myself stayed to Sacrament, George did not. Mr Becher came in. In speaking of Mr Street's defalcations, I said [that] I thought he must have secured an independance. Mr Becher said not a penny. If the statements in the papers were correct [I] could not conceive what [he] had done with the money as the District deficiencies alone were estimated at £23,000 besides a very large sum at the Bank and debts to private individuals and his own income from different offices was £1400 a year. Mr Becher said how did money go, how was it that Harris' accounts were in confusion. I was very very angry to hear Mr Harris' name brought up in *such* association with Mr Street and said that Mr Street had helped to confuse Mr Harris' accounts to suit his own purposes, that I knew nothing of Mr Street's affairs except what was in the public prints but if his deficiencies were as great as stated that I must be convinced before I

[23]Sir William Eyre (1805–59), an officer with the 73rd Regiment, knighted for his services in the Crimean War.

[24]John Hillyard Cameron (1817–76), a Toronto lawyer and M.L.A. for Cornwall (1846–51; 1854–57). See Donald Swainson, "John Hillyard Cameron," *Dic. Can. Biog.* X, pp. 118–124.

[25]Philip VanKoughnet (1823–69), a Toronto lawyer appointed to Legislative Council, Canada West (1856), Chancellor of Upper Canada (1862–67), and of Ontario (1867–69).

[26]Sir George Augustus Wetherall had commanded the First Royals Regiment of Foot when they were stationed at London during the early 1840s. At this time he was stationed in England.

[27]Duke of Downshire (1812–68) was M.P. for Downshire (1836–45), and succeeded his father on 12 April 1845. He and his wife lived near Mary and Shuldham Peard and were effectively their patrons.

[28]Reverend Adolphus Egerton Ryerson (1803–82), Methodist clergyman, reformer, and educationalist became the first president of the University of Victoria College, Cobourg, and Chief Superintendant of Education for Upper Canada (1844–76) and first cousin of Amelia Harris. His daughter Sophia Ryerson married Edward Harris in 1860. See R.D. Gidney, "Egerton Ryerson," *Dic. Can. Biog.* XI, pp. 783–795.

could believe that he had not secured himself. It is the first time that Becher has not shown me the respect of a mother. He left the room in a passion. Why did he bring up poor Mr Harris' name who had been seven years in his grave. If he had snubbed me and said that I was neither just nor generous towards Mr Street I should not have minded it but I was miserable all the afternoon and yet I had taken the Sacrament in the morning. I wrote a very short letter to Mary, & Teresa and myself walked over to the Wilson['s]. Mr Goodhue was just saying goodbye. He is looking very well. Mrs Wilson was at Thomas, Lucy [Wilson] at home. We stayed for tea. Mr Wilson walked home with us. His mind was evidently preoccupied for I never knew him to talk so little. . . .

Oct 5 Mr Griffin, Amelia & myself went to Hamilton upon Mr Griffin's pass to purchase carpets for Mr Griffin's new house & a carpet for Edward's office. The Griffins pd. 7S [7 shillings] per yard for Brussels and 5/6 [5 shillings and 6 pence] for tapestry pure hand & a carpet of each and a beautiful rug at wholesale price or rather at first cost £3.15, retail price £7.10. Mr McInnis [store owner] was very kind. He left Hamilton in the evening for New York. Commercial distress very great both in the States and Canada. We staied all night at the Anglo American, returned to London on the 6th. . . . The Hon J.H. Cameron came in the train as far as Paris with us. He was going with Judge [Robert E.] Burns to attend the Assise at Brantford. I was very glad to meet Mr Cameron. Have not seen him for ten years. He looks better as a middle aged man than he did when younger. His manner is also improved and refined. He has been travelling and living a good deal in England and on the Continent since I last saw him. He recalled the pleasant evenings he used to spend here when my family were all at home. We arrived at Eldon at ½ past 12, found Teresa very lonely. She had invited Ellen Hamilton[29] and Versy Cronyn to dine with them yesterday. We had a letter from Helen from St Louis dated 29th Sept. Baby was ill, had two teeth and two more coming. Mr Portman & Helen both had colds. Had not yet been at the Great National Fair, but seemed to like St Louis. . . .

Oct 8 Commercial distress very great. Continued failures in every town in the United States and Canada.

[29]Ellen Hamilton, eldest of the three daughters of James Hamilton, cashier of the Bank of Montreal. The Hamiltons lived on Ridout Street, a few hundred yards south of Eldon House.

Oct 9 Malcolm Cameron[30] came here to raise money on mortgages. [He] remained to tea and cribbage. He is a man with a great deal of coarse humour and cleverness. Has been religiously taught and *knows* what is right. He intends trying to put George Brown[31] out as representative of the county of Lambton.
Oct 10 Mrs Askin[32] spent the day here. Teresa Askin came in the evening. She is a very amusing girl and kept us laughing all the time she was here.
Oct 11 Got letters from Sarah, Mary and John. Col Dalzell had gone on a tour of pleasure with his sister Lady Emma. I like Sarah's letter. She appears to be a sensible, *good* woman. Shuldham had gone to join his regiment of Irish ragamuffins and tried to get them into some sort of order and discipline. Mary was alone and of course felt very lonely. John was to leave England by the steamer on the 10th. In 14 days he will be here. Mr Griffin and myself went to Church. Versy came in the evening to tea.
Oct 12 Raining very fast. The Griffins were to move today but they cannot on account of the rain. My old servant Betsy Campbell left me today. She has been in my service nearly four years and I think her the best servant I ever had.
Oct 13 The house is all confusion. The Griffins are on the move. I have been busy all day sending off their things. All Mr Street's household goods were sold yesterday and today. They brought nearly their value, the only thing I know of [being] given to Mrs Street was her jam. She sent all her own and her daughter's trinkets to Mr Lawrason to help pay Mr Street's deficiencies. Poor woman she little knows what a vortex she was throwing her jewels into. They had some pretty trinkets, one bracelet that Mr Street pd 90 dollars for. Mrs Street intends remaining in London for the winter. Doctor Anderson has been very kind and says she may live in one of his houses for the winter rent free. It is asserted that Mr Street has nothing, that all has been lost by loans on high interest and in wild speculation. Mrs Leonard [a sister] and Charlotte [her daughter] will live with Mrs Street and they have a little means. Charlie Leonard probably will assist them. Becher says that there is a probability of Minnie's [another daughter] getting

[30]Malcolm Cameron (1832–98), a Goderich lawyer and M.P. (1867–87). See Margaret Coleman, "Malcolm Cameron," *Dic. Can. Biog.* X, pp. 124–129.

[31]George Brown (1818–80), journalist and publisher of the Globe.

[32]Elisa Van Allen of Haldiman County, Colonel J.B. Askin's wife and a very close friend of Amelia Harris, who was her bridesmaid. The Askins, who had eight children including Teresa, had been resident at London since 1832.

the situation of governess in a Southern family and that Willie Street [a son] will get a situation in the customs. Poor things, what a change! I pray God to help them. Several letters from Mr Street have appeared in the papers. He evidently wishes to return if he could be sure that he would not be sent to the penitentiary. He says his defalcations to the *District* are not as great as represented. People do not seem disposed to allow him to return. He was treated so leniently on a former occasion that he hoped it might be the same now. Had he paid his creditors after his former whitewash when he was able to do so, the feeling would have been less hard against him now. The only thing to be said in his favour is that he has an agreeable manner as a man of business and very convivial as an acquaintance and fond of good living.

Oct 14 The Griffins are gone to their own house and will dine there. I have sent up the last load of goods. The house seems very quiet. A reduction of six in our household in one week makes a great change. Edward has a very bad cold and is not at all well. The weather is fine, Indian summer, but I have put up all our stoves and double windows. The commercial distress is making a great change in the prices of everything. Rents are reduced more than a third, wheat was selling last winter for 12S [shillings] currency the bushel, it is now selling for 5 & 6 shillings York. Mutton has fallen from 8^{d} currency per pound to 5^{d} and other things in proportion.

Oct 15 I wrote to Helen this morning, directed to New Orleans. Edward is a little better. The assignment of all the property of Hutchinson & Hammond to Shanley and MacLean for the benefit of *all* their creditors appeared in the paper this morning. The news from India is most disastrous and harrowing to the feelings. Signs of disaffection among the Sepoys and Musselmen have appeared in Madras and Bombay.

Oct 16 . . . I received a letter from Helen this morning. . . . On the 9th they felt the shock of an earthquake and heard a low rumbling noise. There was no damage done in St Louis except a few buildings cracked from the attic to the base, but most of the inhabitants were so frightened that they ran into the middle of the streets for safety, fearing their houses would be down upon them. The first shock was felt at 4 AM, but neither earthquakes or aught else has the power of diverting peoples minds long from the pecuniary distress which is felt in every part of the continent. . . .

Oct 17 Mrs King came in to spend the day. I like Nan. She is not too fine a lady for the country. She seems so anxious to learn how things are done in this country, and to make a good wife. Amelia came in to luncheon. She is not looking well. We are not very lively. Teresa and I played cribbage.

Oct 18 Went to Church. Mr Palmer [curate] preached a very good sermon. The Griffins came to tea and hurried home on the account of rain.
Oct 21 Edward and self dined with the Griffins. They look very snug and nice. Housekeeping is too new with Amelia for her to feel at ease. She seems anxious and fidgety. We played cribbage and came home in the cab.
Oct 22 The steamer *Europa* has arrived at Halifax and John will be home tomorrow or the next day. How glad I shall be to see him. Amelia called. She had just received a letter from Mr Portman. He has not left St Louis in consequence of not getting his money from Murray Osborne.[33] I am very much afraid he will have difficulty in getting it. Mr Portman's detention at St Louis is a great loss to him as the expenses of himself, Helen and the nurse amount to 100 dollars a week at the hotel. I wrote to Mr Portman and advised him to return and endevour to get his money as few can be trusted in these shaky times without risk. . . .
Oct 23 Mr Griffin telegraphed from the Clifton[34] that John was not in the train. I was very glad to get the telegraph, as I should have expected him all night.
Oct 24 John arrived at 1/2 past 6 PM looking tired and ill. I had hoped to see him much better and with less remains of his former illness about him. But he has brought home the same red face and puffy look about the eyes. His eyes are red, bright and glassy looking. Edward and I talked him over after he had gone to bed and we could not deceive ourselves with the hope that his health was restored. He is certainly much better than when he went to England and we can only hope that with care and attention he will continue to improve. He is much pleased with England and with the attention he received from friends. He found Eliza more changed than Sarah or Mary. The Dalzells were at Bruges, the Crutchleys at Malahide [Ireland] for sea air but stationed at Burr. Mary was at Clifton [near Bristol]. Mr Griffin and Mr MacInnis came up with John and dined here of course. Amelia was here also. George & I went to Church. Teresa staid home with Jack. In the evening, Mr Brook, Ellen Hamilton, Mr McInnes, Versy Cronyn, Mr Griffin and Amelia came to tea. Jack went up to Mrs W. Lawrasons to see Murray Osborne about Mr Portman's money £1250. He thinks it safe. Murray said he had sent Mr Portman £250 in gold

[33]Portman was owed money by Murray Osborne, a Hamilton lawyer.
[34]A hotel at Niagara Falls.

and could not get Mr Portman's draft cashed in New York as gold was not to be had for less than 25 per cent premium and even 50 per cent had been given for it. We spent a very pleasant evening but John looks ill.

Oct 28 Went to Mrs Becher's to call after her confinement. Mrs Becher & her daughter both doing well. Called on Mrs Macbeth, Mrs Macbeth and son [Talbot] both doing well.

Oct 30 Got English letters, one from Shuldham & one from Eliza. Shuldham's Regiment ordered to Aldershott. Mary will join him at Farnham. He likes Lord Downshire very much and with good cause as Ld D is very kind to him. The Crutchleys have returned to Burr. Eliza is sending out a parcel by Sophia, Col Crutchely's photograph for me, a dress for Teresa and a petticoat for Amelia.

Nov 3 Amelia called. Teresa went home with her and remained to dinner, which I did not approve of as Mr McInnes was expected to dine with the Griffins and remarks have already been made about him and Teresa. Mr McInnes did not come. His father is dead. Went to the Hamiltons to tea. No one there but the Harrises and Mrs Westcot [neighbour], pretty dull. Mr Hamilton is a good old fellow with a great love of art and a good natured feeling towards everyone.

Nov 4 . . . John's boxes arrived. I was delighted to see Eliza's dear old face and yet it made me feel sad, she looked so much changed. John thinks the photograph makes her look older than she is in reality yet what matters the look, age must come. Eliza sent me a very pretty envelope case and portfolio. John brought Teresa a very nice winter dress from Paris and paper from England for the drawing room.

Nov 7 . . . John went out to audit city accounts.[35] . . .

Nov 12 I have been ill all night and today. No word from Edward who has not returned. Teresa came home although it [was] raining. I was very glad to see her as it is lonely when I am not well. . . .

Nov 14 Edward came home & has great hopes of winning Mr Portman's Chancery suit, but it will be June next or longer before there is any decision. He says times are quite as dull in Toronto as here. Necessity has forced economy. Everyone is trying how cheaply they can live. No word of balls, dinners or parties now. We had letters from Helen and Mr Portman from Col Hampton's [in] Mississippi. They seem very happy there and like the place very much but say nothing about purchasing. They had a very disagreeable adventure on board of the steam boat when about leaving the wharf at St Louis. When nearly

[35]John Fitzjohn Harris had been appointed auditor for London for 1855–56.

all the passengers were on deck bidding good bye to friends or looking at the city, some thieves broke open the outside door of Helen's cabin and locked the inside door and searched for money but found none as the baby who was sleeping in the berth had cried and the thieves became alarmed and made their escape, only taking a very handsome revolver of Mr Portman's. Helen ran to her baby when he cried and found the door locked on the inside. She then ran to the other door which had been opened with a chisel. She found the contents of Baby's trunk over the floor which happened to be the only trunk in the cabin. Their money was in a bag in the upper berth which they did not find. We all have great reason to be thankful that the baby was not *silenced* with a blow or smothered. They broke open the cabin of a young English gentleman, emptied his portmanteaux and walked off with 25 sovereigns. . . .

Nov 15 . . . Dr Cronyn was consecrated Bishop of Huron at Lambeth Palace on the 28th of October. Dr Ryerson and Sophia were present and after the ceremony went to the Arch Bishop of Canterbury to coffee. . . .

Nov 17 John left at 1/2 past 7 for Hamilton and returned 1/2 past 9. Murray Osborne not returned from New York. John saw his brother who told John that Murray Osborne had sent 1,000 dollars to Mr Portman by express and promised to send the other 4,000 dollars to John either tomorrow or the next day. I hope he may keep his word but Murray has behaved very badly. In these times of commercial distress, it is difficult to know who to trust. . . . Mr McInnis was in great trouble. He says his affairs are all right in this country and is gone at once to see what is wrong in England. Edward went to St Thomas and returned at 7 PM. He does not know which way to turn himself to pay for the land he has purchased in St Thomas. . . . I got a letter from my brother Edward [Ryerse]. He I trust has got over the worst of his money difficulties. It is pleasant to hear an old man like him after more than thirty years marriage speaking so affectionately of his wife. . . .

Nov 18 Mrs Cronyn called and asked *all* the family to her daughter Margaret's wedding[36] which is to take place as soon as the Bishop returns. . . . Neither telegraph nor letter from the Osbornes. John is very anxious about Mr Portman's money. He wrote to Mr Snead to know if he had received the 1000 dollars which Murray Osborne says he has sent to him for Mr Portman. John and Edward do not work together in the office as harmoniously as I could wish.

[36]Margaret was to marry Edward Blake.

Nov 21 Amelia came here. Heard from Helen, who is at Col Hampton's. She likes the Mississippi very much. Mr Portman when out hunting [and] was very near being killed by a wild cow. . . . Helen does not say what the arrangement[s] for the future are. Lord Althorpe was with them at the Hampton's and the gentlemen of the party were to leave the next day for New Orleans. John went to Hamilton today to see Murray Osborne about Mr Portman's money which he has promised to remit on Tuesday or Wednesday next. He gave John a check on the Bank but did not wish him to present it before that time. . . .

Nov 23 . . . Jack and Ned have moved into their new office in Carling's building next to the Post Office. Teresa gone to the Griffins to dinner. Mr Wilson called. There is a dissolution of Parliament and a new election to take place immediately. Mr Wilson declines standing. Mr Carling[37] and Mr Becher are spoken of as probable candidates.

Nov 26 Weather moderated. Betsy the cook cut her finger and gone home. Engaged an English girl during her absence.

Nov 27 Humiliation Day appointed by Government to pray our heavenly father to save and protect our brethren in the east from the cruelties of those idolatrous people.[38] A collection was taken up after the service for the assistance of the sufferers. The day was beautiful but no one appeared in good spirits. Ellen Hamilton and Emily Street[39] came to tea.

Nov 28 My new cook is ill and has gone home, which entails household discomforts. . . .

Nov 30 . . . Mr Carling nominated as member of parliament. It is a great shame. Mr Becher is the one that ought to have been sent. He is a Man of Honour, intelligence and education, and he would have been a credit and service to the city. The public monster may have many heads but not much brains.

Dec 5 . . . Mr Wilson came to lunch. He seems himself again now. He has given up politics. I think politics does away with all the finer feelings. Mr Griffin and Amelia called and brought the parcel which Eliza sent. Teresa is charmed with her pretty lace dress and Amelia is

[37]John Carling (1828–1911), brewer and politician, was an influential figure in London society serving as School Trustee (1845), Alderman (1854–56), and was active in Canadian politics from 1857 to 1894.

[38]Another reference to the news of the Indian Mutiny. Gory accounts of outrages and massacres such as that of Cawnpore on 15 July 1857 were given prominent coverage in the contemporary newspapers.

[39]Daughter of W.W. Street.

equally pleased with her petticoat. At first I could not recognize Col Crutchley by his photograph, his moustaches alters him but after looking at it for some time his dear good face seems to return to me. The English mail came in, letters from Mary and Eliza. Eliza *talks* of coming out to visit me, says she would like to come. How glad I should be to see her again before I leave this world.

Dec 6 . . . Vere Foster[40] came to tea. He has just returned from Chicago where he has been looking after his emigrants and is now going to travel about the state of New York and see where he can get work for the poor who are out of employment and starving in the city of New York. He then intends travelling through the Southern states to see where the best opening is for poor Irish emigrants.

Dec 7 . . . The corporation want John to stand for councillor for one of the wards of the city. John says his health is not good enough to enable him to attend to the duties. . . . Versy Cronyn called to say that his father would not be here before Christmas, consequently the wedding is put off until January. . . . Ellen Hamilton told me that Emily Street and Doctor Popplewell are to be married very soon and that Doctor Popplewell had satisfactorily explained to Mr Becher who he is and what he is. Minnie Street expresses herself highly delighted with New Brunswick and that she goes to balls and concerts without number. The papers are full of the elections. As Mr Carling is a brewer, Mr Leonard[41] opposes him upon the temperance ticket, though it is said he is not at all averse to a social glass.

Dec 8 Very busy preparing for a tea party which has gone off very well. Mrs Cronyn and the two Misses Cronyn, the two Misses Blake, Sam Blake[42] and Versy Cronyn, . . . Mr Griffin, Amelia, Ellen Hamilton and Mr and Mrs King were here. They played games and appeared very happy. Mrs King remained all night. The roads are so bad and the night was so dark that she was afraid to go home.

Dec 9 . . . Mrs King remained all day. Mr King came for her just before dark – she appears very nice and amiable and yet I do not like

[40]Vere Foster (1819–1900), an Englishman active since 1850 in promoting emigration to the United States from Ireland. See Mary McNeill, *Vere Foster 1819–1900*, Newton Abbot: David and Charles, 1971.

[41]Elijah Leonard (1814–91) established a foundry in London in 1834. Mayor of London in 1857, he was defeated in that year as candidate for the Legislative Assembly by John Carling. He was appointed to the Senate in 1867. See Christopher Andreae, "Elijah Leonard," *Dic. Can. Biog.* XII, pp. 552–554.

[42]Samuel Hume Blake (1835–1914) was the second son of William Hume Blake, former Chancellor of Upper Canada. He and his brother, Edward, married respectively Sophia and Margaret, daughters of the Reverend Benjamin Cronyn.

her quite as well as I did. She has a glassy staring eye that rather wearies one.
Dec 12 Morning beautiful. Mr Becher called. He feels hurt and disappointed that he was not chosen to represent London. . . .
Dec 14 Amelia and Mr Becher came to luncheon. Mr Griffin much to his surprise received a notification from the Gore Bank that he owed them £470 with two years interest. Mr Griffin says he has paid the whole amount which he owed the Bank, he has proved satisfactorily that all has been paid except £170 and unless Mr *Street* will be *guilty* of doing one *honest action,* Mr Griffin may have to pay this amount over again. Mr Griffin has written to Mr Street on the subject. Mr Street is anxious to return to London and there are people here who are endevouring to smooth the way. He is an unfeeling dishonest man. Ellen Hamilton came to dinner. . . .
Dec 15 Dull and cloudy, wind easterly. . . . Hughes Wilson[43] was shot with a revolver and badly wounded in the head last night. It took place in a brawl in a brothel. His recovery it is said is doubtful. Poor miserable boy – how wretched his poor father must feel. Thermometer at 7 AM 26 at 9 PM 32.
Dec 16 The day beautiful. Went to the Wilsons with John. Hughes very dangerously wounded. Was in convulsion all night. On our return as we passed the house where he was shot. We traced the blood for some distance, as we came over the rail road bridge. The three other men who were wounded came into the town by that bridge. . . .
Dec 17 This is the first day of the city election. Mr Carling is far ahead. Another most shocking event took place last night. Miss Maggie McFarlane drowned herself. The poor girl has been a long time engaged to Mr Garret, an engineer on the Port Stanley Rail Road, and yesterday she received a letter from him breaking off the engagement, stating that he was too poor to marry, having only one hundred and twenty pounds a year. She, poor girl, could not bear up against the disappointment. She left a note for her aunt, Mrs Hamilton, telling her what she intended doing. At five o'clock they called her to dinner, she said she would come directly. After waiting some time they heard her go out of the front door and thought no more of it for some time, when the family became uneasy about her and Mr Hamilton[44] went to Mr Askin's and some other houses to see if she was there. In the

[43]Son of John Wilson.

[44]James Hamilton, Sheriff of the London District was an uncle of Miss McFarlane. He caught a cold while searching for her and died in March 1858.

meantime the note she had left was found and people were searching for her all night. Early this morning George Goodhue[45] and young Givens who had been sitting up with Hughes Wilson were walking on the Bank opposite the Wilson's house when they saw a woman in the river by the side of a log. They got a boat and brought the body of poor Maggie McFarlane to the shore. An inquest was held today and Mr Garret's letters were read. They are said to have been open and manly and have caused no reflection upon Mr Garret. Mrs Hamilton of course is in great distress. Amelia called. Mrs Becher drove me to the Wilsons. Hughes no better, had convulsions all last night. Doctor Anderson says he cannot live. Mr Becher called for a very few minutes. . . .

Dec 18 Ill natured people circulated a report that Maggie McFarlane was in the family way which caused her to destroy herself. Mr Hamilton insisted upon a medical examination to prove her innocence. She was buried today, poor girl. Mr Garret arrived in time to attend her funeral. He was almost mad and wept bitterly at the grave. He wished to see her but Mr Hamilton and his friends would not permit it as she was much swollen and changed. I think they were wrong. Edward was one of the pall bearers. The inquest brought in a verdict of temporary insanity which everybody approved of as it is the general belief that she was deranged when she committed the rash act. Fanny Becher came in to spend the day but was sent for before dinner. Hughes Wilson died at 5 o'clock this afternoon without ever having recovered consciousness. . . .

Dec 19 The first news this morning was that poor Maggie McFarlane's grave had been violated. The sexton going to the cemetery early saw that her grave had been disturbed and on going up to it he found the coffin open and the body drawn half out of it. The first idea was that the act had been done by Mr Garret in a fit of frenzy, but it was found that Mr Garret had gone with his brother to Hamilton yesterday, immediately after the funeral, and no doubt remained but that it was body snatchers who had intended to take the body away by the midnight train. But between 11 & 12 o'clock there was a cry of fire near the cemetery and an immense number of people running about in that vicinity which had disturbed the body snatchers and they had made their escape without the body. This last act sent a chill in every heart. Mr Hamilton offers a reward of £25 for the discovery of the parties who violated the grave. People think he ought to have offered at the

[45]Son of George J. Goodhue.

least £100. Teresa and I went over to the Wilsons. Poor Mr Wilson looks wretched and Lucy also has grief in her face. Mrs Wilson is one of those that the surface is easily disturbed but the water is too [shallow] to hide a deep grief. An inquest was held upon Hughes today. Mr Wilson at first objected but the Coroner (Dr [George] Moore) insisted upon it. Mr Wilson then named the jury-men. John was one. On examining Hughe's head the ball had gone through the skull and lodged in the brain. The jury are to sit all week and examine evidence regarding the murder. . . .

Dec 20 . . . John, Edward and George went to Hughes Wilson's funeral. It being Sunday all the idle people about the town attended. . . .

Dec 21 . . . John was all day upon a coroner's inquest inquiring into the murder of Hughes Wilson. A verdict of wilful murder was found against Hardy, a butcher, who has made his escape to the States.

Dec 22 Mr Carling has been returned member for London by a majority of 560. . . .

Dec 23 Mr Wilson, & Mrs Griffin came to luncheon. . . .

Dec 24 Mr Wilson came to luncheon. He gave Teresa a gold dollar as Christmas box and gave four gold dollars to George . . . Mr Becher and Mrs King came to luncheon. Ellen Hamilton came in the evening and assisted in hanging the pictures. The drawing room looks so nice with the new paper and the pictures. Dr Cronyn arrived yesterday. He is to preach tomorrow.

Dec 25 . . . His Lordship the Bishop of Huron preached his first sermon in his diocese since his consecration. He alluded to the melancholy events of last week (the death of Hughes Wilson & Miss McFarlane). He spoke feelingly and unsparingly. His sermon was generally approved of Mr Becher, Amelia and Ellen Hamilton and Mrs King called after Church. In the afternoon John, Edward & George went skating. . . . Mr Griffin, Amelia, Ellen Hamilton & Mr Des Voeux, Mr Brooke & Mr Douglas dined here. Mr Des Voeux was rather tipsy. He had been drinking before he came here. After dinner we played round games,[46] whist and cribbage.

Dec 26 . . . Edward Blake came up last evening and intends remaining until after his marriage on the 6th. . . .

Dec 27 George and I went to Church. The English mail came in. I had a letter from Mary and from Eliza. They are well and happy. Shuldham wants me to go to England and offers to pay my passage – not

[46]Games played at a round table where there were no partners and any number of players could play.

to be thought of at present . . . Edward Blake[47] came after Church to see John and remained to tea. I wrote to Sarah. Teresa wrote to Capt Knight to congratulate him upon the birth of his son.[48] How sad those congratulations sound to me, where is my poor Chasse and her babies.
Dec 28 John, Teresa and Mr Griffin have gone to Toronto, John on business, Teresa to have a dress made. Amelia came to spend the evening. She is not well. Ellen Hamilton came to tea. Edward is not very well but keeps at work.
Dec 29 Beautiful weather. Mr King came to luncheon. The Misses Blake and the Misses Cronyn called. Margaret [Blake] was paying her farewell visits before her marriage. Amelia came to dinner, she is all right again. This day Mr Talbot[49] the editor of the *Prototype*,[50] was elected member for West Middlesex. He is an Irishman with no property or interest in the country and only four years a resident. He must have talent and a good deal of assurance, which suits or rather carries his class of voters. His opponent was Mr Blackburn,[51] the editor of the *Free Press*. A Clear Grit and equally penniless. Mr Talbot is moderately conservative and decidedly the best of the two. But how strange a thing is popularity. Here is Mr Becher, more than twenty years a resident in London, a man of talent, wealth and integrity and character impeccable. He could not even get a nomination.
Dec 30 Got a telegraph from Sophia, want[s] Teresa to remain. Later in the day got a letter from [Sophia] to the same effect. It came too late to answer. Telegraphed to Sophia that I would rather Teresa come home but I left it to John to decide. We got a letter from Mr Portman who is in treaty for a cotton plantation, price 65 thousand dollars. There are 40 negroes with the plantation, house for proprietor and houses for slaves, good machinery, 700 acres of land, 600 in cotton. Mr Portman wants to draw 15,000 dollars of his money from his investments here to make the first payments. He thinks the produce of the plantation will make the second payment. . . .

[47]Edward Blake (1833–1912) attended Upper Canada College and Osgoode Hall Law School with John Fitzjohn Harris. An admirer of John's sister, Helen, he subsequently married Margaret, daughter of Reverend Benjamin Cronyn.

[48]Edward Knight remarried in 1856, two years after the tragic deaths of his wife, Charlotte, and two sons in 1854. He had two children by his second marriage.

[49]Marcus Talbot (1831–60) became editor and joint editor of the *Prototype* in 1855.

[50]The *Prototype* was a printing house which irregularly published a newspaper in the 1830s and 1840s.

[51]Josiah Blackburn (1823–90), founder and editor of the *London Free Press*, was the Reform candidate for Middlesex East (1857–58). See Elwood H. Jones, "Josiah Blackburn," *Dic. Can. Biog.* XI, pp. 80–82.

Dec 31 . . . It is reported that Mr Street has got a situation on the Milwaukee rail road with a salary of 3,000 dollars a year. Mr [C.J.] Brydge's[52] and Mr Becher's interests in the rail roads have procured it for him. Strange that a man notoriously dishonest and one that cannot return to this country for fear of the penitentiary should get a situation in the country where he can have no claims in preference to many applicants who have. The engagement between Emily Street and Doctor Popplewell is said to be off. Emily says she does not like him. And thus ends 1857. In looking upon the last year, a year of unparalleled commercial distress, how much have I to be thankful for. To me the year has been marked by no misfortunes. John's health is vastly improved, Edward is devoted to his business, George's conduct has met with the approbation and praise of Mr Wilson, Teresa is a good girl, and my married daughters are all well and prosperous and my own health is good and the professional standing of my sons very good and their business on the increase. Oh God, make me truly thankful for all thy mercies.

1858

Jan 1 The morning beautiful, the bells were ringing and the band playing through the streets immediately after 12 o'clock. We have had only 12 visitors this New Year's day – George Moore & Benjamin Cronyn, Versy Cronyn, [Edward] King & Mr Brooke, the Lord Bishop, the Revd Mr O'Neil, Mr Lawrason and Mr Des Voeux, Dr Brown, Mr Askin & Mr Armstrong. Mr Griffin, Amelia and Mrs Wicksted and Ellen Hamilton came to tea. John took tea at the Wilsons. Mr Street has not yet got a situation and Mr Blackburn the editor of the *Free Press*, has not run away.
Jan 2 Received a letter from Mr Portman and Helen. They do not purchase the plantation they were in treaty for. Mr Portman intends returning to St Louis in a few days and says he will purchase there. Helen wants a lock of Teresa's hair to make a necklace. I sent her a lock of mine to make a bracelet they make beautifully in New Orleans. Amelia and Mrs Wicksted called. John, Edward, George and Teresa all went to the Kings for dinner, they did not return until 12 o'clock. The dinner very nice and everybody agreeable. The Griffins and Mrs Wick-

[52]Charles John Brydges (1827–89), managing director of the Great Western Rail Road Company of Canada (1852–62), and later general manager of the Grand Trunk Railway. See Alan Wilson and R.A. Hotchkiss, "Charles John Brydges," *Dic. Can. Biog.* XI, pp. 121–125.

sted dined there also. Ellen Hamilton came up in the evening and Mr Des Voeux. The weather moderately cold.
Jan 3 John, George and myself went to Church. I remained for the Sacrament. Mr O'Neil preached. No one here today. John not very well. I wrote to Eliza.
Jan 5 Edward Blake and Versy Cronyn called. Edward Blake sat all morning with us and returned here to dinner late in the evening. Mr Wells[53] came by the train. He remains with us until after the wedding and is to be the bestman or rather groom's man.
Jan 6 Edward Blake came to breakfast and remained until it was time to dress for the ceremony. I think he was glad to get away from the Cronyns out of all the fuss and confusion of the preparations. . . . At half past eleven we went to St Paul's Church. There were a great number of people in the galleries and Church to witness the ceremony. The bride came in with her uncle Tom Cronyn. She looked very pretty although she is thought plain. She was beautifully dressed in a rich white silk made with double skirts, the waist hemmed with lace and a close fitting lace cap, a tulle veil with a pretty wreath of white roses and orange blossoms and a very pretty bouquet completed her costume. One of the brides maids, Rebecca Cronyn, wore a light blue silk dress with a white opera cloak, wreath and veil. The two Misses Blakes wore colourd drapes with opera cloak, wreaths and veils. Edward joined his bride at the altar and the bride went through the ceremony and received the congratulations of her friends with her usual quiet manner and without any apparent emotion. A large party of about 90 went to the breakfast which was exceedingly good and nice in all its arrangements. I was introduced to the Chancellor Blake[54] for the first time and like him very much. He is almost as young looking as his son. The young married couple left for Hamilton by the 2 o'clock train. Amelia and Mr Griffin came home with us and remained to a tea dinner. Ellen Hamilton, Sam Blake and Versy called. Mr Wells spoke to Teresa about Edward Blake's former attachment to Helen and said he was so fond of her though to her he never told his love. Just before dinner John had a faint turn which continued for more than a quarter of an hour without any apparent cause. This is the third or fourth turn of the kind he has had since he came from

[53]Rupert Mearse Wells (1835–1902) attended Upper Canada College and the University of Toronto with Blake and was his law partner.

[54]William Hume Blake (1809–70) was Solicitor-General for Canada West (1848), Chancellor of Upper Canada (1849–62), and Chancellor of the University of Toronto (1853–56).

England. I cannot tell what causes them, but they distress me beyond measure for they are so like the faint turns his father had during his last illness. May God in his mercy spare my son.
Jan 9 Mr & Mrs Blake called. The Blake family left for Toronto at 2 o'clock. Mr Wells left also. We were all very dull.
Jan 10 John, Edward, Teresa and myself went to Church. Mr Cronyn preached. The weather became very mild & the air excessively oppressive and affected me so much that I was unable to keep awake for some time and then I became quite ill. After the rain began to fall I felt better. John went to the Wilsons, but returned in time for tea. The Griffins came to the Church door and found they were so late that they were ashamed to come in and came here and sat for an hour but left before we came from Church. I finished my letter to Mary.
Jan 12 The English mail came in. . . . There is a letter from Mr Portman to John. He wants 20,000 dollars immediately to make a first payment for a cotton plantation in the State of Mississippi. The plantation contains 700 Acres, has 70 Negroes on it and costs 70,000 dollars. I sincerely hope he may not ruin himself. I hate slavery and would have nothing to do with slaves. . . .
Jan 13 . . . Not a soul here all day. . . . Mr Griffin had a letter from Mr McInnes who wrote in very bad spirits. His partner Mr Holman has nearly ruined him by speculating in American stocks and [he] is returning to Canada to try and make another fortune. I sincerely hope he may succeed for I believe him to be energetic, industrious and worthy. . . .
Jan 14 . . . Edward got a letter from Mr Portman and Helen. They seem quite decided upon buying a cotton plantation near Col Hampton's. I hope they may not ruin themselves, but 70,000 dollars is a large sum to invest in Negroes and 700 acres of land to say nothing of the sin of owning slaves. . . .
Jan 15 A very dull heavy day and rain tonight. Mr Griffin called today and was so nice and agreeable. Old Kitty [ex servant] came in and is in great distress. They are sued for £31. . . . All at Eldon invited to the Hamiltons this evening but George is the only one who has gone. The news from India is good. Lucknow is relieved.[55]
Jan 16 The morning warm with rain. . . . Mr & Mrs King came to

[55]The fortunes of Lucknow during the Indian Mutiny were of considerable interest to Amelia and her contemporaries. The first "relief of Lucknow" occurred on 25 September 1857 after a siege of 87 days. Relieved a second time on 17 November, it was not until 24 March 1858 that the besieging forces were defeated by a force under the command of Sir Colin Campbell.

luncheon. Mrs King remained until evening. Ellen Hamilton called and told us there was a rumor that her father was to be sent to Quebec to take charge of the U[pper] C[anada] Branch Bank there. I should be sorry if Ellen left London but it would be much pleasanter for her at Quebec as London must be very dull at present for young people. Old Kitty came again about their being sued. I tried to get the money for her from Mr King. He is to let me know on Monday. I read Benvenuto Cellini[56] and then George & I played cribbage.

Jan 18 Teresa went to the Griffins. I wrote to Helen. Mr Wilson came to luncheon. Kitty's husband came in again to try and get money to stop the execution against them. Mr King would not let them have any money. John bought their note and gave them 64 dollars for it. He paid that money to Mr Frank, the man that he owes, who has taken his note for the balance and given him a year to pay it in. The poor man went home very happy and thankful. . . .

Jan 19 . . . Mr Becher came out strong against Mr Street and thinks him nearly as great a villain as we do. I think his conscience reproached him a little for the way he spoke to me about Mr Street. Mr Becher expects to lose about £1400 by him. . . .

Jan 21 Clear and slight frost. Amelia and Mr Griffin came to luncheon. Teresa returned from the Kings and after I had gone to bed her brothers were up. George dined with the Griffins. Teresa intends turning her Horse into a bracelet & broach and get Capt Knight to buy them in London, England.

Jan 22 For the first time in my life I went to market with Amelia. She came home to luncheon. We found Mrs Cronyn here. On my way from the market we called at Mr Griffin's and John & Edward's office. I am to go to the market again tomorrow with Amelia and Mrs Cronyn. George and Ellen Hamilton went to the Griffins to dinner.

Jan 27 The first Synod called by the Bishop of Huron met today. The Rector is not yet to be appointed. Mr Askin came here after Church and spent the day. Amelia came to dinner. She is not looking well. . . . The Bishop spoke well and showed that he had a clear head. Mr Becher and Mr Wilson spoke well also. . . .

Jan 30 George left at 7 AM for Toronto to keep Term.[57] He looks upon it as a fortnight's holiday. Teresa sent to Mrs Lyons to make a white silk waist for her lace dress to wear at the Governor's Ball. . . .

Jan 31 . . . The house seems dull without George who is always rioting with Edward when here. . . .

[56]Benvenuto Cellini (1500–62), famous Italian sculptor, artist and writer.
[57]George was continuing his studies to be a lawyer.

Feb 1 . . . Teresa in great excitement, cannot get a sewing girl to let down her dress. She has grown so much that they are all too short. I undertook to make her a lace skirt and Ellen Hamilton assisted in lengthening the skirts of her other dresses. Teresa had a letter from Sophia [Ryerson] who says the ball at Government House is to be a very grand affair. Invitations have been sent to the military at Quebec, Montreal and Kingston. The young ladies are requested to dress in white. George is staying with the Ryersons who have asked the Griffins to stay there also until after the ball. Of the Indian news, General Inglis' description of the defense of Lucknow has created a great sensation. It is a simple relation of facts that comes home to every heart.[58] Mr King came to luncheon and paid Teresa for her horse, and is going to remit the money for her to Capt Knight to buy her a brooch and bracelet. . . . Amelia came to tell Teresa that if she wore any finery he [Gilbert Griffin] would not take her to the ball. Teresa was greatly disgusted that he should think such a threat necessary as of course we wish to dress her as well and as in good taste as we can.
Feb 2 A wet snowy day. . . . Ellen Hamilton came and assisted Teresa to finish her dress and pack trunks, etc. She is a kind good little girl. We dined early. Amelia called and had tea. We played whist in the evening.
Feb 3 . . . Teresa left for Toronto in a great state of excitement. She could not eat any dinner. This will be her first public ball. Dear girl, she is entering a world of cares and crosses. I think I must be bilious today for I feel so low spirited at parting with her, much more so than the occasion requires. I have parted with seven daughters and shall feel alone indeed when the eighth is gone. John, Edward and Ellen Hamilton went to the station with Teresa.
Feb 4 . . . I had a letter from my brother Edward. I was very busy all day and consequently not very lonely. . . .
Feb 6 . . . My brother George [Ryerse] came on a visit.[59] He had not been here for more than three years. He thought I looked old and very much changed & I thought the same of him. I felt very glad to see him. Amelia returned from Toronto. The Ball at Government House went off very well but the rooms were crowded. Lady Head[60] was

[58]Brigadier Inglis of the 32nd Regiment (Duke of Cornwall's Light Infantry) commanded the garrison during the siege at Lucknow.

[59]Both of Amelia R. Harris' brothers, George and Edward Ryerse, lived at Port Ryerse.

[60]Wife of Sir Edmund Walker Head (1805–68), Governor General of Canada (1854–61).

very particular in her enquiries about Mr Des Voeux's matrimonial engagement. Amelia thought it would have been more dignified if the first lady in the country had cared less for gossip. She sent for Amelia three times to question her on the subject. . . .

Feb 7 John, Edward and I went to Church. The Bishop preached. John and myself stayed for the Sacrament. Amelia and Mr Griffin came to tea. My brother went to the Baptist Church. John went to the Wilsons in the evening. Neither John nor I wrote any English letters by this mail.

Feb 8 I had a letter from Teresa – only told me what Amelia had told me about the ball. Edward Blake came in the evening. He has come to attend the first Chancery Court that has been held in London, all Chancery business hitherto has been done in Toronto. . . .

Feb 9 Edward Blake came in early to see John and Edward upon business . . . I wrote to Teresa. . . . Today Mr McInnes leaves Hamilton for New York. He has taken a bottle of graphs[61] to forward to Earl Spencer [Lord Althorpe]. I promised Ld Althorpe that I would send them. . . .

Feb 12 . . . Had a letter from Teresa, wants money to buy a wreath. She seems very happy and enjoys her first introduction into the world. I wrote to Teresa and sent her money. Mr & Mrs King & Mr & Mrs Griffin dined here and then went to see some amateur theatricals got up by the employees of the Great Western. Full house but performance not very good. The Kings stayed here all night.

Feb 13 Ellen Hamilton called. She says Ned Blake told Mrs Wilson that she was to be married to John. I acquit John of any intention of the kind.

Feb 14 . . . We had four letters from the Portmans. I am sorry to say that Mr Portman appears determined to buy the cotton plantation he was in treaty for, and I very much fear he will in a few years find himsef involved and ruined. He hopes now to get the plantation for 80,000 dollars and finds the plantation without a house and destitute of supplies which will involve an immediate outlay and he in total ignorance of how any thing is to be done. . . . John went to the Wilsons. He does not like the report about him and Ellen Hamilton.

Feb 15 . . . Becher came to luncheon. He spoke of the dinner parties in Toronto being sumptuous, particularly with the rail road contractors, Mr Gzowski and McPherson. . . .

Feb 16 Snow and very cold. Mr Becher came to luncheon. We dined

[61]Probably a reference to plant grafts.

at 7 expecting George. He did not come until eight and much to our surprise and pleasure Teresa came with him. Both George and Teresa are improved by their visit to Toronto. Teresa has taken more exercise and consequently has a better colour. . . .

Feb 17 . . . She [Amelia] is not well. I was in hopes that her household cares which compel exertion both of mind and body would benefit her health and she has been better since she has been in her own house but she seems [to be] giving away again and I feel anxious about her. . . . Mr Wilson *blew George up* before all the students for having over staid his time two days. George felt very much hurt. He has been in Mr Wilson's office 4 years and nearly 4 months and during that time has never been absent one week, taking $^{1}/_{2}$ days into count. . . .

Feb 19 Today I completed my 60th year. Oh God make me truly thankful for all Thy mercies. Mrs Plummer[62] came in this morning to tell us that Mr Des Voeux intended leaving John's office and going to Toronto to study. Mr Des Voeux came in a few minutes after Mrs Plummer left to speak to John on the subject. John of course had no objections to transfer his Articles to anyone that he wished to study with but he must change very much for the better in many ways if he ever does much for himself. His engagement is quite off with Miss Matthews, not to come on again he says. He is kind hearted and clever enough but sadly in want of common sense and easily influenced by others for short intervals either for good or evil. Toronto is a bad place for him. . . . All the papers are full of the marriage of the Princess Royal.[63]

Feb 20 Received a letter from Helen mentioning the death of Col Wade Hampton Senior. Mr Portman feels his death very much as they were great friends. I hope his death may prevent Mr Portman's purchasing. One of his greatest inducements to purchase was to be near the Hamptons. . . .

Feb 21 . . . Mr [Charles] Hutchinson gazetted District Attorney. John took tea with the Wilsons.

Feb 22 Mr Des Voeux called to say goodbye. He is gone. . . .

Feb 23 English mail came in. Had letters from Sarah, Mary & Eliza and John had a letter from Ld Portman and Mr Bennett[64] returned the debentures which John had purchased for him and wishes him to sell them. He wants to raise money to purchase his majority. John can

[62] A neighbour on Ridout Street.
[63] Queen Victoria's daughter.
[64] Portman's brother-in-law.

dispose of them at once. Mary sent me a pocket handkerchief, one of 2 dozen which Lord Downshire had made her a present of. She is ailing and [has] not been well since John left England. . . .
Feb 25 Amelia, Mrs King and Mrs Wilson came to luncheon. The weather lovely. The House of Assembly met today. Henry Smith[65] of Kingston chosen Speaker. He is a very coarse vulgar man. Mr Talbot M.P. for Middlesex got Mr Hutchinson appointed District Attorney. It is reported that he threatened to join the Opposition if the appointment was refused and now it is said that he is going to force big John Ferguson on the county as Registrar, an illiterate vulgar Irishman. The Ministry will soon say of Mr Talbot as they did of Col Prince that they might buy him but he would not stay bought. We played euchre.
Feb 27 Mr & Mrs Griffin, Mr McInnes came to luncheon. We had letters from Helen and Mr Portman. They are coming home for the summer. Their buying the cotton plantation I think doubtful, as Ld Portman does not approve of it. The Pacific Hotel at St Louis has been burned. 18 lives lost and many more people injured. It is said a murder was committed by a man belonging to the Hotel and that he set the Hotel on fire. He has been arrested as well as the landlord and one other respected person. . . .
Mar 1 Cold. Mr Gzowski in town. No one called during the day. I wrote to Helen. Teresa went to the Hamiltons to tea and we played euchre. John and I won, luck has changed.
Mar 2 Very cold. Teresa went to the Kings with Edward and the Griffins to dinner. . . . John got a telegram from Mr Portman from New Orleans to say that he would not want his money (40,000$) and told John to reinvest. Ellen Hamilton came to tea. We played whist.
Mar 6 . . . I had a letter from my brother Edward enclosing 60$ the rent of my farm in Woodhouse. . . .
Mar 10 Received a letter from Helen. They have not given up the idea of buying in the south near the Hamptons. Helen will come home in May. . . .
Mar 11 . . . The day beautiful and bright, no one here, we played euchre, John & I were well beaten. It looks absurd a mother and three sons playing euchre every night for two hours. I suppose they think it amuses me, as I am dull not having eyesight to read or see very much by candlelight and it is very kind of them.

[65]Sir Henry Smith (1812–68), was representative for Frontenac (1841–61), Solicitor-General (1854–58), Speaker of the Legislative Assembly (1858–61), and was Knighted in 1860.

Mar 12 Lord Palmerston[66] has been defeated on the Bill for bringing to punishment any refugee or other conspirators to commit murder in or out of Great Britain. I thought the Bill to be both just and honorable but John Bull has taken offence at the threats of the French people in their addresses to Louis Napoleon and will not be bullied into doing what their own good feeling would have prompted them to do. Consequently Lord Palmerston has resigned and Lord Derby[67] has formed a ministry. . . . It is the general opinion that Lord Derby's reign will be short as Lord Palmerston is so very popular. . . .
Mar 13 John has a letter from Mr Portman. His present intention is to purchase 150 acres from Col Hampton and build a house at once. I am very glad he is not going to buy more at present until he sees how he will succeed growing cotton. I shall be very much surprised if he does not come north to live in a few years. . . .
Mar 14 . . . We received a letter from Helen. Mr Portman is very vexed with John for writing to Ld Portman that he did not like Mr Portman becoming a slave owner and also for saying anything about the matters [of] money, he wished his father to think that he invested it. Ld Portman is too good a man of business not to know that Mr Portman must have some one to look after his business when 3,000 miles distant, John answered Helen's letter immediately and repeated what he had said to Lord Portman which could give offence to no one. . . .
Mar 15 . . . John went to the station to meet the Chief Justice Sir John B. Robinson[68] who holds the Assize here which is to commence tomorrow. Mr McInnes [staying overnight], John, Edward & I played euchre. They all cheated except myself.
Mar 20 . . . Chief Justice Sheriff Hamilton very dangerously ill (bleeding of the lungs).
Mar 21 Edward Blake called. Mrs Blake and Edward have come up to be present at the installation of the Bishop which is to take place on Wednesday next. The Chief Justice called and went to Church with George and myself. He returned and lunched with us. . . .
Mar 27 . . . Ld Portman has given Mr Portman leave to draw for another £5000. . . .
Mar 29 We are all invited to a christening at the Becher's Wednesday

[66]The British Prime Minister.
[67]The father of Amelia's one-time fiancé.
[68]Sir John Beverley Robinson (1791–1863), Chief Justice of Upper Canada, speaker of Legislative Council, and president of Executive Council, was a leading figure in the "Family Compact."

evening. Sheriff Hamilton died last night. Mr McInnes came to luncheon. . . . I went to the Griffins to dinner. John, Mr & Mrs W. Lawrason and Mr McInnes dined there also. . . .
Mar 30 . . . The house is in confusion. We have a carpenter making alterations in the Griffin's room and we have plasterers and white washers. . . .
Mar 31 I went to market . . . Sheriff Hamilton buried today. The shops were closed during the procession, which was very large as he was much respected. He took cold the night Maggie Macfarlane drowned herself[69]. He was all night searching for her, and her death prayed upon his mind during his last illness. When a little delirious, his thought was upon her. He would start and ask, "Who saw her jump?"
Apr 1 Mr Wilson and Mr Becher came to lunch. . . . The English mail came in. The *Persia* makes such quick trips. I had a letter from Sarah from Bruges in 14 days. . . .
Apr 2 . . . John, Edward and Mr Griffin walked out to the Kings. They called at the Griffins on their way home and drank a bottle of Goldlock.[70] John came home ill.
Apr 3 John ill. He is not strong enough to take such a long walk. He went to the Griffins in the afternoon. . . .
Apr 5 . . . The Chief Justice came to tea. He had just come from Toronto and was on his way to St Thomas to hold the Assize court there.
Apr 7 The trial of Townsend, the murderer of Mr Nellis and of a constable, closed today, and he was acquitted. This is one of the most singular trials that has ever taken place in the province. Himself, his mother and sisters have resided in the province for years and yet he could not be identified in a way that would not leave a doubt. He called himself Mr Henry, and although there were more than 50 people swore positively that he was Townsend, the murderer, and there were 50 others that swore that he was Mr Henry and not here at the time of the murder. The witnesses in his favour were much less respectable than against him. His mother and sisters swore that he was not Townsend. He has the benefit of the doubt although Judge McLean charged strongly against him and it is the conviction of the country that he *is* Townsend, and [the populace] is strong in the conviction that he is not at liberty but is to be removed to Cayuga to stand another trial for the murder of Nellis. . . .

[69]See Amelia's diary, 17 December 1857.
[70]A brand of whiskey.

Apr 10 Edward went to St Thomas as witness. The Chief Justice was to have spent tomorrow with us. . . .

Apr 12 . . . Edward Horton abused Edward Harris in Court at St Thomas in a most uncalled for manner. Mr Wilson was the lawyer for the prosecution and he showed up Mr Horton in a way that was any thing but satisfactory to him and contradicted all he had said of Edward. Edward was only a witness and could not reply. He returned at night wet and weary.

Apr 13 Teresa and John insisted upon my going to the Griffins to spend the day. I felt as if I was turned out of doors. When I returned in the evening I found the library cleaned and in order and they had insisted upon my spending the day out so that I might not weary myself by assisting them. It was kind of dear Teresa. . . . Mr Wilson came to the Griffins to tell me about the dressing [down] he gave Mr Edward Horton. Mr Wilson could not sit quietly and hear one of my family abused. He is a kind true friend.

Apr 15 Edward and George left here this morning by the 6 o'clock train, Edward for Chatham, George for Woodstock, Simcoe and Toronto. . . .

Apr 16 Fanny Becher is mad about rail roads. She knows all about the trains and all of the conductors. It is a pity her mother does not prevent her making herself ridiculous.

Apr 22 The day beautiful. Dr McKay[71] arrived in time for lunch. The people are annoyed at his remaining with us. They wished him to be the guest of the City. John told him not to feel bound to us but to do what ever he preferred. He came to us and goes to supper after the lecture given to him by the leading men of the city. We asked the Bishop of Huron, Mr Goodhue, Mr Lawrason, Amelia and Mrs Hugueson to meet Dr McKay at dinner. Dr McKay is what may be called a small man with a peculiar head going up straight from the eyebrows to the top of his ears around the head with almost an even fullness and high. He is very plain looking, with a sharp twinkling eye and a soft clear voice. As far as I could judge, I should say he was not brilliant in general conversation but talks very well with one or two. He prefers Canada very much to the United States and prefers the eastern and northern states to the South and will come out strong against slavery when he returns to England. Our dinner went off very well. All excepting myself went to the lecture. . . .

Apr 23 Dr McKay left by the 11 o'clock train for Toronto where he is to lecture tonight. . . .

[71]An Englishman visiting London to give a public lecture on music and song.

Apr 24 The ground covered with snow and the morning is cold and disagreeable. . . . The steamer brings the news that Lucknow is taken without any very severe fighting. Sir Colin Campbell will win a peerage.[72] Doctor McKay told us that he knew Sir Colin Campbell's father who is a shepherd, a very handsome man and very much respected in his class of life. His name is McClaverty. A governess fell in love with him and married him and she had interest enough to get a commission for her son, who without money to purchase and without interest has slowly worked his way up to his present high position. He allows his father £50 a year out of his pay and has done so for many years. Doctor McKay saw his father at the time the city of Glasgow gave Sir Colin a sword and asked him if he was going to the presentation. The old man said he had not been sent for nor had he seen his son for forty years. He was only a few hours distant. It made me sorry for both father and *son.*

Apr 29 . . . Edward and George gone to a ball got up by the young gentlemen of the town. George is one of the stewards. It is the first time he has had anything to do with a public ball. Teresa did not go as it is rather a mixture.

Apr 30 Got a letter from Helen. She will not be home as soon as expected. The steamer (*Falls City*) that they were to come by blew up backing out of New Orleans. A great many lives were lost not only in the *Falls City* but in boats that were near her. Helen wishes herself safe at home and I wish she was safe here. Mr Portman has again bargained for a plantation and will forfeit 5000$ if he draws back. He is infatuated and in a few years will be ruined. . . .

May 1 . . . The [Lord] Downshire Regiment of Militia are to be disbanded which will throw Shuldham out of employment. Col Dalzell and Col Crutchley met for the first time in London and went together to visit Capt Knight and the brothers-in-law like each other, of course, as they are all gentlemen. . . .

May 6 I have been sowing flower seeds all the morning and we finish house cleaning today. . . .

May 8 . . . Amelia brought a letter from Mary who writes in better spirits. She met Sir Richard Airey at Aldershot, and they have made friends, which I am very glad of. Sir Richard has had trials of the heart in losing two sons, and worldly vexations in the public sensure

[72]General Sir Colin Campbell, later Lord Clyde, commanded the forces that relieved Lucknow on 17 November 1857 and recaptured it on 24 March 1858, in the final stages of the Indian Mutiny.

[sic] that filled the papers in regard to his management or *mismanagement* of the troops in the Crimea. All this may have softened his character, but when in this country he was one of the most [dis]agreeable, most selfish, most grasping and heartless men I ever met. When we first knew him, how much we all liked him, and Mary's conversation with him brings the same feeling of regard back. *Query* – is it possible to dislike a person that we once have been truly attached to? I think not. We might disapprove – regret – but never dislike. Mary is going to visit Lady Airey in London. . . .

May 10 Edward got up very early to go with Mr Griffin to Ingersol trout fishing. The morning very cold. He returned 1/2 past 10 PM very tired, very wet, having caught only five small trout, having been thrown from a buggy and narrowly escaped having their necks broken. . . .

May 11 . . . I have changed servants today. Betsy and Jane Cummings are both gone. We took in an English farmer's son who brought a letter from Ld Portman to John until we could get him a place and they refused to make his bed. Consequently I told them to look for other places.

May 14 . . . Edward came in with a telegraph from Mr Portman saying they would be home to dinner, we were all so delighted. At 40 minutes past three they arrived. Helen look[s] very tired, Mr Portman looks very well and the boy is a beauty. . . . Amelia and Mr Griffin came to dinner. . . .

May 16 . . . Amelia feels very unhappy. She knows that Mr Griffin and Mr Portman do not like each other. She should let things take their course, . . .

May 20 Edward gone to Toronto. I wrote to ask Sophia to return with him and spend two or three weeks with us. . . .

May 21 . . . Edward returned from Toronto. He went to a ball at Government House. Sophia could not return with him as she is taking lessons.

May 24 Malcolm Cameron called. He wanted to sell mortgages. . . . Edward and George went to Hall's Mills to fish, caught a few rock bass. In the evening there were the usual fireworks to celebrate her Majesty's birthday. Long may she reign over us.

Jun 2 . . . The papers are full of Dr Ryerson's defalcations. The bank of Upper Canada allowed him interest on some moneys that had remained in their hands over six months. Dr Ryerson was not aware that they intended to do so but when the sum amounted to £1,400 he made use of it and afterwards when his right to the money was questioned he referred the matter to the Government and said that unless the money was in law as well as equity his, he would refund it as he on no account would retain a farthing if not legally his. The ministry have never gave him their decision but told him to keep the money until he heard further on the subject. Now the Committee on Accounts have taken the matter up and he is outrageously abused and will probably lose his appointment.[73]

Jun 4 The 2nd anniversary of Helen's wedding day. Mr Portman made me a present of 150 dollars. . . . The non-practicing cricketers proposed making up [an] eleven and challenging the London Cricket Club to a match to be played on Monday next. The challengers call themselves the Vagabond Club. The challenge has been accepted and the match is to be played as proposed on Monday. George is in a great state of excitement.

Jun 7 . . . [Mrs King] told me about her being in the family way and asked if she ought to engage a nurse at once. I thought three or four months hence would be quite time enough. Mrs King does not improve. She grows careless in her dress and vulgar. Mr Becher called. He would not lend his tent for the day to the cricketers. Mr Griffin gave a supper to several of the cricketers. All from Eldon went including Helen and Teresa. The cricket match was not played out. The Vagabond Club were to have another innings which they are not disposed to take as they know they must be beaten.

Jun 9 . . . Capt Hugueson brought up before the Police Court for striking a shop boy, who came to his front door with bills and parcels and when he was requested to go to the back door became very impertinent and struck the door and Capt Hugueson struck him, for which he was fined five dollars and costs, which were three dollars more. . . .

Jun 11 . . . English mail came . . . [Sarah] wrote from Baden Baden. Col Dalzell and Sarah are in search of a school for their children. . . . Mary was on move to a cottage of Ld Downshire. . . .

Jun 13 At breakfast it was discovered that Edward had not been home as his bed had not been slept in. We supposed that he had gone to the Griffins to dinner and the rain had prevented his coming home. I sent there to ask. He had not been there. We then sent to Mr Parke and to Mr Daniels.[74] They know nothing of him. I was in a dreadful state

[73]Ryerson's appointment was that of Superintendant of Education for Upper Canada and the funds in question had been credited to the Education Department. The correspondence between Amelia Harris and Ryerson on this subject is in the Harris Papers. See C.B. Sissons, *Egerton Ryerson: His Life and Letters*, Toronto: Clarke Irwin, 1947, Vol. 2, pp. 369–94.

[74]James Daniels, a London lawyer who became a London alderman in 1860.

of alarm and thought of the foot bridge and the high water – of his deafness and the railroad – I thought of the *Ercolano*[75] and Chasse, and of my first born, and the morning that he was placed on bed by the sofa, a bleeding corpse.[76] The agony was intense for half an hour. All old wounds seemed to be opened, and I was ill for the day. He had met Mr [Charles] Hutchinson and had gone home with him to dinner. As it rained heavily in the evening he was persuaded to stay all night and as the next day was Sunday he had loitered away the morning, little thinking the commotion he was causing at home. And to look back the whole thing appears absurd, but during the 43 years that I have been a wife and mother, neither husband, son, or daughter have ever been absent a night without saying why and wherefore. . . .

Jun 14 People say that Mrs Hugueson was the daughter of a game-keeper. People cannot let them alone and they are so quiet. Whose business is it if she is a game keeper's daughter. . . .

Jun 17 The Lawrasons gave a pic nic but did not ask us. They gave as a reason that they thought that we would not like to meet the Goodhues. It is strange that people cannot let us decide upon whom we should like to meet. If we did not wish to meet any of their guests we could have declined. We were very glad we were not invited as we dislike pic nics and would not have gone. . . .

Jun 18 44th anniversary of the battle of Waterloo. The horrors of war with all their worst features are now raging in the East and the Plains of Waterloo are visited in peace by the tourists and an inexhaustible number of buttons and balls sold to the collectors of relics, while few remain who took part in that day's, what shall I call it, glory and misery. . . .

Jun 21 . . . Mrs W. Lawrason had arranged to ride with John and Mr Portman but Mr Lawrason went to the office and told John that he would not let his wife go and that his wife went home crying with mortification. Mr Lawrason shows very bad taste in telling of their little squabbles and it appears to me very absurd his forbidding her riding occasionally with Mr Portman and John as he declares he cannot ride with her himself being too heavy for any horse. . . .

Jun 22 Mr Portman, Helen, John and Teresa went to Mrs Bill's party. The evening very hot. The party was one of the best that London can give. W. Lawrason told everyone that he would not [let] his wife ride

[75]The ship on which Charlotte (Chasse) had been drowned in 1854.

[76]Amelia's first child, William, had died in 1822 after falling from a cart. The anniversaries of William's birthday and death are often commented upon in Amelia's diary.

with John and Mr Portman and that she was angry. Remarks are very general about Lucy Wilson's driving to the pic nic with Bill Bailey and their wandering away and not returning until all the people left excepting old Mrs Lawrason and another carriage party who waited for her. Mrs Lawrason spoke sharply to Lucy.

Jun 24 . . . Lady Portman has written to ask Helen to go home for her confinement and the Portmans are inclined to go. I do not know how they will decide. I wish her to remain with me until her confinement is over very much. She would doubtless be taken as good care of with the Portmans as with me, but two months in England could not give her the same home feeling that she has here and it is a long journey to take [in] this hot weather in her situation, with a small child who is in the agonies of teething.

Jun 25 . . . George and Edward as members of the Cricket Club go today to St Catharines to play the club there who has challenged them. George has never seen the Falls and Mr Becher had offered him a pass to go there. This morning I reminded him of his offer and he gave him one, and John gave him money to pay his expenses. So that George has gone on his travels in a great state of delight, with the small drawback of expecting a good beating at cricket at St Catharines.

Jun 27 . . . This is the 43rd anniversary of my wedding day. How fresh and bright and beautiful was that morning. And I, how young I was and full of life and hope. How little I knew of the world or its cares. The world's life had not commenced and now it is nearly over. There are but three living of the 25 that were assembled there that morning and the youngest of the three is 57. I am 60, my family dispersed, my youngest child nearly 19. All are good and doing well. My labours and cares are nearly ended. . . .

Jun 29 We are all invited to tea at the Wilsons tonight to eat strawberries and cream. . . . George is delighted with his first view of the Falls. They have as they expected been well beaten by the St Catharines Club. . . .

Jul 2 Amelia came this morning to say that Capt Rattallack had written to Mr Griffin to procure rooms for the Governor General on Monday evening next as Sir Edmund Head and suite would remain one night in London. I of course wrote at once and asked them here, Sir Edmund and Lady Head and one of the suite. John telegraphed also to Capt Rattallack, who immediately accepted our invitation for Sir Edmund Head. Lady Head does not come. . . .

Jul 4 . . . John went to the Wilsons and returned full of my going to England and taking Teresa and Lucy Wilson with me and they want me to go to the Continent and to remain away a year or two. Mr

Wilson offers to pay more than Lucy's proportion of the expense. It might be a very good thing for Teresa as she could take drawing lessons and learn to speak French but I have not funds and very little inclination to leave my quiet home. The Wilson[s] wish to send Lucy away from Bill Bailey, but I much fear they will not be able to prevent her marrying him. . . .

Jul 5 This morning I was very quietly picking over some strawberries in my usual morning dress when John came in and told me that His Excellency would be here in 10 minutes. I dressed in a great hurry, when another telegraph came saying that he would not be here before 1 PM at which hour he arrived. Mr Hopkins, an English gentleman who is with his daughters on a visit to his Excellency, and Lady Head came with him and remained here as our guests. Capt Rattallack, the Governor's A.D.C. remained here also. I had no more room vacant to offer. Consequently Mr Deeds and Col Bradford slept at the inn but lunched and dined with us. . . . Sir Edmund Head looks better than when I last saw him three years ago. Lady Head could not accompany him on account of her visitors. Our dinner went off very pleasantly. . . . In the evening Sir Edmund Head and myself, Mr Hopkins and Amelia played whist. We like Mr Hopkins very much. About 2 o'clock in the morning the band serenaded his Excellency and disturbed all of our slumbers.

Jul 6 . . . The Bishop of Huron called and remained to luncheon. Major Shanley and Capt Rivers called and turned out the Artillery and Troop for his Excellency's inspection. A salute was fired for his Excellency who of course was full of praise. The band returned and played at our gate during luncheon. . . . I had a long talk with Sir Edmund Head this morning about Dr Ryerson and his appropriating £1,500 of interest to himself. He exonerates the Dr from any intention of wrong but thinks that he ought to write to Mr [Francis] Hincks[77] and get a written acknowledgment that he had told him that any interest which the bank chose to allow him upon any public money remaining in the bank over three months was his (Dr Ryerson's) own. That the public had nothing to do with it as long as all legal demands were paid as soon as presented. Or what would be better, for Dr Ryerson to pay over the money at once, and then petition the House for remuneration for his extra services. I shall write to Dr Ryerson and advise him accordingly. Sir Edmund Head expressed very great surprise that Mr

[77]Francis Hincks (1807–85), Prime Minister in the Hincks-Morin Administration (1851–54).

Portman should become a slave holder and thus lay himself open should he ever return to England to a prosecution for felony by any ill natured person who wished to annoy him. . . .

Jul 7 Mr Becher came to luncheon and complained of the expenses of his house keeping. Said there must be retrenchment, that they were now living at the rate of £1,500 or 1,800 a year. We told him that Sir Edmund Head asked why he was not into the House of Representatives and that John had said he could not get there. He thinks otherwise and says he would only have to hold up his finger to be elected, but I think he is mistaken. Few people can form a right estimate of their own popularity until it is put to the test. He ought to be the city member, but his very expression that he has only to hold up his finger to be returned will be used against [him]. He has made use of it on several occasions and it has already been made use of to ridicule him. Should Mr Becher ever come forward, Mr Wilson will do all he can to prevent his return. I wrote to Dr Ryerson advising him to return the interest to which his right is disputed and told him what Sir Edmund Head said on the subject. I hope Egerton may not be annoyed with me. . . . The thermometer 90 in the shade.

Jul 8 Mr Becher came to luncheon and spoke to John about Mr Griffin's debt to the Gore Bank. Mr Griffin has paid nothing and made no effort to pay any thing. John thought his name was only on notes for £150 but it appears he is endorser for the whole £400. Mr Becher says he dislikes seeing him but says it will have to be done. He will place the note in the hands of some other lawyer. Mr Wilson spoke to me also and says Mr Griffin has over drawn his account at the Bank of Montreal £80 and makes no effort to pay it although repeatedly requested to do so. My poor Amelia. What is to become of her. I think she knows nothing about it. Mr Griffin must have been in debt when he came to London. . . .

Jul 12 Today I have had a piece of very unpleasant information. Dr Farrar talks of giving up my house. If he should continue on it will be at a reduction of £50 a year and £50 out of my small income is a very large item. Teresa and myself will be dependant on my three sons. I also discovered that my son John had paid Doctor Anderson's bill for £47 which had given me much uneasiness as I could not sell any land to raise money and I could not pay it out of my small income. My God reward him for all his kindness.

Jul 13 I received a letter from Dr Ryerson in answer to mine. He received my advice with all kindness and acted upon my suggestions and has made arrangements to pay over the money at once. He will be a poorer man but a much happier one as his right to the money being

doubted would make its possession painful, however convinced *he* might be of his legal right to it. I wrote to him today. . . . Amelia came to tea. I think she knows of Mr Griffin's embarassments. John advanced an instalment for him today and has made some arrangement with the bank. . . .
Jul 14 We had just dined when we got a telegraph from Mr Portman saying they would be home at 4 o'clock. They all looked the better of their trip. They returned from Quebec by the way of Saratoga and the Falls. They thought the company at Saratoga very second class. They saw the Lords Grosvenor & Cavendish and Mr Ashley at the Clifton. They are to be here the last week in August. . . .
Jul 15 Helen and Teresa busy unpacking. Ld Portman has given Mr Portman £4,000 and lends him £6,000 more at 5 per cent to pay for his plantation. It is a great pity, the property is in a slave state. . . .
Jul 17 Received a letter from Dr Ryerson who again expresses his thanks for my advice to him. . . . Dr Ryerson feels that it was my letter that opened his eyes to the false position in which he was placed and he begs of me to regard him as a son in every sense of the word. I wrote to him advising him to suppress a part of his official letter as his enemies would put a very different meaning to one clause of it than what it was intended to convey. . . .
Jul 20 . . . Col Crutchley is removed from the Depot at Birr to the command of the Depot at Belfast. . . . There was a commotion in the House today. Mrs Panton, the cook, refused to tell Mrs Portman's nurse when dinner was ready. I told her if she would tell the house maid that the house maid would call her. But the house maid said she would not mind telling her, only Mary the nurse carried her head so high. I was rather surprised and told both cook and house maid they might leave. They came to their senses and the house maid became willing to do anything, even to tell Mary that their dinner was ready. Mrs Panton is a good specimen of pride and poverty. She was in a state of starvation when she came to me, & I should send her to the same state if I send her away now as her husband is so lazy no one will employ him for more than a day and no one will take her with her child to service. Yet she cannot eat cold meat and will not notify other servants that their dinner is ready. And yet I pity her. She is hardworking and has a lazy helpless husband, one child and another coming. And what is to become of her?
Jul 21 . . . Panton absented himself without leave and got drunk.
Jul 22 John left this morning for Toronto to try and have a Bill altered which is now before the House which if passed into a Law will prevent any lawyer from holding the office of Registrar to the Surrogate

Court.[78] . . . The Portmans go to the Falls on Monday the 26th. They are to pay $50 a week for the cottage and the board of themselves and nurse.

Jul 23 John returned today from Toronto. He went to a ball at Government House and enjoyed himself very much, but did not succeed in getting the Bill altered. He found when he got there that there were two Bills that would have to be altered, and thought it was not worth the time and trouble. . . .

Jul 24 . . . In the House of Assembly, Mr McKenzie[79] [sic] made another attack upon Dr Ryerson. A motion was made to grant a sum of money necessary for the Normal School. Mr McKenzie objected to Dr Ryerson's being entrusted with any more public money until he had paid over the interest which was in his hands. The Premier J.A. McDonald [sic][80] rose and said he had much pleasure in stating that the money was paid, every farthing of it. How glad I felt that Dr Ryerson no longer had a doubtful position, or retained a sum of money however small to which his right was disputed. . . .

Jul 28 John went to Toronto again to try and get the Bill altered which is now before the House which will prevent lawyers from being registrars of Surrogate Courts. Consequently if he cannot get it altered he will have to resign.[81] It is rumourd in the papers that Sir Allan MacNab is to be the Governor of the new Province of Caledonia. The enthusiasm is on the increase about the Gold digging at Fraser's River. Many are going from Canada and the U. States. . . .

Jul 30 . . . J.A. Macdonald's Ministry have resigned and Mr George Brown has been called to form a Ministry. It is very much doubted whether he can command a working majority. The late Ministry were defeated upon the Seat of Government question. They wished to abide by the Queen's decision. The opposition voted against it. Very uncomplimentary to the Queen after asking her to decide where the Seat of Government should be. I went to the cemetery which is neglected. Cows are allowed to pasture there and of course eat off all the shrubs planted about the graves. . . .

[78]This decision was of interest to Amelia as John had held this position for some years.

[79]William Lyon Mackenzie (1795–1861) had been reelected to the House of Assembly in 1851, following his return from exile in the United States in 1849. This must have been one of his last actions as a member. Less than a month later he resigned his seat.

[80]Amelia inconsistently misspelled Sir John A. Macdonald (1815–91) as "McDonald" and "MacDonald," and occasionally gave him his correct name. To avoid confusion he is henceforth rendered here as "Macdonald."

[81]John was not successful and did resign.

Jul 31 . . . I wrote to Dr Ryerson to forward by express some wine that John and Dr Ryerson had purchased jointly when in Paris last summer. We are converting the smoke house into a summer house.
Aug 3 Every body is speaking of the change of Ministry and wondering whether the [George] Brown Cabinet will last a day. A vote of want of confidence passed both Houses by very large majorities today, and the Ministry have requested Sir Edmund Head to dissolve Parliament. He has taken time to consider the subject. . . .
Aug 4 Mr Portman and John rode to the Kings. John was thrown from his horse or rather his horse fell with him and hurt him a good deal. I have had a change of servants. My new cook has come and Mrs Panton leaves today. The Brown Ministry have resigned and their resignation has been accepted.
Aug 5 Great news today. The telegraph fleet has been successful and England and America are united by a telegraph line. A message came today from the Queen to the President and the bells have been ringing merrily. The Governor sent for Mr Galt[82] to form a Ministry but he has declined. It is supposed there will be a dissolution of Parliament. . . . I had a letter from Eliza which gives a glowing description of Irish filth. Amelia had a letter from Mary who talks of coming to this country on a visit. Teresa got her bracelet, broach, locket and ring from the express office yesterday. John paid $22 charges upon articles which cost in England $8, and Capt Knight had paid all expenses as far as New York. The charges were enormous and unjust.
Aug 6 8 varieties of French wines arrived today. Dr Ryerson added one dozen of claret as a present to me. There is six dozen in all. Costs when here, carriage, customs, and all, $64 for five dozen. . . . Mr Portman and John rode again today and John's horse fell with him again but fortunately did not hurt him much. John will sell the horse as soon as he can. Mr Portman brought home two young puppies (Beagles). The Artillery fired a royal salute tonight in consequence of the success of the Atlantic telegraph.
Aug 7 The Macdonald Ministry have returned to office and the Brown party give the Governor General unlimited abuse because he would not dissolve Parliament. . . . A second game of cricket came off today between the English and the Irish. The English won this time.
Aug 9 . . . Edward requested me to note that we have had our first apple pie today. . . .
Aug 11 . . . Mr Hutchinson's marriage with Minnie Street on Tuesday

[82]Alexander Galt (1817–93), Member of Parliament for Sherbrooke, Lower Canada since 1853 and a leading advocate of the federation of the Canadian colonies.

next is no longer secret. Every body is speaking of it and bets are offered that it will never come off. . . . Mr Portman made a great purchase of the late Mr Duff's guns, rifles, pistols, etc worth at the least £200 for $250.

Aug 12 . . . The day was kept as a holiday in commemoration of the success of the Atlantic telegraph. Mr Portman, John and Edward amused themselves firing at a mark with the guns Mr Portman had purchased. In the evening there were several bonfires lighted and the City was partially illuminated. There has been a regular organized band of incendiaries discovered and three or four have been sent to jail for trial. They belong to No [?] Fire Company and they appear to have the object in setting fire to unoccupied houses and barns that their fire company may be the first on the grounds. Their Company has been disbanded.

Aug 13 George returned from Guelph. The London Cricket Club was beaten. They have been very unsuccessful . . . [Mrs Hopten] says she has no love for her native country, Canada, and would not live here for any thing. It appears to me an odd feeling. I have always fancied a love of country innate.

Aug 16 . . . Amelia called today. I saw she was in trouble and have observed several times lately when she called that she looked as if something was wrong, but she said not. Today she told us if we did not some of us occasionally go to her house she would not be allowed to visit us. She said she had a scene every time she came here and it would end in her not being able to come. How sorry I feel for her. Mr Griffin knew how much we disliked her marrying him. Can he think that unkindness to her will make us like him better? We have no reason for not going there oftener excepting that we all like home better than any other place, and Edward and George play cricket when they have any idle hours and Mr Portman and John ride. The walk is too long in hot weather for either Helen or me, and Teresa cannot be induced to go any where often. They know all this and Amelia calls almost every day and air and exercise is necessary for her, and we take both in the garden and terrace, but if she was ill or any thing wrong Mr Griffin would soon find that she was Amelia *Harris* to us though she is *Griffin* to him. Mr Dunn of the Montreal Bank came to tea. We all like him very much.

Aug 17 This is the 41st anniversary of poor William's birthday. How painful was his death, and now how thankful I feel that my first born is in heaven. But it is hard to give up our treasures. Fever, delirium and a long illness to myself followed his death and it was long before I could say, Thy will be done. . . .

Aug 18 Minnie Street was married yesterday to Mr Hutchinson. The course of true love did not run smooth with them for their engagement was on and off publicly half a dozen times at the least besides quiet private quarrels. Poor girl, her conduct throughout has been correct. When Mr Hutchinson first paid her attention she was a child in good circumstances and fair prospects. Now she was poor and dependent, her father an exile from justice. I hope Mr Hutchinson may give up his bad habits and make her a good husband. . . .

Aug 19 We have accomplished our visit to the Bechers at last. Mr Portman, Helen, John and myself went there to tea last night. Mr Ridout of the Upper Canada Bank, Toronto and son were there.[83] Mr Ridout is an old friend of Mr Harris. The appointment of Sheriff and of Registrar have at last been made, and are disapproved of by almost every one. The only recommendation of Mr Glass, who is Sheriff, is his being the brother in law of Mr Carling, the Member, who has lost his popularity and probably his reelection by the appointment as Mr Glass is an ignorant, uneducated man and not popular among his own class. John Ferguson, the Registrar, is an Irish bully, ignorant and very much disliked but was a warm supporter of Mr [Marcus] Talbot's. He is an Orangeman and has a good deal of influence with his own Order and no doubt influenced Mr Talbot's election very much. But there is but one feeling and that is disgust at his appointment as Registrar, as he is totally unfitted for the office.

Aug 21 . . . Mr Wilson and Mr Becher came to luncheon. . . . There was a very good article in this morning's *Free Press* condemnatory of the appointments of Sheriff and Registrar. I soon saw from Mr Wilson's face that he had written it. . . . Helen had a letter from Sarah which offended both her and Mr Portman without cause I think. Sarah said she was sorry they had purchased in the South. She had heard New Orleans spoken of as a city surpassing even Paris and Vienna in wickedness and she cautioned Helen, being herself much the elder, not to become so familiarized with Roman Catholic customs as to lose sight of what we know to be wrong and alluded to the great responsibilities of mothers as guardians and guides to their children. But what appeared to give the greatest offence was her declining their invitation to visit them in the South and immediately expressing her dislike to the Americans both northern and southern and pronouncing them a vulgar people. I think Sarah's prejudices are absurd, but I do not see

[83]Thomas Gibbs Ridout (1792–1861), Cashier, or General Manager of the Bank of Upper Canada, 1822–61.

why they should offend the Portmans. Sarah would have just the same right to be offended because they like the Americans and slavery. Teresa and Ellen Hamilton went to the Griffins to tea.

Aug 23 Mr Ferguson, a nephew of *Big Jim* the Registrar, horse whipped Mr Blackburn, the editor of the *Free Press* this morning for printing the article[84] that appeared in his paper a few days ago. Mr Ferguson was fined £5 and costs and bound over to keep the peace. . . . John went to the Griffins to tea. Mr Griffin feels the death of his brother very much. . . .

Aug 25 This morning eight years I was watching over a dying husband. The weather looks the same and I can scarcely realize that eight years have passed since then. What a day of anguish. It makes me tremble to look back upon it. When I think of all his suffferings and all that we suffered. The time is near at hand when we shall again meet. . . .

Aug 27 . . . Mr Portman and John went to the hotel to arrange a cricket match for tomorrow between the Vagabond Club (supplemented by some visiting Englishmen) and the London Cricket Club, the Strangers play with the Vagabonds.

Aug 28 A continued rain yet no one would agree to postpone the cricket match but played the whole day every one being thoroughly drenched. . . . Mr Portman was too much overcome by his exertions, with no lunch, and had beer mixed with gin to make his appearance. He was very glad to go to bed. . . .

Aug 31 Lord Frederick Cavendish, Ld Richard Grosvenor and the Honb Mr Ashley arrived today on a visit to Mr Portman. They are all very young and very agreeable. . . .

Sep 1 . . . There was a cry of fire just after the ladies left the dinner table and all the gentlemen rushed to see a house and stable burning opposite the Methodist Church and did not return until after 10 o'clock, giving what we chose to declare a very confused account of themselves. . . .

Sep 2 . . . Mr Becher called and told me he had heard from Fanny . . . who had seen a young gentleman who was very anxious to see Miss Harris. Miss Harris [Teresa] of course was very anxious to know who the young gentleman was. Mr Becher said a son of Lord Shaftesbury. I made a face at him as Mr Ashley was close to him talking to Amelia. . . .

Sep 3 . . . Amelia called looking wretched. She would not stay to

[84]The article was regarding Ferguson's appointment as Registrar.

luncheon. When I spoke to her about it she burst out crying and said it would end in her never being allowed to come here, that Mr Griffin thought himself disliked by all, particularly by Mr Portman. I wish he had thought of all of those things before he married. He knew we did not like him and that I did all I could to prevent the marriage. But since his marriage whatever my feelings have been I have treated him with the same cordiality that I have my other sons in law and I have tried in every instance to do what I believed to be right. But I see but too plainly that I can never establish a perfect cordiality between Mr Griffin and the rest of my family. There is no sympathy between them, and when I am dead poor Amelia will be alone. No child can ever secure their own happiness by going in opposition to a mother, even if that mother is wrong. . . .

Sep 7 We dined at three o'clock and our visitors left us at 4. Mr Portman has gone with them to shoot on the Prairies. . . . We like all our young friends, Lord R. Grosvenor the best – he is such a perfect gentleman and seems so good and kind. Mr Ashley is a few years older and more a man of the world, was private secretary to Lord Palmerston and possesses a good deal of information and can be highly amusing and very agreeable. Lord Frederick Cavendish I think has no great flow of conversation and makes himself less agreeable than the other two. Helen and Amelia think him haughty and that he thinks too much of his rank. Teresa likes him and found him very agreeable at times. His education has been neglected. He reads hard now and tries to improve himself, and I shall not be surprised to hear him called clever in a few years. . . .

Sep 10 I feel very much better this morning. The house is so dull without Mr Portman. Mr Wilson came to lunch. He wrote several articles in the *Free Press* condemning the appointment of Mr Glass as Sheriff and Ferguson as Registrar but did not sign his name to them. The *Prototype* wrote an article in defence and said that Mr Wilson amongst others had signed the petition for Mr Glass' appointment. I asked Mr Wilson if it was true. He admitted that he had signed the petition. I could not help remarking that if a person was induced from any cause to make an improper recommendation, I thought they ought to be silent afterwards about the appointment. He, Mr Wilson, spoke of George Brown and said he was a scoundrel. I was surprised to hear afterwards that he had gone to Toronto and voted for him and against his old friend J.H. Cameron. It appears to me that nothing perverts the mind like politics. Mr Wilson's standard of right and wrong was so clear and so high when he first came to London and now he will do what he knows to be wrong for party. . . .

Sep 11 Mr Portman came home this morning. He had had an attack of cholera morbus. He left the rest of the party at Chicago. . . .
Sep 12 George and Teresa went to Church. . . . Mr O'Neil preached his farewell sermon. He returns to Ireland with his family. He is a good man, though not an eloquent preacher. The Church here is so poor that they cannot give him as good a living as he has in Ireland, which he will have to give up unless he returns immediately. . . .
Sep 13 Mr Hamilton called to ask for some money for Mr O'Neil. People are collecting for him. Mr Hamilton says the Rev Mr O'Neil's debts amount to £180 and it will cost him at the least £100 to take his family to Ireland. His friends wish to collect £300 for him but are quite sure they will not succeed. . . .
Sep 14 . . . I went to pay my long promised visit to Mrs Askin. I felt very glad that I did so, she was so glad to see me. I spent a very pleasant day there. Mr Cummings from Chippewa called out there to see me. . . . Mr Cummings looks old. It is a long time to look back when we were young and used to amuse ourselves at Port Ryerse. Mrs Horne had her breast cut off for cancer a few days ago. About this time next year she will die, poor woman. . . .
Sep 19 Teresa, George & I went to Church. A Negro clergyman read the prayers. Edward Blake came early in the afternoon and took tea with us.
Sep 27 . . . Mr Wandesforde[85] sent a portrait of me as a present to Teresa. He has finished one of me for Helen and one for Sarah. . . .
Sep 29 . . . The comet was very splendid as we came home and look[s] larger every night as it approaches the earth. . . .
Sep 30 . . . A great outrage has been committed on the Great Western at Chatham. A southern gentleman was passing through with a slave boy of ten years old. Some negro made the discovery here and telegraphed to the colourd people at Chatham who assembled in a mob of three hundred and when the train stopped at the station they took the boy forcibly from his master although the child cried and did not wish to go. Mr Brydges is much annoyed and intends to prosecute and punish with the utmost rigour of the law. It will turn the American travel from Canada.

[85]J.B. Wandesforde (1817–1902), a Canadian painter, executed most of the watercolours that hang in the drawing room at Eldon House today. During his Canadian years (1847–57), he painted landscapes and portraits, the latter often being rendered from photographs. He was a painter and teacher in New York in the 1860s, subsequently moving to California where he became President of the San Francisco Art Association in 1872.

Oct 10 Helen ill. No one went to Church. Mrs Becher called after Church to ask for Helen. Mrs Wilson called and Ellen Hamilton came to enquire after her. I had a letter from Mary. Amelia and Mr Griffin came down. Amelia offered to remain. I told her I would send for her when I sent for the Doctor Anderson. At 8 o'clock I sent for them both. The baby was born twenty minutes past eleven PM He is a fine boy. There is a little disappointment that they had wished for a daughter. Helen was longer ill and suffered more pain than when Berkeley was born. . . .

Oct 15 Helen not so well, had to be kept very quiet and take medicine. . . .

Oct 16 Helen is much better today. . . .

Oct 20 . . . In searching over some papers today I found the first letter poor Chasse wrote from Rome. How full of life, hope and happiness she was then, poor girl and how soon her and her babes were to rest under the blue waters of the Mediterranean. Why should I regret her every hour shortens the distance between us and yet it seems as if my heart would break when I think of her. Even today at dinner I had to turn away to hide the agony I felt when no one thought or spoke of her. What a fountain the heart is of sweet and bitter thoughts and but little understood even by those most dear to us.

Oct 22 . . . The pictures arrived from Mr Wandesforde. I did not know until they arrived that he was doing a picture of John as a present for me. The likeness is admirable, and it is a delicate attention from Mr Wandesforde that I shall not easily forget. I wrote to him today. . . .

Oct 26 . . . Teresa liked her visit to Toronto pretty well. She thought there was a little coolness with the Ryersons when she first arrived. John could not lend him money.

Oct 28 Mr Ward, the Station Master, was dismissed today. He let a train pass that ought to have been stopped. No accident happened but it was by the mercy of God. Mr Ward told Amelia with tears in his eyes that the agony he suffered for half an hour was beyond description until he heard that all was safe. He felt the justice of his dismissal. Everybody is sorry for him, but it does not do to allow mistakes on the rail road. . . .

Nov 2 Maurice William Portman christened today by the Bishop of Huron. John is one Godfather, the Hon William Portman the other. He was represented by Dr Robertson. . . . I represented the Hon Ella Portman who is the Godmother. Amelia and Mr Griffin were to have been here but said the weather was too bad to come out, but the truth of the matter was that Mr Griffin would not come and Amelia would not come without him. . . .

Nov 3 . . . George's time with Mr Wilson is out today. I hope there may be some opening that he may make his way in the world. . . . Mrs Hamilton gave Teresa a party to celebrate the important event of Teresa's having finished embroidering her petticoat.
Nov 11 . . . Harding was tried and acquitted for the murder of Hughes Wilson. . . .
Nov 13 . . . George went to Toronto to keep Term. . . .
Nov 15 . . . Mr Wilson called. He wanted assistance for some poor people. He does more acts of kindness than anyone I know of. . . .
Nov 17 Heard from Mr Wandesforde who will make copies of all our portraits for Mary of a size smaller than the originals for $20 each. . . .
Nov 18 . . . Mr Scott[86] came to tea. We all played monte. . . . I dislike their playing for money. To play for amusement is all very well.
Nov 21 The gentlemen remained very late at the party last night, it was 5 o'clock this morning when they returned. I felt sorry that they should have disregarded the Sabbath morning, but it was the first time and reproach was useless. It is not likely to occur again. . . .
Nov 24 . . . We decided upon asking some people here tomorrow. I very foolishly allowed myself to feel vexed because there were objections made to three people whom I proposed asking. Teresa thought there would be too many people without a piano as we could have neither music nor dancing. I told Teresa that Helen, herself and John might ask who they liked, that I would ask no one. I should have said that at first and without anger, as I never go out and do not care in the least who they invite as long as they are pleased. My only reasons for wishing the Rivers to be invited was because they had all accepted invitations there more than once. And then we were all unhappy the whole evening. . . .
Nov 25 The party came off I believe to the satisfaction of all. . . . Cards was the order of the evening. The supper was very nice and they all left here at 1 o'clock.
Nov 26 . . . John, Teresa and Edward went to a concert and ball given by the firemen or rather got up by them. Teresa had no intention of staying after the concert but the firemen requested her and John to open the ball and she felt a little elated by the respect shown her. . . . Teresa and Edward returned at a quarter past eleven. . . .
Nov 28 . . . Mrs Lawrason and Mrs D. Askin came to tea. They are two unfortunate women. The husband of one is conceited, coarse and vulgar and the husband of the other is debauched, dissipated and worthless.

[86]The first reference in the diary to William John Scott, Teresa's first husband.

Nov 29 Mr Scott came to luncheon. . . . Mr Portman, Mr Scott and Teresa were invited to the Kings to lunch, but did not go. . . . George is to write in John's office from breakfast until lunch and then study to prepare himself for his examination as an Attorney in February. . . .
Dec 7 Mr Scott dined with us as it is his last day in London.[87] . . .
Dec 8 . . . Mr Scott called to say goodbye, He thinks he will return to London again in February. We were all so sorry to see Mr Portman go but are very glad that Mr Scott is with him. . . .
Dec 10 Mr Becher came to luncheon and has promised to take Helen as far as St Louis. . . . John is applying for the office of Recorder so as to make an opening in his office for George. . . .
Dec 13 . . . Mr Nichol from Vienna and his little son came to tea. It is strange what stupid sons a clever father will have. Mr Nichol's father, the late Col Nichol, was admitted to be one of the cleverest men of his day in the province and certainly his son's talents are not of a very brilliant order but the little grandson I should think would be clever, perhaps true to the old saying [that] talent skips a generation, or is the other theory correct that it requires a clever mother to make clever children.
Dec 14 We had letters from Sarah, Shuldham and Mary. The Dalzells are in constant worry about their money matters. Shuldham is the best fellow I know and he and Mary appear as happy as the day is long. Mr Wilson called, and Mr King came in a great state of excitement to tell us that Mrs King has a son. She has been very ill and the child was taken by instruments but both mother and child were doing well. Mr King looked as if he had suffered almost as much as his wife. . . .
Dec 15 . . . there is a great scandal at Toronto. Miss Shrieber, a young lady of the upper ten, and two other young ladies (Miss Jessop and Miss Barrick) who move in outer circles . . . are all in the family way. The clergymen have thought it necessary to preach two sermons pointing out the immorality of the City of Toronto. Poor girls, how much they are to be pitied. Miss Shrieber has no mother and her father, although a clergyman, I imagine is not a very good guardian for his daughters. Mr Down of the 100th Regt is said to be the seducer of Miss Shrieber. He was known as a notorious profligate, had seduced his Col's wife and was forced to sell out of the Guards. Yet the people in Toronto made a hero of him and his notice was coveted by all the young ladies and not the old more to blame than the young.

[87]Since his first visit on 25 November, Scott had visited Eldon on five occasions, once for luncheon, twice for tea, twice for dinner.

Dec 16 . . . Mr Patten of the Trust and Loan Company dined here. We all liked him. We talked over Kingston 40 years ago, long before he was born. I know of only one person living there now that was living there when I left in 1817, that is old John Marks, a Purser in the Navy.[88]
Dec 20 . . . Edward was in good spirits. He had won his suit against Mr Ferguson, the Registrar, for charging enormous fees to which he was not entitled and he has to refund. We think it very creditable of Edward that he studied the law and discovered that the charges were illegal, an imposition that the whole country have submitted to for four or five years without making the discovery.
Dec 24 . . . I feel not well, lonely and low spirited when I ought to feel only thankful for all God's blessings and mercies to me and mine. God grant me a more penitent, humble, thankful heart.
Dec 25 Helen, Teresa, Sophia and John went to Church and stayed to the Sacrament. Amelia and Mr Griffin called after Church and stayed to luncheon. Mr Becher and Fanny called. Mr Henry Griffin[89] came with the Griffins to dinner. . . .
Dec 30 Helen and Sophia called on Mrs Wilson. John, Edward, George, Teresa and Sophia went to the Bachelors' Ball. The evening was very wet. The rain fell in torrents and the Ball was any thing but pleasant to Sophia and Teresa as the preponderating portion of the company were shoemakers, dressmakers, grocers, etc.
Dec 31 Sophia and Teresa were very tired after the ball. . . . Helen and Sophia walked up to the Griffins in the evening, and so ends the last day of the year. Where shall we all be at the end of the next? May God enable us to put our whole trust in his mercies both now and forever.

1859

Jan 1 Helen, Sophia and I went to Church. The day was mild and beautiful. We had not many visitors, . . . The Griffins dined with us, neither Sophia nor Teresa were well in the evening. The Griffins, George and I played cribbage, John and Edward took tea at Mr Lawrason, Sam Blake and Benjamin Cronyn called.

[88]John Bennett Marks (1777–1872), another Royal Navy veteran, served as purser on the *HMS St. Lawrence* and Clerk of the Royal Naval Dockyard at Kingston. Active in local affairs, he was founder and first President of the Frontenac Agricultural Society, Justice of the Peace, Colonel in the Frontenac Militia, and Director of the Commercial Bank of Upper Canada.

[89]Gilbert Griffin's brother.

Jan 6 . . . John came home from the office again ill. I am very anxious about him. . . .

Jan 7 Helen heard from the Portmans who fortunately received Mr Portman's letter telling him that the report (sent home by Ld Bury) stating that Lord F. Cavendish, Lord R. Grosvenor and Mr Ashley had been murdered by the Indians was not true.[90] Lord Portman was in time to notify all the respective families . . . that there was such a report and that it was not true before they had heard anything of it. . . .

Jan 13 . . . John, Edward, George, Sophia and Teresa went to a ball at the Goodhues. The ball was a very good one and went off very well until about 1 o'clock, when there was an alarm of fire, and it was said that Mr [J.W.B.] River's house was on fire, but it proved to be an empty house next to theirs, which had been set on fire by incendiaries. At first Mr and Mrs Rivers and her sisters were in a great state of alarm – all the gentlemen ran from the ball to the fire in their best coats etc & the ladies came home.

Jan 22 We invited Mr Jackson, Mr Sthalshmit [sic] and Mr Nind[91] to tea. The two former gentlemen came. Mr Nind returned to the Kings. Ellen Hamilton came to tea also and looked very pretty. It is such a pity that her manner is so bold, if she was quiet and retiring she would be liked and admired for she is amiable and clever. Sophia has evidently made a conquest of Mr Stahlschmidt, for he has neither eyes nor ears for anyone but her, and her manner is very good. She has advantages which few girls possess as she is well educated, accomplished and has travelled, that is, she has been to England and on the Continent, and although not very handsome she is pretty and pleasing. I do not know whether Mr Stahlschmidt is a marrying man or whether he is in circumstance to marry, but he is evidently in love, but I think Sophia tries to have too many strings to her bow and encourages Mr Nind who is a non marrying man a little too much. Katherine, the house maid, got tipsy and made confusion at the dinner table. . . .

Jan 25 . . . All the young people were asked to Mrs W. Lawrasons to tea, Sophia and Teresa had many doubts about going but after a great deal of demurring they went, and were sorry they did so. John, Edward and Mrs Duncan Askin were there and Mr W. Lawrason's manners were as vulgar as usual. . . .

[90]That is, the Indian Mutiny.

[91]They were all friends of Mr. Scott. Stahlschmidt was consistently, and variously, misspelled by Amelia. He is hereafter given his proper name.

Jan 26 Sophia left this morning. Mr Griffin, Amelia and Mr Stahlschmidt went with her, they are all going to the Ball at Government House. Mr Stahlschmidt is certainly very much in love. Teresa told me today that Amelia had told Mrs Howel that Sophia's father would allow her £200 a year. This report most probably has come to Mr Stahlschmidt's ears and may influence his admiration for her a little. It is a pity Amelia ever told this. I should like her to get a good husband who would marry her for *herself*. . . . The house seems dull without Sophia. I do not know how it will appear after Helen and her babies are gone. . . .
Jan 30 . . . Dr Ryerson does not look favorably upon Mr Stahlschmidt and will not allow Sophia to have anything to say to him. Dr Ryerson prefers Mr Nind very much to Mr Stahlschmidt, and Mr Nind told Mr Jackson that the only thing that took him to Toronto was to tease Mr Stahlschmidt by devoting himself to Sophia and Sophia has allowed Mr Nind to discover that she prefers him. Mr Nind has neither the means nor inclination to marry, and is only amusing himself. . . .
Jan 31 . . . John and Edward are talking about opening an office in Toronto and that either Edward or George will go there to practice Chancery business[92] and by that means there will be an opening for George either here or in Toronto. . . .
Feb 2 . . . Mr Becher came to dinner and gave Helen and John a pass on the Great Western. . . . John only goes to St Louis. He cannot leave his business longer. . . .
Feb 10 . . . John came home by the 3 o'clock train, very tired having travelled two nights. . . . John left her [Helen] with great reluctance in the care of some friends who are going to N[ew] Or[leans] and have promised to take every care of her and see her safely landed near her own home. Ellen Hamilton came here and dressed and went with us to the [Tecumseh] Ball.[93] There were 5 or 600 people present, and all well dressed and well conducted, which I think speaks very well for London as everyone could go who could pay 4 dollars for a ticket. I as one of the Lady patronesses remained until after supper. The supper was the best and prettiest that has ever been given in London and the music (Pappenberg's Band) was excellent. . . . John came home very soon after I did, that is, about $^1/_2$ past two. It was near 4 o'clock before Ellen, Teresa and George came. Edward did not return until

[92]The Court of Chancery dealt with disputes involving the ownership of property.

[93]The Tecumseh House played an important role in the early social life of London. It opened in 1856 and at one time was the largest hotel in British North America.

eleven the next day and I am sorry to say he had joined a convivial party and drank more than he ought to have done. Ellen slept here.
Feb 11 Everybody very stupid this morning. Edward came home at 11 looking wretched. I wanted him to go to bed and take a good sleep but he would not. I disliked his being seen until he looked better. What a pity it is that young men will ever take the first step in the downward path. It is hard to recover even one false step. There has been scandal afloat about Mrs D. Askin and Bill Bettridge for a long time but no one believed it, but last night her manner gave rise to doubt as to her rectitude with more than one . . .
Feb 13 . . . [John] called on Mr Scott who has just returned from . . . Havana. Edward Blake told us that last year he made $11,000 by his profession and collected $9,000 of it and booked $2,000, which is doing pretty [well] as he has only been 2 or 3 years in practice, but it is said that his charges for agency business in Chancery are enormous. John says he cannot afford to keep him as agent as Ned Blake gets all the money and he [John] does nearly all the work. . . .
Feb 14 Mr Scott sent up several little presents for the different members of the family, a carved ivory card case for Teresa, a sandalwood fan for Amelia, a box of Havana cigars for Edward, some guava jelly for me and a gold half dollar for Teresa. It is very kind of him. . . . He does not look well and said the climate at the south did not agree with him. He likes Mr Portman's plantation and does not dislike slavery as much as he thought he should and said that he should like a plantation down there very much if the climate agreed with him. He told us that Mr Portman led a very active life, that he was on horseback all day. . . . Teresa had a Valentine today telling her she was as poor as Job and as proud as Lucifer. Teresa thought she got off very well not to have more abuse and that if her latter days were as prosperous as Job's she would be content. John had one telling him that he was double faced. I do not think it is just. Edward had two, one which I suppose was in reference to the night of the Tecumseh Ball represented him half tipsy glass in hand. It pained me that such a representation should apply to one of my family if only on one occasion. God grant it may be the last. His other Valentine was simply absurd it represented him as a fop.
Feb 16 . . . Distress in the country is very great. Farmers are buying wheat in place of selling it. The first soup kitchen that has been in London has been established here within the past week and it gives relief to 70 poor families. . . .
Feb 18 . . . Mr Scott called and brought us the *Illustrated News* and *Punch*. . . .

Feb 22 Teresa got a letter from Sophia, insinuating that Mr Jackson is very much in love with Miss Loring,[94] rather a good speculation for Mr Jackson. Miss Loring is said to be a very nice girl with £1,000 a year. . . .

Feb 23 . . . Nancy [Cameron] my old servant called here today. She has the dropsy and came to town to consult Dr Anderson. Nancy lived with me for 12 years and was with me when Sarah, Mary, Eliza and Chasse was married and she was here when George and Teresa were born and she was here when Mr Harris died. Nancy looks to me like a dear friend and had she chosen to remain with me she should never have wanted a home as long as I had one but her only sister moved away and she would not remain so far from her.

Feb 24 . . . John, Edward and George dined with Mr Scott yesterday. Mr King, Mr Nind, Mr Sheffield, Mr Jackson, Mr Stahlschmidt and Mr Griffin made up the party. Mr Jackson got tipsy and used insulting language to Mr [C.A.] Hammond who came in for a few minutes and he abused all Canadians and Canadian lawyers in particular. He said he would not trust any Canadian. John wished he had been strong enough to knock him down, but as he was not he turned his back upon him. At the time Mr Jackson had drunken courage and was disposed to call John out, but thought better of it. . . .

Feb 27 John received a letter this morning from Mr Scott which surprised us very much. It was a formal proposal for Teresa. He in a very gentlemanlike manner said that he did not think it right to continue his visits here without telling us that Teresa was the great attraction and that if we would sanction it he wished to make her his wife, promising to make her a good husband etc. We thought it best not to tell Teresa at present as it would make her feel very awkward when Mr Scott called, and as we told Mr Scott that our acquaintance had been so very short that it would be better for all parties that we should know more of each other, that we felt very much flattered by his proposal and wished him to continue his visits as hitherto, and if our mutual liking should continue and that if he could gain Teresa's consent he should have ours. Such was the substance of John's answer though not expressed in the same words. Mr Portman wrote to Teresa that if Mr Scott proposed for her not to take him. What his reasons & objections are we do not know. As far as we can judge Mr Scott is an excellent match. He has upwards of £2,000 a year and his conduct appears to be

[94]The first reference in the diary to Elizabeth Loring of Toronto, who married John Fitzjohn Harris.

very correct. In personal appearance he is certainly the reverse of handsome but I do not consider beauty an essential in a matrimonial connection. I do so wish that Mr Portman had told us what he knew objectionable about Mr Scott. As it is we cannot help feeling doubtful what we ought to do. Edward took John's answer to Mr Scott and asked him up to tea. George, Teresa and myself went to Church. . . . Mr Scott and Mr Jackson came to tea. Mr Scott looked a little awkward at first but soon got over it. I received him as usual and said nothing. . . .

Mar 1 Teresa and I went to Mr Egan to get our photographs taken to send to Mr Wandesforde. It is a very tiresome business. I sat five times and got three good ones, one for Amelia, one for Mr Wandesforde and one Mr Egan kept. Teresa's were a failure. . . . Mr Scott came to dinner. After dinner Mr Scott and Teresa and George and I played cribbage. Mr Scott I think improves very much upon acquaintance. . . .

Mar 3 Teresa got a letter from Sophia who is very gay. Mr Scott called and brought the *Illustrated News* and *Punch*. Teresa was not well and did not see him. When we were going to bed she told me she would not marry Mr Scott, that she did not like him well enough. Oh Great God enable me to put my whole trust in Thee and to believe Thou will over rule all things for good.

Mar 4 I told John this morning what Teresa had said last night. He said he liked Mr Scott, that he believed him to be an upright, honorable man. He knew he was not a man that would take much with ladies but said Teresa must decide for herself. . . . John, Edward, George and Teresa all went to the [Bachelors'] Ball. Just before Teresa left we remarked how out of humour John was and Teresa asked me if I had told him what she had said about Mr Scott the night before. I told her I had. She said she had thought all day that it was that which had vexed him. I then told her about Mr Scott's proposal, which she had suspected. I then told her how open and honorably he had behaved. I then stated his worldly advantages, and that I believed that he was a worthy man and would make a good husband. Against this is that he is excessively plain and not at all a taking man with ladies but that I considered him superior, far superior, in all that pertains to a gentleman to anyone here. She spoke very rightly and said with her present feeling it would neither be justice to Mr Scott or herself to marry him. She did not know whether she could learn to like him better. I told her to think well and be quite sure she was right before she declined an offer such as in all probability that she might never have again. If we could only see clearly what is right, but we are so apt to be influenced by our own wishes or prejudices and likes and dislikes, too often formed without cause or foundation and which would not bear the test of common sense for a moment.

Mar 5 The Bachelors' Ball, the last of the season, my juveniles decided was a success. There were few strangers present. . . . Mr Scott and Mr Becher came to luncheon. Mr Becher asked Jack and Mr Scott to dinner and they went. A Mr Kirkpatrick[95] from Kingston was there. Both John and Mr Scott thought him a great puppy. . . .

Mar 6 The day lovely. Teresa, George and I went to Church. Mr Scott joined us on the way and sat in our pew. Teresa flutters like a young bird when she sees Mr Scott. She cannot help feeling nervous although he does not know that she is aware of his matrimonial wishes. . . . I wrote to Eliza and told her of Mr Scott's proposal. Teresa wrote to Mary.

Mar 8 . . . Mr Scott came to dinner. Our dinner was very nice but one decanter of wine had been watered *so much* that it was scarcely wine and water. Katherine's [maid] weakness betrays itself too often. Mr Scott was cross and very much out of humour about something. He snubbed us all. He became better humourd before he left but was not very smiling even then. I wonder if he is bad tempered and if that is the reason Mr Portman told Teresa not to marry him. I wish I could hear from the Portmans. At present Mr Scott is in a position in regard to Teresa that no gentleman would hold for very long. He is now held on approbation to see whether *we, not Teresa,* will like him before he is allowed to speak to her. . . . I am very much afraid that Teresa will make a mistake and refuse him without any good reason, and if she does I can read her future but too plainly. She will by and by form an attachment to some young fellow that will take her fancy and marry as she will think to please herself and place herself in a position in which she will never be happy. I can only pray that God may guide and have her in his keeping. In a few years at the farthest I shall have done with all worldly cares but I think I should feel more content and more that my work was finished if I could see her what I believe to be well married. . . .

Mar 10 . . . John asked Mr Dunn and Mr Scott to dinner. Mr Scott seemed in a better humour than when last he dined here. He excused or rather explained his manner on that day by saying he was not well. The next day he confined himself to the sofa. He got letters from

[95]Possibly George Airey Kirkpatrick (1841–99), the son of Thomas Kirkpatrick, and future Lieutenant-Governor of Ontario (1892–97).

England informing him of the death of an old aunt who has left him £4,000 and a remote chance of £50,000 more.

Mar 11 . . . Lucy Wilson[96] called for me and I went with her to the Wilsons. The afternoon was very wet. The house was very gloomy. Mr Wilson was very kind and attentive to me. The dinner was very nice but everyone seemed to wear a look of discontent and unhappiness. Lucy does not look in good health. The children were very well conducted but I felt it a relief to get home again. Who can tell what marriages will prove happy. They were young (that is not old) and married from affection for neither of them had anything and have risen together in the world, and now have wealth and position, and yet I think I never visited a house where there was less happiness. Good temper I believe is the greatest sweetener of this life, and neither Mr nor Mrs Wilson possess good temper. . . . John dined with Mr Scott.

Mar 13 I did not go to Church not being very well. Teresa was the only one that went. Mr Scott sat in our pew. . . . John went over to the Wilsons but returned to tea. He had the same impression that I had, that happiness was not a guest at present at the Wilsons. . . .

Mar 15 . . . I am very anxious about John. Last week he fainted in the street. Today he came in in such distress that he had to have mustard plasters on his back and breast and then as soon as he is a little better away he is at the office with so much to do. I do not think he ever knows what it is to feel well. This cannot go on very long. There will be a break up or he must get relief. If anything were to happen to him I too should die. I could never survive another great sorrow. . . .

Mar 16 Bayard Taylor[97] left this morning at ½ past 6. Teresa, John and George got up to give him breakfast and see him off. He was much amused at an uncomplimentary speech that was made to him last night after the lecture. He took out his watch and observed that he had lectured one hour and twenty minutes. Mr Adams who was standing next to him said he thought it had been much longer. We spoke of Thackeray who is a friend of Mr Taylor's. I said he appeared to have a feeling of hostility towards the titled aristocracy of England and that clever as his works were that they always left me impressed with the feeling that he was not a happy man, but that he was more *sour* than *sad.* Mr Taylor said that Thackeray's lectures on the Georges had

[96]John Wilson's daughter.

[97]Bayard Taylor (1825–78), American traveller, man of letters, and public lecturer. He became famous for his publications and lectures on travels in Africa, India, China and Japan. He also published several novels and volumes of poetry. See Carl Van Doren, "Bayard Taylor," *Dic. Am. Biog.* XVIII, pp. 314–16.

caused him to be cut by nearly all of his noble friends – that Lord Landsdowne cut him, and that Ld Palmerston would have cut him but Lady Palmerston would not allow it. He was with Thackeray when Ld Landsdowne sent him an invitation to dinner. Mr Thackeray said "Ah, Ld Landsdowne has discovered that *I* can do better without him than he can do without me." It struck me as being a very conceited speech.

This evening we had a letter private – Mr Portman says Mr Scott gets drunk, that when going down the Mississippi that he got so drunk that he fell out of his birth [sic] and would not believe it in the morning until he saw the blood on his elbows and knees and that he tells dirty stories which shows a depraved mind and that he *romances* to a great extent. . . . Edward said at once that he did not believe that Mr Scott was a drunkard that he may have been drunk more than once but that he has been in London a good many months and that he has never seen anything that would lead him to think that he was in the slightest degree intemperate. He admits that his conversation is not at all times such as we could listen to but not worse than the common style of conversation of young men. So much for Edward's defence of him. George I think would not be quite content to see Teresa married to him. When John came home and read Helen's letter, he said that he felt satisfied that from many little circumstances that Mr Scott was not a drunkard. Teresa I think felt delighted that she knew why Mr Portman told her not to marry him and she felt herself now at liberty to refuse Mr Scott without having a feeling that she might be doing wrong in refusing a worthy man (though not a very attractive one). So ends this evening's discussion on the subject. . . .

Mar 17 . . . Teresa did not wish to see Mr Scott, but as all his conduct has been most honorable to her the least she can do is to behave like a lady to him. I liked him better yesterday than I ever have before and I think a woman of sense might very soon give him a polish that he would hardly think himself susceptable of. . . .

Mar 18 John ill again. He does not know what it is to have a day's health. . . . We scarcely know how to give Mr Scott his dismissal, and yet it must be done, and soon, for he has done everything that is right towards us, and from our manner and frequent invitations to the house he has had reason to think that his suit was favorably received, but as Teresa has decided that she cannot marry him an explanation must take place. I cannot help wishing that the result had been different, that is, if he is as correct as we suppose him to be. When I die she will find herself very lonely and dependant, but we cannot force the affections and money alone will not make people happy. But money excludes a great deal of unhappiness.

Mar 19 . . . The carpenter came about fitting up the library as a sitting room. The books are getting very much injured by our constantly using the room as a common sitting room and John thinks it best to build a library and in the meantime pack away the books and fit up the room afresh purposely for a morning sitting room. Mr Becher came to luncheon. He told us that Mr Rideout [Ridout] was to have an operation or in other words have his cancer cut out of his tongue today. Poor man, I have never known the knife save a life from cancer. Dr Mott may be a very skillful operator but I have no faith in the operation. . . .

Mar 21 Teresa & I have worked very hard to take a catalogue of the books and removed them from the library. The carpenter comes tomorrow to make some alterations in the library as we are going to convert it into a morning sitting room as John intends building a library . . .

Mar 22 The day beautiful. We have been busy all day finding places for the books. Mr Becher came to luncheon, Mrs Wilson and Mrs Cronyn called. Mr Scott came to tea. I do wish I knew whether he has a weakness for drinks. John, Edward and George all think not. Amelia called for a few minutes only.

Mar 23 The weather beautiful. I had a letter from Sarah and one from Elisa. No one here today excepting Mr Scott who brought *Punch* and the *Illustrated News*. . . . Eliza has had a miscarriage and her baby is only 5 months old. . . . The property which Mr Scott most probably will become heir to has been registered at £60,000. . . .

Mar 24 . . . I was told that someone wanted to see me in the dining room. When I went there I found it was Amelia. Mr Scott had been to see her and told her all his hopes and fears in regard to Teresa. I found that she had been in his confidence from the time he had written to John and John also had gone to her and Mr Griffin and consulted what answer he had better give Mr Scott and John here had advised us not to speak to anyone on the subject as Teresa's decision was so doubtful that it would be best that no one should know anything about it. The consequence is we all looked mysteriously at each other when we might all have consulted what was best to be done if John had only spoken openly. Mr Scott was tired of uncertainty and gave Amelia a letter to me and another for Teresa if I thought best to give it to her. Mr Scott depicted his own unhappiness under this painful uncertainty, and his hopes and fears and promises of being a good husband in a most lover-like way. I sent for him in the dining room and told him I would give Teresa his letter after he left that evening and that I would write to him the next morning. Poor Teresa does not know what to do. If she was quite sure that he did not drink, she would decide in

Mr Scott's favour. Mr Scott told John that both he and Mr Portman were tipsy when they left St Louis. His being once tipsy would not make him a drunkard but then would Mr Portman say what he did unless he had strong reasons for believing what he said. We must know more of him than we do at present.

Mar 25 We decided upon telling Mr Scott that our acquaintance was too short to venture a life's happiness upon, and that at the end of 2 months if he chose to renew his proposal and that if she then thought as well of him as she does now that she would accept him and that in the meantime they were both at perfect liberty to withdraw. I asked him up to luncheon and told him Teresa's and our decision. He said that he would consent to whatever she proposed, that he was too much attached to her to give up the slightest chance of ultimate success. Teresa had been up to the Griffins in the morning to have a talk with Amelia. She was so much excited and agitated that she was almost hysterical and could not go down to see Mr Scott or Mr Griffin who came to luncheon. We intend writing to Shuldham and asking him to go to Roxboroughshire and make some inquiries about Mr Scott's antecedents, for if he is really as good a man as all of my sons and the Griffins think him and as wealthy as we know he is it would be folly in Teresa to refuse him, but if he should be intemperate in his habits it would be madness to marry him if he was as rich as the Rothschilds.

. . .

Mar 27 . . . I wrote to Shuldham and asked him to make inquiries about Mr Scott. . . . Mr Scott feels very awkward. . . . He does not quite know what position he is to take in the house.

Mar 28 The Griffins, Mr McInnes, Mr King and Mr Scott came to luncheon. Edward has gone to Toronto to attend to his Chancery business. Teresa went to the Griffins. Mr Scott was there. He wanted her to accept a ring from him but she declined, as if she does not accept him at the end of 2 months it would have to be returned and if she accepts him, then it will be time enough to give the ring.

Mar 29 We are all invited to tea tomorrow evening at the Bechers. Neither John nor I are well enough to go. I wrote to Helen. Teresa went to the Griffins and they walked home with her. Mr Nind has got himself rather in disgrace. Out at the Kings the other day he offered a ring as a prize to the lady who would make the best shot with a rifle. Mrs King, Mrs Whitehead, Mrs Howel and I believe Miss Whitehead and Miss Hamilton were the ladies who contested for the prize. I do not know who won it, but Mr Nind incautiously confided to one of his friends that the ring was given to him by a lady of easy virtue in London. The story has got about, at least a dozen people know of

it, and he is in a great state of alarm for fear the ladies who contested for the prize will find it out, which they are quite sure to do.
Mar 30 . . . Edward brought very little news from Toronto. Dr Ryerson intends writing a history of Canada and wants information from all who can give it and expects a good deal of assistance from me.[98]
Mar 31 The party at Mrs Becher's was rather successful. Mr Scott was there, his manner to Teresa is very gentlemanlike. He does not compromise her in the least. . . . We got letters from Helen and Mr Portman, things are not going well with them on the plantation. All their cotton fields are again under water. There will be no crops again this year. . . . She says they have been too prosperous and that they must have a reverse. Mr Portman writes private to John and says let Teresa marry Mr Scott if she likes him but be sure that he has the money he says he has. Now it is evident enough that it was from a momentary impulse caused most probably by Mr Scott's not liking the South that made him write to Teresa not to take him if she had the chance. . . .
Apr 1 . . . We had letters from Sarah, Mary and Eliza. Sarah advises us to find out who Mr Scott is before we give him any encouragement. . . .
Apr 3 Amelia returned last night. John and Mr Scott are to come home on Monday.[99] They remained to go to a party at Mrs Widders and they and Miss Loring were to dine at Dr Ryerson's on Sunday. Teresa and I went to Church and remained to the Sacrament. Teresa then went home with Amelia and they all came here to tea and brought Mr Jackson with them. Mr Jackson is in great hopes of marrying Miss Loring.
Apr 4 . . . John came home from Toronto at 9 PM. He thinks Miss Loring a very clever girl but rather *strong-minded*. . . . Mr Price[100] is very attentive to Sophia, and we are all much in hopes that he will propose for her as it would be pleasing to both her father and mother. . . .
Apr 5 . . . Mr Scott gave Teresa a small diamond ring very pretty but not very *good* and a bracelet of the new metal called almoninam [aluminium]. It is very pretty. Mr Scott came to tea. I thought him very agreeable.
Apr 12 . . . Mary and Eliza are rather in favour of Teresa's marrying

[98]The outcome was her "Historical Memorandum," published in Ryerson's *The Loyalists of America*.
[99]They were in Toronto.
[100]David Edward Price (1826–83) is mentioned several times in Sissons' *My Dearest Sophie*. Price represented Chicoutimi, a lumber town founded by his father.

Mr Scott but acknowledge that they know nothing about him. Mr Scott and John went out riding and Mr & Mrs W. Lawrason, Mrs Vansittart,[101] Mr Jackson and Mr Scott spent the evening here. W. Lawrason, Mr Jackson, Mrs Vansittart and myself played whist. Mr W. Lawrason, John, Mr Scott and Teresa played cribbage. John lost his temper because Teresa did not attend to the game. The evening was pretty stupid, they went away at 12.

Apr 14 . . . John got a letter marked private from Mr Portman and requesting us not to show it to Teresa. Of course it was about Mr Scott but saying only what he had said before. I dislike any thing private but John thought it best not to show the letter as Mr Portman was positive in his request. . . .

Apr 18 . . . My brother Edward [Ryerse] arrived. . . . He wished to consult about the sale of his Harbor, and wishes John to go to Port Ryerse on Friday to draw up articles of agreement. I am very glad that he is about to sell the Harbor as it has already involved him in debt.

Apr 19 My brother and I lunched with the Griffins. Amelia's housekeeping does her credit. Both house and table are exceedingly nice. Mr Scott and Mr Jackson called at the Griffins when we were there. Mr Scott had lunched here. . . . I got letters from Mary and Eliza. They both think that Teresa will be a great fool if she refuses Mr Scott unless we are satisfied that his conduct is not what we can approve of.

Apr 21 We were all very busy cleaning the drawing room and rehanging the pictures when I got a note from Amelia telling me that Mr Griffin had seen Mr [Francis] Hincks (the Governor of Barbados) in Toronto and that he was coming up to see us and would be here by the 10 PM train. Consequently it was necessary that we should exert ourselves to get our house in order. Mrs Askin came in to spend the day, but when she saw the state of confusion we were in she returned to come again. . . . John and Mr Griffin met Mr Hincks at the Train. Amelia was here. Mr Hincks is looking very well but older and his hair has whitened a good deal since I saw him three years ago but he has lost none of his cleverness nor have his eyes lost their brilliancy. Report says that he is to succeed Sir Edmund Head as Governor General of Canada, but many think it would be a dangerous experiment to place one who had so lately been a leader in politics in the country at the head of affairs as he must have many enemies as well as friends. He has one saving trait in his character that qualifies him better than most men for a difficult command. He appears to forget all opposition

[101]Mrs. Vansittart, a visitor from Woodstock.

and endevours by a kind cautious manner to convert his enemies into friends. Consequently his political opponents are not as violent in their opposition to him as they generally are to a successful oppositionist.
Apr 22 Mr Hinck's reception by the public in London was not very warm. A deputation came over from St Thomas and presented an address to him. I think he was never wonderfully popular in London. . . . Mr Griffin, Amelia, Mr Scott and Mr Hincks, the nephew, to dinner. We had to dine at three as he had to leave at $^1/_2$ past 5. We were much gratified by his visit as his time in the country is very limited. His family went direct from Barbados to England, and he is on his way there. Mr Scott remained to tea.
Apr 25 Teresa got a note from Amelia asking her to go to Brantford with her and return in the evening. I gave her leave to go but they went to Hamilton in the place of Brantford, saw Mr McInnes, got some gloves and returned through a heavy rain. Mr Wilson called, but I found the evening very lonely. I wrote to Helen. I think Teresa for some cause unknown to me is deciding against Mr Scott. I pray God to guide her right. As far as I can see and judge I should feel much more confident in her marrying him than I did. We have all decided that he is much more of a temperance man than an intemperate one and as we have now known him for eight months we think we should have discovered any habit of exaggeration, but all his statements appear to be correct and his connections good. But how weak is human judgement in all things. How often I feel this most painfully in my endevour to do right, again I can only pray that God may guide us.
Apr 28 . . . Mr Scott gave *Dr Syntax*[102] to Teresa. We suspecting that he was very close had given hints that we would like the book. Teresa expressed a great wish to read it, not that we cared a farthing about the book only we wished to see if he could give, and when the book came we all felt ashamed and could not help feeling that we were the mean party. I always feel contempt for people who give hints for presents. Teresa went to the Griffins. Mr Scott and Mr Jackson called there, and they with the Griffins walked out to the Peglar's Green House. Mr Scott gave Teresa a very pretty bouquet, when they returned. They all dined with the Griffins. John went up to walk home with Teresa.
Apr 29 Mr Scott and Mr King came to luncheon. Teresa not well her

[102]William Combe's "Dr. Syntax" books were very popular: *Tour of Dr. Syntax in Search of Picturesque*, 1812; *Second Tour of Dr. Syntax in Search of Consolation*, 1820; *Third Tour of Dr. Syntax in Search of a Wife*, 1821.

long walk was too much for her. I got a letter from my brother Edward. He is afraid that he has done a bad thing by selling his Harbor. Amelia and Mr Scott came to dinner. The day beautiful. I put some flower seeds into the ground. The aurora was splendid in the evening.
Apr 30 . . . I got letters from Shuldham, Mary and Sarah. Sarah surprised me by the announcement that she was again to become a mother after nearly eight years respite. Shuldham has gone off delighted like a school boy on a holiday to make enquiries about Mr Scott. Both Sarah and Mary think Teresa will be very silly to refuse Mr Scott unless there is something really objectionable in his character. They laugh at the idea of objecting to him because he is ugly, and it is true a plain face wins upon one if there is kindness and goodness with it, and beauty soon loses its charms if kindness and goodness are wanting. Mr Scott returned after luncheon and brought me some English letters to read and also a letter from Mr John Scott wherein he speaks very highly of Mr Scott who is here. Mr Scott brought other congratulatory letters from some of his lady friends. He has evidently led them to believe that his engagement was a reality not a *fancy* and he will be in a very awkward position if Teresa refuses him. He brought a very handsome watch and chain and 3 rings, one rubies and diamond, one emerald and diamond and one pearls etc, all 3 good and pretty and offered them to me for her acceptance. I advised him to keep them for 2 or 3 weeks until her decision was known or in other words until we heard from Shuldham. Mr and Mrs John Scott sent out an agate bracelet and shawl broach, the best and handsomest of the kind that I have ever seen. Those also were offered for her acceptance and declined. He then asked me if I would take charge of them for the time being, which I did. . . .
May 1 . . . The Griffins and Mr McInnes came to tea. Mr McInnes looked very much as if he felt disappointed when he looked at Teresa. I am sure he thinks that Mr Scott has been accepted. . . .
May 7 Our visitors, Miss Loring, Sophia and Mr Price have arrived. Miss [Blanche] Widder stays with Amelia. They came up with Mr Griffin and Mr Scott. I think them all nice lady-like girls and I like Mr Price. . . .
May 8 We got English letters this morning. Shuldham went to Hawick and made enquiries about Mr Scott and all he heard was in confirmation of what Mr Scott has already told us, so that all objections on my part will be withdrawn and now Teresa must decide for herself. Mr Price, Miss Loring, Miss Ryerson, Teresa and Edward went to Church. I told Teresa to ask Mr Jackson to return to dinner. He begged to be excused and behaved in a very stiff manner. He walked home with

them from Church, Teresa and Sophia taking great care to let him walk with Miss Loring. At the gate Teresa again asked him to call during the afternoon and to come to tea, all of which he refused almost rudely. We cannot understand it unless he fancies John is trying to cut him out, but he need not fear. Even if John had any designs upon Miss Loring he would not interfere with Mr Jackson. . . .

May 9 . . . Miss Loring and I had a long talk about him [Mr Jackson]. She says she will not marry him, that she knew very little of him and had not thought of him in a matrimonial light. I told her I thought he would propose for her if he had an opportunity and it was for her to accept or refuse. I told her that Mr Jackson's intentions were honorable and that he wished to pay her the greatest compliment that a man could pay a woman. At the same time *I* knew he would be a *very* bad match and if he does not tell her his true position I should feel duty bound to do so before she accepted him if I saw that she looked favorably upon him. He cannot return to England and is liable to arrest even here. His character is free from reproach as far as we know but it would be madness for a girl to marry a man inextricably involved and without a six pence. . . .

May 10 . . . George left for Toronto this morning to pass his examination for attorney. God grant that he may pass. He was very low-spirited and nervous, poor fellow. Mr Becher has promised me that he will be there on Monday at the last examination. . . .

May 11 I got a letter from Helen who is not well. I wrote to her to come home as soon as she could. The water in the Mississippi has not subsided and there has a further rise commenced. They apprehend great disaster the whole length of the river. I got letters from my brother Edward who is in trouble about his Harbor. Edward will have to go down and see about it. . . .

May 12 The Griffins, Miss Widder, Mr Scott and Mr Stahlschmidt came to luncheon. Mr Jackson called and accepted our offer of making some jelly for Mr Drake who is ill. A riding party was arranged. Mr Scott, Mr Jackson, Edward and Mr Dunn were the gentlemen. Mrs Becher, Miss Loring and Sophia were the ladies who were to go. John would not go as Mr Jackson is evidently so jealous of his attentions to Miss Loring and he is of such a violent temper that we were afraid that he might commit himself in some way that would make Miss Loring feel very uncomfortable and thought it best for John to avoid a collision, but Miss Loring decided that her manner to Mr Jackson should convince him that his attentions were disageeable to her and when he offered to put her on the horse she preferred the assistance of the groom. At the same time she declined John's assistance and Mr

Scott's, but Mr Jackson rode off in a fury and went throught the streets like a madman. We congratulated her upon having freed herself from his attentions. He behaved so rudely that she need not acknowledge his acquaintance and I cannot ask him here as long as she is my guest. After they were all gone John went out with Teresa and gave her a lesson upon riding. . . .

May 13 Ned and Sophia were to have gone up this morning for Miss Widder and then to have gone hunting ferns but Sophia thought better of it. Ned went and Miss Widder returned to breakfast. Mr Scott came to breakfast and they arranged a driving party to call at the Kings. Mr Dunn was to take Amelia and Miss Widder, Mr Scott and John were to take Miss Loring and Teresa and Ned was to give Sophia a buggy drive but poor Ned had to go to Long Point to arrange the Port Ryerse Harbor business and Mr Griffin took Sophia. Both Sophia and Miss Widder like Ned's attentions and Ned has a secret weakness for Sophia. They are both nice girls. Miss Widder without being handsome is a stylish lady like looking girl and Sophia has always been almost as dear to me as one of my own daughters. Mr Scott came to luncheon and I told him that he had our willing consent to marry Teresa if he could gain hers. We have all learned to like him, & I believe if she marries him she will secure her own happiness. We have been a long time coming to this decision, but we heard so many things unfavorable to him, that we could not give our consent without knowing more of him. Mr Scott came to dinner.

May 15 This is John's birthday. Mrs W. Lawrason sent him such a pretty bouquet with a line of congratulation. John gave Miss Loring the bouquet and I showed her the congratulations. John thought I was wrong, and that Miss Loring ought not to have known that the bouquet was given to him, but I know I was right, for Miss Loring if she placed any value on a compliment from him could not help feeling that he had paid her one in giving her a bouquet that was given him on his birthday by a person that he had great regard for. Had he given it and said nothing when its history became known, which it certainly would, both Mrs Lawrason and Miss Loring would have been offended. He should either not have given it at all or he should have had no reserves about it. Open straight-forward conduct, even about a bouquet, is always the best. . . .

May 17 . . . George returned from Toronto. He had passed his examination and was sworn in an attorney. I felt so glad. Our party went off very well with two exceptions. Mr. Johnston & Mr Barton got tipsy. I will never ask them here again. If a gentleman *can* forget himself once in that way he may a second time. The band played very well.

The supper was very good and all the ladies looked nicely dressed. All the guests were away at 3 o'clock and we were in bed at 4.
May 18 The servants had the house nearly righted when I came down stairs at $^1/_2$ past 10. All our party went to Mrs W. Lawrasons to luncheon. Afterwards Miss Loring and Sophia returned their calls. Mr Scott came to dinner. Amelia and Miss Widder called. Ned and Miss Widder went for a drive. Sophia dined at the Griffins. Edward went to the Station to meet Mr Price and called at the Griffins on his way home and brought Sophia. We all had supper and hurried to bed, very tired.
May 19 Mr Price brought me 2 pairs of moccasins and some bark work for Teresa and 3 nets for the hair, one for Sophia, one for Teresa and one for Amelia. I spoke to Sophia this morning about her flirting with Mr Stahlschmidt and Ned, and told her how very foolish she was – that Mr Stahlschmidt could not marry if he would, that he was poor, and that Edward however much he might like her was not within 2 or 3 years of matrimony and in that time his feelings in all probability would change towards her, that it would be folly in her to refuse a good offer upon the mere hope that at some future time Edward might propose for her. I told her that I thought Mr Price's visit was to her and that I liked him very much, that I thought he possessed great energy of character and that he was an honorable good man and would make a good husband. She answered me curtly that she did not like him and could never like him well enough to marry him. I told her to think well what she was doing, and that if she was determined that she would not marry him, she was right in not giving him any encouragement. In my opinion she is a little foolish flirt, and that Mr Price is well without her as she would never make him a loving good wife. . . .

After dinner they all went to a party at Mr Watson's and came home at 2 o'clock. Something seemed wrong with Miss Loring and Amelia made her tell what it was. Miss Loring had got a letter from her mother cautioning her against Jack. James Morris[103] had told Mrs Loring that we were all match makers and that John was on the look out for a wife with money. Mrs Loring advised her daughter to return home. Amelia told Miss Loring that John had property and income enough of his own to support a wife and that she thought him in every respect as good a match as there was in the country and as for asking her here to marry her to John she might be assured that John would not propose for her in his own house and that we knew that our con-

[103] A visitor from Toronto.

nections were better and our position as good as that of anyone in the country, and that *we* thought we paid anyone a compliment that we asked to the house, and that our invitations were few and select. Miss Loring is a very nice girl as far as I can judge upon so short an acquaintance and I certainly think that if John makes love to her he has had no discouragements from her. She has appeared as well pleased to listen as he was to talk. She proposed going home on Saturday. We told her if she must go George would see her home. John gave her a beautiful eye glass which he bought at Tiffany in New York. She seemed much pleased and took it conditionally that is if her mother approved. She made some decision about going out riding with John. We at once met her views, offered to give up the riding party or that Amelia would ride with John, but she did not give up the riding party and *rode with John.* I hope she is not acting, as John is no flirt and she certainly has *met* all his advances, and if she is merely amusing herself I shall feel very, very sorry for him.

May 20 . . . Ned says he will give her [Sophia] up for a simpleton if she refuses Mr Dunn who would certainly be a very fair match but *I* should infinitely prefer Mr Price to him. . . . Mr Scott continues his devotion to Teresa. I wonder when she will decide either to accept or refuse him.

May 21 . . . I like Miss Loring very much. She is a girl of very good abilities but there is a something wanting, I hardly know what it is, probably it is the want of a mind superior and more experienced that her own to guide her, she being an only child has had her own will all her life and has never been encouraged to read. Yet she is very anxious to acquire knowledge. . . . Jack will propose for Miss Loring and certainly she gives him all the encouragement he can wish for. Things went wrong with Mr Scott and Teresa today. When Mr Scott came to dinner he had evidently taken a very little too much wine. It alarmed me, as he had been accused of intemperance and I told her when she was going out riding that if he urged her to give an answer not to give him one today. I felt vexed at his appearance and wish to know how it had occurred. John told me that he had been in Mr Scott's room and he had opened a bottle of Burgundy and he supposed that Mr Scott had taken a glass too much [and] coming out into the hot sun it had affected him which I believe was the case. But sure enough Mr Scott urged Teresa to give him an answer and said if she would wear in the evening a ring which he had given he would take it as an acceptance or her not doing so as a refusal. He looked at her hand as he was going away and saw that the ring was not there and said good night without making a remark. Sophia says she will not have Mr Dunn and her manner is very correct towards him. Mr Dunn told Edward without hesitation that he admired Sophia more than any girl he had seen and that he would try to win her unless Ned was a candidate for her hand. Ned pleaded not guilty of any matrimonial intentions towards her and said that she had been looked upon in the light of a sister ever since she was a child. At the same time Mr Ned knows that she likes him better than anyone and that if he would propose for her that she would think of no one else. She told me this only a few days ago. It is a curious world we live in, and the course of true love never runs smooth. Edward cannot marry at present but I believe in his heart he likes her as well if not better than anyone else, though he is very sweet upon Miss Widder just now, and both her and Sophia are very jealous of his attentions to each other. He is very like a donkey between two bundles of hay. He would like them both.

May 22 We all got up very late and had to eat a hurried breakfast in time for Church. Miss Loring, Sophia, Edward, George and myself went. Sophia went home with Amelia to dinner. Mr Scott dined with us. He looked very low-spirited and accepted my invitation to dinner with hesitation. . . .

May 23 Our visitors leave today. Miss Loring got up very early and dressed herself very nicely. I knew she wanted to spend an hour or 2 with John. I went to his room and told him to get up and do the agreeable, which he did. I think there is no doubt but Miss Loring is to be had for the asking, but would it be wise to propose until he knows more of her. Mrs Loring is said to be a weak silly woman. Miss Loring admits that her mother is no guide to her. It has always been my theory to judge the daughter in a great measure by the mother and although Miss Loring seems a nice girl with good abilities yet there always appears something not easily understood about her and although naturally clever yet her mind is very uninformed. There is very cool calculation in all her actions and I should think a disposition to closeness, beyond economy. Yet I like her better than any girl I have seen, and I hope and pray oh how sincerely that if John marries her that she may make him a good wife. If her mother is only a woman possessing good common sense, and good principles, I should have no fear, but early impressions are strong let them be good or evil, and it is more than probable that an infantile mind that is left to be filled up by chance impressions will receive more wrong than right ones. Both Miss Loring and Sophia appear sorry to leave. Mr Griffin and Edward went to Toronto with them and came back by the return train. Amelia came here on her way home from the station. Mr Scott and Mr Stahlschmidt came with her and stayed to luncheon. Mr Scott looked wretched. I never saw anyone look more miserable. I could not help telling him to cheer up, that faint heart never won fair lady. I asked him to come to dinner which he did. We were much amused with Mr Stahlschmidt, who is really in love with Sophia but pretends that he has transferred his admiration to Blanche Widder. . . .

May 24 Mr Scott and Amelia came to luncheon and remained to dinner. Mr Griffin dined with us also. We have a fine household. Mr Scott is in love with Teresa (I wish she was in love with him). John is in love with Miss Loring, this is mutual I believe. Ned and Miss Widder are very much in love with each other for the time being and George looks on with supreme disgust and thinks they ought all to put on cap and bells. Edward, Amelia and Teresa had an animated discussion with me about John's wishing me to leave the house as soon as he married. I told them that I had always said that if Teresa married, George had his profession, and if John married that I would go to England if I could muster up courage to leave my own home, but that I well knew that when I went out of the gate and turned my back on my house and home associations that I bade *adieu* to peaceful content. Here I believe I am respected by all who know anything of me and I have a few friends who are strongly attached to me. For me to leave all that I know of friends and country with a conviction of a doubtful return, I know will be a hard struggle although I go to see my daughters. I have never in my life left home even for a few hours without reluctance. I have often said that I thought it best for young people to be by themselves for some time after marriage. It is upon this suggestion, I think, that John spoke as urgently as he did for me to leave at once should he marry in the autumn. I expressed my dislike to a winter voyage and said if Helen wished me I would go for the winter with her to the South. Edward spoke very warmly and very kindly and said John could not mean it, and said that if John or any one of my children ceased to cherish me with the greatest tenderness or ever forget that I alone had borne them through every difficulty and made them all what they were, ill luck would befall them, and that if any one of them knew that John even hinted that I had better go visiting when he got married that he would be cut by every brother and sister that he had and that not one would write or speak to him except on business, and I am quite sure that such would be the case. How little children know a mother's heart or how much love it contains. I know what John's manner ought to be to me. He ought to humbug me into the belief that I was his dear and much loved mother and that his first thought would always be to make me happy and comfortable and that he felt quite sure the first wish of his wife would be to make me happy. My going or staying would be all the same but a person likes to be flattered. I have never intended to stand in his way if it was left optional with me. But this is my home while I live. When I die it shall be his, if I leave it for a time for his or my pleasure I shall return, should I live when I am weary of wandering, and should John and his wife prefer taking another house to having me in the house with them they must do so and I must get some other child to come and care for me in my old age. It appears to me so strange that my presence should disturb the happiness or that my absence should be necessary to the happiness to a son that I have loved so much or that he would take a wife who objects to his mother. I have always endevourd to smooth difficulties and I am sure I shall try to make none for John and his wife.

May 25 Mr Scott called this morning. I think Teresa has decided in his favor. I told her I should be very glad to see her married to Mr Scott if she liked him well enough to make him a good wife, but that she must reflect seriously while she is away and if she felt any repugnance to him and could not like him well enough to marry him to write to me and I would break it to Mr Scott, and that she had better not come home for some time. On Sunday she must give a decided answer either one way or the other. Her and Amelia have gone to Toronto. Teresa is to stay at the Widders who give a grand ball tomorrow evening and if she takes Mr Scott she will come home on Saturday. Mr Scott came to luncheon. . . . I got a letter from Helen who is better but not well and will not be able to leave the plantation before the middle of June. I had a letter also from Miss Loring. It was a very nice letter but a little flowery.

May 26 John, Edward and Mr Griffin have all gone to Toronto to Mrs Widder's ball. . . . I enjoyed the day's quiet with George. After dinner he went pruning the trees of dead branches. We walked on the terrace until late, then came in to tea and cribbage. George was very much afraid that I would feel lonely having no one sleeping on the same floor with me. He is so thoughtful, kind and good.

May 27 We expected Edward home at 3 o'clock but he did not come until 9 PM, and then we talked until 12. I think he has got pretty well over [his] love fit. He says Mrs Widder is a d__ old humbug. I believe there has never been but one opinion on that subject. Her ball went off very well. John and Miss Loring were very devoted to each other.

May 28 Mr Becher came to luncheon. I never saw him in such a low spirit. He said everybody said that Teresa was to be married to Mr Scott and asked him, but he knew nothing about it. I told him I could not tell him that she was going to be married as she had not when she left home made up her mind on the subject, but was to decide while away and if she refused Mr Scott she would remain some time in Toronto. John and Teresa came home at 9 PM. They both looked very happy and well pleased, John with his prospects and Teresa with hers. She *has* decided in Mr Scott's favor. I hope she will be happy. . . .

May 29 . . . Mr Wilson paid me an hour's visit before Church. He also asked me about Teresa and approved of the marriage that she is going to make. He spoke of his daughter [Lucy] and young [Bill] Bailey and is evidently much disappointed with her choice but from her delicate state of health he is afraid to offer violent opposition to her wishes. I asked him if he did not think it would be much better to take Mr Bailey by the hand and give their marriage his consent and countenance, that his character was not only irreproachable but that he was liked by all who knew him, and that as his son in law with his approbation and countenance he would hold a very different position from what he held now, and there was no reason why he should not succeed in business and accumulate wealth as well as others. He assented to what I said and I think B. Bailey and Lucy will receive no more opposition from Mr Wilson. . . .

May 30 . . . Amelia and I had a long talk about John. She says John felt hurt at my misunderstanding his wish that I should go to England as soon as he married. He knew my daughters wished me to go, and that he thought, the sooner I went, as I am getting old, the better I would be able to go, but that while he lives the best room in his house would be mine and that he would not marry any woman that would not look upon me as a mother. I felt sorry that I should for a moment [have] doubted his right judgment, his affection I knew he could *never* withold from me. The future in this world, can never be very bright to people who have seen sixty years. Bereavements, old ties severed, separations, with all the infirmities of old age, feebleness, feverishness, weakened intellect, and selfishness is what we all have to look forward to – but I make one constant fervent prayer, that I may receive God's many blessings which are given to me with a grateful heart, and that I may never be the cause of sorrow or unhappiness to any one. Teresa is going to marry Mr Scott. I feel that I have influenced her in this decision. God help me if she should prove unhappy. How am I to know whether I do right or wrong. Had I influenced her to decide against him would that have been right. I have believed that it would not, and she trusts so much to me that decide herself she would not. We find it hard to choose the right when the way is clear before us, how are we to choose it when the way is dark. I wrote to Mr Scott of Edinburgh and to Mrs and Miss Loring. On Saturday evening Basil

Hamilton and a lad by the name of Murray who is a very bad character broke into Mr Wilson's office with the intent to rob but were discovered and when Mr Carroll attempted to take them, Basil Hamilton made free use of his knife. It all appeared in the paper this morning but from delicacy towards Mr Hamilton they did not say whose son Basil was and from the same feeling Mr Wilson has not had them arrested. Basil has been allowed to run wild about the streets for years. Mr Scott came to tea.

Jun 1 John has been very much fretted today. He got three dunning letters from Mr Becher, one on Sunday morning, one on Tuesday evening and the third this Wednesday morning for a debt of mine for money borrowed of Sir Richard Airey. Mr Becher's last letter was not only uncourteous but sneering, almost insulting. John was making arrangements to get the money but could not do so until after the 31st as he had to put in a note at the bank for it, and has now paid Mr Becher the whole sum £174. I feel so sorry that he should all his life have a weight of debt upon his shoulders. It is true he will be compensated in the end, but now there is nothing but a sacrifice of property, which would fall on my sons, as my daughters get almost nothing, could enable me to meet even a small debt. I often feel that the mortification which I have to endure when I have to go to my sons for money is necessary to keep my proud heart humble. Joys and sorrows, pleasures and pains, all alike will come to an end by and by.

Mr Scott came to luncheon and he, Teresa and John went out riding. He gave his horse – Chatham – to Teresa and told her if John married Miss Loring that he wished her to give it to Miss Loring as a wedding present. Nothing could be kinder or more generous. He certainly was calumniated when he was called stingey. A distant cousin of his, a Mrs and Mr Alexander from Toronto, dined with us. They seem very good people but are not in a very aristocratic circle. Amelia and Mr Griffin dined here. I got a letter from Mary. She is getting stronger and in better health. In the evening Mr Becher sent me a plate of strawberries, the first of the season, and a note endevouring to make a joke of John's annoyance. Becher is evidently very sorry but he was much to blame. His manner of dunning was ungentlemanlike and uncalled for. That he has wanted money badly himself I am sure. It was not Col Airey's interest alone that was concerned or he could simply have told John that we must pay a higher interest, or pay up. I am very sorry but one unkind act must not do away with the mutual kindness and friendship of years.

Jun 2 . . . We got a letter from Mr Portman who appears to be pretty tired of the South. He says he is 20 years older within the last six months and that he has had nothing but trials and vexations since he has been there. The flood, his wife and children ill, his negroes ill and a stupid nurse. . . .

Jun 3 . . . Mrs Street and family have left London to join Mr Street in Chicago. Poor woman, her life has not been made a very happy one. . . .

Jun 4 . . . My journal came under discussion and Edward said it did not contain one kind word of any one individual. Can this be so? I must endevour to correct so great a fault and look at people's good qualities more and their bad ones less.

Jun 5 Teresa and I went to Church. It was Sacrament day. At one time all of my family that were old enough used to attend the Sacrament table, now only Amelia, Teresa & myself, and occasionally John. It is with sorrow I say this. . . .

Jun 8 . . . There is to be a ball at Government House tomorrow evening. . . . John is going to Toronto also with the intent of going to the ball, and to see Miss Loring and to propose for her most probably. I sincerely hope all may end well. . . .

Jun 9 Today Doctor King was to be hanged for poisoning his wife, the feeling in the country is very strong against. . . . Edward and Mr McInnes returned from Long Point. . . . Mr Griffin and Edward were highly amused with the primitive manners of the Long Pointers and delighted with the beautiful country that they passed through. . . .

Jun 11 . . . John returned by the 3 o'clock train. He enjoyed his visit to Toronto very much. If he has proposed for Miss Loring he has not told us of it. . . . John again urged me to go to England this autumn. He thinks I would enjoy a visit there, and that it will be my only chance of ever again seeing my daughters and their families and that I shall very soon be getting too old to go. All this I know and would be very, very glad to see my children, but the thought of leaving my home sickens me. I was ill and feverish all night and am far from well this morning. My dislike to leaving home is almost a disease. At this moment I think I could look at the road to the cemetery with more pleasure than the road to England, yet I shall go to England but never return. Only once for 20 years has the thought of going to England given me pleasure and then only for a few moments. A few days ago Mr Scott told me that there was four miles of walk at Teviot Bank[104] and that it was so very pretty. For a few minutes the feelings of youth returned and I thought how I should like to wander about alone, and then the conviction returned that even a walk to Amelia's fatigued me

[104]Mr. Scott's residence in Scotland.

so much that I did not get over it for two days. My days for sight seeing and enjoying anything but quiet are passed. I could wish to die amongst familiar objects even if the faces I have most loved were away, but God['s] will be done. He is everywhere and with his help I will give up all my own wordly wishes and I will try never again to put down my thoughts on this subject. . . .

Jun 12 . . . I wrote to Eliza and Sarah and told them to expect me in England in October. . . . Mr Scott is very anxious to have the wedding day named. I said it might be either the 18th of August or the 1st or 8th of September. Mr Scott wants Teresa to go to Teviot Bank before the Autumn destroys its beauty but Teresa would rather spend a month visiting places of note in the States. I think the 1st of Sept will be the day, and then they can go to England after the equinoxial gales are over.

Jun 14 I got a letter from Eliza enclosing a note from General Kenna[105] with information about Mr Scott. . . .

Jun 16 I got up at 5 and was at the station in good time. No one in the house was up but the servants. John heard me close the gate and followed me down. Amelia met me at the station. When we arrived at Hamilton we went to the Anglo American[106] and breakfasted and then went to Mr McInnes and made our purchases. He was very kind. We dined with him at his mother's and then went out driving and saw the water works. There are a great many splendid views about Hamilton. . . .

Jun 18 George started at six for Hamilton to play a cricket match between Hamilton and London. Edward returned from his fishing excursion[107] with his usual luck, having caught nothing. Mr Becher called and asked the Eldon party to tea at Thornwood. . . . The Misses Gzowski and Fanny Becher called. The Misses Gzowski are much improved in looks and manner but are too noisy and speak too loud. I do not think it possible for a young girl to be lady like unless she has a gentle quiet manner. . . .

Jun 26 . . . It is very painful to me to [see] such disinclination upon the part of John, Edward and George to attend divine service. I cannot account for it but fear that I have in some way neglected my duty. . . .

[105]Thomas Kenna was commissioned as an ensign in 1799 and after service in Holland, Egypt, Sicily and Spain had risen to the rank of Lieutenant General by 1851. A close friend of the Crutchleys for many years, he served briefly with the 63rd Regiment in the mid 1860s. He died in 1869.

[106]A Hamilton hotel.

[107]He had been to Dorchester.

Jun 27 . . . John came home at 10 PM looking very tired but very happy. He has proposed and has been accepted by Miss Loring. I believe no arrangement has been made as to the time of marriage. I am very glad and rejoice in his prospect of happiness. I think highly of Miss Loring and sincerely hope she may make him a good wife . . . every man ought to be married before they are 30. . . .

Jun 29 . . . I received a letter from my cousin Dr Ryerson telling me that Miss Loring had called upon them and told Sophia that she is going to be her cousin, that John had proposed for her, and gave them to understand that although delighted with his offer yet in the excitement of the moment she had not given him the decided answer which she ought to have done and that she wished Sophia to write and say that she, Miss Loring, wished John to write to her and also to her mother. I had tried to impress upon John that either too much or too little had been said, but he has written today most fully to Miss Loring and her mother. . . . We were discussing the letters to Miss Loring and her Mother when in walked Helen and Mr Portman. . . . The Portmans came back looking very happy and seemed to be well pleased with the South, notwithstanding flood and fevers. . . . Helen brought up a pretty dress for each of us of foulard silk.

Jul 1 John this morning got his answer from Mrs & Miss Loring. It was as we knew it would be a cordial acceptance, and an invitation to visit them immediately. . . .

Jul 2 . . . John has gone to Toronto to arrange all about his marriage. . . . Edward and George went to the opera. Last night was the first time an opera as ever been given in London.

Jul 3 . . . I told Mr Scott that I wished I had told him to return next summer to marry Teresa and he was in a great fright and told Mr Griffin that he thought I wanted to put him off again and that if so he should pack up and be off altogether. I was glad when they told me what high dudgeon he was in and thought that if Teresa wished to break with him she could do so. I told her to act for herself and if she could not marry him with all her heart and make him a good wife to break off the engagement, that Mr Portman said as long as he has a home she should have one. I told her not to be influenced by John's going to be married or by the wishes of anyone but do as her own heart dictated and she has chosen to marry Mr Scott. It is now her own act. God grant she may be happy.

Jul 4 Helen and Teresa have been very busy all day preparing to go to Toronto to get Teresa's trousseau. John gave Helen £50, it will take all of £50 more besides the £50 worth bought at Hamilton. . . . John returned from Toronto. His marriage with Miss Loring is all arranged and announced but the day not named. In talking over matters with Mrs Loring it appears that Miss Loring will have at her mother's death over £12,000 so that she will be very well off indeed, but that is a very secondary consideration to her being a nice wife.

Jul 9 . . . The Portmans, Teresa & Mr Scott came home by the 9 o'clock train, hungry and tired. . . . Dr Ryerson was as kind as he could be and professes a great liking for Mr Portman and wants him to stand for a Member, and several of the Ministry wish it also. Mr Portman has every requisite to make himself popular, if he chooses to take a very little trouble. He may be a member or anything else he wishes to be. Mr Portman does not estimate Blanche Widder very highly. He says she has no conversation excepting of the most frivolous kind. Sophia they all think a very nice little girl but all agree not liking Mrs Loring. They think her a good deal like old Miss Watson and if she is as good a woman we may touch her faults lightly. They say she talks a great deal about *high Society,* having been accustomed to such high society. People can generally tell by our manners and conversation what sort of society we have been accustomed to. . . . Teresa could not make all the purchases she wished. They could not find anything in silk or any other material fit for a wedding, nor was there a dress maker in Toronto that they could trust a dress with to be made, and now they will have to go to Detroit and see what can be done there.

Jul 14 . . . Edward went to the Griffins in the evening and found they had moved. He followed them to their new house. Mr Griffin said that he hated Mr Portman, Mr Scott, John, Edward and George for not going to assist him to move his furniture. The weather was rather too hot for people for volunteer labor that they were unaccustomed to.

Jul 20 I got a letter from Eliza who does not respond very warmly to my proposal of going to England this fall. She evidently thinks there is something behind – untold – and says I am wrong to give up housekeeping as my remaining here would be beneficial to both John and his wife. . . . Mr Portman and Helen are full of plans for a house. . . .

Jul 26 . . . Mrs Cronyn called. The Bishop is going to the seaside and will not return before the 1st of Sept for which I am very sorry as I would very much prefer him to marry Teresa as he has married all her sisters excepting Mary. He was absent when she was married and Mr Brough officiated. I got a letter from Sophia saying that she had got the dress and wished me to send the money which I did immediately £10 – by post. . . .

Jul 30 . . . All the family are sorry that John does not take a house for himself when he marries. There is but one feeling that his manner to me has not been what it ought to be, and they think my old age will not be made as comfortable as they think it ought to be. Had John taken a house Mr Portman would not have built, but for my sake would have remained here during my life, and kept the family together. Helen would have assumed all the duties of housekeeping and all the expenses, Edward, George and myself contributing enough for our keep. I should as a matter of course prefer my daughter to live with me to a daughter in law, however kind and agreeable she might be, but as John is eventually to have this place I have always looked forward to his bringing his wife to live here, and as I know that he has arranged to do so, I do not think I should be doing right without some just cause to say that he should not do so, although on a former occasion when his intended bride refused to live with me, he had no hesitation about leaving me to get on as best I could with three unmarried daughters and one son not out of his time. Should he again urge me to leave the house before Mr Portman has given out the contract for his house I should feel that I was too indifferent to the future, not to exchange the son for a daughter who has always been kind and who would watch my declining years with tender care. . . .

Jul 31 Teresa and George went to Church. John and I had a long talk about the future. He thinks the whole family turn against him as soon as he thinks of marrying. He is mistaken. All the family wish him to marry, and like all they know of Miss Loring, but as it is a proverb that sons are only sons until they have wives, and his urging me to go to England, and saying that I must go as it was best for him and his wife to be alone when they are first married, it was sounding a note of alarm, and all the family instantly became jealous and watchful of any arrangements that were to affect me. They all said my going or staying must depend upon my own wishes and not upon the will of anyone else. But we are all glad he is going to marry and are pleased with his choice and as far as it depends upon the members of the family we will *all* endevour to make them both happy. Mr Scott came to dinner and Amelia came to tea.

Aug 1 Things did not go so smoothly today. Mr Scott showed temper in an argument with John upon English taxation and we know so little of Mr Scott that we are all ready to take alarm at the slightest indication of anything wrong. Mr Portman said he was very much out of humour in the morning and complained that he had been detained here shilly shallying at a loss of £100 a month. I told Teresa and she spoke to him and told him not to suffer such loss on her account, that he could go to England whenever he chose. Mr Scott was very unhappy and said he had spoken in jest, but altogether we did not quite like it.

It is painful to be doubting as to the right or wrong of this match within two weeks of the wedding day. But so it is. Mr Scott was here at luncheon and dinner. John had a long talk with me and agreed to take my wild lands,[108] that is John, Edward and George, and pay my debts, which amount to about £1,200. . . . He spoke about our housekeeping after his marriage and said that he was willing that Edward, George and himself should equally divide the profits at the office provided they equally shared the expenses of the house. I think nothing could be more fair or generous.

Aug 4 Sent plate etc to Thornwood for Mrs Becher's party. Mr Wilson came to luncheon. After dinner all the family insisted upon my going to the party. . . . Mr Scott engaged the City Hall omnibus which will take us all. The Bechers took a great deal of trouble to endevour to give a nice party. They had a tent on the lawn for a gentleman's dressing room, and a part of the verandah curtained and sofaed, but trusted to amateurs and the piano for music, which was a mistake. They ought to have had the band. The supper was very good but the *sherry* was execrable. Fanny Becher looked very nice and lady like. She is by far the nicest [unmarried] girl in London. The Misses Gzowski looked very nice also and were very plainly and prettily dressed. Though nice cheerful good tempered girls, there was something about them I cannot describe what, that seems to negative what ought to be pleasing. The Becher's party was as good as they could give in London but it must be confessed that the general society is not of a very high tone. . . . I went to chaperone the last Miss Harris for the last time. I think it will be a *very long* time before I go to another party. . . .

Aug 6 . . . Teresa was not well and was in very low spirits. Mr Scott had said that he had asked his cousin Miss Beatrice Scott to live with them, and Teresa naturally enough did not like it. She said that when she came to know Miss Scott she might like her and be glad to have her with her but to be forced to live with a person that she might not like, who was much older than herself and who would feel herself entitled to approve or disapprove of whatever she did, was more than she would undertake to bear. She spoke to Mr Scott who drew in and said that he had only asked Miss Scott to be at Teviot Bank when she arrived and that most probably they would not remain a week there. I do not feel quite happy about her marriage and yet I know not what to object to. We cannot get a wedding dress from New York and I do

[108]The reference here is to undeveloped property. Amelia Harris had been awarded 200 acres at Port Ryerse as the daughter of a United Empire Loyalist. Her wild land holdings would principally have come to her from John Harris' will.

not know whether she will have one made of tulle or put off the wedding until the 1st of September. Helen and Teresa were both speaking to me about John's being dilatory in business. Helen says Mr Portman is much vexed because John has not made out his sister's accounts, and that unless John is more punctual in his accounts that both himself and Ld Portman will take their business out of his hands, and Teresa says that Mr Scott thinks him so procrastinating, that if George is equal to managing his investments he will give his money to him or otherwise he will employ a lawyer to search title and invest for himself. It made me feel very sorry. I do not know what John can be thinking of. If he cannot keep the accounts made up to the day he should employ assistance. People that place money in his hands have a right to know all about it. I am quite sure that Mr Becher will not manage it better for them. I believe John has done as well as it was in his power to do by *all* the money in his hands and that he is truly honest and upright. But it is unpardonable his not having his accounts ready when called for and made up punctually. They complain of Edward and he loses their confidence by never giving a satisfactory answer. Their hopes seem to rest upon George. I wish he would think less of cricket and look more after his bread.[109] It is not the loss that Harris and Brothers would sustain by the withdrawal of *their money*[110] but it would destroy all confidence and ruin the firm in that way. There is nothing but care, vexations and anxieties in this world. Oh that I could realize the happiness of a firm well grounded hope of a happy future.

Aug 13 I could not sleep very well toward the morning and waked up with one of those depressing feeling[s] that I used to have during my days of deep sorrow. I could not restrain myself from crying and to avoid waking Teresa I got up and went into the little spare bed room and on my knees I sought support and comfort from my Saviour. . . .

Aug 15 We had much trouble getting our things from the Customs House but Mr Strathy at last allowed them to pass by paying $6^1/_2$ dollars duties. . . . John is not well and not good humourd and when Teresa asked him if he would get her things from the customs he said he would *have nothing to do with them.* He did not say what was the fact that he had no time but that George would look after them, which

[109]George Harris had become an excellent cricketer and represented London in matches against Hamilton, Toronto and Brantford.

[110]A substantial proportion of the Harris Brothers' accounts involved the investments of members of the family resident in England, notably the Dalzells, the Peards, and Edward Knight, the first husband of Charlotte.

he did. Teresa was very much hurt. . . . Mr Scott wrote such a kind letter to me asking me to live with him and said that it would add so much to the happiness of himself and Teresa. Nothing could be kinder than this letter, and I am sure that he wishes what he says. John read the settlement and Mr Scott's will to me. He settles £10,000 Ster[ling] on Teresa which is left to her disposal to will if she survives him, and by his will should he die without children he leaves her the entire income of all his property during her life. At her death it is to go to some of his relatives. If she has one child she is to have £500 a year during her life besides her jointure. If more than one child, it is to be £300 a year for life. Nothing could be more liberal. John seemed very sad and out of spirit when he read the will to me before he went to bed. He and Teresa had had some cross words brought on by her asking Ellen Hamilton to the wedding. He said he would withdraw his name from being executor to the will and from being trustee in the settlement. I hope he will not as we all have entire confidence in him and he does not know how much his illness has changed him. . . . But whatever his words may be his acts are right. I many times think he has not a long life before him, and whom I have always looked to as the head and support of our house is now one cause of trouble and I know it all arises from ill health. But from whatever cause it arises it will make him unhappy when he is married, for a young wife naturally expects her husband to be cheerful, joyful and good tempered, and if they are not the natural feelings, they cannot long be assumed after marriage. . . .

Aug 16 Teresa's wedding dress arrived from Mrs Lyon's in Toronto. It is tulle very prettily trimmed with lillies of the valley and orange blossoms. . . . John and I had a long talk in the garden. He too feels unhappy and dissatisfied with himself and all around him but with him ill health is the cause of all. He wishes to do all that is right but his manner of doing things is often offensive, and he complains that we are all cross and that Edward's temper has become very disagreeable. I must speak to Edward. It has been strong family affection and a loving bearing and forbearing of each other's faults that has made our family what they are, and it is always best to look at things as they are, and let each one open their own eyes to what is wrong in themselves and endevour to correct it. . . . Being sour and discontented cannot improve our position let it be what it may. But good temper and smiling faces lightens the heaviest burdens. . . . It is said of some men that they will make more friends when refusing favors than others will in granting them, which is quite true. Some people make friends of all who know them, others may be liked very well until they are known when a selfish or uncourteous manner will make people lose sight of their better qualities. . . . Teresa is away *for ever*, never to be mine again. . . .

Aug 18 How wretched I felt this morning. I got up as soon as I could see and wrote to Sarah and Eliza. . . . I could only come into my room occasionally to see Teresa, and her spirits sank as the hour approached for her marriage and departure. Sophia came over to see us and then returned to the Griffins to dress. Mr Portman, Edward and George breakfasted with Mr Scott. The guests were punctual in their attendance at one o'clock but the ceremony did not take place until two. Teresa's spirits gave way altogether towards the last and it was some time before they could get her sufficiently composed to come downstairs. I saw the necessity of commanding my own feelings and did so to the best of my power but Teresa and Mr Scott pronounced their vows very feebly. She looked very nice. The breakfast was very good and pretty and went off well. There was a good deal of speechifying. Mr Scott returned thanks when the bride's health was drank and made a very good speech, and Edward spoke very well and amusingly when he returned thanks for the brides maids. Mr Becher proposed my health in a very kind and complimentary manner to me, but introduced the subject of the approaching marriage of John and Miss Loring and urged its taking place at once. Had he made a slight allusion to it it would have passed very well, but he dwelt upon it until it became painfully embarrasing to Miss Loring and all present. The brides maids were dressed in tarlatan trimmed with blue and they looked very pretty. They were Miss Loring, Sophia and Fanny Becher. . . . Our guests were Mr & Mrs Wilson, Mr & Mrs Becher, Mr King and Mr Wandesforde who arrived this morning and Miss Smith[111] who arrived a few minutes before the ceremony commenced. The clergyman, the brides maids and our own family made up the party. Mr Wilson sent his carriage to take them to the station and Mr Brydges gave them a car to themselves, which was very kind of him. Mrs Harris, the cook, threw an old shoe after them for luck and Teresa was gone. The Griffins and Mrs Widder came back to supper. I retired very early. Amelia, Helen, Mr Portman and Sophia were so kind to me. Sophia came and took Teresa's place in my bed. Mr Portman knew how sad I felt. He came in so affectionately the last thing and kissed and said good night. How wretched this world would be to us if there was no one to love us and for us to love. . . .

[111]Elizabeth Loring's aunt.

Aug 19 . . . I have always advised my sons to look at the mother before they made love to the daughters. . . .
Aug 21 . . . From my window I saw sitting on the terrace such a cheerful looking party Mr Portman, Helen, Mr Wandesforde, George and Amelia. I could not resist joining them. We voted ourselves a couple of bottles of champagne and some wedding cake. . . .
Aug 22 . . . Mr Portman telegraphed to Mr Scott to take a room for him at the Cataract[112] if Blondin[113] walked the rope again on Wednesday. Mr Scott answered, all right room taken. . . . Helen and the children have succeeded in having good photographs taken for Mr Wandesforde to paint from. . . .
Aug 23 . . . I had a long talk with Edward about the general ill humour that pervaded the house, which if not checked will not only destroy our domestic happiness, but destroy the family. Our strength has ever been in our unity. All admit that the evil complained of exists and that we are none of us exempt from blame. We cannot correct each other, but each one *can* correct themselves, and those bickerings and fault findings about each other must end. If we cannot commend we had better be silent and if we cannot live lovingly together we must separate and do so to *prevent* disagreeables and not wait until ill feeling is established. Now I know that our hearts are all right towards each other, but each one fancies some little petty grievance which would vanish like vapor before a general good humour. . . .
Aug 25 . . . [Mr Portman] says Mr Scott and Teresa are very spoony, and that she acts the spoilt child to perfection. She has never had money at her command before and I hope she may not become extravigant.
Aug 26 . . . I had a long talk with John and advised him to take a house for a couple of years at all events. The more I see little things developing themselves the more I am convinced that we should not all live happily here, and it is placing his young wife in a wrong position. She cannot come here and be head as long as I am equal to managing my own household, however willing I might be to resign in her favor. The other members of my family would not accept from her. . . . I do not like Mrs Loring and she would naturally wish to see her daughter often and her visits would always be an annoyance to me. John thinks that it will not be best for us to live together, but he wishes me to live

[112]A hotel at Niagara Falls.

[113]In 1859, Jean François Gravelet, more commonly known as "Blondin," was the first to cross the 2,000 feet wide Niagara Gorge by tight-rope, and was the first of many daredevils who attracted thousands to this famous tourist centre.

with my daughters and he live here. If I did so Edward and George would leave also and the family would be broken up. But I cannot leave my home, and feel truly thankful that one of my daughters and a son in law is willing to live with me and to take care of me in my old age. . . .
Aug 28 . . . After dinner John and Miss Loring came to my room and John told me that he had decided upon taking a house for a couple of years at all events. I felt very glad because I think it best. Mrs Loring will naturally wish to be with her daughter and when she becomes infirm it will be her daughter's bounden duty to take care of her and have her with her. I feel that I could not live with her and I too shall be glad to have *my daughters* to care for me as no one else can. A son, however kind he may wish to be, cannot be to a mother in her old age and illness what a daughter is. Nor can a daughter in law, however good, be expected to bear and forbear as one's own child, and yet it is painful to me to see John go. Blessed as I am . . . in *my* children, yet I can never be without anxiety and care.
Aug 29 Last night there was an aurora of unusual beauty which continued all night illuminating everything like a bright moonlight and changing colour from bright red to a milk-white. It radiated from the centre of the heavens. I got up several times in the night and looked out the windows, and could see the flowers in the garden and move about with ease in my room without a candle, although there was no moon. . . .
Aug 30 Mr Portman offered John a house to live in rent free for one year as a wedding present and we, that is Miss Loring, myself, Mr Portman and John, went to see the house and I believe John has decided upon accepting Mr Portman's offer. He thinks by expending £25 upon it that it will be more comfortable than any house he can get. . . .
Aug 31 . . . They [John and Miss Loring] have decided that they like the house the Griffins used to live in the best. I advised John not to think of himself for a moment, but to take any house which Miss Loring preferred. . . .
Sep 1 This morning Miss Loring and Miss Smith returned to Toronto. John escorted them down and will remain there a few days. We all like Miss Loring and believe that she will make John a good wife. . . . I shall not see Miss Loring again until she returns here a bride as I will not go to the wedding if I can avoid it. Weddings in my own family call forth many painful feelings to me that I shall be glad to make any excuse to remain at home. . . .
Sep 4 . . . He [John] has arranged that his marriage shall take place on

the 3rd of November. . . . I wrote to my brother George about Nancy [Cameron] who goes tomorrow to him to be treated for the dropsy. . . .
Sep 6 Amelia came this morning to take care of Helen. We were all very busy all the morning and fussing getting Helen ready to leave. They went by the 4 o'clock train and expect to be in New York tomorrow night. . . .
Sep 7 . . . Mr Wilson came to luncheon. He was in great good humor. He said some complimentary things of Edward and spoke very kindly of John. He was laughing at Sophia about getting married and said that I believed that marriages were made in heaven, but that his own was made in the other place. . . .
Sep 11 . . . Some evil person last night cut our cow in a most brutal manner. It looks like the full blow of an ax on the ham. We had to send for a cow doctor to sew it up. The poor animal seems to have lost half her flesh during the night. I did not think I had an enemy in the world that would have done me an injury. The family and servants suspect William Golby, my discharged servant, who when drunk is of a vile temper. Almost anyone but himself would be afraid of the dog. . . .
Sep 15 John continues very unwell. I am seriously alarmed about him, and doubt his living very long. Also there is Mr Griffin's debts. Amelia until today has been kept in ignorance of how much he owes, but as there was a prospect of his creditors suing him, John and Edward thought it necessary to tell her. Poor girl, how my heart ached for her. John and Edward have arranged that Mr Griffin shall live upon £300 a year until their debts are paid, and divide the remainder of his salary amongst his creditors. Poor Amelia will find £300 a year very little for their support and to educate the boys. She consented at once to sell her piano to meet a first payment and expressed her regret that she had not known from the first her true situation and I can do nothing to help her.
Sep 21 Sophia got a letter from her father, who is becoming anxious for her return, which I am not surprised at for he must be very lonely without her. She is a dear girl, and I have suffered much less at parting with Teresa than I should have done had she not remained with me. John asked me this morning about going to his wedding. Miss Loring has written as she had heard I did not intend to go. I would rather not go but will go if my staying away is to call down a remark but weddings in my own family have become painful to me as each marriage is a child gone. Although I am glad they are going to be married and *wish* them to marry yet I cannot help feeling that they are no longer mine, and that I am old and lonely. It is not selfishness for rather than have John's marriage broken off I would give up my home

and go anywhere. But about his wedding, Nancy being away, I felt that both Helen and I could not leave the children and that they would rather see her young and cheerful face there than mine, but we will make any effort rather that hurt anyone's feelings. . . .
Sep 23 . . . Sarah [Dalzell] has a daughter and is doing well, they call her Charlotte [Carrie] after dear Chasse. And I got a letter from Mary who very much to my surprise is going to have another child. . . .
Sep 26 . . . Amelia and Mr Becher came to see Miss Steers off. She returned to Louisiana to her charge as governess. Governesses in the southern states are much better paid for their services than in the North. Miss Steers gets $1,500 a year and $2,000 is not an unusual salary. In the north governesses never get more than $400 a year and very few so much. From $100 to $300 is the usual salary. Miss Steers possesses more energy than any woman I have ever met. She has struggled through poverty and lived for several years upon the smallest sum possible that she might have the more to give her father and mother. After their death she saved money that she might travel for a couple of years. She visited England and went the usual line of travel on the Continent. She perfected herself in French, studied German and Italian, and although she had learned singing from childhood and sang very well indeed, yet she took lessons in Italian singing. She acquired a speaking knowledge of the different languages that she studied as well as a reading knowedge. She is the best read woman I have ever met. . . .
Sep 27 . . . John is not well, never well. This evening he told me that he would *not pay* for the things which he told me to get at McInnes for Teresa amounting to $270. For an instant I felt myself in a position where I did not know how to turn as I would never incur a debt that I saw no means of paying. On this occasion I did not feel under any obligation to John as I knew that Mr Scott's investing would much more than pay for *all* that he gave to Teresa, and Ned told me that if Mr Scott would give *him* the £10,000 to invest, that he would not only give Teresa her trousseau but a couple of hundred pounds in her pocket. I had told John this, and he said of course he would give her all that she required, . . . I looked at him with sorrow, as I feel and know that ill health has destroyed the even balance of his mind. A few minutes afterwards, he denied more than half of what he had said and I am sure that *he believed* that he never had said what he did. He said of course Harris and Brothers would pay the bill, and spoke right and kindly of Amelia and Mr Griffin and expressed his conviction that Mr Griffin was *really* trying to pay his debts. How sad it makes me as the conviction daily comes that John's health is getting worse not better.

I dreamed a few nights ago that we were both travelling in the same carriage, that he got out first, that I drove a short distance and got out also. I many times think that his journey is near an end as well as my own. I know well that when he stops on the road I shall go but very little farther.

Sep 28 This morning when I spoke to Edward about Mr McInnes' bill I found that it was already paid, that John had paid it: how strange – he must have confused it with something else. His memory seems to fail him so very much. Edward got a letter from Mr Scott. They are still at New York, but intend coming home before they go to England. . . . Mr Portman is looking about the place and having everything cleaned, repaired and put in order. Eldon will look like a new place. . . .

Sep 29 John and I had a talk about a decisive arrangement being come to in the office as to what proportion of the profits each one was to have. John thinks he ought to have $1,000 a year more than Edward or $600 from the business and he himself retain the profits of the Registry to the Surrogate Court. My own opinion is, that it is about what he ought to have. Out of the rest of the profits to pay George $600 a year for two years and then the profits of the office to be divided equally between the three brothers, with the exception of the $1,000 a year extra to be paid to John. I am sure they will do much better together than they will separate and if the firm continues prosperous there will be a good living for them all. May God bless them and keep them united. . . . Sophia and Edward took a long walk. From all appearances I should think that Edward has serious thoughts of matrimony, and should feel very glad if he were out of debt, with a moderate income, just enough to support them. But it would be madness of him to think of marrying before he is out of debt. He would place himself in the position that Mr Griffin is in, which even a man blinded by love could not think pleasant. I like Sophia next to my own daughters and shall be glad to have her as a daughter but not to see her with the cares that Amelia has. Amelia came down in the evening and sat stitching while the rest of us were amusing ourselves. She would not let me give John's house linen to a workwoman but does it herself to earn some money. . . . She might better have lived and *died* as the engaged of Lord Stanley than accepted the fate that she has.[114]

Oct 1 After breakfast this morning Edward led me into his room and told me that he had proposed for Sophia and been accepted, and now

[114]In the fall of 1848, the son of the then Lord Stanley proposed to Amelia. See Chasse's diary 26 October 1848.

comes the anxiety whether her father will approve of it. I fear he will have difficulties in that quarter. I am so fond of Sophia and so pleased that Edward has chosen so well, that I shall use all my influence to arrange things with her father. Helen, Mr Portman and myself when discussing it thought it best that I should go to Toronto tomorrow or the next day and tell Dr Ryerson everything, make a statement of his debts and his prospects and get Dr Ryerson's sanctions or disapproval of any arrangements we wish to make. Edward wishes to be married in 6 months. To that I will not consent even if Dr Ryerson would, which I am sure he will not. *He, Edward, must* pay off that unfortunate debt which his land speculation has led him into before he marries and finds himself involved in expense which will take all his income. . . . Dr Ryerson is very fond [of] and very ambitious for Sophia, and did not like Edward when he was living in Toronto, and whether he will give his consent at all to the marriage is doubtful. I think they may both do worse than marry. Edward is a good tempered warm hearted young fellow who I think will make a good husband, and whose prospects are fair for making an independence. . . .

Oct 4 . . . Sophia got a letter from her father this morning telling her she had better return home as I was no longer alone, and we feel that it is better she should go. Since Edward has proposed to her, it is not right that she should remain here in hourly intercourse with Edward unless she had her father's sanction – and Edward does not wish to speak to him until he can lay a full statement of his affairs and prospects before him – which he intends doing when he goes to John's wedding. Sophia will return the end of this week without seeing Teresa.

Oct 7 . . . at the gate we met with the telegraph boy with a telegraph from Mr Scott to say that that they would be home by the 3 o'clock train. . . . Amelia called just before I went out and told me that Mr Griffin had been at St Thomas yesterday and that Mr Ermatinger had shown him some of the proof sheets of the life of the late Col Talbot, wherein Mr Ermatinger had spoken most disrespectfully of Mr Harris.[115] We are of course all very much hurt and annoyed that 9 years after he is in his grave, that his name should be brought forward in a way to hurt all our feelings. At first it was decided that I should write to him in a friendly manner and request to see the proof sheet where Mr Harris is mentioned and then request him to withdraw what is

[115]Edward Ermatinger's *Life of Colonel Talbot and the Talbot Settlement*, (1859) was rewritten by Ermatinger's son, C.O. Ermatinger, and published as *The Talbot Regime or The First Half Century of the Talbot Settlement*, (1904). The contentious section is to be found in pages 86–89 in the first volume, and in pages 144–45 in the second.

offensive to us, and if he should not do so for John, Edward, George and Mr Portman to go over and do the only thing left for them to do give Mr Ermatinger a horsewhipping. Mr Becher came to luncheon and we spoke to him about it. He said that he had known for several months what was going to be published, that he [Mr Becher] . . . had written to Mr Ermatinger condemning the remarks upon Mr Harris and others and advising him to withdraw those sheets, but Mr Ermatinger said it was too late now and that it could not be done. Mr Becher thought my writing to him would be useless but that Mr. Ermatinger's scurility was beneath our notice. I met Mr Wilson and told him about it. He said if it was him and his father that was spoken of disrespectfully that he would beat old Ermatinger within an inch of his life. Amelia came to dinner and felt disposed to go to St Thomas and endevour to see what had been written. The Scotts arrived at 3 o'clock. Teresa looks the same as when she went away, only improved and more womanly and she looks so happy. Mr Scott looks very tired and not very well but very happy and contented. I am so glad they came home before going to England. I now feel at rest and satisfied that Teresa has done a wise thing and got a good husband. She now is as fond of him as he is of her. . . .

Oct 8 I felt so happy and thankful this morning to again see so many of my children around my breakfast table. . . . Mr Griffin called. Teresa gave Amelia two twenty dollar gold pieces in place of a tea set of china which she had spoken of giving to her. Poor Amelia put her head on Teresa's shoulder and cried. Mr Griffin asked Mr Scott to take *up* the note which he had endorsed for £50 and begged of him not to tell John anything about it. How completely that system of falsehood destroys all confidence. John and Edward were endeavoring to arrange his difficulties and asked him to make a full statement of all his debts and Mr Griffin said he had done so, and then we discovered this £50 which he had borrowed of Mr Scott, and we cannot be at all sure that there are not more debts untold. Poor Amelia, what a fate to be tied to a man in whose words she can have no confidence. Mr Scott is so sorry for her.

Oct 10 . . . I wrote to Mr Ermatinger expressing my regret that one whom we had for many years considered as a friend should publish anything of Mr Harris that would hurt our feelings, and telling him how reluctant I was to believe it, and asking him to allow me to see the proof sheets in which Mr Harris' name is mentioned.[116] . . . John

[116]Amelia Harris' letter is in the Harris Papers.

got a letter from Col Phillott, who says there are to be two new Regiments raised in Canada and wishes to know whether George would like a commission in one of them. It is very kind of Col Phillott to look out for him, but his professional prospects are much better than any he would have in the Army. An Ensign with only his pay and no means of purchasing his steps[117] has not a very brilliant prospect before him.

Oct 14 . . . All the morning we were all very busy getting Teresa's things ready and her trunk packed. Amelia came early and remained until Teresa left. Mr Becher and Fanny came in when we were at dinner to say good-bye to the Scotts. . . . I have tried for the last two days to nerve myself for the parting hour with Teresa, and had strength given me to bear it pretty well, but with her young arms around my neck and her warm face to mine I felt that it might probably be our last embrace. If so I pray God to have her in his keeping and that we may meet in a better world. She has a kind good husband and every prospect of happiness in this. They left here at 4 PM. All at Eldon (excepting myself), the Griffins, Mr Becher and Fanny saw them off at the Station. John went with them as far as Hamilton. . . . How desolate a house looks after one of the household have left. There is the empty room, the vacant chair at the table, the fragments of discarded etc thrown about and the familiar step and cheerful voices no longer heard.

Oct 17 George left London for Hamilton by the six o'clock train to play the great cricket match with All England's Eleven. . . .

Oct 20 George came home by the night train, not at all cured of cricket. He made a very good catch and his play has been praised in the papers. One of the English cricketers said that anyone who could make that catch was worthy of playing with All England's Eleven. We cannot help feeling pleased that he was praised even for his play at cricket, and yet we think it would have been better for him had his play been a total failure. . . .

Oct 22 . . . The dentist (Stone) came and drew two teeth for me. He put some liquid which has lately been discovered for deadening pain around the gums, and it certainly had the effect, for I am sure that I felt much less pain than I should if it had not been applied. . . .

Oct 29 I was all the fore noon endevouring to write to Col Dalzell who fidgits too much about his money, which John has invested for him. It is all safe and well invested, but he is always fearing some-

[117]A reference to his prospects for promotion.

thing wrong if his accounts and remittances are not to the day. . . .
Oct 31 The weather looks a little less like January than it has done. They were enabled to have their boat race which has been postponed from week to week for fine weather. The prize was a pewter mug (the Club too poor to give silver), to each man in the winning boat. The first race the bets were 10 to 1 against the boat George was in. The second race 5 to 1. George's boat won all three races although he has never pulled an oar a dozen times in his life. He came home pleased because he had won when no one expected him to do so. He will have to give up these amusements. A man whose future independence depends upon his own exertions should have no time for them. . . . John came home in the evening . . . he says Elizabeth's wedding dress is the prettiest dress he ever saw. The lace veil cost $75. . . .
Nov 4 John and I had another talk about the Griffins. I told him I thought it would not be right of him to avail himself of the first excuse to sue Mr Griffin and secure himself, which he says he will do. Edward and John have induced other creditors to withdraw their executions and wait, Mr Griffin making such payments as he can quarterly. In failure of such payments they will then proceed against him. . . .
Nov 6 . . . Mr Becher is going to send me a pass to go to Toronto to John's wedding. . . .
Nov 7 . . . Edward told me that John and him had a long talk last evening about their affairs and that John had proposed that his liabilities, Edward's and mine should all be assumed by the firm of Harris and Brothers and that my wild lands, Edward's St Thomas property and all lands that John has purchased in his own name should be held by the firm as common property and that when they could each make in the firm £500 a year that the £250 which he was to have according to the first arrangement with Edward is to be given up and they are to share alike and that in a year or two George is to come in on equal terms. . . .
Nov 8 . . . The Bishop, George and myself went with Mrs Becher and Fanny in the Director's car. . . . We read, had luncheon, and talked at our ease all the way to Toronto. . . . When we arrived in Toronto we found Helen and Sophia at the station waiting for us, with Dr Ryerson's carriage. . . . George went to the Rosser House. Dr and Mrs Ryerson appeared very glad to see me. Immediately after dinner Dr Ryerson and myself went to the Library, and I spoke to him about Edward and Sophia. I stated Edward's hopes and fears and prospects as nearly as I could. He did not say any thing for some time and then laid great stress upon Edward's deafness, which precluded all hope of his ever taking part in political life, and in the end decided that it was

rather an advantage than a disadvantage to keep clear of politics. Sophia was in a state of great agitation to know what her papa would say. I told her that I could not say positively what his decision would be but that I did not anticipate much opposition. . . .

Nov 9 . . . The morning wet and very gloomy. Dr Ryerson met me early and said that he had thought over all about Edward and Sophia and would give his consent to their marriage, that is when he [Edward] is free or nearly free from debt. I thanked him and when Edward came in a few minutes afterwards, I told him what Dr Ryerson had said. He then spoke to Dr Ryerson himself and then to Mrs Ryerson. Mrs Ryerson showed a good deal of feeling and could not speak of Sophia's leaving without crying. She told us that Sophia was extravagant in her ideas and that she was afraid that Edward would not find it as easy to support a wife as he imagined. . . . The bride went through the service very well and looked rather more self possessed than John did. Her dress was Honiton lace and very pretty, only a little too much colour. I would rather see a bride pale than flushed. Her dress and veil cost about £70 Sterling. They were married by the Bishop of Huron assisted by the Revd Mr Stinson,[118] a gentleman that I do not like. I should think there were a hundred people at the breakfast, nearly all of the elite of Toronto. There was scarcely standing room and yet the breakfast went off very well. Everything was very nice. John got through his speech pretty well and Edward caused the people to laugh but I could not hear what he said. Dr Ryerson returned thanks for the mothers of the bride and bride groom and complimented us very highly. The Bishop took in the bride to breakfast and John took in the bride's mother. J.H. Cameron as host took in Helen and Sir James Macaulay[119] took me in. Mrs Loring had all the presents laid out for inspection in the drawing room and the things were very pretty. But *we the Harris'* would have preferred not making a display of them. . . . When we returned to Dr Ryerson's Helen was fatigued and ill and had to pack up to return to London by the 4 o'clock train. Edward felt very happy that all was arranged with Sophia. Both he and George went home with Helen. They could not be away from the office. . . . About 12 miles from Toronto, John and his

[118]Joseph Stinson (1802–62), an English Methodist leader who presided over the Canadian Conference (1858–72). He was an active and influential participant in the development of Methodism in Upper Canada. See G.S. French, "Joseph Stinson," *Dic. Can. Biog.* IX, pp. 749–751.

[119]Sir James Macaulay (1793–1859), Chief Justice of the Court of Common Pleas (1849–56) and a judge of the Court of Error and Appeal (1856–59).

bride joined them [Edward, George] they had driven that far. They stayed at Hamilton that night.

Nov 11 . . . After dinner Blanche Widder asked Sophia to go to her room with her and when there she asked her to tell her whether it was true that she was engaged to Edward or not. Sophia told her she was. Blanche was silent for a moment and then kissed her and wished her every happiness. We both felt sorry for Blanche as we felt quite sure that she herself likes Edward. When we came away she told Sophia to remember that she was to be brides maid.

Nov 16 . . . Becher came to luncheon. He remarked to me about Amelia's looking so very unhappy, and asked if it was Mr Griffin's embarassments that fretted her. I said yes. He said how absurd that thousands of people were in debt and got over it, that it entailed no disgrace. So I should say if Mr Griffin's conduct had been truthful and upright. . . .

Nov 21 Mr Griffin left for England this day. He goes to Chicago first and takes the mail through and is to sail from Portland [Maine] on Saturday. Early today I commenced sending up John's property and at one o'clock I went to his house to unpack and arrange and came home at night very tired. . . .

Dec 1 We got a telegraph from John saying that they would be at home at 5 o'clock. . . . John is looking much improved in health, Elizabeth was looking very well but very tired. . . . They dined with us and then took possession of their own house. It seemed so strange to see John go away to another home. . . .

Dec 4 I got a letter from Mary who wants her brothers to draw up a settlement which Shuldham is willing to make upon her and her children. He had not the means of making a settlement when he married and now she is afraid she may not survive her approaching confinement. . . .

Dec 8 John and Elizabeth came to breakfast. Elizabeth wanted to see how my omelets were made as her cook's were a failure. . . .

Dec 10 Elizabeth came this morning to arrange about going to Church tomorrow. She is afraid that John will not be well enough to go. . . . Dr Ryerson arrived at 5 PM. . . .

Dec 11 I went with Dr Ryerson to a little Methodist chapel in the outskirts of the town. . . . He is an eloquent and sound Preacher but he did not know the congregation that he was to address and his sermon *probably* was not appreciated as highly as it would have been had it been delivered in the Church in North Street. His appearance in the pulpit is most pleasing and one feels that what he says comes from his heart. . . .

Dec 12 . . . [Mr Portman] came home tired and hungry having travelled all night. Berkeley is so fond of his father. He seems content to show his own love even when his papa does not notice him. He will pat and kiss his forehead, hang about his neck or run between his legs when standing up. . . .

Dec 18 . . . I got a letter from Eliza and Edward got one from Mary. They make a good many remarks about Mr Scott and his want of manner. They are severe upon his lying upon the sofa in the drawing room and his coming to dinner with *a net string* around his neck in the place of a white tie, and also about coming to breakfast in slippers after two days acquaintance. Poor Mr Scott has not passed muster very well. . . .

Dec 21 . . . Teviot Bank is to be sold on the 11th of next month at auction, and Mr Scott expects to be able to send early in May £25,000 for Harris and Brothers to invest, which will be a great thing for them. . . .

Dec 23 . . . Mrs Sewell wanted her daughter to come up with Amelia [from Toronto] but Amelia had the courage to tell her that Mr Griffin was too much involved for her to increase their expenses in the least, and that she could not invite anyone to visit her. I was very glad that she had the courage to tell the *truth.* As I looked at Amelia I felt the full force of a parable in Scripture and thought she was a precious jewel in a *swine's snout.* Poor girl, I pray God that her trials in this world may lead her to lay up treasures in Heaven. Sophia looked so nice, and so happy.

Dec 24 . . . [Amelia] had a long talk with Mr Portman about Mr Griffin and his affairs. . . . she cried as if her heart would break and said she had been some days with only one meal a day and yet she would not come home for her meals. All the money she gets she pays out until she has not a shilling left to buy food. Mr Portman told her *he and we* did not like Mr Griffin and would not give money for his support, but that she should share in any and every thing belonging to any of us. She does not know how he has spent his money. . . . She said Mr McInnes signed a check and told her to fill it up for any sum that she might need. How kind of him, when he is already a loser of $700 and knows what a vagabond Mr Griffin is. We all feel so sorry when we look at her. She [is] such a favorite with every one and so gentle, so agreeable and so kind and good, and to think of all the family that she is the one unhappy one. Melancholy thoughts for Christmas Eve when I have so much to be thankful for.

Dec 25 A lovely morning. Sophia gave me a very pretty sachette. I gave the servants dresses and there was a general giving of little presents. Helen told me that Mr Portman had last night given Amelia a check for $50. Helen told him she would rather he gave it to Amelia than her. He would not give her anything as long as she lived with Mr Griffin, but that he would not talk with her and keep his promise. It is a large present and very, very kind of Mr Portman. . . . All from Eldon went to Church this morning except myself. . . .

Dec 28 Mr Wilson and Mr Becher came to luncheon. We were discussing Mr Ermatinger's *Life of Col Talbot*[120] in which Mr Wilson has been mentioned in not the most flattering way. . . .

Dec 30 When at breakfast this morning, Amelia sent a message that she wished Edward to come and see her. It frightened me so that I did not get over it the whole day. I knew she must have some fresh trouble. . . . We have discovered that Mr Griffin has borrowed 60 dollars off Mr King, $600 off Mr Ritchie. No one can tell where his debts end. Their things will be sold for taxes very soon if not paid. . . . Amelia dined with us. Our dinner was nice, but Edward acquitted himself very badly at the head of the table, and neglected our guests so much that it spoiled our dinner. I felt very vexed. After dinner we played monte and whist.

Dec 31 . . . and so ends the year 1859 and great are the changes in the Harris family. During the year, Teresa married and gone. John married and in a separate establishment, Edward engaged and to be married in a few months, the Portmans given up the intention of living in the South and have arranged to live with me during my life. Business prosperous and every thing satisfactorily arranged in a partnership with my three sons. How much to be thankful for, and yet there is a heartache remaining. My poor Amelia's future looks dark indeed. I can see nothing before her but poverty, disgrace, and wretchedness caused by a worthless husband. I pray God to give her strength to bear her hard lot and I hope her troubles in this world will cause her to lay up treasures in the next.

1860

Jan 1 Sunday the thermometer 10 below zero. Miss Widder, Sophia and Edward went to the Church. I was afraid to venture out. I asked John and Elizabeth to dinner but they declined on account of the cold. John came and sat with me for some time. Amelia came after dinner. . . . I left Edward and Sophia in the drawing room, the rest of the party in the sitting room and came to my room. . . .

[120]See Amelia's entry for 7 October 1859.

Jan 5 . . . Something was wrong between Edward and Sophia. They both looked unhappy but Edward looked miserable. Helen spoke to him. He said he did not know what was wrong with Sophia but that her manner was quite changed towards him. Helen told him that Sophia was equally unhappy, that she was crying whenever she was alone. Helen when she came upstairs sent Sophia down to him. I hope Sophia will not prove of a sullen stubborn temper. It would make him very unhappy. He cannot cherish anger long, nor could he bear it from another. If he thinks that I am not pleased with him he will come to me and ask if I am angry with him and what for. He is unhappy if he imagines there is the least unkind feeling towards him and if his wife should wear a cold manner to him for three or four days at a time I do not know what the effect would be upon him but certainly not good. He would not mind a quick temper, who said *all* and *more* than they thought, and then kiss and make friends. He is one of the best tempered fellows I have ever known although he possesses keen sensibilities.

Jan 9 . . . I thought a good deal about Sophia's having shown so much temper to Edward, and at last decided that I would speak to her. When she is once married I could say nothing. I told her she was wrong and advised her as she valued her own happiness and the happiness of her husband never to go to sleep angry nor never let her husband leave the house estranged from her, that very few men would bear a sullen disposition, and that I was sure Edward would not, that if she had cause for vexation to express her displeasure and then let it be over. She took what I said in very good part and acknowledged that she had been wrong, and I hope she may be more guarded in the future. I think she is of a good disposition but she felt a little jealous of Edward's attentions to Blanche [Widder] and then she could not get over Edward's ungallant speech when they came late to the dinner, *that* he could see what had detained Blanche but could *not see* what had detained Sophia (who was not so immaculately dressed). . . .

Jan 10 . . . When Sophia comes to London again it will be as a bride and I hope she may be a happy one and make her husband happy – his wife ought to be kind and good, to soften his affliction of deafness, and I hope she may be more than hearing to him. . . .

Jan 11 Edward was invited to dine with the John's today and as I had not yet been there I thought I would go with him. Mr Portman told John what I intended and he invited the Portmans and Amelia. Elizabeth called and invited Nancy to go and attend upon the table as her own servant is very awkward so that we made up a family party. It was very strange to the cook to have *no* dinner to get at Eldon. John's house and house keeping shows an inexperienced housekeeper, she will learn after a time how much happiness as well as comfort depend upon trifles. . . .

Jan 14 . . . When any thing is said that hurts Edward it pains me as much as it does him. From his deafness he cannot understand half that is said and very often makes inapplicable remarks, but if he had his hearing as the others have theirs there is not one of the family that could get the better of him, for he has natural wit and a quick apprehension. He works hard and encounters many disagreeables in the office during the day. At home I have always endevourd to cheer and encourage him, and have had the gratification of feeling that his conduct in the Office and out of it is just, generous and honorable and may a mother's best blessings rest upon him.

Jan 17 I got a letter this morning from Shuldham telling me of the birth of a son and Mary doing well. . . .

Jan 20 Edward wrote to Sophia disapproving of her dancing five times in one evening with her former admirer, Mr Killaly[121] and then allowing him to walk home with her and her cousin Enid Duggan. Edward wrote a very kind but a very proper letter to her, as her flirting manner is neither creditable to her nor to him. . . .

Jan 22 . . . Edward got a letter from Sophia in answer to the one which he wrote to her. . . . She is sorry and mortified and a little vexed, but I think she will be more guarded in the future. She wishes to do right but is very fond of admiration. . . .

Jan 24 . . . Mr Becher called and wants me to go to his reading of a selection from Thackeray's and Dickens' works on Thursday evening.[122] . . .

Jan 25 . . . Edward frightened me so much about John's state of health that I have not yet got over it. Edward said they, the three brothers, went on the ice to skate and Elizabeth went with John to look on. She spoke to Edward about John and said she could not help feeling very much alarmed about him. He had not had one well day in the last fortnight. Edward told me that he had had the same feeling for some time, that John was getting worse, and what can be done for him.

[121]One of the sons of Hamilton Hartley Killaly (1800–74) who was M.P. for London (1841–44), member of the Executive Council (1841–43), Chairman of the Board of Works (1841–46), Assistant Commissioner of Public Works (1851–59) and Inspector of Railways (1859–62).

[122]According to Becher's diary, he and Thackeray were distant cousins. See M.A. Garland and O. Miller (eds.), "The Diary of H.C.R. Becher," *Ont. Hist. Soc., Papers and Records* XXXIII, 1939, pp. 116–143.

Edward told Elizabeth to keep him from the office as much as she could, not to let him come until late in the day, and then to call for him early in the afternoon. It sent me to bed with a heartach[e]. . . .
Jan 31 . . . After tea we had a dull game of casino, got up to please me because they thought I was vexed because they played without me the previous evening. I played because I knew they would think I was cross if I did not. Amelia played (when she wished to go home with the children) to make up a table for me. Mr Portman played because others played though he only cares to play with Helen, so the game of casino was not very bright, every body played because they thought they ought to. . . .
Feb 2 . . . I did not feel altogether content with what Dr Ryerson[123] seemed to expect from Edward. His ideas seem large. He thinks Parke's house is the only house fit for him to take that he has seen. At the same time he gives Sophia *nothing* to commence with excepting her piano. At the same time he appears to expect her to walk into a good establishment, although we have told him that Edward has everything to make by his own industry, and for them to live quietly and economically for several years is *absolutely* necessary to their future welfare. Dr Ryerson told me that both Mr & Mrs Widder would be very glad if George would propose for Blanche. I told Dr Ryerson that I liked Blanche but that George could not think of marrying for three or four years but if people would only let things take their course such a thing might come to pass as his proposing for her.
Feb 6 I went to see Elizabeth and found her in bed but better. She is very anxious about John's health and wants him to spend the next winter in Rome. She proposes that Edward shall go into their house and live during their absence in place of taking a house and furnishing it for himself. . . .
Feb 7 Mr Portman and Helen drove out to the farm. I got a note from Elizabeth again urging the necessity of John's going away for change of air and rest from work. John called for a few minutes and seemed rather surprised at the way we were disposing of him and his house. . . .
Feb 10 . . . Mr Griffin did not come home until 12 today. . . . Edward came to me and asked whether it would not be best for him to go and see Mr Griffin, that he had to speak to him on business and he thought it would be better to keep on speaking terms. I told him to act for

[123]Dr. Ryerson was visiting at Eldon for several days while attending school conventions at London and St. Thomas.

himself and do what he felt was right. Both him and George went to the Griffins in the evening, but did not look very cheery when they returned and had very little to tell. At all events they told very little. . . .

Feb 12 . . . Mr Portman got a very civil note from Mr Griffin, sending him the half of a Stilton cheese. Amelia had asked him if he would accept it from her and Mr Portman said he would but today it came altogether from Mr Griffin. Of course Mr Portman wishes to have as little to say or [do] with him as possible. At the same time on Amelia's account he dislikes to treat Mr Griffin as he otherwise would, but Mr Griffin has too little delicacy and is too pushing to give Mr Portman up easily. Mr Portman did not answer the note and had not decided whether he would accept the cheese or return it when in walked Mr Griffin and Amelia on their return from evening service. He shook Mr Portman's hand most cordially and was so sorry he, Mr Portman, was not in when he had called the day before, and hoped he would accept the cheese, was sorry he could not send him a whole one. Mr Portman took the cheese but went to his room as soon as he could make his escape. . . .

Feb 19 The 62nd anniversary of my birthday. I went to Church with Helen and Mr Portman in their sleigh. The Bishop preached on charity. Edward called at the John's and said that he is going to Toronto on Tuesday to return on Thursday. . . . The Griffins called on their way from Church (evening Service) and had supper, he goes tomorrow to Chicago. I wrote to Mary.

Feb 20 . . . On Saturday evening Edward very foolishly by way of bullying George accused him of cheating at casino. George and Mr Portman were playing together. George denied the accusation and I scolded Edward for making it. Mr Portman said he would not play with him again. After they all left the room I told Edward that an accusation of false play should never be made at cards. Though we do not play for money, even if the accusation was true the only notice a gentleman should take of it would be not to play again with the misbehaving party. He said he was only bullying George. I thought he ought to be as gentleman like to his brother as to any one else if not more so. I had lectured Edward and thought there was an end of it. But this evening when I proposed a game of casino Mr Portman said no, he was not going to play. I felt so hurt and sorry that I could not say a word. What little things disunite families, and I feel that I am the cause of this break, for I have encouraged our playing and have several times had my doubts whether I was right, as it was keeping George from reading. . . . Edward comes home tired with office work and after dinner sleeps on the sofa, taking cold, and I thought casino would amuse him as well as myself. But I have been wrong and my intellect is not and must not depend upon cards even for the amusement of an hour. So good-bye casino.

Feb 27 Mr King called this morning and appeared a good deal excited. He wished to see Mr Portman at the office and they went away together. Helen and myself wondered what was up. After some time Mr Portman returned and told us they wanted him to stand for the East Riding of the County of Middlesex, which he has consented to do should Mr [Marcus] Talbot resign his seat or should it be true that [he] is lost on Board the ill-fated *Hungarian*.[124] Mr King, Mr Whitehead and several others have already commenced a canvas for him. I cannot say that I am glad that he is going to enter public life nor do I know that I am sorry, yet I doubt whether it will lead to their happiness. They have so much now to make them happy that it seems like a venture in which they may lose more than they can gain. Yet he is young and needs employment. . . .

Feb 28 When Mr Portman came to breakfast this morning he was rather out of conceit of standing for Member, and some letters which he received from Col Hampton about renting and purchasing his plantation decided him upon withdrawing from the list of candidates, . . .

Feb 29 . . . George told us when he came to luncheon that Mr Griffin's things would be sold today for taxes. . . . No help that John or Edward could give him would save him from ruin. No reliance can be placed upon his word or his principles. Edward went to see Amelia after dinner. . . . Edward thinks she does not know anything about the probability of their things being sold for taxes. . . .

Mar 3 I was ill all night. I dreamed about dear Chasse & thought she was at home with me looking as gentle and loving as she always was. I thought she had been engaged to Capt Knight but had been estranged from him for some time but was endeavouring to win him back again, and he because Chasse had cast him off had devoted himself to other ladies but was willing to return to her and with the inconsistency of dreams I knew that Chasse was dead and that I saw him [Knight] for the first time since her death and that he looked so strange. He was dressed in black evening dress, with knee breeches, black silk stockings and dress shoes and his face looked nearly as black as his dress. We did not speak. This was a dream of indigestion, and it is the only time I have dreamed of Chasse since I heard of her death. I would be

[124]An Atlantic steamer recently reported lost at sea. Marcus Talbot (1831–60), elected M.P. for East Middlesex in 1857, was on board and was drowned.

willing to be ill another night to have the same dream of her. . . . Mr Becher called. He has just returned from Quebec. He is going to offer himself as a candidate for the East Riding of Middlesex, but he said if Mr Portman would stand he would withdraw. Mr Portman said he would not stand, but he did not know that he could support Mr Becher as he stood pledged to support the candidate nominated by his party and unless Mr Becher should be the man named he could not support him. Mr Becher is [the] one who ought to go, he has the interest of this part of the country at heart and he stands well with the government. I do not know how it is but he does not stand well with the general class of voters. Mr Portman, though a stranger, stands very much better, and it is thought would be returned almost without opposition if he would consent to go. The Great Western wish to get Mr Becher in the House to advocate their interests. . . .

Mar 5 The electioneering still continues. A large number of conservatives insist upon Mr Portman's standing. Many of Mr Becher's friends who would prefer him think it useless to bring him forward as he could not get in and it would be the means of returning a Grit.[125] Mr Adams[126] is making himself very busy with Mr Portman's private character and says that he dare not return to England. If Mr Adams was worthy of notice he would get a horse-whipping. . . . Berkeley[127] had his cap and cloak on and was allowed to play in the garden but by some means he got the gate open and made for Dundas St. It was not very long before he was missed, and after searching about the garden Helen thought Mr Portman must have taken him with him, but sent the servant man to see. Mr Portman returned quickly but had not seen the child. We then became alarmed and commenced a search for him in earnest. Helen heard that he had been seen at the upper end of Dundas Street, and Mr Portman found him on the track of the railway. John, Edward and George and myself were all in search of him and met Mr Portman with him and he handed him over to me and ran home to tell Helen that he was found as we were afraid of the consequences with her in her situation. Master Berkeley was as happy as a king and had enjoyed his run wonderfully. . . .

[125]The "Grits" or "Clear Grits" were one of several reform-minded political factions in the late 1850s and early 1860s from which the the Liberal Party developed. The modern Conservative Party in Ontario can be said to have derived from an alliance of several "Tory" factions and other regional interests in the mid-1850s.

[126]Probably the man referred to in Amelia Harris' diary 16 March 1859 as the commentator on the length of Bayard Taylor's lecture.

[127]Maurice Portman's two year old son.

Mar 6 . . . Mr Becher vexes us by being quite sure of his election when everyone else says he will not get in. He says it is unnecessary to take any trouble, that he thinks that there will be no difficulty, that he is sure of being returned. His absurd security makes even his friends lukewarm. Today there has appeared in the *Globe* a letter from a sister of Mr Talbot regretting that she could not get ready to come out with her brother in the *Hungarian* so that there is no longer a doubt about Mr Talbot's being drowned, poor fellow. . . .
Mar 7 . . . They are all excitement about the election. Mr Becher is coming out tomorrow with his address. He brought it here this evening for us to see. It is a very good address and noncommittal. I never saw anyone so deceived about their own popularity. He thinks people will be but too happy to have the opportunity of returning him. He will not electioneer and will not ask anyone to electioneer for him, . . .
Mar 8 Mr Portman was away early this morning electioneering for Mr Becher and was very successful excepting at Bricksville where they tore up Mr Becher's address. . . .
Mar 9 . . . Mr Portman is very busy electioneering for Mr Becher. I dislike elections and have good reason to do so as at the Township elections the Radicals made it the test with their candidates that they would not support Mr Harris in office because he was a Conservative. . . .
Mar 10 . . . Mr Portman met Mr Whitehead who told him that the Conservatives were holding a meeting at a tavern and that they would not have Mr Becher at any price, and that they had met him to again request Mr Portman to come forward and if he would *not* do so, they would get someone else. Mr Portman came back to the house to ask what he had best do. Helen is very reluctant that he should come forward at this election, but as we all rather wish him to do so at the next, we do not think it would be wise for him to offend all his supporters, and if they brought forward another candidate they would feel in honor bound to support him at another election. Taking all these things into consideration Mr Portman decided upon standing and called at Mr Dunns to tell Mr Becher the state of affairs and that he had agreed to stand if he got the nomination at the Convention. If Mr Becher got the nomination he would give him all of his support. Mr Becher seemed very much surprised and said it was very extraordinary. . . . Mr Becher's conduct has ever been honorable and upright, and his worst enemy can only say that his manner is finikin and that they do not like him and will not have a lawyer. I feel sorry for Mr Becher. He is the man that ought to [stand]. He is an old resident, a good Man of Business, Honorable, and has the interest of this part of the country at heart. At the same time I cannot help feeling pleased at the very

great compliment paid to Mr Portman, who has only decided upon making Canada his home within the last year and who is very young and almost totally unknown to the voters. . . . Mr Portman's conduct had been open and honorable. But as we did not wish the shadow of a doubt to exist in the minds of any one on the subject we wished to get the opinion of some disinterested person on the subject. We of course thought of Mr Wilson although he was named as an opposing candidate, but we knew that that would not prevent his seeing things as they would appear to others and giving a correct opinion and one that might be relied upon, and we were not disappointed. He said there was no injustice to Mr Becher or anyone else, if he accepted a nomination, his party having refused Mr Becher and insisted upon his standing. He advised Mr Portman not to send out an address until after the nomination nor to make his appearance in the electioneering field but to write a letter to some of his leading supporters giving a summary of his political views and have a number of lithographed copies so that his supporters might have something to show to the voters that they might know in some measure what the views are of the man they are asked to support, and then if he is nominated to come into the field with all his energy, not lukewarmly. Mr Portman will take his advice. . . .
Mar 11 . . . After dinner Mr Portman and John drove out to Becher's and told Mr Becher what he was going to do, and that if Mr Becher got the nomination he would support him. Mr Becher said he would not try for the nomination, but should stand independently of it. Mr Portman told him that he hoped he would believe that he had electioneered for him in all sincerity without any intention of standing himself. Mr Becher said, of course, my dear Sir, of course. He had not the slightest feeling about it if Mr Portman could reconcile it to himself. I did not like the expression as it showed but too plainly that Mr Becher was annoyed. . . .
Mar 13 Mr Portman went out early and did not return until near six o'clock. . . . He was told that some worthless vagabonds were attacking his private character. I cannot help noticing the difference in people's manner before Mr Portman consented to come out. A very many people urged him to come forward and said the country would support him, that Mr Becher was unpopular and could not get in, that he was disliked for his manner and that they would not have a lawyer and that Mr Portman had only to say that he would stand, and he would be returned without any doubt or difficulty. But now the tone seems a good deal changed and many whose support was spoken of as decided and positive are now considered doubtful. But such is the world. . . .
Mar 17 Mr Portman was out all day with electioneering friends. About

5 o'clock he sent Helen a note that he had to go to St John's to a meeting. Edward and John went also. . . . [They] did not return until past 11 PM. They were very much excited. Mr Becher made a violent attack upon Mr Portman and made statements which were not correct and Mr Portman told him they were *false*. . . . The meeting terminated very much in Mr Portman's favor and although he feels very grateful to his many friends, yet he will avail himself of the first good opening to retire. He had no idea he would have to submit to the abuse and misstatement that meet him in every turn. . . .

Mar 19 . . . Amelia called on her way to attend a meeting of ladies to consult about making up a purse for the Rev Mr McLean [St. Paul's]. Some propose giving him a silver inkstand. We think it would be much better to give a curate who has but £100 a year the money. He can do very well without a silver inkstand.

Mar 21 At 1 o'clock this morning Mr Portman awakened me and said that Willy had the croup. I hurried out of bed, we sent for Doctor Anderson and put the child in a warm bath. The Dr prescribed for him and remained until he was better, and then went home and I again went to bed. In a very short time Mr Portman came to me again and told me that Helen was ill. I again hurried out of bed, dressed myself, and found it was 4 o'clock. The doctor was again sent for and at a quarter past 5 the child was born. A fine boy, weighing 8½ pounds without clothes. Helen is wonderfully well, there was a shadow of disappointment as to the sex of the child, as we all wished for a daughter, but . . . he was as warmly welcomed and thankfully received as if he had been a girl. Amelia came and remained during the day. John, Elizabeth and Mr Griffin called. Mr King called to inquire, to congratulate and to urge Mr Portman to attend *if possible*, a meeting of Militia men and voters. . . . [Several] friends had promised that Mr Portman would go there, so that the constituency could see and become acquainted with the man they were asked to vote for. . . .

Mar 22 The doctor called, Helen is going on well. Elizabeth called and saw Helen. Amelia sat with us until 4 o'clock. Mr Portman went to the meeting in Westminster. John and Elizabeth came to dinner and then Mr Portman, John, Edward and George went to an election meeting. . . . Mr Griffin gave a Shakespeare reading in the Mechanics' Institute. . . . He reads well and the house was crowded. Helen and Baby both doing well.

Mar 23 . . . Mr Becher assuring me of his continued regard for me, . . . I answered it assuring him of my unchangeable affection for him, . . . Helen was very well until 5 PM when there was a little appearance of milk, cold chills were followed by fever and violent afterpains. In the course of two hours we sent for the doctor three times. He gave her some medicine which relieved the severe pain and I went to bed hoping she would sleep.

Mar 24 The opium Helen took deadened the pain but kept her from sleeping and she felt very feeble and miserable this morning. We had to send for the doctor again this evening to check the effects of the oil she had taken. I hope she will be better tomorrow. Mr Portman did not leave her today, though people urged him to attend meetings, he would not go. Edward wrote a capital parody upon Mr Becher's address, it is very clever and a great success, written in gentlemanly style and not offensive to anyone. . . .

Mar 25 . . . Helen is a little better but very weak and listless and without appetite. . . .

Mar 26 . . . Helen appeared better this morning but very nervous and restless.

Apr 15 I now must write my journal as I best can from memory.[128] Such weeks of sorrow and despair the heart can only feel, words cannot express. On Monday the 26th we hoped that she was better. She always seemed a little better in the morning. I had asked Dr Anderson the evening before what I should give Helen to eat she had lost all appetite and refused every thing. I had offered her during the day some chicken broth, but she had refused it and had taken nothing but toast [and] water. She would not touch gruel nor any light nourishment that I could offer her. He told me to give her a piece of chicken in the morning. I asked if a little mutton chop would not be better and easier of digestion. He said, yes, perhaps it would, and that I had better give her the mutton chop. Late in the evening of Sunday night she consented to drink some barley water.

On Monday thinking she was better about 10 o'clock I took her a little mutton chop. She cut it, minced it, took a little in her mouth, but said she *could not eat it*, that she could not choke it down, and told the nurse to take it away. I then had a custard baked and brought it to her. She tasted it and shoved it away, she could not eat it, it was so sweet. I asked her if she thought she could eat a little boiled rice. She thought she could but when it was brought she could not even taste it. Amelia came with a little chicken broth which was almost a jelly and some arrowroot that was made very nice. The doctor came very soon after. Amelia asked him if Helen might take the broth. He said no, she required something more solid. She told him it was the essence of chicken and asked him to taste it, which he did, and oh yes that is just the thing for her. He then looked around and saw the tray and said,

[128]After a long interlude, Amelia recounts the events of Helen's illness and death.

have you been giving her meat, although he had told me the night before to do so. I said I had taken her meat but she could not eat it. He then went in to her room and said she was going on all right and that there was not the slightest cause for any uneasiness about her. She told him she had tried to eat some chop but could not choke it down. Notwithstanding the doctor's assurance I was dreadfully alarmed and my anxiety was to be seen in my face. The doctor told Amelia that Helen was only nervous and must be kept quiet and that I *must* be kept out of the room, that my anxious looks would injure her. I told Amelia that I did not betray my feelings before her. Amelia said Mamma your face is perfectly frightful. You must not go in. . . . She was taken with dysentry during the day and she disliked anyone attending to her but myself on those occasions, and it was only when required that I saw her this day, but I observed and remarked to the doctor that she kept folding the sheets and arranging the bed clothes just as her Papa did the day before he died. The doctor was sent for as soon as the dysentry commenced, he gave her opiates, I believe, which partially checked it. Her face was very flushed and she was very restless, but the doctor assured us she was doing very well and going on all right. Late in the evening he gave her some more medicine, some thing to soothe, he said.

[March 27] She slept a little and on the morning of the 27th we were again told that she was better and going on all right, and we tried to believe what we were afraid to doubt. But when I saw her altered face, the deep purple under her eyes, her flushed face, and her pulse at 128, I went to the library and told Mr Portman he must telegraph for Doctor Hodder, a well known doctor in Toronto.[129] Amelia came downstairs while I was speaking and said Helen would like to have Hodder. He was telegraphed for immediately. We hoped he might catch the evening train and be here at 9 o'clock, but he did not get the telegram in time and answered that he could not be here until the next day. I then said, send for Doctor Brown.[130] We cannot have her die with only Doctor Anderson to attend her.

[129]Edward M. Hodder (1810–78) maintained a large practice in Toronto and was professor of Midwifery and Diseases of Women and Dean of the Faculty of Medicine, University of Trinity College. See W.G. Cosbie, *The Toronto General Hospital: A Chronicle*, Toronto: Macmillan, 1975, pp. 52–55.

[130]Vesey Agmondisham Brown (1824–95), an M.A. of Trinity College, Dublin, served in the Crimean War as medical officer, and came to London as part of the military establishment there. He subsequently associated himself with a local militia, The London Field Battery, and retired as surgeon in 1895. See Edwin Seaborn, *The March of Medicine in Western Ontario*, Toronto: Ryerson, 1944, pp. 175–79.

Doctor Brown was sent for and came. He says it was near 10 PM but I thought it was near 9. Doctor Anderson had paid his afternoon visit and said she was going on all right, that there was not the slightest cause for alarm. He said I was old and nervous and easily alarmed but that Helen was in no danger. Edward who had just returned from Nissouri ran out as Doctor Anderson passed the window and asked him if Helen was in any danger. He repeated to Edward what he had said to us – that she was going on all right. Our anxiety was so great that Amelia went to Dr Brown and Edward went to Dr Woodruff and both described her symptoms as nearly as they could. Both doctors said she had puerperal fever and that she was in a very dangerous state. As soon as Amelia returned we sent for Dr Brown, and then sent to ask Doctor Anderson to meet him, which he refused to do. Doctor Brown was shocked that Doctor Anderson had never examined her abdomen, which was painfully sore to touch. He put on six leeches and then for two hours her bowels were fomented with hot water in which hops and poppy seeds had been boiled. After that a linseed poultice was applied. She then slept a very little.

[March 28] In the morning a telegram came from Doctor Hodder saying that he could not be here until 5 PM. Doctor Brown then put on 12 more leeches and the hot fomentization were continued until five o'clock when Doctor Hodder arrived.

Doctor Hodder and Doctor Brown had a consultation, the fomentations were discontinued, and they commenced with stimulants. They gave her port wine and beef tea and then pure brandy and beef tea. The doctors declared her life in great danger, but said they were not without hope. Who can tell the agony of that night. We watched and prayed and wept, and hoped. Amelia and Mr Griffin, John and Elizabeth did not leave until all was over. The Bishop had called during the day and had had prayers with my dying child. He asked her several questions which she answered satisfactorily and collectedly. Mr Portman never left her, her heart was so full of love, she threw her arms around my neck and said, Oh Mamma if I should get well and I hope I shall we must all love each other even more than we ever have done. I was on my knees in the library when I felt Becher's arm around me. He said Amen to my prayers, but I did not then know that he had refused to come in as long as Mr Portman was in the house. He came to the kitchen to inquire and Mr Griffin insisted upon his coming in to see me. My God, my God how severe are Thy chastisements, and my heart how stubborn and hard it is. Edward went in to see the sister that he would have given his life to save. She kissed him again and again and pressed his hand. John kissed her on the forehead but she pulled him down and kissed his face many times. George she kissed and said God Bless you Georgie dear, God Bless you. Mr Portman she caressed constantly and uttered words of love. Amelia and Ann the nurse were constantly with her, Dr Brown was in attendance all night. Doctor [Hodder] went to bed with directions to call him if necessary. He said if she lived until the morning she might recover. Oh with what agony we watched the first dawn of day, and she was living and again we hoped.

[March 29] Dr Hodder left for Toronto. He told us Helen could not be in better hands than Doctor Brown's. About 11 o'clock Doctor Brown told me there was no longer any hope, that she must die, and that I might see her. They had kept me out of her room for fear my grief would injure her. I do not remember the hour when I received the last embrace. Her lips and face were getting cold, her senses were perfect, she clasped her chilly arms around my neck and pressed me to her bosom with a good deal of strength. Those around the bed dragged at my clothes and pulled me away. How much agony and despair a person will live through. That weary night came to an end, and her spirit fled as the day dawned. To the last she was loving to her husband and those around her. She took her ring off her finger and put it into Amelia's hand, and then several times held her hand to see if she had it on. Helen did not ask for her children and when Mr Portman asked her if she would like to see Berkeley she said not tonight.

[March 30] All is over. Helen my beloved child is dead, and the rest of my life is dreary. All my children are good and loving, but those that are gone have left a vacancy that can never be filled. Mrs W. Lawrason has been here for two days, and she, Amelia and Ann laid Helen out in her last robe of white. Mr Portman wrote to Mr Becher and said that political differences should be forgotten and asked him to come in, which he did, and they made friends. . . .

[March 31] Every body has been good and kind and sympathizing and another day has passed and now arrangements are making for the funeral. Mr Hutchinson, Mr Wilson, Mr King, Mr Plummer, Dr Brown and Mr Becher, chief mourners. Oh what a host of misery. The Bishop, Mr McLean and Mr Brough called and had praying. Tomorrow Helen is to be buried, tonight the coffin came home, made of walnut, lined and cushioned, and my poor Helen looking perfectly beautiful as she lay nestled in her coffin in her long sleep of death. How willingly would I have rested my weary head and aching heart by the side of her. This night I took leave of her. Mr Portman went many times to take a last look of his loved and loving wife.

[April 1] Another night has passed. This morning Mr McLean christened the baby (in Edward's room) Maurice Vidal so as to unite their two names in their child and then the coffin was placed in a leaden one and then in a shell. A grave was bricked up, and all that remained of Helen, the wife, the mother, the daughter, the sister, was placed in her last resting place, and we, who can tell our wretchedness. They say an immense concourse of people attended. I have a very imperfect recollection of all that passed for the two or three following weeks. Sophia was telegraphed for and arrived on the 31st and was a great comfort to us. Mr Portman withdrew his name as a candidate for a member for the East Riding of Middlesex. Edward Blake came to the funeral. He was one of those who loved her when living and mourned her when dead. Mr Portman, Amelia and John wrote to the absent members of the family on the first. I wrote to each one of them as I could afterwards. Dr Ryerson came up on the 7th and remained until the 9th. On the 13th I received the following letter from Dr Anderson

Madam,

I never thought it would have been my duty to address you in the way I feel in justice to myself compelled to do now, in reference to statements which you and certain other members of your family have made and industriously circulated regarding my attendance and management of the late Mrs Portman.

Fair and just criticism of the conduct of professional men and those holding public appointments, I consider right and proper. You have held public offices yourselves, and have been subjected to some just criticisms, and had some of your friends acquainted with the facts of the case, displayed the same industry and malevolence which you have shown towards me on this occasion, you might now feel a little more charitably disposed, but when criticism descends to misstatements, exaggerations, and malicious insinuations, it ceases to be criticism and becomes personal malice.

In the first place you will recollect, that Mrs Portman had a very short and easy confinement, and progressed in her recovery as favourably as any woman could have done, showing no symptoms or indication of any latent or visible disease, and she continued to do well until you gave her some fried meats, mutton chops, I believe, without my knowledge or consent, which she told me herself she could hardly swallow. They never digested, became putrid in her stomach, producing nausea, restlessness, gripping and flatulency and which terminated as you know in a violent and debilitating diarrhoea.

This after going on a considerable time gave way to the usual remedies, but left her in other respects but little improved. She had nervous excitement, great anxiety, and restlessness and other symptoms indicating the approach of puerperal fever to the grave nature of which I called your attention at the time, and I had just commenced the treatment of it, when I was suspended, although I had received a note from Mr Portman, sometime after Mrs P had begun the use of the medicine, saying she was a great deal relieved from taking it.

I was suspended and by whom, by a person who does not pretend to understand or practice that department of the profession, and who is not met by any respectable member of the profession within the city and has obtained his present position (whatever that may be) by traducing and vilifying his professional brethren rendering him apparently a fit subject to your patronage. What happened to Mrs Portman after this I do not know. I have heard, however, that leeches had been applied to her which in a strong robust woman might have been admissable, but to a person of her weak constitution, debilitated as she was from the diarrhoea, must have depressed her beyond the powers of rallying.

In concluding this note, I must say that I never attended a case, where I was more conscientiously satisfied with the correctness of my opinion as to its nature or to its management as far as I could control it, and I will also say, and with all the solemnity of which I am capable, that Mrs Portman's sickness and death are solely attributable to the improper food given to her by you.

This case shows strongly, the danger to such persons who have over solicitous and anxious relations for their nurses particularly if they have a book.

Yours, Alexander Anderson

P.S. In reference to members of your family joining with you in the slander to which I have alluded, I exonerated Mr Portman. I believe him to be a gentleman, and he could never stoop to the meanness of placing a man in a false position, and then traducing his character when he could not defend himself. A.A.

[Amelia Harris continues:] God help me, I am accused of killing one that I would have given my life to save. Every member of the family was shocked and outraged beyond expression. Mr Portman took the letter to Mr Wilson and he wrote me the following

Westminster 13th April 1860

My dear Mrs Harris

I was shocked at reading that letter – and I need not say what the first impulse was, but the sadness of your bereavement – and respect for her whom we deplore, must repress what under other circumstances would have demanded and received prompt notice. I shall not suffer myself to remark upon the letter for it breaths the very spirit of the evil one, but I do feel that it will best become you and the family not to notice or reply to it.

As to the reflections thrown upon you in reference to the treatment of the dear departed, and which are well calculated to tear open the yet bleeding wounds, there is this answer and this consolation that you could but do, and did what you anxiously and trustfully thought was for the best and in regard to reflections cast upon him and by him wickedly thrown back upon you. We cannot but feel and say this, that God in his Goodness carries out the merciful designs of His good providence in His own way, and that we are prone to ascribe to causes we dimly see and imperfectly know that which was His merciful dispensation, and we humbly hope that in good time all that appears dark and mysterious will be made clearer and rebound to His glory.

I can but sympathize with you again dear Mrs Harris on this new and aggravated affliction, which you must and will bear as becomes a christian, trying to fight the good fight, and gain the crown the redeemed shall wear.

Affectionate, John Wilson

[Apr 14] Sophia returned home. A number of people called and expressed their indignation against Dr Anderson, and advised my sons not to notice the letter but the most of them would finish by saying: *if it was my Mother* – and then stop. We are all so wretched and unhappy. John & Edward looked for Dr Anderson with a horse whip but he was not to be found.

[Apr 15] Edward Blake came to tea. He appears to think that he has as much right to be sad as any of us.

Apr 16[131] Mr McLean called and stayed to dinner, in speaking of Dr Anderson he as a clergyman would urge that no notice should be taken

[131]Apparently Amelia resumed her diary on 16 April and over the next month recorded in it a total of ten letters, six of them addressed to the Editor of the *London Free Press*. Even though not written by her, these letters are an integral part of Amelia Harris' journal.

of the letter but occasionally he would forget himself and clench his hands and say *if it was his mother* – John, George and Mr Portman said Dr Anderson must and should be horsewhipped. Edward was averse to it, but Mr Portman said he would leave it in their hands until the next day, and then he would act, that Helen's mother should not be insulted with impunity. Mr McLean was in the next room during this discussion. I went to him and thought that John and George had gone out but John had not. George had gone to Dr Anderson's office, found him there and requested him to apologize to me for his insolent letter, which he refused to do. George then slapped his ears, knocked him down and spit in his face and came home as if nothing had happened. Mr McLean had left when he returned. Every body were pleased with George and were only afraid that he had not thrashed him enough.

Apr 17 George expected to be brought before the police but no notice was taken of it today. Doctors Harper and Catermole called upon Dr Anderson and made him apologize for saying that no respectable medical man would meet Dr Brown, as they were both in the habit of consulting with him constantly.[132]

Apr 18 At 8 o'clock this evening George was summoned to appear tomorrow morning at 9 AM. We have a wet nurse who comes three times a day to Baby, neither nursing nor the food satisfies him. We are endevouring to get a nurse who will give up her own baby and come into the house and take entire charge of him, night and day. Our present nurse is most extortionate, she asks five dollars a week for nursing Babe [sic] three times a day and Mr Portman has to give the cab man a dollar a day for bringing her here and then poor Baby is wretched between nursing and feeding.

Apr 19 George and all the gentlemen part of the family went to the Police Court this morning. George did not intend to deny the assault but to read Dr Anderson's letter to show his provocation. Mr Portman attended to make oath that Dr Anderson ordered the mutton chop and Ann the nurse attended to make oath that Helen did not eat it, but Dr Anderson pleaded illness and did not attend, and the trial was postponed until tomorrow morning at 9 AM. George asked Mr [James] Daniel to conduct his defence, Mr Wilson being absent.

Apr 20 They all attended the Court again but Dr Anderson did not appear, people said he would have been mobbed if he had. George was

[132]James Cattermole (1807–90). See Edwin Seaborn, *op. cit.*, pp. 191–93. Seaborn makes several references to the "Portman" case.

dismissed, unless he had a fresh summons. George then published the following letter:

To Editor of the *London Free Press*:

Sir:

Doctor Anderson having summoned me to the Police Court for assaulting and beating him, and having twice failed to appear, I have been unable publicly to justify myself, and I therefore beg you will afford me an opportunity of doing so in the columns of your paper.

The accompanying letter which Dr Anderson addressed to my Mother, provoked me to take the law into my own hands. I may have been wrong in doing so but I first asked him to apologize for writing such a brutal and cowardly letter, and I could not restrain myself when he refused. I cannot enter upon the medical statement in his letter. I would merely say that the attack upon my mother was my provocation, as Doctor Anderson must have known that he had stated therein what was false, but made for the wretched purpose of endevoring to remove the bad impressions which must assuredly be entertained of him in consequence of his treatment of my sister and of placing the responsibility of her death on my mother. Mr Portman heard Dr Anderson order the *fried meat*, or mutton chop for my sister, and the nurse and others know that she never ate a single morsel of it.

I therefore leave the public to judge between us, appealing every man to ask himself whether he would or could have acted differently under similar circumstances.

I am, sir,
Your obedient servant
George B. Harris
Eldon House, London, April 1860

Apr 21 A letter appeared in this day's paper from Dr Brown to Dr Anderson. Dr Brown has been shamefully treated by Dr Anderson, but my poor Helen, my darling child, has been the victim. How could I ever employ so bad a man as Dr Anderson. How could I have been so blinded as to trust her precious life to such a brute? Oh I sincerely and fatally believed that midwifery was one branch of his profession that he understood.

A requisition has this day been presented to Mr Portman signed by

500 voters requesting him to allow himself to be returned as member for East Middlesex. The requisition is highly complimentary, and very kindly and nicely expressed:

To the Honble M.B. Portman:

We the undersigned beg to offer you our heartfelt sympathy for the irreparable [loss?] which you have sustained, and exeedingly regret to hear that in consequence of your bereavement, it is your present intention not only to retire from the contest for our representation in Parliament, but likewise that you propose leaving the country and extend to us but little, if any, hope of welcoming you amongst us again, except in the capacity of a visitor.

During the short period of your residence in this neighborhood you have made many true friends, and during your canvas for our suffrage, you cannot fail to be aware that you added largely to their numbers daily. We therefore duly appreciating your society as a good neighbor and politician, are unwilling that you should leave us without an earnest request on our part that you will reconsider your intention of absenting yourself from us for ever. And should the election of East Middlesex be deferred, as it probably may be for some months, that you may return to this country, when time will have eradicated (as we trust it may) some of the pains of grief under which you are now suffering, and again consent to aid our cause by allowing yourself to be nominated as our candidate for the ensuing election. We trust that you will give this, our requisition, due consideration, and should you then grant our request, we on our part promise you our most hearty support during your absence and will endevor to prove on your return that we have not worked in vain.

Signed by four hundred voters and many more names not yet in on the 23rd April, Mr Portman returned the following answer:[133]

Gentlemen:

I feel quite unable to express to you the deep feelings which your more than kind address has stirred up in my mind. For your sympathies with me in my loss, I thank you most sincerely.

[133]The letter was addressed to J. Mahon and the Electors of the East Riding of the County of Middlesex.

Could I forget for a moment the heavy affliction under which I am suffering, I should do so on seeing the large number of warm friends and supporters I have in this country, and I would not hesitate to allow my name to be used in any way that seemed best to them. But I feel at present totally unable to enter into public life, and I must therefore with the greatest regret respectfully and regretfully [decline] your invitation to come forward for the approaching Election. Many causes lead me to this decision. The first and most weighty is, that I have sustained the loss of one, the nearest and dearest relation a man can have, and I feel as it were that I have to commence life anew, and cannot decide hastily upon my future career.

I am about to leave Canada for England and I cannot positively say that I shall ever return, otherwise than as a visitor. But wherever my lot in this world may be cast, and whatever my future may be, I shall ever carry with me the most grateful remembrance of the many acts of kind and disinterested friendship I have received at the hands of my friends as well as many with whom I regret to say I was not acquainted. In taking leave of you all, which I now do, I assure you with the most heartfelt sorrow, I find one bright spot always before my eyes, and that is the assurance you have given me that I carry with me the sympathy and kindly feeling of so many. I am sorry that in the short time I was before you in a public capacity and endevoring to gain a most enviable position I should have met with any whose political zeal should have led them to forget the kindly and generous feelings that should always exist between neighbors, though they may temporarily be opposed to each other in politics or interested in the success of a rival candidate.

Should I live to return to this country, I hope, and indeed feel sure, that, although I cannot on this occasion accede to the wishes of you all to contest the election, I shall find your hearts and good feelings to me personally unchanged, whatever may then be your political views.

I am, gentlemen, Yours most truly
Maurice B. Portman

Edward returned today from Toronto. He went there on the 20th to visit a dentist.

Apr 24 Today Mr Portman and John left for Columbia, South Carolina. Mr Portman wished to arrange the sale of his plantation, make the deed etc, and also see Col Hampton before he left for England but he could not muster courage to go alone, and John is so ill and works so much that we urged his going as the change and relaxation might do him good, and we also wished him to consult a doctor in New York. Elizabeth and I drew up a statement of his case from the commencement of his illness until now as nearly as we could and gave it to Mr Portman that he might show it privately to the doctor. John certainly has not improved in his health in the last year. He was much stronger last spring than he is now. A wet nurse came today and will take entire charge of Baby. She has left her own baby with her sister. We give her 16 dollars a month and pay for her washing.[134]

Apr 27 . . . As I write now from memory I can only recollect that people have called from day today and that all is sad and gloomy. I sit before Helen's picture until I fancy I see her arms around my neck and her lips pressed to mine.

Apr 30 . . . Mr Portman's letter confirms my fears about John's health. He was examined by Dr McCready in New York and he wishes to see him again with another medical man on his return from Columbia. The Dr appeared to think that John was in a very bad way.

May 1 . . . I copy a second letter of Dr Brown's to the editor of the *Free Press*.[135]

May 3/4/5 George got a summons again from Dr Anderson to appear at the Police Court on the morning of the 4th, which he did. We all thought it best that he should make no defence, but admit the assault and pay the fine, which he did. The Police Court was crowded with Dr Anderson and his friends and Dr Brown and his friends and a great number of George's young friends were present. I believe it was the intention of George's friends to have paid his fine, but the Mayor said he would take time to consider of it, and the next day when he was called up and fined 20 dollars including costs, there were very few present or that knew anything about it. Dr Anderson was very much disappointed that George made no defence as he had gone prepared to introduce a great deal of matter, so as to have it published in the police reports.

Today we got our English letters. Poor Helen, how she was loved and how sincerely mourned. The blow came heavy as I knew it would

[134]At this point, Dr. Brown wrote to the *Free Press* the first of two long-winded and self-serving letters in response to Dr. Anderson's original one. This prompted Anderson to write a second time, which in turn occasioned a response from Brown. Amelia Harris also recorded a letter condemning Anderson from Gilbert Griffin's father, a medical doctor.

[135]It is twice as long and is as equally self-serving and self-centred as the first.

to poor Teresa, for she loved her best of her sisters. Teresa and Mr Scott say they will come to me immediately. I hope they may. Poor Eliza expects her confinement in a few days, and I fear for her life poor girl.
May 8 Admiral Vidal[136] called and urged me to visit him, and would scarcely take a refusal. I will never leave Helen's children for a day while they are under my charge. . . . Mr Portman who says he will either take the children with him [to England] or stay with them, that he cannot be separated from them. They had a very rough passage from New York to Charleston and were very nearly lost. They will come home by rail and hope to be here on Saturday.
May 9 . . . I dreamt such a frightful dream about [Eliza] on the night of the 7th. I thought she had a figured muslin night cap on, very much trembled and some sort of dressing gown, but she looked so pale and so thin, the corners of her mouth drew so painfully when she smiled, and her figure looked so very thin that I remarked it to her more than once. I was awakened several times by thunder and storm but each time I closed my eyes I had the same dream and saw her looking so pale and thin. My poor daughter, if you should go too I am afraid to think. Mr Wilson called today, it is a very long time since he has been here.
May 11 I this morning copied Dr Griffin's letter written to his son Gilbert on the 26th of April 1860.

> My dear Gib:
> I received poor Mrs Harris' sad diary[137] and read it with great sorrow, as you must well remember that I felt and still feel that your poor mother's [Helen's] fatal illness was misunderstood and not in fact treated at all. But all regrets are useless, when the grave has closed over those who are dear to us as life itself.
> I have also in my possession papers containing the letter of Dr Anderson, and that gallant young man George's sensible letter. He acted right, and if he had shot the scoundrel, it would have found many to excuse him.

[136]Alexander Vidal, a colleague of John and Amelia Harris on the Owen Hydrographic Survey, and close family friend. See Robin Harris, "The Beginning of the Hydrographic Survey of the Great Lakes and the St. Lawrence River," *Historic Kingston* 14, 1966, pp. 24–39.
[137]It is improbable Gilbert Griffin had provided his father with the actual diary and, therefore, he is probably referring to correspondence that had chronicled the series of events.

A more heartless blackguard letter it has never been my fate to read – and based on a falsehood too – he [Dr Anderson] may speak and write of malice etc, but he has furnished the world around him, with a more potent weapon against himself than any of his maligners could have invented. It is his letters widely circulated, I hear, through the country. I have heard but one opinion of his character. I wish Dr Brown had written a better letter, if he is capable of it, few men are. He should have confined himself to the case in point, no one cares to know the history of himself and his doings. . . . I gave the matter to a medical friend of mine to read, his remark was, it is to be hoped there are not many Dr Andersons amongst us. They must be badly off for medical men in London C.W. I gave the diary etc to Lavinia to read & the letters as they appear in the papers.

With kindest regards to Mrs Harris and Mr Portman and love to you Amelia. I am etc

George Griffin

Mr Portman and John arrived at 1/2 past 3 PM very tired and glad to get home. . . . Mr Portman brought a picture of dear Helen done by Mr Wandesforde but it is not like her. . . . Mr Portman read his letters which kept him awake all night as I knew they would. Oh Helen, how dear you were to us all.

May 12 Mr Portman looked wretched this morning. His Mother and family are so urgent (and so kind) that he should take the children home that he has decided upon taking Berkeley and Willy, but will not go until after the Scotts arrive. Lady Portman says the children shall be as her own as long as she and Lord Portman live. Sorry as I am to part with them I know it will be for their benefit that they should go. The baby will remain with me for a year or two if not longer. I am afraid to think of the future. Helen gone, Mr Portman and the children going, what a change in my home and feelings. Helen, my child, my child, how lonely you have left your Mother. . . .

Cornish[138] went to Edward and wanted him to ask Mr Portman to propose him at the nomination on Monday next. Edward spoke to Mr Portman who declined, as his feelings were too deeply wounded by his recent affliction to allow him to take any part in the election. . . .

[138]Frank Evan Cornish (1819–1878), settled in London in 1819, became a lawyer, and was called to the bar in 1855. After serving as Alderman (1858–6) and Mayor (1861–64), he moved to Winnipeg in 1872 and became its first Mayor in 1874.

May 14 . . . Dr Brown has published another letter to Dr Anderson. Mr Portman and Edward secreted the paper and did not tell me of it, but Mr Wilson came in and he asked me if I had seen it and expressed his regret at its publication. . . . We were hurt and distressed to find this evening that Dr Brown was publishing my diary of poor Helen's treatment by Dr Anderson. Mr Portman called on Dr Brown but he was not at home. He then wrote a note to him forbidding him to publish it, and then went to the *Prototype* office and found it was already in type. He stopped its publication for the present. After dinner Mr Portman went to the Griffins and Dr Brown came there. He has written to the *Prototype* to stop the publication altogether. It was the most outrageous thing of Dr Brown to publish my diary without my leave, and when *I had told him* I would not allow it to be published. He says Edward gave him leave, but in an indirect way. It must have been in a very indirect way but Dr Brown fears that his professional reputation is attacked by Dr Anderson and that the publication of my diary would place things in their true light, and if he could have *smuggled* it before the public he would have done so regardless of our feelings, and when once done we could not undo it. I have been all day in trouble about George. He has not been very well of late. . . .
May 16 . . . Mr Portman got Doctor McCready's opinion of John's case today. He has consulted with Doctor Medcalf of New York, and both think there is a malignant tumor (cancerous) forming in John's side, but advises that he shall not be told this as hope will do more for him than medicine. He gives directions as to John's diet, air and exercise, and hopes that he may be mistaken in the nature of the tumor forming. If so John may live a dozen years, if not he will not live a year. . . . Mr Portman and Edward went to Dr Woodruff[139] and showed him Dr McCready's letter. He said he had never examined John and had never suspected the existence of such a disease, but that he would call upon him tomorrow and endevor to examine him.
May 18 We have been all day consulting what we were to tell John and how we are to induce him to put himself strictly under medical treatment without showing him Dr McCready's letter. It is hard to tell him that the doctor thinks he must die, we came to no decision and have told him nothing. He has a slight diarrhea hanging on him ever since his return from the South, it is accompanied with great pain. Edward has given up going to England, and talks of being married very quietly about the last week in June. . . .
May 19 . . . John called and we spoke of Dr McCready's letter to him,

[139]William Woodruff was to become the Harris family doctor in the 1870s.

but did not tell him what Dr McCready advised I should not be told. We urged him to see a doctor in London who would communicate with Dr McCready, which he promised to do. I told him that Dr McCready considered him very seriously ill. I could not tell him more. He seemed to think very seriously of all I said. Elizabeth was here but she seems to have gotten over her alarm about him. . . .

May 23 John sat for an hour with me, and asked me all about our arrangements for Edward's marriage, and seemed to wish to know whether Edward and Sophia were to live here permanently. I told him no, there living here now was only a temporary arrangement, that I at present could come to no decision about the future. I did not know what the Scotts would wish to do. . . . I told him I could not help preferring a daughter with me to a daughter in law. . . . A man I think may like a mother in law almost as well as a mother, but not a woman. I told him if I left Eldon I should give the house up to him, and that if he got ill so as to be confined to the house he must come home, let who would be here, that if there should be no other room vacant he and Elizabeth should have mine, and I would move to the library. I asked him if he would not rather be here if he was ill and he said that he would. He spoke about his health and about Dr McCready. I told him that Dr McCready spoke far from encouragingly about him, and said that there was a tumor forming in his side. He said he knew that, that Dr McCready had said as much to him, he wondered what the nature of the tumor was. I told him upon the nature of that tumor depended life and death. He said he knew that also. I told him we all hoped for the best, and although many who were strong and healthy might go before him, yet he ought to be prepared, that we had so recently felt that in life we were in the midst of death, that if we did not take warning from it, all warnings would be useless. I trust he is looking beyond this world for home. I wished him to see Dr Brown or some medical man, not that they should prescribe for him but to see if they agreed with Dr McCready as to his disease. Dr McCready advises but little medicine. Air, exercise and but little work, with a regulated diet is all that can be done. Nature must do the rest. We both spoke very composedly, yet my heart was ready to burst. . . . The election is over today. Mr Crick is returned by a majority of 170 over Becher who polled many more votes than it was supposed would be polled for him. Cornish had only 380 votes, Crick had a majority of six hundred over him. John went out and polled his vote for Mr Becher.

May 25 . . . Mr Becher and Cornish are already electioneering for the general election and Mr Portman's friends want him to come out. He says he will do so if they will insure his return but that he will not come out to divide Conservative votes and to ensure the ruin of the Conservative cause. . . . I shall be glad if he is returned, as it will insure his return to the country for a time at all events. . . .

May 26 Edward had a talk with me this morning, he wants Amelia to go to England and stay there until next spring. He says he will find the means or rather that her brothers and sisters will. He thinks her looking ill and says that if she remains here she will never look better. I wish very much that she could go, she came here this morning and I kept her busy. . . . There was a meeting of Mr Portman's friends today, he has placed himself in their hands, . . .

May 28 This morning Mr Portman went to see Doctor Brown to ask his opinion of John. He says there is no malignant tumor forming in his side, but that his spleen is very much enlarged and so is his liver and that nothing can be done for him, and he doubts his living a year. . . .

May 29 . . . In this morning's paper Mr Becher announces himself a candidate for the next election and hopes no one will be ungenerous enough to oppose him after his having lost the last and having expended a great deal of money, time and trouble. I suspect people will say, that is his lookout, not theirs. Amelia went to a meeting at Mrs Goodhue's. Old Mrs Lawrason proposed that a collection should be made to buy a present for the Bishop [Cronyn] as well as a collection for Mr McLean. She said nothing had ever been given to the Bishop during his long service here. Her proposition was opposed. . . . There was a great deal of sparring between Mrs Wilson and Mrs Lawrason on Church matters. . . .

May 30 . . . Mr Portman [received] six pictures of Helen from Mr Wandesforde today and they are all very good likeness, there was only one coloured one, and that he made me a present of. . . . He gave one of the others to Amelia, which is very, very kind as she is unable to pay for one.

May 31 . . . John came here today and we had a long talk. He is perfectly aware of his state of health and has thought of every arrangement that he can make as to his affairs. He says Elizabeth must sign a release of dower to prevent difficulties in the office. He says her own means are ample and that he does not think it necessary to leave what little property he has to her, that if she had a child of course he should leave everything to the child, but should he leave no child he should wish the most of his property to return here. He said he should [leave] some books to Elizabeth. He named [John] Ruskin and one or two others, but the bulk of his books he wished to return here and go with the other books. His pictures he said were mostly of his own drawing and he wished them to return to his family, as Elizabeth of course would marry again and his own family would value them most. He wished all the things which had been in use in Eldon to return here. He named his papa's chest of drawers, his own dinner service and breakfast service which have his crest on them. I thought Elizabeth might wish to keep them but if he wishes them to return to his own family he had better name a sum for them to pay Elizabeth for them. All the rest of his furniture was bought for his house, and they would have no association with him for us, that everything in the house bought for the house would be Elizabeth's. He spoke about the marriage license[140] and wondered whether it would be possible to get the office transferred to one of his brothers, and said if it could not be done before his death that it would not be given to one of them afterwards. He spoke about this place, and said there would be much here to remind us of him. . . . I thought I could not live away from Eldon, but now everything and every feeling seems changed. . . . I did not know but a change of scene would be absolutely necessary for my existence. Can anything be more sad than the above conversation with a beloved son 30 years of age with good worldly prospects, and yet feeling that death was near at hand. I told him that Dr Brown said there was no tumor forming in his side. He grasped a hope at once that people might live long with an enlarged liver. I could not tell him that Dr Brown thought there was as little hope of his living over a year as Dr McCready did. I too some times think that doctors may be deceived and have a hope that he may get better. If I could only feel an assurance that he would get better, I think the joy would be almost too great, it would be almost like receiving one from the dead. . . .

Jun 9 . . . When Amelia came I spoke to her about her going to England, as Mr Portman had spoken to me about it in the morning. I had always fancied there was some hesitation with Mr Portman about taking her and I could not make it out, as I thought it would be a great relief to him to have her to take a mother's care of the children, and in every way would be and would appear much better, than if the children went home with their father and only a servant to look after them, and as her going would not increase his expenses, there seemed to me a little mystery about it that I could not fathom. But today it was all explained. He would like Amelia to go with him very much,

[140]The granting of marriage licenses had been a perquisite enjoyed by John Harris from the early 1830s until his death and constituted a modest but steady source of income. The office was passed to his son, John, following his death. One of John's last actions before going to England was to request that the right to issue marriage licenses be granted to his brother, George.

but he would wish it to be *our act,* independant of him, as he knows that Mr Griffin would say that his wife had gone away to take care of Portman's children, and that he has already called her head nurse, and that should anything happen to her while away, that he would be reproached during his life for it. I had not thought of Mr Griffin in the matter further than his saying yes or no, but I know very well that he would say all that Mr Portman says he would. As for myself I should care but little for it. Who ought to be head nurse if she is not? Under present circumstances, can she do too much for her sister's husband and children? We shall all soon be wide apart, and what Mr Griffin may say will be of small account. It is to be decided on Monday whether she is to go or not. . . . Mr Scott wants to know if I can put up with a butler if he brings one out; I can, unless he is a very fine gentleman. Mr Portman attended his election committee this afternoon, . . . Mr Portman shall run even if it ensures the defeat of both candidates. . . . Edward got angry when at dinner because John thought he had left the office earlier than he did – their time differed – it was a matter of not the slightest consequence, I feel very sorry to see Edward who used to be quoted as one of the very best tempers in the world, giving way to a *hard temper* which will, and is growing upon him, and will soon become beyond his control. How painful it is to see those one loves do foolishly.

Jun 10 . . . John and I had a long talk upon religious subjects. I feel so thankful to find that he is thinking so seriously of the one all important subject. . . .

Jun 11 . . . John came to luncheon. I noticed that after John eats or when sitting down that he unbuttons the lower buttons of his waistcoat and also the buttons of his waistband, he seems swollen and it appears to give him ease. . . . Amelia had a long visit from Mr McLean this morning. He seems to be aware that there exists a feeling of jealousy towards him, and acknowledged to her that he did not feel as comfortably situated here as he had done . . . the nurse who is to go to England with the children came this evening.

Jun 12 Amelia called on her way to Toronto. Mr Portman left here at 5 PM to attend an election meeting at St John's. . . . Amelia left the money she had collected for Mr McLean (54 dollars) to be sent to Mrs Goodhue. Mrs Wilson called after the meeting of the ladies who were collecting and their return should [be] only $203. . . . The paper is to be changed into gold and presented to Mr McLean in a purse. I asked Mrs Wilson to stay to tea which she did. She spoke of Mr Portman's coming forward as a candidate. . . . I said that I disliked elections, but that in his case I thought it might have a tendency to divert his mind and make him forget his troubles a little, and in addition to that it was his father's wish. . . . She talked nearly all the time about the past and the loved ones that are gone, and of John. John and Elizabeth called on their return from the farm and stayed to tea. Elizabeth is very much troubled about the tale her cook has told her mother about Charlie, her groom and [the] house maid. Cook says there is an improper intimacy between them, which Elizabeth does not believe but feels hurt at the report. I advised her to be very cautious how she listened to reports of Roman Catholic servants against Protestant ones. At the same time for her own sake and the sake of those under [her] care she should keep a watchful care over her household. . . .

Jun 13 I got a letter from Eliza and one from Sarah. Sarah is at Ostende and Eliza is doing well. She made an effort and wrote herself that I might see that she was able to write. Mr Portman left in very low spirits to attend another election meeting. John and Elizabeth came to tea. John looked ill, he complained of a bad headache, the veins on his forehead were like cords. After bathing his head some time with cologne water, the veins relaxed and he was relieved. I felt more alarmed than I wished him to know. The doctor says from the state of his liver he is very liable to a rush of blood to the head and that death would follow very quickly. I saw in the evening that he was only thinking of his death in all he is doing now. He is trying to get all the intricacies of his business made plain and straight for Edward and George and the accounts of his clients all correct and plain. He expressed his regret that Edward gave way to temper in an uncourteous manner in the way he does. He says he dislikes asking him a question as it generally brings on an argument and angry words. John says he is trying hard to conquer his own ill temper, which to do him justice, poor fellow, has only come with his ill health. Edward has no excuse of that kind, though Dr Ryerson did make his deafness an objection to his marrying Sophia and said that deaf people always become querulous and suspicious. Surely deafness is a sufficient misfortune without voluntarily making themselves and all about them miserable by bad temper. My dear Edward think of this and guard against rude speeches to people and never again kick anyone from the door. Let the man be what he may, he is still one of God's creatures possessing the same natural feelings that we do and if people do any thing that requires chastisement let the proper authorities correct. I wrote to Sarah.

Jun 15 . . . Mr Becher called and brought me a cucumber. We did not speak of politics. . . . Mrs Goodhue called to ask me to sign an address to be read when the Ladies give the purse to the Revnd Mr McLean. . . .

Jun 17 Mr Portman and George did not get home until 2 o'clock in the morning. Their meeting was not a very successful one, as there were mostly Grits in the neighborhood. . . .
Jun 18 . . . John called and seems better. When we were at dinner he sent for me to look at his new horse, I liked her because she is very like the first horse Mr Harris owned after we were married. . . .
Jun 21 . . . Mr Portman sent in to town to ask his friends to go out in the evening to support him, as there had been a sort of mob fight during the day, and he anticipated another attack during the evening. Two or three wagon loads of his supporters went out. . . .
Jun 23 Mr Portman dined at home today for the first time this week. Edward and George went with him to attend his last meeting. John wished to go but I objected as he is not well enough either to endure excitement or exposure. . . .
Jun 24 Mr Portman, Edward and George did not come home until 3 o'clock this morning. . . . at 4 o'clock the fire bell rang and they all went to the fire. It was broad daylight when they returned and went to bed. At breakfast no one was sufficiently recovered to appear. The meeting had been a very stormy one. Mr Becher was there and again made a personal attack upon Mr Portman and was very abusive. He turned many of his friends from him, who at once gave their support to Mr Portman. Mr Becher made a very ridiculous speech which everyone laughed at, and introduced a story about cats which called forth numberless meows. . . .
Jun 27 . . . it is now settled that [Edward] is to be married on Saturday the 7th. . . . Mr Portman asked today if there was a picture of me that he could have. I showed him the one that belonged to Helen. . . .
Jun 30 . . . There was a very large meeting of Mr Portman's friends today, it was said they numbered between two and three hundred of the most respectable farmers in the country. They are all on his committee and have pledged themselves to do all in their powers to secure his election. Mr Portman had luncheon provided for them and pledged himself to return and go to the Poll if they supported him as they had promised to do. Every one appears to regret his going away. . . .
Jul 1 Mr Portman, Edward and George went to Church. I asked John, Elizabeth, Mr Griffin & Amelia to dine with us as it is the last Sunday that Mr Portman will be here, and the last Sunday that Edward will dine here as a bachelor. Mr Griffin made himself disagreeable and sent to know if his two boys were to dine here. I said they were not asked, but that they could come, and they did come. John looked very ill, and Amelia looked unhappy. Mr Griffin was cross and rude, and we all thought it will end by his not letting her go to England, but if he does

prevent her going without a reasonable reason for doing so, all the Harris family will cut him. He has been false and untruthful in all his conduct to her, and ever since her marriage he has made her a slave to himself and children, and now after consenting that she should go to England, and she ready to go, Mr Portman and her brothers paying all expenses, if he prevents her going from ill temper and tyranny, we will never speak to him again. He left the tea table in the sulks. She followed him and tried to make peace, her tearful eyes told too plainly how unhappy she was, she had to go home with him, and he jesting and looking as bland as if he only thought of making her happy. How little happiness there is in this world. . . .

Jul 4 . . . John and Elizabeth came to luncheon. Elizabeth in a very kind way told Amelia that she wanted her to do something for her in England. Amelia said, that she would do anything in the world that she could. Elizabeth put 5 sovereigns in her hand and said she wanted her to buy something pretty for herself (Amelia). It was very kind of Elizabeth and Amelia felt it so. . . .

Jul 5 The day of separation has come. . . . Slept very little. Who can describe the wakefulness caused by a disparing heartache. When Helen died I knew that a separation from her husband and children must follow, but that knowledge has not made it less painful. Willy is much better and both children were pleased with the excitement of going to England and yet the poor little fellows felt there were sadness about it. . . .

Jul 6 No little voices this morning to waken us, all silent and dreary. Edward left at 12 noon to go to Toronto. Tomorrow he is to be married, and although his wedding will be sad and gloomy, yet he has every reasonable prospect of happiness. He marries with the willing consent of her friends and his own, we are all fond of her, and know that she has been well educated and that she has good religious principles. I pray God to bless them both and give them many years of happiness. John and Elizabeth dined here. John left for Toronto at 3 PM. Elizabeth will remain with me until he returns. . . .

Jul 7 . . . Mrs Cronyn called, she looks very poorly, I should not be surprised if she did not live very long. She is a good woman and the change with her would be a happy one. She says that Edward and Sam Blake have bought a yacht, and I do not think she approves of it very much. She spoke of the Gzowskis and says Mr Gzowski is very kind and is always asking her to go there and stay, but some way she does not care to go, she thinks they are changed, and she fancies she likes the Gzowskis poor better than she likes them rich. . . . John and George returned at 10 PM and Edward is married. I pray God to help him and his wife and to have them in his keeping. The wedding was very quiet and every thing very nice and the bride looking very pretty but a feeling of sadness over it all. We had all anticipated such a happy merry wedding which there would have been had dear Helen been there. . . . John looked better and in good spirits. He pulled Elizabeth on his lap and gave her a kiss and told her what a great girl she was at packing his trunk. When he arrived in Toronto he supposed of course that everything required was in his trunk. The first thing that enlightened him on the subject was a telegraph from Elizabeth to Edward which in mistake was given to him, asking Edward to [provide] a sponge and comb for John as she had forgotten to put his in his trunk. John said he smiled but thought he could do very well without the sponge as he could use his course towel, but when he opened his trunk he found the course towel had been forgotten also. He afterwards wanted to write, and took out his dispatch box but found it empty, the portfolio, ink and pens had been taken out and Elizabeth had forgotten to put them in. He thought then that he would wash and get rid of the dust, but found Elizabeth had put up only one shirt and if he wore it that evening he would have no clean one for the wedding next day. When he was going to bed he looked for his night-shirt and found that that had been forgotten. He declared with something of his old humor, that Elizabeth had only packed up an empty dispatch box and a pair of boots, and she looked very much like a child that had been caught idling. . . .

Jul 13 . . . I got a letter from Sarah who is very urgent that John should go to the German baths. Elizabeth is very anxious that he should go abroad. John talked the matter over very seriously with me. He says if Dr McCready is right and there is a malignant tumor forming, his leaving home is useless. He has only to remain at home, linger, suffer and die, but if Dr McCready should be mistaken and Dr Brown right who says there is no tumor, then there is a possibility that his life might be prolonged. Then the question is, shall he act upon this chance and try the baths or remain where he is. I felt that hope was not extinct and advised him to go, though the thought of his getting ill and dying from home is frightful. Elizabeth is herself almost an invalid, and is no nurse even if she were well. We almost decided upon John's going immediately.

Jul 14 . . . we asked [Mr Becher] . . . if he knew where John A. Macdonald was. He said at Quebec and asked what we wanted of him. John said he wanted to get Edward appointed his Deputy in the Surrogate Court, and the issuing of license[s] transferred to George if possible for a year or two. Becher immediately offered to write to Mr

Macdonald on the subject, and sat down at once and did write. The offer was made with great apparent kindness and earnestness and it was difficult to refuse his letter, but George was annoyed and said that he would have nothing to do with it. I do not know whether John will send the letter. Becher has behaved so badly to Mr Portman, and unfeeling to dear Helen, that we do not, any of us, wish to have anything to say or do with him, more than to be on speaking terms. I shall never enter his house unless it is in a case of illness. Mr Becher proposed taking me to Woodstock or Ingersol to meet the Scotts. I declined with a shudder. He then wanted to drive me to the station, this I declined also. I do not wish to meet Teresa publicly, nor do I wish to accept his civility. He went to the station to meet the Scotts and met them with the same cordiality as in former days. . . . The Scotts arrived at 3 PM. Teresa looks very thin and tired, Mr Scott looks much the same. Our meeting was painful, we felt the absence of the loved ones, but I am so glad to have them back with me. . . .

Jul 21 Edward and Sophia arrived this morning at 4 o'clock, very tired but looking very happy. They have my room until theirs is ready for them which will be on Tuesday next. I have a bed in the nursery for that time. . . .

Jul 25 John & Elizabeth came to breakfast. . . . The Bechers called upon John yesterday but did not see him. Mr Becher then wrote a very kind note taking leave of him, and sent him a rest for his head to wear in the train. John and Elizabeth left here a quarter before 12, and the parting is over. How painful it is God only knows, or whether we shall ever meet again in this world. . . .

Jul 27 This morning I went to John's house, packed and sent to Eldon the things that were to be kept, and arranged what things were to be sold. I was there from 10 AM until 5 PM. It has been a dreary day. A few months ago I was fitting up his house for his bride, then the world seemed bright. Helen's smiling face looked in upon me, bringing grapes and cakes for my luncheon, now she rests in the grave yard, and John has gone in the search of health almost without the hope of returning. . . .

Aug 9 Mr Wilson and Becher called. Mr Wilson spoke to me about the marriage license. . . . I got a joint letter from Mary and Eliza, they had seen Amelia, Mr Portman and the children. Amelia slept the night after arrival at Princess Gate [with the Portmans]. The next day Lady Portman invited the Crutchleys and Peards to luncheon, and Amelia gave up the charge of the children and returned with the Crutchleys. Lord and Lady Portman were most kind and poor little Berkeley took to his

grand pappa and grand mamma most affectionately. Willy was more shy, it was painful for Amelia to part with the children and Mr Portman, they neither of them had time to write to me.
Aug 19 I finished my letter to Lady Portman and one to Mr Portman and also one to Amelia. I write a little each morning during the week and then close the letters in time for the mail on Monday morning. . . .
Aug 24 I am no better today, felt very faint when I got up and could not sit up to wash Baby.[141] It is the first time anyone else has washed him, and he made *loud* objections to their doing so today. Teresa rushed in in her night dress to see what was the matter. . . . John had arrived in London where Mr Portman met him. Col Crutchley and Mr Portman insisted upon his seeing a doctor, who gives very little encouragement, but urges his going to Harrogate [Yorkshire] for six weeks. I am sorry that he has not gone direct to Carlsbad [Germany] as he intended when he left home. My hope rested on those hot springs, now I expect to see him home in a few months to die, yet they have all acted for the best and his life is in the hands of God.
Aug 30 . . . I got English letters from Elizabeth, one from Mary and one from Mr Portman. . . . John is under Dr Budd's care. Dr Budd pronounced him incurable but thinks his life may be prolonged for a time. He is now trying the acid treatment, and the waters of Scarborough. Mr Portman has taken advice from Dr Budd also. His liver is out of order and he is not well. . . . At dinner Edward spoke harshly to George about some license money and made all at table feel uncomfortable and me unhappy. Edward speaks to George in a way that no gentlemen should speak to another. Mr Portman wishes to give up his trusteeship for Teresa's settlement. Mr Scott will appoint George.
Sep 5 The Orangemen put up an arch at Kingston decorated with all of their flags & the Roman Catholics presented it in a complaint to the Duke of Newcastle, who would not permit the Prince to land unless all party distinctions were done away with. At the last accounts the Orangemen had not given way and the Prince had not landed. . . .
Sep 6 The Prince did not land at Kingston but came on to Belville [sic]. There is a strong feeling of regret throughout the Province that any thing so disagreeable should have occurred . . . I went to the cellar to attend to the unpacking and putting by of Mr Scott's wine, having had closets made that will lock up so that he can have the key of his own wine.
Sep 7 The Orangemen from Kingston followed the Prince to Belville

[141]Portman's youngest child, Maurice, had remained with Amelia Harris.

[sic] and joined their Bretheren there. They would not give way but decorated the arches with their flags and insisted upon joining the procession and wearing all their badges. The Prince would not land but steamed on to Cobourg where they had no party distinctions and all united in giving him a most enthusiastic welcome. . . .
Sep 8 The Prince is at Toronto and is most joyfully welcomed.[142] No Orange demonstration. . . .
Sep 10 Great excitement about the Prince's visit, people hard at work at arches and getting ready to illuminate. Sophia got a letter from her father wishing her to go to Toronto. Edward and her go tomorrow morning at six. I have been very busy all day attending to putting up curtains and making brandy peaches.
Sep 11 Edward and Sophia left at 6 this morning. The weather is not very propitious for putting up arches and decorating the town, but the town is all bustle, every body is busy, and a great number of people are in from the country. . . .
Sep 12 Edward and Sophia returned at 4 PM, they both had a private introduction to the Prince of Wales at the Normal School.[143] Sir Edmund Head introduced them, of course they were much gratified. The Prince and suite arrived by the Grand Trunk a 1/4 after 4 o'clock PM, and the Londoners gave him a royal and enthusiastic welcome, and have made as much display in the way of arches, devices, flags, processions, etc, as their limited means would admit of. The city has been crowded with people from the country. Sir Edmund Head and General Bruce came to see me, as soon as they could leave the royal party after their arrival. Sir Edmund looks very much changed and broken and has not recovered the loss of his son. General Bruce is very much aged since last I saw him, but is so kind and gentlemanlike. There has been a great rumpus amongst the ball committee today, 17 out of 30 met, and proposed that Mr Becher should be master of ceremonies instead of Mr Griffin, who is first named, and has taken all the trouble of decorating the room. Everything has been managed

[142]*The Tour of H.R.H., the Prince of Wales through British America and the United States by a British Canadian*, Montreal: John Lovell, 1860, provides a day to day, and dance to dance, record of the daily progress of the 1860 visit of the future Edward VII to the main cities of Newfoundland, Nova Scotia, New Brunswick, Prince Edward Island, Quebec and Ontario (including Toronto and London) and, under the title of Baron Renfrew, to the main centres in the north-western United States.

[143]The site of the levée at which the Prince received local dignitaries in Toronto was the Normal School, which Egerton Ryerson, as Superintendant of Education for Upper Canada, had established in 1847 for the training of teachers for the common schools. It was on the site of what is now Ryerson Polytechnic University.

by him or the ball would have been a failure. Mr Becher has done nothing but make himself disagreeable. Of course Mr Griffin was annoyed, and so were many others who do not care for Mr Griffin, as well as his friends. They felt that he had been badly treated. Though I dislike having anything to do with the ball, yet I feel sorry to see him treated so scurvily.[144]

Sep 13 The illuminations last night were pretty, in short the people have done their best, but will not bear comparison with larger and richer cities. At $^1/_2$ past 9 the Prince left for Sarnia, and returned again at 4 PM and held a levée. Mr Scott, Edward and George were presented. Mr McInnes went with them, and was presented also. Today a larger number of the ball committee met and undid what was done yesterday in regard to Mr Griffin's being master of ceremonies. They appointed 4 masters of ceremonies giving them power of choosing a chief, whose orders the other three would obey, Mr Griffin, Mr Becher, Mr [James] Daniell and Mr Scatchard,[145] were the 4 chosen. . . . Mr Daniell and Mr Scatchard chose Mr Griffin as chief, and all things were going on smoothly again. Mr Pennefather[146] and Mr McInnis dined with us. Mr Pennefather told Sophia a good many anecdotes about the ladies of Toronto. Mr Widder[147] wrote to Col Irvin[148] hoping that he would consider his daughters, and endevor to have them dance with the Prince, and the gratitude of the Widder family would be secured for ever to His Royal Highness. The report is that Mrs Widder wrote to the Duke of Newcastle, but it is not true, the letter was to Col Irvine, but shown to all the royal party, and Mrs Widder very much laughed at. The Prince danced with Miss Widder and Mrs Widder was so overcome with the honor that she sank into a seat, breathed very heavily, put her her hand on her heart, and was going to faint [when] people formed a circle around her, fanned her, and gave her the usual restorative, the whole scene was rich and absurd in the extreme. The Prince has danced with Miss Powell of Niagara at three different balls, and some person remarked it, when one of

[144]H.C.R. Becher's account of the Prince's visit to London is recorded in his diary for 13 September 1860. See M.A. Garland, *op.cit.*

[145]Thomas Scatcherd (1823–76), London lawyer and politician, M.P. for West Middlesex (1861–67) and for North Middlesex (1867–76). See William Horton, *Memoir of the late Thomas Scatcherd.* ... London, Ontario, 1878.

[146]A member of the Prince's suite.

[147]Frederick Widder (1801–65), the father of Sophia Ryerson's friend, Blanche, came to Canada in 1839 with the Canada Company. His home in Toronto was Lyndhurst Lodge.

[148]Member of the Prince's suite.

the royal party explained it. Sir Fenwick Williams[149] is a friend of her mother's, and said that he would procure her a dance with the Prince at any ball she went to, and he had done so. Miss Powell and her friends are of course very much pleased and elated, but the royal party made rather disparaging remarks upon her putting herself so forward. She always kept a position either on or very near the dais. They say that the Miss Widders sat on the dais all the evening at the ball at the Crystal Palace in Toronto, so as to be at hand in case the Prince wished to dance with them, but he did not. It was at the ball at Osgoode Hall that he danced with Miss Widder.

Sep 14 . . . The ball to the Prince was a success. Miss Isabella Meredith[150] was thought the belle of the room. Mr Becher succeeded in offending every body, he would be the master of ceremonies and usurped Mr Griffin's duties, Mr Griffin's expostulations were useless. He must either give place to Mr Becher or have a row in the ball room. Mr Becher altered the list of ladies who were named as partners for the Prince, and brought forth his own friends, and this has given mortal offence to all those who were not danced with. They threatened to kick Mr Becher. Every body is pleased with the Prince. . . .

Sep 15 . . . Mr Portman is not well, and would be very glad if he had not pledged himself to return for the election. Sarah had been on a visit to her sisters in England and felt hurt when with them. She thought that her separation of 14 years had made her a stranger to them and that they did not love her as they did each other. [I] felt sorry when I read her letter for I know what she suspected was true. Mr Becher called, and asked me what I had heard about the ball and said that he had heard that Mr Griffin was annoyed with him. I said yes, that I was told that he had usurped Mr Griffin's duties, and that Mr Griffin gave way rather than have a row in the ball room. Mr Becher tried to explain, but did not place himself in a better light. He told me that people abused him, and threatened to kick him. George attended a meeting of the ball committee in the evening. Mr Becher was present, and was abused by everyone. . . .

Sep 21 Mr Becher called this morning, and says the Prince was worried with the constant crowds in Hamilton, that retarded all his move-

[149]Sir William Fenwick Williams (1800–83) was born in Canada but educated at the Royal Military Academy at Woolwich. Commissioned in the Royal Artillery, he rose to the rank of General by 1868 and Commander-in-Chief, British forces in Canada (1859–65). He was appointed Lieutenant Governor of Nova Scotia in 1865.

[150]Isabella Meredith (1841–1907) was the second daughter of John W.C. Meredith. She never married.

ments, and in a great degree prevented his seeing any thing, or going any where. The Prince and the Duke of Newcastle lunched at Dundurn[151] with Sir Allan MacNab, there were only three other guests, Mr McInnes was one of them. The Prince has rather a great flirtation with Miss Powell of Niagara, she attended the ball at Cobourg, and danced with the Prince, then she danced with him at the two balls in Toronto and again at Hamilton. Much to the annoyance of the Duke and General Bruce, who expostulated with him, he would sit in corners with her, and get as much alone as he could. At Port Dalhousie, Mr [Philip] VanKoughnet asked the Duke if Miss Powell might come on board the steamer. Certainly not, he said. Mr VanKoughnet bowed and said he had only done his duty. I do not know whether the Prince had requested him to ask, but Miss Powell did get on board, and gave the Prince a bouquet, and had an interview with him in the wheel house, where the Duke and General Bruce discovered them. . . . In landing at Detroit, Mr Pennefather was thrown from the carriage into the river. He sank three times, and was fished out just in time to save his life. He had dispatch boxes in his hand and never loosened his grasp of them.

Sep 23 I got letters from Mr Portman, Mary & Eliza. . . . They are all very anxious that Amelia should remain in England for the winter. . . . Mary was with the Knights and Mrs Knight told her how much Chasse was beloved by them all, and how good she was. . . .

Sep 28 Mr Scott and George left today for the Prairies to shoot. It is the first time that George has been away upon an excursion of pleasure excepting a few days at the Falls. The house is very lonely without them. . . .

Oct 7 . . . Mr Griffin came to tea, and read part of a letter from Amelia to me which told of her being at the Packingtons. I said I was afraid that she would be very short of money. He said if she had not forced herself out of her proper sphere, she would not have felt the want of money. Had she not married him she would not have felt the want of money, nor would she have been out of her own proper sphere. I did not venture to answer him, but I felt a very choking sensation.

Oct 10 Edward made complaints about George, that he was not exact and systematic about his accounts. I felt much troubled, and spoke to George. George says that Edward is unreasonable and unjust in his accusations. He always seems to me to be too ready to accuse George of doing what is not right. . . . I am afraid that George is not as exact

[151]Dundurn Castle, Sir Allan Napier MacNab's residence in Hamilton.

and punctual in all his transactions as I could wish him to be. At the same time I think that Edward's manner of speaking to him and of him are very wrong. A young man and that man a brother, who at the age of 24 years, has never, numbering all his idle days, spent a month in pleasure, nor one night in *bad* company, and whose worst fault is not being a perfect man at business, and even that fault rising very much from the want of experience, he having been but one year and a half out of his time,[152] such a young man should be led not driven. I feel that I can do nothing, but counsel both parties to the best of my knowledge, but I cannot help feeling troubled. . . .

Oct 18 . . . Nancy [Cameron] has almost made up her mind to have an operation performed.[153] . . . I shall write to Dr Ryerson to make every inquiry at the hospital at Toronto. . . .

Oct 26 . . . Nancy went last evening and asked Dr Anderson to give her a written statement about his treatment to her, and also of her care that she might show it to the doctors at the Hospital in Toronto, but he declined. I felt sure he would not. He is not sure enough of his own practice *and is* sure enough of his own ignorance to avoid laying it before the public. . . .

Oct 29 . . . Edward Ryerse sent me a box of chestnuts and wrote to me also. He says George [their brother] is very unhappy with his wife, and they talk of a separation, poor man to have such misery in his old age. . . .

Oct 30 . . . The accounts from John are not very encouraging – he had a tooth drawn and the bleeding could not be stopped for two days. The doctor became greatly alarmed, and would not let him lie down or go to sleep. He, the doctor, remained with John all night. . . .

Oct 31 Mr Griffin and a Dr Landor[154] from England called. Dr Landor has come out with the intention of remaining in London, and following his profession if he has any encouragement. He is highly recommended by Dr Skae of London, England, and looks a gentleman-like man. . . .

Nov 8 I got a letter from Mr Portman. Mr Scott got one from Mary. Mr Portman is not well, and is very unhappy and low spirited. He intends coming out in May. He says that Mr Griffin does not write to Amelia and that she is unhappy and wretched. How they all dislike Mr

[152]A reference to his apprenticeship.

[153]She was suffering from dropsy.

[154]Henry Landor (1815–77), a British doctor who came to Canada in 1860, was in general practice until 1868, and became Superintendant of the London Asylum for the Insane (1870–77).

Griffin. Mary thinks Amelia will return this month, that she will be afraid to remain any longer. Mrs Watson asked all at Eldon to a party this evening excepting myself, but of course no one goes, it would be very strange if the family could go to a ball, and dear Helen lying so near in the cemetery, yet this feeling with them must wear away, and all things go on, as if poor Helen had never been. With me it is different, my feelings can never change, until we meet in another world.

Nov 11 The morning bright and beautiful. George not well, thinks he has rheumatism in his knee. We sent for Dr Woodruff, who gave him some linament to rub on it. Teresa, Mr Scott and I went to Church. I felt ill after my return. George's knee became so painful that we sent again for Dr Woodruff, who leeched it. He cannot move, and I insisted upon his coming into my room, so that I can attend upon him at night. We put up a small bed for him. The Dr says he has inflammation in the joint.[155] . . .

Nov 14 . . . Mr Griffin called, he had a letter from Amelia, . . . She talks of coming out the last week of November or the first week in December. Mr Griffin also brought a letter for me to read from Mr Portman to Mr Mahon about his election. Mr Mahon does not quite like it. Mr Portman says he will not be a tool of any party but if he is returned, he will endevor to do his duty as their representative. I thought Mr Portman expressed himself very well and very right, only not quite clear enough. A member *must* be with one party or the other to be of any use. If he belongs to no party, he might as well be out of the house for all the good that he can do. Mr Wilson tried that, and was a failure. . . . John A. Macdonald and some others at the Ministry are in town. They are making a tour of the province before the meeting of parliament. The public dinner given to them is to come off tomorrow.

Nov 15 We moved George and made his bed. His leg is very much swollen but not painful. The Dr told us to leave off the hot poultice today, and that his leg was only to be kept still and warm. Mr Scott and Edward have gone to the Ministerial dinner, and will return I have no doubt very much disgusted. All public dinners in this country are low and vulgar, yet political people have to court the mob.

Nov 16 The dinner is called a success, a great many people were there. The Ministry stayed until very late and were very tipsy, they were John A. Macdonald, Mr Van Koughnet, Mr Morrison[156] & Mr Sid-

[155]He was to be incapacitated for nearly two months.

[156]Joseph Curran Morrison (1816–85), a Toronto lawyer, was M.P. (1850–57; 1860–62), Solicitor General (1860–62), and Chancellor of the University of Toronto (1863–76).

ney Smith[157] at the hotel. They knocked each other's hats off, tore each other's coats, and did several equally clever things. They were not by themselves, there were a number of their entertainers joined their drunken sport. Mr Hutchinson had to be sent home in a cab. Mr Scott and Edward came home early. Mr Becher got very much snubbed. He went to the dining room during the day and asked what seat was reserved for him, and was told that he must take his seat as he could with the crowd. When dinner was announced, he came with the Ministry leaning on Mr Morrison's arm to the private door, which was reserved for their entrance alone, and Mr Becher was turned back to make his way by the public entrance as he best could. The committee would not allow him to have one word to say about the dinner. . . .

Mr Mahon called avowedly to talk over Mr Portman's letter but in reality to find out whether Mr Portman really intended to return and stand for East Middlesex or not. I assured him that he did, unless his friends became luke warm, and I hoped they would behave honorably by him, and let him know if they thought he would not be returned, so as to save him from the expense and mortification of a defeat. He said they certainly would do so, but assured me upon his honor that it was his firm belief that he would be returned. Mr Mahon does not like the Orangemen, nor the way that J.A. Macdonald has spoken of the Duke of Newcastle, and is very anxious that Mr Portman should not pledge himself in any way to them, and he thinks of Mr Hutchinson as we do, that it is fortunate for Mr Portman that he has resigned. He says that Mr Hutchinson has no standing and but little influence, and [is] a very bad manager in money matters, though honorable and true in his friendship. . . .

I got a letter from Amelia. Mr Griffin watched at the office for it and brought it to me and said he wished to hear what was in it. I felt very awkward for fear she might have written something that she did not wish him to see, but fortunately she had only written what I was glad to shew him. She said that Mr Griffin had not written to her for five mails, and that if she had returned as he wrote to her to do on the 4th of October she could not have paid half of her visits, and that he would have been the first one to reproach her for coming. Mr Griffin said that he had *never* written to her to come out on the 4th of October, that she was the best judge when she ought to return. That no one on this side of the Atlantic could know how many inducements she might have to remain, that the reason he had not written to her was

[157]Sidney Smith (1823–89), a Cobourg lawyer, M.P. for Northumberland (1854–61), and Postmaster General of Canada (1858–62).

that she herself had written to him that she was coming out on the 3rd of November. . . .

Nov 19 . . . The Premier, J.A. Macdonald, did not leave town until today. Mr Jackson saw him at the station. When he left Mr Jackson looked as if he knew a good deal, so I suppose J.A. has been on a spree. They give him a public dinner tonight in Hamilton. What a pity to see such men at the head of affairs in Canada.

Nov 23 . . . Teresa and Sophia have been very busy learning to make minced pies, the cook made bad paste, and has caused the pies to be a failure. Our cook is a very good woman but a very poor cook. . . .

Nov 26 . . . I got a letter from Mr Portman, who speaks of Eldon as his home with so much feeling. . . . He wishes he was well out of the election, and so do I. When the Ministry attended the public dinners throughout the country, and I heard of the drunken debauchery of some of them, and see the daily papers full of charges of bribery and corruptions of others . . . ,I feel as if I would rather see Mr Portman resting by the side of poor Helen, than associated in acts and deeds with people like our present Ministry. . . .

Dec 6 This is Thanksgiving Day. Sophie and Edward went to Church. Teresa was so unwell that we sent for Dr Landor, who says all her complaints arise from weakness, and he says that she has a feeble, thready pulse. He advises her to continue Dr Simpson's tonic, to take cod liver oil once a day, to drink two glasses of wine, and to live *well*, that is to eat strong, wholesome food and to take open air exercises – good advice I should think.

Dec 8 . . . Elizabeth has succeeded in making herself *disliked* by all my family in England. Amelia saw Sir Edward and Lady Head who were most kind to her, and want her to return to Canada with *them* in January. . . . Mr Scott yesterday gave me a pretty second, mourning, black, silk dress, as a Christmas box. . . .

Dec 21 Nancy looks a little better this evening, though very weak. The nurse came this afternoon, poor Nancy has been kept up today with brandy and beef tea and champagne. I was very sorry to hear from Sophia and Edward that Dr and Mrs Ryerson do not live happily together, they even speak of a separation. . . .

Dec 24 I have been busy all day preparing for Christmas. Mr McLean called and prayed with Nancy, who is very near her end. Jane [servant] nurses her most tenderly. I feel thankful that she is here. Dr, Mrs Ryerson and Charlie[158] arrived this evening. I feel very weary and low spirited.

[158]Dr. and Mrs. Ryerson's son.

Dec 25 Christmas morning, and sad and melancholy it seems to me. Poor Nancy died a quarter before seven this morning, one who was very strongly attached to me is gone. At 6 o'clock AM Jane sent in for me, and I remained with Nancy until she breathed her last. A few minutes before her death she looked up, and I said to Jane I think she is conscious, I said Nancy do you know me and her lips said yes. A few minutes afterwards her soul had gone to heaven, I trust. Teresa was with us, she had never seen any one die. I assisted Jane to lay her out and prepare her for the grave. I put one of my nightgowns upon her and we scalloped a cambric sheet to put around her in the coffin. This has been a very trying painful day to me. Mr Scott and Teresa went to Church. Edward had to go to the undertakers and had to send a messenger to Komoka to notify Nancy's friends that she was dead, and that she was to be buried by the side of her aunt in Lobo.[159] Sophia would not go to Church because Edward could not. Dr Landor and Mr Griffin came to dinner. Dr Ryerson, Mrs Ryerson, Miss Beatty and Charlie, in addition to our own family, made a large party. Mr Becher called after Church. . . . What a year of sorrow and wretchedness 1860 has been to me. Shall I see another Christmas?

Dec 26 This morning the undertaker came with poor old Nancy's coffin. It was very nicely made of walnut and lined. Her uncle and friends came from Lobo for her body and took it there to be buried. . . .

Dec 28 This evening we got English letters. . . . John declares himself to be much better. . . . They have all seen Mr McInnes and I believe Amelia will remain and come out with him.

Dec 29 This is Sophia's birthday, she is 24 years old today. My housemaid Mary gave me notice today that she wished to leave when her month is out. I am sorry and glad to part with her. There is no one in the house that likes her but myself, and my liking is because she is a clean, tidy girl, but she has such an unhappy temper that she keeps an ill feeling always in the house. . . .

Dec 31 The last day of the year. All are busy preparing for the New Year. Mrs Ryerson, Sophia & Louisa are making cake. They are to receive tomorrow. Teresa & I cannot feel in spirits to amuse visitors. Mr Griffin called, Mr Scott and Teresa drove out. I played chip with Edward, when I went to my room and thought of this day nine months I felt as if I should go mad. I could not restrain myself but cried as if my heart would break and went to bed ill.

[159]Komoka and Lobo were villages located near London.

1861

Jan 1 The New Year, every one says a happy New Year. God grant that it may be happier than the last and I pray God to give me the grace to bear His chastening hand with meekness and to make me truly thankful for all His blessings. I was ill all night. Hot and feverish and all day I have been so depressed that I can scarcely keep from crying. This day nine months Helen was buried and it appeared to me that I was living that day over again. Mrs Ryerson, Sophia and Miss Beatty received visitors but Teresa & I saw no one excepting Mr Wilson and Dr Brown. Mr Scott asked Mr Jackson to come to dinner but he declined. Mr Scott and Edward made a few calls. George made a good many calls . . . I do not know who all called here, but the Bishop of Huron and the Revnd Mr Beatridge, Mr Lawrason and the two Mr Reids, Mr Hamilton, Capt Taylor, . . . Dr Landor and Mr Jackson Mackorn Wilson, Mr Thomas, Mr Dempster, Mr Templeton, George Moore, Mr Mills, [and] B. Cronyn.
Jan 3 I got a letter from Mr Portman and one from John. John says his health is certainly improving. He is very much vexed with Mr Griffin for ordering Amelia to come home at once, and telling her to bring him a present, when he has not given her a dollar since she has been in England. Poor Amelia, she has chosen a hard lot. Mr Griffin says she is to leave England on the 10th. . . . Mrs W. Lawrason on New Year's Day complained to Mr Scott about Amelia's staying away so long and she pities Mr Griffin very much. Mrs Lawrason has a right to her own opinion on all subjects, but it is sometimes extremely rude to express an opinion about what does not concern her.
Jan 5 Mr Griffin called here. I thought he looked rather down. He is pressed again for money, and wants Edward or Mr Scott to let him have $150, but it is perfectly useless trying to pay his debts. He will never spare upon himself. He knew this debt was owing, yet he could buy a sofa and easy chair in Toronto. . . .
Jan 7 . . . Mr Cornish is 48 ahead of Mr Daniel. It will be a disgrace to the city to have Mr Cornish as Mayor. A man who is notorious as one of the greatest scamps in this city, not one good action can be told of him.
Jan 8 . . . Report says that John A. Macdonald (our Prime Minister) promised him that he would make him a Judge of one of the counties if he would prove his popularity by getting himself elected Mayor of London.
Jan 9 Last night . . . some other rowdies went to the Tecumseh where some of Mr Daniel's friends were going to have a supper, and they

without provocation beat Mr Blackburn, the Editor of the *Free Press* and Frank Smyth very severely. Their faces were cut open so that the doctor had to be called in. Those vagabonds are some of Mr Cornish's friends. . . . Dr Ryerson sent me *The Characteristics of Women* by Mrs Jameson.[160] It is a beautiful edition for the drawing room table.
Jan 13 . . . Dr Landor vaccinated Baby . . .
Jan 20 . . . Dr Landor called at Eldon and told Teresa that she ought to go to a warm climate to spend the next winter. What he said rather alarmed us about Teresa's state of health but in the evening Mr Griffin called and alarmed me dreadfully. He said that Dr Landor . . . thought she ought to go to a warm climate immediately, that she was in a most delicate state of health and that he feared some internal disease. Mr Griffin asked me if I knew what Dr Simpson[161] had treated her for. I said that I did not. He then told me that Amelia had written to him, that she had been treated for cancer of the womb, which he had told Dr Landor, but Amelia had told him not to tell me. Of course I was half crazy and have not felt more wretched since Helen's death. . . .
Jan 21 . . . I asked him [Dr Landor] about Teresa. He said he had never told Mr Griffin that she ought to go to a warm climate at once, that she ought not to go before next autumn, and that Mr Griffin had *never* told him that Dr Simpson had treated Teresa for cancer of the womb, & he said that Teresa had no disease, only a very delicate constitution. That he had never said anything of the kind and that there was no such thing known as cancer with a person under 30 years of age – was it to torture me that Mr Griffin told this falsehood. . . .
Jan 23 . . . All at Eldon have been invited to a ball at the Goodhues the evening of Hetty's wedding, on the 7th of February and all have declined; 10 months is too short a time to forget Helen. . . .
Jan 24 Mr Wilson called this morning and rang the bell for the first time in his life. It is so long since he has been here that he forgot that he was accustomed to walk into the house like one of the family. . . .
Jan 28 ... Edward spoke tonight of taking a house and Sophia told Teresa that she would rather be in a house of her own, so I suppose they will in a few months go by themselves. I shall feel very sorry to see them go, but they must do what will conduce most to their own happiness.
Jan 31 . . . Edward and George work in the office every night until 11 o'clock, it is too much, they will lose their health.

[160]Mrs. Anna Brownell Jameson (1794–1860) was an author of several volumes including the two volume study, *Characteristics of Women*, London, 1854. See Clara Thomas, "Anna Brownell Murphy (Jameson)," *Dic. Can. Biog.* VIII, pp. 649–651.
[161]An Edinburgh physician.

Feb 1 . . . I was playing chess this evening when I had such a sudden strong feeling at my heart that I thought myself dying for a minute. I have had a strong feeling at my heart several times, but never for such a long duration. I had to go to bed. Teresa sent for Dr Brown who was not at home.
Feb 2 Dr Brown called this morning, I felt better but not well. He told me to drink wine or porter and gave me a tonic . . . We got English letters from Mary and John & Elizabeth. Poor John prefers Canada to England, the sight of much poverty in England distresses him.
Feb 4 I am not very well. . . . I got a letter from Mr Portman, he has decided upon leaving Berkeley and Willy with Mary[162] during his visit to this country.
Feb 6 . . . I wrote a long letter to Mary. Edward has gone to Sandwich on law business. . . .
Feb 7 This day has been the most disagreeable one of the winter. It is very cold with strong N.W. wind and a heavy snow storm and tremendous snow drifts. The trains are all delayed. . . . The Goodhues give a large ball tonight but it is paying dear for a ball to go out [on] such a night as this. . . .
May 4 There is a very long blank in my journal. On the 11th of February I was taken very suddenly ill, fainting and becoming cold. Dr Landor and Dr Brown attended me. They gave me brandy and put mustard on both of my legs for some hours. . . . Sleeping or waking I had that pain at my heart which seemed to affect my brain. The doctors examined my heart and said it was [not] diseased and that my heavy afflictions had caused my illness. They also said that they could do but very little for me, that my recovery depended much more upon my being able to conquer and suppress my grief . . . Dr Brown seemed to give me up to Dr Landor very much. I had a second attack about a fortnight after the first. During both attacks I thought I was dying and although I felt and still feel a strong hope that my Saviour will receive me, yet I trembled when I thought I stood on the very threshold of eternity. I sent for the Bishop and his conversation and prayers enabled me to face death with more composure. All my friends have been kind and attentive excepting Mrs Becher who has neither called nor sent to ask after me. Amelia returned from England on the 19th of February (my birthday).[163]

[162]His sons were to stay with the Shuldham's in England.

[163]There is a further gap in the diary and Amelia resumes her entries on 2 June. A daily account of that period is contained in Sophia's diary who was then living at Eldon House. In the meantime, Maurice Portman had arrived from England.

Jun 2 . . . Dr Landor came to tea. I felt better in the afternoon but was taken ill when going to bed and had to send for Dr Landor who had just gone home. All my family are most kind but Teresa's attention never flags. . . .
Jun 3 I felt better this morning. Dr Landor called and changed the tonic I had been taking for nearly four months. . . . Mr Scott, Teresa and myself drove out to the Kings. The country looked fresh and beautiful. . . . Mr Wilson was here. . . . He does not like Mr Becher and says that he will not be returned, even if he is the only candidate. There was a meeting of a few Conservatives today. . . . Amelia got a letter from Eliza telling us how very ill poor John is. He cannot raise his arm and cannot live many days. He tried to write to me to ask me to let Elizabeth have a room at Eldon when she wished to stay here and said she had been such a good wife to him. . . .
Jun 6 . . . Mr Portman's withdrawal as a candidate for East Elgin has caused great excitement. Many of the electors will not hear of his withdrawal, and are determined to nominate him and to insist upon his standing. The meeting tomorrow most probably will decide and that decision most probably will have a very great influence upon his future life. . . .
Jun 8 A political meeting took place today. Mr Portman was a good deal excited but went to it. Mr King and some others called upon Mr Portman. The electors have decided upon holding a convention, and Mr Portman has assented to stand if he should be the candidate chosen. Mr Becher says he will give way for anyone else, but he will oppose Mr Portman. . . .
Jun 9 . . . Mr Portman read his address to us all. Dr Landor, Mr McInnes and Mr Des Voeux all thought it a very clever, well written address. I wrote to dear John, . . . Mr Hutchinson and Mr Jackson came here about 10 PM and remained in Mr Portman's bedroom until 12 o'clock discussing the programme of the election and what was necessary to be done this week.
Jun 10 . . . Mr Wilson came to luncheon. . . . He was rather sorry that Mr Portman had consented to come forward. He said there was not a more corrupt or a worse place in the world for a young man than Quebec and that Mr Portman would be more than a man if he escaped vice in some shape if he went there. Will the memory of Helen and his love for his children preserve him? God grant it for their sake as well as his own. . . . Mr Portman returned at 10 PM. I was in bed. He was in very good spirits, his day's electioneering has been very successful. He does not wish Edward nor George to take any part in his canvas. Edward has had some disagreeable affairs of Mr Portman's to arrange which has made him unpopular with some of Mr Portman's

supporters, as Edward bore all the odium of not allowing great bargains being made out of Mr Portman, or in other words allowing him to be cheated. Mr Labatt returned with Mr Portman and they had supper here.

Jun 11 In this morning's paper Mr Balkwell announced that he was coming forward as a candidate, and he will take a good number of Mr Portman's supporters, which lessens his chance of getting the nomination. [Portman] took an early breakfast and started with Mr Des Voeux to visit some of his supporters in the Township of London but was less hopeful than last night. After driving out a few miles he found that several of the people he wished to see had come into London to attend an Orange meeting, and from what he heard from some of his friends, he thinks that all chance of his getting the nomination is gone. . . . Mr Portman went in the afternoon to see how the Orange meeting went off. The Orangemen say they will support Mr Portman if Mr Cornish does not stand, and he came back a little more cheery. . . .

Jun 12 This day 10 years dear Chasse was married. . . . People appear to be getting a little common sense . . . they think that Mr Portman is the strongest man and are inclined to support him only. Such has been the communication to him this morning. His calls in London appeared to be satisfactory. . . .

Jun 13 Mr Portman's electioneering prospects appear to be brightening. The different parties appear to be uniting for his support. Now that he has entered into the election I should dislike very much that he should be defeated. . . .

Jun 14 . . . Mr Becher is determined to oppose Mr Portman. . . .

Jun 15 . . . Mr Portman has been in a great state of excitement all day about the election. The convention met and have chosen him to stand as their representative. There was a good deal of loud talking and angry feeling called forth. I am very glad that Mr Portman has got the nomination, though there is very little chance of his being elected. But we should all have been mortified if he had not been the favorite. . . .

Jun 16 Last night at 12 PM Mr Becher sent the *Prototype* to Mr Portman with his letter in it offering to resign if Mr Portman would, and to let some new candidate be named in the Conservative interest, so as to save the riding. Mr Portman and all at Eldon only wish it were possible for him to do so without compromising himself. Had Mr Becher made that proposal before Mr Portman was nominated, he would have acceded to it at once, but now his supporters will not allow him to withdraw . . . Mr Portman went over to consult with Mr Wilson. Mr Wilson says that he cannot resign without the consent of the delegates who have nominated, but advised him not to spend money nor be persuaded that he could get in against Mr Becher and Mr Craik.[164] . . .

Jun 17 Mr Portman went with Mr Labatt after luncheon into the Township to hold meetings, . . . Mr Wilson says *he will not* stand for the City. . . . The general opinion has been *today* that Mr Portman will be returned notwithstanding Mr Becher's opposition. Dr Landor told me that Mr Becher was in a very precarious state of health and that the excitement of the election would be most injurious to him. How people wear their days away with passion and excitement not knowing how near death may be to them. . . .

Jun 18 This is the anniversary of the Battle of Waterloo. Few that took part in that fearful fight are now living and where are they all? Where we must all appear very soon when all our hopes and fears and heart burnings will be over. . . . I had a long talk after lunch with Edward about poor John's affairs. He thinks it is very hard upon him to have to pay John's debts and to make up all losses to people by John's mistakes in investing. I have reflected most seriously upon it and it must be done even if it takes years to set everything right. All John's mistakes were from his being compelled to work when he ought to have been caring for his life. . . . I was surprised to see what a change making money had made in Edward's sentiments. When he first took John's business he was poor and involved but his views of matters were honorable and his intentions were all right. He not only saw the present but he looked into the future and felt that present difficulties honorably combatted and conquered would secure future respect, confidence, and independence. He was much more decided in his opinion that no client should lose by Harris and Brothers than John was. . . . I paid all debts, just and unjust, when I had a large and helpless family and would have done so had it left me without a home to have saved my husband's name from reproach, and there must be no reflection upon John when in his grave, even if it takes the home I then saved to pay his just liabilities although they may not be recoverable by law. John left the foundation of the best business in London. . . . When Edward went to St Thomas, John's business was too small to provide and Edward's getting a bank solicitorship John considered him successfully established. And although we looked upon the events which induced Edward to return here as misfortunes at the time, yet they have proved for otherwise and his coming into the office when he did has been the saving of the family . . . Edward has managed the business well and has been successful beyond his most sanguine ex-

[164]Robert Craik, the sitting member for East Middlesex and a Radical.

pectations. . . . I have thought it best to write on this subject at full length as no one can know every circumstance as well as I do and I also trust that whether I am living or dead that neither of my sons will act contrary to what I conscientiously believe to be right, however great the sacrifice may be to them, firmly believing that God will bless those who act uprightly. . . .

Jun 19 Mr Portman has been very much engaged all day with different parties about the election. Mr Wilson came to luncheon. The address from the Radicals of London was presented to him last night but he declined standing as a candidate from private reasons. The truth is he is known to take charge of his business and he cannot afford to leave it. I had a long talk with Edward about the liabilities of Harris & Brothers and he spoke as he ought to and said everything should be paid. I wish very much that he could sell his pet farm for it will be a sinking fund to them as long as they keep it. Mr Griffin and Amelia called. Mr Portman and Mr Scott went out at 5 PM to attend a meeting at Montgomery's Tavern. The meeting was very satisfactory to Mr Portman as the people were almost unanimous for Mr Portman. Mr Becher was there and behaved almost like a mad man. He abused Mr Portman in a most violent manner. Mr Portman kept his temper and would not reply to his personalities by which I am sure he will gain popularity. . . .

Jun 21 Mr Carling has been elected for the city of London by acclamation today, and Mr Becher has withdrawn from the contest of East Middlesex and he is to support Mr Portman and Mr Portman and [his] friends are to support Mr Becher in Malahide for the Upper House. I am very glad that the contest between Mr Portman and Mr Becher is over. Mr Becher has behaved like a foolish mad man throughout. . . . Mr Portman, Scott and many others went to a meeting in Dorchester. Mr Becher being a director of the Great Western went with them and had a special train for Mr Portman's service. Mr Becher spoke and electioneered for Mr Portman unsaying all he had said before. I am sure no one can ever again have much respect for Mr Becher or put faith in what he says. . . .

Jun 26 Dr Landor came to see Sophia. He thinks she has benefitted very little by his treatment.[165] . . . Mr Portman went to Belmont to attend a meeting which was a great success. There is I think very little doubt but what he will be elected. The Grits are circulating most scurilous articles about him. . . .

[165]According to Sophia's diary, she had been consulting with Dr. Landor for six months, but we do not know exactly what her illness was.

Jun 28 . . . English letters came in just before we went to luncheon. Amelia gave me one from Mary in which she said that poor John still lingered on in the same way, but when I looked around the table at luncheon I saw they had other news. When George left the room I followed him and asked him if all was over with dear John. He told me it was. I had been in expectation of this news for months and knew that it must come. Yet the certainty that he is gone, and that we can never again exchange a thought in this world is hard to bear. I thank my heavenly Father that I feel more humble and resigned than I have hitherto felt. John left this world in peace, looking to a happy future, putting his trust in our Saviour's love. Time with me must be short when I hope to meet all my loved ones again where sorrow never comes. John's heart like his dear father's and Helen's was full of love when near death. All other feelings seemed to be dead. John requested that a lock of my hair and a lock of Elizabeth's might be buried with him. His death took place on the 14th of June and he was buried on the 20th in East Hampstead Church yard by the side of Mary's baby. This was his own request. Even in the grave he wished to be near some of his family. Col Crutchley arranged all about the funeral. . . .
Jun 29 I was ill how could I be otherwise. Dr Landon called but I did not see him. . . . Amelia sat with us the most of the day. Another beloved one of our number gone.
Jul 1 The nominations came off today. The Sheriff declared it a tie between Mr Portman and Craik, but Mr Portman said the Conservatives were evidently out numbered, and that Craik had a majority although Mr Portman's supporters would number 2 to 1 over Mr Craik's, who had come into London to attend the nomination, but many of them had taken shelter in the inn during the heavy rain and were absent when the show of hands was called for. Mr Portman was vexed and mortified, as we all were. Mr Portman has had but little to gratify him this day. He listened to abuse and the cry of Mrs *Hunt* and came home thoroughly wet and disgusted. . . . Next Monday must decide who will be best supported. . . .
Jul 2 . . . Mr Wilson came to luncheon. Amelia made an attack upon him for supporting Mr Craik. He was vexed and said she ought not to speak of him or mention his name, as she ought to know that his party [the Radicals] had urged him to electioneer against Mr Portman and that it was his regard for Mr Portman and our family which prevented his doing so. But the least said on the subject was the best. . . .
Jul 3 Mr Portman left Eldon at 9 AM and did not return until long after I was in bed. Amelia and Mr Wilson were here at luncheon. Mr Wilson asked who was Mr Portman's legal adviser and said that Mr

Portman ought to be very careful what he did, for should he be elected the Radicals if they could get the slightest opening would prosecute and endevor to unseat him. I asked him what he meant. He said Mr Portman had been getting a number of flags and that it was contrary to law, . . . but he should be very sorry if Mr Portman laid himself open to his enemies in any way. It is very kind of Mr Wilson to give those warnings. . . .
Jul 4 Mr Portman did not come home until 3 o'clock this morning and was off again at 11. He was thankful to Mr Wilson for his hint about the flags, and has suppressed them all. . . .
Jul 6 Mr Portman looked very tired and worn this morning. He has gone again this evening to attend the last meeting. Edward went out early this morning electioneering and has not yet returned. George has gone to attend a meeting at Montgomery's Tavern. Mr Wilson came to luncheon. He gave Mr Portman some hints about calling on people who have influence but would wait to be asked to exercise it. Mr Wilson certainly wishes that Mr Portman may be elected and seems quite sure that he will be. . . .
Jul 8 . . . Mr Portman was away before 7 o'clock. He was in a great state of excitement. Mr Scott took charge of a waggon and drove voters to poll in London. Burns [manservant] took charge of another waggon. Edward and George were out all day. Mr Becher voted for Mr Portman but has been rather luke warm in his support. He has just done enough to preserve appearances. . . . At the close of the polls Mr Portman had a majority of 142. . . . All appear to think that Mr Portman's election is safe. . . .
Jul 9 . . . Mr Griffin came at 1/2 past 5 to tell us that Mr Portman was returned by a majority of 306 and the procession was expected to arrive in town about 1/2 past 6. Teresa, Sophia and Amelia went to Richmond St to witness Mr Portman's entry as an M.P.P. I heard the band playing and went to the gate to see the procession which was very large come down from the Church and when they saw me they cheered and waved their flags. I felt glad that Mr Portman was returned and felt hopeful that it would be for good and he looked so pleased, so young and handsome, and I could not help contrasting the long line of carriages, the cheering and excitement with the two or three lowering John into his solitary grave away from his home. I thought of dear Helen too and how pleased she would have been to see her husband. It is hard to feel joyful with all those thoughts rising in one's heart. Mr Jackson, Mr Griffin and Amelia came to supper and everybody seemed glad and joyful. The bells rang and bonfires were lighted in the streets, and the people may well be proud of our new member for he is a nice good fellow. . . .

Jul 13 . . . The declaration took place today and Mr Portman was declared the member for East Middlesex. Mr Duggan and Edward both said that Mr Portman spoke well and made a good speech, and I am sure he will acquit himself well in the House. . . . The Grits entered a protest against Mr Portman's election accusing him of bribery, but I imagine their protest will amount to nothing. . . .
Jul 14 . . . Dr Landor came to tea and Mr Portman told him that he intended trying to get a grant of money for a lunatic asylum in London. Dr Landor who had charge of an asylum for 10 years offered to give him some suggestions on the subject. . . .
Jul 20 . . . Mr Portman has been annoyed and fretted beyond measure today, teamsters who carried voters to the polls & others who electioneered for him now demand pay and they make most exorbitant charges and threaten violence to his committee if they are not paid, and the Grits are watching Mr Portman to get some opening to unseat him should he pay anything illegally. . . .
Jul 21 . . . Mr Portman told me that he had received a letter from his father which was not very satisfactory. His father wishes him to marry again very soon. He says that Lady Portman is not strong and not equal to taking charge of his children. . . .
Jul 23 . . . A letter came from Mr Hutchinson asking for another $1,500 to pay election expenses. Mr Portman was very justly annoyed, as we all were, all charges have been most extortionate. In short he has been regularly swindled out of a large sum of money. . . .
Jul 27 The death of Col Wade Hampton was in the papers today . . . but news from the States is so incorrect that we trust this is not true. Should he be dead it may affect Mr Portman very seriously, as he owes Mr Portman a large sum of money. . . .
Aug 3 . . . All is hurry and bustle with Edward, Sophia and Mr Portman getting ready to leave. . . . Sophia visits her father and mother during Edward's visit to England. Edward goes to seek relief for his deafness. . . .
Aug 5 . . . We are all packing up and getting ready to go to the Falls tomorrow. Amelia came and packed my trunk. . . . My leaving home seems such an event that I do not know how to realize it.
Aug 8 Baby is not very well, his teeth trouble him, and he feels the want of his home comforts. . . .
Aug 11 . . . After dinner Mrs Duncan[166] asked me into her room, she talked a good deal about Mr Portman. She said that he spoke as if his returning to Canada was very doubtful, that he hoped to get an ap-

[166]An American guest at the hotel.

pointment on the Southern Legation if England acknowledged the South. . . .

Aug 19 I commenced a letter to Mr Portman and put my drawers to rights. . . . George commenced moving into his new office.

Aug 21 . . . Elizabeth is very anxious to live at Eldon, but it is quite impossible that she can do so. . . .

Sep 2 Mr Scott and Mr Griffin left at 11 AM for Clinton to shoot partridge and quail. Mr Jackson called with invitations . . . to a ball at the Kings, given in commemoration of Mr King's having passed as a barrister, of course the Scotts and George declin[ed]. . . .

Sep 25 . . . Dr Ryerson arrived at 10 AM. . . .

Sep 27 . . . Dr Ryerson returned this morning to Toronto. I got letters from Sarah, Elisa and Mary and also from Lady & Sir Edmund Head. . . . Edward was to leave England on the 21st. He seems to have made a very favorable impression upon all his friends, Sarah & Col Dalzell went to Paris with him. [Elizabeth] is coming out with Edward. . . .

Oct 1 . . . Mr Scott and Teresa went to the station at 10 PM to meet Sophia who has returned and is looking wonderfully well. . . .

Oct 8 . . . All our old friends have been very civil to Edward. Capt Knight & his brother came to London to see him and Capt [Arundell] Neave came on purpose to dine with him at the Crutchley's.[167] Mr Portman came from Bryanston[168] to bid him good bye. Shuldham and Mary came to Chelsea to say good-bye also. . . .

Oct 9 Edward came home at 2 PM. Isabella Meredith returned from Ireland under his care. Elizabeth went to Toronto from Hamilton. . . . He brought dear John's watch and chain for George. . . .

Oct 13 . . . Sir John [Beverley] Robinson came home from Church with Teresa and dined with us. . . .

Oct 15 . . . Mrs Wilson told us of Lucy's[169] engagement to Bill Bailey. . . .

Oct 19 . . . Becher came to luncheon. It is the first time he has broken bread in the House for nearly two years. . . . Teresa gave us a great fright in the evening by having a fainting turn, which she is not subject to. She became cold and the symptoms were very like one of my attacks. I sent for Dr Landor in a great hurry. He said it was her stomach which was out of order. . . .

Oct 20 . . . Dr Landor called in the morning to see Teresa and in the afternoon he brought Mrs Landor and two of his little daughters. . . .

[167]Their home at Chelsea, England.
[168]Lord Portman's home in Dorset.
[169]Lucy was Mrs. Wilson's daughter.

Oct 21 . . . Miss [Isabella] Meredith called. She is certainly very pretty but she is not the gentle retiring beauty I fancied from what I saw of her in Church. She is sparkling and self possessed. . . .
Nov 1 Elizabeth arrived today. She looked very much distressed poor girl. . . . Edward bought the City Hotel for Mr Portman today.
Nov 5 Mr Scott is thinking seriously of buying the City Hotel from Mr Portman. He thinks from the present upward tendency of all property in the city, that it may be a good speculation. . . .
Nov 6 . . . Elizabeth let Amelia and Teresa read her journal during John's illness and death. I had not the courage to ask to see it. Elizabeth is certainly very unselfish about John's things, she asked to retain very little for herself.
Nov 10 . . . I believe Sophia scolded Edward for being so very attentive to Miss Meredith. Edward means no harm, but he is very wrong. He has a good wife and he should make her happiness his only study.
Nov 17 . . . I read the service and one of Jeremy Taylor's sermons in my own room. I never read any sermons that had the power of retaining my attention more than his, yet I do not quite like many of his sermons. Yet they are like the conversation of a very clever man, they rivet the attention, although we may not be able to comprehend or agree with *all* that is said. . . .
Nov 18 . . . Elizabeth told me today that she thought she ought to have all John's furniture that was left unsold. I told her I would be guided by John's wishes. From the memorandum which John dictated the day before he died, I thought he wished me to keep the things which had belonged to Eldon before he was married. I wished her to read it over again, and to tell me whether she did not think that was what he intended. She said she remembered it perfectly, but thought that he only alluded to the chest of drawers that belonged to his father, but in his memorandum he says there are several things. I can only understand those several things to be what he had purchased for Eldon House but took them away with him when he married. I should wish to give her every thing that John wished her to have, at the same time I should wish to keep those things that he wished should remain at Eldon. . . .
Nov 22 Mr Wandesforde arrived last night and went to the Becher's. He will remain with us until tomorrow, when he intends returning to Hamilton. He is getting a good deal to do. He is to paint a portrait of John for Elizabeth, and another for Teresa, and Edward wishes to have my portrait painted. . . .
Dec 7 . . . We all wish not only to love but to respect John's wife. People can not always love as they wish, but it is in the power of

anyone to command the respect of others. . . . Dr Ryerson arrived this evening, and brought a pair of ponies, a sleigh, phaeton & harness. All excepting the sleigh are a present to Sophia, it is a very nice present and very kind of him.

Dec 16 Elizabeth left us this morning. I felt sorry to see her go, *she is John's wife*, and yet I felt glad that her visit was over. I wish she had not sent that account into Edward. She at last gave up all claim to the things that John wished to remain at Eldon, but Edward will send her nearly all the things that she wanted. . . . The British Government demands an apology from the American Government, and that Mason and Slidell shall be given up to the British flag again.[170] Troops are to be sent to Canada, and the militia are advised to organize & drill. Mr Scott is trying to get up some volunteer companies.

Dec 21 Mr Scott & Mr Mahon both got letters from Mr Portman. He is in a great state of excitement about the war, and wants a company of riflemen raised for him at once. . . .

Dec 25 Christmas brings a saddened cheerfulness to us now. I am afraid even to write the thoughts that never leave me. . . . The news of Prince Albert's death, which reached us yesterday, makes every heart ache for our much loved Queen. Little presents have been given to all the servants, and Teresa, whose tender care of me is unfailing, gave me a pattern of very pretty silk for a dressing gown. . . . Amelia gave Baby a very nice picture book of her own make. The Scotts, Edward and Sophia went to Church. I read the service in my own room. . . . Mr Scott gave the dinner and used his own plate. . . . Mr Griffin sent a beautiful wild turkey. . . .

Dec 31 . . . Tomorrow will be the New Year, the past year has been one of sorrow & sickness to me. God grant that it may make me humble and penitent and bring me nearer to Thee.

1862

Jan 1 Firing guns & ringing bells have ushered in the New Year. How many who are now cheerful and merry will be numbered with the past

[170]In 1861, the Confederacy sent James M. Mason and John Slidell to England and France respectively to negotiate formal recognition of the South. On route, their vessel, the *Trent*, was intercepted by an American naval vessel, the *San Jacinto*, and Mason and Slidell were taken prisoner. In response to British and French pressure, President Lincoln ordered the release of the detained commissioners on 26 December. See Brian Jenkins, *Britain and the War for the Union*, Montreal: McGill-Queen's University Press, 1974, Vol. 1.

before the next New Year? The Scotts had a breakfast party. . . . Edward & Mr Wells drove to Lobo. . . . Sophia received visitors, but there were very few, only 14 called. Neither Teresa nor I would receive so soon after John's death. . . .
Jan 5 . . . There appears to be a good deal of jealousy among the volunteers. The men all want to be officers.[171]
Jan 18 . . . This is Mr Portman's birthday, today he is to leave England, I shall be very, very glad to see him. I have such strange feelings & I never see any thing but *death.* When I go out driving and meet people, they all seem travelling one road to the grave. Some reach there sooner, some later, but the end of all is the same. What folly to care so much for this world, when the one care should occupy us, to be ready for the call which must come, and if we are only ready, what joy awaits us. . . .
Feb 10 There is a long blank in my journal.[172] I have been ill and unable to write. I thank God that I am better, and for all his mercies, I try to be truly thankful. Though I have many and heartbreaking sorrows, yet how few are blessed as I am, surrounded as I am, with the devoted affection of my children, my every want and wish attended to. That God will bless them here and here after is my constant prayer. Mr Portman returned on the 1st, looking himself again. Baby without actually remembering him seemed to identify him with his pictures and to receive him at once as his Papa. Many thing[s] happened during my illness. Teresa and Sophia have both been ill. Amelia had to come and turn housekeeper and nurse for two days. General [Alex] Russell, and his staff have arrived. It is said that 2,000 troops are to be stationed in London, all the public buildings have been taken for Barracks and rents have doubled. . . .
Feb 11 I feel a little better today. Dr Landor called. Mr Wilson came to luncheon. George with Mr Griffin has gone to the oil springs,[173] . . . She [Amelia] asked Teresa if she knew how much Mr Griffin owed Mr Scott. She said she did not, but said that she would find out. Teresa asked Mr Scott, who gave her Mr Griffin's note, and told her to make Amelia a present of it, which she did. Amelia said she could not take it, and Teresa threw it in the fire. Amelia made an effort to

[171]See the several entries in Sophia's diary for December, 1861 that refer to the raising of volunteer militia companies by Mr. Scott and others as the prospect of war with the United States excited the community.

[172]There are no entries between 21 January and 9 February.

[173]This is the first reference in Amelia's diary to the discovery of oil that was to excite the Harris family and the local community for the next few years.

command her feelings, but I know she gave way to them when she reached home. . . .
Mar 20 Once more I resume my journal.[174] I have had a long and severe illness, but it has pleased God to spare me yet a little while and I must go. Mr Portman left us on the 13th [February] for Quebec to attend to his Parliamentary duties.[175] J.A. Macdonald wishes him to take office and form one of the Ministry. It is complimentary to him and we should all feel rejoiced if his reelection could be secured without a ruinous expense to him. He has decided upon taking Baby to England with him this summer. I pray God that it may be for the best. I many times think that I am quite reconciled to parting with him, but when I feel his dear little warm embrace, I know that the trial is not over. . . .
Mar 21 . . . The pictures came today from Mr Wandesforde. The one of me is a total failure, and the [one] of John which he painted for Teresa is a failure also, the one of John for Elizabeth is good, the one of Mr Scott is very good, and so is the one of George. . . .
Mar 24 . . . Mr Portman is to second the address today. I hope he may acquit himself well. He makes no allusion to his taking office. . . .
Mar 31 . . . Leather the architect called to get directions about the plans for the addition to the house.[176] The *Globe* honors Mr Portman with a little abuse.[177] I read Mr Portman's speech with pleasure, and felt glad that he had acquitted himself so well. He has talent enough to take a high position, all he wants is industry, and determination never to swerve from an upright and honorable course.
Apr 3 I got a letter from Mr Portman. He writes in low spirits that Mrs Hunt['s] scandal has followed him to Quebec.[178] It seems strange that one false step of his life should meet him at every turn, although since then his conduct has been correct and his married life was exemplary, whilst hundreds of married men sin daily and the world takes no notice of it. . . . Mr Becher appears quite sure of his election. The

[174]Amelia resumes her journal after another interruption extending back to 12 February.

[175]The House convened on 20 March at Quebec City.

[176]W.B. Leather was a London architect and civil engineer.

[177]Portman's speech, seconding the address to the Throne, is quoted in an editorial in the *London Free Press*, while the editorial in the *Globe* of 31 March commented, "Neither matter nor manner afforded the slightest hope that Mr. Portman would ever serve his country efficiently as a legislator. East Middlesex was never worse represented."

[178]At the age of 19, Maurice Portman was cited as a correspondent in a divorce action in Britain, an incident which his opponents used to embarrass him.

Radicals have tried hard to get someone to oppose Mr Carling, but have failed. . . .

Apr 7 Mr Carling elected by acclamation. Edward went to Toronto to bring Sophia home. . . . There is another piece of gossip about Mr Portman, I shall request my *own family* not to repeat anything of the kind to me, and should anyone else venture to repeat anything against him to me I will take good care to offend them. Those falsehoods are only told us to annoy us, as people well know that anything said to lower him or make him ridiculous must hurt us, and one of those stories (although I know them to be untrue) always deprives me of a night's rest. I have no unmarried daughters for people to scandalize, & now they think to hit us through Mr Portman. May God ever bless & keep him and his.

Apr 8 . . . Edward and Sophia came home at 9:30 PM looking very tired. Edward went to see Elizabeth. He said he felt sorry for her, & thought that she looked cheerless & lonely. She had furnished her room with John's things as far as they would go. She has made Edward & George her executors and left them each £250 as a legacy, independent of any charge for their troubles as executors. This is Berkley's birthday . . . he is five years old today and has been more than two years motherless. It is Mr Scott's birthday also, he is 35 today.

Apr 10 . . . Edward has let his farm[179] to Mr Ocelton for 5 years. He is to pay £25 for the first year, & the rent is to be increased £5 each succeeding year. Mr Scott & Edward drove out to the farm to take an account of the stock. . . .

Apr 13 . . . Mr Portman told us that if the Militia Bill passed there would be situations in it that might suit Col Dalzell or Shuldham, & advised Edward to write to them at once and enclose a draft of the Bill, and if they would like to have an appointment to send an application to him, to be given to Lord Monck[180] as soon as the Bill passed. Edward wrote at once, it would be strange if they should get appointments, and return to this country, a member of Parliament has a good deal of power if he plays his cards well.

Apr 15 Mr Portman & I looked over our accounts, & arranged what money we are to pay him. I take the breakfast set at cost, without duties or freightage. George is to take the drawing room furniture & Edward takes the dining room chairs, pays for painting house, eaves,

[179]Edward's farm at Lobo.
[180]The Governor General.

troughs, and the rooms in the garret. Mr Portman takes nothing for what he has done to the stable & several other little things, amounting, I should think, to about $200. If I were rich the balance should be the other way. . . .

Apr 16 Edward came to my room last night after I was in bed. I feel sorry to find that his nervous system is so much like my own, and that he feels so acutely. He told me he felt there is something wrong in him, and that what the fault is he cannot tell. He says that since he came from St Thomas that he tried in his business, and by the rectitude of his conduct, to gain the confidence and respect of his clients, but he feels that he has not succeeded. I assured him that neither Mr Portman nor Mr Scott even thought for one moment that they were injuring or doing any thing that could injure him in the least, but I could not heal the wound. . . . He said if I thought that he viewed the transaction wrong that I had better state all the circumstances to Mr Wilson, and ask him what was right. He told me to remember what talk it made that Becher was losing his business. . . .

Apr 17 The day very wet. Amelia got a letter from Sarah who talks of coming out this summer. My illness has alarmed her, but when she hears that I am better she will not come, but put it off for a more convenient season which never comes. General Russell, Major Bowles, Capt Hewitt,[181] Capt Ramsbottom and Amelia dined here. The dinner was a success. . . .

Apr 18 . . . Mr Portman spoke of not returning to England this year, that is if he accepted the offer of being a director on the Grand Trunk, but whether he was in jest or earnest I cannot tell. . . .

May 11 There is another long break in my journal.[182] I have been too ill to write. . . . Yesterday Col [Edward] Wetherall spent the greater part of the day here. It is 18 years since I last saw him . . . we had a long talk about old times and old friends. Capt Hewitt came to tea. Col Wetherall & a number of other officers are appointed by the British government to select the proper places for fortifications on the Lakeshore and in the interior, in case of war with the United States.[183] . . .

May 13 . . . Capt Hewitt called and remained from 3 PM until 6. Sophia is making him a racing cap. Capt Leslie called. . . .

[181]The first reference in Amelia Harris' diary to Captain Edward Osborne Hewitt, Royal Engineers.

[182]There are no entries between 19 April and 11 May.

[183]Members of the commission of military experts despatched by Lord Monck to survey frontier fortifications and defences.

May 15 . . . All at Eldon are invited to a ball. . . . Sophia wishes to go. Edward asked me if I had any objections. I said not one. There is no reason why she should not lay off her mourning and go if she wishes to do so, and he ought to go with his wife although it may be a little sooner than he may wish to go after his brother's death. . . .
May 16 . . . Dr Ryerson came up this afternoon to spend a few days with us. He has a most violent cough & is looking ill and miserable. I hope the change of air may do him good.
May 19 Dr Ryerson wished to go home but I insisted upon his remaining until Saturday. . . . I got letters from Eliza & Sarah, [who] has given up the hope of ever visiting me, she says she is too poor to incur the expense. . . . Eliza writes a gossiping letter but is hurt that Mr Portman has never once written to her. . . .
May 21 . . . I got a letter from Mr Portman who seems to be enjoying himself at Quebec, but hates the political life he has entered, & I should be surprised if he did not, for the Government nor House of Assembly stand high either for gentlemanlike manners, honesty or morality. The telegraphic news today is that the Ministry have resigned, having been defeated upon the Militia Bill, I imagine the true cause of their defeat has been the intemperance of J.A. Macdonald. He has not been sober for the last fortnight and totally unable to attend to his public duties. . . .
May 22 . . . Dr Ryerson & Sophia went to see the artillery parade this morning. This afternoon they drove out to the farm. Edward drove Capt Hewitt out also. . . . On their return they went to see the Armstrong guns. Capt Hewitt came to tea, I did not see him but went to bed. . . . The Opposition are trying to form a Ministry. J.A. Macdonald and Mr Sicotte to be leaders of Upper & Lower Canada with what success is not yet known.[184]
May 25 Last night there was a great fire in Dundas Street, three houses belonging to Mr Wilson were burnt, and one other house. The offices of Harris & Brother were in great danger. All the books and papers were taken out. Teresa & Sophia were at work all night assisting to remove and take care of papers, every thing was taken to Becher's old office. This morning all were too wearied to go to Church. . . .
May 26 I told Sophia this morning about the remarks that had been made upon her & Capt Hewitt and that their flirtation had been dis-

[184]Louis Victor Sicotte (1812–89), lawyer, politician, judge, and fervent "Patriote." He joined J.S. Macdonald in forming the new government which was to last until May, 1863.

cussed. . . . I told her what Ellen Hamilton had said to Teresa and also what Mr Scott & Mr Griffin had overheard. I also told her that she was foolish to have invited Capt Hewitt a seat in our pew. She had placed herself in an awkward position. Now people in the Church will watch Mrs Edward and her beau and make their remarks accordingly, & she was wrong to make for & give Capt Hewitt a racing cap, had she made the cap for him & he bought it at the bazaar it would have been alright. I suppose she thinks that she has the right to the disposal of the seats in the pew, because Edward & George have paid the rent for the last two years, but she ought not to forget that Mr Harris paid £30 for the pew & that I & John have paid the rent for 15 years. . . . I was pleased with Sophia this evening, she showed good sense by not being offended by what I said to her. I thought her more amiable and nicer than I have seen her for some days, and she seemed to feel herself one of us again. . . .

May 27 Col Witherall called this morning. All the Commissioners on Fortifications have returned to London and are on their way to Port Colbourne to endevor to get a steam boat to make the round of the Lakes & enable them to report upon harbor defences. The whole party went as far as Paris in the same car with Amelia & myself. . . . Dr Ryerson met us at the station at Toronto and drove me direct to the house of Dr Adams the homeopathic physician. He prescribed diet & fresh air and infinitissimal globules. . . .

May 28 We went to Palmer's to get photographed, it was a very fatiguing businesss. I took a picture of Helen when she was 17 to get photographed as I think Mary & Eliza would remember her by that picture better than the later ones. Amelia went to Mrs Loring to borrow the large picture which Elizabeth had taken of John, as I wished to have that photographed also. Amelia found it in Elizabeth's drawer rolled up, crushed and torn at the edges, even Palmer said, what a pity. It is strange that she should pay $50 for a picture that she does not think worth framing. Elizabeth is in a boarding house at Niagara and it is whispered that she does not intend living with her mother again. . . .

May 29 . . . Dr & Mrs Ryerson came with us to the train, no people could be kinder than they have been to us. I am fonder of Dr Ryerson each time that I see him. . . .

May 31 . . . It is decided that George is to go to England. He is to sail from Boston on the 11th of June. . . .

Jun 1 . . . Mr Scott told us today that he had decided upon their going to England in August. . . . Edward, George & Capt Hewitt rode to the farm. Capt Hewitt returned to tea.

Jun 9 The parting is over and George is on his way to England. Edward was most kind and affectionate towards George on his leaving and did everything he could to make his trip pleasant. . . . The House is prorogued today, so I trust we shall soon have Mr Portman with us. All the family excepting myself went to the station to see George off. Teresa Askin was there and exalted in having the last kiss. Capt Hewitt has been very kind in giving George letters of introduction to his friends, and in writing to them about him. Amelia & Mr Griffin were here all the morning assisting his packing. Mr Griffin, Amelia and Mr Wilson came to luncheon. Mr Wilson told us that the present Ministry wants him to be chairman of a committee of three to investigate the accounts of money expended on the Ottawa buildings.[185] He either said that he had or would decline. I said all that I could to induce him to act. He has legal as well as local knowledge & in his investigation he would be just & generous & do nothing factious or ungenerous, but it would be shameful that a million of dollars would be expended in excess of the estimates, and no enquiry made into it. The Ministry could not have chosen a better man than Mr Wilson, and he will be wanting in his duty to his country if he declines. We were much amused a few days ago at his telling us that the govt had offered him the Deputy Judgeship under Judge Small & he to be judge after Judge Small's death (it being supposed that he is in bad health) with a present salary of £250 a year and by way of a finale old Small wrote to him congratulating him upon his elevation. Wilson could not help laughing at the idea of his coming in second to old Small with a salary of £250 a year when he is making by his profession nearly £2000. . . .
Jun 12 . . . Capt Hewitt called. He seems to be a very extraordinary man, very rich according to his own account, and full of adventure. He was chased for a mile and a half once by a ghost, and although he rode at full speed it kept close to him. . . .
Jun 16 Amelia received a very nice kind letter from Capt Dalzell of the Guards. . . . He is engaged to Mary Ross and although he expects opposition from his family yet he hopes when he pleads his case personally to gain his consent and to be able to return in a few months to be married. . . . Mary Ross is very young, only just from school. She is the daughter of clever parents and I believe a very nice girl but

[185]A special Commission of Enquiry into the construction of the Parliament Buildings at Ottawa was appointed on 21 June 1862 by the Governor-General-in-Council. It consisted of John Wilson (Chair), Joseph Sheard, Victor Bourgeau, and David Stark. The Commission presented its report to the Provincial Secretary on 29 January 1863. See NAC RG II, B(a), Vols. 837–43.

she is a colonist and that will be an objection and if she has no money that will be a very great objection as Capt Dalzell's father looks very sharp after money. . . . This is told in confidence & not to be repeated at present.[186] . . . No word from Mr Portman. Mr Carling told Edward today that Mr Portman had gone on some pleasure party, and would not return to Quebec until Tuesday, but what Tuesday it may be we do not know. He should have written.

Jun 17 Mr Scott & Teresa left for Lake Superior. Mr Scott intends fishing for some days at the Sault, and they will return by way of Collingwood. I try to feel cheery about Teresa's going, for I know that she will leave for England very soon, but her absence makes the house very solitary to me. . . .

Jun 20 . . . poor Col Dalzell has had another attack of hemorrhage from the lungs, but not so severe as the last, but I very much fear that he is not long for this world, as several of his family have died in the same way. We all hate to be asked by everyone where Mr Portman is, and what is detaining him, & giving such knowing looks as if they know, although we do not.

Jun 21 . . . In the evening I had a long talk with Edward, he is not very happy and thinks that Sophia is foolish in her intimacies and that she will be the subject of gossip. He spoke very kindly and very correctly. She had made arrangement[s] to go to a ball at the Gzowskis on Wednesday, without having told Edward, and Capt Hewitt is to go down to it, and as remarks have already been made about him and Sophia he thinks she had better not go, and I think he is right. Young married women cannot be too cautious in avoiding remark. . . .

Jun 22 . . . Capt Hewitt called and Edward and him walked to the Cove. Capt Hewitt remained to tea, we had a long talk about things past, present & to come.

Jun 23 Amelia called, she had a letter from Charles Griffin who said he had seen Mr Portman on Friday last, and that he talked of leaving Quebec on Monday (today), but that he was enjoying himself so thoroughly that he did not think he would get away unless by a *fluke* . . . a telegram came from Mr Portman to Mr Scott, asking him not to go to the Sault until his return, which would be Saturday at the very latest, & that he was very seedy. Why did he ask the Scotts not to go to the Sault, if the Griffins told him they had gone, and what did he wish us to understand by being very seedy – not that he is ill or he could not be leading the gay life that he is. If he is seedy from dissipa-

[186]A reminder that Amelia Harris' diary was read by all members of the family.

tion he has the remedy in his own power. . . . Sophia says Dr Ryerson has a large dinner party on Friday, but she does not tell Edward that she had invited Capt Hewitt to it before she left London. In Toronto the gossip is that Mr Portman is very much in love with some girl in Quebec, who is supposed to look like Helen. I hope he may get a good wife and be happy, and be truthful and honorable in all his actions for the sake of his children and for his own sake. . . .
Jun 26 . . . Mr Wilson came to dinner. He said that I had induced him to act on the commission for investigating the accounts of the Ottawa buildings. If so the country is indebted to me for a good commisioner.
Jun 28 This morning at $^1/_2$ past four I was surprised and delighted to see Mr Portman. He had come up by the night train, he acknowledged that he had behaved badly. Wounded affection is willing to accept any excuse and still trust and hope for the future, but I cannot help feeling how totally the remembrance of the past and all home ties and every thing that has been near and dear to him, had been obliterated for the time. When I saw that during his long absence he had never once thought sufficiently of Baby to bring a slight token of remembrance, not a toy, not a picture book, not even a paper of candy, it seems strange with a warm heart like his and possessing such kind and loving and tender feelings, there is something wrong some where, and I fear that during his sojourn at Quebec, that he has only carried the character of an agreeable man of pleasure. The thought carries a chill to my heart, for I know so well what he might be, and I have hoped so much that I at last expected him to be all that I wished. I still hope on, and pray that God will awaken him to a true sense of his responsibilities in this world, and lead him to live here as if there were an hereafter, that God may bless and keep him is my constant prayer. . . . Mr Portman, Amelia & I talked steadily from the morning until bedtime.
Jul 1 . . . Mr Portman and myself had another long talk about his marrying. I think he has made up his mind to marry soon, and although I advised him to reflect seriously, and be guided by cool judgment, and not be carried away by sudden passion or impulse, . . . yet I fear that it will be impulse & passion that will lead him at last. If it were not for the children I should feel less anxiety, yet I could not help feeling anxious for his happiness had he no children. I have a horror of Quebec society. I believe the House of Assembly to be one large brothel, and few members go there without feeling its contaminating influence. Mr Portman read my journal, and at luncheon he upbraided me with not believing him. When I asked him if he was in love or engaged, he said no, but I felt that there might be some mental reservations, . . . and also that his love was not what he had felt so

that he might without telling me an untruth answer me as he did. But today he spoke in a way that I cannot doubt his truthfulness, and confirmed what he before said, unless I believed him to be totally without principle, which God forbid that I should ever for one moment have cause to think. I will endevor to be silent on the subject of his marrying, unless he speaks to me. He knows what I think on the subject and the sort of women that are my aversion, then why should I say more. How sorry I was that Baby was not a girl, how thankful I now feel that he is a boy. Oh God, enable me to put my whole trust in Thy wisdom and mercy, and oh God I pray thee to bless and keep those motherless children. The remains of my first born son and daughter arrived here today. William was buried this day forty years. Amelia [Ellen] was buried the previous October. I was afraid the grave yard at Port Ryerse might be desecrated, and I wish them to lie near their father and sister, and therefore had them taken up and brought here, whilst poor John rests far away and poor Chasse sleeps beneath the deep until God bids the sea give up its dead. It brought strange sad feelings back after forty years to have the remains of these children once so dear to me again with me. . . .

Jul 2 The excitement of yesterday made me ill. I could not sleep and felt low & depressed this morning. . . . Edward opened the coffin of my children, and I looked once more upon the remains of those who were once so dearly beloved, so loving and so beautiful. I took a tooth from each of them to wear in a locket. After having been forty years in the grave, we are together in this world and shall soon meet in another.

Jul 3 . . . after Edward left me I had an uneasy sleep with that constant working of the brain until two o'clock, when I woke in great distress. I felt that I could not of my own will shake off those cares & anxieties, nor could I live under them. My burden was too great for my strength. I got out of bed and knelt by the window and prayed God with my whole heart to enable me to put my whole trust in Him, and to give me strength to bear and to submit to His will. I felt so ill and faint that I thought (without terror) they will find me here on my knees, dead, in the morning. I was unable to get into bed, and I recollect nothing until 5 o'clock when I awoke. I had had one lucid connected dream, which I very seldom have. I thought I was in the backyard, and that mules were drawing in a hearse. There were no horses to it, and the hearse & feathers looked old and faded. At the same time I heard the band in front of the house. I was surprised that Edward should have thought this necessary for the reinternment of my infants, and felt sorry. I knew the funeral was not quite ready and turned to come in, as I entered a large room, not like any in this house. I saw John coming to meet me. I knew that he was dead, but oh so glad to see him as he advanced towards me. I tried to see what change had taken place. He said if they have a wedding why did they not let it be very quiet[?] I said oh John it is not your wedding, it is your funeral; do you know you are dead[?] He said oh yes, and spoke quick & cheery. He asked me if the girls had come from England; I said yes. If we had made friends with the Bechers[?] Yes; if the new Ministry had got a rattling[?] Yes; I said John, my beloved John, are you happy[?] He said oh yes & that he had died slowly and resignedly. At this same time he seemed lying on a bed, I was bending over him, with my arms around his neck, and his arms around mine. I felt his frame so thin in my arms, and there was his high forehead, and his hair long and thin hanging over his head as in life. The room seemed to be filling with people and I was taken from him. As I awoke, feeling the pressure of his arms around my neck, I felt almost happy that I had seen him so vividly even in a dream. I turned to look at the clock, it was 5 AM. I went to sleep instantly, and slept soundly and sweetly, and rose up more hopeful to meet my poor Edward's unhappy face. He had no letter from Sophia. Mr Scott & Teresa came home by the 3 o'clock train. They saw Sophia at Toronto, she told them she was not coming home for 6 or 8 weeks and that she was going to the sea shore with her father and mother. She looked very bright and happy, and told them how much she was enjoying herself. The Scotts had a very pleasant trip to the Sault, and brought home a good many specimens of ore from the copper mines. . . .

Jul 4 I persuaded Edward not to go to Toronto until he heard from Sophia. He did not sleep last night, and was half mad. How heartless Sophia has behaved, and the worst of it is by the advice of her father. I have been dreadfully alarmed all day from the state Edward has been in. I am afraid of convulsions or brain fever. I telegraphed to Dr Ryerson to *bring* Sophia by the early train tomorrow. Before his answer came Edward got a letter from Sophia telling him that she was going to the sea side, thanking him for the money he had sent, and telling him he need not send any more, as her father would defray her expenses, and then followed a long list of things she wished to have sent down. Not one regret at not seeing him nor a wish that he would go down before she left. Its cool indifference almost maddened him. He decided upon going to Toronto at once. I was afraid to let him go alone, and Amelia volunteered to go with him. Poor fellow, I never saw any one so frightfully unhappy. How unworthy she is of so good, so kind & so devoted a husband. All he has asked of her was not to go to a ball without him, where a gentleman was to be, with whom she had been a subject of remark. Her father requested that she might go & Edward at once gave his leave. Then Dr Ryerson stepped in between his daughter & Edward and wrote an absurd, wicked letter which Edward would not answer, and this has led to estrangement on her part, and intense misery on his. She preferring her pleasures to her husband's happiness in which she is justified and supported by her father. What the end will be who can tell, but I fear happiness is gone from both of them. . . .

Jul 5 We were very anxious to get a telegram from Amelia this morning. About two o'clock it came, saying that all was right, and that they would all be home tonight. I do not know how matters have been settled, but I pity poor Edward. . . .

Jul 6 Last night Edward and Sophia came home at 10 PM. Mr Portman came at 4 this morning. Edward brought his wife home, but parted most unpleasantly from Sophia's father and mother. I will endevor to write down all the particulars when I feel equal to it. . . . Amelia came in the afternoon looking better than I thought she would, after all her fatigue and mental anxiety, going to Toronto with Edward and being abused by Mrs Ryerson, and travelling all night, in this excessive hot weather. Capt Hewitt called. I asked him to stay to tea but he declined, as he was going to Church. Sophia and Edward went to Church also, and Capt Hewitt returned *with them* to tea. . . .

Jul 7 I spent a wretched night and rose up ill. Sophia does not come near us, where we are she is not, perhaps it is best so with the feelings she entertains towards us. Her father & mother could not have spoken of us as they did, if it had not been the expression of her feelings. This is the second anniversary of her wedding day. . . .

Jul 8 I drove to the farm with Edward, he says Sophia is becoming a little more sane. He declares that she shall never see one of her family until they take a very different view of the duties of a married woman to what they do at present. Dr Ryerson told Edward that every lady in history (French History I suppose) had an admirer. Edward doubted whether they had happy husbands, however happy their admirers might be. Dr Ryerson gave Sophia the handsomest riding habit he could get and he also wishes to buy Teresa's saddle for Sophia and it was all arranged before she left Toronto, that when she returned to London, that Edward was to buy a pair of good saddle horses, and that Sophia was to ride Capt Hewitt's horse, and Capt Hewitt was to ride with them. Edward & Ellen Hamilton were to ride the horses Edward was to purchase and then the riding party would be perfect. Today when Edward was sitting in his own room with Sophia, a note came from

Capt Hewitt to Sophia, saying that he had been in the country to look at a pair of horses which he thought might suit Mr Harris, etc etc. Edward asked Sophia if she thought him rich enough to keep four horses, or fool enough to keep them if he was rich enough. He insisted upon her writing a note to Capt Hewitt as he dictated, which was to say that Mr Harris had no intention of purchasing *any* horses. He also told Sophia that if he has to take a house and live by themselves, he should return the horses that he has. Sophia then promised him that she would never write another note to Capt Hewitt or see him again if he wished it. Edward said he wished her to behave to Capt Hewitt as she would to any other gentleman, so as not to draw down remarks upon her. Edward told me Sophia was not going to the Becher's party.

Jul 9 Edward came to my room very early in the morning, his face looked haggard and anxious. I found out afterwards that Sophia was going to the Becher's party, although for reasons connected with her health she ought to have remained quietly at home. Mr Portman and Edward have been engaged a part of the day over Mr Portman's accounts. A difference of opinion arose as to which of them was largest around the shoulders, waist and hips. . . . Edward is largest around the waist & hips, they wished me to note this down in my journal. The Scotts, Mr Portman, Edward & his wife & Amelia went to the Bechers. I wrote a very long letter to George.

Jul 12 Edward not at all well this morning. Last night when he was looking so ill and wretched on the sofa, I told Sophia that I had been afraid that he would be ill, that she little knew how much he and we had suffered, that I had feared brain fever and even suicide. She did not say a word. . . .

Jul 22 I have had another ill turn and have been unable to write regularly, and I now can only put down those things that have made a deep impression. Edward has been very ailing as well as myself, but I believe it is mind that affects him more than disease, and I sometimes look at him with astonishment to see how cheerful and smiling he looks, when I know the bitter heartache he is enduring. Dr Ryerson continues to write to Sophia as if she was the most injured person, and he tells her to pray to God to support her through her trials, and Sophia continues to flirt as much as she can with Capt Hewitt. We do not encourage his visits. On Sunday the 13th Sophia asked Edward to drive her to the farm in the afternoon. He knew there was some motive besides the pleasure of the drive with him. They had not gone far when Capt Hewitt overtook them, and asked leave to join them. He said he knew they were going to the farm, and would like to go with them. He rode by the side of the carriage, and when they were at the farm Sophia was so devoted to Capt Hewitt that Edward spoke to her afterwards, and told her what her manner was. She asked him why he did not speak to her at the time – she is to be pitied. How can she think that to be wrong which she has always been taught to believe right and to flirt and to excite admiration she has believed to be the great object of life. . . . Miss Griffin and Charles Griffin[187] are on a fortnight's visit to the Griffins. . . . Mr Portman appears delighted to have the Griffins here and spends the most of his time with them. I cannot understand Mr Portman, he is so changed. He used to be so kind and affectionate and so loving, and he has been so dearly loved, and through that very affection he has had the power of hurting me more than any one ever has had out of my own family and now the struggle comes to kill the feeling I have cherished and to subdue the power which I have given him to hurt me. When he came from Quebec I spoke to him as I always have done of what I approved and what I disapproved, but what I said was more in support of my own belief that good could not come of evil, and that sin and sorrow were inseparable. He appeared to take all I said in good part and although I saw from the first day that he arrived here that he was determined to return to Quebec, yet it was no business of mine, . . . [I] was not at all surprised when he decided upon going to England by the Canadian steamer, although he had declared again and again that *nothing* would induce him to go by that line. But now he recants all that he had said, throws by all his fears & prejudices *to save a few dollars*. The fare is less and the steamer sails from *Quebec*. I have not, and shall not, make a remark, but straws cast on the water show the current. Though at first I only suspected, yet now Miss Griffin tells Amelia of his attachment there to a Miss Hale, & he unintentionally admitted to me that she was the young lady that report said he was in love with. Miss Griffin does not speak very highly of her. She says she is a fine voluptuous looking woman, and that her connections and the Prices are determined that Mr Portman will marry her. Miss Griffin says if he chooses to make a fool of himself she does not care. Is it not strange to hear Helen's husband and one we love so dearly spoken of in this way? The report came here that Miss Hale was engaged to an officer, a Mr Jackson of the 17th, but Miss Griffin says it is not so, nor has D. Price proposed for her as Mr Portman was led to believe. But all those reports were intended to make Mr Portman grasp at a prize which so many coveted, and it certainly had a great effect upon him. For the

[187]Gilbert Griffin's sister and brother.

day he heard that Miss Hale had accepted Mr Jackson he scarcely knew what he did or said. . . . I have never heard of Miss Hale before I heard her name coupled with Mr Portman's, but I do not like what I have heard of Quebec society, and from Miss Hale's mother having married a second husband 20 years younger than herself, when she had grown up daughters, and that second husband a brute. I should not argue much from her parentage, and the way they appear to be trying to lead Mr Portman into this marriage does not say much for the young lady herself. . . . Mr Portman must be the best judge of his own happiness, or of what requirements will make him happy in a wife. The children are in God's hands, and I try to say from my heart, thy will be done. The day that Mr Portman made the admission regarding Miss Hale, he did it so unintentionally, and looked so embarassed, that I laughed at him, as I would have done at any other man in love, but it was but a few minutes before memory reminded me that in this very room it was that Helen told me Mr Portman had proposed for her. How vividly she came back to me as she then looked, and now she had been but a little more than two years in her grave, & I, her mother, was laughing at Mr Portman for being in love – it is all right and natural that he should forget (and replace) Helen, . . . His marrying may be the best thing he can do, but it cannot bring pleasant thoughts to me, nor can I help feeling anxious about the children, so I will not speak of it to any one. Since the discussion about Miss Hale, Mr Portman's manner has changed towards me altogether. He scarcely speaks to me, and never comes into my room. I am unconscious of having said or done anything to annoy him.

On Saturday last Teresa heard there was a Camp Meeting near Komoka and as she had never seen one, she wished to go and asked Mr Portman if he would go with them. He gave a sort of half assent. I told her she had better get a decided answer, for if he went we would all have an early dinner. He said he would go & we dined early, and when the carriage was ready, the Scotts sent to the Griffins for Mr Portman thinking he was there, but he was in his own room and said he would not go. The Scotts were rather put out as they would have liked to have him with them, and they also depended upon him to show them the way. . . . When Mr Portman came downstairs he said he had told them the way. I said he ought to have told them that he was not going sooner. It was the only remark I made. . . . He came down at $^{1}/_{2}$ past six and was going out. I told him we would have tea at 7. He said alright but did not tell me not to wait for him. He did not return until after I was in bed. The next morning nurse came into my room in a state of great consternation, and said Mr Portman was gone, and his bed had not been slept in. I went into his room and found it was true. I then went to Teresa who was as much surprised as I was. Mr Portman had returned before she went to bed, and had said nothing of going away. We searched his room to see if he had left a note of explanation for me, but there was none. I thought it very strange and felt much hurt. I told Teresa to write to Amelia and see if she knew what it all meant. Amelia said he had gone to the Falls by the night train and would be back at 3 PM. When I saw Edward and Sophia they told me that Mr Portman had gone to their room to borrow a travelling bag, and that he had told *them* that he was going to the Falls. When he returned he did not come to my room and greet me as he always had done, but merely glanced into the door as he passed. I went into the hall and told him that he had caused a great commotion in the house when it was discovered that he was gone. He said very little excepting that he had been at the Falls and that Col Hampton was not dead as had been reported.

Since then Mr Portman has been towards me so cold and distant, I cannot comprehend the cause. I have never by word, look, or act, since I have known Mr Portman meant an unkindness, nor do I think when he allows himself to reflect that he can say or think otherwise. I thought he has always been so kind and good a husband to Helen, that after her death I gave him the same warm love I had felt for her, and our mutual sorrows had made him very near and dear to me. What the cause or motive of his present coldness may be I cannot tell. Some times I think he fancies I will oppose his marrying, and that he will gradually break with us before that takes place, but he need not fear one word of opposition from me. From my heart I wish him every happiness. . . .

Jul 24 This morning Mr Portman came into my room as usual. I gave him my hand and asked him if we were friends. I pulled him towards me & kissed him, I could not keep from crying. I asked him what had caused his coolness towards me. He denied being so, but said he had been in a bad humor for two or three days. . . . Edward took me out for a drive. He is happier than he has been for some time past. He thinks Sophia takes a more common sense view of things. She is to be pitied for she has never been taught what her duties in this world are, either towards her God or her husband. . . .

Jul 25 Another anniversary of dear Helen's birthday. . . . Mr Portman has been more like his own dear self today, and yet there is something wrong with him. He as Miss Griffin says is easily influenced by those about him. This would be all well if he only associated with the good. I feel daily more convinced that the good cannot associate with the impure without suffering from it in some way, particularly women, they must avoid the very appearance of evil. I daily feel more thankful that my family never had intimate friends or associates. . . .

Jul 27 Teresa, Edward & Sophia went to Church, I read the service in my own room. Edward & Sophia are getting on very badly & I am afraid their disagreements will end in a separation, which will be to the great scandal of both, but Sophia is the one that will most justly suffer, . . . as she has exposed herself to scandal with Capt Hewitt. . . . Capt Hewitt called. Sophia has told him of the remarks made about him & her. It appears to me that she must have laid aside a good deal of womanly delicacy before she could have named such a subject to him. I do not quite like his manner when he knows the remarks that are made and when Dr Ryerson has asked him his intentions. He cannot think his visits here can be agreeable either to Edward or to the rest of the family and he ought to avoid Sophia in place of seeking her on all occasions. Mr Portman had letters yesterday from his father and mother. They did not appear to be very satisfactory. Amelia tells me that his father insists upon his marrying immediately and wants him to go to England and marry a woman with money. . . .

Jul 28 . . . Sophia complains to every one she talks with of her hard fate & tells them how much she dislikes living here. I went to her this morning and asked if she would rather have a house to herself, or live here. She said she would rather live here if the Scotts left. If they remained she would rather go by herself. I told her that however reluctant I might be to part with Edward, yet whenever she wished to leave I would insist upon his going. . . .

Aug 4 Mr Portman left today for Quebec on his way to England. . . .

Aug 6 . . . Edward drove Baby and me out. He wants me to make a new will and only entail Eldon House upon him & George, if they are without children leave it for the survivors of them to will as they think best. By my present will it will go to Sarah should they die without children. . . .

Aug 9 Sir Allan MacNab[188] died yesterday after a very short illness, it is said of gastric fever. Another of our leading Canadians is gone. Few of his contemporaries are left. Sir John Robinson and Chief Justice McLean are still amongst the living. Sir Allan's name will long be remembered in the Province. He has been a consistent politician

[188]Allan Napier MacNab (1798–1862), M.P. for Hamilton (1841–57) and Prime Minister of Canada (1854–56). After living in England from 1857 to 1860, he had returned to Canada in 1860 and was elected as representative for the Western division.

and an agreeable companion, a true friend to the city of Hamilton, always furthering her interests to the utmost of his power. His principles were conservative and unwavering in his habits, he was extravagant, always living beyond his means, but a kind husband and an indulgent father. The all exciting subject is the American Conscription.[189] To avoid it the Americans are coming into the country by hundreds. . . .

Aug 11 Capt Hewitt called and paid Sophia a visit of an hour & a half. She did not tell any of us that he was here. . . .

Aug 15 I went out driving with Baby and made three calls, the first I have made for three years excepting in the case of sickness or sorrow. I called upon Mrs Innes & her mother, Mrs Clarke.[190] I knew her 45 years ago, she was then Janet Cummings, and have not seen her since until today. We parted in our teens and have met old gray headed women. She was a pretty little girl of thirteen when I last saw her. She used to spend a great portion of her time with me and was a great pet with all the gentlemen at H.O.[191] Kingston. I was 19 when I last saw her. . . . I called the Lawrasons, . . . I then went to the cemetary and took Baby to his mother's grave.

Aug 16 . . . Edward and Sophia . . . did not enjoy the ball at the Streets[192] very much. . . . Amelia would have enjoyed herself if Mr Griffin had not been in one of his disagreeable humors. He took it into his head to be jealous of J.A. Macdonald, who took Amelia in to supper and paid her a good deal of attention. Amelia had only seen him once before in her life and that only for a few minutes. He is a clever man whose moral character I despise. At the same time, from the position which he has held and will most probably hold again in the country, it would not do for Amelia whose husband holds a public office, to be rude to him, and she felt, from her own age, character and connections, that she could hardly suffer in the estimation of the world by talking with J.A. Macdonald in a public ball room for an hour or two. . . . He spoke very well of Mr Portman and said that he was a general favorite. . . .

[189]Faced with a serious shortage of manpower, on 17 July 1862 the U.S. Congress passed the Militia Law that extended federal powers and compulsory enlistment in the Militia. Conscription was subsequently introduced by the Enrolment Act on 3 March 1863. Of some 776,000 men drafted, 161,000 "failed to report," many fleeing to Canada.

[190]Mrs. Clark was a friend of Amelia Harris during her days at Port Ryerse and Kingston.

[191]Hydrographer's Office.

[192]The Streets lived in Niagara Falls.

Aug 18 . . . Amelia told me part of her conversation with Mr Macdonald about Mr Portman. He said that he hoped Mr Portman would get married while in England, that he was afraid that he might marry in Quebec and said that he was very much in love with Miss McFarlane, and he but little knew what a connection he would be forming if he married her. He said Mr Portman worked hard and was steady in the House until after his [Macdonald's] Ministry went out, that after that he had not much to do, and he gave himself up to Quebec society, which, from the free and easy manner of the Quebecans he supposed had a charm for Mr Portman, but if he was not led into matrimony that he would get over his liking for it after a short time. This is the conversation of J.A. Macdonald *sober*. He condemns and despises what in drunkeness and debauchery he gives himself up to. How melancholy that men of sense and talent, who know the right, will yet choose the wrong. . . . J.A. Macdonald spoke of John to Amelia in the highest terms, as an excellent young man of great intelligence and promise.

Sep 8 It is over. Teresa and Mr Scott are gone. God only knows whether we shall ever meet again in this world. They seemed to wish almost that they had never thought of going. Sophia was very kind in assisting Teresa. Amelia was here all morning doing every thing she could. Amelia and Edward went to the station with them, Sophia remained with me. . . .

Sep 11 . . . In the evening Sophia showed me a set of agate buttons which he [Capt Hewitt] had given her, they were very pretty. I asked her if Edward knew that he had given them to her, she said, of course he did. . . .

Sep 19 The result of the election is known and Mr Becher has been defeated by a majority of 209. I am very sorry. It is strange that a correct, moral man should be so much disliked. . . .

Sep 20 . . . The Declaration of the Members elected took place today. Mr [Elijah] Leonard's speech was said to be unmanly and insulting to Becher and that Becher did the pathetic, forgave his enemies, blessed the public, friends & foes, and cried and made a fool of himself. . . .

Sep 23 Elizabeth arrived last night after I was in bed, she is looking very well. She is really handsome, by far the finest looking woman that I know of. . . .

Sep 25 Mr Wilson called. He has just returned from Ottawa. . . . [He] says had he known what the Ottawa investigation would lead to he would have had nothing to do with it. . . . He says there will be a great exposure & many of his friends and acquaintances will be placed in no enviable light. Mr Wilson told me today that he would have offered himself as a candidate for the Upper House, for the Malahide Division, but that Becher came to him and would have made it a personal quarrel. . . . Becher could not deny what Mr Wilson said, but he thought from their long friendship that Wilson would not oppose him. Mr Wilson said their friendship was a very one sided affair, that when it suited him (Mr Becher), he would make claims upon it, at other times he would cast it to the winds, . . .

Sep 30 . . . The report that Mr Portman intends resigning his seat is still kept alive, although I have had it contradicted in both papers. It causes a good deal of ill feeling towards him. How well the Radicals play their game. They think they could carry the riding now if they could only provoke him to resign.

Oct 6 . . . Poor Edward is in trouble again tonight. He saw a letter from Mrs Ryerson to Sophia telling her that Capt Hewitt had arranged to send a horse to Toronto on the 18th, the day Sophia is to go down for her to ride. Mrs Ryerson says Dr Ryerson has bought another horse and she would rather Capt Hewitt did not send his. No allusion to this arrangement has ever been made to Edward, though I think it is evident that she expects to meet Capt Hewitt there. Mrs Ryerson wishes *her to write to Capt Hewitt's groom* and tell him not to take the horse down.

Oct 7 . . . Sophia gave him [Edward] her mother's letter to read, but suppressed the sheet about Capt Hewitt's horse. This deception looks very bad and Edward cannot help feeling that it is so. . . .

Oct 8 . . . Edward this morning spoke to Sophia about the arrangement made for him to have Capt Hewitt's horse when in Toronto and about her suppressing the part of her mother's letter alluding to it and telling him that was all of her mother's letter. She justified her conduct & her father's conduct regarding Capt Hewitt and almost maddened Edward and he made use of language towards her father & towards her which he ought not to have done. I know that he has had great provocation from her father, but he should never forget that he is Sophia's father and whatever he may do or say he will have to answer to a higher power. . . . When she got that letter she should have gone to Edward and showed him the letter in place of suppressing it and telling him an untruth about it, and told him that she knew nothing of the arrangement which her father had mad[e] but that she would not go to Toronto until after Capt Hewitt returned to London. I told her then that Edward could not have blamed her, I told her also that when a woman lost her husband's confidence that it would take years of rectitude and truthfulness to regain it, but that it was worth the trouble, that they were both young, but a little over two years married, and that nothing could separate man and wife but *death or sin*. . . .

Oct 9 . . . Sophia looks very unhappy, but Edward looks wretched. . . .
Oct 10 . . . The whole day has been one of mental misery to me although I had a very great pleasure in getting letters from nearly all my absent ones (Col Dalzell, Sarah, Mary, Mr Portman, George & Teresa) and they were all well & happy as far as I could judge. I saw this morning that things were getting worse between Edward and Sophia. . . . I this morning felt so alarmed to see the state Edward was in that when Mr Griffin came I spoke to him. He afterwards spoke to Sophia, and when he came downstairs he told me that Sophia wished to go for Edward, that she was going to ask his forgiveness & to promise never to see Capt Hewitt again. Edward came up after a short time and peace seems to be restored, but Edward looks exhausted and wretched. . . . I was in a great fright again in the evening for fear peace might again be disturbed. In the spring, Sophia spoke to Capt Leslie[193] when he was going to England about getting a [riding] habit for her. Mr Griffin was present at the time and accidentally mentioned it to Amelia. Something was said to her about it when she [Sophia] denied having spoken to Capt Leslie about it. Now his letter comes proving that she was untruthful and [for] Edward to see this immediately after his reconciliation must give him very unpleasant feelings.
Oct 12 This morning when alone with Edward I asked him if he felt happier. He said, yes. I asked him if he thought it would last, he said he could not tell. He thought she had really given up Capt Hewitt, but that yesterday she had got another letter from her Mother kindly written as regarded him, but wanting Sophia to go down on Tuesday, telling her there was to be a sort of family meeting, that her grandfather's house was to be sold and that her Aunt Beatty and Aunt Spencer had come to pay her grandmother a visit before they left the old residence and they wanted her to go down. Edward said, What am I to do, it is only two days since our reconciliation has taken place, and then she agreed not to go to Toronto until Capt Hewitt's return, and now she wants to go on Tuesday. I told him he had better let her go, that if she wants to be his wife to the end of his days, she would have to stand the test of Capt Hewitt's admiration, and of her family's influence against him, that what ever her father or mother did his tongue was tied. . . .
Oct 13 . . . Edward told me this evening that he had opened a letter

[193]Captain Leslie, an officer in the Royal Artillery, and his wife, were close friends of Amelia and Gilbert Griffin.

from Dr Ryerson to Sophia full of abuse towards him. It was a letter no father ought to have written and no wife ought to have read. He told Sophia so and advised her to burn it without reading which she did at once in his presence. Sophia had told her father that Edward was going to return the horses, carriage, etc which Dr Ryerson had given her and it was that which called forth his abuse. . . .

Oct 17 . . . This morning he [Mr Griffin] got a letter from Dr Ryerson thanking him for acting a brotherly part towards Sophia and going over the same ground & justifying himself about Capt Hewitt's horse. The letter was ungrammatical, badly expressed and deficient in common sense. I begin to think that his brain is affected as he has suffered much in his head for a year or two past. Perhaps we judge him harshly when we think him so wrong headed. He may not be capable of seeing what is right. Mr Griffin read his answer to me and it was very good indeed. He spoke kindly of Sophia but did not justify her conduct, and he represented things in rather a different light from what Dr Ryerson has viewed them. . . .

Oct 19 . . . Edward has been busy all day writing to Sophia. He seems a good deal softened although he wrote strongly. He could not read his letter or speak of Sophia without crying. . . .

Oct 20 . . . [Amelia] told me that Mr Griffin told her this morning that the day he spoke to Sophia it was her intention to have left for Toronto without saying a word to Edward. In short, that she intended to leave him for good. She told Mr Griffin that she was perfectly miserable, that Edward constantly abused her relations and constantly praised his own and that she could not stand it. By Mr Griffin's advice she made friends with Edward. Edward certainly has spoken of her father *to her* in a way that cannot be justified under any circumstances though Edward certainly has had great provocation. It is not often that a father will take part with his daughter's lover against her husband but still he is her father, and Edward ought not to abuse him in the way he does to her. I wish I had known yesterday what Amelia told me today. I would have tried to have prevented him mentioning her father in his letter to her, but it is too late now. I shall not be surprised if she never returns to him. Perhaps if he lives over 5 or 6 months he may be happier without her than with her, but I fear he will be broken hearted. . . .

Oct 21 . . . Today he [Edward] wrote another long letter to Sophia going over pretty much the same grounds that he did on Sunday. Amelia and I advised him not to send it as it could do no good. He took our advice and wrote a more chirpy letter & made no allusion to Dr Ryerson or to any thing that was disagreeable.

Oct 25 . . . Edward got a very indignant letter from Sophia rather taunting him with being poor and not able to keep horses, & says she does not wish him to incur any expense on her account. But that if he will not let her exchange the ponies for a riding horse why he can keep the ponies but if he cannot afford the expense to send them down and her father will sell them and she will give her father the money to pay for the grey mare and her father will keep it for her and that will be an additional inducement for her to visit Toronto. Edward wrote back a very kind and jovial letter pretending not to understand any of her bits of ill humor. . . .

Oct 28 . . . My first inquiry in the morning was, had George returned. No, he was not here. When I was about half dressed there came a tap at my door and in walked George. I was so glad to see him, he looked thin and not as well as I had hoped to see him. . . . George has returned very much pleased with his sisters, and estimates them very highly. He thinks Col Crutchley one of the best men in the world & I quite agree with him. . . . Edward got a letter today from Sophia telling him that her father and Capt Hewitt had gone to the Bay[194] to shoot, that Capt Hewitt had lunched there that day and that he had got an extension of leave until the 15th of November. She told him that he *must not* send the horses down, that when her father returned *they* would decide what was to be done with them, that if the horses went down, the phaeton and sleigh *must* go too. Her letter was very unwifely. It was what I could fancy a mistress might write when she was about getting a new lover and wanted to get rid of an old one. Edward had engaged a groom to take the ponies down and bought a ticket, but stopped them & wrote to Sophia that he would keep the ponies until the 15th, but *he had decided* upon not keeping horses this winter. When Sophia left he requested *her* not to see Capt Hewitt. She has lunched with him. Dr Ryerson wrote to Mr Griffin that Capt Hewitt was not to return until December. He was in Toronto on Monday the 27th, how long before that we do not know. His horse that was to have gone for Sophia's use has been in Toronto some time. Whether Sophia has ridden him or not I do not know, but one thing is certain, both her and her father are acting very foolishly. . . .

Oct 30 . . . George has returned to the office and is hard at work. . . . He [Edward] told me that Sophia said Mrs Loring was most anxious that Elizabeth should remain here all the winter & wondered if I would ask her. I wish people would let my household alone. Edward and

[194]Long Point Bay.

George went to a ball given by the 63rd. They both looked very nice when they went away.
Oct 31 The ball went off as well as it could where there were very few gentlemen & still fewer ladies, though there were plenty of people there. . . .
Nov 1 . . . When Sophia left she was to return on Tuesday the 4th, now she wishes to remain until after a ball on the 11th. Edward told her it was a farce asking his leave to stay or what she should do or not do. He had quite made up his mind that she would stay away as long as she chose and do what she liked, and return when it suited her purpose to do so. . . . He says it is like beginning a new life, all his old hopes of happiness and plans for their future are gone, that he must endevor to strike out something new for himself alone.
Nov 2 . . . I asked her [Elizabeth] to come for six weeks, they are up today. I have said nothing about her remaining longer but intend to ask her to extend her visit to the beginning of December, but I will not ask her to make her home here. If Sophia does not return no daughter in law shall again call Eldon House home while I am living.
Nov 6 . . . There was a letter here from Sophia. Its contents were as light and as frivolous as she is. She takes no notice of his not having given her leave to remain to the ball, nor does she make a remark upon his saying that it had been long since she had in any way been influenced by his wishes, but tells him about their daily riding parties of young girls and officers and about her having jumped nine fences in one day, and asked him if he could not leave his business for one day and come down to the ball, that it would do him good, but not one word about coming home. Edward thinks he will not write to her again. . . .
Nov 10 I got a letter from Teresa & Edward got one from Mr Scott, requesting him to send home at once his chest of plate & linen. It made me feel quite ill as I felt the next news would be that they did not intend returning. . . .
Nov 12 . . . Things now seem to have come to a crisis and Edward wishes me to go to Toronto tomorrow and to see if I can convince Dr Ryerson that he is doing his best to ruin his daughter, both soul and body.
Nov 13 Edward wrote out my instructions. . . . When I arrived in Toronto I put up at the Queen's Hotel to avoid Capt Hewitt who was staying at the Rossin. I at once wrote to Dr Ryerson asking as a *favor* that he would call to see me the next morning between 8 & 9. . . . There was a tremendous noise at the Queen's Hotel all night. Cabs driving up. People running in and out. I decided in my own mind that it was the noisiest hotel I had ever been in.

Nov 14 This morning the noise was all explained. Last night the Rossin House was burned down. 4 or 5 lives were lost. . . . Dr Ryerson came at half past nine and remained until a quarter to two. . . . He told me that he had arranged to bring Sophia as far as Paris on her way home the next day. I fancied that Capt Hewitt was to take charge of her the rest of the way as his leave would be up and unless he got an extension he would have to return to London. Dr Ryerson told me that he held a bond from Edward to make a settlement when he had anything to settle of three hundred pounds a year upon Sophia and that he should enforce it to the utmost that the law would allow. I said the whole [thing] was a bad business. He said he had always found Sophia truthful and that he believed her incapable of deception. I wish I could say the same. He justified or excused everything Sophia had done and refused to believe what he could neither excuse nor justify. . . . We shook hands and parted probably never to meet again. On my return I met Edward at the station. He was very much excited and I had nothing pleasant to tell him. There was not one softening word. I told him every thing. . . .

Nov 15 . . . He got a letter from Sophia the day I was away telling him how dissipated she was & that Capt Hewitt was to dine there that day. Edward returned the letter. . . .

Nov 17 Edward sent the horses, sleigh, harness & phaeton to Toronto to Dr Ryerson today. . . . Elizabeth is very kind and good, and is improving herself in every way. She reads books that will form and improve her mind and as she reads she makes notes so that it will be impressed upon her mind and she is improving her French. . . .

Nov 19 . . . Elizabeth has advised, and Mr Griffin approved of Edward's writing to Sophia to explain what her father seems not to have understood that he does not wish her to return unless she will cut the acquaintance of Capt Hewitt and promise never to go to Toronto without his leave, nor see her father & mother until he is willing she should do so. If she will agree to this she can return at once to Eldon or he will take a house and fit it as soon as he can. He has written to this effect but I doubt her submitting to such terms. Capt Hewitt returned last night. Mr Griffin saw him today and delivered my message that I did not wish him to call again at Eldon & Edward requested him not again to see or have any communication with his wife. Capt Hewitt said that he knew that he was the unintentional cause of trouble between Edward and his wife which he very much regretted and he regretted also that he had given pain to a family from whom he had received so much kindness. He spoke highly of me and hoped that I would not feel it necessary to cut him in public.

He said the Ryersons & Mrs Edward [Sophia] had been so kind to him that he could not promise to cut them without an explanation, that he would go to Toronto tomorrow night to see them and on his return he would tell Mr Griffin whether he would cut them or not. This sounds very cool to me. It appears to me that if he was the honorable man he professes to be and if he felt the respect for the family which he professes to do, that when he found that he was the innocent cause of unhappiness to any of us that he would of himself at once withdraw, but of course Sophia is to decide that point and the only thing left for Edward to do is if Sophia returns to his protection, to horse whip Capt Hewitt if he speaks to her. If she remains with her father Edward must let her father take the responsibility of her actions. Any man is a fool that fights a duel for a false or a frivolous woman. . . .
Nov 21 . . . Sophia is safe with [Capt Hewitt] as far as any criminality goes. He will flirt, but he is wise enough not to commit himself or entangle himself with a married woman, it is fortunate for Sophia that her lover has more prudence than she has.
Nov 22 Edward got a letter this evening from Sophia. She tells him she felt for some months before she went away that she would be much happier in her father's house than at Eldon and that she will not leave her father at present to return to him but says at some future time she may if he asks her. . . . Her letter is evidently dictated by her father. . . .
Nov 23 . . . Capt Hewitt wrote to Mr Griffin enclosing the copy of a letter which he had written to Dr Ryerson, in which he said he had gone to Toronto to endevor to restore peace and that he had done so by the request of Mr Griffin who on this occasion represented the family at Eldon, and requesting Mr Griffin to see him. Mr Griffin wrote to Capt Hewitt requesting him to disabuse Dr Ryerson's mind of the impression that the family at Eldon either wished or induced him to go to Toronto and Mr Griffin begged him to recollect that he had distinctly told him that he went contrary to his wishes and approval. Mr Griffin also declined seeing him. . . .
Nov 24 . . . Mr Griffin showed me the correspondence between himself & Capt Hewitt. Capt Hewitt's last letter was alright. He declines all his invitations to Toronto and will hold no communications with Sophia whatever, and we are to recognize him in public. So the matter stands at present. If Sophia returns in less than a year it will not be for the happiness of either her or Edward. She must have time to reflect and to feel what it is to be separated from her husband, that is if she is capable of seeing and feeling as most women would. . . .
Nov 27 . . . Elizabeth & I have been busy packing up Sophia's things to send them to Toronto. Mr Griffin came in & thought we were

wrong to send them without her writing to ask us to do so. He said it was like shutting the door in her face. I thought differently, I think they ought to be sent. Her father wrote to request that *all* her things should be sent to her. . . . After Mr Griffin left us he went to Edward and advised him not to send them. Edward consulted me. I would not advise him but told him to do what he thought best. The result is that the things are not to go at once but to wait and see what two or three weeks will bring forth. They remain packed ready to go. . . .

Nov 29 . . . I got another letter from Dr Ryerson. He abuses Edward as usual and praises Capt Hewitt.

Dec 2 Amelia had a visit by appointment today from Capt Hewitt. She discovered that Edward and Sophia have been the amusement of the Barracks for some time. Their conversation not of the most agreeable kind was overheard at a ball at the Barracks and on some other occasions, she also discovered that Capt Hewitt had not a very high opinion of either the doctor or Mrs Ryerson and he admitted that all our family and Teresa in particular were abused in the grossest manner. . . . I answered Dr Ryerson's letter and made my answer very short and curt. . . .

Dec 3 Elizabeth got a letter from Sophia requesting her to lock up and send down all her *belongings*. There was nothing in the [letter] but directions about her things. We finished packing today and *all* her things are in readiness to go. . . .

Dec 6 I got letters from Mr Portman, Teresa & Dr Ryerson. . . . Dr Ryerson's letter was in the same style as his former ones, only he is more vicious towards me. He says Sophia has improved so much in health and looks that every body observes it, and he says it is owing to her happiness in being freed from her husband and being away from Eldon. . . .

Dec 19 . . . Edward and George did not return from the Barracks until 3 AM. Edward and Capt Hewitt exchanged bows. They sat opposite each other at dinner and fate threw them together at the whist table. . . .

Dec 22 Elizabeth left this morning for Toronto, she is to return in about a fortnight. . . .

Dec 23 . . . I am very glad to find the Scotts intend returning next summer. Eliza says Mr Portman will not leave England before the 10th of January. . . .

Dec 25 Christmas has passed with all its remembrances. I went to Church with Amelia. Mr Griffin, Amelia & the two Griffin boys dined with us. . . .

Dec 29 I received a very nice letter from Elizabeth. Sophia & Col

Robertson of the Engineers had driven over in Sophia's carriage and called upon her. Sophia was handsomely dressed & looked very pretty and very happy. When Elizabeth returned the call she found Sophia and Colonel Robertson in the back drawing room on a sofa very sweet, looking over a photo book which Col Robertson had given her. . . .

Dec 31 A lovely day. Amelia came here early and we were very busy . . . Mrs Cronyn called & Mrs Goodhue and Mrs Thomas called. Amelia remained all day. I wrote to Mary and so ends the year 1862. It has been a sad year to poor Edward and leaves him but little hope of future domestic happiness. Sad thoughts will arise if I sit here alone. Edward & George both gone out yet I try to forget my sorrows and look to the end which must be near and to feel grateful for all God's kindness and blessings to me. . . .

1863

Jan 1 A lovely morning. Edward & George wished me to receive visitors, they dislike having the house shut up, so I have admitted all who came. . . . The Bishop was my first visitor, then Mr Hamilton, Mr Askin, [G]eorge Moore, who staid to luncheon, the Revnd Brough, & the Revnd Mr Long called. The Revnd Mr McLean, Mr Griffin, N. Montserratt, W. Lawrason called. Amelia spent the evening here. Edward went to the Griffins to smoke. George did not return from visiting until 12 at night. He spent the evening at the Askins & so ended the first day of the year.

Jan 6 . . . I got a letter from Mr Portman and one from Teresa & Mr Scott. Mr Scott has made me a present of his carriage. . . . He says he will come out next summer and return every winter for hunting. Much as I wish them here I would rather they did not come if it is only to spend the summers here and the winters in England. Teresa is not strong enough to stand the wear and tear of such travel. . . . Mr Griffin told Capt Hewitt that his interference was unauthorized and disapproved of and Mr Griffin wrote in strong language to Dr Ryerson on the subject but Edward had no power to prevent Capt Hewitt's going to Toronto & Sophia was then separated from him and under her father's protection. Edward might have horse whipped Capt Hewitt or called him out, either act would have branded Sophia with guilt and it must be borne in mind that we did not then, and do not now think her criminal, and we then much more than now looked forward to the possibility of a reunion.

Jan 7 Edward sent Sophia her quarter's allowance of $50 through

George on Monday. Today the acknowledgement of the sum received arrived, enclosing some studs and a solitaire[195] of Edward's which had been sent with her things. Sophia requested George to give the enclosed to *Mr Harris*, not even to Edward. . . .

Jan 14 Mr McInnes left this morning. He invited me to his wedding.[196] . . . We read Mr Portman's speech at an agricultural meeting in England published in the *Times*. He abuses Canada when here but I am glad to see that he speaks up for her when away.

Jan 16 . . . Dr Ryerson says Nordheimer[197] will call in a few days for Sophia's piano, either to sell it here or to send it to Toronto to sell. We would rather it was not sold here as people will think that Edward is selling his wife's piano and we do not like to say a word as we would not willingly let them think that they could do anything that would annoy us. I shall be glad when every article that Sophia has any claim to is out of the house. . . .

Jan 23 . . . I got a letter from Elizabeth. She is at Barrie and will not be here until the end of the month. She sent up a large box of pictures which arrived today. As she is to remain here but two months I cannot imagine why she sent them. . . .

Jan 25 . . . Mrs Askin came in after Church and remained all day and told me so much scandal. She asked me if it was true that Edward and Sophia had separated. I said Sophia would not return soon. Then, she said, the reports are true. I said, what do people say for I have no chance of knowing. She said it was reported that Sophia flirted very much with Capt Hewitt and that Edward and her had quarrelled and that he had sent her home to be out of the way of Capt Hewitt, but that Edward was mistaken if they thought that she was out of his way for Capt Hewitt went to Toronto. But no one appeared to throw any blame upon Edward. . . .

Jan 26 . . . Mr Griffin had a letter from Capt Hewitt saying that the two months were up in which he had pledged himself not to go to Toronto and that he intended going there on the 30th to a ball. Mr Griffin replied that he had nothing further to do in the matter but if Capt Hewitt had the feelings of a gentleman for Sophia's sake he would not go to Toronto while Sophia is there and separated from her husband. His going will confirm all the scandal about Sophia. I think we shall all cut him on his return. . . . Becher asked me if there was any truth in the report that Edward and Sophia had separated. I admit-

[195]A reference to jewelry.
[196]He had been visiting Eldon for two days.
[197]A music company in Toronto.

ted that it was true and told him some of the causes laying the blame upon her father as much as I could. He thinks there is temper on both sides and that it will all come right again. There must be a great change in the feeling . . . of both parties before things can come right. . . .
Jan 29 . . . George came in with a very unpleasant piece of news. The present Ministry have appointed another issuer of marriage licenses for London – Mr Moncrieff. It will make the income of the office very small, not over £700 a year. I wrote to Sandfield Macdonald[198] about it but I suppose it will do no good.
Jan 31 The Chief Justice, Sir John Beverley Robinson, died this morning. As a Canadian of Honor, talent and integrity, he stood first and there is one universal feeling of sorrow that he passed away. . . .
Feb 1 . . . Dr Ryerson wrote to me by Elizabeth and returned my manuscript, microscope and hydrostatic balance.[199]
Feb 3 I got letters from Eliza & Teresa. I am sorry to find that Mr Portman was seriously hurt by his fall when hunting. . . . Mr Wilson came to breakfast & luncheon. He is annoyed about the issuing of the marriage license being given to Mr Moncrieff, at least his having been appointed to issue as well as Edward and he has written to Sandfield Macdonald about it, which is very kind of him.[200] He goes to Toronto tomorrow to attend Sir J. Robinson's funeral and he will call upon Sophia and speak to her about signing her dower.[201] . . .
Feb 4 . . . He [Mr Portman] is unable to return in time to attend the present session of Parliament and if his constitutents are discontented he has placed his resignation in the hands of Mr Labatt. He will not return before the end of May. I am very sorry not to see him for so long a time, at the same time I shall not feel sorry if his parliamentary career is ended in Canada though his supporters will be very much annoyed.
Feb 5 . . . Elizabeth took down the Scott's pictures and hung up her own. I felt vexed at first and asked her what was to be done with the

[198]John Sandfield Macdonald (1812–72), Prime Minister of Canada (1862–64) and Prime Minister of Ontario (1867–71). See Bruce W. Hodgins, "John Sandfield Macdonald," *Dic. Can. Biog.* X, pp. 462–469. Amelia Harris had various idiosyncratic spellings of both J.S. and J.A. "Macdonald."

[199]The manuscript referred to must have been Amelia's "Historical Memorandum" written at Ryerson's request in 1859; the scientific instruments had probably belonged to her husband.

[200]Wilson had been instrumental in obtaining the appointment for John Fitzjohn Harris in 1851 and for Edward in 1861.

[201]"Dower" is the portion of a deceased husband's real property allowed to his widow during her lifetime. The "barring of dower" was the legal process by which the wife relinquished this claim.

Scott's. She said she would hang them up also but she cannot and I will put them away. I suppose she wants to see her pictures hung up some place. . . .

Feb 6 . . . Sophia returned the deed today with the dower barred without one word of reply to George. I suppose Mr Wilson has induced her to sign it.

Feb 7 . . . I asked Mr King about the meeting that was called to decide whether they would accept Mr Portman's resignation or not. They have declined accepting it and have written to him, hoping that he will return as soon as he can. The reasons for not accepting his resignation are first that they like him and secondly that if there was a new election a Radical would be returned as the Conservative interest would be divided.

Feb 13 . . . Mr Wilson's report of the Ottawa buildings has gone in. The Commission of Inquiry will cost £3,000 and they have saved to the country four hundred & fifty five thousand dollars, the unjust payment of which Mr Killaly who was at the head of the Board of Works had sanctioned and the late Government let it pass rather than brave the exposure which has now taken place. The present Government had no scruples in exposing the mismanagement of the last and their selecting Mr Wilson as Head Commissioner was proof of their good judgement. . . .

Feb 17 Mr Wilson came to luncheon. The Ministry have refused to pay his expenses when on the Ottawa Commission. . . .

Feb 25 . . . I got a letter from Teresa. They talk of returning with Mr Portman and he talks of returning the last day of May. . . .

Feb 26 . . . Mr Portman appears to be very happy. Mr Scott says Lord Portman has made good all Mr Portman's losses in this country and the South. If so I do not wonder that he feels happy.

Mar 2 . . . The Scotts appear to be very unsettled as to what they are going to do this summer. They now talk of Germany. I do hope they will come home and not go back for a year at all events. . . .

Mar 8 Edward returned at 5 AM cold and tired but getting up the Port Ryerse Harbour Company has been crowned with success. All the stock has been taken and the company has been organized, directors appointed & people are now ready to enter into it and think it will pay well. . . .

Mar 10 This day has been kept as a public holiday.[202] A salute has been fired by Mr Shanley's Artillery. Different processions parading

[202]The Mayor had declared 10 March a public holiday to commemorate the marriage of the Prince of Wales. He invited all businesses in the city to remain closed.

in the streets. Bonfires in the evening and a ball at the Tecumseh [House] at night. . . . Mrs Askin spent the day with us and remained all night. . . . [She] has heard a good deal of gossip about Edward and Sophia. Her news comes through Mrs Greer[203] who corresponds with Sophia and Mrs Greer tells all she hears to her friend Mrs Taylor, who tells Mrs Lundy, who tells Mrs Askin, and so the gossip goes losing nothing on its way. Sophia speaks of me as bad, and she detests Teresa & Mr Scott and Amelia worse than any of us and Mr Portman nearly as bad as the worst of us. Sophia says she will never return to Eldon as long as the old woman (that is me) lives. I do not think she will. Mrs Greer also said that Dr Ryerson's brothers were strong in their condemnation of his conduct in regard to Edward, and Mrs Greer. She justifies Sophia in her dislike to all the Harris family, yet condemns her conduct towards her husband, and Mrs Askin says she has never heard one word of blame attached to Edward in regard to his separation. . . .

Mar 11 There was a row at the close of the ball last night. The Mayor, Cornish, was drunk and he insulted Major Bowles of the 63rd, knocked him down and pulled off his medals. Today he was brought up before the Police Court and fined $6, when he ought to have been fined as heavily as they had the power. Mr Jackson as he went out of court said that this is pretty justice. The Court ordered him back and fined him a dollar. George passed a hat round and four or five dollars were collected instantly. . . .

Mar 18 I felt very ill today. Edward would send for Dr Landor who said nothing could be done for me. It is not disease, it [is] sorrow and age that ails me. Amelia came to luncheon. Mr Griffin called and brought me a quail. Elizabeth got a letter from Sophia today. Sophia wishes her to send down her bathing dress and she also wants to buy Elizabeth's saddle as she hears that Elizabeth is talking of going to England. Sophia's letter speaks of nothing but pleasure present and anticipated. . . .

Apr 3 Good Friday. Edward Blake and Mr Wells called early as they intended going away by the 12 train. We persuaded them to stay and have an early dinner and go by the 3.40 train which they did. E[dward] Blake walked for one hour with me in the garden. We talked about Edward & Sophia. I told him that we had all avoided the subject

[203]Mrs. A. Greer, Sophia's cousin, was the adopted daughter of John Ryerson, an older brother of Egerton Ryerson. She had been living in London for some years with her husband.

and preferred that people should form their own opinions but that I had no objection to speak with him about it. . . . He said he felt so sorry for Edward. I asked him *what was* said of Sophia in Toronto. He implied that from her conduct she was considered a woman of light character and that people thought the strongest part of it was that her father knew and encouraged her in her conduct. He said that Col Robertson was always with her and at her father's. . . . I said something about my doubting their ever living together again for any time. Mr Blake quite started and looked and spoke as if he thought that things had passed the point of reconciliation or return. I have always felt that it was poor Edward, but it is poor Sophia. . . .

Apr 4 Today the address from the City of London to the Military in disapproval of Mr Cornish's conduct was presented. Becher did not accompany the party of presentation. He said he was too busy but the truth is that he is afraid of Cornish's influence with the Orangemen in case of an election. Although Becher says that he is done with politics, I think he has not yet given up the hope of a seat in the House of Representatives, but he will never be elected. . . .

Apr 13 Mr Griffin called. He had been told by Capt Houssen yesterday that the Engineers were ordered to Kingston. This is the first withdrawal of troops, the rest I suppose will follow before very long. . . .

Apr 18 . . . Amelia, Elizabeth and I went to the Wilsons for tea. His greenhouse and gardens look very nice but desolate & the inside of his house is dreariness itself. Everything looks soiled and neglected. The house looks as if it is without a mistress. Mrs Wilson is expected home the end of the month.[204] . . .

Apr 20 Elizabeth and I commenced taking an inventory of everything in the house that there might be something to refer to in case of fire. . . .

Apr 21 . . . [The Scotts] have given up coming to Canada this summer and go to Germany by the doctor's advice that Teresa may use the baths. . . . Mr Portman thinks he will not come out this summer. I am both sorry and glad, sorry that I shall not see him and glad that Maurice will remain with me for another year. . . .

Apr 27 . . . Mr Wilson is going to stand for the Upper House in the St Clair Division in the place of Malcolm Cameron. Mr Wilson has so often told me that he had done with politics, that I asked him why he had come out. He said he supposed few would believe him, but that

[204]Mrs. Wilson had been in wretched health for over a year and was currently at Clinton Springs, a spa near Ottawa.

his only motive was to keep either Murray Anderson or Buckley out.[205] They are or were candidates but they will not come forward now as they would have no chance against Wilson. Mr Wilson says he will not ask for a vote nor spend a dollar.

May 2 . . . In the evening George and Mr Robertson (R.A.) started to go to Komoka in a skiff. It took them until 11 PM to get three miles down the river. They speared no fish. They landed, tied up their skiff, walked home arriving here to find themselves locked out. They were cold, wet, hungry and tired. George squeezed himself through the skylight in the back kitchen and then let his friend in. They made a descent into the cellar and got something to eat & drink and then George found that his bedroom door was locked and he could not get into his room without disturbing the servants . . . he made shift as he best could until morning.

May 4 Elizabeth left this morning for Toronto. She was very sorry to leave and I was very sorry to see her go but she ought to visit her mother. . . .

May 7 Col Lysons arrived this morning.[206] We asked him to stay at Eldon. . . . Col Lysons naturally looks much older but in manner he is much the same and seems to possess the same active energy. . . .

May 8 . . . Sarah's letter has made my heart ache. . . . Harris Brothers' investment of their money has not been as successful as we all had hoped. We thought that ten per cent would be the least that they would get for their money and both John and I encouraged them in that belief. For a time it paid that, and then a crisis came and mort[ga]ges fell in and the land[s] at present are unsaleable. For the last two years Edward has not rendered their account and now they find a great diminution of their small capital and poor Sarah's wail of sorrow went to my very heart. Edward is not without blame. He should have kept them fully informed as to the state of their affairs, but he has hoped that lands would rise in value and that their account would come all right. . . .

May 12 There is to be an immediate dissolution of the House and a new election. . . .

May 18 . . . [Ellen Hamilton's] engagement with N. Montserratt is on

[205]Wilson subsequently withdrew his candidacy.

[206]As a young lieutenant, Daniel Lysons, Royal Welch Fusiliers, was stationed at London in the early 1840s and was one of the participants in the 1843 steeplechase depicted by Lady Alexander. A letter of 1853 indicates that he proposed for Amelia but was discouraged by her mother from pursuing the matter further. His memoirs were published in 1896.

again but they are not to be married for three years. She will then be past 30. . . . I advised her if anything occurred to break the engagement again to think no more of it. He is younger than she is and he is constitutionally indolent and his getting on very well is doubtful. . . .
May 23 . . . Edward and George went to a political meeting. Mr Carling spoke of the way that Mr Wilson had spoken of him and alluded in a very gentlemanlike way to Mr Wilson's public and private life, showing that he was not the one to cast stones.
May 26 . . . Mr Wilson came to luncheon. We talked about elections. I made strong objections to members of the Upper House taking part in the elections of the Lower House. He declared it to be right and proper. I cannot agree with him and think that members of the Upper House ought not to be party men. He has always told me that he was a Conservative in heart although circumstances had united him with the Radical party but that he despised them and now he voluntarily identifies himself with them, when every right and honorable feeling should make him eschew all *parties*. I told him I did not like his speech about Mr Carling. . . .
Jun 1 . . . Just as I was going to bed last night Nicholas Montserrat came and wished to speak to me privately. He wished to ask me what I thought of his breaking his engagement with Ellen Hamilton and whether I thought he ought to do it as although she had agreed to wait three years for him, yet that there was no prospect of his being able to marry at the end of that time as he has to give what he made by his profession to his father. I asked him why not marry at once and give a certain portion of his earnings for a certain number of years to come to his father. I told him that Ellen would be quite willing to do that and she was an industrious, prudent, economical girl and would make a good wife and that if he broke with her he would never get so good a one. But he made a great number of difficulties and decided that marriage was impossible either now or at the end of three years. I told him that if a man was truly and sincerely attached to a woman and looked forward to calling her his wife as the greatest happiness in store for him and if he had a good profession, health, youth and energy, that he would conquer all difficulties. The only danger was that he would be too hopeful. I said I thought Ellen was much fonder of him than he was of her. He said he felt ashamed to acknowledge that it was so. Poor Ellen, how bitter this conviction will be to her. I then said one thing was quite certain, that if he had made up his mind that he could not marry, that he ought at once to tell Mr Hamilton so as well as Ellen. Should they marry, I felt there would not be much happiness for Ellen.

Jun 7 . . . The gossip today is that Capt Hewitt has proposed for Miss Biscoe and that they are to be married. She has been staying for some time at the Bechers & Capt Hewitt has been very devoted to her.
Jun 9 . . . Capt Hewitt has proposed for Miss Biscoe and has been accepted. Miss Biscoe has returned home. Capt Hewitt will have to return from Halifax for his Bride. The R. Engineers left London today for Halifax. . . .
Jun 15 . . . Mrs & Miss [Rebecca] Blake called here. I thought Miss Blake both pretty and pleasing. I have seen no young lady for a long time that I have admired so much. I wish George would take a fancy to her.
Jun 16 . . . People seem amused at Col Robertson and Capt Hewitt having changed divinities. Col Robertson used to be an admirer of Miss Biscoe and now he is devoted to Sophia and vice versa with Capt Hewitt.
Jun 19 Mr Carling has been returned by a majority of 36. . . .
Jun 25 . . . Mr Portman is not coming out and wants me to send Maurice home with Sarah. Her letter excited me so much that I was unable to sleep. The last link is broken between Helen's husband and her family in Canada. . . . The sooner Maurice leaves the better for the longer he remains with me the more attached I must become to him. Dear little fellow, Helen's life, but he must be with his father and brothers.
Jun 26 . . . Mr Wilson & Becher lunched here. Mr Becher leaves for England on Monday next. The Great Western Railway business is taking him there. Mr Wilson had seen Sandfield Macdonald who told him of the way that Dr Ryerson [had] spoken of Edward and asked him about it. It was a repetition of what Miss Griffin told Amelia that Dr Ryerson had said, that Edward had treated her with such brutality that he had to take her home . . . that London was too dull for her, and that she was so dreadfully in love with Capt Hewitt that she had no love left for her husband, that she would sacrifice husband, character and her fortune rather than give up Capt Hewitt, and flirting and put up with the dullness of London. The time will come when she will bitterly repent her folly, and worse than folly her weakness.
Jul 7 This is the 3rd anniversary of Edward's wedding day and he has been nearly a year separated from his wife. This morning he got a letter from Sophia marked private wanting him to go to Toronto today to meet her privately, that is, unknown to her family. She commences the letter Dear Edward and signs it Yours, S.H. Harris. Edward has taken no notice of the letter. From the style in which it was written it was impossible for him to notice it. It was quite as if she looked down upon him from a pinnacle. . . .

Jul 10 . . . I got a letter from Eliza and Amelia got one from Mr Portman who is going into a Bank at Chester. Ld Portman has enabled him to become a partner but he dislikes it and I am sure will not remain there long. He would be much happier if he could or would attend to business of some sort. An idle life can never be a happy one.
Jul 11 Sophia wrote to George today acknowledging the receipt of fifty dollars and wished him to send her thirty dollars in addition as fifty were not sufficient for her quarter's expenses. Edward is neither able or willing to increase her allowance. . . .
Jul 14 I got a letter from Col Dalzell & Sarah from Montreal. They will not be here for some days as they intend going to Ottawa and they intend stopping at Kingston and Toronto. . . . Mr McInnes came by the last train.
Jul 15 Mr McInnes remained to an early dinner. He looks very happy but matrimony has made a great change in him, all his thoughts seem to revolve on a different axis. I was very busy all the morning making cherry brandy, etc and had quite given up the Dalzells for another day or two, when Edward called me and told me that Sarah was here. I was less affected than I thought I should be at seeing her after 16 years absence but she is so changed that I could not for some time realize that she was my Sarah. She is looking wonderfully well and has grown very stout. After a short time one feature after another seemed to return to me, even her voice is changed. Col Dalzell looks delicate and of course older but he is very little changed. His voice is the same and I should have known him anywhere but Sarah I should not. . . . There was a most splendid borealis tonight. There was a bright path all across the heavens from west to east.
Jul 16 . . . Mr Wilson called very early to tell me that he had accepted a judgeship and that he should leave London in one month & reside permanently in Toronto. . . . He seemed almost to regret his acceptance of the judgeship. . . . Almost every lawyer in town is trying for the solicitorship,[207] and Edward amongst the members. . . . I am very sorry Mr Wilson is going to leave the city. He is one of the early settlers and one of our oldest friends. . . .
Jul 17 Mr & Mrs Askin, Mr & Mrs Wilson all made separate calls upon the Dalzells. Edward went to Hamilton to endevor to get Mr Buchanan's[208] interest in an endeavour to procure the solicitorship for the Bank of Montreal. . . .

[207]Solicitorship of the Bank of Montreal.
[208]Isaac Buchanan (1810–83) was a leading merchant and M.P. for Hamilton (1857–67).

Jul 21 Col Dalzell generally breakfasts in bed. . . . After luncheon Sarah and Amelia went to return calls and took Maurice with them. . . .

Jul 22 . . . Mr Wilson called, we spoke about his leaving his place. He said all regret was over, he had no one to leave his place to. His sons were worthless, and who had Lucy married, but he said, we won't speak of it, it is over. He then spoke of Sophia. After a little hesitation he said to me, I wonder if I dare tell you what they say of her. I said, I should think it very strange if he did not tell me all that he knew, but he would not say anything more and when I urged his doing so he turned if off by repeating things that he had already told me. There was evidently something that he is afraid to risk telling us. We shall hear of it after a time. . . .

Jul 27 The Griffins came early and made a communication that surprised me very much. Amelia is in the family way. After having been more than seven years married and childless, she has now become pregnant and at the age of 40. I have always felt very thankful that she had no children, . . . This accounts for her ailments this spring & summer which have caused so much uneasiness. I wish I could divest myself of anxiety about her confinement. . . .

Jul 30 . . . Mr Abbott of St Thomas is appointed solicitor of the Montreal Bank in London. He is a bad character. The appointment is no compliment to the other lawyers who applied for it. . . .

Jul 31 We had a dinner party today. Mr & Mrs Wilson, Capt & Mrs Leslie, Capt Fitzroy & Mr Griffin and Amelia. The dinner went off very well, thanks to Sarah and Col Dalzell. Sarah took the trouble of seeing to everything about the dinner and she makes people talk and sees that every body is amused in some way and Col Dalzell is always so gentlemanlike. . . . Mrs Wilson wishes to go to Nice with the Dalzells, or rather she wishes to go as far as Paris with them.

Aug 1 . . . Col Dalzell not well, . . . Sent for Dr Landor who told him that he had tubercles on the lungs which alarmed him very much. Dr Landor thought them so slight and unimportant that he did not hesitate to speak of them and when he spoke to us he assured us that Col Dalzell had no ailment as far as he could tell to prevent his living to a good old age. He said diet, air, and exercise was all that he required and the more cheerful he kept the better.

Aug 4 . . . Mrs Loring wrote to Sarah wanting her to endevor to reconcile Edward and his wife. Sarah thinks Edward old enough to manage his own affairs and has no intention of interfering. . . .

Aug 6 . . . There has been a cricket match between London & Detroit. The Yankees were badly beaten . . .

Aug 14 This has been a wretched day to me. . . . There has been disagreeables between George & Edward and I have had so much trouble that the least thing breaks me down. Dr Landor called. Ill as I felt I went with *all* at Eldon to a heavy tea at the Wilsons in the hope that the little change would do me good, which it did. Every thing looks so nice at the Wilsons. The grounds are in such good order, they have such beautiful flowers and shrubs and every thing seems so abundant. They are most successful with their bees and have such quantities of honey. They gave me a box of beautiful honey. As I look around at every thing which seemed conducive to worldly comfort I felt that they were not happy. Their children have been a failure and they feel themselves alone in the world.
Aug 20 Edward left for Port Ryerse. The present Ministry have done away with the Customs there and it is not longer a Port of Entry which will be a great injury to the place. Edward will get up a petition to the House of Assembly to endevor to have the Customs House officer reappointed. . . .
Aug 23 Edward came home this morning. He is in hopes to get the office of Customs restored to Port Ryerse. The Warden of the District is going to call a council and take action about it. All the merchants are indignant. . . .
Aug 27 . . . Edward wished me to ask the Scotts to come out. He is anxious that I should not be alone at the time of Amelia's confinement. Mrs Landor came to tea. . . .
Aug 31 . . . The Griffins returned from the Falls and dined here. They enjoyed their trip very much and saw a great number of old acquaintances; the Gzowskis, Camerons, Boultons, Plumbs and a number of others. The Duggans were at the Falls and spoke to Amelia. Sophia and Col Robertson came to the Falls with the Duggans but after remaining for a few days they returned to Toronto. Of course people made remarks upon Sophia's conduct, yet she seems to retain her footing in Toronto and is invited to all the parties. Mrs Boulton told Amelia that Sophia had a good many young lady friends who even got up parties for her to cheer her up. Mrs Boulton also said that she never in her life saw any young woman so wholly given up to pleasure, that she was the gayest of the gay at all parties and places and that last winter she was at the skating rink every day and always accompanied by Col Robertson, and that he is always with her riding, driving or walking and yet people countenance her. . . .
Sep 4 Elizabeth arrived last night at 11 o'clock. We were all in bed, she is looking very well. We spoke of Sophia and Elizabeth said she was a woman who conducted herself in such a way that she would not

be intimate with her nor would she be seen walking or driving with her. She says that Sophia is totally unchanged and that unless she alters that a reconciliation would be hopeless and useless. I told Edward all Amelia had heard about when she was at the Falls. I was wrong in telling him. He was not so well after it & I had to send for the doctor in the evening. Elizabeth told me *about* her lover but not his name. I am afraid he is not a good match for her. He has been unsuccessful in the lumbering business and did not succeed as an editor of a paper. He then studied Law but has not yet got into a good practice and has nothing.[209] She speaks well of him as a worthy good man. . . .

Sep 14 Elizabeth left us this morning. She has returned to her water cure at the Clifton Springs. . . . She now thinks she will spend part of the winter in Toronto and part in London. . . .

Sep 22 Amelia & Edward Blake came to luncheon. Edward consulted him about trying for a divorce from Sophia. He thinks it would not be possible to obtain one unless he could prove her criminal, which he cannot. . . .

Sep 26 . . . Ld Portman is trying to get Shuldham an Adjutancy of Militia. If Shuldham gets it it will . . . be a very great assistance to them. . . .

Sep 28 . . . The usual croquet party met & played. Mr Griffin has celebrated their doings in verse and it is very clever.[210] . . .

Oct 5 Edward & the Dalzells have gone to Long Point. . . .

Oct 13 Sarah came into my room this morning in a great state of alarm. Col Dalzell had a hermorrage [sic] of the lungs. This is the third attack in three years. . . . Dr Landor thinks that he will be as well as usual in the course of a week but it tells us very plainly how uncertain his life is; poor fellow. Lord my heart ached for him as he lay trembling between this world and the next. Sarah behaved very well and commanded her feelings better than I could under such circumstances and she is a devoted and tender nurse. . . .

Oct 17 . . . Edward returned from Long Point not well and out of spirits. There were a good many disagreeable things took place be-

[209]Elizabeth's fiancée was William Edward O'Brien (1831–1914), brother of Lucius O'Brien, the painter. Both brothers attended Upper Canada College. Edward was called to the bar but never practised. He was the M.P. for Muskoka (1882–96), and was active in the militia, commanding the York and Simcoe Regiment during the North West rebellion of 1885.

[210]The verse is to be found in the Harris Papers entitled, "Croquet, A Macaulay Flower, (Which can't be beat) Cabbaged by G. [Griffin], London, Canada West, 1863."

tween him and the Dalzells on their way to and when at Long Point. They were all to blame but Edward the most so because they were our guests. I am very sorry. Edward said he would do whatever I and Amelia thought he ought to do. I told him to say nothing to Robert [Dalzell] about what had passed as it would not do to excite him but to offer him his hand and say that he was sorry to see him ill but to Sarah he should say that he was sorry for what had passed. I believe he did as I told him but all tender love and intimacy is over between them. . . .

Oct 22 . . . Amelia came here for a few minutes in great alarm thinking that Boyo[211] had dyptheria. Dr Landor had been called in and pronounced his sore throat dyptheria. . . .

Nov 2 Edward has been very ill all day and in great pain. The Dalzells lunched with the Griffins. In the evening George brought me a letter from Sophia to Edward. Edward was so ill and excitable that I dare not give it to him until he is better. I opened the letter, for the first time she admits that she has injured him and wants him to use *his own* unbiased judgement and go to Toronto to see her. She finds herself cut and now she would fain come back to him. He shall follow his own unbiased judgement for I will say nothing to him.

Nov 6 . . . When we were at breakfast Sarah said something about their accounts. I said that I felt it my duty to tell her that if Col Dalzell drew for a thousand pounds and said that he must have it that Edward would send it to him. She said that Edward would be very wrong to let him overdraw his account. I said that Edward could not help it, that Col Dalzell was the last man in the world that would allow any one to tell him that he was not to do as he liked with his own money. She flew into such a passion and told me that I was unjust to Robert. She forbade my speaking and said she would not hear what I had to say, that she had rather not hear it and begged that I would not say another word and rose to leave the table but sat down again. When she calmed down a little I told her that if Col Dalzell told Edward to send him all the interest that was due him he would send that amount and no more, or if he said let me know if the sum I want will encroach upon my principle, of course Edward would tell him. But when he writes and says that he must have such a sum and that he *cannot* do without it, that he is ill and has doctor's bills to pay besides rent, education and various other things, Edward has no right to say that *he will* not send it. Not one of his clients would allow him

[211]The Griffins' son.

to exercise that power over their money and I am quite sure that Col Dalzell would not. Sarah said she thought her brothers were friends but she found they were only men of business, and I should not like to write down what else Col Dalzell said Edward was.

The Griffins spent the day here. . . . There were the Dalzells, Amelia, Ellen Hamilton, George & myself at Table. There was something said about Mr King & Jackson and some allusions to their quarrel. Some one spoke of Mr Jacksons having struck Mr [E.A.] King. I do not know how the remark happened to be made nor do I know who made it but Col Dalzell took it up warmly and said that Canadians certainly had a code of laws that would not pass in England. He wanted to know what Mr King did. George said Mr Jackson was very sorry for it and apologized. Ah, he [Dalzell] said, that would not do amongst English gentlemen. We said they were both Englishmen and not Canadians, that Mr King had an Oxford education and was highly respected at Oxford. He still said that such a thing could not be got over in England. George tried to explain and defend Mr King and told Col Dalzell that he did not know anything about it (that is, the quarrel between Mr Jackson & King) and that circumstances altered cases. Col Dalzell turned upon him looking perfectly furious and said that he, a gentleman by birth, and who had lived amongst gentlemen all his life, knew what gentlemen ought to do, . . . implying that George was no gentleman. . . . George at once apologized and said that he did not intentionally say any thing to offend him. Col Dalzell's face was perfectly frightful but the subject was dropped, but any one would have said that George had behaved more like a gentleman than Col Dalzell. Col Dalzell afterwards spoke to Mr Griffin about it and said that George had attempted to *tell him* what gentlemen ought to do and that he had found it necessary to set him, George, down. As they were to leave the next day, we tried to look as pleased with everything as we could, but that sort of temper would kill me. I was so ill that I could scarcely hold my head up. It was our last dinner together and we all tried to be as cheerful as we could. Mr Griffin was here nearly the whole day doing anything that he could in the way of getting the packages ready and spending the last day with Maurice. The dear little pet, how hard it is to part with him. I was head and heart weary when I went to bed.

Nov 7 This morning I was so ill that I could scarcely sit up. It has been a sad day to me. My poor baby is gone, the last earthly tie with Helen is broken. The poor little fellow went away half sad half happy with excitement. It was a strange parting with Sarah. I could not wish them to stay for had Col Dalzell's health become worse he would have thought it the winter here that caused it and after his impressing upon me that neither Edward nor George were gentlemen and that they did not know how to treat a gentleman, it could not be pleasant for them nor for him. Sarah is a strange compound of right and wrong, affectionate, warm hearted and generous to a fault, passionate, constantly saying and doing many foolish things, extravagant and economical, capable of any self sacrifice, and with all she has had a hard lot and much to bear. I think either of her sisters would have sunk under what she has borne and her future has nothing bright in it as far as I can see.

The leave taking was painful. They left at 12. Mr Becher got the Directors' car for them as far as the Suspension Bridge.[212] My poor Baby, how solitary the house is without him . . . that I am never to see again. . . .

Nov 9 . . . I gave Edward Sophia's letter.[213] He is so much better that I thought I might venture to do so. He said very little about it. I said not a word. . . . After some time I asked him what he intended to do. He said either send the letter to Blake or take no notice of it. He thought there was no change in her and that her letter was in much the same style as her last one. . . .

Nov 18 Sandfield Macdonald called and expressed great [regret] about having appointed another issuer of marriage license and said should the office become vacant he should not make another appointment. He had no idea that it affected me in any way. . . .

Nov 24 . . . George came in with an astounding piece of information, that Sophia had arrived and was at the Greers. In the evening a note was brought to Edward from Mrs Greer asking him to go there. Edward wrote to Mrs Greer that he had heard his wife was there and as he wished to avoid seeing her, he declined her invitation.

Nov 25 This morning early Mr Griffin sent down a note to him from Sophia saying that she had come up to tell Edward how sorry she was *for what* she had done wrong, but that he need not be afraid for she had no intention of forcing herself upon him. Edward answered her note, I thought harsh, though just. Amelia & I talked it over during the day and we thought that if either of our husbands had written such a note it would have crushed us and that we could not have forgiven them and all day we felt softened towards her thinking how wretched she must feel and had she come during the day to see either Amelia

[212]The bridge at Niagara Falls.
[213]Amelia had been holding this letter since 2 November.

or me we should have received her kindly. In Edward's note he refused to see [her] but said should he think it judicious in a couple of years he might see her, and then if he had formed any plans for the future he would let her know, and as to her duty being at an end, it rested with herself to decide. In her note she said if he refused to see her, her duty was at an end. Just before we went to bed another note was brought to Edward. His note had not the slightest effect upon her. She pretended she could not understand it excepting that he refused to see her which she urged him to do. The tone was more penitential but with as little heart or feeling as her former notes. Both Amelia & myself might have saved our sympathy for she is incapable of deep feeling and has not a spark of true affection for her husband. . . .

Nov 26 This morning Edward wrote to Sophia declining an interview but told her that when she returned to Toronto she could at her leisure write at length all she wished to say to him. Mr Griffin went at her request to see her. She cried a good deal, laughed a good deal and told him some gossip. Mr Griffin spoke very plainly to her and told her that people thought lightly of her not only in London but in Toronto. She told him that for the first nine months that she was in Toronto that she did every thing which she thought would annoy Edward, that she was so irritated and that she wished to let him see that she was happy and enjoying herself. She spoke of having been at the Cataract House with Col Robertson . . . but she said for the last three months she had tried to do what was right and that she would do anything Edward wished her. She talked of going to England for a couple of years and of spending some time with her Aunt Beatty at Cobourg and also with Mrs Hardy at Brantford, and she turned around with a giggle to Mr Griffin and wanted to know what she was to do about Capt Hewitt while he was in Toronto. Mr Griffin said if she did not know how to behave herself properly it was useless for him to say any thing. She said when her father returned from Long Point he would certainly ask Capt Hewitt to dinner. Mr Griffin said it would be compromising her in a shameful manner and that he thought her father had given her the worst possible advice throughout. *She thought* he had. She said she was very fond of Edward, fonder than ever. The conclusion that Mr Griffin came to was that she was a fool, without sense of principle or one spark of affection for Edward. She is beginning to be looked coldly upon in Toronto and it would suit her convenience to return to her husband, which Mr Griffin told her was impossible until she had proved by her conduct that she was not only sorry for what she had done but that the public voice approved of her altered conduct. He advised her to return to Toronto and not to write to Edward until she could say from her heart that she was sorry. . . . Her sorrow will never be for bringing scandal upon herself and misery to her husband, but because she finds herself dropped and shunned and that her days of pleasure are past. She has gone as wrong as she could without being criminal though she is accused of criminality. I believe the accusation is false. She left at 3 PM for Toronto. . . .

Dec 1 . . . Shuldham has succeeded in getting the Adjutancy that he was trying to get. We are all very glad as it will give him employment and £275 a year in addition to his income. . . .

Dec 3 . . . He [Mr Wilson] told us what Mr Greer said of Sophia, that she had run herself out in Toronto and that now she does not know what to do with herself. Her determination to do every thing that could or would annoy Edward has brought scandal upon herself and has failed in bringing Edward to her feet. People in Toronto look cool upon her and her Mother, she says, is so cross and disagreeable that she cannot live with her and that her father's feelings have become very much changed and softened towards Edward and that he will no longer interfere or advise her how to act and that now she would be glad to come back. In all this I see nothing to encourage poor Edward. He was right in not seeing her, she has changed her views from circumstances not caused by affection for him or sorrow for the wrong she has done him or the disgrace she has brought upon herself and him.

Dec 12 Edward has been ill all the week. He has required constant attention. He has been leeched and poulticed steadily. . . . The much talked of Pioneer dinner took place on the 10th. It was well attended and went off very well. I have written to no one this week nor have I received any letters.

Dec 15 I got letters from Mr Wilson and Elizabeth both in reference to Sophia. Sophia had written to Mr Wilson wishing to see him and he called upon her. He told her how very badly she had behaved and the view that people took of her conduct. She admitted that she had been in love with Capt Hewitt and that she had left her husband on his account, but said that if Edward had done the same sort of thing that she would have forgiven him. Her conversation with Mr Wilson makes us almost think worse of her than we have done. The great thing that makes her wish to return is as far as I can see, that she finds her Mother's house very unpleasant. Mr Wilson held out no hope that Edward would receive her at present. Elizabeth's letter is much in the same style that Sophia wished to return and that she confides all her plans to Mrs Loring. Sophia told Mrs Loring that she was regretting before her Mother that she had no one to ride with now that Col

Robertson was ill. Mrs Ryerson said, but Capt Hewitt will soon be here and you can ride with him. . . .

Dec 16 . . . The Dalzells and Baby had arrived at Chelsea and all well. Mr Portman was overjoyed to see his boy. . . . Teresa came up to London to meet him. Nurse returned today . . . and says she will never, never nurse another child. Mr Portman was very liberal to her and gave her five pounds for going home with Baby and he gave her £29 to pay for a first class passage back. She was taken by a family as nurse coming out and they paid her passage so that she saved her money and only spent £3 in Rail Road fare. She has been a kind and an affectionate nurse to Baby. . . . Fanny Becher is to be married on the 9th of next month to Capt Bruce late of the 63rd. . . .

Dec 21 . . . This evening Ellen Hamilton called and told us that 30 of the oldest officers of the Bank of Upper Canada were dismissed, her father amongst the members, after having been more than 30 years in the Bank, without having a complaint against him. . . .

Dec 25 Christmas. Very quiet. I went to Church & Mrs Askin came in after Church and remained until after dinner. Then I went up to see Amelia. Mr Wilson did not come up, nor did he send an excuse. I am afraid he is ill. This has been I think the loneliest Christmas I have ever spent.

Dec 29 I went up to see Amelia, being quite alone is neither good for her or me. We spoke of the death of Ld Elgin[214] and felt that we had lost a kind friend. Years ago he told Amelia that from boyhood it had been the dream of his life to be Governor General of India and there he rests from all his labours. . . .

Dec 30 Mr Griffin when in Toronto went to see the Leslies and found them very kind and hospitable. He did not see Sophia and heard very little of her. She had been staying with Mrs Loring and the Leslies had asked Mrs Loring to dinner and she had declined going unless she might take Mrs Edward so the Leslies asked Mrs Edward to go also but they do not admire her much.

Dec 31 . . . I went to see Amelia, she is looking better . . . and so ends 1863. In looking back upon the year how much have I reason to be thankful for and yet how much mental anxiety I have suffered from various causes, but I feel that God has brought me nearer to Himself in all my thoughts and hopes. I write this with a grateful heart and my prayer is for faith, humility and humble trust in the mercies of our Saviour.

[214]James Bruce, eighth Earl of Elgin (1811–63), Governor General of British North America (1847–54).

1864

Jan 1 New Year's Day. Bitterly cold the thermometer at 22 below zero and blowing a gale. I did not go to Church and there was little visiting. Mr Wilson came from Toronto very cold. He remained to dinner. He had sent his letter to Sophia but had heard nothing more from her. Col Grant and Capt Armstrong of the Canadian Rifles called. Ellen Hamilton came in the evening and so ends the first day of the year.
Jan 2 Mr Griffin called and brought me a letter from Elizabeth in which she announced her engagement to Mr O'Brien. We feel sorry for he is poor and we have not heard him very well spoken of but she thinks him one of the best men in the world. Poor John is soon forgotten but I hope she may be happy. Poor girl, she had not much happiness in her first marriage. John ought never to have married. I had letters from Teresa and George had one from Col Dalzell. George had given him an overcoat to wear on board ship. It was not a very good one but it was the only one George could give. . . . George wished him to take his plaid which was new, thick and warm but Col Dalzell declined as it was an overcoat that he wanted. Col Dalzell sent the coat back by nurse and tonight his letter to George was cool, sarcastic and impertinent. He says he has returned the coat as the cut and style would not do in England and that he thinks it would be a sin to deprive George of it and that it is a pleasure to him to think how comfortable George will be in it this winter. The truth was he wanted John's beautiful fur coat which Edward has. Both him and Sarah gave a great many hints for it but it was the last coat that John bought and wore. . . . Col Dalzell wanted [it] and he was bitter that he did not get it. . . . Col Dalzell is a frightfully selfish and bad tempered man and Sarah has had a hard life with him. . . .
Jan 6 Amelia was delivered this morning of a still born child, a son. She has had a very hard labor but the Dr says she is doing well. Edward & George knew last night that she was ill but would not tell me. They went out with Ellen Hamilton pretending to see her home and then went to Amelia's and remained until twelve. The child was born at two this morning. Edward went there very early. Doctor Landor called to tell me about her. He called in Doctor Harper[215] when he found there was difficulty. It was a face presentation which, I believe, is considered one of the worst. The death of the child will be a great disappointment to them. I think but little of the child. I feel so

[215]Dr. Alfred Harper had recently established a practice in London.

thankful that her life is so far safe. The Dr advised me not to go to Amelia until after he had seen her, when he would be able to judge whether my going will agitate her. I went up and found Amelia almost better than I expected to see her. That wonderful strength and courage that is generally given to women in labor had not entirely left her. The reaction had not yet come. She was excited at seeing me and would talk so I thought it best to leave her. Her heart was full of love and she wanted to kiss and caress me all the time and she sent her love to her sisters and told me to tell them all that she gave up her baby without a murmur. . . . Mr Griffin brought the baby to me on a pillow, it looked so pretty and so sweet with its little cold face but there was nothing there to make a mother's heart glad. It had come and gone. I went home and wrote to Sarah and Mary. Dr Landor told me that Amelia behaved so well, that she never lost her courage, and did everything as she was told, but that Mr Griffin broke down and they had to turn him out of the room and he remained outside of her door until it was over. No one can be kinder or a more tender nurse than he is. . . .

Jan 7 . . . Edward had Mr Harris' grave opened and Amelia's baby was placed on her father's coffin. Mr Griffin has not left Amelia all day. Mrs Askin called. . . .

Jan 11 . . . Ellen Hamilton came in the evening to tell me that her father is made President of a permanent Building Society which they think in a year or two will give him an income equal to the one he lost.

Jan 16 I got letters from Teresa and Sarah. Sarah's letter was very unsatisfactory, complaining of her brother's management of their affairs and of their poverty. I went to see Amelia who is going on well. . . . Ellen Hamilton says she cannot come here any more for her mother says she comes to see Edward and George & she cried with vexation and mortification. . . . I had a letter from Elizabeth who seems very happy in her love for Mr O'Brien and hopes to be married within the year. The dead are soon forgotten and their places filled with others. It is better so.

Jan 17 George came home.[216] . . . He met Sophia in the street, a stiff bow was the only recognition. . . .

Jan 18 . . . Edward sent a box of two dozen pairs of gloves as a present to Fanny Becher and I sent a dozen of very nice hemstitched pocket handkerchiefs, which Ellen Hamilton worked very prettily. Mr

[216]George had been in Toronto on business since the 14th.

Becher called and asked me to send them all the plates I could spare which I did.

Jan 19 The great wedding[217] is over and the day has been very disagreeable, a high wind and heavy snow storm. . . . Edward and George went to the wedding. Edward thought that Mrs Becher and Fanny were scarcely civil to him but it may have been accident or fancy. . . . Capt Hewitt was there. . . .

Jan 20 Mr Wilson came this morning. . . . He told me he had dined at the Ryersons last week, that Dr Ryerson had wished to see him previous to the dinner party and that he had spent two hours with him, Dr Ryerson all the time talking about Edward and Sophia. He makes out Sophia a perfect angel. Mr Wilson asked him if he understood his, Mr Wilson's, position towards our family, that he was a friend and should always remain so. The Dr said he knew that. Then Mr Wilson asked what the purpose of this conversation was, whether he wished it to be private. He said no, he might make what use he pleased of it. He spoke of the bond which Edward had given to make a settlement upon Sophia and said that he would enforce it when the five years were up. He asked Mr Wilson if he knew what allowance Edward made Sophia. Mr Wilson said he did. Dr R[yerson] said it was not sufficient to dress her. Mr Wilson said some women could dress upon it.

Dr R[yerson] said Sophia could not dress upon less than £75 a year and keep her station in society. He also said that Edward was putting his property out of his hands into mine and had sent a number of deeds to Sophia to sign away her dower and that she had not refused but that he had kept a list of them all. Mr Wilson thought the most of the lands which Edward had deeded were lands which he had held in trust and that he was quite sure that he had never made any property over to me. Mr Wilson was right about the land, nearly all were held in trust by Edward and Sophia could be made to sign them by the Court of Chancery but it would give him a great deal of trouble and expense. Dr Ryerson spoke of the scandal about Col Robertson and Sophia and said that Col Robertson was a most gentlemanlike, well read, intelligent, agreeable person. . . . Dr Ryerson said Sophia wished to return and if a reconciliation could be brought about he would oppose it as he did not wish to renew his intimacy with our family. I suppose he thinks from Edward's dislike to him that he is an obstacle in the way of their reconciliation. As Mr Wilson was going away, I

[217]The marriage of Fanny Becher and Captain Bruce.

said Sophia is right in cultivating the Leslies and if she behaves herself as well as she is now doing, she may in some measure reestablish herself in Toronto. Mr Wilson quite started as he turned around upon me and said, why she drives out every day with that fellow Robertson, . . . I have been feeling very soft towards Sophia for some time and have thought that perhaps she would behave herself more correctly, but she cannot change. . . . Ellen Hamilton came in the evening and told us more about the wedding. The servants were all tipsy and when the gentlemen went for their coats they pelted them with bread & potatoes. Mr Becher was very vexed when he found out. . . .

Jan 21 Mr Becher called, he is very much pleased with everything about the wedding. He says Fanny has a great number of very handsome presents, that a package arrived only this morning from Mr Brydges containing a very handsome bracelet and broach worth not less than £25 or £30. . . .

Jan 29 I had letters from Mr Portman and Eliza, all well. I went to see Amelia who is gaining strength very slowly. Miss Steers arrived about 2 PM and we talked incessantly until we went to bed. . . .

Jan 31 . . . I have dreamt of my little pet[218] the last two nights and in my sleep have seen him looking ill and miserable. I hope my little darling is well.

Feb 3 . . . I have sent Jane [maid] to stay with Amelia until her cook returns. I went to see Amelia and wanted her to come to Eldon for a few days but Mr Griffin objected, he thought she would get cold.

Feb 4 . . . Capt & Mrs Bruce called. It is the first I have seen Capt Bruce. He is very nice and gentlemanlike looking. Fanny looked wretchedly ill but very happy. . . .

Feb 6 . . . I am very lonely and miss my little Maurice so much. I never felt so utterly solitary when he was with me.

Feb 9 . . . Edward got a cab and brought Amelia home today, she looks weak and listless as if she had no interest in anything. . . .

Feb 19 My birthday. In looking at my past life it seems like a waste of 66 years, that in all that time I have never done one truly good thing. . . . I got a letter from Sarah and Amelia got one from Mr Portman who is leading a very gay life, going with parties from one noble mansion to another, a favorite every where.

Feb 21 Edward & I went to Church. Amelia was there for the first time since her confinement. She returned thanks for her recovery. Mr Hill of the 63rd came in with George. Mr Wilson walked in very unexpectedly in the evening. I felt so glad to see him. He found his

[218]Her grandson, Maurice Portman, junior.

house so cold & damp that he is going to remain here during his stay in London. . . .
Feb 23 . . . the murderer Greenwood hanged himself last night with a rollen towel. He was to be hanged this morning at 10. He was a horrid wretch. Another Canadian steamer is lost, the *Bohemian* almost in the Harbour of Portland. It is thought to be from gross mismanagement. Fortunately there are but few lives lost.
Feb 24 . . . Col Crutchley is now a General. . . .
Feb 29 I got letters from Mr Portman and Mary which were fished out of the *Bohemian*. . . .
Mar 4 George had asked some people to dinner but Lewis Ryerse[219] came to spend the day and George put off his party until tomorrow. Lewis is a rough genius with a great deal of brains. . . .
Mar 7 . . . Mr Griffin's reading Shakespeare at Goderich was a great success. It gave about $60 to the Church fund.
Mar 11 Amelia returned and Elizabeth with her. I do not think Elizabeth is looking as pretty as when she was last here. . . . Amelia saw Sophia. Sophia wrote to ask if she might call to see her and Amelia said yes, but there was no allusion made to the past. . . .
Mar 15 There was a great fire last night. Five shops were burned in Dundas Street. . . .
Mar 22 We were horrified this morning to see in the *Free Press* all Mr Lawrason's household furniture offered for sale at auction without reserve on the 28th. It is long since I heard they were in difficulty, but we always hoped they would pull through it. I am sorry, for they are such kind, charitable, good people. The Griffins came to luncheon. . . .
Apr 1 . . . The Lawrason's things were sold on the 28th for taxes. It is said that a good many things were bought in for them and that they will remain in the house until it is sold which it must be as Mr Lawrason has made an assignment of every thing to Mr Shanley for the benefit of his creditors. It is said that he owes over $100,000 dollars and that although his property is worth more, that it will not bring so much when brought to the hammer. . . .
Apr 2 I wrote today to ask Judge and Mrs Salmon to spend a week or two with me. He is dying with consumption. I wish much to see him once more. . . .
Apr 4 . . . Col & Miss Wilson arrived from Long Point and remained with us. They have come up for the 63rd Ball.
Apr 5 Miss Wilson is a nice little girl, full of life and unaffected and appears as innocent as if she had just come out of the Garden of Eden. . . .

[219]Son of Edward Ryerse.

Apr 6 . . . Judge Salmon sent a message by Col Wilson to ask me to go to see him as he wished to see me once more. I was glad that I had written to him before I got his message as it showed him that I too wished to see him. I told Col Wilson to tell him that if he could not come to Eldon that I would endevour to go to Simcoe early in May. . . .
Apr 8 . . . General Crutchley has been offered the command at Gibraltar and will go there in June. They will leave their two little boys in England, Percy at school and Charley with Mary for a year, and then he will go to school. . . .
Apr 15 . . . Dr Landor called with a Prologue which he said he had written and submitted to the committee of the Shakespearean festival if they chose to have it read.[220] Edward felt sure it was not his own but copied from some author, and sure enough he found it word for word in a Prologue & Epilogue from two of B[en] Johnson's plays. I should not have suspected Dr Landor of copying it without acknowledging. It is pity that he has done it for he has lost with us all.
Apr 18 . . . Ellen Hamilton came in the evening. The First Building Society have offered Mr Hamilton the Secretaryship with £200 a year and he, poor man, feels doubtful whether it would be honorable to accept it and leave the one that was nominally got up for him with a salary of £50 a year which will be utter starvation to himself and family. . . . Edward thinks as I do that it is a duty to his family to take the £200 a year. . . . Each party are studying their own private interest in some way and he will be very foolish if he does not look to his.
Apr 22 Mrs Leslie & Mrs Knapp went to the Barracks to practice with Miss Grant and others for the concert. Mr Galloway & Robertson R.A. came to luncheon. They intended to have played croquet in the afternoon but it came on to rain. I had a large afternoon tea party. . . . In the evening all of the Eldon party went to see Merchant of Venice murdered. The performance was even worse than they expected.
Apr 26 . . . Mr Griffin's father died this morning. . . . Ellen Hamilton came here to go with the Eldon party to the ball. Both Mrs Plumb and Mrs Leslie were very handsomely dressed. George wore a fancy dress[221] – Spanish – and looked very handsome in it. . . .
Apr 27 . . . The Eldon party did not return from the ball until 4 o'clock. Mr Galloway and Mr Robertson returned with them and the gentlemen had a little convivial party of their own which enabled them

[220]A festival organized at London by the London Dramatic Association to mark the 350th anniversary of Shakespeare's birth. A second theatrical, consisting of readings from Othello, Macbeth and the sonnets, was reviewed in the *London Free Press*.

[221]A photograph of George in fancy dress is in the Harris Papers.

to go to bed without candles, but gave Mr Plumb and Edward most violent head aches. Edward kept the sofa all day and Mr Plumb was scarcely well enough to return home but they and the Leslies left by the 12 o'clock train. . . .

May 5 . . . George showed [Mr Wilson] the correspondence between Dr Landor and the Shakespearean Committee. He thought it reflected very little credit upon Dr Landor. . . . Dr [Landor] say[s] he must bear the odium of plagiarism as he best can but that he did not intend to pass it as his own, but he did not say this until after the appropriation had been discovered.

May 6 . . . Mr Griffin returned today disgusted with everything he had seen in the States. He brought his pocket full of rings taken from federal soldier's letters in the dead letter office at Washington. The rings are sent by the soldiers to mothers, sisters and friends in the letters. They say they are made from the bones of Rebels' legs. They are worse than savages. . . .

May 20 . . . I asked both Amelia and Mr Griffin to dinner, as we expected the Scotts early. . . . I cannot help thinking that Teresa has grown taller. She has a better colour and looks in better health than when she left. I am so glad to have her back but the time will soon come round when they will leave me again.

May 25 Miss Steers came up and was very vexed with Mr Becher whom she expected to see here but he had just left for Toronto without notifying her although he knew she was coming to see him on business. She is not satisfied with her accounts nor the way he has managed her money. . . .

Jun 1 . . . Edward, George & Montserrat have dissolved partnership. I feel very sorry for Montserrat for he is honest and honorable but indolent. I think his indolence is constitutional. . . .

Jun 6 Edward & I went to Long Point. We drove in a buggy from Paris to Simcoe. . . . We found Judge Salmon ill in bed. . . . Mrs Salmon looks anxious and care worn. The two daughters are very nice girls and promise to be very pretty.

Jun 7 . . . Miss Wilson called & Col Wilson took me for a drive around the town of Simcoe. I had not been there for ten years consequently saw very great improvement. . . .

Jun 8 . . . Poor old Perry[222] called to see me and she looks very old. . . . Col Wilson drove me to Port Ryerse. We went by the way of Vittoria. Ten years has made but little change in Vittoria. We came

[222]Perry, an old servant of the Harrises.

past my old home and it looks sadly changed. The house is almost tumbling down. It is 30 years since we left it and there has been no repairs. 40 years is considered the age of a frame house. . . .

I found Edward and Patty[223] looking better and in better health than I expected. Edward Harris & my brother Edward and I went to the graves of my father & mother and thought of their landing at Port Ryerse in 1796 when there was not a dozen settlers in a range of 200 miles and my father's pointing out the spot where he would be buried. Those pioneers were wonderful stout hearted people in their day. We went out to the Point and looked at the warehouse and down upon the Harbour. There was an immense quantity of lumber ready for shipping and it has the appearance of a busy little place. My brother George asked me to dine with him tomorrow. Emily[224] called. She looks older but otherwise is not much changed. Her husband is a very idle worthless fellow.

Jun 9 Edward Ryerse drove to Vittoria. I went as far as my old home with him and then walked back. The drawing room was less changed than anything else. The verandah was gone and all traces of the flower garden and the outside of the house looked most dilapidated. In this old house I had spent many happy years and nine of my children were born here. I went to George's to an early dinner. Poor George, I feel so sorry for him. He is quite alone in his old age. His wife is a detestable woman and has turned his children against him and in his own house no one speaks to him, looks after him or cares for him. He looks dirty and neglected and yet he has been a kind, good, religious man. He is not far from a better world. I went to Edward's for tea. William Ryerse[225] and his daughter came to see me. My brother Edward drove me out to Simcoe. I found Mr Salmon not so well. . . .

Jun 10 Mr Salmon exerted himself to get up to breakfast. . . . [I] called at Col Wilson's. His house looks like the house of a gentleman and Miss Wilson shows very well in her own house. . . . We left Judge Salmon's at twelve noon for home. We stopped at Arnold's nursery garden, not much to be seen excepting a splendid view. Paris is a very pretty town. We arrived home at 9 PM. . . .

Jun 25 Thermometer 91 in the shade . . . George left for Barrie to attend Elizabeth's wedding.

Jun 26 . . . Mr Portman will not come out this summer.

[223]Her brother, Edward Ryerse, and his wife.
[224]Probably a cousin of Amelia Harris.
[225]Amelia's nephew.

Jun 29 . . . Mr Wilson says that it is generally believed now that Dr Ryerson's brain is softening which accounts for his strange conduct. He went from Toronto across the lake to Port Dalhousie in a small boat quite alone. No persuasion could stop him. Every body thought he would be drowned but he arrived safely, went through the Welland Canal and up Lake Erie to Long Point Bay where he spends a great portion of his time. . . .
Jun 30 . . . The Griffins, Scotts and Edward went to Port Stanley to a pic nic given by the Artillery. . . .
Jul 1 The pic nic went off very well but they were all too tired to go to the Boat Club one today. George returned last night. Elizabeth was not married until the 29th. George was pleased with Mr O'Brien's father and family. He said they looked like gentle folks but poor. He thinks Mr O'Brien a very good man but with very little of the gentleman in his appearance. It is a strange match of Elizabeth's but she is a strange woman. Amelia came to dinner, George went to the B.C. pic nic.
Jul 3 . . . Much to our surprise Vere Foster,[226] the Philanthropist who has spent so much of his time and money in bringing immigrants to this country and the States called. He has not visited this country for the last six years but has come now to look after the immigrants he brought out and to see how they are getting on. Those he brought were mostly Irish servant girls and were married and doing well. . . .
Jul 19 . . . Amelia & I went to the Falls. The Scotts, Leslies, Miss Creighton, Miss Perkins & Col Peacocke [16th] were there all in great spirits.
Jul 20 Mr Griffin and Miss Sewell arrived from Quebec. . . . Capt Hogg & Mr Robinson of the 16th joined the party. All very cheerful and merry playing bowles, billiards, croquet, muggins, drinking tea at all hours and in all places, dancing in the evening, and each one trying to be agreeable. . . . They all dined by themselves at 7. I dined at 3 with the Mob. I do not like late dinners. There are a great number of people here, mostly Southerners, some very pretty girls amongst them. Mr & Mrs Ludlow are here, they are common place people and she is not at all pretty.
Jul 21 The party went to the American side and had their photos taken in a group.[227] . . .
Jul 22 Mr Becher came to the Falls. He & I went to Buffalo. I bought

[226]See Amelia Harris' diary, 6 December 1857.
[227]The photographs are in the Harris Papers.

a silver plated jug, price in green back $18, in Canadian money $7.20 ct. I bought shoes & boots in the same way. Those that would cost me $2 & $1.50 a pair here cost me 62 ct there, that is in Canadian money. . . .

Jul 26 . . . Mrs Plumb drove me about to show me all the localities that I used to know 54 years ago when I was a child at school in Niagara. The town was burned in the war of 1812 & 14 and has never recovered since. All business has gone to St Catharines and all the old families are dead or gone. I could only hear of one person living there whom I had [known] and that was Mr McCormack. We hunted him up. The world is sadly changed with him, poor man. His wife has been long dead and he is poor & lonely in his old age. Mrs Plumb returned with us to the Falls and went to her mother's.

Jul 27 Spent the day much as usual, each one amusing themselves in their own way. In the evening a telegram came from Mr Gambier wanting us to return to London as the 47th Regt theatricals were to come off tomorrow evening. Consequently the Scotts and Griffins have decided upon going home tomorrow. I am very glad as there is so much noise that I cannot sleep here.

Jul 28 Miss Sewell & I breakfasted early and went to the museum and were very much gratified. I bought a few trifles for the Portman children. We left the Clifton [House] at twelve and arrived home at $^1/_2$ past 4 and found all well. They were all too tired to go to the theatricals. . . .

Aug 4 I have been ill in bed since the 30th. Dr Woodruff has attended me and today I am much better. Teresa has been the same kind nurse and the household has gone on as usual.

Aug 5 We have had letters from Sarah, Mary & Eliza and Mr Portman. Sarah complains of poverty. They wish to withdraw £12 or 1500 to buy a house and for fear their money may be lost in this country. Mary likes Dorsetshire and seems to be making friends and acquaintances as fast as she can wish. The Crutchleys like Gibraltar and seem pleased with everything about them. Mr Portman has decided upon running the blockade and going to the South to endevour to get the money owing him. I think he wishes to marry Alice Pitt. He will come to Canada before he returns to England.

Aug 18 The anniversary of Teresa's wedding day and I am thankful to say that her marriage appears to be a very happy one. . . . I got a letter from Mary who is in great alarm about the Yankees taking Canada and she wants £2,000 sent home for fear it may be lost. Col Dalzell has had another attack of bleeding at the lungs.

Aug 19 . . . It appears to me that there is less probability of war than there has been for years. When the Yankees have to pay $1,300 for a substitute, it is not probable that they will provoke another war.[228]

Aug 31 . . . Edward got a letter from Sophia written as she ought to write, expressing her sorrow for her misconduct, her love for him and asking him to take her back, promising to make him a faithful, good wife. . . .

Sep 1 There was a presentation of Colours to the Volunteers today by the Ladies of London. Mrs Mitchell, the druggist's wife, was deputed to present them. They are of silk and said to be very handsome. All the City were assembled to witness the ceremony. . . . Edward wrote to Sophia & asked her to see Edward Blake preparatory to her return. He looks happier than he has for some time.

Sep 2 Mr Griffin and Amelia called. Amelia looked wretched and Mr Griffin looked sullen. He would not play croquet, consequently she would not. I asked her what was the matter. She said Mr Griffin made her life miserable, that he would not allow her to speak to a soul, that she was not allowed to ask even her own sister to the house, and that he reproached her with coming *here* to see the officers, and he said that if Capt [W.B.G.] Cleather [47th] came to his house he would insult him. . . . She says that if she ever did anything wrong in thought, word, or deed that she should feel it less, but for him to be jealous of her when she is past 40 years of age is too humiliating. Her marriage has been a very unhappy one & will remain so, I suppose to the end. . . .

Sep 3 . . . the civilians gave a dinner to the officers of the Garrison. . . .

Sep 4 . . . Mr Hall of the 47th called. The dinner last night was a great success, every body seemed pleased and satisfied. Nearly all the officers attended and there was not one objectional person amongst the civilians. . . .

Sep 6 George & some of the officers have been teasing me to let them have a party this evening. This morning I consented and they have invited all the young people and have engaged the Canadian Rifle Band. The day has been a very busy one taking up the carpet and providing supper. . . . The rooms were filled and the supper was nice and the party went off very well. . . . The Review today was a great success, it is said there were 30,000 people present.

Sep 12 The troops got their marching orders today and are to leave on

228Reference to practise of buying-out of military service following the introduction of conscription in 1863.

the 14th. We are all so sorry to have them go. London will be very dull without the red coats. . . .
Sep 13 . . . He [Edward] got a letter from E. Blake about Sophia urging him to be reconciled to her and wishing him to go down. I believe Sophia repents what she has done & I think Edward ought to take her back as we believe her not to have been criminal but her conduct was such that it is very hard for Edward to forgive. Forget he cannot. . . .
Sep 14 Capt Cleather, Mr North & Mr Hall[229] had breakfast here at six AM and the Regiment [47th] marched at 7, bidding a long adieu to London. It is very doubtful whether there will ever be any more British soldiers stationed in London as the home government say they will not defend the colonies. . . . The regiment marched in very heavy rain but it appears that Col Lawrie had no option, he had to go.
Sep 17 . . . Edward returned from Toronto. He made it a condition before he would see Sophia that the bond which her father holds for a settlement should be given up or assigned to someone else. Sophia was willing to do anything, to sign any document that would secure Edward from further annoyance from herself or her father. Edward Blake was counsel and advisor, he said that Dr Ryerson was very violent and very abusive towards Edward and Mr Blake thinks the Dr a bad man. Dr Ryerson at first refused to give up or assign the bond or to allow Sophia to act in the matter, but Edward said he would never see her until Dr Ryerson's interference and power of influencing her was at an end. Dr Ryerson at last agreed to assign the bond to Mr Wilson as Edward said that not one shilling of his money should ever go to her by compulsion, that he would leave the firm and country first. After Mr Blake, Mr Wilson, Sophia & Dr Ryerson had pledged themselves that all the arrangement should be carried out as Edward wished, Edward consented to see Sophia at Mr Blake's and saw her there for an hour. She appeared to be truly sorry for all her misconduct and was anxious and willing to return to him upon any terms that he was willing to take her. She told Edward that she would never get a civil word from her mother in consequence of her return to him and that her stay at her father's would be very unpleasant to her as her father was angry with her also.
Sep 24 Mr Cornish is being tried today for bigamy. He has long been not only a disgrace but an injury to the town. . . .
Sep 29 . . . Edward gets letters constantly from Sophia. They are not

[229]Members of the 47th Regiment.

very satisfactory. She is the gayest of the gay. He thinks he has bought the elephant, that she is unsuited to an office man who has to work and economize. There are but too many unsuitable marriages. . . .

Oct 13 The day very fine, put up the hall stove. . . .

Oct 19 . . . Mr Scott and Edward came home at 4 AM this morning very tired of course. They brought home 90 ducks and gave a good many away at Port Ryerse and Simcoe. There was a letter here from Edward Blake. Dr Ryerson refuses to transfer or to give up the bond. Edward was foolish enough to . . . make a settlement, if Sophia signs the document she agreed to sign it will nullify the bond. If she does not I doubt her returning to Edward and the consequence will be that Edward will hold no property. Every thing will be in George's name and then let them do their worst. Edward as in duty bound would leave all he has to Sophia should her penitence be real and she return and become a good true wife but he says he will never give her anything by compulsion, that she by her conduct has forfeited all claim to the provision of that bond and now that by her future conduct she must establish a new claim upon him which he would be but too glad to respond to. . . .

Oct 21 Edward has gone to Toronto. He has business to do for Mr Scott and he wishes to see Blake about his own affairs concerning Dr Ryerson and Sophia. . . .

Oct 22 . . . Edward was very much hurt to find that Sarah had told Mrs Wilson that Edward and George had so mismanaged their money and that they had lost so much that they should withdraw it all as soon as they could. The statement is untrue . . . [and] will be very injurious to Harris Brothers coming from their sister. She little thinks what injury such a statement may do men in business. May God forgive her. . . .

Oct 31 The Scotts are gone. I have seen Teresa most probably for the last time . . . & I feel very lonely. . . .

Nov 1 . . . We commenced our house cleaning and we are getting Edward's room ready for Sophia.

Nov 2 Got letters from Shuldham, Mary, Mrs Knight, and Amelia had one from Eliza. There is a probability of Mr Portman's being here in a few days. If he hears discouraging accounts of yellow fever at Bermuda he will come to Canada. Mrs Knight sent me such pretty photos of Capt Knight, herself and children, her little daughter must be a beauty. Eliza continues to like Gibraltar. . . . I had a long talk with Edward this evening about Sophia. He doubts any happiness being in store for him. Dr Ryerson will not transfer the bond for marriage settlement, but intends proceeding upon it as soon as the five years are up. It will cause great annoyance and publicity even if he cannot recover anything upon it.

Nov 9 . . . Charley Leslie is not better. Miss Dewar wrote to Edward to ask if Sophia must come home on Saturday as Capt Leslie wished her to remain with them. She has been very kind in sitting up with the child & in nursing him. Edward of course wrote to her to stay as long as she could be of any use to the Leslies or as long as she wished.

Nov 10 . . . Old Lincoln is reelected President. The election took place without disturbance but gold rose immediately 12 or 14 per cent. . . .

Nov 12 Charley Leslie died this morning. A worm crawled out of his mouth before he died and now it is thought that his death was caused by worms. . . .

Nov 16 . . . Mrs Cronyn called. She spoke about Sophia's return and thinks it will never answer for her to live at Eldon and I begin to feel more and more that it would be better for Edward to take a house. But I dislike to urge it upon him as I know that he is [convinced] that we all are poor and that we can live much cheaper together than separately but peace and quiet should be preserved at any sacrifice. . . . Capt Leslie had a post mortem examination of little Charley and find that his death was caused by worms and the doctors had treated him for congestion of the brain and said the disease is caused by the bad air from bad drainage of the house.

Nov 17 Edward went to Toronto. He is to bring Sophia home with him. . . .

Nov 19 . . . Edward and Sophia returned at 1/2 past 9 PM. Sophia looked a little awkward, more as if she had returned to a household that she had condemned than as if she herself had ever done anything wrong. Nor do I believe that she think she has, and I cannot help feeling that she returns more from the conviction that from a worldly point of view it is the best thing that she can do than from either love or duty. When she came in I met her in the hall and she stood still and mute. I kissed her and asked her whether she would come to the drawing room or go to her own room. She came to the drawing room for a few minutes then went to her room and returned to supper. After supper I retired and so ends her first day at Eldon.

Nov 20 . . . We, that is, Amelia, Edward, George & myself had decided before Sophia returned that she would not go to Church the first Sunday as her going away was associated with so much scandal and her having had no intercourse with her husband for two years. We thought she would rather remain quiet for a week and allow people to think of her as returned before she made her public appearance, but to our great surprise she insisted upon going to Church. Edward made excuses which she over ruled and he is determined that she shall do just as she pleases. When George found that Sophia was going to Church he thought there was such a want of nice feeling that Edward ought not to let her go. It was against my will and judgement to do so but I told Edward that George thought she had better not go. Edward said he thought that it had never entered into Sophia's head that she ought not to go and that he would not say a word. I felt that I had made my first mistake in speaking. George walked me to the Church door and then returned. . . .

Nov 25 The first news that I had this morning was that Mrs Becher was dead. . . . As soon as I heard the sad news I called for Amelia and we went out there. The whole family seemed in a state of stupor as if they could not realize what had so suddenly come upon them. She was a fond mother whatever her other faults may have been. . . . Mrs Cronyn called to ask about Mrs Becher. . . .

Nov 27 . . . Mrs Becher was buried at 3 PM. Edward and George went as mourners. It is now said that drink was the immoderate cause of her death. . . .

Dec 8 . . . Mr Becher came to luncheon, . . . he had just received a letter from Sir Richard Airey who said that he had made a very strong representation to the Horse Guards on the impolicy of removing all the troops from Upper Canada and also of leaving the great extent of country west of Hamilton without a nucleus of regular troops for the Militia to rally around in the case of invasion. He says he shall exert all of his influence to keep the troops in Upper Canada.

Dec 13 Mr Griffin has gone to Woodstock to have a public reading for charitable purposes. George has gone to Sarnia for a land sale.

Dec 16 There appears to be a very great probability of war with the Yankees. If so, the country will be over run and then what will become of the money entrusted to Edward to invest, the mortgages paid up most probably in green backs which will be worthless. Am I never to be free from care and trouble? The thoughts of such a possibility keep me from sleep. . . .

Dec 25 George, Amelia & I went to Church. Amelia & I remained to the Sacrament. The Church had no green decorations. I do not recollect ever seeing the Church without them on Christmas Day before. It did not appear to me like Christmas. Amelia & Mr Griffin called in the afternoon. Edward gave Sophia a very pretty ring. He had sent to New York for it.

Dec 31 Amelia and Mr Becher came to luncheon. Mr Becher told us his housekeeping was much less expensive since his wife's death. He said that she had no idea of the value of money and that the waste in his house was very great and that Miss Leonard[230] had set right many things that were wrong. I am sure that he finds his home much more comfortable and satisfactory. . . .

1865

Jan 1 George & Sophia went to Church. . . .
Jan 2 There is a great contest going on today for the mayoralty. People are making a great effort to put out Mr Cornish and hope to succeed although Mr Glass, the opposing candidate, is very unpopular. People vote less to put Mr Glass in than to keep Mr Cornish out. Today has been kept as New Year's day. We have had very few visitors. . . .
Jan 3 Mr Cornish is no longer Mayor and we are all very glad. . . .
Jan 6 . . . George was at a party at the Goodhues last evening. I think he has a liking for Minnie. . . .
Jan 13 . . . There is a great probability of war with the Yankees. Every paper is full of war excitement.
Jan 22 Last night the City Hotel was burnt. The stables and two or three offices attached to the hotel building escaped. Every thing was taken out of the offices. All Harris Brothers' books and papers were brought here. Mr Scott who owns the buildings would have lost very little had they all been burned as they were pretty well insured but the hotel being gone he can get but little rent for the others and the taxes are heavy. His insurance on the hotel is $10,000. . . . There is a suspicion that the City Hotel was set on fire. . . .
Jan 29 All at Eldon went to Church excepting myself . . . a letter from Eliza who gives a glowing account of the pleasures of Gibraltar. . . .
Feb 2 Mrs Ermatinger & Miss Warren called. . . . I was very glad to see Mrs Ermatinger, it is several years since she has been here. . . .
Feb 14 . . . George went out in the evening. I sat up until 11 for him and then went to bed but could not sleep. The front door was left open for him. At 1 o'clock I got up and bolted it. At ½ past 1 he came home. I let him in. I could not sleep. I do not like his being out so late at nights. No good can come of it, there are no houses that he can go into unceremoniously to tea and there are no young men of a class that he can spend evenings profitably with at taverns. I am so helpless, I can only tell him that he is taking a wrong road and pray for him. Oh that God would keep him right.

[230]Becher's sister-in-law.

Feb 15 I have been ill all day . . . I had a talk with George in the evening. He promised all I wished but feels that he is old enough to do as he pleases without being called to account. True he is old enough to be more than he is, to be a barrister, to have a formed character and to give up unprofitable companions and to only have manly, gentlemanly and praiseworthy pursuits.
Feb 17 . . . George is in a state of excitement about the Bachelors' Ball this evening. He is one of the bachelors and the expenses are going to fall very heavily on a few of them. It is great folly, their giving the ball. Edward and Sophia returned this evening from Toronto. They seem to have enjoyed their visit. Edward discovered that there is a panic amongst the military about coming to London. They feel that it will be banishment and no one wants to come. It is that horrid Regiment, the 63rd, that has given London a bad name. It used to be the favorite station. . . .
Feb 18 Both Edward & George thought the ball one of the best that has ever been given in London. What is a very uncommon thing, every body appeared to be pleased. Mrs Cronyn called. . . .
Feb 19 My birthday. I am now 67, a very few more birthdays remain for me. Shall I ever see another. How short and unsatisfactory even a long life appears to look back upon. All at Eldon went to Church excepting myself. I had the service in my own room – and wrote to Teresa. Amelia came in the afternoon and brought me a pretty hyacinth in flower. . . .
Feb 21 . . . Elizabeth arrived at 10 PM. She has not improved in appearance. She looks coarse and dresses her hair badly but she looks very happy.
Feb 24 I got a letter from Louisa Portman telling me of Lady Portman's death, so peaceful, humble & loving. Louisa took Maurice's little children in to see her. She blessed them and told those around her to take care of those poor children. Poor children indeed, they have lost a second mother and God only knows whether their father will ever return. Lady Portman was so good a woman that all who knew her felt that death is a gain to her. Mr O'Brien went to the Griffins to dinner. Elizabeth did not go. She was not very well and feared a miscarriage.
Mar 7 Elizabeth was to have gone at 7 this morning but the cab did not come & she missed the train, consequently did not go until 4 PM. I like Elizabeth and am glad to see that she is happy in her second marriage. . . . George & Edward went to the skating carnival and were much amused. There were between two and three hundred people there, about 80 of them were in costume. This is the second skating

carnival of the season. It is very money making to the rink as all who enter pay 25 cents each.
Mar 17 . . . Mrs W. Lawrason spent the evening with us. She says that old Mrs Lawrason does not know that their house is sold and the family are afraid to tell her. She is in such a delicate state of health. Poor old people, they are much to be pitied being sold out of house & home in their old age. . . .
Mar 28 . . . Edward sold some of his St Thomas lots for $2,500. It is much less than they cost him but it is more than he expected to get unless he kept them for a very long time. Everyone thinks it a very good sale.
Apr 6 . . . it is Assize Week and a great many strangers are in town. . . .
Apr 15 The telegraphic news of this morning is very shocking. President Lincoln was shot last evening in the theatre when sitting with his wife and party.[231] . . . Canada as well as the States is horrified at the crime.
Apr 22 Edward & Capt Leslie were off very early to Wyoming to the oil springs. They returned in time for dinner, very much gratified with what they saw. Capt Leslie slipped into an oil vat about a foot. He recovered himself before he went deeper, or rather people caught hold of him and prevented his going deeper, but he had no sooner opened the door than the whole house was scented with the aroma of the crude oil. . . .
Apr 25 . . . The left wing of the 16th arrived today. We were all glad to see the red coats again. . . .
May 3 Mrs Wilson came in and spent the day with us. She says Ellen Hamilton is the worst tempered girl she ever saw and speaks very unkindly of her, but I am on Ellen's side as I have seen a great deal of her without discovering her bad temper. Not so with Mrs Wilson. . . .
May 6 . . . I was very ill in the night and had such a bad attack of night mare without any of the usual frights of horrid animals or pressure on the chest but simply that I was conscious that I could neither breathe or move. I was in great agony & tried in vain to move my head. There seemed bright streaks of light about me without my being awake. I was quite able to think & I have long expected to die suddenly, I thought the call had come when all at once the circulation returned, but I felt very weak and ill with a strange feeling about the heart & I feel weak and ill this morning. . . . I have been ill all day. Mr King came to dinner. Mrs King called.

[231]Several newspaper clippings have been pasted into the diary.

May 10 Yesterday all day Amelia was ailing and confined herself to the sofa. She felt so weak that she felt she had better go to bed before her visitors arrived. As soon as Mrs W. Lawrason appeared she went with Amelia into her room. She had scarcely got into her room before symptoms of a miscarriage appeared. The Doctor (Landor) was sent for but his skill could not prevent the misfortune. The party left early supposing that Amelia was not very well but not knowing how very ill she was. I saw her today. She looks very weak but I hope with care will soon gain strength again. The great danger is that she has been so weakened by her last confinement and now again by this miscarriage that she may go into a decline. This misfortune is a great disappointment to Mr Griffin as well as herself but if the misfortune ends here we shall have great reason to be thankful. . . .
May 11 . . . Mr Wilson and Becher came to luncheon. After Mr Wilson left, Becher and I had a long talk about their speculations about his marrying again. He laughed at all their surmises & says if he ever does marry, the lady must have money, that he cannot afford to marry without it. . . .
May 17 There is great oil excitement amongst the oil speculators. It is thought that oil will be found in abundance in and near London. . . .
May 19 Edward drove out to the Walsh farm with an oil speculator who sees indications of oil. He wants to sink a well on the 25 acres with the right to buy it in one or two years as may be agreed upon. If he finds oil he will pay $300 to $1,000 per acre for what would be then worth $100,000. If they found no oil they would not buy. I will not bond it. I will wait until a well is sunk some where near and if they find oil the 16 acres will be *mine* to sell at my own price, and if there is no oil found in the vicinity I shall be no worse off than I am at present. . . .
May 23 Amelia got a short letter from Mr Portman from Columbia[232] dated the 12th of May. He hoped to be here nearly as soon as his letter. There was very little in his letter or I suppose it would never have reached us but it gave us the information that he was alive and well and would be soon with us and that was what we were most anxious to hear. For where life is so little valued as in the South, we could not but fear for his safety. . . .
May 24 . . . We had a great fright. Leonard's old foundry[233] was *set on fire*. Fortunately the wind was favorable to us or Eldon would have

[232]North Carolina.
[233]The foundry was located at the southeast corner of Fullarton and Ridout Streets.

been in great danger. Our garden fence is very much injured and all the pretty forest trees killed which added so much to the beauty of Eldon and which will take a quarter of a century to replace. I feel very thankful that Eldon has escaped. . . .

Jun 8 . . . Dr Ryerson is in town attending a Methodist conference and will be here for a fortnight. We do not know how to act. Sophia naturally wants him to come here and we, none of us, want to see him. But he is Sophia's father and she is Edward's wife & I think it best to bury the past as much as we can and as we have a dinner party tomorrow I think we had best ask him to dinner and if he comes receive him as any other guest and then we can get on to a sort of civil footing without ever alluding to the past, which will not bear talking over.

Jun 9 Dr Ryerson has dined here. It was very difficult to get Edward & George to consent to his being invited. They both said they would not dine here if Dr Ryerson came and then, of course, I would not ask him. Sophia looked very disappointed but behaved very well and left every thing to me. At last Edward and George agreed to do any thing that I wished and said they would dine here and be civil but I believe they thought Dr Ryerson would not come. It was two o'clock before we came to a decision & we were to dine at 7. Sophia took the note and he came and we received him as any other guest and every thing went off very well.

Poor man, I think there is no doubt about his brain softening. I asked Sophia if she suspected it. She said no, but told me several things which convinced me she must know it. She says that people frequently ask her father if his brain is not softening. It is a very strange question to be asked. It is very much like saying, what a fool you are. . . .

Jun 17 . . . The croquet party with the Bechers could not commence play until 5 o'clock and they did not finish the game until nearly 9. The Bechers won. The whole Becher family was here including Miss Leonard. It is the first time for many years that our families have met in social intercourse as they have at the last two games of croquet.

Jun 20 Amelia came to luncheon. Sophia had a croquet party in the afternoon. . . .

Jun 21 Miss Geddes & the Griffins played croquet. . . .

Jun 22 . . . We had another croquet party today. . . .

Jun 23 Miss Geddes, Miss Brough & Amelia came to luncheon. They played croquet for a very short time. Mrs Edward Blake called to ask Sophia, Edward & George to go to the Bishops to a croquet party tomorrow. The Goodhues give a party tonight, George is the only one invited from Eldon.

Jun 26 Sophia had another croquet party. . . .
Jun 27 This is the 50th anniversary of my wedding day and the tenth anniversary of Amelia's. The Griffins & Eldon House people went to play croquet at the Bechers. The Bishops beat Eldon. George did not go to the Bechers until late. He was playing cricket with the London Cricket Club against the garrison. It is more than seven years since I have been at the Bechers. . . .
Jul 5 Mr Becher came to luncheon and afterwards drove me out to the cemetery to see the vault which he has built and has placed Mrs Becher and child in it. I want to have one built for my family and think that one like his would do very well. . . .
Jul 22 . . . Mr Portman arrived this evening. He looks changed, looks thinner and older. It is three years since I last saw him. He has witnessed a great deal of distress in the South. . . .
Jul 28 . . . After luncheon I went to pay a long promised visit to Mrs Askin. There was no one home excepting Mrs Askin and Teresa and they appeared to be very glad to see me & repeatedly expressed their pleasure at my visit & I felt very glad that I had gone there. Mr & Mrs Askin are old and every thing about the place looks like age and narrowed circumstances. . . .
Jul 30 . . . Mr Portman, Edward & I had a long talk about oil and Mr Portman and Edward are much inclined to use their best efforts to get up a company and to enter onto the oil business, that is if they can see their way clear and have a reasonable prospect of making money for themselves & stockholders and not losing it for either. The suspicion is that George Brown and Mr Gzowski being with Becher to buy Port Talbot is a humbug, that it is oil speculating that they are about and it is whispered that Becher sent a man to England on Saturday last to carry out their plans by getting stock taken in a company which they are forming. There can be little doubt but what large fortunes can and will be made by oil.
Aug 1 Edward went to the oil springs to see if he could bond any land but failed. Land in that region is selling at very large prices & no one will agree to bond it for longer than a month which would not give Mr Portman time to go to England & raise money. But I have not lost hope about making our fortunes by oil as I think it will be found on our lands. . . .
Aug 3 Mr Pepper, one of the oil millionaires, came here today to see Edward upon business. Two years ago he was a poor farmer working hard for his living and now his *share* from one well amounts to $60 a day and there is room on his property to sink 100 more. The wealth from the oil wells is almost fabulous. . . .

Aug 6 . . . Edward was vexed with George last night and called him a *donkey* for devoting himself to Fanny Goodhue all the evening. Fanny is a very good girl but I should not think there was anything in her to attract George further than she talks about her sister Minnie. George is certainly fond of Minnie but fortunately she does not care for him. She is in such wretched health that the chances are she will not live very long. Probably her state of health makes it impossible for her to love anyone. I have thought favorably of the girl because George liked her and he has always with one exception shown refined feeling and nice taste in his liking for ladies. He seemed to have a thorough contempt for boldness or levity. It is strange to me that all three of my sons should have in succession liked and flirted with a woman that I think worse than lightly of. George now likes Mrs Duncan Askin and writes to her as his dear cousin, yet she has walked so near the precipice that it is difficult to believe that she has not made a step over it. Am I wrong in my dislike or rather disapproval of her? Not unless all sense of right is changed and that vice is virtue and that it is right and praiseworthy for a woman to entertain her lover when her worthless husband is dying in the room over her head. Yet I have been civil to her but not very willingly. . . .
Aug 7 . . . Mr Portman read my journal and was much more excited and vexed than he ought to have been as I only noted what passed without a remark of my own. Mr Portman never ought to be vexed with me, I have loved him as my own child and have wished him as well, and have been as sorry to see him act foolishly and do wrong as if he had been my own son. There was croquet here today. . . .
Aug 18 . . . [Sir John Michel[234]] enters warmly into the oil speculation and told Mr Portman to put his name at the head of his list for £1,000 and he also told Mr Portman that if he wanted money to draw upon him to any amount. This was particularly kind. I suppose he thought that Mr Portman, having been so long in the South might be short of money. . . . Mrs Askin came in and spent the day with me. Mrs Cronyn and Ellen Hamilton came to dinner. Teresa Askin came in the evening for her mother and she looked so amused when she saw Ellen here. Mrs Askin went with me to see Amelia and as soon as we got outside of the door at Eldon she told me that Teresa had heard that Ellen was in great hopes of being Mrs Portman, that Mr Portman had flirted with her at the pic nic and that she believed he was in love with

[234]Sir John Michel (1804–86), administrator of the Government of Canada (1865–67).

her and that she had no intentions of throwing cold water upon his feelings. Mrs Askin said she felt much inclined to laugh when she saw Ellen walk in pretending not to know that Mr Portman was at home. Mr Portman was cautious and did not flirt openly and I only observed the sweet looks & softly modulated voice when he spoke to her. It is a shame for him to turn her head.

Aug 25 . . . Mr Egan the photographer came and took photos of the drawing room, small sitting, my bedroom and one from the hall door. . . .

Sep 3 . . . No one from Eldon went to morning service. All went in the evening excepting myself. I read the service in my own room. Mr Portman says that Amelia & I would speak ill of an angel if the gentleman part of the family paid them much attention. I think he is unjust. At all events we have never been tried in that way. I think that neither Mrs Bill [Lawrason] nor Dora Bettridge have claims to the angelic. I have some times thought that I am not very fond of women but upon self examination I believe there are more good women than there are men & I have felt a strong friendship for more women out of my own family than I have for men, but of our acquaintance in this world, there are but few either men or women, that we entirely approve of or entirely condemn. I have been very fond of a few women & when with them have felt that I was inferior to them in everything that was good and think of them now as numbered amongst the bright spirits who have entered into their rest. Mr Portman says that I always used to speak well of Ellen Hamilton but that as soon as he paid her attention I condemned her at once. He misunderstands me and he ought not. I like Ellen for her many good qualities & if Mr Portman told me that he wished to make honorable love to her, however disappointed I might be in his choice of a second wife, I would invite her here if he wished it and would treat her with all the respect that I should wish a woman to be treated that he loved. But it requires no great stretch of imagination to realize how painful it *must be* to me to see idle love making here when I have known him only as a loving husband and father, and here where his wife died. My feelings may be very foolish but they are not imaginary. They are too dreadfully real. Three times they have brought me to the verge of the grave and they have left me a wreck, a feeble old woman, feeble in mind and body. I only knew Capt Knight as a husband to my poor Chasse for a few short hours, yet when Capt Knight & Henrietta spoke of coming out it cost me a painful struggle to ask them and to think of the Mrs Knight that he took away and of the Mrs Knight that was coming in her place & to see her in Chasse's seat at Church & table. I felt that the Knight's regard for us, called for all the return that I could make & I asked them. I could see them anywhere else with less pain than here. Those feelings are struggles of the heart. They are real, whether every body have them or not I cannot tell. I love Mr Portman as one of my own children and am as rejoiced as he does right & as sorry when he does wrong as if he was one of them.

Sep 6 I have been ill with a very bad cold and unable to write but I do not know that anything very particular has occurred. . . . Becher came to luncheon today & the Killerys called. Mr Griffin brought me some very nice grapes. When I am ill he always brings me any nice little thing that he sees that he thinks I would like or any book that he thinks would amuse me. It is a kindness for which I feel very grateful. Mr Portman . . . will leave for England on Friday. I shall be sorry to see him go. I now when saying good bye always feel that it may be for the last time.

Sep 7 This has been a long & gloomy day to me. I have been very ill and feel so lonely. The change of the last few years seems to me so great. I had so many leaning and depending upon me, now all are gone & I am old and helpless & have to lean upon others. It is the natural result of old age. We all have to journey the same road. It would not be called the *dark valley* of the shadow of death if the approach to it were not gloomy. . . .

Sep 9 My cold continues very bad. Mr Portman left at 12 for England. I could not speak when he bid me good bye. I watched him as he walked to the gate & thought most probably it was the last look I should ever have of him. . . .

Sep 19 My brother George came up today & returns tomorrow. . . .

Sep 20 . . . My brother left by the 4 PM train. He looks very old & is much changed more in intellect than looks. Sophia & George went to the ball. Mr Manning of the 47th called.

Sep 21 The ball went off only pretty well. The 16th band took offence about the supper and would not take any. It is said that there was plenty to eat but all solids. Today Edward drove Sophia & I to the Exhibition Grounds. There was an immense crowd. We did not attempt going into the building. . . .

Sep 28 . . . Minnie Goodhue's engagement to Ben Cronyn is announced. . . .

Sep 29 George passed his examination at the Military School today. . . .

Oct 7 . . . I got a letter from Elizabeth who *is not* confined.

Oct 17 George went to Port Stanley with the V[olunteer] Battery for artillery practice. . . . There has been numerous burglaries lately and last night another was attempted at the house of Mr Glackmeyer, but he was aware of what the gang of burglars intended and was prepared for them. Two or three of the police were secreted in his house. Mr Glackmeyer himself went out and went to a saloon, the resort of the suspected parties. Henry Schram challenged him to billiards & when Mr Glackmeyer attempted to go Mr Schram would use all his arts to detain him. Mr Glackmeyer played his part well and watched one after another leave the saloon and knew that they were going to rob his house. He had not long to wait, when the police came in and made several arrests, but I will enter the printed report. It was a melancholy sight to see six or eight young men, sons of the most respectable people in the place, marched handcuffed to the jail, and they have all been led into their evil ways by that son of the evil one, Henry Schram.

Oct 30 Schram was found guilty by the jury and is now safe for the Penitentiary but I fear it is too late to save those young lads who are under his influence. . . .

Nov 1 . . . Schram has 14 years, Claypole 5 & Kerr 3 years in the Penitentiary.[235]

Nov 3 . . . Elizabeth has a daughter & is doing well. . . .

Nov 6 I took my hour's walk. The ground is covered with snow & it is quite winter weather. . . . Edward got a letter from Mr Portman who wishes him to go to England immediately about getting up an oil company. Edward says he will endevor to go in a fortnight.

Nov 10 . . . I got letters from Mary, Eliza and Mr Portman. Poor Eliza has had a dreadful anxious summer at Gib[raltar]; out of a 1,000 patients 500 have died with cholera. . . . Edward went to see Hicks' well where they have struck oil. This is great news for London for it proves that there is oil in the valley of the Thames as far up as this and there is reason to believe that it will be found much farther up.

Nov 11 There was great excitement last night, Hicks' well struck oil. Edward was at a meeting in town when the news came in at 8 PM. The oil men & many others made a rush out and got horses, buggies & any conveyance that was at hand and all started for the well, the oil men hallowing to each other, Oil, Oil. Edward drove there with Mr Hicks the chief owner of the well. When they came within a quarter of a mile of the well they left their horses etc & made a rush through

[235]Excerpts of the *London Free Press* reports of this incident are pasted in the diary. Two of the "young lads" were Basil Hamilton (son of James Hamilton) and William Wilson (son of John Wilson).

the woods yelling Oil, Oil, tumbling over logs & stumps. When they arrived at the well they found that the oil was a fact and then Edward said it was the funniest thing he ever beheld, singing, dancing, drinking, with the chorus of Oil, Oil. He returned at twelve & today the city has been in a state of great excitement. Mr Becher came to luncheon. He tried to sham coolness but was in as great a frenzy as any of us. The stock for the test well below the jail was all taken in a very short time and was at 75 per cent premium at night. . . . The 60th Rifles are ordered to London. It is supposed to be on account of the threatened raids of the Fenians. Information has been received that they intend to make a night attack on the banks in Toronto.[236]

Nov 25 . . . The 60th Rifles arrived this evening.

Nov 29 Mr Plumb called and is rather disappointed that Edward has not made him head & soul of his contemplated oil company. . . .

Dec 3 . . . Edward has been in a sad humour all day about Magee's[237] not returning from Volunteer duty & he was very violent towards George. . . .

Dec 4 . . . Amelia not well and has to keep quiet.[238] Mr Griffin told me what Edward said about George at his house. He talks more foolishly than I could have believed. . . . George told me in the evening that he should tell Edward that he would leave the office in a year, that he worked hard and endevored to do all that he could but that he could not stand Edward's language to him and it is such that I cannot write it down. George is very low & he knows that they can do better together but thinks they may perhaps be better friends apart. When I objected to his proposal he asked me what I wished him to do, if I wished him to remain and put up with such language constantly used to him. What could I say to a man of 29 years of age? My trials are not to end this side of the grave.

Dec 12 . . . I got letters from Mr Portman, Sarah & Teresa. Mr Portman's letter was very nice & cheery. He is very anxious for Edward's arrival & very full of oil. . . . Becher was here at luncheon and is giving Edward all the assistance that he can in getting up his oil company. He is preparing everything for him to take to England.

[236]An American-Irish movement to form an independent Irish State in Ireland, which resulted in a series of American invasions of Canadian territory during the 1860s and 1870s.

[237]James Magee (1846–1939), a prominent lawyer, was a law partner of Edward Harris. See Henry James Morgan, *The Canadian Men and Women of the Time*, Toronto: William Briggs, 1912.

[238]Amelia is pregnant with her third child.

Dec 14 Edward left today for England. He felt low & anxious about his success. I felt sorry & glad to see him go, sorry to part with him, yet anxious that he should make money so as to secure an independence. Sophia went with him as far as Montreal on her way to Quebec. They remain from Saturday until Monday at Montreal with Sir John & Lady Michel. Col Peacocke goes with them as far as Toronto. Amelia came to luncheon. It is the first time that she has been out for nearly a month. She looks very miserable. Mr Griffin & Becher came to luncheon also. Ellen Hamilton came in the evening and will remain with me during Sophia's absence. Magee returned this morning before Edward left in time to receive his instructions which we were all very glad of.

Dec 23 The show of meat today at the market is said to be very fine. The Yankees were astonished. They do not make any unusual display in the markets at Christmas. . . .

Dec 25 The day bright and lovely, . . . Mr Griffin sent me a dozen half pints of champagne as a Christmas box. Ellen went to Church with me. There was a large congregation. We remained to the Sacrament. I found Mr Griffin and Amelia at Eldon. They remained to luncheon. We are all, including Edward and Sophia, invited to dine with the Hellmuths[239] on the 28th, only Mr Griffin and George accept. We dined with the Griffins today, no one there but themselves, George & I. Every thing very nice, and so has ended the Christmas of 1865.

Dec 30 Amelia came to luncheon. Miss Warren came over to spend the week with me. Ellen & Selina Hamilton came in the evening to tell me about the Strathy's party. Things were in a pretty primitive style. Drinks were in black bottles and in the refreshment room tea cups served as tumblers. They had no wine, only beer, gin, rum, whiskey & lemonade. . . .

Dec 31 Miss Warren & I went to the morning service, George went in the evening. Amelia came to Eldon for a very short time. I wrote to Mary and Edward.

1866

Jan 1 New Year's Day. The weather beautiful, thermometer 28, no snow. I have had the following visitors: Bishop of Huron, B. Cronyn,

[239]Isaac Hellmuth (1817–1901), founder and first Principal of Huron College (1863), founder of Hellmuth Boys' College (1865) and Hellmuth Ladies' College (1869), succeeded Benjamin Cronyn as Bishop of Huron (1872–83).

R. Brough, Capt Collins 16th, Capt Hawlayn, Col Barrows, Mr Hutchinson, Mr Walker, & Mr Stewart, Aleck & Harry Becher, Dr Hellmuth, . . . Capt Rogge & Mr Robinson 16th, Amelia & Charley Griffin. Ellen & Selena spent the day here and so ends the first day of the New Year. May our Heavenly Father bless us & have us in His keeping.

Jan 4 . . . I heard from Sophia who is very gay and is not coming home as soon as she first intended. . . .

Jan 12 . . . The ball at the Johnson's last evening was a pretty rowdy affair. George went with a party of 12 in one of the Cootes' long waggons. The driver was tipsy when they returned and upset them very close to the Johnson's house and they had to walk home & carry their buffalo robes. Mr Brownrigg [60th] took off his dress boots and ran home in his stockings. It was 5 o'clock in the morning when they got home.

Jan 16 . . . I had a letter from Sophia. She wants to stay longer at Quebec. I do not know why she should bother me about her staying. I have neither the wish nor power to control her actions, but the letter that I got from Major Leslie about Sophia's staying was certainly a surprise. It was most insulting to me and most uncalled for. Sophia had written to ask me when she had better come home. I said that she was not in the least needed at home but thought that she had better leave Quebec this week and stay for a few days with Lady Michel at Montreal and a few days with the Sandfield Macdonalds at Cornwall & a few days with her mother so that she would be in reach of Edward's letters when they arrived. In answer to this I got an abusive letter from Major Leslie. It was such a letter as I could not answer. I asked Amelia to write and say that I had no wish to hurry Sophia home & that Edward's letters could be forwarded to her. In Sophia's second letter she asked me to telegraph whether she can stay. She had already received what I have written above but that was not what she wanted. She wanted me to tell her to stay so that if Edward was not pleased she could say, your mother told me to stay. I telegraphed to her, – Stay of course – and she has got her last letter from me.

Jan 18 Amelia was not well enough to come to Eldon. I went to see her. I very much fear she will have another miscarriage. . . .

Jan 25 Last night George & Miss Warren went to the 60th ball. They did not return till 4 this morning. . . .

Jan 31 Teresa Askin came and took me with her mother to get our photos taken. We in 1814 were bride & brides maid. . . .

Feb 23 . . . Edward returned at 1/2 past 7 PM looking very well but his getting up an oil company has been almost a failure. He says the

Portman children are very much grown & that they are very fine boys but very unruly. They have been too much indulged. . . . Teresa sent me half a dozen silver salt cellars & spoons. Dear Teresa, she is always so kind & good. Edward could not go to see Sarah nor Mary. Mary & Shuldham came to London to see him. The Dalzells he did not see at all and they are very angry with him. I feel thankful he has returned in safety to us.

Feb 27 . . . I have rheumatism in my shoulder. . . .

Mar 5 I have been ill all day. Edward & I, last night and this morning, discussed many subjects. When we come into contact it always makes me ill, whether I am wrong or he is wrong the result is the same. . . . I wrote to Mary. . . . Sophia had visitors. . . . I did not see them. Sophia refused to go to the pic nic today because Edward was away & George would not go. But as she went to all parties when Edward was in England & George was not with her, I do not see why she should object now. . . .

Mar 8 Sophia's new dresses arrived today. They are very handsome and very expensive. The duties & carriage from N[ew] Y[ork] was $37, that included a dress sent by Teresa to Amelia. It is a very pretty dress & a very nice present. . . . There is a great scare about the Fenians, 10,000 volunteers are called out. Official notice has been sent by the American authorities at Chicago that an attack will certainly be made upon Canada before the 20th of this month. . . .

Mar 13 . . . Oil has been struck at McKenzie's farm which is not far from Edward Walsh's farm & Becher's bank property. A Yankee company talk of buying the whole off Becher & Edward. They all drove out today to look at it. . . .

Mar 17 There is a great stir today about Fenians. The soldiers are confined to Barracks & kept on the alert. Guards are placed at all the bridges. It may be a very proper precaution but I do not think there are Fenians enough . . . for them to venture upon any outrage. . . .

Mar 21 . . . I begin to find myself very much in the way here. Sophia is never content unless she is visiting or has visitors & she is making Edward dissatisfied with all I do & say. I will write to Mary & Teresa and if they wish me to go to England, I will go after Amelia's confinement. I hoped never to leave my home until I went to the cemetery but looking at everything I think it will be best to go. George will have to leave next, if it would do him any good I will stay on, but it would not, and this constant worry is more than I can bear. . . .

Apr 3 The day very fine. Mrs Landor came over and wants me to hold a share in the City Oil Well for her and to keep it secret. She has a little money of her own and she says Dr Landor's necessities would make him sell it if he knew it. It is only 20 dollars. Edward says he could sell her a share but thinks it will be a loss as he thinks they will not find oil. He will only consent to hold her 20 dollars and if there should be oil she shall have her share. If there is none he will return her the money. . . .

Apr 5 Edward left for Port Ryerse at 12 noon. Mrs. Henderson called to see Sophia. Sophia paid visits. I was alone with my memories, books & work.

Apr 23 Edward worried me until I became frantic. I do not know whether I had hysterics or what ailed me. I lost all command of my feelings. Edward is so changed towards me. I know it does not originate with him but I cannot stand it. Every thing I say or ever have said or done is wrong. He must either change his manner or it will kill me unless I leave.

Apr 24 . . . I went to the Griffins & remained all night. It is the only night I recollect sleeping out of my own house since I have lived in London. That is, I have slept in no other house in London. I have been away from London several times. I would not have told Amelia of the disagreeables we have at Eldon but both Edward & George had told her. It can do no good telling anyone about our family disagreeables. My outraged feelings may arise a good deal from my being ill and feeble. The time is past when I could see clearly and act with firmness, but things may soon end to the relief of all parties.

Apr 28 . . . Mr Griffin asked me if Amelia could come here and be confined. . . . Of course I would be glad to have her here but could not say that she should come without the consent of others. I spoke to Edward and he was very nice & kind about it and said whatever was best for Amelia & *me* must be done. I am such a weak, nervous creature that he fears the effect that her sufferings would have upon me, that if she was not in the house it could be kept from me until all was over. I do not myself know the effect that it would have upon me. If her sufferings were short I might bear it pretty well, but if they were protracted as they were the last time the end might be more fatal to me than to her. Edward & Mr Griffin are going to consult Dr Landor. I wish she could be with me, but must leave it for others to decide.

May 9 The weather lovely. The carpenters are busy putting up a verandah. The Griffins dined here as they will not have a cook until Saturday. . . .

May 18 . . . Edward got very disagreeable letters from Mr Portman & Scott about the oil company. If Edward could only make lots of money for them all they would then be content or perhaps they think that he ought to make more. . . .

Jun 1 The Fenians this morning invaded Canada. They crossed the river from Buffalo below Black Rock. It is telegraphed that there are about 1,500 of them. 1,000 Volunteers & some companies of the 16th have gone to repel them. It is to be hoped that we shall have a good account of them by tomorrow. The Military & Volunteers are all ready for a move here. The garrison had arranged for a pic nic. . . . but on account of the Fenians no one was allowed to leave the Barracks, so the pic nic was turned into a dance in the mess room. Edward, Sophia & George went. . . .

Jun 2 2 companies of the 60th & two of the 16th left at 2 this morning for the frontier. The Toronto Volunteers have been engaged. Several killed & wounded on both sides. Particulars not known. There is intense excitement in the city this evening. Col Shanly's Battery of Artillery and three companies of Volunteers left for Sarnia. George is with them. He belongs to Col Shanly's Battery. George left such a desolate feeling behind him. The house & grounds look lonely but the loneliness was in my own heart.

Jun 3 Few people in London I imagine slept soundly last night. All were so anxious for news. I went to Church and walked around to see Amelia who is pretty well. There was great excitement during the service. Capt Gore sat in our pew. In the middle of the Litany he was beckoned out. Soon after the bugle sounded & then half the congregation left. After another short interval the bell rang in alarm. Sophia looked so anxious that I told her she had better go home, which she did. There were very few left in the Church. When the service was over it was pouring with rain. No one in the Church knew what the cause of all the alarm was. It was very exciting. There had been a telegram from the Stipendary Magistrate from the militia at Windsor to say that 5,000 Fenians had crossed there in half an hour. Capt Gore's Battery and two or three companies of the 60th were in the cars when another telegram came saying that the first was incorrect, that no Fenians had landed. Consequently the troops were ordered back to Barracks and then came a telegram from Port Colbourne saying that all the Fenians had escaped across the river at Fort Erie excepting 700 who were intercepted by the American War Steamer, *Michigan.* Now it remains to be seen what the American government will do with them. I wrote to Teresa and sent all the papers & telegrams that I could get hold of to the different members of my family. . . .

Jun 4 Every one is anxiously looking for news. No great reliance is to be placed upon the accuracy of the telegrams as one generally contradicts another. The Fenians are all out of the country but troops (British) are concentrating about Prescott where an invasion is apprehended.

The companies of the 60th & 16th returned this evening from the Niagara frontier. I have heard nothing from George or of his Battery. . . .

Jun 5 . . . The Fenian excitement continues but not so absorbing as it was. There is a great feeling against General Napier & Col Peacocke. It is said that Gen Napier was drunk and that Col Peacocke delayed so that the volunteers at Ridgeway were sacrificed. . . .

Jun 6 There are many flying reports about Fenians gathering at different points for the purpose of invading Canada, but what they intend to do is very doubtful. . . .

Jun 7 I heard from George this morning, quite well, does not know when he will get back. I sent him some things. . . .

Jun 9 . . . Edward got a telegram at 1/2 past 5 PM from Mr Portman saying that he would be here at 6.20. . . . When he arrived he was tired & I thought he looked much changed, but after he had washed and changed his clothes he looked more himself. I am very glad he has come though his mission here is one of great mortification to Edward & of course to me. It is the oil company's total disapproval of Edward's management and a withdrawal of confidence from him & the same feeling with Mr Scott & Peard in regard to their private affairs. Mr Portman, I trust, will be able to see that all of this is unjust and without cause but nothing can do away with the pain and mortification that has been inflicted. It appears that Edward's report in some way has laid him open to this. Mr Portman has the power of taking the whole management of the company from Edward and closing the company by selling if he can and thinks best. Edward will be very glad to have it all off his hands but not with the loss of character. One thing is certain, there is nothing to be discovered in Edward's management derogatory to his character unless they are determined to think ill of him as he has not made a farthing by the company & has not even made a charge for his time & trouble & would not unless the company was a success & paid the stock holders well. The closer the investigation the better, where there is nothing wrong to discover. Consequently I am glad that Mr Portman has come to relieve Edward from a responsibility which he should never have accepted. He has said, ever since his return . . . that there was only someone to act with to share the responsibility. I laughed at him and said, what can there be wrong in the management of four or five thousand pounds, more than half of it owned by yourself & brothers-in-law. But I am very ignorant of the world & its ways.

Jun 12 . . . I see that Edward's report to the oil company has not been as explanatory as it ought to have been but he thought there were but

few stock holders besides his own family & that they could doubt his *honesty* never entered his head & he thought that they would understand his motives & explain any thing that was not clear. He has been wrong & has put it in their power to view his actions in a different light, which they have not been slow to do, & now in place of standing defiantly upon his conduct as honest & upright, he has to accept the admission of his uprightness as a good natured interpretation of what he has done, & why, because what he has written is not sufficiently explained. But what he has done cannot be found fault with. . . .
Jun 13 . . . George came from Sarnia on two days leave looking very brown. . . .
Jun 18 . . . I had another discussion with Mr Portman & Edward about Edward's report. Edward has acted uprightly if he has written foolishly. The only thing that I see that he can do is to make a plain statement of facts & let the Board judge him accordingly. George returned in the evening with his Battery from Sarnia. The Volunteers are all returning to their homes until their services are again required.
Jun 24 Sophia went to morning service. George went in the evening. The Bishop, in the morning, preached a farewell sermon upon resigning the Rectory. Dr Hellmuth read him out & read himself in as Rector in the evening. . . .
Jul 4 This morning a message came to me that Amelia had a son & was doing well. About an hour later another message came saying that they wanted me to dress the baby. I wondered that the nurse had not dressed him. When I went there I found there was another baby coming. The boy was born a quarter past seven and at a quarter past nine a daughter was born. Both very fine children. After they were dressed I weighed them; the boy weighed 8 lbs. and the girl 9 lbs. Amelia is doing very well. Of course the babies have caused great excitement in [the] Harris family. . . .
Jul 12 There was an Orange procession today, but no row. Sophia spent the day at the Griffins. Amelia is going on all right & the babies are doing well. . . .
Jul 26 I got a letter from Teresa. It is private so I burn it . . .
Jul 29 . . . The 16th all leave London. I cannot shake off a feeling that something will happen to prevent Sophia & George going to the Falls on Thursday. I have not much faith in gloomy presentiments, they generally arise from a disordered stomach.
Aug 13 Sophia had a croquet party today. [Edward] had a letter . . . to say that No. 1 well had struck oil. We hope it may be in paying quantities. . . .
Aug 24 Edward & Capt Leslie went to Bothwell. The pump at

Edward's well is not yet fairly at work so that we do not yet know if there will be oil or not. . . .

Aug 30 All the Eldon house party excepting George & myself went to the artillery pic nic at Port Stanley. The day proved very wet & they had to amuse themselves in the tents as they best could. Mr Portman & Bessy Dewar went away in the rain & did not return until the trains were about leaving. All parties felt themselves scandalized. Yesterday he wanted Sophia to ask her here in the evening but Sophia declined. He then went to Mrs Todd,[240] & asked her if she would do him a favor. She said with pleasure if she could. He then asked her to invite him & Bessy Dewar to tea after the pic nic as it would be pleasanter for Bessy to spend the evening in town than to go directly home. Mrs Todd declined and said that Bessy was a girl that she did not admire & that she would not ask a lady to her house that she did not approve of. Mrs Todd went to Mrs Haughtain & [told] her of Mr Portman's request & said that she thought it the greatest piece of impertinence that she had ever heard of, but Mr Portman was not discouraged for he asked Mrs Travers to invite them which she did & they spent the evening there & he had the pleasure of escorting Bessy home late at night.

Aug 31 This morning Mrs Leslie told Mr Portman that she should speak to Mrs Dewar about Bessy's conduct, that she felt herself a friend of the family & that she should certainly speak to her and tell her that Bessy was bringing scandal upon them all. Mr Portman did not like it & went to Amelia & told her that if she would, she could prevent Mrs Leslie's saying any thing to the Dewars that he would have nothing more to say to Bessy. Amelia came to Mrs Leslie & she promised to say nothing in acceptance of Mr Portman's promise to have done with Bessy. Mr Portman calls Bessy a little devil & speaks lightly of her as every one else does.

Sep 4 Last evening Mr Portman was tipsy & cross, so Sophia tells me. He said that he was snubbed & not well treated in the house & that he would not stay here, that he would to go the Tecumseh. She asked him if I ever said any thing to him. He said no, but that every thing that he did was found fault with. . . . He did not come down to breakfast until we were all done and at prayers. Mr Portman, the Leslies & Sophia went to the Dewars to luncheon. . . .

Sep 9 . . . Amelia's twins were christened at the 3 PM service. Dean Hellmuth christened them. The boy is called Edward Scott. Edward &

[240]Wife of Captain Todd of the 60th Regiment.

Mr Scott are godfathers, Gilbert Griffin stood proxy for Mr Scott. Miss Griffin was God mother for the boy, Mrs Leslie standing proxy. The girl was christened Helen Teresa Amelia. Mr Portman stood God father, Sophia & Teresa God mothers. . . .

Sep 22 Edward went to Bothwell. No oil yet. Prospect rather gloomy. . . . Mr Becher wished his prospect of oil at Bothwell was as good as Edward's. I wished they were better. . . .

Sep 26 . . . There was a row at the Barracks a few days ago between Mr Cunningham & his friends & Mr Portman & his defenders about Bessy Dewar. They accused Mr Portman of not doing what was right for one gentleman to do towards another. Yesterday Mr Cunningham cut Mr Portman but in the afternoon they made friends & Mr Portman dined with him. Mr Cunningham had proposed for Bessy two days ago & had been refused as she hoped to get Mr Portman. Yesterday he proposed again & was accepted, as I suppose she had lost hope of Mr Portman. I suspect Mr Cunningham will have cause to regret his acceptance for she is a girl that every one speaks slightingly of, & her conduct has been such that correct people could not help condemning her. I am most thankful that Mr Portman is out of the scrape.

Sep 30 I told Mr Portman this morning that he was not acting honorably by Mr Cunningham. . . . He did not defend himself. I thought he was angry but I believe he was not. He told the Griffins what I had said & they advised him to go to England. They told him that I was quite right in what I had said, but he would not have gone to the Dewars if he had not drank too much and when in that state he says & does every thing that he ought not to do. He told us at dinner that he was going to England in two weeks. . . . George went to the Askins to tea. He says that Miss Ronalds is the nicest girl that he has seen for a long time.

Oct 3 . . . George has been walking with Miss Ronalds & spent the evening at the Askins. He has spent every evening there since Miss Ronalds has been there, that is, since Friday last. . . .

Oct 4 George still devotes himself to Miss Ronalds. He took her & Teresa Askin out driving & then spent the evening there. . . .

Oct 6 George has proposed for Miss Ronalds, been accepted and has gone to Sandwich with Miss Ronalds and her lady friends to ask mamma's consent. He looked very happy this morning. May God's blessing rest upon him. . . .

Oct 8 . . . George returned looking very happy. Mrs Ronalds has given her consent to his marrying her daughter. They do not wish the engagement to be announced until next month. He is to go to Windsor on Saturday next & spend Sunday with them when some further arrange-

ments may be made. He has always been a good son & I hope he has made a good choice & that he may be as happy as I wish him. . . .
Oct 16 Mr Portman dined at the 60th mess & did not return until 5 AM. He won at loo,[241] $37, *all bad.*
Oct 24 George returned in the night. I believe all is settled between him and Miss Ronalds but I have no idea when they think of marrying. I hope not for some time. I told him what Mr Wilson told me about there being insanity in the family.[242] It appeared to have no terrors for George. . . .
Oct 25 Mr [James] Montgomery arrived at 12 last night. . . . [He] told Sophia that the Ronalds were in straightened circumstances & that Miss Ronalds had nothing now but after a time she would have a little property. I would not care if she is a nice girl. If George only had income enough to marry upon, which he has not. . . .
Oct 29 . . . Mrs Cronyn died this morning, she was 69 years of age. She was as far as her life appeared to others, a good woman. . . .
Nov 10 . . . Portman returned at 6.30 looking very well & his manner to us was very amiable, very different from what it has been since he came from England. He was more as he used to be. I think his short absence has worked a cure about Bessy Dewar & his infatuation is at an end.
Nov 13 . . . Mr Portman and Mr Townsend lunched with Amelia. Amelia was once engaged to Mr Townsend. It is 15 years since, but I believe he is still attached to her. He is an honorable, good man, though a Yankee. He is married & has 4 children.
Nov 14 There was a great excitement last night. The American Astronomer said there would be a meteoric shower such as appeared in 1833, but no meteors appeared. It is hoped that they will appear tonight. . . .
Nov 16 . . . I got a very kind letter from Ld Stanley saying that should it be in his power to do anything for Col Dalzell that he would.[243] . . .
Nov 21 . . . Amelia & Mr Becher came to luncheon. . . . Amelia was helping Mr Portman pack his things. He has spent his last evening in London with the Dewars, the last I expect that he will ever spend here.
Nov 22 Mr Portman did not return until 4 o'clock in the morning. Bessy Dewar is a very bad girl. She wanted him to take her as his

[241]A card game.

[242]Lucy Ronalds' grandmother, Elizabeth Lucy, the only daughter (and sole heir) of William Robertson (1781–1806). He had made his fortune in the late 18th century as a fur trader based at Detroit. After bearing four sons, she spent much of her later life in several asylums in England until her death in 1892.

[243]Lord Stanley's eldest son had also been engaged to Amelia and their relationship is described in Charlotte's Diary.

mistress but he declined. How wickedly he has spent this summer. . . . What an example he sets to Helen's poor boys. . . . He left at 12 noon for England. . . .

Dec 3 Mrs Askin spent the day with us. . . .

Dec 10 The thermometer this morning stood at 12. The ice took last night so that the gentlemen have had their first skating today. Capt Thompson & Edward went this afternoon to try the ice. . . . Edward & Sophia have gone to the opera.

Dec 12 . . . Edward has a bad headache today. Mess dinners do not agree with him. . . .

Dec 15 . . . The skating party came back to afternoon tea. . . . George has gone this evening to Windsor to see his lady love. . . .

Dec 17 . . . Col Peacocke sent Amelia a sewing machine as a present & such a nice kind note with it. . . . She was very anxious to have one. . . .

Dec 24 . . . Amelia is ill in bed with cold, altogether it is like to be a dull Christmas. I asked the Griffin family to dine here but no one can come. Edward ill from cold also but went to the office today. Mrs Thomas called to get Sophia to go to the Church to help decorate, she went for a short time. . . . Another Christmas eve has come and from Thy many blessings, Oh my God make me more truly thankful.

Dec 25 Christmas & all its memories. I have tried hard to be cheerful. The Griffin family were not well enough to dine with us so we dined alone. Sophia went to Church. Edward was not well enough to go out. I read the service in my own room and then went to see the Griffins. The twins are dear little babies. I have not seen them for nearly three weeks & they have grown so much. Amelia has just received a parcel from England containing two pretty dresses from Mary for the babies. . . . In the afternoon we had so many visitors to early tea; the two Miss Merediths from Port Hope, Bella [Meredith] and Major Garnier, Capt Elmhurst, Capt Truell and Capt Lynes. In the evening Edward, Sophia, George & I played a quiet game of euchre & so has ended Christmas of 1866.

Dec 26 Mr Wilson came up to spend Christmas. . . . We had a great many visitors. . . .

Dec 31 A lovely day. The thermometer 28. I am not very well. George has gone to Windsor to see Lucy. She is to come Saturday. . . . I do hope that they may feel mutually pleased with each other. Mr Becher came to luncheon. He sent me a couple of dozen of Sauternaia[244]

[244]Bottles of wine.

Christmas box. He is very kind to me. Mrs Wilkinson called & so ends 1866. Where shall I be at the end of 1867? Oh God have mercy upon me & keep us all from evil and make us to love Thee and serve Thee with our whole hearts.

1867

Jan 1 . . . George telegraphed to have his dress clothes sent to him so we suppose there is to [be] a ball at Windsor. . . . Eliza says the Scotts are coming to Canada next spring. They have not said a word of it to us. . . . Eliza is sending a Moorish tray to Amelia. Mr Thomas[245] told Mr Griffin that George had proposed for Minnie Goodhue two or three times since he has been engaged to Lucy Ronalds. I am sure it is a falsehood and George will have to clear this up when he returns. There have been a good many calls at Eldon today. . . .
Jan 3 George returned last night. We told him what Mr Thomas had said about him & Minnie Goodhue. George called upon Mr Thomas & asked him about it, he said Minnie had told him herself. George told him that Minnie must be under a very strong delusion. He assured Mr Thomas that he had not proposed for her & that he had only seen her twice or three times since his engagement to Miss Ronalds. He said if he was not engaged that he should care very little what was said, but that it was due to Miss Ronalds that it should be contradicted. He said that before he was engaged that he used to walk & flirt with Minnie after she was engaged to Ben Cronyn. It was no concern of his if she chose to flirt with him. He told Mr Thomas that he did not walk with her three times out of ten that she would ask him. . . .
Jan 4 Mr Becher & Wilson came to luncheon today. Mr Wilson has been taking a trip over to Buffalo, Cleveland, Detroit & Chicago to show the Fenians that he is not afraid of them.[246] In Toronto a few days ago, he got an invitation to a ball given by the Fenians at Cincinatti & a note accompanying it telling him that if he would go over to the ball & bring the Crown Officer with him they would endevor to give them a good time & that the proceeds of the ball was to go

[245]F.W. Thomas, Manager of the Bank of Montreal in the 1870s. He married a Goodhue.

[246]In 1866, Judge Wilson was selected to preside over the trial of sixteen persons captured in the abortive Fenian invasion of June of that year. The Crown prosecutor was James Cockburn, Solicitor General of Upper Canada. Nine of the sixteen were sentenced to death, but in all cases the death sentence was commuted. See Colin Read, "John Wilson," *Dic. Can. Biog.* IX, pp. 843–844.

towards clothing the Fenian Army so that they might make a good appearance when they came to Canada and appeared before his Lordship. His life has been threatened several times by the wretches. . . .

Jan 5 I am very unwell. No one knows how miserable I am & it is all mind. Sarah's poverty, illness & complaining distress me more than I can tell. How I wish Edward could send them all their money.[247] This morning Mr Griffin came & gave me the benefit of his complaints against Edward & George. He said they had done him all the injury that they could, that he had lost $2000 by them. . . . I had a note from Lucy Ronalds, she is coming to us on Monday for a very short visit. . . .

Jan 7 Mr Griffin & Amelia came to see Lucy on her arrival. George & Sophia went to the station to meet her. Lucy was very nervous & felt very much excited when she first arrived but when she became more at her ease she was very nice & pleasing & I feel very well satisfied with George's choice. She certainly does not want for sense. She has very pretty eyes & an intelligent face & I hope that George & her may be happy in their marriage.

Jan 8 . . . We all like Lucy, she improves on acquaintance. George took her for a drive & this evening they have all gone to the Ball given by the garrison. . . .

Jan 9 They did not return from the ball until nearly four this morning. . . . Lucy looked very nice but hers was rather a country get up. She is not pretty but she does not make the most of herself. She thinks herself so plain that it does not matter, but a little attention to dress & carriage would make her look very well. Mrs C. Goodhue & Mrs Dempster called. . . .

Jan 11 There were more than 100 people at the Thomas' ball last night. The supper was beautiful & everything was very nice but Mrs Thomas was unable to appear as just before the guests arrived one of the children was declared to have the scarlet fever. Mr Thomas did not appear for some time but left Capt Williamson to do the honors. The guests proposed leaving but Capt Williamson entreated them not to do so as Mr Thomas would be very much hurt if they did. When the band began to play Mr Thomas came down, he said that he could not resist the music. The whole thing was a little odd. As soon as Amelia heard the word scarlet fever she left instantly for fear of carrying infection to her own babies.

[247]Reference to Edward's responsibility of administering and investing the funds of the Dalzells, Crutchleys, Scotts, Maurice Portman, and Edward Knight, his relatives in England.

Lucy was paid no attention last evening. No one but George, Edward & a Mr Cromby asked her to dance. I felt a little hurt that not one of the officers who have been at the house so often should have shown her any attention but she is only a country girl & not pretty and they only study their own amusement. I think she has plenty of sense & hope that she will make George a good wife. She went home today and George went with her. . . .

Jan 21 The Thomas' youngest child died yesterday of scarlet fever and their other two children are very ill & were prayed for in Church. . . .

Jan 23 . . . The Thomas' have lost another child with scarlet fever, they have but the one left. . . .

Jan 25 . . . Amelia had letters from Eliza & Mr Portman. Mr Portman saw Mrs Glyn & says that she is much admired, that he danced with her and was teasing her about being in the family way. She told him that she could tell him how to keep from getting *kids* if he would promise secrecy, which he did. She then told him not to try to get them. I should call it *fast* conversation between a young married lady & a gentleman. Mr Portman says that he is coming out again next summer. . . .

Jan 29 The dining room chimney took fire this morning. We were afraid the house would be burned. I threw sulphur on the fire until I was nearly suffocated. We have much reason to be thankful that the house is safe. . . .

Feb 4 Old Mrs Moore died today. Mr & Mrs Askin and myself are now the oldest people in London. . . .

Feb 19 My birthday. Today I enter my seventieth year. Time is nearly at an end with me. God grant that I may depart in peace. We had to dinner today, in addition to the guests staying in the house,[248] Mr Griffin & Amelia, Capt Spears who is going to the South with Major Leslie, Mr Ledget of the 60th, & Mr Smith of the 53rd. The dinner went off very well but I was glad to make my escape & go to bed but I must not forget to note the kind presents that I received on this my birthday. George gave me *The Land and the Book*, a work on Syria & Palestine, Amelia gave *Meditation* by Henry Alford, Major Leslie gave me *Spare Hours*, all nice works. Mr Griffin gave me a basket of geraniums to hang in the window. . . .

Mar 11 . . . The Fenians are threatening us with another invasion.

Mar 12 . . . The officers of the 53rd have been notified that the

[248]The guests were Miss Warren and Miss Ella Beatty from Cobourg and Major Leslie.

Fenians were going to blow them up. They searched through all the cellars today but found nothing combustible. It is all a hoax.

Mar 13 . . . George laughs at our alarm but it is not a time to treat any information about what the Fenians contemplate doing with indifference. . . .

Mar 15 . . . The Fenian excitement is on the increase, troops are on the move & volunteers are to be called out. . . .

Mar 20 . . . George has gone to Windsor to see Lucy. I do not think he is as fond of her as I could wish. . . .

Mar 22 . . . A ring that George had asked Teresa to buy him for Lucy arrived today. It is very pretty, saphire & diamonds. . . .

Apr 13 Amelia came early to see me, she had a letter from Mr Portman telling her that he is engaged to be married to his cousin Eva Portman and that his father entirely disapproves of the match & that his engagemnent had the effect of making his father very ill, so that he was near dying. Ld Portman dislikes Eva's mother, disapproves of her & disapproves of cousins marrying. . . . I fear that it is a bad business altogether. She has no money & Mr Portman has not the means of marrying or rather of supporting a wife unless his father gives it to him. I wish he were well married but to a woman that his father could approve of. A parents approval carries a blessing with it & opposition to parents seldom prospers. . . .

Apr 15 . . . I had a letter from Mary. She approves of Mr Portman's engagement & says that Eva is a nice, amiable, pretty girl.

Apr 22 . . . My brother Edward arrived this evening. He is looking very well. He has held the office of Inspector of Licenses[249] for 29 years without having a complaint against him, now he is called upon to come to London to be examined by the Heads of the Department to see whether he is competent to hold the office.

Apr 24 . . . My brother Edward commenced his examination today. . . . I wrote to Col Bell today to ask him to come to Eldon. His wife has eloped with Capt Holyroyd of his own Regmt, the 23rd W[elch] Fusiliers. We knew Col Bell years ago when he was stationed in London with his regiment. We're all so sorry for him & thought the change of a short visit to Eldon might cheer him up, but this afternoon I see by the papers that he has gone to England.

May 15 . . . George returned from Windsor last night. There is some difficulty about the settlement with Lucy. George says the law gives the woman the entire control of her own property and he wishes Lucy

[249]Office held in Port Ryerse.

to keep the control of hers and not place it in the hands of trustees to manage well or ill as they may think, but without her being able to interfere. I should not be surprised if the marriage never took place. . . .
May 21 Heavy rain all day. George left for Windsor early this morning to see Lucy & to come to some final understanding as to what she intends doing. After he left a letter came from Lucy, it had not been well sealed and it was open & I read it. She has decided upon breaking her engagement with him. The misunderstanding is about the settlement. Had the letter come before George left I suppose he would not have gone.

The Griffins called. Amelia had letters from Mr Portman & Eva Portman. They were both very nice, kind letters, Eva's particularly so. Mr Portman says that Teresa wrote to him scolding him for not having written to tell me of his approaching marriage. He says that he did write but he knows very well that he did not. I read a letter from dear Sarah today. She is very unhappy & her letters always make me feel wretched.
May 22 . . . George returned in the night. His engagement with Lucy is all right again. I believe he agrees that Lucy shall have her money settled upon herself in any way that she likes.
Jun 4 . . . When I am well I can always find occupation & the time passes quickly but it hangs heavy when I can neither work nor read. . . .
Jun 6 . . . The Scotts arrived. Amelia was here when they came. They are both looking so well & we are glad to see them. Edward met them at Paris and came up with them. How glad, how very glad I am to have Teresa home once more.
Jun 7 The Griffins & babies were here all day & the house seemed like it used to be. Mr Becher came & played croquet. The Scotts trunks arrived, they had been left at Boston. Teresa has such quantities of beautiful dresses & trinkets. Mr Scott gave me a very pretty fan & Teresa gave me a set of ivory handled hair brushes . . . she has brought a quantity of things for Amelia & the babies. . . .
Jun 11 . . . Capt Williamson & Capt Northey made me such a nice present today & in such a nice way. They sent to England for a beautiful bible, the handsomest edition that I had ever seen & gave it to me in the memory of the many pleasant Sunday evenings they had spent at Eldon. . . .
Jun 14 . . . Mr Ronalds called to see George. He is Lucy's uncle & I suppose we shall know now whether the engagement with Lucy will come to an end or not. There is still some hitch about settlement.
Jun 15 All quiet today, no croquet. All is arranged, I believe, between George & Lucy & the settlement seems to be satisfactory to both

parties. John Ronalds, Mr Montgomery & Edward are the trustees. Lucy has the power of willing her property & if she dies George is to have the income during his life. He returned to Windsor with Mr Ronalds.

Jun 28 There is disagreeables about croquet between Edward & Mr Griffin. Edward & George think they ought to play sometimes. . . . Mr. Griffin looked on at the game for the first time since we have had a croquet ground without playing. Amelia played.

Jun 29 . . . Col Peacocke left . . . we were sorry to see him go. Edward & George gave the Scotts a very handsome robe, the skin of a polar bear, I think. Teresa was very pleased to get it. . . .

Jul 1 This is Dominion Day, the first day of Confederation. There has been a review today of the Military & Volunteers. The most of the people have celebrated the day by going on excursions as it is a public holiday. . . . Edward went to Port Stanley. He wished to see the steamer the *City of London*. Mr Becher came to luncheon and arranged that we should all go with him to Port Talbot on Thursday. . . . George returned from Windsor late in the evening.

Jul 2 The news today is that the Mexican Republican Chief has shot the Emperor Maximillian.[250] There is a general feeling of horror at the deed. . . .

Jul 4 Mr Becher got up a small party to go to Port Talbot; Capt Williamson, Capt Truell, the Twins, Miss Grant, the Scotts, Sophia, myself & Becher. We went to Port Stanley by train & then in three carriages to Port Talbot. There came on a heavy shower & we had to take shelter in a farm house for an hour when it cleared up and we went on. The only change that I saw about Port Talbot was in the trees which are so much larger. It is nearly 18 years since I was last there & then I went with John & Helen to see Mrs Airey after the death of her eldest daughter. The place has a solitary look to me. Col Talbot used to give an interest to the place by the eccentricity of his life. I am glad to have seen it once again. We got home at 7 PM very well pleased with our day's excursion & very tired.

Jul 25 Sandfield Macdonald & Mr Carling called. Sir John A. Macdonald sent his card. They are going through the country on a political tour. . . .

Jul 26 . . . Mr Scott had a letter from Shuldham who has been invited

[250]Maximilian of Austria (1832–67), an Hapsburg Archduke, became Emperor of Mexico (1864–67) with the support of Napoleon III of France. Under pressure from the United States, the French withdrew their support of Maximilian, and a popular uprising under Benito Juarez deposed him. He was executed in June 1867.

to Mr Portman's wedding which is to take place on the 3rd of October.

Aug 1 Croquet has been the order of the day. . . . Major Leslie, now Col as he has got his promotion. George played cricket with the Vagabonds against the 53rd and were well beaten.

Aug 2 . . . Mr Leget took photographs of the house & different views from Eldon. . . .

Aug 5 . . . Major & Mrs Gordon called & invited all the Eldon party to croquet on Friday. . . .

Aug 11 I have been ailing all day. Sophia & Edward went to the morning service, the Scotts went in the evening. The Griffins [and many others] came to tea. . . .

Aug 12 Teresa's birthday. She is 28 today & looks not more than 20. . . .

Aug 15 Teresa was taken very ill last night with common cholera. Dr Landor was called & gave relief. He thinks she will be all right tomorrow. . . .

Aug 20 Teresa gave a croquet party. The Gordons & the Grants came to luncheon. Major Granier, Capt Collins [and others] & the Griffins came later to croquet. . . .

Aug 25 The 17th anniversary of Mr Harris' death. What painful recollections this day brings. . . . George is preparing every thing for his departure. He appears very happy in the prospect of his marriage. . . .

Aug 31 . . . George's bachelor days are approaching a close. Next Thursday he is to be married & then I shall be alone, all my children will have those who are dearer to them than I am. They all will have left father & mother & will cleave unto others according to God's ordinance & I shall soon go where they must follow. I hope George will be happy and that he will make his wife happy.

Sep 3 . . . Teresa & Amelia packed up George's things for his marriage & trip to England. The house had a very lonely feel after he left. . . .

Sep 4 Amelia came to see the start for Windsor. We, that is, the Scotts, Edward & Sophia, Capt Collins & myself left here at 12 noon & George met us on our arrival at Windsor. Sophia & George went with me to Mrs Ronalds. The rest of the party went over at once to Detroit to the Biddle House. Lucy & her Mother met us at the door. Lucy looks very nice & very happy. Mrs Ronalds is a particularly pleasing old lady. I remained with them all night. George & Sophia went to the Biddle House & joined the rest of the party. Everything in the Ronald's House is very nice but very plain. Their neighbours appear to be very kind in offering any assistance about the breakfast & sending them quantities of flowers. Lucy has not many presents.

The front of Eldon House. Amelia Harris, her son George, Amelia Griffin, Sophia (white dress) and Teresa sitting. Gilbert Griffin preferred the window. (c. 1860)

The golfers. Milly with her brothers, Ronald (dark suit) sitting, and Ted on the lawn and an unidentified friend. (c. 1880s)

A leisurely day at Eldon. Milly and her father, George Harris. On the boat: a friend, Ronald, and Ted holding the paddle. (c. 1880s)

Little Ted and governess at Raleigh House in 1885.

Milly in the grounds of Eldon House. (c. 1890)

Lucy (sitting with child) entertains a group of friends. (1890)

"Col. Talbot's Den," oil by Eliza Harris. (1850)

Lady Alexander depicted the conclusion of the military steeplechase held on May 9 1843 on the flats of the Thames River just below Eldon House.

"Go it Chasse," sketch by Eliza Harris. (c. 1846)

"Moving Day," sketch by Eliza Harris. (c. 1848)

The library at Eldon House as it looked in the 1880s.

The symbol of time and continuity. The clock dated 1760 which belonged to the Ryerse family remains at Eldon House among other beautiful pieces of furniture inherited from the Ronalds' family.

Tea party at Eldon House. From left, fashionable Sophie, Lucy, a friend, Edward seated, Milly and George. (c. 1884)

The new generation at Eldon House: (left) George Harris and Lucy Ronalds, and their children Milly and Ronald. (c. 1888)

She has a few pretty little things given her but nothing of much value. I was very tired and went to bed early.

Sep 5 We all got up early as the marriage was to take place at half past 9 AM. The guests were not very distinguished looking. They looked like a good sort of country people. George & the London party were punctual, all but Edward who had some bother with the Customs House about George's trunk & he did not arrive until the ceremony was over. Lucy looked very nice. She wore a white moire antique with white wreath & tulle veil. She wore a set of pearls that had descended to her from her grand mother, they were worth over £200. The brides maids wore white alpacha & did not look nice. They were very badly made and looked *very* countrified. The breakfast was served by an American confectioner from Detroit & was very nice but everything in Yankee fashion, the woodcocks were stuffed, etc. The gentlemen said the wines were good. Mr Swinyard happened to be at Windsor & most kindly gave the young couple the Directors' car to go to the Falls in. They had it all to themselves & left in *state* & comfort but there is always some mishap & between Edward & George the key of George's trunk was left behind. He telegraphed for it & it was sent by mail but he would not get it until tomorrow and in the meantime he could neither get a clean shirt or night shirt. . . . After they left we all returned to Detroit. I had never been at Detroit. We dined there, walked about, looked into the shops & saw a little of the city. Moving in the streets, I did not see one person whom I could recognize as a gentleman or a lady by their appearance. Sophia was very ill before we left, so ill that I almost despaired of her being able to come home. Edward got a lower berth for her & me in the sleeping car & we reached home at 12 midnight, very tired but Sophia was better. I felt very sorry to see George married, the last of my family who was unmarried & yet I wished him to marry & I like his wife but it is like severing the last tie with my *children*. They are now all off and no longer mine in the same sense that they were.

Sep 15 Edward, Sophia & I went to the morning service. The Dean preached. My hearing is so bad that I heard none of the lessons & very little of the sermon. . . .

Sep 23 . . . The Scotts returned.[251] . . .

Sep 26 Capt Northey, Capt Collins, the Griffins & Bella came to croquet. . . . Mr Scott gave me a very pretty water jug & a pair of tumblers.

[251]They had spent a week at Niagara Falls.

Sep 27 . . . She [Mrs Askin] brought me a bignonia plant. . . . & the Griffins came to croquet. . . .

Sep 28 Mr Becher came to luncheon . . . the Griffins came to croquet. . . .

Oct 3 Today Mr Portman is to be married to his cousin Evelyn Portman. I wish them every happiness. . . . Mr Griffin came to croquet.

Oct 4 Teresa gave a dinner party. . . .

Oct 5 Mr Scott & Edward left at 3 PM for Long Point Bay to shoot ducks. . . .

Oct 6 Teresa, Sophia & I went to Church. . . .

Oct 9 Rain. Mr Becher came to luncheon. . . .

Oct 14 We had a great number of visitors today. Mr Scott and Edward returned at 12 noon. Edward was at the Bay but a very short time and consequently killed a very few ducks only 7 or 8. He had to attend to his business at Port Ryerse. Mr Scott brought home about 20 brace. . . .

Oct 15 Teresa lost her umbrella when out fern hunting & the same party went to hunt for it today but could not find it. . . .

Oct 16 The weather lovely . . . the Griffins, Bella, Capt Collins & Capt Towell came to croquet. Mr & Mrs Hutchinson called. The Scotts dined with the Griffins. . . .

Oct 19 Amelia's birthday, 44 today. Mr Griffin, Charley and Teresa have made their presents, but I have given her nothing but best wishes . . . my cold very bad, I am just able to sit up. . . .

Oct 21 Capt Collins called & invited all the Eldon people to a luncheon tomorrow at the 60th Barracks. . . .

Oct 23 . . . The first letter received from Mr Portman since his marriage. It was very unamiable towards our family. He does not speak nicely of Mary & from his own showing she had been totally neglected at the wedding breakfast. Edward he abused like a pickpocket. I had a letter from George written in a very different style. . . .

Oct 25 Sophia spent the day & evening at the Bazaar. Capt Collins & the Griffins came to croquet. After dinner the Scotts & Bella went to the Bazaar.

Oct 28 I got a letter from Mary describing Mr Portman's wedding. All went off very well only Mary was not taken in to breakfast and felt very much hurt. . . .

Nov 3 . . . tomorrow Teresa will be gone, it is very hard to part with her, & with the feeling that I shall never see her again.

Nov 4 The parting is over, Teresa is gone. It is a severe trial to me & yet I feel very thankful that I have had her with me for 5 months of my last days. . . . I got a letter from Elizabeth. She is at St Catharines

under the care of Dr Mack & expects to remain there for 2 months. She seems in very low spirits and not happy.
Nov 5 . . . I miss Mr Scott also but he is not my child. . . .
Nov 14 Edward left for Port Ryerse, Sophia called at the Merediths & Bella much the same.[252] I got a letter from Teresa from Halifax.
Nov 15 Amelia not very well, I went in a cab to see her. Bella no better. . . . I was very ill last night, indigestion. . . .
Nov 20 I have been ill all day. Edward left early for Sarnia & returned again in the evening. . . .
Nov 22 . . . Dr Ryerson came to spend a day with Sophia. He is looking well and his health is very good. . . .
Dec 4 . . . Mary is pleased with Lucy and likes her.
Dec 17 Edward got a telegram from George who is at N. York and will be at home on Thursday. We had a dinner party today . . .
Dec 18 . . . George & Lucy returned at 6 PM. George looking older & thinner, Lucy looking very well & improved in every way. They have not been able to get a statement of Lucy's affairs from the trustees after waiting a long time, now they promise to send it. I doubt her ever getting any thing. Not one of her relatives in England made her a present.
Dec 21 George & Lucy have gone to Windsor. . . .
Dec 24 I got a letter from Lucy saying that they were going to stay with Mrs Ronalds over Christmas. Mr Becher came in and surprised us all with little presents. . . .
Dec 25 Christmas day. . . . Sophia is ill in bed with cold & swollen face. . . . Mr Griffin, Amelia, Gilbert, Charley & Capt Collins dined with us. Not a very lively party but Christmas cannot be a very cheery day to me. In some way this day more than any other recalls the changes that have taken place & one's thoughts go back painfully to the dead & absent & I think of the time when the table was surrounded by bright little faces and I could give pleasure as well as receive it. The young Griffins wore long tailed coats for the first time & looked nice & gentlemanlike. Edward went to Church. Mr. Becher called & talked about his first years in Canada. He has been reading his old journal.
Dec 31 . . . I had a letter from Sarah. She is in Italy. Col Dalzell is very weak, bleeding at the lungs. The probability is that he will not live very long & she, poor thing, is poor & unhappy & wretched. Poor, dear Sarah, it is not in my power to do anything to comfort or assist you. . . .

[252]She had been ill for two weeks.

1868

Jan 9 . . . Lucy told me she was in the family way with many blushes.
Jan 14 . . . Edward & Sophia, George & Lucy have gone to the 53rd ball.
Jan 15 They were all pleased with the ball. Lucy did not dance fast dances & came home at 1/2 past 1 AM. Sophia came at 3. Sophia left for Toronto. . . .
Jan 28 . . . George has taken the house that Capt Grant is living in. They are to go into it the first of April. . . .
Feb 1 . . . We had a small dinner party . . . Mrs Hamilton's dress was of a style quite new to me. I suppose it was fashionable but certainly it was not becoming. . . .
Feb 3 Lucy left at 12.30 for Windsor to spend a fortnight with her mother. . . .
Feb 9 Edward & Sophia went to Church. Col Hawley [53rd] was notified that the Fenians were going to blow up St Paul's Cathedral & he kept the soldiers from the morning service. At the 11 o'clock service Edward observed that he had never seen so few people at Church. After the service Capt Northey told them of the report but both services went over without an explosion. In the afternoon Capt Truell & Capt Elmhurst & Mr Fyfe called & they tried to make a joke of the report & said the soldiers were kept from Church because it was snowing. They hate to be laughed at for being so easily frightened. When Capt Northey came in the evening he tried to make a joke of it also. I think he was sorry that he had said anything about it. . . .
Feb 19 My 70th birthday. . . . Many might not think it a subject for congratulation that three score years and ten had passed away & that the end of time must be very near, yet I have never met any one person who would wish to live their life over again just as they had lived it. . . .
Mar 13 Rain again today & we are having another flood. George left for Toronto. . . . He has gone to buy some furniture for his house. . . .
Mar 17 George left for Toronto . . . He did not buy half his things when last there. He go[es] to see a homeopathic physician as I wished him to do. He is never quite well & the Alapathy [sic] Doctors do him no good. For years they have said tonics & exercise but he remains the same.[253] His ailments are very like poor John's were. The water is nearly as high as I have ever seen it. . . .

[253]Homeopathy (the treatment of diseases by administering minute doses of a remedy that would produce symptoms of the disease treated) and allopathy (the treatment of diseases by using agents that produced effects different from those of the disease treated) were both referred to in this age of pre-scientific medicine.

Mar 18 . . . George returned. He went to see a doctor who has promised to put him all right very soon. . . .
Mar 31 . . . We were very sorry to bid Capt Truell good bye as he will not return and he is a great favorite with us all. . . . Mr Thomas gave Capt Truell a farewell dinner party of 12 gentlemen. Before the party broke up Mrs Thomas had a son. Neither Mr Thomas nor any of the guests knew anything of what was going on upstairs. . . .
Apr 2 Lucy & Sophia were at George's house all day getting things in order. . . . [Heard] the news of Bishop Cronyn's being married to a lady in England with lots of money. He went home last autumn quite broken hearted about the loss of his wife but seems to have found consolation at 66 years of age. . . . George and Lucy have gone to their own house. Eldon is no longer their home. . . .
Apr 4 . . . There is a good deal of excitement in town about the Bishop's marriage. People think that he would have been more respected if he had not married.
Apr 7 . . . Today we have heard of the assassination of Darcy McGee. He was returning at 2 AM this morning from the House of Assembly at Ottawa & as he was opening the door of his lodging he was shot through the head, the ball lodging in the door & was killed instantly. The Government have offered a reward of $10,000 for the discovery of the assassin, a Fenian, no doubt, as his life has been threatened by them.
May 12 The 60th are gone & we're all so sorry for they were all such nice people. . . . Mr Becher came for a moment to say good bye & told Amelia to take great care of me. He, I think, is almost as fond of me as he would be of a mother. . . . I went to see Lucy. It is the first time that I have seen their house. The house is not large but could not be nicier or more comfortable, & if Lucy is not content there the cause must be in her disposition & not in her surroundings. But she appears very happy & as bright & busy as a bee. . . .
May 15 Elizabeth with two children & nurse arrived at 12 noon. . . . [She] is very unhappy. The husband is high tempered and the mother is old 74 & has a teasing worrying disposition, & it has driven Elizabeth nearly mad. She tells me that her mind for some months was very much impaired & though better she needs tenderness & quiet. Her oldest little girl is a very fine child. . . .
Jun 14 . . . The Bishop of Huron has returned with his bride. People say that she is a nice looking young woman about 30 years his junior. . . .
Jun 15 Edward & Sophia went to George's before 6 AM this morning. Lucy gave birth to a daughter at 1 AM this morning & is doing well.

Dr Landor was with her. Edward went to the Station to see the 53rd off. He took a bottle of whiskey & a cake to Col Harrane. We have all been in a state of excitement all day in consequence of Lucy's confinement. . . . The town appears very dull without the 53rd.
Jun 16 . . . They have given the baby my name, Amelia. . . .
Jun 18 . . . Today Lucy and the child are so well that she and Mrs Ronalds have decided upon doing without another nurse. The Griffins came to croquet. . . .
Jun 28 Edward went to the morning service, Sophia sat with Lucy while Mrs Ronalds went to Church. . . .
Jun 29 46 years ago William was killed, even now the memory of that day is painful. Sophia spent the morning with Lucy then made some cards and had a croquet party in the afternoon. . . . In the evening Edward and Sophia went to a musical party at the Deans. . . .
Jul 2 . . . The Bishop of Huron & bride called. She is not so young looking as I imagined, & the Bishop's beard has grown much darker in colour since he left for England. . . .
Jul 4 The thermometer 90 in the shade, I have found the heat more oppressive today than I ever remember to have felt it.
Jul 7 . . . Edward got a letter from Mr McInnes today. It appears that Mr Griffin has been altogether untruthful & has not paid Mr McInnes any thing for a very long time & now Mr McInnes intends suing him for the whole amount of his debt. He has agreed to take half if paid at once but it is more than 2 years since he made that offer & Mr Griffin has paid nothing yet, though he told me & told George that he had paid all, excepting one or two hundred dollars. Poor Amelia.
Jul 8 Dr Landor left today to take charge of the Lunatic Asylum at Amherstberg, his family will . . . join him in a couple of months. I am glad that the family are at last free from poverty.
Jul 9 . . . Mrs Ronalds brought the baby for me to see, it is a nice little infant. . . .
Jul 18 More trouble. Mr Griffin had assigned an insurance upon his life to Edward by way of security for his debt & was to keep it paid up. Edward made the inquiry for two or three years & found the insurance had been regularly paid. For the last six years he has taken it for granted that Mr Griffin paid it, but on writing to enquire finds that it has not been paid for the last five years so Edward has not the slightest security. Mr Griffin is most unprincipled & untruthful.
Jul 28 The excessive heat appears to be over but the drouth continues. The paper says that there has been cholera at New York & one case at Hamilton. . . .
Jul 29 . . . George & Lucy had their baby christened today. Its name

is Amelia Archange.[254] Edward is God father, Sophia & Mrs Ronalds God mothers. Dean Hellmuth christened the child. The Griffins, Edward, Sophia & myself were the only guests. The child was christened at home & the Dean remained to lunch. . . .
Aug 7 No rain, the gardens are all destroyed. . . . Mrs Landor called to say good bye, she goes to Amherstberg to live. . . .
Aug 8 Sophia left this morning for Toronto. . . .
Aug 13 Dr Landon called, he says that no one can imagine the state of the Lunatic Asylum at Amherstberg when he took charge of it. He never saw brutes treated as badly as those poor lunatics were.
Aug 19 I had one of my old dreams that I was going home. My home always seems to be on the old farm at Port Ryerse. . . .
Sep 1 . . . Mr Bond of the 69th called & abused London most violently, it was the most stupid disgusting place he had ever been in. Sophia & I turned his rudeness into ridicule & laughed at him. . . .
Sep 4 Last night in my dream I was going home. For nearly 50 years I have had this same dream (with slight variations) at intervals. . . . Bella Meredith & Anna from Port Hope paid a long morning visit. . . .
Sep 14 . . . Sophia has gone to Mr Becher to a croquet party. . . .
Sep 15 Sophia went to the W. Merediths to croquet. . . .
Sep 16 . . . Whalen who shot poor Darcy McGee is found guilty and sentenced to be hanged on the 10th of December next. The country say it is a righteous verdict & sentence. . . .
Sep 17 . . . Mr Becher came to early dinner. He is just appointed Solicitor to the Bank of Montreal which will give him £300 or 400 a year, a nice addition to what he is already making. Sophia had a croquet party. . . .
Sep 25 George has gone to Chatham. He lost the train twice. He is appointed agent to the Ronald[s] estate & has gone on that business. . . . Edward dined with Col Simpson last night. The Artillery have not much of a Mess.
Oct 2 Sophia has been out all day getting subscriptions for the luncheon out table at the Bazaar. . . .
Oct 8 Sophia has been at the Bazaar all day & not yet at 9 PM at home. Edward left this morning early for Toronto. . . .
Oct 9 Sophia at the Bazaar again today. She did not return until nearly 12 o'clock last night. Edward returned from Toronto late last evening. . . .
Oct 10 Sophia has finished her labours at the Bazaar today & she is very tired. . . .

[254]One of the diarists in this volume.

Oct 11 . . . George finds the Ronald[s'] property of more value than he supposed.
Oct 22 . . . I have had my old dream of going home. Last night in my sleep Capt Owen was with me in the old house at Kingston but Mr Harris was away. I am always in my dreams expecting & waiting for him to take me home.
Oct 27 Mrs Skae called to say good bye. George returned last night from Chatham. He & Lucy called to see Mrs Ryerson who arrived today. The order has come today for the removal of the 69th Regiment. They are to leave London on the 10th & go to Montreal & two companies of the 29th are to come here until the spring when all the Troops are to leave here. It will be a great loss to London and leave the place very dull.
Oct 30 Amelia & Lucy called, Mrs Ryerson & Sophia went visiting. . . .
Oct 31 I got letters today from Mary & Teresa. . . . Mrs Ryerson & Sophia spent the day at the Griffins & have gone this evening to George's. . . .
Nov 10 Dull heavy day. All the 69th left this morning & four companies of the 29th arrived. . . .
Nov 11 George called & Amelia came to tell me about her troubles about her cow. Elson, the butcher, has treated her very badly. He has bought two cows for her. They are both so savage that the girl cannot milk them. . . .
Nov 14 Mrs Ronalds, Miss Askin, George & Mr Skae called. Dr Woodfall & Miss Lightfoot came to practice duets . . . Miss Lightfoot[255] spent the evening here. She seems a nice girl but has the American education & shows no deference to age. When she calls here, if there are a half dozen in the room I am always the last one that she speaks to and she makes a point of never listening to a remark of mine. Dr Woodfall looked surprised today when she shook hands with him, before she noticed me. That is quite [the] American manner.
Nov 24 Sophia left this morning for Toronto, she goes for a fortnight with her mother. I dined with George & Lucy, it was Mrs Ronald's birthday. . . .
Nov 25 A Memorandum of what we the Ryerses & Ryersons know of our Ancestors.[256] . . .

[255]Miss Lightfoot is from Mobile, Alabama.

[256]The four pages of the memorandum are written into Amelia Harris' diary at this point, dated 26 November 1868, and signed by her.

Nov 26 . . . George has gone to Chatham again to attend the Ronald estate. . . .

Dec 21 Poor Mrs Plumb died yesterday. A telegram came today asking Edward to go to the funeral on Wednesday. We all share their sorrow. Little Scotty Griffin has scarlet fever. Amelia is very much alarmed but the symptoms are very favorable so far. . . .

Dec 24 Mr Becher called & gave me *Scriptural Portraits* by Dean Stanley as a Christmas present. He thinks of me on all occasions and is very kind. He gave Sophia a little cap for a good girl. George called. Edward returned from Mrs Plumb's funeral. . . . The body was placed in a very handsome coffin with a plate of glass extending the whole length of it, & she was dressed in white satin as if for a party with a bouquet in the hand & natural flowers about her & wreaths on the coffin. Mrs Plumb looked very natural and like her living self. All her sisters & children came into the room to take a last look at her before the coffin was put into the shell. Mr Paterson thought it a strange custom for the female friends to come publicly to take a last look at one so much loved. . . .

Dec 25 Christmas Day. Edward & Sophia went to Church. I read the service at home. George called & gave me a book, Professor [Louis] Agassiz' *Exploration in Brazil*. All are kind to me. We had only George and Miss Lightfoot to dine. Mrs Ronalds was not well & the baby was not very well. Lucy would not leave her but came in the evening after baby went to sleep. . . .

Dec 29 A poor wretched Englishman, a man with a large family, was hanged today for the murder of his neice. Hundreds of people came to see the execution. He denied his guilt with his last breath.[257] . . .

Dec 30 I heard from Amelia this morning, little Helen has the scarlet fever. We cannot yet tell whether it will be light or malignant. . . . Col Simpson is very much aged since I last saw him & he looks as unhappy & miserable as his worse enemy could wish him to look. Miss Akin is really dead & the supposition is that her death was caused by her trying to procure [an] abortion. She sent for Col Simpson & he went to New York twice to see her & now she is gone, poor wretched girl, & Col Simpson will probably try to make peace with his wife, that is if she has never heard of his inconstancy.

Dec 31 The last day of the year. How many of the young and healthy

[257]An editorial in the *London Evening Advertiser* on 29 December 1868 condemned this public execution of Thomas Jones. It noted that this was the first such public execution in London since that of seven "traitors" in 1837.

have been called away since last New Year's eve and many old and feeble are still here. Oh that God would enable me to give Him my whole heart. . . . Helen Griffin is ill with scarlet fever but not yet dangerous. Edward went to a card party last night at George's & did not come home until four this morning.

1869

Jan 1 Mr Griffin wrote to Edward this morning asking what he had done to give offence & wishing to make friends. Edward told him how he had been treated after having stood between him & his creditors more than once & paid more than $16,000 for him, that after having assigned an insurance upon his life to Edward as security he had let it lapse without saying a word & that he had deceived him in almost every money transaction that he had ever had with him. As Mr Griffin could not deny one of his statements, he has not answered Edward's letter & they are as they were but poor Amelia is suffering from the estrangment & poor little Helen will not recover, the symptoms are growing worse. I have not been well today & did not see visitors, very few came only . . . Ellen, Selina[258] & Emmaline Hamilton. . . .
Jan 3 It is all over with Helen. I went there early this morning & remained all day. . . . She was conscious all the time & died at a quarter past 9 PM. Mr Griffin feels very deeply that Amelia's sorrow is more distressing as her health & life is in danger.[259] The servants have all shown a great deal of feeling. . . .
Jan 5 I went to see Amelia this morning at 10 o'clock. Mr Griffin, his son Gilbert & the nurse Anna had just gone with poor little Helen to the cemetery. Amelia of course, was in great distress but she had slept last night. . . . Dr Woodfall has been very kind. . . .
Jan 25 . . . Mr Wilson arrived at 6 PM most unexpectedly & intends remaining for a few days. I thought him looking wretchedly ill. He says that he has what is called the bright disease[260] & seems to know that he cannot live long.
Feb 14 . . . Dr Ryerson[261] was very tired & wanted rest. Sophia has [a] bad cold. George & Lucy called. I enjoyed the day with Dr Ryerson who is looking better than I have seen him for several years.

[258]Selina Hamilton, often referred to as "Selena" by Amelia.
[259]Amelia was pregnant again.
[260]Probably a reference to Bright's disease, named after Richard Bright (1789–1858), an English physician.
[261]Dr. Ryerson was visiting at Eldon.

Feb 18 Today we have had much more company than usual. Dr Ryerson arrived in time for breakfast. Edward is ill with a violent headache. Sophia went in the afternoon with her father to his school meeting.[262] Mrs W. Meredith and Bella sat with me for a couple of hours, then Dr Woodfall called. Miss Warren came to spend a few days with us. George & Lucy came to tea & spent the evening here. Dr Ryerson, Sophia & Miss Warren went to another of the school meetings this evening.

Feb 22 . . . Mrs Warren came over this evening to spend a week with us. I had not seen her for nearly 30 years. George came to tea.

Mar 4 Mr Becher sent me six bottles of very excellent sautern. We have had a dinner party today. . . . The news is today that Mr Whitaker of the 53rd has been shot in the neck at Quebec. He is not yet dead but insensible & cannot move. The assassin is a young man of 17 years of age, whose sister it is said that Mr Whitaker violated after having made her insensible from chloroform, having saturated his pocket handkerchief with it. He afterwards promised her family to meet her at the church & marry her which he did not do & her brother took the law in his own hands & shot him & then gave himself up. This is the statement in the *Globe*. Challoner is the name of the lad who shot Mr Whitaker.

Mar 12 . . . Amelia was taken ill today. I went to see her . . . she gave birth to a daughter a few minutes after 5 PM. Dr Brown attended her & she is so far doing very well. Both Mr Griffin & Amelia seemed a good deal excited. They were rejoiced that the child is a girl but it made them think of the poor little darling that is gone. Little Scotty is in a great state of delight that he has got a baby & will give it his hammer which is his most valuable possession.

Mar 15 Mr Wilson called here today. He is looking very ill much worse than when last here. I should doubt his living very long. Col Simpson came to luncheon. . . . Amelia going on well, . . . Mrs W. Meredith & Bella called, I had letters from Mary and Teresa.

Mar 22 . . . George leaves for Chatham tonight. . . . Miss Lightfoot is going to spend a few days with us. She intends returning to Mobile on Monday next. I think she has not been very happy as Governess with Mrs Cleveland. . . .

[262]As Superintendant of Education in Upper Canada, Ryerson held five public meetings throughout the province to explain legislation which he was on the point of introducing in the Legislature. These tours have been described in detail by C.B. Sissons in his *Egerton Ryerson: His Life and Letters*. For the 1869 tour, see Vol. II, pp. 564–74.

Mar 28 Easter Sunday. Sophia & Miss Lightfoot went to church. . . . George, Lucy, Major Ledyard came to afternoon tea, Edward Blake called. I am always glad to see him. Edward & Mrs Lightfoot went to evening service so late that they only heard part of the sermon. . . .
Apr 4 . . . Edward called to ask after Mr Wilson. He is very ill. I went to see him in the afternoon. He thought that he would not have lived through the last night. . . .
Apr 8 Sophia had a musical party this afternoon. . . .
Apr 10 J. Sandfield Macdonald called. He is in London selecting a site for a Lunatic Asylum. We are in hopes that he will buy a lot that belongs to Edward. . . .
Apr 11 Sophia went to church and dined with the Griffins. I had service at home. Edward went to see Mr Wilson who is very little better. George & Lucy called. Mrs Askin is ill which I am very sorry to hear. Sundays seem long & are lonely to me. I cannot read all the time. My thoughts dwell on those who are gone and become sorrowful.
Apr 17 I went to see Mr Wilson who is very ill. He was glad to see me & said he wished so much to spend 3 or 4 days at Eldon, that it always gave him a pleasant feeling to come here. I spoke to him about preparing for the change which is more at hand with him. He said that he could not speak about dying to any one as he could speak to me. When I came away I said that glad as I should be to hear that he was getting better, I should be much more rejoiced to hear him say that he was ready & willing to die. He gave me his hand and said that he was both. I feel most thankful to have that assurance. . . .
Apr 20 Mr Wilson no better. There is a heavy flood. Mr Blackburn[263] came to ask me some particulars of Mr Wilson's early life, that he might write a short obituary of him in case he dies. . . .
Apr 28 I shall be very glad when our house cleaning is over. . . .
Apr 29 . . . I went to see Mr Wilson & Mrs Askin. I found them both changed very much for the worse. I should doubt Mr Wilson's living many weeks or days. He seems very much resigned & willing to go & I think it is very doubtful whether my dear old friend Mrs Askin will ever again visit Eldon. I trust that she too is ready and willing to go.
May 4 Edward had to go to Port Ryerse about the Harbour although we had a dinner party. George had to take his place. I lunched at the Griffins. The baby has grown much & is such a good nice little child. . . .

[263]Owner of the *London Free Press*. See Amelia's diary, 29 December 1857.

May 5 Amelia's baby was christened today by Dean Hellmuth. Tom Street stood God father, Eliza & Teresa God mothers, all by proxy. The Dean, Dr Woodfall & myself were the only ones there & we remained to luncheon. . . .
May 7 . . . [Edward] himself would be always kind and indulgent to me if he was not influenced by her [Sophia]. I endevor to give way in every thing and it is contrary to my sense of right ever to say one word to Edward against his wife. Today I have almost made up my mind to go to England for a time with Mr Becher but it will be almost like death to me to leave my house and the graves of those who were so dear to me. . . .
May 23 I went to church & then to George's to dinner and then called at the Griffins on my way home.
May 24 The Queen's birthday. Not much doing in London. Most of the people went on excursions. Lucy called to say goodbye she has gone to Windsor for a fortnight. . . .
May 28 Rain. No one here today. Judge Small died this morning.
May 30 Edward & I went to church. Mayor Ledyard came to dinner & spent the evening here. Mr Wilson is much worse.
Jun 3 Mr Wilson died this morning at 5 minutes past 9. I have lost an attached friend. Amelia & myself went over to take a last look at a face that had always a smile for us. Mr Elliot is appointed Judge in the place of Judge Small.
Jun 4 Poor Wilson was buried today. Three judges & several law officers came from Toronto to his funeral. The shops were closed & there seemed to be general wish to show to his remains every respect. I should think there were 100 carriages of different description that followed his remains besides an immense concourse on foot. How desolate Mrs Wilson must feel tonight. Mr Becher came to dinner. Amelia, Bella Meredith & myself went to Edward's office to see the funeral pass & that is the last of our poor friend. . . .
Jun 7 . . . Lucy returned & came to dinner. . . . We then went to Mrs Askin's . . . then called upon Mrs Cronyn. . . .
Jun 9 There are races today. Mr Becher came to luncheon. Tom Galt is made Judge in the place of Mr Wilson. Mr Becher will not own that he is disappointed. . . .
Jun 22 . . . Amelia & I went to the Hamiltons & took some flowers for Nicholas. . . .
Jun 24 Got a letter from Teresa. They, my daughters, all want me to go to England. Mr Scott offers to pay my expenses. I am glad the letter did not come until Mr Becher had left. I am afraid the temptation to see them all once more would have been greater than I could

have resisted & I know that I ought not to be an expense to my sons in law, as I could give my daughters nothing. . . .

Jul 1 Dominion Day. Shops shut but no particular celebration. Amelia came & we went to see poor Nicholas Hamilton who I think is dying. . . .

Jul 2 . . . Dr Landor called today. He is in London upon some business connected with the Asylum. . . .

Jul 3 Amelia not well today. Nicholas better & talks about getting well. Lucy & George came to afternoon tea. She looks as if she had been ill. . . .

Jul 8 Mrs W Meredith & Bella called. Amelia paid her usual visit. I got a letter from the Revnd Mr Rogers telling me that the church at Port Ryerse is commenced. He sends me a lithograph picture of the late Revnd George Okill Stuart, Rector of Kingston & one of the earliest settlers of that place.[264] Poor Nicholas Hamilton died at 1/2 past 6 this evening after 11 weeks of intense suffering.

Jul 12 There was not a very large Orange procession today & no disturbance. . . .

Jul 16 George, Mr Thomas, Mrs Dougal & Sophia played croquet.

Jul 17 Mr Swinyard played cricket today. The Hamilton Club beat the London Club. Edward Blake sent me a check for $20 for the church at Port Ryerse which is very kind & liberal of him. Amelia called. Mr Carling, Mr Swinyard & George came to dinner. Lucy & Mrs. Dougal came in the evening.

Jul 18 . . . Mr Griffin returned from Niagara. He says that Mr Plumb is very low & desponding. He has Mrs Plumb's chair placed at the table every day & will allow no one to take her seat. The children have to speak in a subdued tone as if some one was ill or dying in the house and he will not allow Mrs Plumb's pet servant Maria to be treated as a servant. She is to take her meals in the nursery with the children & is to be his medium of communication to the servants & she is not to buy anything for herself. He will see that she is properly clothed. He is doing all this out love to his late wife but the chances are that it will end in his making Maria his wife though I imagine such a thought has never yet entered his head.

Jul 19 Edward left this morning for Port Ryerse. Miss Warren came over & remained to dinner. . . .

[264]George Okill Stuart (1776–1862), Rector of St. George's, Archdeacon of the diocese of Kingston (1839–1862), and Dean of the diocese of Ontario (1862). See A.J. Anderson, "George Okill Stuart," *Dic. Can. Biog.* IX, pp. 770–771.

Jul 24 . . . Lucy & Amelia called to say good bye to Sophia who left for Toronto. She is going to Portland [Maine] for a month with her father and brother. Edward went to Port Stanley & returned at 7 PM. . . .

Jul 31 Mrs Ronalds returned from Windsor to George's today. This evening we have had a tea party. . . . Genl Bragg is a fine gentlemanly old man & Mrs Bragg is one of the most ladylike Southerners that I have seen. Her mother's family were very rich before the war but have been much reduced. They did own 250 slaves.

Aug 2 George left today to go to Paris, Hamilton & Toronto. . . .

Aug 3 Mrs Malcolm Wilson, Mrs Ronalds, Lucy & Amelia called. There is a great menagerie & circus in town. Edward has gone to it this evening.

Aug 4 Lucy went to Toronto this afternoon with Mr Griffin. George will be there to meet her. . . .

Aug 7 Thermometer this morning stood at 42. We had fire in the small drawing room. Lucy returned last evening from Toronto. Mrs Ronalds & Lucy called this morning. Lucy gave me a bottle of lavender water. . . .

Aug 19 . . . Sir Francis Hincks is at Ingersol. Edward telegraphed to ask him to stay here when he came to London. He accepted & will be here at half past 10 this evening. I am not well enough to sit up for him & George will have to receive him. Edward had to go to Bothwell today & will not return until an hour after his arrival. . . .

Aug 20 Sir Francis Hincks arrived at ½ past 10 last night. . . . I prepared some supper for him & George did host until Edward returned. I was very glad to see Sir Francis & he looks as young and as well as he did 10 years ago. Amelia who is a great favorite of his, spent the day with us. Mr Swinyard[265] . . . called. . . . Edward took Sir Francis to call upon the Bishop of Huron & Mr Goodhue. . . . They went also to the Ladies School to call upon Dean [Hellmuth] who called here but could not dine with us. The Bishop & Mrs Cronyn, Mr & Mrs Thomas, Mr Swinyard, Amelia & George made up our dinner party which went off very well. . . .

Aug 21 Sir Francis left at 9 this morning. He gave me unasked $20 for the Port Ryerse church. . . .

Aug 27 The boat race between the Oxford crew & the Harvard (American) crew came off today, the Oxford crew won . . . all at Eldon spent last evening at George's. They had a small party. . . .

[265]An officer of the Grand Trunk Railway.

Sep 4 Mr Plumb had a long talk this morning about Mr Griffin's & Edward's quarrel but we could see no way of making peace. It makes me very unhappy on Amelia's account. My heart ached when she came here tonight, to feel that she could no longer come here as one of the family but could only come at odd times to see me. . . .
Sep 6 . . . George goes to Chatham today. . . .
Sep 8 I am not so well today. . . .
Sep 9 George returned last night & has gone again today to Chatham. Egerton Ryerson came up last night & he, Sophia & Emma have gone to the Walkers to croquet. . . .
Sep 10 Sophia had a croquet party this afternoon & they all remained to heavy tea. . . .
Sep 18 George returned from Chatham. Mrs Ronalds, Lucy & Amelia called. Edward left for Simcoe. . . .
Sep 20 . . . Dr Ryerson arrived this evening.[266] . . . Mr Becher came to luncheon, he is looking tired & ill from fatigue on his journey to England. He gave me a pretty box of needles.
Sep 21 Sophia & I went with Dr Ryerson to see the Exhibition & I was much gratified. . . . Prince Arthur, Sir John & Lady Young & a number of other great people arrived in London this afternoon. Mr Glackmeir's house has been taken for the Prince. . . .
Sep 22 J. Sandfield [Macdonald] arrived in time for luncheon. . . . Our dinner party were only Mr S. Macdonald, Mr Walsh & George, the Gzowskis & Mr Swinyard called.
Sep 23 . . . Sandfield lunched with Mr Carling who gave a grand luncheon to the Governor General & party. The Prince, the government party & a number of others went out to the Ladies School to witness the opening. . . .
Sep 24 . . . The ball went off very well last night. The Prince was not allowed to select a partner which was rather hard upon him. Sophia had the honor of being selected to dance with him first, after the daughter of the Mayor. Lucy danced with him later in the evening. The Prince has won all hearts by his unaffected, pleasing manner. Amelia called to discuss the ball as she did not go. . . .
Oct 1 Amelia & Miss Griffin came to luncheon. Lucy called & she was not in a very amiable humour. Edward had not taken or sent her letters as soon as he ought to have done. He told me that he went half way to her house with her letter & met a client & had to return to the office. . . .

[266]Dr. Ryerson was in London for the opening of the Ladies' College by Prince Arthur on the 23rd September.

Oct 2 . . . [Lucy] left at 12 noon to go to Chatham & will remain there until Monday. George is there. She told Edward to take her set of pearls to Toronto for Sophia to wear at the McPherson's ball which is very kind of her. I have had seven young girls from the Ladies School to spend the day with me. . . .
Oct 5 Edward left at 6 AM for Toronto to attend the McPherson's ball given to Prince Arthur. . . .
Oct 7 Edward & Sophia returned last night very tired but very much pleased . . . Sophia's dress which her father gave her for the ball is very handsome. . . .
Oct 14 George Goodhue was buried today.[267] Edward went to the funeral. . . .
Oct 26 . . . Mrs Thomas called, Mr Goodhue is very ill but will not allow Mrs Goodhue nor anyone to sleep in his room at night. He has his door locked & barred and there he is alone with his *safe*. Mrs Thomas said that he is afraid of being robbed. . . .
Nov 3 . . . We have had two young girls from the Ladies School & a boy from the College to spend the day with us. . . . They all ate as only school girls & boys can eat. . . .
Nov 7 . . . The Cathedral was opened today & there was a great gathering of clergymen there. The Bishop of Michigan, the Bishop of Toronto & other strangers. . . . [It] has been repaired and there has been no service there all summer. . . .
Nov 14 Edward left for Port Ryerse. George returned last night from Chatham & came here to breakfast. He went to the Askins & remained all night as Lucy was there. Mr Askin is so very ill. George went again after breakfast & returned this evening. Mr Askin died at $^1/_2$ past one PM & Lucy has remained with them. Sophia has taken charge of Lucy's baby. Another of my oldest friends gone.
Nov 15 I went to sit with Mrs Askin who is ill in bed. Both Mrs Askin & Teresa bear their loss with more composure than expected. I went in to see Mr Askin. He looks younger than when alive. . . .
Dec 2 . . . Sophia & Lucy walked over to see Mrs Askin who is better than Sophia expected to see her though in very low spirits.
Dec 10 I have finished reading a second volume of the *Christian Classics*. If God would only make me as good as the least of those celebrated. . . .
Dec 22 Superintended the making of a cake for Christmas & New Year. Mr Becher came to luncheon & gave me two books. . . . He is very kind. George called, he left for Chatham. . . .

[267]Son of George Jervis Goodhue.

Dec 25 I am not very well. All my children are kind to me. All have brought an offering of books & such nice books & I shall have quite a library. Ellen Hamilton called. She tells me that Mr Hamilton is in the last stages of consumption. She asked me for some religious books for him to read. . . . George & Lucy dined with us. Amelia called, & so ends Christmas Day of 1869. I pray God to give me a thankful heart for all His mercies.
Dec 27 . . . Dr Beaty came this evening & will sleep here. He has gone to the station to meet Dr Ryerson who came by the 10 PM train to pay us a few days visit. Edward has gone to a dancing party at the Glasses & I go to bed before Dr Ryerson comes as I cannot sit up late with impunity.
Dec 30 . . . Sophia asked some people to dinner to meet her father. . . .
Dec 31 I got letters from Eliza & Mary. Colonel Crutchley's Aunt Hester is dead and Evy Portman[268] is ill, she had a miscarriage & is very weak & ill. Dr Ryerson returned home today. Amelia called & so ends 1869 & I am still here & pray God to make me more humble more thankful & enable me to serve Him better. I give Him my *whole heart.*

1870

Jan 1 Frauline Smidt spent the day here. Our visitors were Mr Becher, the Dean [Boomer], Mr Brough, Mr Fitzgerald, F[rank] Cronyn, . . . Mr & Mrs Thomas spent the evening here & we played euchre.
Jan 12 Mr Goodhue died last night, leaving property to his family in money & mortgages amounting to a million of dollars. His object in life has been to get money but we hear no mention of his deeds of charity.[269] . . .
Jan 13 I got a note from Mrs Thomas asking for a pattern for a widow's cap for her mother. I sent her a cap and asked Mrs Goodhue to accept it. Mrs Goodhue sent her sleigh for me to go & take a last look at Mr Goodhue. His face could only bring back kindly recollections to me. I did not see Mrs Goodhue. . . .

[268]Mr. Portman's second wife.

[269]Goodhue's will left an estate valued at $650,000, with provisions for his widow, children, grandchildren, and some charities. The estate was to remain intact until the death of his widow. The children attempted unsuccessfully to have the will broken by provincial statute. See F.H. Armstrong, "George Jervis Goodhue," *Can. Dic. Biog.* IX, pp. 323–324.

Jan 21 . . . George has gone to Toronto to see Sandfield Macdonald and to try and get the deeds of the Ronalds' land which he has.
Jan 22 Frauline Smidt came to dinner and gave Sophia a lesson in German. . . .
Feb 8 . . . Lucy & Mrs Ronalds, Amelia and Miss Grant called. Sophia and Mrs Meredith went again today collecting for the Church Society. We have heard the sad news that Teresa Askin died yesterday at Chatham at the house of her brother Dr Askin. . . .
Feb 19 My 72nd birthday. I thank my God for all his mercies & they are many. Amelia & Scotty, Ellen & Selina Hamilton, Mr Ronalds, Lucy & George all called. . . . George & Lucy gave me a little statuette of Our Saviour, & Mrs Ronalds a supply of papers & envelopes which is most kind. . . . Mr Thomas was at the same card party with George & Edward & did not get home until nearly 4 o'clock this morning when he found that Mrs Thomas had given birth to a little daughter at 11 o'clock last evening. He sent Sophia today a further gift of $40 for the Church Society in acknowledgement of the blessing conferred upon him.
Mar 1 A very quiet day. No one here but Amelia. . . . I have had a very strange feeling this evening when walking in the hall. I felt as if dear Chasse was near me. The feeling was strange, unlike anything I have ever felt before and seemed so real that I expected to see her. Cold chills went over me. I wonder if I am well. I felt as if our hearts met in the warm love of former days. Dear darling Chasse.
Apr 5 . . . Mrs Page gave me an astounding piece of information this morning, that she was going to be married. She has been with me as cook for more than nine years & as she must be 60 years of age. I thought she was safe from matrimony & that she would remain with me for the rest of her days. She is a good cook. I fear I shall not be able to get another as good. Yet I cannot regret her marrying as she will get a comfortable home for her old age & will be her own mistress. . . .
Apr 14 Our order of groceries from Montreal arrived, also the lace curtains which Sophia bought in Toronto. . . .
Apr 22 . . . In the morning I assisted Jane in making a wedding cake for Mrs Page. . . . Mrs Ronalds returned from Windsor & brought little Amelia back with her. . . .
May 2 Today Mrs Page was married to Mr Goff. I am afraid she has done a foolish thing as people say that he is very ill tempered & miserly and that he did not treat his last wife well. . . . I told Mrs Page that she might be married in our dining room & that she might ask her friends to come & that we would give them tea, coffee, cakes & wine

which we did. Mr Goff brought two sons and their wives, & Mrs Page's daughter, her husband & their son & daughter were here. The Rev Dr Cooper, Baptist minister, married them & Mrs Cooper rather a nice Scotch woman came with her husband. Amelia came & we treated them all as if they were very honored guests. . . . I have engaged another cook this evening but I fear that she will not be as good as Mrs Page.

May 3/4 . . . Our new cook has come & has proved to be another failure. She seems to be a very good sort of woman but now confirms that her knowledge of cooking is very small indeed. . . .

May 10 . . . Our new cook came. I sent her away after four hours. She did not even know how to boil asparagus. I am to have another cook tomorrow upon trial. . . .

May 11 Mr Becher drove me to see the Askin's old place. I felt a strong wish to see [the] place once more. It gave me a very depressing feeling to see the empty house and the neglected garden and they gone who always gave me a welcome. . . .

May 14 . . . Our new cook is not a success, I do not think we can keep her. . . .

May 16 I was ill all night & dreamed the old dream of endevoring to go home. The home I am endevoring to go to is always the place of my birth. This is three times within the last week that I have dreamed the same dream & have dreamed it at intervals for 50 years. . . . Old Page came this evening to see us. She seems delighted with her new home & her old husband.

May 21 . . . Mr Becher came to early dinner. Our pudding had to be sent back from table, it was not cooked. Our cook is a failure. She is very cleanly but cannot cook. . . .

May 23 I have engaged another cook to come on the 1st of June. . . .

Jun 1 I have spent the afternoon at the Griffins. It is the first time that I have been there since October last.

Jun 9 Sophia & Miss Warren went to the races in Mr Thomas' carriage. . . . Both Sophia & Miss Warren won some money at the races. I cannot approve of races.

Jun 15 I left London with Mr Griffin, Amelia, children & nurse in the Director's car which Mr McInnes, Director of the G.W., kindly placed at our disposal to take us to Niagara. Sophia, Edward, George, Mr Thomas, Mrs W. Meredith & Bella came to the station to see us off. Amelia & myself leaving home seemed such a great event in our little circle. . . . At Hamilton, Mrs McInnes & Gilbert Griffin met us. Mr McInnes was very kind in anticipating all our wants. Mrs McInnes is near her confinement. G. Griffin came to the Suspension Bridge with us and returned by the next train. Mr Plumb and his children met us at the bridge. . . . The Plumb's house & grounds are in nice order & the household appears to be well managed but Mrs Plumb who gave a charm to every thing is gone. Mr Plumb's great anxiety appears to be to have the house in the same order as she used to have it.

Jun 18 . . . We drove to the lake to see the regatta, which was not much to see, one yacht arrived & at anchor & two others in sight. The town of Niagara is the most desolate looking place I have ever seen, 60 years ago it was a thriving, prosperous looking place. The County Town has been changed & all trade has left the place.

Jun 21 Mr Plumb drove Amelia, myself, the two Girls and Scotty to Clark Hill.[270] The drive was very pleasant & the scenery beautiful. We found Mrs Street looking much better than I expected to see her. She is 76 years of age but not too old to make herself agreeable. Her table is served in the style of 40 years ago & I should think the same Delft and dish covers were still in use but it is the kindly feeling & not style that makes a home pleasant. Mr Street was not at home. . . . Mrs Street has invited Amelia & children to spend a few days there. We returned to Niagara at 8 PM.

Jun 24 . . . I had letters from Sophia & Mary. Mary complains that the expense of educating George & starting him in the world is drawing very heavily on their means, & she feels poorer than she has ever yet done. Mrs John Scott, the widow of Mr Scott's cousin has given Mr Scott £10,000 to buy a place with, a very nice present.

Jun 27 I left Niagara at 10.30 AM. . . . The Station Master, by Mr McInnes' direction, handed me into the Directors' car and I was the sole occupant as far as Hamilton. There Mr M[cInnes] met me, took me for some refreshment & then gave me a seat in the Pullman car with only three others. Thanks to Mr M[cInnes] I returned home in comfort & without cost. Edward met me at the station. . . .

Jun 28 . . . Lucy was confined this morning with a daughter. We are all a little disappointed it is not a son but feel very thankful that she is doing well. We have just heard that Mr Swinyard was out boating yesterday with two gentlemen & six of his children. The boat upset in a squall & three of his daughters were drowned, the oldest 15 & the youngest 6 years of age . . .

Jul 5 Edward left this morning for Port Ryerse to be present at the opening of the Church built on the reservation made by my father in 1795. . . .

[270]Thomas Street's home.

Jul 23 Dean Hellmuth called. We had a long talk about the Pope's infallibility. He preaches tomorrow upon that subject. The two absorbing subjects of conversation at present [are] the war between France & Prussia & the Pope's declaration of infallibility.

Jul 26 Last night I had my same old dream about going home. I now find by close observation that this dream always precedes indisposition of mind or body. . . .

Jul 28 Edward returned at half past 10 PM. He had been at Hamilton to see the Directors of the Great Western about getting up an opposition to granting the bonus asked of the Township by the Southern Railway of a million of dollars. Edward has been busy all day getting placards printed & he is going with others tomorrow to distribute them. . . .

Jul 29 Edward left very early and went to Elgin to prevent the people giving a bonus to the Southern Railway. This is the 34th anniversary of George's birthday. He had his little baby christened today, named Charlotte Adelaide by the Revnd Sweatman. The party invited were Mr Griffin, Amelia, Mr & Mrs Sweatman, Miss Garland, Mr Becher, Mr Walker, Sophia & myself. Edward absent . . . dinner was very nice. I had letters from Mary, Eliza and Sarah.

Aug 4 Mrs Ryerson arrived at 10 PM last night & will remain with us for some time. Mr Becher came to luncheon. Mr & Mrs Vidal, Mrs Ronalds, Lucy, Amelia & Capt Prince called.

Aug 13 . . . I had my old dream of trying to go home. The home I try to go to is always Port Ryerse near my birth place.

Aug 14 . . . Edward told me this evening that there had been a great row between Lucy & George because I wanted Amelia & husband asked to their christening & George asked them. Lucy had made up *her* party without them. I am so sorry I said a word. I thought they might be vexed with me but I never dreamed that it might cause vexation between George & Lucy. I knew Lucy did not like Amelia but I did not know that the feeling was so deep & strong. Much as I should like to tell Amelia I think it best not to do so. I am afraid if such trifles can disturb their domestic peace, that there is not much happiness in store for George & Lucy.

Aug 21 Mr Thomas gave me a book of photographic views by Notman.[271] It is a costly & handsome present. . . .

[271]William Notman (1826–91), the prominent Montreal-based photographer and businessman. See Stanley G. Triggs, "William Notman," *Dic. Can. Biog.* XII, pp. 787–791.

Aug 22 Mr Thomas is making his arrangement for opening a branch of his bank [Molsons] here. Mr Griffin is to be the agent & Edward the solicitor. . . .
Aug 23 I had my old dream again trying to go home, packing up my things for the move. I hope I may be in readiness when the hour does come that I am to go home. . . .
Aug 24 There was a heavy rain last night from 7 till 1 AM & I have never seen the water rise so high in so short a time. It is now as high as I have ever seen it. Our fences are gone & a third of the hay that was cut and on the field is gone. The corn & potatoes are under water & the potatoes will all rot. Our loss, I suppose, will be $150. . . .
Aug 25 This day 20 years ago Mr Harris died. What a day of sorrow it was to me yet how many years I have survived him & how many bereavements & trials I have had since then & I am still here. . . .
Aug 26 . . . Jane has just told me that she is to be married on the first of October. I am very sorry to part with her. She has been with us nearly ten years and has been a very excellent servant. . . .
Sep 2 I asked Lucy to call upon some southern ladies that Judge Bragg wished Sophia to call upon. Mr Becher took us out for a drive. We went to the Lunatic Asylum, not in the building but drove past it & then out to the Ladies School & we went through the Dean's new house. It is the best house I have ever been through & nearly finished. The situation is beautiful. The Dean certainly deserves the thanks of the Londoners for all that he has done for the place. He tells me that both the Ladies School & the Hellmuth College have as many pupils as they can take. We then called at the Bechers. . . .
Sep 15 . . . Jane's sister Bella came today. She is to take Jane's place when Jane is married. . . .
Sep 25 Edward left by the early train for Hamilton. . . . [and] returned at 5 PM. Major & Mrs Evans. . . . called & went to evening service with Edward, Sophia, Mrs Warren & Mr Thomas.
Oct 1 My housemaid . . . left us today to be married to a farmer. . . . She is a good girl & has been an excellent servant. I am very sorry to part with her. . . .
Oct 9 . . . Last night I had my old dream of endevoring to go to my old home at Port Ryerse. It is strange that I had the same dream when I was living there of being away or living at some other place & endevoring to go home. I have had the same dream at short intervals for more than 40 years.
Oct 11 . . . Edward has bought a billiard table which is being put up in the library. . . .
Oct 18 . . . Sophia left for Long Point Bay on a visit to her father.

Edward went with her as far as Ingersol and sent her across to Port Rowan in a buggy. George returned to Chatham. Lucy & Amelia called, Ellen Hamilton came in the evening. She has spent the summer at Quebec, Montreal, Brockville & Toronto & has just returned. I felt very glad to see her. I have not been well all day.

Oct 21 . . . George called. I told him that Edward did not like his speculating. He said he would not speculate again as long as he was in the firm of Harris Brothers.[272]

Nov 5 . . . I do not dine with the family any more. They dine late. It suits Edward's business but I cannot dine late. It makes me ill, so I get some sort of dinner of any thing that I can get. I wish I had the means of keeping my own house.

Nov 17 Miss Warren has gone today to the Asylum to remain. Edward left for Port Ryerse. . . . Lucy called & sat with me for some time. I asked Mrs Landor to come here and remain until her house is in readiness for her. . . . Mrs Landor appeared very glad to come and I am glad to have her as I am quite alone.

Nov 22 I have felt better today than I have for a long time, . . . Baby Griffin continues a little better but I fear she will never be well. Ellen Hamilton paid me a long visit & told us a great secret. That her sister Selina, is to be married to Capt Prince in February if not sooner. She has my best wishes for her happiness. . . .

Nov 23 Mrs Landor has gone to her own house, it being at last habitable. Edward returned last night very tired. He has been trying to prevent some townships in Norfolk from giving a bonus to the Southern Railway. He is working with the Great Western. . . .

Nov 25 . . . George came this evening & he & Edward are playing their first game of billiards on their table.

Dec 9 William Wilson, a son of the late Judge Wilson, died suddenly yesterday at the age of 27 . . . having wasted his life by intemperance & other vices. . . .

Dec 11 . . . I had my old dream last night of going home but last night for the first time in my sleep I got to my old home at Long Point & Mr Harris was there. In all former dreams I have always been on my way & trying to go home.

Dec 14 I sent this morning & asked Mrs Askin to come & remain with me until Sophia comes back, & she came, dear old lady, & here she is. Lucy came & sat some time with us. . . .

[272]The speculation was probably in purchases of land. George was to withdraw from his partnership in Harris Brothers in 1871.

Dec 19 . . . [Amelia Griffin] told me that some ill natured, shameless person had written an anonymous letter to Capt Prince saying everything that is bad of Selina Hamilton, accusing her of being unchaste, and Capt Prince felt very unhappy about it. Mr Griffin, whom he consulted, told him to burn the cowardly letter & not give it a thought, that some unprincipled people who could not be discovered, had been in the habit for years of writing to & about everyone. It is most shameful. . . .

Dec 21 I have been up nearly all day but am weak & ill. . . .

Dec 22 Still confined to my room. All my friends are so kind coming to see me. Mr Becher sent me the last volume of Macaulay[273] that I wanted so much. Lucy brought me grapes. . . .

Dec 24 . . . They are all so kind to me & no one could have treated me with more tenderness than Sophia has since I have been ill. . . .

Dec 25 Edward & Sophia went to morning service. I felt better & went downstairs to dinner. Sophia had a nice fire made in the drawing room. I went there, in a few minutes I found the chimney was on fire & the house consequently was all in confusion. . . .

Dec 26 I have changed my room for the room opposite as it is warmer & less drafty. Mr Becher called & brought me a Christmas present of a very pretty flower pot. He is very kind to me. Amelia came & brought me a present from Mr Griffin of *Rob Roy on the Jordon*, a very amusing work. Mr Griffin is always thoughtful & kind to me. Sophia had a sort of *impromptu* dinner today under many difficulties. Shops all shut (holiday), meat all frozen, difficulty in getting fish, the cook in bad humour. . . . George & Lucy dined here. Mr Thomas made me a present of a woven shawl & a book of lectures & essays by Professor Seeley.[274] My friends are all so kind.

Dec 28 . . . I am better but feel very low spirited tonight. I have the blues. . . .

Dec 31 The last evening of 1870. How much I have to be thankful for during the past year & yet it has not been without its trials. The thought will arise, shall I live to see the close of another year. My daily prayer is that I may be ready & willing to go when called. George called, his baby is better. Amelia called. Edward & Sophia have gone to dine with the Walkers.

[273]Thomas Babington Macaulay (1800–59), English historian, author, and statesman.

[274]Sir John Robert Seeley (1834–95). Amelia is referring here to his *Lectures and Essays*, London: Macmillan and Co., 1870.

1871

Jan 1 New Year's day, all is quiet. Sophia went to morning service, I had service in my room. . . . George & Lucy called, Amelia & Gilbert Griffin called. George went to see Mrs Askin & took her a book as a New Year's gift. Mr Dobell came in the afternoon & paid a long visit. He did not impress me as very gentlemanlike or very agreeable. He sings very nicely. Ellen Hamilton called, she looks tired, worried with the preparations with Selina's wedding. Harry Becher called, he looked so well & handsome. He and all the Londoners are excited about the municipal elections tomorrow. Mr Thomas called for a few minutes to tell us that he could not come here tomorrow, all the Goodhue's connections are jealous of his coming here. I think that he prefers Eldon to their house.

Jan 2 This day has been kept as the New Year's day for visiting. . . . Mr Becher came in & then Dean Hellmuth. Mr Thomas & Mr Becher shook hands very coldly. They have an intense dislike to each other. Mr Thomas thinks that Mr Becher has treated him very badly & made a poor return for all his kindness. . . .

Jan 3 Edward & Mr Thomas went to Tillsonburg. Mr Thomas wishes to see if it will do to start a branch of the Molson Bank there. . . . I had letters today from Mary, Eliza . . . and from Mrs Thomas. . . .

Jan 4 I heard from Elizabeth today. Her mother & her do not get on well together & they have separated. Elizabeth & her family have gone to live in a small cottage on Col O'Brien's Estate. I fear they are very poor. I think all Elizabeth's money is gone & her husband is one who never succeeds in any thing excepting spending all the money he can get. George & Lucy are in a great state of fright. Their nurse has gone home ill with scarlet fever & neither George nor children have had it. . . .

Jan 8 For the second time last night in my dreams I had got home. The first time we were only there. Last night I was fitting up the drawing room white, all white looking so pretty. In many hundred of my dreams I have been trying to go home but have always been unable to reach there until in my last two dreams. Perhaps when the third dream comes I may be home in earnest. . . . I feel ill today. . . .

Jan 10 . . . old Mrs Lawrason called to see me, the poor old lady had to climb the stairs as I could not go down. . . . Louisa Campbell arrived tonight on a visit of a few days to Sophia. She is a very nice lovable girl.

Jan 11 I am better today but had a very disturbed rest last night. . . . Amelia paid her usual visit. Egerton Ryerson arrived at 10 PM. He will pay us a visit of a few days & make Miss Campbell's visit less stupid.

Jan 14 I was very ill again last night. Dr Woodruff was called in this morning but I am much better tonight. Becher paid me a long visit today. He told me why he opposed the Bill giving the Goodhue heirs the property, setting Mr Goodhue's will aside. He acted according to the advice of Chief Justice Draper. . . .

Jan 15 . . . [Mr Thomas] told me several things about Mr Becher that does not tell in his favor & which I was very sorry to hear. Mr Becher assured me that he was not opposing the heirs of the Goodhue estate in getting their money from interested motives. Every body seem to think to the contrary. He goes to Toronto again tomorrow to try & prevent the bill passing if he can. Mr Thomas goes to Toronto tomorrow also & will remain there until the bill is passed or thrown out.

Jan 16 . . . Edward left for Toronto this morning also to see if he could influence any Member to vote for the bill to give the heirs of the Goodhue estate their money. His friendship for Mr Thomas induces him to do this. George has gone to Chatham. . . . George engaged Mr McGee[275] to make additions & alterations as to his house as Edward thought if he built it all this year that he ought to arrange about it at once. . . .

Jan 17 . . . I had a letter from Mary describing her daughter Helen's first ball & how much they enjoyed it, both mother & daughter. . . .

Jan 18 Sophia got a telegram from J.S. Macdonald saying that Edward wished her to go to Toronto today by the 12 o'clock train. She went of course. . . .

Jan 20 Mrs Askin's 77th birthday. She is stronger & has more life than I have who am four years her junior. . . . Dr Ryerson is very dangerously ill. Edward brought me a letter from Sophia. It will be impossible for her to leave her father for some weeks. Doctor Ryerson was so glad to have Sophia with him that he cried for an hour after she arrived. The bill about the Goodhue estate has not yet come before the House. Mr Becher is making most strenuous exertions amongst the Members to prevent its passing. Mr Thomas is becoming very low about it. . . .

Jan 21 . . . Mrs Ronalds called to say good bye, she has gone to Windsor to remain for some months. . . .

Jan 25 Mr Becher sent me another printed letter in which he calls Mr Thomas a *liar*. I do not know how it is all to end. Lucy & Amelia came to see me. Louisa declined driving with Harry Becher today. She

[275]A local contractor.

says she does not care for him but young girls say that even of those they like. . . .
Jan 26 . . . I heard from Sophia. Her father is a little better. His recovery depends upon care & good nursing. Bella came to ask Edward to take her cousin Annie to the ball tonight, which he is going to do.
Jan 27 Edward thought the ball stupid. Louisa said she liked it very much. Harry Becher I suppose made it pleasant for her. He drove them to the Ladies School today and she has gone to spend the evening with the Merediths. . . . Sophia sent Edward Mr Thomas' reply to Becher's charge of falsehood. It is very gentlemanlike & yet very much to the purpose. Versy Cronyn bears testimony to the truth of all of Mr Thomas' statements & there is no doubt but the bill will pass to give the heirs the money. It is a great pity that Mr Becher offered such violent opposition.
Feb 1 The weather is very mild. . . . Mrs Askin returned home in the morning to entertain Col Askin's adopted daughter. She returns to Eldon again this evening. Amelia, Lucy, Bella &. . . . Anne Meredith called. The Goodhue will . . . is the all engrossing subject of conversation. . . .
Feb 2 Mrs Askin returned home this morning, ill. . . .
Feb 4 Sophia sent me a glove box & stretcher which I wished to give to Selina Hamilton as a wedding present. Lucy called. George has gone to Chatham. Amelia & Ellen Hamilton called. I have again freshened my cold.
Feb 6 I am a very little better. . . . Lucy & Amelia have sat with me at different times. Selina Hamilton, Bella, Mrs W. Meredith & Mr Becher paid me a long visit. . . .
Feb 7 . . . Miss Leonard called. Mrs Askin returned home tonight in very low spirits. . . . She is a poor feeble lonely old woman. . . .
Feb 8 I had a note from Mrs Landor. . . . Amelia & her children, Lucy, George & Mr Becher came to see me. Edward & George have had more words tonight. How painful it is to me.
Feb 9 . . . I am & have been very much worried with the disagreements between Edward & George. George told Lucy of his troubles & difficulties & she behaved like a duchess as she is. I think people wonder very much that Sophia remains away when I am so ill and no one to look after the house.
Feb 10 I am a little better this evening. Amelia, Lucy, Bella & Mrs W. Meredith have been with me, that is one of them all day. Mr Becher and Judge Hughes called & Misa, my old servant. Mr Griffin had a note from Dr Landor who writes very discouragingly of Miss Warren whom he says has not improved in the least for the last week.

Feb 11 I continue to improve a little. . . . Lucy & Amelia & Mr Becher were my visitors today. Lucy turned out all Edward's clothes which were full of moths & would soon have been all totally ruined.
Feb 13 I felt miserable until 4 PM. . . . Amelia & Mrs Lockhart came to see me. . . . Amelia had a letter from Mr Portman who writes in good spirits. He says he is making lots of money. . . . Edward heard from Sophia who speaks of coming home on Saturday. . . .
Feb 14 Mr Howel died on Sunday at the age of 42. He was an officer under Col Crutchley in the 23rd. Lucy wrote to me this morning that both her children were ill last night. George is to be home tonight. . . . She [Amelia] is the greatest comfort to me. . . . Mr Thomas wrote. It would have been much better that he had left it unwritten. The purpose of the letter was to tell Mr Becher that he would cut him in future & that he would never on any occasion recognize him. Mr Becher's answer was very sarcastic. He said that he hoped that he would keep his word.
Feb 15 I am much better. George returned last night & Lucy & the children are better. Mrs Ellis & Capt Prince called. . . .
Feb 17 Amelia & George came to see me. I am so troubled that Edward & George do not get on well together any more. It will make my last days miserable. Sandfield Macdonald called to see me. I asked him to come to my bed room as I could not go out. He is looking well & I was very glad to see him. He is staying with Mr Carling. Edward has gone this evening to see him. Goldwin Smith[276] lectures in London tonight.
Feb 18 I have been very busy mending all of Edward's clothes. . . . George called & we again discussed our troubles. . . . Sophia returned. . . .
Feb 19 My 73rd birthday. Lucy sent me a couple of very pretty caps as a present & George brought me the history of the Great Railroads.[277] Mr Becher came to see me & wish me many happy returns of the day. How absurd to make that wish to a person of 73 years of age. . . .
Feb 20 . . . Dean Hellmuth called to see me. He does not like Mr Becher & condemns his conduct about the Goodhue Estate Bill. . . .
Feb 21 Capt Prince & Selina Hamilton were to have been married today but she took diphtheria & the marriage had to be postponed. . . .

[276]Goldwin Smith (1823–1910) migrated to Canada in 1871 and commenced a career as influential author and journalist. He was a cousin of Elizabeth Loring O'Brien (widow of John Fitzjohn Harris).

[277]Possibly J.M. & E. Trout, *The Railways of Canada*, Toronto: The Monetary Times, 1871.

Feb 22 Mr Becher sent me a brace of partridge. I asked Mrs Askin to come and dine with me in my bedroom. . . . She came & we enjoyed our dinner. . . .
Feb 23 . . . George and I have had another talk about the differences between him and Edward. George looks so miserable. My heart aches for him. He says people stop him in the street & ask what is the matter with him. I can only pray that God may guide them to what is right.
Feb 24 . . . I looked over my old letters and burnt a good many & wrote a memorandum of what I wish done with my clothes and some trifles about the house. . . .
Feb 25 I was ill during the night & have felt ill all day. Edward & George's difficulties are helping to wear my life away. . . .
Feb 27 . . . It is suspected that Harry Becher is engaged to Louisa Campbell.
Mar 2 Edward talking of our affairs & of George gave me a pain at my heart & a sleepless night. . . .
Mar 4 The country is in a real state of excitement about the coming election. Mr Cornish is going to oppose Mr Carling in the City.
Mar 5 . . . It was pleasant to go even downstairs after a month's confinement.
Mar 8 . . . Mr Cornish seems to have more support than was anticipated. It will be a disgrace to the City if he is returned. . . .
Mar 11 . . . a letter from Teresa, Mr Scott has been seriously ill. . . .
Mar 14 . . . W. Meredith came to play billiards & Edward kept him for dinner.
Mar 16 Edward's birthday. He is 39 today. . . .
Mar 28 I again resume my journal. I have been very ill with cold, fever & other ailments, but am now much better. Dr Woodruff attended me & Sophia has been a most kind nurse. Amelia has been ill . . . Lucy has been here almost every day & all are most kind. The weather keeps very cold & there is a great deal of illness about. Selina Hamilton was married on the 22nd to Capt [Robert] Prince of the 53rd & they are away on their wedding trip. They were married in Church & Selina had 7 brides maids & 7 grooms men. The Princess Louisa was married on the 21st.[278] She had 8 brides maids but only 2 grooms men. . . .
Mar 29 . . . I gave directions about drawing my Will & in addition to my Will I wrote a letter to Edward telling him what my wishes are regarding Eldon. . . .

[278]Princess Louisa married Prince Arthur, Queen Victoria's second son.

Mar 31 . . . I signed my will. . . .
Apr 3 McGee commenced building the front verandah. Harris[279] came to work for the summer but he smelt strong of whiskey & I think he was not quite sober. If he indulges in that way he will not do for Eldon. . . .
Apr 8 Lucy's baby is dangerously ill. Sophia has been there the most of the day. I asked Mrs Askin to remain until Monday & she is so glad to stay. She said more than once today that she was glad to be here. . . .
Apr 14 I was out this morning pruning rose bushes. I feel so thankful to be able to get out. . . .
Apr 15 . . . Amelia came twice today to see me. How desolate I should feel if she was away.
Apr 17 . . . I tried to pursuade Becher to resign the trust to the Goodhue estate but he says it would be cowardly & shirking his duty to resign now. Sophia has gone to a public reading by Mr Griffin this evening.
Apr 19 . . . Sophia very busy making underclothes. . . .
Apr 24 . . . finished trimming the rose bushes. . . .
May 1 Painting & house cleaning still going on. . . .
May 18 . . . An English gentleman, Mr Chamberlain . . . called. He is travelling through the country & stopped in London by the request of the friends of the late Lieut Winyatt [sic] of the 83rd Regiment, who was drowned in 1841 in the Thames.[280] His brother wished him to see what state his tomb was in. . . .
May 29 Sophia & I left for Toronto. . . . We received a kind welcome from the Ryersons. . . .
Jun 1 Went to Notman[281] & had our photos taken. Cost $11 for nine cabinet size & 12 small cards if they are good. I am very much aged since I was last taken. . . .
Jun 3 Dr Ryerson took me out driving & showed me all the places of note about Toronto. Toronto has become a large city since I drove about it 18 years ago. There are handsome buildings & nicely kept plans in all directions. . . . The Methodist Church looks very imposing. Dr Ryerson says it will be the handsomest Church in the Dominion. Its cost will be over 100,000$. . . .

[279]A gardener and no relation to the Eldon House Harrises.

[280]Wynniatt's death is related to the Eldon House ghost story which is referred to in W.T. Stead, ed., *Real Ghost Stories*, being the Christmas Number of the *Review of Reviews*, November 1891, p. 67.

[281]Notman's photographic studio in Toronto. See Amelia's diary, 21 August 1870.

Jun 7 The pass came this morning & we left Toronto at 12 noon & were delayed for more than 2 hours. . . . We had to go round in omnibuses. It was near 8 PM when we got home. I was very glad to be at home again. I enjoyed my visit as much as I could but I do so much dislike going from home. I found all well & the place looking very pretty. . . .

Jun 10 . . . Mrs W. Meredith dangerously ill with measles. I had a letter from Sarah. Mary Dalzell was presented at the last drawing room.[282] Her mother was much pleased with her appearance and thought her almost handsome. . . .

Jun 16 . . . Edward & Sophia left this morning, Edward for Montreal, Sophia for Quebec . . . & expects to be away for a month, Edward is to return in a few days. . . .

Jun 22 Our garden & grounds are looking prettier than I have ever seen them. . . .

Jun 25 . . . Edward went to morning service. Miss Warren returned home with him & spent the day here. She is looking much better. She told me that she had received a proposal of marriage from a Mr. Coone, a Commission Merchant of Chicago. From what she told me of him I advised her by all means to accept him. . . . Amelia tells me that Gilbert [the son] is engaged to Miss Brown of Hamilton. *Gilbert* says she is a very nice girl, her father is rich & can do a good deal for the young people if so inclined.

Jun 30 . . . George is very low this evening. His house is costing him so much more than he expected. Edward heard from Sophia who is not well. She intends remaining in Montreal boarding at a convent and having medical treatment for some time. . . .

Jul 1 Edward left for Buffalo. . . .

Jul 3 Dominion day was celebrated today & the foundation of the new hotel which is to be built opposite the Sulphur Springs, was laid with great ceremony. . . .

Jul 11 . . . Mr Griffin is going in about a fortnight to British Columbia in an official capacity to make postal arrangements. He is to go to Ottawa first. . . .

Jul 15 Mr Becher . . . is in great trouble. His daughter Conny is very ill. He telegraphed today for Dr Hodder. . . .

Jul 18 . . . Mrs Beddome called about the trunk that she was to take to Sophia. I could not give her Sophia's address as the only address

[282]A reference to Amelia's grand-daughter, Mary, who was presented to Queen Victoria.

that I know to her is through the Molson Bank, & as people are making ill natured remarks about her & Mr Thomas of the Molson Bank, I would not give Mrs Beddome that address, as it would have been confirmation strong to all the evil reports. . . .
Jul 19 Dean Hellmuth was elected Coadjutor to the Bishop of Huron today. . . .
Jul 24 Mr Griffin & Amelia came, it is the first time Mr Griffin has been in the house for years. I am very glad he came. He left at 5 PM for British Columbia. . . .
Jul 25 Edward left for Detroit & he is going down the south side of Lake Erie. Mr Howard is with him & they wish to see what prospect there is of selling brick as they are disposed to commence brick making at Port Ryerse. . . . George tells me that he has left the firm of Harris & Brothers. He is going to open a land office. I hope he may make a competence.[283]
Jul 28 There is a disturbance in the kitchen. . . . The cook is so bad tempered that the house maid will leave if she remains & no servant will live with her so that she will have to go. . . .
Jul 31 . . . I got a letter from Sophia today, enclosing one from her father in which he expresses his disapprobation in very strong terms of her conduct in regard to Lilly Beatty. Sophia, when last in Toronto, treated her cousin Lilly Beatty with great coldness because she thought her brother Edgerton [sic] was fond of her.[284] Sophia said, if he married her that she would never speak to him, & she told her mother that she would never again go to her house if Lilly was there. Dr Ryerson tells her in strong language that neither she, nor any one else shall dictate to him who he shall invite to his house. I told Sophia that she was wrong at the time & that her brother would choose his own wife & that her opposition would be much more likely to make the match than to prevent it, & now her father says that if Edgerton chooses to marry Lilly, he will not oppose it. I wrote and advised Sophia to write an humble, affectionate letter to her father and acknowledge how wrong she had been in what she had said in her opposition.
Aug 2 . . . Amelia had a letter from Mr Portman. His son Willy has entered the Navy as a Midshipman.
Aug 10 Gave two dollars towards buying a Bishop's Robe for the Coadjutor, the Bishop of Erie. . . .

[283]George conducted a modestly successful business, G.B. Harris & Company, until 1894.
[284]Egerton, usually referred to as Charley by Amelia, married his cousin, Lilly, in 1875 and they had six children.

Aug 13 . . . Mr Carling came to see Edward after we were all in bed.
Aug 15 . . . Ellen Hamilton called this evening with a request that I should present the address with the Bishop's Robes to the Bishop (Dean Hellmuth). I had much rather not, but will do it if Edward wishes that I should.
Aug 17 . . . This has been a busy day with me. I went to the Rectory and presented the address & the Bishop's Robes to Dean Hellmuth. There were not many there. I think I read the address very well. . . .
Aug 22 . . . Ellen Hamilton brought her lover, the Revd Delven, to see me. He seems a very gentlemanly man but I should not think him very clever. . . .
Aug 24 . . . Dean Hellmuth was consecrated Bishop today with the title of Bishop of Norfolk. There were a great assemblage of clergy present, the Metropolitan, Henden, the Bishop of Ontario, of Toronto, of Michigan, of Ohio . . . besides many clergymen of lower grades. The day was so hot that I was afraid to [go] as I knew the Church would be full. . . .
Aug 25 . . . 21 years today since Mr Harris' death & I am still here.
Aug 29 . . . Edward gave me a snub at tea again tonight. Almost always when any one is here at table he snubs me in some way. I shall leave the table and the house if it is repeated much oftener. I left the table this evening as soon as I could without drawing attention. Amelia came to tell us that Lucy's uncle, John Ronalds died on the 6th of August, aged 41. His death will most probably leave her in undisputed possession of all the Ronald[s'] lands in this country, worth $200,000, that is when the grandmother dies.[285]
Sep 8 I went up to George's house with my brother. . . .
Sep 12 . . . very busy today canning peaches & house cleaning. . . .
Sep 17 There was a very disagreeable attack made upon me this morning by Edward and Sophia. I do not know why but a message came to me that George's baby was ill. I felt afraid that the paint had affected it. Edward said if the child died Amelia & the Merediths would say that the paint killed it. I said, every body would say it, & then they both turned upon me & said a good many disagreeable things which I had better not write down, but how much I wish I had a few hundreds a year. Yet I suppose there are those who would give me a comfortable home for the rest of my days if I would give them the

[285]Elizabeth's will, made in the 1820s, left her estate in equal parts to her four sons and, in the event of the death of any of them, in equal parts to the survivors. If all four predeceased her, the estate passed in equal parts to the granchildren then living. There were at one time seventeen grandchildren, but only one, Lucy, was alive when the grandmother, who had been in an asylum since 1849 in England, died in 1892.

house & what things that are mine within it when I died, but it would be only bitter necessity that will induce me to make such an arrangement, & the very necessity I think will kill me if it ever comes to pass. . . .

Sep 22 . . . The Bishop of Huron died this morning, he has been long ill. Mr Blackburn called to see if I knew any thing of him that could be mentioned in the obituary. I told him all that I know of Mr Cronyn's coming to the country.

Sep 24 . . . Edward & I went to the morning service. The Cathedral was draped in black out of respect for Dr Cronyn. . . .

Sep 28 . . . [Mr Becher] wants me to spend the winter in the Southern States, which I will endevor to do if I find myself suffering from the cold as I did last winter. . . .

Oct 4 I went to see a poor sick woman, Mrs Richmond, the mother of our servant boy, Willy & found her dying. She was very, very poor, but had seen better days. Her husband had kept a shoe shop & was very well off but was murdered & robbed, it was supposed by one of his workmen who became suddenly rich but there was no proof to convict him. Mrs Richmond was most anxious that I should take charge of Willy. I put him to a trade when he was 17 years of age. I will do what I can for the boy. . . .

Oct 25 . . . I have decided to spend a fortnight with Amelia & a fortnight with George and Lucy. . . .

Oct 28 I am getting slowly better. . . . There is a great scandal about Mr Hendman & Mrs Laidlaw. They were turned out of the hotel at Guelph. He is a respectable & wealthy man of business & she has worn a cloak of pity.

Nov 16 Thanksgiving day. Amelia went to morning service, I read the service in my room. . . . W. Meredith & Mrs Meredith came to dinner. We played whist.

Nov 24 . . . tomorrow I return home having spent a very pleasant fortnight. I shall find my own home lonely when I return as there are no children to enliven Eldon, yet it is my own home & I dearly love it. . . .

Dec 3 Edward went early to see Mr Carling. Miss Warren came from Church & spent the day here. Mr Griffin called, George & Lucy left for Chatham. . . .

Dec 6 All Edward's negotiations have come to naught & the Council have cancelled the agreement to sell the Port Stanley Rail Road stock. Edward is much disappointed. . . .

Dec 8 . . . The telegram this evening is that the Prince of Wales is dying, the announcement has shocked everyone. . . .

Dec 19 . . . The J. Sandfield Macdonald Ministry has been defeated today, & Mr [Edward] Blake will be called upon to form a Ministry. . . .

Dec 25 Christmas day. Edward & Sophia went to morning service. I read the service in my own room. Mr Griffin called & gave me a bottle of lavender water & gave Sophia a beautiful book of hymns illuminated. Amelia brought me a pair of partridges. Mr Becher & young Becher from Ottawa called. Mr Glass, Mr Dalton & Mr Millan & George & Edward played billiards. George, Lucy & Mrs Ronalds dined here. Charley Griffin called & so ends Christmas 1871. . . .

Dec 29 . . . Edward returned from Toronto in time for Sophia's party which commenced in music & ended with a dance. . . .

Dec 30 The Misses Daniel[286] returned to the Ladies School today. They are both nice girls with love affairs already upon their hands, as they are both engaged without their parents' knowledge. Harry Becher went in strong for Louisa Campbell last evening. He will get a nice wife if he gets her. . . .

Dec 31 Sophia went to morning service. Miss Campbell came home with her & spent the day here. She is one of the very nicest girls that I know. . . . The last evening of 1871, the year has been one of many blessings. I pray God to make me more thankful of His mercies.

1872

Jan 1 A lovely day. Edward & George both very busy about the Election of City Council Men. They wish to put in men who are in favor of leasing the Port Stanley R. Road to the Great Western. Most of the men whom they wished in have been elected but they were unable to keep out Mr Smith who is antagonistic to their views. Amongst the callers today there was only one old friend, that is Mr Becher, & he is almost one of the family . . . all [the rest] young people, most of them new people to me. I did not go into the drawing room to them. That old brute Mason used insulting language to Edward today & came so close to him that Edward struck him across the face. I do not know how Edward has borne so much from the old villain. . . .

Jan 2 I got a letter from Mr Portman, the first one for a year & a half. He sent a photo of Berkeley & Willy, they look fine handsome boys. . . .

[286]They had stayed overnight.

Jan 3 . . . [Mr Becher] has trouble with his girls. He got a bill today from Beattys for $350 for things bought by the girls since last July without his knowledge.

Jan 12 . . . Harry Becher called for the Misses Campbell & took them for a drive. I suspect his suit will have a favorable termination. He & Louisa Campbell are very happy together. He told me that his father knew about Florry's flirtation with Mr Furness & had put a stop to it.

Jan 15 Mr Walker has got up an oil company in England. Harris & McGee are appointed Solicitors. . . .

Jan 16 Conny Becher came this morning to tell me of Harry Becher's engagement to Kate Campbell. He is a lucky fellow. He gets the nicest girl I know for a wife, & she will have money also. . . .

Jan 17 I was startled, shocked & distressed this morning by seeing Florry Becher's marriage to Mr Furness in the paper. Mr Becher is in Toronto. It will be the severest blow he has ever had. Poor wrong headed girl. She little knows what she has done. She has made a run away match. . . .

Jan 18 . . . Conny called for a few minutes this morning. She told me her father was to be home this evening and that Kate Campbell was coming with him . . . she will do more than anyone else to soothe their outraged feelings at this time. . . .

Jan 20 . . . [Becher] very depressed and had remained away as long as he could. . . . he could not bear the thought of coming home & Florry gone. . . . This morning he came the back way to his office as he did not wish to see any one. Florry has not yet written a word to any one of them, nor asked her father's forgiveness. . . .

Jan 22 . . . Mr Becher came to see me. He is heart stricken. Seeing his anguish has made me ill. He is not vindictive towards Florry but he is utterly crushed. She wrote to him today, not a penitent letter but that if he would only forgive her it would make her *perfectly* happy. I like Mr Furness' letter better than hers. . . . Conny has come out well under this trial & is a great comfort to her father. . . . Mr Campbell has assented to [Harry's] marriage with his daughter but not until he has £400 a year. . . .

Feb 13 Since writing the above I have had a severe fit of illness. I was taken on the night of the 28th with cold chills, vomiting & bowel complaint. When the chills left, fever set in & continued for a week. Since then I have been getting better. Dr Woodruff attended me & every one has been most kind. Sophia has been a most kind & tender nurse, nursing me when she was scarcely able to be out of bed. Amelia spent nearly all her time here for the first week & has done all her loving heart would permit her to do for me, & Lucy has been most

kind. . . . I have had many kind inquiries since I have been ill & am now able to come downstairs. Heavy rain today which was much wanted & has nearly filled our empty cisterns. Edward hired a man today at 15 dollars a month & sent away the boy. . . .
Feb 21 Lucy called. Her trustees have increased her allowance to £200 a year which is a great thing for them, it was only £60 a year before. . . .
Mar 14 I walked on the verandah today, it is the first time that I have been outside of the door since early in November. . . .
Mar 23 . . . Elizabeth has lost her second child, Esther, four years & a half old. . . .
Mar 27 . . . I am overjoyed at the news that Eliza's letter contains. She and her daughter Carrie are coming to visit me. . . .
Apr 15 . . . Edward & Mr Walker went to see the Bishop. The Bishop wants their support at the Vestry tonight about building a Cathedral. Mr [Mc]Innes & Versy Cronyn have got up an opposition to the Bishop. . . . [George] goes to the Vestry tonight to support the Bishop. . . .
Apr 18 . . . I have finished reading Ld Campbell's *Lives of the Chancellors* & I have commenced Pepy's diary. . . .
Apr 25 . . . I went to town today to choose a paper for the pantry & an oil cloth . . . the paper hangers have come at last. I had a great many visitors today, Lucy came early. The Bishop called. . . . My bedrooom has had its spring purification today.
Apr 26 Went with Edward to get paper for the small drawing room. Dr Landor advised us not to put up the green we had bought as greens were poisonous. Lucy sat some time with me . . .
May 8 This morning Conny & Alice Becher came to say good bye, they leave for England tomorrow. Mr & Mrs Furness met them here. Mr Becher asked Florry to dine at Thornwood last evening but would not have Mr Furness. . . .
May 17 Mrs Furness spent the day here. She looks sad & out of spirits. Tomorrow Eliza & Carrie are to leave England. . . .
Jun 1 Eliza & Carrie have come at last to my great joy. I have been so excited today that I have been quite ill. Eliza, of course, looks older but she is the same dear old Eliza that she ever was, & Carrie looks what she is, a dear good girl. . . . Mr McInnes has been most kind to them. His agents have watched over them from N. York to London. He sent a Pullman car to Rochester expressly for them with a luncheon etc. . . . Edward went to the Clifton to meet them. Sophia has been most kind . . . Amelia, Mr Griffin, George & Lucy were here to meet them. . . . An old friend of ours, John Sandfield Macdonald died

today. He has been a long time in indifferent health & he has overworked himself in the public service.

Jun 5 Eliza & I walked the verandah all the morning. The foundation stone of the new Cathedral was laid today.[287] Yesterday the Honble John Sandfield Macdonald was buried. He was a leading man in politics for over thirty years. Over two thousand carriages followed him to the grave. He leaves about the same number of friends that political men usually leave. His private friends are many. For thirty five years we have been friends. . . .

Jun 6 Eliza & I spent our time talking. It is such a pleasure to have a child back again after so many years. . . .

Jun 21 Not well & have trouble with our servants. The cook has given notice today & I do not know where to get another. . . .

Jun 26 Edward, Sophia, Eliza & Carrie left at 12.30 for Detroit. . . .

Jun 28 The Eldon party returned home at midnight very tired & hungry. They enjoyed their trip to Detroit pretty well. . . . The Great Western people have invited all the Eldon House party to go to the Falls for two or three days. The English Directors of the Great Western are to be entertained there before leaving for England. . . .

Jul 3 Edward & Sophia returned last night or rather this morning at 4 AM. They, the Crutchleys & Amelia dined at the Plumb's yesterday, & Edward & Sophia came home by the night train. The others returned this evening. . . . The Great Western Directors paid all expenses until Monday noon. . . .

Jul 16 There is to be a great political meeting tonight. Sir John A. Macdonald & Sir Francis Hincks are here. Sir Francis called to see me. . . .

Jul 21 . . . Eliza thinks very highly of Lucy & thinks George most fortunate in getting such a wife and I agree with her. Eliza thinks Edward has no faults. . . .

Jul 30 . . . I am getting a nice tombstone for Mr Harris' grave.[288] It is to be placed over the grave tomorrow. Mrs Ronalds called. Mr Griffin came to croquet. . . .

Aug 2 Their visit is over. Eliza & Carrie are gone & I shall see them no more. It has been a wonderful joy to me having them here & Edward has done every thing in his power to make their visit pleasant.

[287]According to Orlo Miller, *Gargoyles and Gentlemen*, (p. 118) the cornerstone of Holy Trinity was laid on 6 June 1872. Actually, it was the cornerstone of the Chapter House, which was later to be joined to the Cathedral by a cloister, and which was officially opened 2 November 1873 at a cost of $27,000.

[288]The father, John Harris.

Mr Griffin goes with them to Quebec & then will see them on board the train at Montreal for Boston. . . . Edward went as far as Hamilton with them. . . .

Aug 8 Dr Landor came for me & I spent the day at his house. I was glad to see them so comfortably situated & looking so happy. They were so very poor before he got the appointment of Superintendant of the Lunatic Asylum. I used all the influence that I possessed with my friends in power to get the appointment for him. Went to the Asylum & through several wards. It is painful to see so many poor creatures bereft of reason. They seem to be well cared for but the most of them have a very unhappy look. . . .

Aug 10 . . . Lucy returned from Sarnia with her poor sick child. The doctors say that her brain is affected & that she will never be better. . . . Mr W. Meredith has the nomination for the local Parliament. There is a good deal of dissatisfaction about it. It is thought & said that Mr Walker[289] has not had quite fair play.

Aug 16 . . . Mrs Ronalds worse. All hope of her recovery given up. The priests have been with her, annointed her & I believe have given her extreme unction. She has always been a dear, kind, affectionate, self sacrificing woman & beloved by all who knew her. Her brother was telegraphed for & has come. Amelia & Sophia have been with Lucy all day & will remain until all is over. . . .

Aug 17 Mrs Ronalds died at 9.40 last night. Lucy is in great distress. . . . Mrs Ronalds is to be buried at Sandwich in the R. Catholic burying ground where all her departed relatives are buried. Edward went up this evening with the body. The funeral is to take place tomorrow. It was thought best that George should remain with Lucy & try to comfort her. . . .

Aug 19 Edward came home at noon after having seen poor Mrs Ronalds in her last resting place. They are to have high mass in the Church at Windsor tomorrow for the repose of her soul. The prayers of the righteous avail much but it must be before death as the tree falleth so it will remain. I have no faith in the R. Catholic religion. Father B. impressed upon Mrs Ronalds just before her death that her not having made her daughter Lucy a R. Catholic might exclude her from heaven. What a power those priests have & how unscrupulously they use it. . . .

[289]John Walker (1832–89) came to London in 1867 where he became involved in manufacturing and the oil refining industry. He was elected M.P. for London in 1874, but the election was declared void as a result of Walker's electioneering tactics. He was declared ineligible to contest the by-election, and was defeated in the election of 1878.

Aug 20 . . . Lucy is looking over her mother's trunk today. Found $2,500. Mrs Ronalds requested Lucy to give to Mrs Ronalds' mother $200 & $100 to each of her sisters & brother & $50 to each of her 4 God children. . . .
Aug 23 . . . Edward went to Toronto to see a celebrated doctor for curing deafness & Edward has hope that he may yet recover his hearing.
Aug 26 . . . The election for Ontario came off. Mr [W.R.] Meredith & Mr [James] Durrand were the candidates. Mr Meredith was returned. Mr [John] Walker ought to have been the Member but Mr [John] Carling tricked him out of it. The Bishop, the Honble Dr Tupper[290] & Mr Walker lunched here. The Bishop expressed himself very strongly about Mr Walker's having withdrawn.
Aug 28 The Honble Dr Tupper called. He is to return here this evening & remain all night. . . .
Aug 30 Mr [David] Glass is elected & at this moment he is the happiest & the vainest man in the Dominion. Sophia called at the Carlings. . . . George & Lucy left for Windsor this morning. . . .
Aug 31 . . . Edward and Sophia have gone to Toronto. Edward to see the doctor about his deafness. . . .
Sep 7 . . . Tom Street died yesterday.[291] . . .
Sep 19 Harry Becher is married today to Kate Campbell of Simcoe. The Becher family are delighted with the match. . . .
Sep 25 Edward left at 12 noon for Toronto, it is his last visit to the aurist & he goes to a ball at Government House. Tonight the Governor General, Lord Dufferin & Lady Dufferin are to be there. . . .
Sep 28 . . . I wanted Sophia to ask Amelia & Mr Griffin to dinner today. She positively refused to do so but said I might invite them which I did, but I feel *hurt* to see with what unwillingness any of my children are ever received here in my own house but I am dependent & must bear & forebear during the rest of my life. . . .
Oct 8 I wrote last night in the bitterness of my heart, & this morning I tore it out. Why should I have a record of what pains me?[292] . . .
Oct 10 Lord & Lady Dufferin & suite arrived today & went to the Exhibition & then to the Ladies School & [Hellmuth] College. Mr

[290]Sir Charles Tupper (1821–1915), physician and Father of Confederation, represented Cumberland in the Nova Scotia Legislative Assembly (1855–67), became the Prime Minister of that province (1864–67), and Prime Minister of Canada in 1896.

[291]Thomas Street (1814–72), lawyer, businessman, and represented Welland in the Union Parliament (1851–54, 1861–67) and House of Commons (1867–72). On his death, he left an estate estimated at $3 to $4 million.

[292]Several preceding entries have been removed from the diary.

Carling & Mr Walker, Edward & others went with them. They are the guests of the City & the City is very jealous of any interference with their visitors. We wished to ask Ld & Lady Dufferin here to stay but found it would not do even to ask them to dinner. There were some arches erected of a very indifferent sort but there was some very fine fireworks tonight & a torch light procession & there is a ball tonight. Edward & Sophia have gone to it. . . .

Oct 11 Edward & Sophia did not enjoy the ball very much. There is a new set who pushed themselves forward, who a few years ago were tailors & soap boilers but now they wish to take the lead. . . .

Oct 22 I have been very busy today seeing to the house cleaning & looking after the apples for winter stock & sending some to Amelia & George. . . .

Nov 13 . . . The Honble Mr Tupper & son came to visit us.[293] . . .

Nov 22 . . . The Scotts left England on the 7th for Egypt. . . .

Nov 25 . . . Edward came into my bedroom with the morning paper, announcing Mrs Askin's death. My poor, dear old friend died yesterday morning. . . . She died at Chatham at her sister's. . . .

Nov 27 Mrs Askin was buried today. . . . Edward & George were pall bearers. We were attached friends as girls & have remained so through life. Dear old lady, we shall not be very long apart. . . .

Dec 7 . . . The North Shore Transportation Company have voted Edward $1,500 for his services as President of the Company. Very handsome of them.

Dec 9 . . . George left early to go canvassing for voters as he has been induced to offer himself as Councilman. . . .

Dec 25 . . . George, Lucy, Mr Griffin, Amelia & Mr Becher called. George & Edward played billiards. . . . I thought our Christmas brighter than usual, yet pleasing and painful. Thoughts come to me as I come to my own room. Eliza's visit was a great pleasure, Mrs Askin's unhappy death a pain. Shall I never see another Christmas?

Dec 31 . . . 1872 is nearly at an end & I am still here. My old friend Mrs Askin has passed away. God give me a humble trusting faith & that I may be ready & willing to go when the call comes.

1873

Jan 1 We have had very few visitors today, only Mr Walker, Mr Griffin, Harry & Frank Becher & Dick Brough. Amelia called. George & Lucy come this evening. . . .

[293]They remained until the 18th November.

Jan 6 I got a nice long letter from Teresa from Cairo. . . . Today the election for Aldermen came off. George did not get in.[294] The people will not return a gentleman. . . .
Jan 8 . . . Edward wished me to enter into my journal that the port & sherry wine that he got last summer from Smith was not good. The sherry tasted of the cork & the port was generally condemned. . . .
Jan 22 . . . The first train on the Loop Line ran to Simcoe yesterday. The railroad will make a great change in the Long Point country. . . .
Feb 2 . . . Mr & Mrs Walker . . . came to tea after evening service. The Walkers looked very happy. Mr Walker feels that being Vice President of the Pacific Railroad not only gives him a good position but will enable him most probably to become a millionaire. . . .
Feb 6 . . . Amelia Harris [Milly] spent the day with me. She is a dear little chatter box. . . .
Feb 15 I had letters from Mary, Eliza & Teresa. Teresa had arrived at Thebes. . . . I heard from Sophia also. She cannot understand why it is that Mr Thomas has not called to see her. Mr Walker thinks as I do that he is afraid to go. His wife does not like Sophia. . . .
Feb 20 . . . [Lucy] gave me the pleasing intelligence that she is again to become a mother. . . .
Feb 21 . . . Bella tells me that Port Hope Annie has a proposal from a *very rich* American, a millionaire in fact, & a highly respectable worthy man. I should think she had better accept without hesitation. I wish Bella & Mr Griffin would give up walking together. People say such horrible things about them. . . .
Mar 7 . . . George Peard[295] has got a Commission in the First Royals.
Mar 8 I saw in the papers today that Elizabeth has lost both her children. I feel sorry for her. . . .
Mar 10 . . . Mr Becher came to luncheon. We advised him to marry & asked him why he did not try for Miss Gordon, a young lady of 40 or more, & said to have £2,000 a year. I should not be surprised if he did try for her. . . .

[294]There were four candidates for the three alderman seats in Ward 2 for 1873: S. McBride, who received 314 votes, Thomas Beattie, 299, Smyth, 267, George Harris, 235. All addressed the electors after the closing of the poll. Smyth, who narrowly defeated Harris for the last position, identified himself as a "True Reformer." Harris remarked that "although the defeated candidate at the present time, owing to his tardiness in consenting to run, he would offer in good time next year and had not the slightest doubt but that he would be returned at the head of the poll." *London Free Press*, 7 January 1873. He did not let his name stand in 1874.

[295]Son of Shuldham and Mary.

Mar 18 . . . Peters[296] came about the plans for the new billiard room & kitchen. The plans were approved of. I intended to remain in the house with one servant during the alterations but this is objected to by Edward & Sophia & I shall have to turn out much against my will. I would willingly have put up with any inconvenience rather than have left my home even for a month, but to go out for three or four months I feel as I shall never come back.
Mar 29 . . . Lord Carnwath is dead. The title is almost certain to come to my grandson as there are only two old men without sons between Robert Dalzell & the title.
Apr 17 . . . I have done a little gardening. . . . Sophia went to see Lucy, little Amelia is here for the night.
Apr 19 . . . Mr Becher called. He had a letter from his sister in law about sending me a cook. I am to send money (£15) to pay the passage out & am to keep it out of her wages. She will come out immediately. I am very glad for we do not know where to get a cook. . . .
May 12 Sophia left . . . for Toronto. The cook wishes to leave at once & it may be a month before the one arrives from England. I do not know how to manage as we expect visitors. I tried hard to persuade her to stay for another month. . . .
May 15 . . . Brickmakers arrived from England & are to work for Edward at Port Ryerse. Eliza sent them out. The cook has got over her tantrums & says she will stay as long as I want her. . . .
May 21 Edward returned from Ryerse. He found his English brickmaker & family settled & apparently contented. . . . Our English cook is to leave England tomorrow & will be here about the 2nd of June. . . .
May 31 I went to the Griffins . . . then went on to see Lucy who keeps very well. Her house is looking so very nice, she seems to have every comfort about her. . . .
Jun 4 Dr Ryerson arrived last night after I was in bed. He is looking wonderfully well. . . .
Jun 6 Our cook from England arrived today. . . .
Jun 7 Our new cook who is not a very good cook feels discouraged & is sorry she left England. . . .
Jun 11 George came at 7 AM to tell us that Lucy had just given birth to a boy. The child was born at half past six AM. Lucy is going on well. . . .

[296]Samuel Peters, a prominent London architect, was responsible for the major renovations at Eldon House in 1877.

Jun 21 My first news this morning was that George's house had been entered & all or nearly all their plate stolen, worth from $800 to 1,000 dollars. George was [away] from home. Mr [George] MacNab, one of Edward's partners, slept there. Lucy ill in bed. The nurse & servant girls were moving about the house until twelve o'clock. Lucy was very wakeful & the nurse was up two or three times during the night, yet they heard nothing & the little dog who is very wakeful did not bark. The police suspect the servant girls, who are sisters. The plate ought to have been taken to Lucy's room & was not. A reward of $200 has been offered for the discovery of the thief. . . .
Jul 1 Mr Bowman[297] called early this morning, his face beaming with pleasure to tell us that George's plate was at Cleveland. A detective had taken possession of two or three hundred dollars worth and knew where there was more of it. George telegraphed to them to keep the man whom they had arrested & that he would go there today. He has gone to identify the plate. Our new cook came today, I hope she may prove satisfactory. Florry Furness came to luncheon. . . .
Jul 4 George returned from Cleveland. He has left a man in jail there who calls himself Stanley. He had $190 dollars worth of his plate in his possession. He could not discover the rest of the plate. It is doubtful whether he can do any thing with the man. He says that he bought the plate at Fort Erie & it will be difficult to prove to the contrary. . . .
Jul 10 . . . Sarah Hawkins that was taken up being suspected of the robbery at George's is committed for trial. The rest of the family are discharged. George A., Mr Campbell & wife are here for billiards.
Jul 26 . . . Lucy asked me to be God mother to their son. I advised a younger person but she was so urgent that I consented to stand. . . .
Jul 29 George's boy was christened today by the Revnd Dean Boomer. Name George Henry Ronalds. Sponsors Mr Walker, Edward, & myself. The guests were Mr & Mrs Boomer, the Griffins, Edward, Sophia & myself. Miss Askin is on a visit to the Georges; the baby is an uncommon fine child.
Jul 30 I got letters from Eliza & Mary & Carrie [Crutchley].[298] They are so exultant that the Harrow 11 have beaten the Eaton boys at cricket. Percy Crutchley made the second best score amongst the Harrow boys. It seems strange to me that there can be so much rejoicing over a game of cricket. . . .
Aug 22 Mr Becher paid us a long visit. We want him after a reason-

[297]A local policeman.
[298]These letters are in the Harris Papers.

able time to propose for Mrs Robinson & see if she will accept him as a fourth husband. He is inclined to do so as she has between six & eight hundred thousand dollars of her own. . . .
Aug 28 . . . Edward Blake called, . . . Old Edward Blake holds a Radical meeting at the City Hall tonight. I do not like his politics.
Sep 1 Engaged a cook & hope she may prove satisfactory. . . .
Sep 8 Barnum's Grand Show. Thousands of people have come in from the country to see it. Edward & Sophia went this morning. The smell of the animals made Sophia ill. She has not yet got over it. . . .
Sep 13 . . . I had a letter from Sarah. Her son Robert was married on the 19th of August to Miss Emily [Hippesley]. Her father is rich & has settled £600 a year upon them. They all seem pleased with the match, though Robert is poor. Even when he inherits the Earldom he will still be poor. . . .
Sep 15 . . . Mr Becher called. He is very anxious to sell his place & wishes Mr Walker to buy it, but Mr Walker declines. . . .
Oct 2 . . . I called at the cemetery. I have had the ground about Mr Harris & Helen's grave made level & sodded & Helen's tombstone cleaned. . . .
Oct 9 Our new cook came today. I hope she may be a success. . . .
Oct 26 . . . Dr Anderson is very ill, not expected to live. I proposed sending to inquire but Edward thought that he had behaved so shamefully towards us all & to me in particular[299] that I ought not to notice him. But as I have forgiven him & every one else all the evil they have ever done me & as there has never been any unkind feeling between Mrs Anderson [and myself], I sent over quietly in the time of her trouble to ask after her husband. She sent her love to me & thanked me for sending & said that her husband was very, very ill. I felt glad that I had sent, that he might know that I had forgiven him as I hope to be forgiven. Mr & Mrs Walker, George & Lucy came to heavy tea.
Nov 1 . . . The Montgomeries dine at George's & Edward & Sophia dine at the Bishop's where there are a large party of clergymen staying there. . . .
Nov 3 I have been quite ill all day. Mr Becher came to luncheon. The Bishop of Huron & Mrs Hellmuth, the Bishop of Quebec & Mrs Williams, the Bishop of Ontario & Mrs Lewis, Mrs H. Becher & Amelia came to afternoon tea. [Others] spent the evening. I shall not go down to the drawing room. I feel too unwell.

[299]A reference to Helen's death in 1860.

Nov 6 Thanksgiving Day. Sophia went to the Chapter House service. Mr Becher & Amelia called. Edward lunched at the Walker's, he & Sophia have gone to dinner at the Bishop's & then go to the Ladies School. . . . I wrote to Eliza.
Nov 8 Sophia has been very busy all day preparing for her dinner party tonight . . . [list of guests]. The dinner was good, & the attendance was good. . . .
Nov 15 . . . The workman finished putting up the furnace today & it seems a great success. The house is almost too warm. Sophia had a luncheon party today . . . [list of guests].
Nov 22 . . . Mr Becher lunched with me. He & Conny leave for England on the 3rd. He seemed rather out of sorts. Lucy & children spent the afternoon with me. I was so glad to have them with me & to see Baby. He is such a fine boy. . . . The day has passed pleasantly with me, I have felt better & have not been so much alone.
Dec 2 . . . The paper for the dining room came. It is not nearly as handsome as the paper that was on the room, but it appears that red paper has gone out of fashion & there is none to be had. . . .
Dec 4 Last night there was almost a hurricane with very heavy rain. This morning there was a flood, the waters are as high as they have ever been known. The wind has done much damage, several buildings are blown down. . . .
Dec 11 Dr Anderson was buried yesterday. He received extreme unction & absolution from the priests & was attended & prayed with by the Rev Mr Scott of the Scotch Church & said that he was going to join them. The Rev Mr Scott & the Rev Mr Innes both attended his funeral. . . . The bells were tolled at both the Episcopal & the R. C. Churches. The whole ceremony seemed very uncommon.
Dec 24 . . . Lucy sent me such a quantity of paper & envelopes, enough to last me the rest of my days & Mr Walker has given me such a beautiful edition of *Plutarch's Lives* in 5 volumes, a magnificent present & Sophia has given me a very pretty lace pocket handkerchief. . . .
Dec 25 Christmas Day & I am still here. I wish I could feel more humble & thankful for my many blessings. I wish I could serve God with all my heart, all my soul & all my strength, each night I feel my own unworthiness & how far I fall short of the true Christian I wish to be. . . .
Dec 31 Mrs Cunningham called to say good bye, they leave London today not to return. His employment as Engineer has collapsed with the Huron & Bruce Rail Road. Mr Griffin & Amelia called, Dr Ryerson returned home. Mr Walker & Edward have gone to a political

meeting, there is to be a dissolution & a new election & now politics is the all engrossing subject . . . & so ends 1873. What will the next year bring forth. I pray God to bless and keep us from every sin & enable us to do what is right in His sight.

1874

Jan 1 Sophia made ready for visitors who did not come. In former years the house used to be crowded all New Year's day but now there are no young people here to attract the present youthful generation & the older visitors are either too old to visit or are gone to another world. Mr Phillips is our only New Year's visitor for 1874. Mr Walker, Mr Griffin & George can scarcely be counted as they are daily visitors. . . . I wrote to Mary.
Jan 2 . . . The town is all excitement about the election. Mr Walker is coming out to oppose Mr Carling. . . . Amelia called & Lucy, Edward, George and Mr Walker have gone to an election caucus.
Jan 5 The Municipal election took place today, all is excitement. Mr Walker's coming out as a candidate is causing a great deal of hard feeling & abuse. Mr Carling is a strong man & there will be hard fighting. . . .
Jan 6 . . . At the election meeting last night Mr Walker made a speech approving of Mr Glass & said he should give him his support.[300] I do not . . . see how any man of honor can approve of Mr Glass' political conduct. Edward made a speech last night & spoke of Mr Carling in a way that I highly disapprove of. . . .
Jan 8 . . . I have a great dislike to elections of all [sorts]. I have a dislike to courting the mob. . . .
Jan 11 . . . Mr & Mrs Walker, George, Lucy & Edward Blake came to tea & spent the evening here. Edward Blake is a good deal changed. His mind is absorbed in politics but my regard for him is quite independent of all wordly doings or prospects.
Jan 13 Elections, elections, I hear nothing but elections. . . .
Jan 17 . . . The election fever is unabated.
Jan 20 Mrs Harry Becher confined this morning after a very severe labour. The child taken with instruments, but is like to live, is a boy. . . . Bella bet six pairs of gloves to one that Mr Carling will be returned by a majority of one hundred. . . .

[300]David Glass was twice elected Mayor of London. He was M.P. for Middlesex (1872–74), M.L.A. for St. Clements, Manitoba (1886–88), and Speaker of the Manitoba Assembly (1887–88).

Jan 21 . . . [James] Magee[301] is here getting ready some election articles against Mr Carling. Mrs Walker called today looking as placid as if her husband was not all excitement in an election contest.
Jan 22 We are having another flood. This is the third one this winter. I have lived in London nearly forty year & this is the first time such a thing has occurred. . . .
Jan 25 . . . George & Lucy came to afternoon tea. Mr & Mrs [F.H.] Cumberland,[302] Mr & Mrs Walker, Archie Campbell & Wife & Mr Geddes came to heavy tea. Amelia called. We have people here too often on Sunday. I do not think it right to keep servants at work, *extra* work on Sunday.
Jan 28 . . . The election excitement continues. Mr Meredith asserts that Edward told something about Mr Walker which Edward in today's paper positively denies. Party feeling is very high. . . .
Jan 29 The election came off today. Mr Walker is returned by a majority of 62. Mr Carling's defeat is most unexpected by himself & supporters. There has never been so much excitement at any previous election in London. Mr Glass is defeated also in the East Riding of Middlesex. Sophia, Mrs Walker & several other ladies spent the day at Edward's office where they could get a good look at the voters. Amelia called & Lucy spent the afternoon with me. . . . Harry Becher early in the day made some offensive remarks & was knocked down & his eyes blackened. He was driving about the streets afterwards with his head bandaged. Mr Magee & Mr Geoffrey[303] are here.
Feb 4 . . . Lucy spent the evening here. I had a letter from Elizabeth.
Feb 5 . . . Mrs Anderson called. It is 15 or 16 years since I have seen her as Doctor Anderson & myself were not friends but there was no unkind feeling between Mrs Anderson & me. She justified my coolness with her husband but said she could not prevent Doctor Anderson's doing what he did. Mr Walker has gone with Sophia to meet Mrs Ryerson at the station. Sophia ought to have declined his escort. I am sure it is not pleasing to Mrs Walker.
Feb 9 Mrs Ryerson & Sophia went to Lucy's to luncheon. . . . Mr Geddes called. Sophia played accompaniment to his songs. . . .
Feb 10 Sophia very busy all day arranging about their dinner party. . . .

[301]Edward's partner. See Amelia's diary, 3 December 1865.
[302]A Toronto architect.
[303]Joseph Jeffery (1829–94), whose name Amelia variously spelled as Jeoffrey and Geoffrey, was one of the founders, along with Edward Harris, of the London Life Insurance Co. He is hereafter rendered in this text as Jeffery.

Feb 23 . . . I am alone, but my happiest evenings are when I am alone, then all is peace. I can live in the past & can hope for a future where the weary are at rest. Oh God bless my children & pardon all their sins. . . . & pardon all my sins & receive me into Thy Kingdom for My Saviour's sake.
Feb 27 . . . Sophia has a tea party tonight. . . . I thought the evening very stupid.
Feb 28 It has been an unpleasant day to me. Edward is in trouble & out of humour. Amelia came twice to see me. What should I do without her.
Mar 3 . . . Angus and Mary were married tonight. They went to Mr Scott's parsonage with the grooms man and brides maid, were married & then returned here to supper & have separate rooms here tonight & go to their own home tomorrow. They are both very happy & full of hope. Here they have lived in plenty without care. Now they will find a change when they have to pay their rent & supply all their wants out of 24 dollars a month.
Mar 9 . . . George came in the morning & we had a long talk about money matters which has made me ill. . . .
Mar 12 . . . Amelia called, it is little Teresa's birthday, she is five years old today. . . . I have heard some very painful domestic news today. It appears that every day brings me some new trouble.
Mar 16 Edward's birthday, 42 years old today. . . . Sophia had a tea party, this evening. . . .
Mar 17 We have not had a solitary visitor today. . . .
Mar 19 Mr Bridges came today about laying our grounds in front of the house. . . .
Mar 20 Contracted with Mr Bridges to lay out the grounds, make or rather newly arrange flower beds & transplant roots & shrubs & sod between the beds. . . .
Apr 7 Busy white liming the ceilings. Mr Griffin & Amelia called, Lucy came to dinner. . . .
Apr 17 Mr Becher, Conny & Fanny Grant called.[304] Mr Becher looks ill. They had such a rough passage coming out of 19 days & were very nearly lost. They saw nothing of the Scotts or Crutchleys & feel hurt that neither of them called or invited them to their houses & Eliza feels hurt that they did not call to see her. . . .
May 2 . . . Bella walked as far as the gate but would not come in. She is offended with Edward about the election. Our house maid Kate left

[304]They had been on an extended visit to England.

us today without saying good bye. She has a vile temper & will never stay long in any place. . . .

May 10 . . . The first time I have been outside of the gate for 8 months. . . .

May 12 I have been busy all day & my looking after things & lending a helping hand offends both Edward & Sophia though Sophia is not well & *never* looks after any thing in the kitchen or garret or cellar or back premises. She attends to the marketing, orders dinner & looks after the front part of the house & is very fond of entertaining her own friends. I dislike waste & cannot bear to see so much without making a little effort to prevent it in some degree. . . . It is a great misfortune for a widowed mother to have to live with her married children. It is often misery to both parties. I have felt half crazed all day & went to bed at 8 PM. . . .

May 15 . . . I got a telegram from the Scotts to say that they will be here at 6 AM tomorrow. I hope they will cheer us all up. . . .

May 16 Mr Scott & Teresa arrived at six this morning looking not changed or older than when they left here seven years ago. We are so glad to have them with us once more. They have brought us all such handsome presents, to myself a beautiful black velvet dress, a joint present from Eliza & Teresa, a very handsome gold ornamental cross for Sophia . . . a locket & charms for little Teresa [Griffin] and pretty sashes & Mr Scott gave Scotty [Griffin] a silver watch. They gave Lucy a pretty travelling clock. . . .

Jun 6 Mr Becher came to luncheon. We had a long talk about Mrs Robinson. He will I think propose for her. . . .

Jun 16 . . . Mr Becher came to luncheon. He says now that he will not sell Thornwood. He, I think, must be contemplating matrimony. . . .

Jun 17 Sophia went for a drive with Mr Walker, which I think very unwise. . . .

Jun 20 . . . Mr [R.M.] Wells[305] told us that Mr Plumb is engaged to Miss Reynolds of Ottawa. She is a young lady of 25 & he must be near 55. Miss Reynolds is said to be a very nice girl but she must be nice indeed if she is ever to equal the late Mrs Plumb. . . .

Jun 24 . . . Mr Walker came in for a few minutes this evening & made a bare faced excuse to follow Sophia out for a few minutes. . . .

Jun 26 I never feel well any more. Without any particular disease, I am always ailing. Mr Walker took Mr Scott for a drive, Lucy & Amelia were here to afternoon tea. . . .

[305] A Toronto visitor.

Jun 27 59 years today since I was married & I have been nearly 24 years a widow. . . . [Becher] is in a great state of delight. Captain Becher in England [a cousin] has just written to him asking leave to propose for Conny. As it is a match in every way satisfactory he has given his consent & I do not think that Conny will withhold. . . .
Jun 30 I had a letter from Sarah today giving me a very pleasing piece of intelligence. Her daughter Mary is to be married the first week in August to Major [Thomas] Leith, a Scotch gentleman with an estate of £5,000 a year & will eventually have 9 or 10 thousand a year. He is well connected, highly respectable & in every way a good & desirable match. Sarah & indeed all the connection are highly pleased. Teresa & Amelia returned calls. . . .
Jul 3 . . . Dr Landor called. Miss Warren has been replaced as Matron of the Lunatic Asylum. She is to retain half her salary (two hundred dollars a year) & live at the Asylum, to keep her present room & have her mother with her. It is not probable that she will live longer than a few months & then what is to become of her mother who is without money or friends to assist her. . . .
Jul 12 . . . Teresa told [Gilbert] Griffin that he ought to contribute something to enable Amelia to go to the sea shore with Scotty & he said he would give 50 or 100 dollars toward their expenses & go with them to Portland [Maine] & see them established at some cheap good place for bathing. . . .
Jul 13 There has been a great gathering of Orangemen today, a thousand came from Cleveland & their brethren met them here & they have paraded & made speeches, & they have a ball tonight. . . .
Jul 16 Mr Becher called, he sails for England on the 25th. Conny goes with him. He goes to propose for Mrs Robinson & to be married if she accepts him & Conny to be married to Capt Becher of the [East] India Company Service. . . .
Jul 17 Mr Becher has most kindly given Amelia fifty dollars toward her expenses going to the sea shore & Bishop Hellmuth has given a letter to the Bishop of Maine asking them to show every attention in his power. . . . Mary Peard doubts the marriage of Mary Dalzell taking place. Col Dalzell & Sarah are most foolishly making a difficulty about the settlement which is most liberal, it sounds like madness to me on the part of the Dalzells.
Jul 24 . . . Major Leith has been most liberal. She has £500 a year pin money & twelve hundred a year & a . . . house to live in should she be left a widow. . . .
Jul 28 I got a letter from Eliza, Mary Dalzell was to be married today, we have all reason to rejoice that she is making such a good match. . . .

Aug 1 . . . J.H. Plumb is apparently one of the happiest men I have ever seen. He is pleased with himself & all his children & has much cause to be content for his children are clever & good, & I hope they will remain so, but as yet they are untried by the world. Mr Walker has a dinner party tonight, Mr Plumb, the Scotts, the Edwards, Mr Griffin & the Georges dine there. . . .
Aug 4 I had letters from Mary Peard & Mary Dalzell. The Dalzell family have been most generous upon the occasion of Mary's marriage. Lady Emma gave £300 towards the trousseau, Lord Carnwath gave the wedding breakfast & the Hon Col Harry Dalzell gave £80 toward the lace wedding dress. I am so glad. . . .
Aug 24 The Scott's visit is over. It commenced with months, then weeks, days, hours & minutes & now they are gone. It is a great trial parting with them, it is not probable that I shall ever see them again. I am now well on in my 77th year & they have gone for a trip around the world. They go to San Francisco, then to Japan, China, India visiting all places of note & will not return to England for nearly two years & will not again visit Canada for some years after their return. . . .
Aug 27 . . . About 1 o'clock this morning Mary & Emily [servants] were just done washing up in the pantry when in walked a drunken man. They were very much frightened & ran to Edward's room. Sophia put on her dressing gown, went downstairs without alarming any one & took the man by the arm & marched him out of the house. She certainly showed a good deal of courage. . . . I had a letter from Mr Becher today telling me that he would be married to Mrs Robinson before I received his letter. I am very glad for I think he has a nice wife & will be happy with her. His daughters like her & she is rich. Mr Plumb says she is worth £160,000. . . .
Sep 8 . . . The election trial is still going on. There is no doubt but Mr Walker will lose his seat & it is possible that he may be disqualified from offering for reelection until there is a new Parliament. There is no doubt that there was a great deal of money spent to procure his return. . . .
Sep 10 Mr Walker has lost his seat but is not disqualified for running again. He called today in great spirits. He feels quite sure of his reelection. . . .
Sep 11 . . . [Edward] gets a great deal of condemnation for advancing money for Mr Walker's election. I wish he had not done it. . . .
Sep 15 . . . The household has been busy today preserving & canning peaches. . . .
Oct 17 I got a note this morning from Amelia telling me that Teresa has scarlet fever. I went as soon as I could to see her. Mr Griffin

thought I had better not go in to the room where the child was. Sophia is so afraid of the infection. . . .
Oct 18 My first communication this morning from Amelia was that Doctor Woodruff had been called in, that Dr Brown had been there all night & that the child's life was despaired of. Another note at 1 o'clock saying there was little hope. At 7 o'clock in the evening the child died. Poor Amelia my heart aches for her. . . .
Oct 19 Amelia's birthday. What a sad day to her, her little darling lying dead & the sun shining so bright, it ought to be all gloom, to suit our feelings. . . . Dr Ryerson wrote a letter of condolence to Amelia . . . I wrote to Eliza.
Oct 21 . . . After the child was buried yesterday, Mr Griffin asked the man who has charge of the cemetery to rake off the little plot of ground which had been disturbed by digging the grave & make it look tidy as he should bring Mrs Griffin up before dark to see the grave. When Amelia went there she was so surprised to see the little grave all surrounded with pretty flowers. The man had brought from his green house many pots in bloom & foliage plants & sank the pots in the earth & every thing looked so pretty & bright. A perfect little flower garden, & it was the poor man's own kind heart that prompted the delicate act. Amelia feels that she can never forget it while she lives. Scott who has been staying with Mrs Hammond since his sister's death has returned home & his presence cheers his father & mother a little. . . .
Oct 22 Mrs Ryerson returned to Toronto at 1 PM. She found Eldon too dull with only poor stupid me here. . . .
Nov 11 Edward & Sophia packed up to go to Toronto today but could not go as Edward is detained as a witness in George's trial which is to come off tomorrow. He is prosecuted by the servant that was in the house when his plate was stolen. He suspects her of being concerned in the robbery & had her arrested but could not bring sufficient proof to have her convicted & now she brings a suit for malicious arrest. . . .
Nov 14 . . . Miss Hawkins who brought the suit for damages against George was non suited much to our relief, Mr Rock[306] was in hopes of getting damages. . . .
Nov 23 Edward's conversation with me this morning was not very pleasant. I try my best not to think of it. Each day I feel any tie I have in this world lessening. I am afraid to write what I feel lest I should feel sorry for it afterwards. . . .

[306]Miss Hawkins' lawyer.

Dec 8 . . . Mr Walker comes every afternoon for an hour to play billiards with Edward. . . .
Dec 9 What a dull place this world is to me. How I wish to leave it. Oh great God give me humble submission to Thy will in all things. . . .
Dec 11 . . . Dr Ryerson arrived at 6 PM. We had a scratch sort of dinner as our cook is drunk. Edward ordered her off tonight, but we persuaded him to let her remain until morning. She is a bad one. I feel sorry for her son who seems a good boy.
Dec 12 Dr Ryerson & I had a long religious conversation this morning. It was what I very much wished for. . . .
Dec 15 George's children have scarlet fever, both Amelia & Ronald. Charlotte has come to us. She as yet shows no symptoms of it. The attack as yet is mild but we are all in a great fright for the disease in the City is so malignant. So many children have died & George has never had it. . . .
Dec 22 I had a letter from Mr Townsend enclosing photos of his three eldest children. . . . [He] is very anxious that Amelia should visit them but she cannot afford the money required. . . .
Dec 25 Another Christmas has passed & I am still here. . . .
Dec 28 . . . The fever is very malignant in many places. We hear of deaths almost every day. Mr Holmes of the Great Western has lost four children in two weeks. . . . Charlotte is going on well, the fever is very mild. . . .
Dec 31 This day has not been a pleasant one to me. There is trouble about business between Edward & George & their troubles are mine. . . . George & I had a long talk in the library.

1875

Jan 1 I am not well today. I am so worried about affairs over which I have no control. I cannot say that I have spent a happy new year. We have had a very few visitors. . . .
Jan 3 . . . Edward sent nearly all the Dalzell's money home by tomorrow's mail. . . .
Jan 6 . . . George called to consult me about his supporting Mr Durrand at the coming election.[307] I rather encouraged his joining the

[307]James Durrand was the son of James Durrand who established a successful building and contracting business in 1854 in London. He ran for Parliament in 1875. See Nancy Z. Tausky and Lynne D. DiStephano, *Victorian Architecture in London and Southwestern Ontario: Symbols of Aspiration*, Toronto: University of Toronto Press, 1986.

new party, Canada First,[308] with Mr Blake as leader. It will eventually become the new Conservative Party. The old Conservative Party is broken up & dispersed since out of power.
Jan 7 George called this morning to get my pension papers & to draw my pension. . . .
Jan 12 . . . The scarlet fever still rages. Poor Mila, our old servant has lost two little daughters within the last ten days. . . .
Jan 16 The Judges gave their decision today upon Mr Walker's case about bribery at his election & have disqualified him as a Member for the Dominion during this Parliament. I saw him after the decision was known & he looked very troubled & well he might for it is saying that he took a false oath, as he took an oath that he did not know, that his friends were buying votes. . . .
Jan 18 The election came off today. Mr [W.R.] Meredith is returned by a majority of 150 very much to the astonishment of Mr Durrand's friends & supporters. This is another great blow to Mr Walker for he has electioneered for Mr Durrand & supported him with all his strength. I think it is a pretty plain hint to Mr Walker that if he had not been disqualified that he would not have been reelected for London. Edward has taken very little part in this election but feels very disappointed at the result. . . .
Jan 22 I have just finished reading Greville's diary, three volumes.[309] They are very amusing but not equal to Pepys. . . .
Jan 24 . . . George left in the morning for Detroit. He has gone with a party of curlers to play a game or match with the Detroit curlers. . . .
Jan 31 . . . Mr [Archie] Campbell's partnership with Harris & Magee ends in May & will not be renewed. Mr Campbell is going into partnership with some Lawyer in Toronto. I do not feel sorry.
Feb 2 . . . I am reading Josephus.[310]
Feb 3 . . . Mr Walker & George came for a game of billiards.
Feb 8 . . . If I should live through this winter I think I will go to the Peard's next summer & remain there the rest of my days. Hard as it will be to leave home & the graves of my husband & children, yet it will be for my own peace & the happiness of the house. I feel that I cannot stand another Canadian winter. The cold is intense for people nearly 80 years of age. . . .

[308]Canada First was an intellectual movement founded in 1868 to promote Canadian nationality.

[309]Charles Cavendish Fulke Greville (1794–1865), political diarist, eldest son of Charles Greville, grandson to the fifth Lord Warwick. The 1875 edition of his diaries referred to by Amelia were for the years 1817–37.

[310]Josephus (37–100AD), a Jewish historian.

Feb 15 At the observatories they have compared the degrees of cold & the cold has been greater on January 1875 than it has been for the 60 previous Januaries. . . .

Feb 18 . . . The city election for the Dominion Parliament came off today. Mr Fraser[311] the Conservative candidate, & Mr Samuel Peters,[312] the Reform candidate. Mr Fraser has been elected by a majority of 133. . . .

Feb 19 My birthday. I am 77 today & am not quite forgotten. Mrs Landor sent me such a pretty bouquet. Lucy sent me a pretty bouquet & a Japanese ornament for my dressing table, very pretty & useful. Amelia's bouquet is to come tomorrow. Amelia called. Mr Griffin took cold yesterday & is ill today. George & Lucy spent the evening here. Mr Walker called & gave me a kiss for my birthday.

Feb 20 . . . There is such a sameness in my life that there is very little to record. . . .

Feb 22 . . . Edward not well. His kidneys very much out of order. . . .

Feb 27 . . . Sophia returned at 6 PM looking all the better for her month's visit. . . .

Mar 1 A heavy easterly snow storm, all the trains slowed up, a general strike of all the employees on the Grand Trunk. . . .

Mar 3 . . . [Amelia] is the only person we have seen today.

Mar 10 . . . There has been a row in the house today with the servants. Mrs McKenzie (the cook) has too much temper for the peace of the establishment.

Mar 13 . . . Eliza . . . is very anxious that Amelia & Scotty should go to England & spend the summer with them. . . .

Mar 14 . . . Mr Walker looks very depressed. He & Edward walked for a long time on the verandah. I think the pending law suit about his oil company is worrying him. . . .

Mar 18 Arch Deacon Fuller was elected yesterday Bishop of Niagara.[313] . . . I had a letter from Mary & Shuldham wishing me to go to England & end my days with them. The thought of going & leaving my own dear old home where I have had so many joys & sorrows made me nervous & almost ill. . . .

Mar 28 . . . George came to see me, & Edward spoke to me about my going to England. He does not like the idea of my going. George is

[311]James H. Fraser (1841–99), a Conservative candidate in 1874, elected in 1875.

[312]The London architect.

[313]Thomas Brock Fuller (1810–1884), clergyman, bishop, and author. Archdeacon of Niagara since 1867, he was consecrated first bishop of the diocese of Niagara on 1 May 1875. See Richard E. Ruggle, "Thomas Brock Fuller," *Can. Dic. Biog.* XI, pp. 326–327.

more willing to make the necessary arrangements, but I much doubt whether I shall muster courage to leave Eldon. . . .

Apr 5 Edward surprised me by telling me that he & Sophia were going to England in early May & that they will be away over three months. Edward has business & the trip I hope will do him good as he is far from well. . . .

Apr 20 Mrs Furness lunched here. She would be glad to separate from her husband. I advised her to use her influence & try to keep him from drinking & to make the best of every thing, that a woman should only leave her husband when she was afraid of her life. . . .

Apr 22 . . . Amelia is in trouble & all our feelings have been most cruelly outraged. She has for some time sent Scott who is a very delicate child to Mr Rhymer's school. He is one of the youngest boys there, being only 8 years old, & most of the other boys are from 10 to 14 years of age. Scott is praised by his Master for learning his lessons better than any boy in school. The bigger boys feel this as a reproach to themselves, & they constantly play tricks upon him. A few days ago they rubbed his face with a dead cat. The child, after he came home, fainted away, & the day before yesterday when they had an intermission of ten minutes & were in the play ground, young Gleghorn, who is a very bad boy 10 years old, said, let us hang Scott Griffin & the boys made a rush for Scott, dragged him to the rope of the swing, put it around his neck & pulled him up off his feet. Young Groden rushed to his rescue, took him down. Mrs Rhymer took him into her room & after he recovered himself a little sent him home. Dr Woodruff thought it a mercy that the child had not been frightened into convulsion or idiocy the delicate nervous child that he is. All night he was in a hot fever & talking in his sleep about the school. Amelia said she never closed her eyes all night. . . . He was ill all day yesterday. Today he is getting a little over it. I had a letter from Mr Becher who does not return to Canada until the end of June.

May 6 They are gone. Edward & Sophia left for England. . . .

May 15 . . . The Scotts have become tired of travelling & intend returning to England in June. . . .

May 17 George & Lucy & the children have come to Eldon to remain until Edward & Sophia return. . . .

Jun 11 . . . Dr Woodruff called to see me. I think Edward must have told him to look after me. . . .

Jun 27 The 60th anniversary of my wedding day. What a long life to look back upon, & how many regrets it calls forth. If I only looked to the one thing needful, how much happier my life would have passed. I have thought too much of this world. . . .

Jul 12 . . . The Orangemen walked today. No excesses were committed . . .
Jul 15 George had a letter from Edward telling him the painful news of Mr Scott's death. Edward has not yet heard the particulars but it appears that Mr Scott died from typhoid fever crossing the Red Sea.[314] Teresa is well & expected in England in a few days. How little we know what a day is to bring forth.
Jul 16 A letter from Mr Littledale who was travelling with the Scotts arrived today. He wrote to Edward by Teresa's request and said that the Scotts embarked at Bombay on the 30th of May. Mr Scott was quite well at the time but the ship's baker died & afterwards Mr Scott became nervous & dreaded the journey across the Red Sea. Then he became ill & would be better & worse alternate days, & then he became delirious. The night before he died he became sensible for a short time & called Teresa three times. He died at 1 PM on the 16th [of June]. The health Officers made difficulties about letting the ship pass through the Canal[315] but Mr Littledale gave the Egyptian doctor a large tip & he gave the required certificate. . . . Mr Littledale bought lead and had a coffin made but feared that they would not be able to bring the body to England. It will be a great grief to Teresa if they are unable to do so. It is most fortunate that Teresa has a friend with her at this time of bitter trial.
Jul 21 I had a letter today from Edward. Teresa had not yet arrived in England, but was expected at Liverpool on the 6th of July. She was bringing Mr Scott's body to England. General Crutchley had made arrangements about the funeral which was to take place on the 8th. . . .
Jul 27 We had letters today from Edward, Eliza, Sophia and Amelia. The English [letters] speak of Teresa and her sorrow & of Mr Scott's funeral. Teresa will live at Wick Hill.[316] Mr Scott has left every thing to her during her life & £10,000 absolute and all the furniture, horses, carriages etc. . . .
Aug 30 George and I left . . . for Simcoe where my brother Edward was to meet me at 6 PM. . . . He is looking better than I expected to see him. . . .
Aug 31 I was early up & glad to see the old place once more & to get a glimpse of the beautiful lake, most probably for the last time. The house & everything in & about it looks as if two very old people lived

[314]See Harris Papers, St. Littledale to Eliza Crutchley, 16 June 1875, for an account of Scott's death.
[315]The Suez Canal.
[316]In Bedfordshire.

there. There was no renovation in or out of doors but the kind & loving welcome was the same that it had ever been.

My poor old brother George came at night & again in the morning to see me. He too has become subject to fits. It is strange that those two old men should be afflicted in this way in their old age. . . . I went with George to Church & to the graves of my father & mother & then on to the cliff where there is now a brick yard where there was once such a pretty private walk & now all is broken up into streets with small cottages on them, I have taken my last look at my old home & have no wish ever to go there again. Edward drove up past my own old house which is in a very tumble down state & the place looks very much as if the owner had not lived there for forty years.

We called at George's. His house looked nice. His wife is not a nice woman, his daughter rather pretty & very bright looking. The son is not good & both son & daughter are taught by their mother to show no respect to their father, & he is most shamefully neglected. Edward then drove me to the lake shore & home. Mr & Mrs Holmwood came to tea. Mr Holmwood is Edward's Man of Business there & manages the Harbor. Mrs Holmwood is a very active, energetic woman & manages the Church matters, gets up bazaars & keeps it out of debt & attends to the Sunday school.

Sep 1 Got up early, took a last and loving look at the place where I was born & spent 36 years of my life. . . . [George] & I arrived home at 1 PM. Lucy met us at the station. . . . I think the trip has done me good, for I feel much better than before I left. . . .

Sep 15 Mrs McKenzie, the cook, has given Lucy & me what she calls a piece of her mind. She has potatoes to sell & I wanted to know the market price . . . as her potatoes are [a] good 5 cents a bushel more than the market price . . . & got into a fury & vented herself first upon Lucy & then upon me. I look upon her more as Sophia's servant than mine or I should send her away. . . .

Sep 22 Lucy & children have gone to their own house today & Eldon seems so quiet. I felt sorry to see them go. . . .

Sep 24 Mr Griffin had another of those faint turns caused by his heart being diseased. He seemed so much better since their return that I hoped he would have no more of them. . . .

Sep 28 . . . They [Edward and Sophia] have returned safely. . . .

Oct 8 The Man has been picking apples all day, the weather is getting cold. . . .

Oct 11 . . . . Sophia went to see the Walkers. Mr Walker returned with her to see me. He is looking much better than when he went abroad in May. . . .

Oct 16 I got a depressing letter from Mary. They are in debt, they owe £300. Educating their children & fitting George out for his regiment they have incurred a debt which they find it hard to pay. . . .
Oct 25 . . . I had a letter from Eliza. Teresa does not ask the Griffins to go there for 4 or 5 months. She has gone through so much during Mr Scott's illness & death that she is afraid to undertake the responsibility of taking charge of another invalid. I am sorry that I wrote to ask Teresa to ask the Griffins there. Teresa evidently thinks Mr Griffin much worse than he is.
Oct 30 . . . The Post Office clerks sent a deputation to Mr Griffin congratulating him upon his being well enough to return to his office & asked his acceptance of a present from them as a testimonial of their respectful regard & whether he would take in money or name some thing that he would like to have to the amount of one hundred & fifty dollars. He declined with thanks, & when they urged his acceptance, he said, if they would make Mrs Griffin a present that she would be very happy to receive it, & Mr Griffin is to tell them on Monday what she would like to have. . . .
Nov 3 The Lieut Governor of Ontario M(McDonald) [sic][317] & Capt Grant his A.D.C. called here today. B. Cronyn, the Mayor was with them. The Governor has come to visit all the public institutions. He was asked to stay at Eldon but he declined on this occasion as he felt himself public property, but he is to stay here on his next visit. . . .
Nov 22 Edward & Sophia left for Toronto by the 9 AM train. They go tomorrow night to a ball at Government House and stay with the Gzowskis until after the ball. Then Sophia will go to her father's for a fortnight. . . .
Dec 17 . . . I have ample time for reflection & I try to improve it to gain that peace of mind which surpasses all understanding. . . .
Dec 23 Sophia had an at home today. Out of over 100 invitations 27 people came & upon the whole we thought it a success. . . .
Dec 25 Another Christmas has passed. Edward & Sophia went to morning service. I had service in my own room. Mr Walker & Mr Becher called & the Griffins. George & Lucy came to dinner. The Griffins would not come. The Walkers sent me a pretty card basket. George gave me Smith's *Explorations in Assyria* & Edward gave me *Masterpieces of Italian Art.* Ellen Hamilton came to tea & so ends Christmas 1875.

[317]Donald Alexander Macdonald (1817–96), M.L.A. for Glengarry (1857–67), M.P. (1867–75), Postmaster General (1873–75), and Lieutenant Governor of Ontario (1875–80). He was John Sandfield Macdonald's brother.

Dec 31 The last day of 1875. . . . I have been ailing & lying down the greater part of the day. . . .

1876

Jan 1 The weather continues very warm, thermometer 66 in the shade. I believe there were a few more people called today than last year. . . .
Jan 4 . . . Mr Cammy McDonald was elected Mayor yesterday, a drunken, dishonest lawyer. He was in John's office [at] one time. Edward sent him about his business. Mr Walker says the new Mayor has not been drunk for a year. . . .
Jan 14 Edward & Sophia have gone to the ball given by the Walkers at the Tecumseh. . . . Lucy came down this evening. She is in trouble. She has discovered that the cook she engaged to go to her tomorrow is a drunken, worthless character, a woman that we once hired & sent her away after she had been here four days.
Jan 15 The Walker's ball was a great success. . . . Edward and Sophia did not get home until nearly 3 AM. . . .
Jan 25 . . . I have been busy all day looking over old letters & have not the courage to burn them.
Feb 2 . . . I have just heard of the death of my eldest brother George J. Ryerse at the age of 82. He has been a good man. . . . I trust and hope that he has gone to a better world. He has been so infirm for the last few years of his life that his death is a happy release. . . .
Feb 4 . . . The Gzowskis arrived at 6 PM. They are both looking much older than when I last saw them. We had at dinner, besides the Gzowskis, the Bishop of Huron [and] Mr & Mrs H. Becher. . . .
Feb 17 Edward and Sophia have left today for England. . . .
Feb 19 My 78th birthday, Mrs Landor & Lucy, each sent me pretty bouquets. All are kind. The Griffins & George dined with me. Mrs Walker called. I had a letter from Mary. Edward & Sophia are now on the ocean.
Feb 21 . . . George, Lucy & the children have come to remain with me until Edward returns. . . .
Mar 6 Goldwin Smith has come to London to lecture for the Young Men's Christian Association. He stays with Mr Cameron, editor of the [London] *Advertiser*. He called here today but was not admitted as I was ill in bed. . . . Dr Woodruff called again today but is afraid to give me much medicine. . . .
Mar 15 Lucy went with Amelia [Milly] to her dancing lesson. . . .
Mar 21 . . . I got a letter from Sarah & Sophia. . . .
Mar 29 . . . A telegram from Edward, he sails for Canada on the 13th

of April. We do not know whether Sophia will come with [him]. His business is satisfactorily settled. . . .

Apr 5 I had a letter from Edward & Sophia which we were all so glad to get. Sophia does not return with Edward but will come with her father in September.

Apr 16 Easter Sunday. Lucy went to morning service. I as usual read the service & a sermon in my own room. I continue very ailing & can scarcely keep up. . . .

Apr 25 . . . Edward & George returned at 6 PM. Edward is looking very well & has been very successful in doing all that he went to England to do. . . .

Apr 27 I have been ill all day. Edward sent Dr Woodruff to see me. The Bishop of Huron called. . . . George & Lucy returned to their own house today. I felt so sorry to see them go. Lucy has been so kind & attentive to me. She is a dear good little woman. The house is so quiet without the children.

May 16 . . . The house is in a great mess. They have taken up the dining room floor and have put supporters under the house. . . .

May 17 . . . a horrid mess yesterday but today is worse. They have taken down all the plastering in the upper & lower hall, & the dust is something frightful. . . .

May 23 . . . General Crutchley's brother died on the 6th after a very long illness. . . . The Sunninghill Estate[318] falls to General Crutchley, & his brother has left him every thing he possessed, an income not less than £12,000 a year. . . .

May 30 I bought a cow today for 50 dollars & sold the one we had for 42$^1/_2$. The one we bought is a new milk cow, and the one we sold is not. . . .

May 31 The plasterers finished the hall today. . . . I was in the garret the most of the day seeing things put to right. . . .

Jun 1 . . . The Honble Malcolm Cameron died this morning at Ottawa after a long illness.[319] As a politican he was a failure. He lost the respect of both parties. . . .

Jun 15 Little Amelia's birthday. Her mother has given her a small party. We unpacked the groceries which Edward & Sophia bought off the Co-operated Society in England. . . .

Jun 20 . . . Painting is still going on & papering is still to be done. . . .

Jun 28 I had a letter today from Major [Thomas] Leith telling me that

[318]Near Windsor Great Forest.

[319]See Amelia's diary, 9 October 1857.

I am a great grand mother. His wife . . . gave birth to a daughter and is doing well. . . .
Jul 4 The last workman and painter left today & the house is all in order. Both Parlor Maid & house maid have given notice. It is a bother. . . .
Jul 5 I took an early dinner with the Griffins. I think it is a year since I have been there. . . .
Jul 6 Mr Becher came to luncheon. He sent me as a present a basket of champagne, half-pint bottles. He is very kind. . . . I wrote to Sarah, Mary & Mr & Mrs Portman.
Jul 23 Edward & Sophia returned at 7 PM. Sophia is looking much healthier & stronger than when she went to England. . . .
Jul 26 A workman has been putting three brackets in the drawing room, a mirror in the little morning room & one in the spare bedroom over the chimney piece, all bought by Sophia in England, and all very pretty. . . .
Jul 27 George, Lucy & the children left this morning for New York & the sea shore.[320] . . .
Aug 7 There has been a division made in the Post Office Inspectors Department, & there has been three offices made where there were only two, & several of the offices that Mr Griffin had the supervision of have been placed under the charge of another Inspector. The Post Office at Hamilton is one that has been taken out of Mr Griffin's division, & the Post Master & Clerks in taking leave of Mr Griffin have sent him a very handsome silver-plated tea service: tea pot, coffee pot, two sugar basins & a cream jug with a very complimentary address, expressing their regret at parting with him. Mr Griffin looked so pleased & grateful I feel glad for him & Amelia. It is a little drop of pleasure amidst all their troubles & worries. . . .
Aug 12 Teresa's birthday. Mr Becher called & asked me to go there for dinner with Mrs Wilson & Ellen Hamilton, I declined [because of] the great heat & not well. . . .
Aug 25 26 years today since Mr Harris' death, many of them have been weary years to me. The end must be near, my hope is in Jesus. . . .
Aug 29 . . . I went with the Griffins for a drive. We went past the [John] Wilson place & the Askin place. I wished once more to see the places where those to whom I was much attached had lived. Their grounds have been laid out into lots & sold & a good many very nice

[320]They returned on 17 August.

houses have been built & the old homes are all changed. We drove to the cemetery and saw the graves of those we love. When we returned we found Mr Walker & Mr Geddes here playing lawn tennis. . . .
Sep 3 I & Sophia went to the morning service & remained to the Sacrament. I think it is more than a year since I have been at Church. The Church has been carpeted & very much improved in appearance. The memorial window which the Griffin's have put up in remembrance of their little daughter is very pretty. . . .
Sep 8 Lizzy Plumb came to show Sophia how to cover tennis balls. . . .
Sep 15 Amelia went with me to do some shopping. I never was fond of shopping & I have not grown to like it. I feel so old & so done with this world & all that is in it. The great change from this world to the next must be near, I look for the change without fear and with a humble trust in our Saviour. . . . Alice Becher, Carrie Maclean & H. Meredith were here to tennis. . . .
Sep 26 The first day of the Western exhibition. . . .
Oct 6 . . . Yesterday as I sat reading near the fire, a spark flew out & set my dress on fire. When I discovered it it was in a blaze. The material of dress and petticoat was of silk. Had it been of cotton, I should have been unable to extinguish it. . . .
Nov 13 I went to the Georges & lunched at the Griffins. Mr Griffin no better, not as well as he was a week ago. I begin to fear that he will not recover. . . .
Nov 15 The Honbl J. Hilliard [sic] Cameron died yesterday.[321] For many years he has been a prominent man in the country, leading Conservative, a Member of Parliament & Queen's Council & very much respected. . . .
Nov 18 Edward & Sophia are very well pleased with the ball. Sophia went in Calico as Marie Antoinette & she is said to be a great success & the most stylish looking woman in the room. . . .
Nov 20 Sophia had her photo taken in her fancy dress.[322] . . .
Dec 11 Amelia called. Mr Griffin much better. . . .
Dec 12 . . . Mrs Ryerson & Sophia returned calls. . . .
Dec 18 Mr Becher came & invited Mrs Ryerson, Edward & Sophia there to dinner, they have gone. Sophia had a letter from Miss McDonald inviting her & Edward to a ball at the Government House on the 11th, the Dufferins are to be there. . . .

[321]See Amelia's diary, 2 October 1857.
[322]There is a copy of this photograph in the Harris Papers.

Dec 24 . . . Amelia & Gilbert Griffin called. It is more than a year since I have seen him. He looks old & changed & out of spirits. His not being able to get anything to do has told upon him. . . .
Dec 25 Christmas Day. Edward, Sophia & Mrs Ryerson went to morning service, I read the service & the sermon in my own room. Mr McGee, Mr Walker & young Jeffery called early, Mr Becher came to luncheon. G. Griffin & Mr & Mrs Billet called. George and Lucy came to dinner. Little Scott saved up his money and gave me two nice minipocket handkerchiefs. . . .
Dec 29 . . . Edward had a letter from Eliza telling him that Teresa is going to be married to Mr Littledale.[323] We hope it is not true. He is 10 or 12 years younger than her.
Dec 31 Sophia went to morning service. I had service as usual in my own room. Amelia, Mr Jeffery & Mr Walker called & so ends the year. My prayers for the last week have given me great peace & I feel truly thankful to Our Heavenly Father for all His mercies.

1877

Jan 1 Lovely weather, good sleighing. . . . We have had a good many visitors. . . . Miss Landor called & asked for a bottle of our port wine for her father, who Dr Brown fears will not live many days. He will leave a very large family with very little to subsist upon. . . .
Jan 5 I had letters from Teresa & from Sarah, both telling me that Mr Littledale had proposed for Teresa, & that she had accepted him. The only objection is his youth. He must be nearly ten years younger than Teresa. How can she be so foolish as to marry a man so much younger than herself. Sarah writes very sensibly about it, advising our making the best of it. She speaks very highly of Mr Littledale. . . .
Jan 6 Dr Landor died this morning. . . .
Jan 10 . . . Edward & Sophia left here for Toronto. . . . They had accepted invitations to dine at Government House to meet Ld & Lady Dufferin on the 10th & to attend a ball on the 11th, given to Ld & Lady Dufferin, and they could not well avoid going. . . . I had a letter from Mary, & Amelia had one from Eliza. They both speak of Teresa's engagement with regret. They cannot approve of it but are trying to make the best of it. . . .
Jan 26 . . . Mrs Landor called today. She has to leave her comfortable

[323]St. George Littledale had assisted Teresa at the time of the tragic death of her husband. See Amelia's diary, 16 July 1875.

quarters[324] on the 10th & to commence her struggle with poverty & privation. . . .

Feb 11 . . . There is a revivalist preacher of the Church of England, the Revnd Mr [W.S.] Rainsford, who has services in St Paul's Church. He draws immense crowds. Hundreds of people cannot get even standing room & have to leave. I hope there may be a real awakening amongst the people. . . .

Feb 17 . . . Teresa is to be married on the 1st of March to Mr Littledale. They go to Kashmir on their wedding trip. . . .

Feb 20 . . . Mrs Landor told her [Amelia Griffin] that Teresa had written to her such a kind letter & sent her fifty dollars. Teresa was attached to Dr Landor. . . .

Feb 25 Lucy was confined last night. At 10 PM, she gave birth to a fine boy & is doing well. George came to tell me. . . .

Mar 26 I have been ill & unable to write my journal.[325] . . . All my friends have been very kind in calling. On the 23rd Dr Ryerson came up for the night. I felt very glad to see him.

Apr 12 Commenced taking down the old kitchen and preparing to build a large addition to the house. . . .

Apr 16 A great deal of work going on, digging cellars under the new addition & work on the lawn. . . .

Apr 24 The place is in a great state of confusion with workmen digging cellar, working on terrace & in the garden. . . .

May 1 I am at George's. Our house is so broken up that I have taken up my quarters here until the kitchen is moved and becomes habitable. . . . (The cook) and Mary, the Parlour Maid, will remain here until our house is in better order. Edward, Sophia, the House Maid & Man Servant sleep at Eldon. . . .

May 7 George & Lucy left at 8 AM for New York en route for England expecting to be away three months. They sail in the Cunard steamer *Scythia* on the 9th. The house has been very lonely all day. The children have been very good. Amelia is one of the best children I have ever seen. I have a very sore eye & feel ill in other ways. . . .

May 15 My eyes have been so sore that for the last week I have been unable to read, write or work today. . . . Mrs Bailey (Lucy Wilson) died on the 12th (consumption) at the age of 37. . . .

May 27 Edward & I had a long talk & not a very pleasant one. . . . Mr & Mrs [Elijah] Leonard called to see me. It is many years since I

[324]She has been living in a house on the grounds of the Asylum.
[325]She had been ill since 14 March.

have seen Mr Leonard. He looks aged & ill. Mrs Leonard looks young and fresh for her age (58). It is the first time I have ever seen her. Mr Leonard from working in his foundry is now a Senator & an *Honorable*, a very good man but retains the manners of the foundry man. . . .

Jun 13 I returned to Eldon today. Sorry to leave the children but glad to return to my own room. Amelia [Milly] came with me & will share my room until her Papa & Mamma's return.

Jul 24 On the 18th Sophia, little Amelia & I went to Dundurn[326] to visit Mr McInnes. . . . It was very quiet, only Miss Saunders who is governess & housekeeper, two small children under seven . . . & Mr McInnes who goes to his office at 9 AM & returns at 1/2 past 6 PM. . . . Mrs McInnes is in an asylum hopelessly insane, a malady that first came upon her when only nine years of age, & before she was married she was more than once sent to England & placed into a private asylum. Yet it was kept quiet, but few knew it, & at a lucid interval when she was with her parents[327] returning to Toronto, Mr McInnes came with her & fell in love & proposed & the Robinson family allowed him to marry her without telling him of her malady. After the birth of her first child she had a return of her malady & wished to go back to the asylum in England. She then told him of her previous attacks. He told me that he felt as if she had plunged a knife in him & turned it around. He was very fond of her. They have six children. She has had many intervals of sanity when she would return home but now the doctors declare her to be hopelessly insane. I think Mr McInnes feels that the Robinson family did not act honorably by him in not telling him that she was a lunatic. She costs him £600 a year at the asylum. He looks very unhappy & I think is getting into bad health. . . .

Aug 26 I went to the morning service with Amelia. I think it is the first time I have been at Church for two years. I did not feel much fatigued. . . .

Aug 28 . . . George & Lucy returned at 7 PM. George looking very thin but in good spirits, Lucy looking much improved in health. . . .

Sep 25 We had a dinner party tonight. . . . We have used the drawing room for the first time. . . .

Sep 28 . . . Mrs MacKenzie, the wife of the Premier,[328] called. She looks a good, kind, plain Scots woman of humble birth which she is. . . .

[326]Dundurn Castle in Hamilton, formerly the residence of Sir Allan Napier MacNab. See Amelia's diary, 1 October 1857.

[327]Chief Justice J.B. Robinson.

[328]Alexander Mackenzie was visiting the Exhibition in London.

Oct 7 . . . Edward and George returned from Long Point last night. Edward brought 40 ducks & George 50. . . .
Nov 30 . . . The upholsterer from New York who made the furniture for our new drawing room called to see the effect when in its place. He was on his return from Chicago.
Dec 25 Another Christmas has come & gone & I am still here. Friends are kind & I have tolerable health. . . . All my grandchildren who are in London called to see grandmamma & to get a trifle in pocket money. . . .
Dec 29 I am better today, but not well enough to go down and see the visitors at Sophia's at home. About 100 people were here. . . . They tell me the at home was a success.[329]
Dec 31 The last day of the year has nearly passed. During the past year there has been no death in the family, the members who have been ill are comparably well & the affairs of the family as far as I know are prosperous. May God continue His blessings. . . .

1878

Jan 2 George has a dinner party tonight. Edward has gone. Butler, our servant man, got drunk last night & remained away. Edward dismissed him today. . . .
Jan 12 I had a letter from Mary [Peard] who hopes to be with me by the end of May. . . .
Jan 29 George came early to see if I was all right. Then Lucy & Mrs Dougall called. I read the morning paper then write letters or work at fancy work, then take my half hour walk on the passage,[330] then dine, work on, read until visitors come. . . .
Feb 19 My birthday. 80 years old today. I had quite an invasion in bouquets & congratulations. The Griffins brought me a very handsome bouquet & Mrs H. Becher, Mrs W. Meredith, Mrs Landor & my little grand children all sent me bouquets equally pretty. Mr & Mrs [John] Walker gave me a book, a work on China, & Lucy gave me a magnificent present of one hundred dollars to make up a sum which I wish to send to Mary.[331] . . . Mr [James] Hamilton remembered my birthday & called with Ellen. He is an old acquaintance but I do not see him

[329]The extensive renovation of Eldon House in 1877 was primarily undertaken by Edward Harris. By this time Sophia was the effective chatelaine.

[330]The Harris family referred to the verandah at Eldon House as the "passage."

[331]The Peard's financial position, like that of the Dalzells, was always marginal, whereas the Crutchleys and the Scott Littledales were extremely well-off.

often. They remained to afternoon tea. The Griffins, the Georges, the Walkers, Mrs H. Becher, Mrs W. Meredith & Mrs Beddome[332] came to afternoon tea. Edward left this morning for Toronto. I have felt so ill all day that it has been a great effort to keep up.

Mar 5 Edward had a range put in the kitchen today, much to the cook's disgust, who thinks she will not like it as well as the coal stove. . . .

Apr 16 Mrs Ermatinger from St Thomas called to see me. I was glad to see her after so many years. She is past 70 & we are both looking forward to our home beyond the grave. . . .

Apr 18 Edward went to Hamilton today to meet the stockholders of the Long Point Company.[333] There has been great mismanagement in the Company & the President & Directors oppose an investigation which Edward & other stockholders insist upon & are determined to have. If they throw the case into Chancery there is more than forty thousand dollars unaccounted for. . . .

Apr 29 . . . The Bechers return today from their travels. Mr Becher came in for a few minutes to see me. George & Lucy have given up their house to the workmen & have taken another house for two months.

May 2 I am ill & ailing. I try to keep up & think that perhaps I am not as feeble as I fancy, but a little exertion or a short walk on the verandah sends me to the sofa. I feel that the end can not be far off [but this] gives me no fear. I have a firm trust in my Saviour. How sincerely I pray for the conversion of my children and that we may all meet in a better world.

May 24 Not much excitement this Queen's birthday, only a Base Ball match in which the Tecumseh Club has been beaten by the Buffalo Club.[334] . . .

May 27 . . . [Becher] says the receipts of his office this year over & above all expenses are $20,000 to be divided between the three partners. . . .

May 30 I went to see George, it is the first time that I have been outside of the gate for more than six months. . . .

[332]Wife of F.B. Beddome, owner of an insurance agency, was an almost daily visitor at Eldon House during Amelia Harris' final decade.

[333]A duck shooting club, founded in the mid 1860s, many of whose members were from the United States. Following an internal investigation, "The Club" was reorganized and Edward became President.

[334]Professional baseball was introduced to London in 1867. In 1878, "The Tecumsehs" were the winners of an international tournament and were called "World's Champions."

Jun 12 Mary [Peard] arrived today . . . much to our surprise. We did not expect her until evening or tomorrow. She came from N. York in 14 hours. I did not know her, 25 years has made a great change in her, yet she is looking very well. Her features & manner came back to me. I was walking in the garden when she arrived & she came & put her arms around me & I knew it must be Mary. . . .
Jun 22 . . . Mary & Sophia returned calls. Lucy, the Griffins, Mr [Mc]Innes & Mr Walker called. . . .
Jun 24 Mary, Edward, Sophia & I went to George's to lunch with Lucy. The Griffins were there also. After luncheon Mary & Sophia paid visits. . . . .
Jul 1 Dominion day. The heat very great. Mr Walker came to luncheon. The Griffins called. Mary & Sophia walked to the Georges. . . .
Jul 12 A great number of Orangemen assembled in London today. They went to Church quietly & afterwards amused themselves in Salter's Grove & then dispersed. . . .
Jul 31 . . . Mr Becher drove Mary & myself to Thornwood to lunch. We remained there until 5 PM. We had a very nice luncheon & they are all so kind to me. If I was their mother they could not treat me with more tenderness or more affectionately. It is a pleasure to see the mutual happiness of Mr & Mrs Becher. . . .
Aug 25 Mary went with Amelia to morning service. I read the service in my own room. It is Mary's last day here. The probability is that she will never again see Eldon, & it is almost a certainty that I shall never again see her. Mr & Mrs Becher called to say good bye & the Walkers called. . . . Amelia spent a great part of the day here. George & Lucy called. . . . My goodnight to Mary was a sad one. Edward & Mary sat up until 2 AM.
Aug 26 The parting is over. Mary, George & Lucy left at 4.40 AM. Amelia came to breakfast & went with Edward to the station. Mr Griffin also went to the station with them. It has been a long, weary, painful day though the friends I love best have called. Amelia spent most of the day with me. . . .
Sep 17 This has been a most exciting day throughout the province. The elections for the Dominion Parliament have taken place. The general result is not known but Mr Walker has lost his election for London. Mr Carling has been elected. Mr Carling is Conservative, Mr Walker Reformer. . . .
Nov 5 I had letters from Mary Leith, Mary Peard & Teresa. Col Dalzell died on the 19th of October & was buried on the 24th. I have so long expected his death that I thought I was prepared for the news, but it came like a blaze, and I have been ill all day. He died very peacefully, sur-

rounded by all who were most dear to him, his wife, his children & his brother & sister. They all took the communion together. . . .
Dec 25 Mrs Ryerson not well enough to get up this morning but came down to dinner. This Christmas [has] not gone off as pleasantly as usual. Mrs McKenzie the cook got into one of her rages and threatened to leave at once. [She] would not let the new house maid go into the kitchen. Sophia gave Mrs McKenzie her wages & told her to go at once if she wished to do so. Then Mrs K. would not go. Amidst all her ill temper she sent in a very good dinner. The gas was frozen & would not burn in the hall nor dining room so that we had to light candles. The Bechers called and Mr Becher brought me Stanley's *Travels Over the Dark Continent.* It was not the edition I wanted, & I was ungracious enough to tell him so. But he had asked me to say what I wanted regardless of price. The edition that I had expressed a wish for was beautifully got up, good type, beautifully illustrated & with maps. All thought I was wrong to have said any thing, that I ought to have taken the edition offered & not have shown that I was disappointed. He would have taken the book back & try for the other. I felt so sorry about the whole thing, it is the last time I will tell anyone what to give me. The Griffins & Georges came to dinner. It is the first time that Scott has been at a dinner party. Dr Ryerson has aged very much since I last saw him. I was so ill that I had to leave the dinner table and go to bed.[335]
Dec 31 The end of the year. Great God make me truly thankful for all the blessings and mercies of the past year & have me in Thy keeping for ever more.

1879

Jan 1 . . . Sophia had 30 visitors, I only saw a few friends. . . . George & Lucy came in the evening, Amelia called in the morning & had a letter from Sarah & Mr Walker.
Jan 5 . . . The Georges and Amelia called. . . . [Charlotte] poor little darling, she seems all right today.
Jan 14 . . . Mrs [Harry] Becher last evening, when walking home with Lucy, insisted upon knowing why Lucy never went to see her. Lucy after some hesitation told her that when she had recognized her gold thimble that Mrs Becher's servant had taken, & that Mrs Becher had

[335]Dr. and Mrs. Ryerson were visiting Eldon for Christmas. Amelia is probably referring to Stanley's *Through the Dark Continent*, or, *The Sources of the Nile* ... that was published that year.

said she would send the thimble to her the next day, that she Mrs Becher had taken no further notice of it, & still retained the servant. Mrs Becher was very angry, said many things that would have been better left unsaid & left Lucy in a passion. . . .

Jan 15 Lucy met Mrs H. Becher this morning & bowed to her. Mrs Becher cut her dead, would not look at her. It is a pity that families should quarrel & be at emnity for trifles. I think Lucy is not to blame. . . .

Jan 17 Edward left for Simcoe at 6 AM and returned at 7 PM. George left at the same hour for Hamilton with the London Curling Club to play a match with the Hamilton Club. . . .

Jan 24 Charlotte had return of those fits last night & is very ill. George is at Chatham. . . . Mrs & Miss Taylor called & old Page came to see us. I am so troubled about dear little Charlotte.

Jan 26 I read the service in my own room & read Dr Farrar upon eternal punishment & do not like the work. . . .

Feb 13 Carling's splendid Brewery was burned this morning, loss supposed over $300,000, insurance $75,000. It is said that he is ruined.[336] . . .

Feb 22 . . . Mrs H. Becher came to afternoon tea. I spoke to her about the coolness between her & Lucy. She seemed to regret it as much as I do. I asked her when she met Lucy to offer her hand & [hope] that Lucy would take it but on no account to allude to what is past, nor attempt to talk matters over but let the past be forgotten. She promised to do so.

Mar 6 . . . Mr Becher showed me a letter from Christopher Robinson announcing his engagement to Lizzie Plumb. He is a very good fellow but 30 years older than Lizzie. . . .

Mar 18 I had a letter from Mr McInnes this morning telling of his wife's death. She died . . . in a lunatic asylum in the States. She has been a hopeless lunatic for several years. Her death must be a relief to her & all her friends but from Mr McInnes' letter it seems to have awakened all the old love in his heart. . . .

Mar 20 . . . A good many Toronto people attended Mrs McInnes' funeral, only one of her brothers, Mr Christopher Robinson, was there. Edward was asked to be one of the pall bearers. Mr Becher continues ill or ailing, & has decided to go to some part of the southern States until the weather becomes warm. . . .

[336]The fire caused over $100,000 in damages, for which $65,000 was covered by insurance. The walls of the brewery were not destroyed and the business was back in operation in less than three months.

Mar 31 I had a telegram from my brother [Edward Ryerse]. His wife [Patty] died this morning. I have felt her death more than I thought I would. Her death has been expected for some weeks, yet the certainty that all is over gave me a great shock. . . . Edward will go to her funeral on Wednesday. . . .
Apr 4 A foot of snow fell last night & the day is very cold. Edward ill with cold not well enough to go to the office. The Georges, the Griffins, & Mrs Walker called.

> The best of what is known as Mother Shipton's Prophecy was first published in 1488 and republished in 1641:
>
> Carriages without horses shall go and accidents fill the world with woe. Around the world thought shall fly in the twinkling of an eye. Water shall yet more wonders do, how strange yet shall be true. The world upside down shall be, and gold be found at the root of a tree. Through hills man shall ride and no horse or ass be at his side, under water men shall walk, shall ride, shall sleep, shall talk. In the air men shall be seen in white, in black, in green. Iron in the water shall float as easy as a wooden boat. Gold shall be found and won, in a world that is not now known. Fire and water shall wonder do, England shall at last admit a Jew. The world to an end shall come in eighteen hundred and eighty one.[337]

Apr 12 Edward today told the Mayor & Corporation that if they wished it he would [arrange] that Eldon House & servants be placed at the service of Lord Lorne[338] & the Princess Louisa during their visit to the city in September next. Edward & Mr Jeffery & two other gentlemen left this afternoon for New York on business. . . .
Apr 23 Here I am at George's & Lucy is so kind to me & has been bathing my swollen foot. Edward is having a bow window put in the dining room, which upsets the house generally and house cleaning is going on also, & Lucy has kindly asked me to remain with her & make a long visit. . . .
May 1 Mrs O'Brien [Elizabeth] arrived today. She could not go to Eldon. The house, from the changes . . . which are being made, is too upset to receive her, so Lucy has kindly invited her to come here, as

[337]This excerpt is rendered in Amelia's hand. See Amelia Harris' diary, 19 June 1881.
[338]The Governor General.

her visit is mostly to me. She is looking very well but naturally older. It is ten years since I have seen her. . . .

May 10 I returned to Eldon today after having spent eighteen very pleasant days with George & Lucy. I felt quite sorry to leave them. The more I see of Lucy, the better I like her, but I like my own, old home. I did not think I could ever have felt as happy as I felt for the last fortnight away from my own home. Lucy brought me home. Amelia & Mr Griffin called.

May 14 The painting etc in the dining room goes on very slowly, workmen disappoint. They have so many jobs in hand that they work a day here & a day there & are a vexation. . . .

May 31 . . . The Honble George Brown called.[339] He is a fine looking elderly gentleman & the Editor of the *Globe* newspaper, a staunch Reformer, I might say the head of the Reform party. . . .

Jun 5 The election is over & Mr W. Meredith[340] is returned by a Majority of 447 over Mr Magee.[341] . . .

Jun 6 The election news is that the Reform Ministry has been sustained & they are reelected with a large majority. This is a great disappointment to the Conservatives. . . . I have today finished my *Recollections of an Early Settler* & shall send it to Doctor Ryerson, & if he chooses to insert it in his forthcoming history, he is at liberty to do so.[342]

Jun 10 Mr Cabot, Edward & George left by the 8.40 train this morning to attend a meeting of the stockholders of the Long Point Company. . . .

Jul 1 Lovely weather. The city has been nearly empty all day all the people are on excursions either down the river or to Port Stanley or Cleveland. . . .

Jul 5 Mrs Becher called for me and took me to hear the band. There were a great number of people there & most of the elite of London. The park is in a very primitive state, it will be many years before there will be shade trees to make it pretty & pleasant. Two or three times I could scarcely restrain my tears as I thought of the past, before be-

[339]"George Brown of the *Globe*" (1818–80). For a fleshing out of Amelia's terse vignette see J.M.S. Careless, "George Brown," *Dic. Can. Biog.* X, pp. 91–103.

[340]William Ralph Meredith (1840–1923) was elected M.P.P. in 1872; he was leader of the Conservative Party from 1878 to 1894, when he was appointed Chief Justice of Ontario. He was Chancellor of the University of Toronto, 1900–23.

[341]Edward's partner. See Amelia's diary, 3 December 1865.

[342]It was included in Ryerson's *The Loyalists of America and Their Times*, Toronto: William Briggs, 1880, Vol. 2, pp. 229–256.

reavement & separation had taken place in the family, & I used to attend the band with my husband & surrounded with sons & daughters.

Jul 19 George, Lucy, & children & nurse & self left London at 8:40 for New York. Edward & Sophia left at the same time for Boston & then go to some place for sea bathing. After Edward establishes Sophia, he will return home. We, that is George, Lucy & self travelled all night & reached the Bervoort House at 7.00 AM. . . .

Jul 21 We have very comfortable quarters at the Bervoort House. Lucy went shopping in the morning. I spent the morning reading the *History of the Jesuits* by Nicolini. We dined early & then took a drive in the Central Park. The park is very beautiful. I do not recognize a place that I knew when I was here 25 years ago. Kate [the nurse] took the children to the menagerie and they declared when they returned that they had never spent such a pleasant day. Lucy called upon Doctor [?] to consult him about Charlotte. His opinion of her case is as satisfactory as we could expect but her restoration to health will require close attention & constant care for three or four years. His fee was $20, & he has written to Dr Woodruff to carry out his directions.

Jul 22 . . . He [George] seems much inclined to go to Newport but has not decided. . . . Teresa has just arrived looking very well, a little older [but] she looks cheery, in good spirits & happy, yet she is changed as if trouble had left its impression. Mr Littledale does not look as young as I expected to see him looking. His elder brother who spends his life yachting, looks the color of mahogany with a peculiar manner. In the evening George went with them to Gilmour's Gardens where they have arranged to meet some of the passengers by the *Bothnia*.[343] . . .

Jul 23 I rather like St George but I must know more of him before I can decide upon all his merits . . . we did our packing this evening. The Littledales go on to San Francisco and return to Eldon the end of Sept or the beginning of October to spend 6 week[s] or two months at Eldon, & we go to New London. . . .

Jul 24 . . . We are in a cottage, clean, quiet & comfortable. We dine at the Hotel.[344] The table & attendance good. . . . George got a telegram from Edward who says Sophia is not well enough to be left alone at Monquite & that he will take her to Rye Beach where she may be with the Griffins. . . .

[343]The ship in which they had recently crossed the Atlantic.

[344]They stayed at the Pequot House.

Aug 19 . . . We bid a last good bye to our friends & left the Pequot House at 3 PM. Came by boat to New London & then took the train to N[ew] York & arrived at the 5th Avenue Hotel at 8 PM. For the first time since I left Eldon I felt ill which ended in a sort of common cholera. I took 4 drops of chlorodine & slept.
Aug 21 . . . the grandest hotel I have ever been in, of course expensive, $5 a day, but all our wants supplied.[345] . . . They sent Kate, Amelia [Milly] & Charlotte to London by the night train. We leave tomorrow night if I am well enough to travel.
Aug 23 . . . Edward, and Mr and Mrs Walker met us. How glad I am to get home and how pretty Eldon looked, and now our travels are over & George, Lucy & I go to separate homes. How kind, tenderly and generously they have treated me I can never forget. I do not think there is a kinder hearted, better woman in the world than Lucy is. May God ever bless her & hers & have them in His keeping. George . . . has been to me kind, loving & affectionate but he is my son, my own flesh & blood. Lucy is & ever has been equally kind, affectionate & devoted without my having any claim upon her. Her thoughtfulness for all about her is a marvel to me. . . .
Sep 15 Had a letter from Teresa which I was very, very glad to get. She has not been well & ought not to be where she is, she is camping in the Rocky Mountains amongst rattlesnakes. Her dog has been bitten by one. . . .
Oct 3 The Littledales arrived this morning at 8.50, Teresa looking much better than when I saw her at New York. Mr Littledale & St George seem to have enjoyed their hunting. I am so glad to see Teresa. . . .
Oct 16 . . . Edward leaves very early in the morning for Long Point Bay for duck shooting. Mr Littledale goes with him, & will remain a day or two, & then return to England. . . .
Oct 23 . . . Teresa thinks my flannels not thick enough for the winter. She went with Amelia into town & bought me a fit out of warm under clothes & two flannel petticoats so nice & made me a present of them. So kind of her. . . .
Nov 16 . . . The parting is over. The Griffins, George & Lucy went to the station to see the last of Teresa & St George. My good bye to Teresa was a sad one as it is more than probable that we shall never again meet in this world. Sophia went to the station with them. . . .

[345]They remained at New London until 19 August when they returned to New York by train, staying at the 5th Avenue Hotel.

Dec 25 We were to have dinner with the Georges but I was too ill to go. I felt so sorry for it is not probable that I shall be here another Christmas. I may never again meet all the family assembled but I was so ill from cold that I could not go. I bathed my feet, took some gruel & went to bed & spent a very restless night. Amelia, Scott, the Georges & the Walkers called.
Dec 31 Mr Griffin has had an increase of salary of $200 a year. It is a welcome addition to a small income. . . .

1880

Jan 1 A lovely day, we have not had very many visitors. . . .
Jan 19 My brother Edward Ryerse arrived at 2 PM. . . . He is looking better than I expected to see him. . . .
Jan 20 . . . My brother left at 2.30 PM for Ryerse. His life is very lonely since his wife's death. He could not speak of her to me without tears. . . .
Jan 27 . . . Lucy heard of the death of her grand mother Askin.
Feb 1 . . . Edward & George went for a walk. Edward with a thin hat, & he got his ears rather badly frozen. After rubbing them with snow, Dr Woodruff ordered a poultice of raw potatoes grated & put on very cold. It has certainly done wonders for his ears. They look red but not so sore as I expected. . . .
Feb 6 . . . Miss Dodds commenced her lessons in cooking today. . . . Nearly all my friends go. . . .
Feb 19 My 82nd birthday. . . . I have had a good many visitors, friends who make a point of remembering my birthday and calling upon me, many of them [15 or more mentioned] with an offering of flowers or some little present. . . .
Feb 27 I have been too ill to write up my journal, but am better tonight. . . .
Mar 12 Dr Ryerson who is a cousin of Sophia & second cousin to me is here. . . . He is said to be clever.[346] The ear & the eye are his specialties. My eyes have been so weak yesterday & today that I have been unable to read.
Mar 15 [Mr Griffin's] sister Sophia Griffin died yesterday at 6 PM. . . . Cancer is a horrid disease. . . .
Mar 29 . . . I dreamed last night that I should not live until the end of the year. . . .

[346]George Sterling Ryerson (1854–1925), a physician, one of the founders of the Canadian Red Cross Society in 1896.

Apr 7 Lucy called to say goodbye as they leave tomorrow on a trip to Philadelphia, Washington, Baltimore & New York.[347] . . .
Apr 29 This has been a day of pain & misery to me. Mr Griffin is again in money trouble in a way that reflects discredit upon him & through him upon his connections. Edward has paid four hundred dollars to stop proceedings. . . .
Apr 30 . . . Amelia and Mr Griffin came to see me. Mr Griffin denies all the statements made against him in the papers & says that he has not touched any Post Office funds & that he owes Mr Lawless nothing & that he has not been suspended from office. Edward says his statements are untrue. . . .
May 9 . . . The Honble George Brown died this morning. He was shot on the 25th of last March by a discharged employee with a revolver. . . .
May 14 . . . [Lucy] told me that she was again pregnant. . . . I was pleased. . . .
May 22 Edward & Sophia took a sudden start this morning & have gone to Port Rowan. . . . George came for me at 3 PM and here I am with them for a week. . . .
May 26 I have had a great shock today. Mr Griffin is to go to Kingston upon reduced salary. Of course it is not for his good management of the Post Office. His conduct, I fear, has been very bad, borrowing money & getting into debt. . . .
May 28 I went this morning to see Amelia. Our interview was a peaceful one but on the whole less so than I expected. She tries to think that every body concerned is more to blame than her husband, and it is best that she should think so. Their having to leave London is a trial to us both. God only knows how great yet we have both come to the conclusion that it is best that they should go. If she remained here our intercourse could not be otherwise than under restraint & painful. Parting with Amelia and Scott is a hard trial to me in my old age. . . . She wishes me to stay for a longer time here, as she would feel more free to visit me here than at Eldon, & Lucy & George are so kind & have urged me to remain longer, & I think I will remain until the 1st.
Jun 2 I packed my trunk and intended to return home but Lucy & George would not hear of my going. Amelia paid her morning visit. How my heart aches for her. She has been paying some debts. She has discovered that Mr Griffin owes more than a thousand dollars, & how much more we do not know. Yet she tried to make excuses for him &

[347]They returned by 21 April.

tries to think that he has been the victim of circumstances. I wish I could think well of him.
Jun 7 I have been busy looking over old letters and burning a great number. . . . [Amelia] has commenced packing to go to Kingston. Almost every day we hear of some dishonorable act of Mr Griffin that was unknown to us. . . .
Jun 8 Mr Griffin left yesterday for Kingston to look for a house. . . .
Jun 11 . . . Mr Griffin has returned from Kingston not very well pleased with his prospects. Rent of houses are higher, taxes less, gas dearer and water rates higher. . . .
Jun 16 . . . I rang the bell and disturbed the house. Edward sent for Dr Woodruff who said it was not much. . . .
Jun 23 . . . The firm of Becher, Street & Becher divided twenty seven thousand dollars last year, it is doing good business. . . .
Jun 25 Mr and Mrs Becher called for me to go to Woodlands, the new cemetery and to the water works. We drove there in a cab & returned in the steamer. The grounds of the cemetery are very pretty. . . . Spring Bank was crowded with children picknicking from different schools. . . .
Jun 29 Amelia came to show me the address from the Post Office clerks to Mr Griffin expressing their regret at his leaving & giving a purse of $120 in gold to Amelia. I am very glad not for the money but for the address. One of the clerks gave Amelia a pretty toilet ornament, a silver stand with bottles of perfume and a trinkets case. . . .
Jun 30 . . . Scott passed his examination for the high school which we're all very glad of.
Jul 2 . . . [Edward] says that he & George will send Scott to the Military School at Kingston[348] & pay for his education if Amelia will consent to it. . . .
Jul 5 . . . I had a letter from Teresa. They are just starting for Norway on a three month's tour.
Aug 24 I had a letter from Mr Griffin. He wants Amelia & Scott to come to London for the winter, Scott to go to the Hellmuth College & Amelia to live at Eldon & with the Georges. It is an arrangement which will not answer. . . .
Sep 4 . . . Lucy has heard of the death of her Uncle Robert. . . . Lucy gets some money & a small house by his death & some plate. . . .
Sep 10 . . . Great improvements are going on in the house. Edward is getting the pipes in to have the house heated by steam, & he is having the roof raised over the servants' hall so as to make a bedroom for the man.

[348]The Royal Military College which opened in 1876.

Sep 18 . . . [Lucy] was confined at a $^1/_4$ before 9 AM & had a fine son & was doing well. We are all so glad & hope that she may have a good recovery.
Oct 5 The trial of the supposed murderers of the Donnellys going on today.[349] . . .
Oct 11 Mr Shawn sent cheque for the year's rent of my farm at Port Ryerse $125. . . .
Oct 15 . . . the steam apparatus is so far in readiness that the steam has been turned on today. The smell for the moment is over oppressive but they tell us that after today that smell will cease.
Oct 24 . . . George called highly pleased with his sport at Long Point for the last five days. The ducks he shot averaged 97 a day, one day he shot 149. . . .
Nov 22 . . . The steam not yet in order. I had the stove put up again in my bedroom. . . .
Nov 24 Much to my surprise my brother Edward walked in today. He had not written that he was coming. He looks old & much broken since I saw him one year ago. He is now 80. . . .
Nov 25 My brother has sat with me all day. Most probably it is the last day we shall ever spend together. . . .
Nov 27 Goodman, the cook's husband, commenced work yesterday. He has been a butler and I should think a very good indoors servant, but to be with his wife he is willing to do all the work done by our man servant. . . .
Nov 29 Dr Ryerson arrived. . . . He looks old & feeble.
Dec 4 Dr Ryerson returned to Toronto by the 2 PM train. He looked better when he left than when he came. . . . I wrote to Amelia.
Dec 12 . . . Edward told me he had to go to England on business for Lucy & that Sophia would go with him & that they would be away for two months. I felt quite stunned with the news, as it involves our shutting up the house & my going to George's during their absence. . . .
Dec 13 The thought of Edward and Sophia going to England kept me from sleep last night. Consequently, I feel unwell today, arrangements have already commenced. Cows are to be sold & servants discharged. If it was summer I would not mind but I dislike leaving my comfortable home in the winter. . . .
Dec 21 Life is dull & lonely, yet all my wants are well supplied, old age must be lonely to a widowed mother, & children away. . . .

[349]The well known murder trial held at the London Court house. See James Reaney, "James Donnelly," *Dic. Can. Biog.* X, pp. 234–235.

Dec 24 Mr Griffin sent me some views of the house I lived in when in Kingston in 1816 & 17.[350] It is very nice. . . .
Dec 25 Xmas is over. I have not felt well & consequently not very cheery and looking back upon past years & the changes that have taken place brings painful recollections. . . . George & Lucy dined here. I had several presents & cards.
Dec 28 I came to George's today after luncheon & shall remain here until Edward & Sophia return from England. I had a very melancholy feeling in leaving my dear old home but my welcome here is so kind that my heart will be cold if I did not respond to it. Edward & Sophia came here to dinner. I am not very well.
Dec 29 My room very warm, comfortable & pleasant. . . .
Dec 30 Edward & Sophia left for England at 2 PM. . . .
Dec 31 Cold continues. Heard again from Amelia. . . . Mrs Beddome called. Another year has gone. I pray God to have me in His keeping & to make me thankful for all His mercies.

1881

Jan 1 The weather has moderated. . . . I had a letter from Amelia who is better, no word from Edward. I felt so ill that I had to lye down & saw no visitors until late & then only the Hamiltons, Col Taylor & Henry Meredith & his brothers, Tom & Lewellan.
Jan 3 . . . [They] Sophia & Edward had a cold, disagreeable journey and arrived at N. York without their luggage and they were afraid that they would have to sail without it.[351] . . .
Jan 4 George left at 6 AM to go to Sarnia to a curling match. . . .
Jan 12 George went to Chatham to curl. . . .
Jan 17 George went to St Thomas to curl. Mr Thomas called, he is looking well. . . . Ben Cronyn stands high in his estimation. He says Mr Carling is to be placed in the Upper House. . . .
Jan 20 . . . George curling with the Toronto Club. . . .
Jan 21 A heavy snow storm. George curling with the Toronto Club, Mrs Walker & Bella came to afternoon tea. . . .
Jan 24 I got a letter from Edward mailed in Queenstown. They had a very rough passage to England. George has gone to a Masonic meeting. Wrote to Mary.

[350] Called the "Hydrographer's House."
[351] Their luggage arrived and they sailed on the 2nd, arriving at Liverpool on the 11th.

Feb 5 George & Lucy reported favorably of the ball.[352] Lucy made some calls today & went to Mrs Labatt's . . .
Feb 19 My 83rd birthday, all well, the day bright & beautiful & my friends so kind. I had letters from the Griffins & a very pretty book containing coloured views of Windsor [England] & its neighborhood & then Mrs Landor came with her annual offering of pretty flowers . . . a pretty white woolen shawl from Lucy, a drawing very well done from Amelia [Milly], a bouquet & cards from Charlotte, Ronald & Baby. . . . Lucy asked several to an afternoon tea, Mr & Mrs Walker, Mrs Taylor, Mrs W. Meredith from Toronto, Bella, Mrs Landor & Ellen Hamilton came. In the morning the Dean & Mrs Boomer & Mrs Smallman called. Lucy had a very nice birthday cake & the day passed pleasantly.
Mar 13 Lucy & children went to morning service. I read the service in my own room. George went for a walk. Mr & Mrs Walker & Mr Hutchison called.
Mar 22 Edward & George returned.[353] . . . He brought a box of plate that Lucy has inherited from her great uncle [Ronalds] & there is a great deal of household goods on the way for her. . . .
Mar 24 I returned to Eldon this afternoon & was very sorry to leave. George & Lucy are so kind. . . .
Apr 6 . . . Edward & I had letters from Sophia. She has taken her passage for the 15th of May. . . . Wrote to Amelia.
Apr 8 . . . I went to George's to see . . . some of the things Lucy had inherited from her great Uncle. There are glass, China & a great number of things that are curious & valuable & there are a great many things that are not worth their carriage. However, she is fortunate in having more good things than she knows what to do with. . . .
Apr 15 . . . George left for Long Point for goose shooting.
Apr 21 . . . George returned. . . . He shot ten geese, very fine birds.
May 5 Had a letter from Amelia who was very weary, moving into another house. I also had a very kind note from Dr Ryerson with a book of portraits of distinguished residents in Canada.[354] . . .
May 9 . . . A good many of Lucy's boxes of furniture from England were unpacked in the kitchen yard today. There are a great number of very handsome & valuable things[355] & a good deal of trash. . . .

[352]The Bachelor's Ball at Tecumseh House on the 4th.

[353]George had gone to New York to meet Edward.

[354]Probably John Charles Dent, *Canadian Portrait Gallery*, Toronto: John B. Magurn, 1880, still in the possession of the Harris family.

[355]The boxes included much of the dining room furniture and some of the four poster beds now at Eldon House.

May 20 . . . Edward bought a coal oil stove for cooking. We do not yet know how it will answer.
May 25 A most dreadful accident happened last evening. The steamer *Victoria* was over loaded with excursionists coming from Spring Bank. She upset & broke to pieces, & two hundred men, women & children were drowned. The city is in a state of gloom. It is the most frightful occurrence that had ever taken place in the province. The greater portion of those drowned are young between the ages of 6 and 22. Mr [J.W.] Meredith is amongst the drowned. . . .
May 26 The shops have been closed & the City are to wear a badge of mourning for a month. Coffins could not be got in London sufficient for the dead & they have been telegraphed for to Toronto, Hamilton & other places. Funeral processions have not been out of sight from early morning until dark. We are constantly hearing of heart rending incidents. It is a dreadful calamity. . . .
May 27 Edward went to Mr Meredith's funeral as one of the pall bearers. The gloom still hangs over the city. People cannot yet settle themselves to business. . . .
May 28 . . . London is sinking into its usual calm & people have returned to their work. The dead are soon forgotten by the public. . . .
May 29 I read the service in my own room. Edward went to morning service. In all the Churches, allusions were made to the great loss of life by the upsetting of the *Victoria*.
Jun 4 . . . Sophia arrived at 6 PM looking very well. She brought a cook & butler with her. The butler is a mistake & does not suit our establishment. George met Sophia at the train. Edward & Percy are to be here on Tuesday next.
Jun 7 Edward, George & Percy[356] returned tonight. . . . Percy is a nice gentlemanly looking young fellow & appears to be a very great favorite with all who know him. I am so glad to see a grand son & one that I may justly feel proud of.
Jun 13 Percy [and Edward] . . . for Galt to attend an Agricultural Show. . . . They are to lunch at Government house tomorrow. George . . . and Percy will leave for Quebec & the Salmon River where they intend spending a fortnight salmon fishing. . . .
Jun 19 There is great excitement throughout the province with uneducated and superstitious people fearing that the world will come to an end today from Mother Shipton's Prophecy & the conjunction of the planets.[357] . . .

[356]Percy, the second son of Eliza and General Crutchley.
[357]See Amelia Harris' diary 4 April 1879 on the subject.

Jun 20 People's alarm is quieting down as nothing unusual happened yesterday. . . .
Jul 1 I find my life very lonely. My eye sight is failing so much that I can neither read nor work at fancy work as formerly & as I only go to George's at long intervals & go no where else & see so very few people. . . . As long as I can read I care not about being alone but the end cannot be far distant. I trust my Saviour will receive me. . . .
Jul 2 An attempt has been made today to assassinate President Garfield. Two shots were fired at him by a man . . . wounds may not prove fatal, but he is in a very dangerous state.[358] . . .
Jul 20 Percy, Edward & George went at 4 PM to play lawn tennis at Mr Street's.[359] Isadore Hellmuth, the champion player in Toronto, was there. Percy beat him with ease. I doubt whether there is any one in the province that plays as good a game as Percy. . . .
Jul 29 St George & Teresa arrived at 6 PM. Teresa looking very well. St George looks rather delicate. I was so glad to see them & dear Teresa, who can take the place of a daughter. . . . Teresa brought nice presents for myself for Amelia, Scott, Lucy & the children & a pretty travelling clock for Sophia. . . .
Jul 30 . . . George & Lucy came in the morning to see the Littledales & again at 4 PM to see them off. The parting is over & they are gone on a wild excursion to the Yellow Stone River with an English gentleman, a Mr Shaw a great sports man, who spends much of his time hunting. They intend camping out & the gentlemen will spend their time hunting. . . . It will take them two weeks to reach the hunting grounds & two weeks to return which will leave them not much over a month for their sport. I wonder that Teresa likes going but she does. They intend returning early in October & will remain here two weeks. Teresa's maid remains at Eldon until their return. . . .
Jul 31 . . . It is arranged that I am to go to George & Lucy's tomorrow . . . [when] Edward, Percy & Sophia leave. . . .
Aug 10 Edward called early. He had sent away his butler with the assistance of the police, as he refused to go. His wife, (the cook) has gone also. She would not remain without him. She is a very good woman & a good cook but her husband is worthless. Edward expects further trouble with them. . . .
Aug 17 My first born, had he lived, would have been 64 years of age today. . . .

[358]U.S. President James Garfield was shot on 2 July 1881 and subsequently died on 2 September 1881.

[359]The son of W.W. Street, a practicing lawer.

Aug 22 Edward called early to make arrangements about the removal of the [Griffin] children & Lucy & Amelia went to St Paul's cemetery & attended to the disinternment and then went to Woodlands & saw them placed in their new graves. They both returned looking wearied and exhausted. Of course it has been a trial to Amelia to have her children disintered & placed in new graves. Lucy has most kindly paid all the expenses of their removal as a present to Amelia. Lucy has my heart felt gratitude for all her kindness to Amelia & myself. She has made Amelia's visit a great pleasure to her & to me. [Sophia's] father is very ill. She will go to Toronto tomorrow. . . .
Aug 24 I returned to Eldon this morning & have found the day very long & lonely after leaving Lucy's cheerful household. . . .
Aug 26 Sophia returned at 1.50 PM to give evidence in regard to the butler & cook. Edward gained the suit. The jury gave them just what Edward had offered them. . . .
Aug 31 Edward, George & Mr Walker left at 6 AM for Long Point to shoot teal. The company allows its members to shoot during the first week in Sept & then there is no more duck shooting until the 1st of October. . . .
Sep 3 I had a letter from Egerton Ryerson. Sophia arrived safely. Dr Ryerson better.
Sep 24 Edward got a letter from Charley Crutchley.[360] He had just arrived at New York and was on his way to Texas with a Mr & Mrs Adair, who own a ranch. . . . They want Charley to give up the army & take to cattle breeding. Charley will visit us in November. . . .
Oct 12 A telegram came at 11 PM last night saying that Dr Ryerson was worse & asking Sophia to go down immediately. She left at 6 AM this morning. . . .
Oct 17 Dr Ryerson very much the same. . . . The Littledales will be here the end of the month. Teresa is heartily tired of hunting & says she will be very glad to see the London station. . . . Edward has arranged that I am to go to George & remain until Sophia returns. I would rather he had let me *propose going*. . . .
Oct 28 . . . Sarah tells me that [her daughter] Maude is to be married to Launcelot.[361] She is much pleased with the match. She likes him very much. He has three or four thousand £s a year. She, Maude, refused a much better match in point of money, a gentleman worth 30,000£s a year. . . .

[360]Charley Crutchley was the older son of Eliza and General Crutchley.

[361]Colonel Launcelot Rolleston (1847–1941) of the South Nottingham Hussars, later commanded a militia regiment in the Boer War and was awarded the D.S.O., and the K.C.B. in 1911.

Oct 30 . . . the Littledales arrived. . . . They brought such a nice saddle & haunch of venison from a deer of St George's shooting. . . .
Nov 3 George returned last night, Edward & St George returned today [from Long Point]. Amelia arrived. . . . It is a great pleasure for me to see so many of my children together once more. . . .
Nov 9 Mrs Street & Ellen Hamilton . . . Mrs Furness & Emma Street & Bella & Mrs Landor called. We, that is the Littledales & Amelia dined with the Georges. W. Meredith & wife dined there [also]. The dinner very nice.
Nov 12 Amelia & the Littledales left this morning by the 8.40 train, Amelia for Kingston, the Littledales for England. The parting was sad as I never expect to see them again & their visit has been made very painful to us all, but it is over & has left me with a heartache. George & Lucy are a comfort to me. I do not know what I should do without Lucy. Sophia returned at 2 PM. Her father a very little better but Sophia has no hope of his ultimate recovery. Sophia looks worn & ill.
Nov 13 I had a long & disagreeable conversation with Edward. . . .
Dec 16 Edward left for Hamilton. . . . The London Whist Club dine with Mr Broughton & play against the Hamilton Club. . . .
Dec 22 I came to George's . . . & shall stay until after the holidays. . . .
Dec 25 Christmas. I am still here. Few of my age are left. Lucy went to early morning service. I read the service in my own room. I had more cards & presents this morning. Col & Mrs Walker called. Edward & Sophia came to dinner. Sophia not well. Her coming was an exertion.
Dec 30 . . . The [Masonic] Ball is said to have been a success but it is a new generation that now fills the ball room. . . . The Whist Club met at Eldon tonight. . . .
Dec 31 The card party at Eldon did not separate until 3 AM. Mr Broughton & Macfie dined at Eldon. . . . Edward & Sophia called here today [at George's] & so ends another year. . . .

1882

Jan 1 George & Lucy went to morning service, I read the service in my own room. Mr & Mrs Walker, [and others] called. . . .
Jan 2 The calls for the New Year were made today. Edward & Gilbert Griffin were the first, then D. Glass & Son Chester, J. Landor, Mr Morrison, Mr B. Macfie, Mr Mahon, the Rev Mr Brown, the Bishop of Huron & the Rev Mr Innes & Mr Lawrason. I believe those were

all. I had a letter from Amelia. E. Meredith,[362] barrister, is voted Mayor for London for 1882. Wrote to Mary.

Jan 4 We have had several visitors today, Mrs Beddome, Mrs Smallman, Mrs B. Macfie, Bella & Ada Meredith. Sophia called but would not come in. Mr & Mrs Walker & Mr Jeffery dined here. . . .

Jan 5 The weather has moderated. Edward & Sophia called. George has gone to the Walkers to play whist or cleve.

Jan 7 Sophia called early. Mrs W. Meredith & Bella came to afternoon tea. Edward called. George & Lucy dined at the Walkers.

Jan 8 Lucy went to morning service. I read the service in my own room. Edward & George went for a walk. The Honble E[lijah] Leonard called especially to see me. Mrs Walker called.

Jan 9 I am not very well. I had a strange sensation almost insensible for a few seconds. I think I shall die very suddenly before very long. I had a letter from Sarah & Charlie Crutchley & cards from the Crutchley family & a letter from Mr Becher.

Jan 11 A light snow fell last night but no sleighing. . . . Sophia is better. Neither Lucy nor I am very well. Mrs H. Becher, Bella, & Edward called. Wrote to Amelia.

Jan 12 I have been so ailing that I have been unable to keep up all day. I had English letters from Mary Peard, Eliza & Mary Leith. I wrote to Mr Becher.

Jan 14 Dr Woodruff called to see me & gave the old medicine, ammonia. It is the only medicine he has given me for the last five years. George & Lucy went to Mrs Glass' at home which was well attended & went off very well. Bella & Edward sat with me. Wrote to Col Charles Crutchley & Teresa.

Jan 15 Lucy not well, did not get up until evening. I read the service in my own room & read sermons by Dr [Isaac] Watts which I like very much. Edward & Sophia called. Wrote to Mary Leith & Amelia.

Jan 18 George left . . . for Toronto with the London Curling Club to play a match. Mrs Meredith . . . Mrs Beddome, Mrs Fitzgerald & Edward called. I had a very nice letter from Berkeley Portman.

Jan 20 . . . Lucy paid visits. Bella, Mrs W. Meredith, Mrs Walker & Edward came to afternoon tea. George has gone to a whist party to the Walkers.

Jan 21 Bella called early about doing some shopping for me. Mrs MacMahon & Mrs Walker came to afternoon tea. . . . wrote to Sarah.

[362]Edmund Meredith (1845–1923), a brother of W.R. and Bella Meredith, was Mayor of London in 1882 and 1883.

Jan 23 A cold snow storm. I had letters from Sarah, Maude [granddaughter] & Mr Becher. I am quite well today. Mrs & Miss Landor & Edward called. Wrote to Eliza.

Jan 26 Mrs Hellmuth, Mrs Glancy, Miss Crooks & George lunched at Eldon. Mrs Walker called here. Charlotte not well.

Jan 27 Sophia, Mrs Percy, Mrs W. Meredith & daughter called. I had a letter from Elizabeth. Edward called. Mrs Glancy, Miss Crooks, Mrs McMahon, Mr Pipon, Mr Thompson & Mrs Ramsay dined here. The dinner very nice. Everything went off well. Wrote to Amelia.

Jan 28 I am not very well. Lucy had a letter from Amelia & I had one from Mary who seems to have as much trouble in getting good servants as we have in this country. Lucy had a ladies' luncheon party. Mrs Beddome, Mrs Percy, Mrs Williams, Bella & Ada Meredith, Mrs B. Macfie called.

Jan 29 . . . Wrote to Berkeley, Elizabeth & Mary.

Jan 31 Had a letter from Amelia . . . [usual callers]. Wrote to Sarah & brother E[dward] Ryerse.

Feb 2 Lucy had a photo of herself & baby taken. She went in the afternoon to make calls in Westminster. Mrs Beddome called here. Mrs H. Becher & Edward came to afternoon tea. Mr Peters the architect died this evening.

Feb 3 I had letters from Eliza & Teresa all ailing. All like Mr Rolleston [Maude's husband]. . . .

Feb 5 Lucy & George went to morning service. I read the service in my own room. Edward paid me a long visit. Mr Ellis came from Church with George & Lucy & dined here. Sophia & Mrs Walker called.

Feb 6 I seldom feel well any more. Mrs Hellmuth, Mrs Glancy, & Mrs G. Hellmuth called. Lucy made calls. . . . Wrote to Amelia.

Feb 7 Warm like a day in April. Edward called. B[enjamin] Cronyn gives a dinner to more than a hundred people tonight at the opening of the new Club house. George & Edward have gone. Wrote to Eliza.

Feb 8 I was ill all night & coughed incessantly . . . feel a little better this evening. The Club dinner was a success. . . .

Feb 9 Feel a little better but not well. Sophia called this morning. Lucy lunched with Mrs McMahon, a ladies' luncheon party. Mrs Glancy called she brought her twin little boys to see me. They are certainly very fine handsome children. Wrote to Becher.

Feb 11 My cough continues bad. Bella & Edward our only visitors. Sophia got a telegram saying her father was not so well & wishing her to go to Toronto on Monday.

Feb 12 Lucy went to morning service, I read the service in my own room. Mrs Walker called. Sophia & Edward called, Sophia to say goodbye.

Feb 13 Sophia left for Toronto at 8 AM. Edward paid his usual visit. Wrote to Amelia.

Feb 14 Edward had a letter from Sophia. Her father is very ill. We should not be surprised to hear of his death any day. My cold is a little better. Lucy's tender care & prescriptions have done me good. . . .

Feb 15 My cold better. I had letters from Sarah, Mary & Teresa, all well and appear to be well pleased with Maude's approaching marriage. Mrs Beddome, Mrs Birrell, Miss Birrell, Bella and Ada Meredith & Mrs Morrison called. Edward paid his usual visit & brought Sophia's letter for me to read. Her father very low.

Feb 16 Had a letter from Amelia & Edward had one from Sophia. Her father is very, very ill. His death may be expected any day. I feel ill & miserable.

Feb 17 Dr Ryerson was supposed to be dying last night but has rallied & is still alive. I had a letter from Mr Becher. Lucy & Edward had letters from Eliza. Mrs W. Meredith called. Wrote to Maude Dalzell.

Feb 18 Lucy celebrated my birthday today in place of tomorrow (Sunday) by giving some of my friends an afternoon tea with such nice cakes. I had a letter from Amelia & a pair of pretty vases & a number of birthday cards from different friends. . . . Mrs Jeffery [sic] called, Mrs Labatt called to see Lucy about her daughters going to school in England with Amelia.[363] Mrs Beddome, Mrs Walker, Mrs Bowleby, Mrs W. Meredith & Bella came to tea. . . . Sophia telegraphed for Edward to go to Toronto. He went by the 1.40 PM train. Dr Ryerson is not expected to live over the night. My cough is bad. I wrote to Amelia.

Feb 19 We got a telegram from Edward. Dr Ryerson died at 7 AM surrounded by his family. He has led an active & a useful life. Baby [Lucy's youngest son] not well. Lucy did not go to Church. I read the service in my own room. Mrs Jeffery called. Mr & Mrs W. Meredith brought me such a pretty bouquet for my birthday. Bella called. . . .

Feb 20 Dr Ryerson is to be buried on Wednesday the 22nd. Edward will remain [in Toronto] until after the funeral. George will go down tomorrow to attend it. My cough very bad today. Baby a little better. I had birthday cards today from Mrs Campbell [of Simcoe] & Mrs H.

[363]Two of the Labatt daughters and Amelia Archange, "Milly," did attend a school in England in the fall of 1882.

Becher & very pretty flowers from Mrs Landor. Ellen Hamilton & her cousin, a Miss Somebody from Chicago, & Mr Ellis called. Wrote to Sophia & Mary.

Feb 21 I had a letter from Edward telling me the particulars of Dr Ryerson's death. When it was known in Toronto the flags on all the public buildings were only raised half mast high & the House of Assembly adjourn tomorrow to attend the funeral. George left at 6 PM to attend the funeral tomorrow. Charlotte, Ronald & Baby all have colds & mine is scarcely better. Bella & Emma Street called. Wrote to Teresa.

Feb 22 Had a letter from Edward & from Teresa. Teresa sent me patterns for wool work. Sophia not well. My cold is no better & Charlotte & Baby's cold are very bad. Bella called to say good bye. She goes to Toronto tomorrow for two or three weeks.

Feb 23 I had letters from Sarah & Mary. They are all excited about Maude's marriage. George & Edward returned by the 6 PM train. Edward dined here. Lucy made some calls. Sophia is to return on Tuesday next.

Feb 24 I have felt so ill today that Dr Woodruff was sent for. I am better this evening & the children are better. I had a letter from Amelia. They are all well. Mrs Walker & Edward called. Wrote to Amelia.

Feb 25 Heard from Sophia. She is not coming home for another week. Maude Dalzell is married today to Mr Rolleston of Watnell Hall, Nottinghamshire. I pray God to bless them. Mrs Beddome & Miss Glass called. Mr Griffin called. Edward came to dinner. I sent papers to all my daughters in England containing a biographical sketch of Dr Ryerson's life.[364]

[Amelia Harris closed her diary on 25 February 1882. She died four weeks later on 24 March 1882.]

[364]The sketch was probably one that had been published in a Toronto newspaper. While this is the last entry in Amelia's diary, two days later, on 27 February, she dictated a "Memorandum" to Lucy.

The Diary of Sophia Howard Ryerson Harris (1836–1898)

Sophia Howard Ryerson, the daughter of Egerton Ryerson by his second wife, Mary Hamilton, married Edward William Harris, the son of John and Amelia Harris on 7 July 1860. The event is described in Amelia Harris' diary.

"Sophie's" diary is brief, covering only the period between 1 September 1860 and 31 December 1861.[1] It is, however, a pleasure to read, her polished style and organized mind producing clear and interesting vignettes of personal interactions and of the society of her time, centred on the family living at Eldon House.

After her marriage, Sophie and Edward moved to Eldon House and her diary is a record of her early days as a young wife, and is full of allusions to the happiness and novelty of a marriage in which she felt fulfilled. She adapted herself comfortably into the ways of the Harris family and enjoyed their friends. Nevertheless, Sophie maintained a close relationship with her own family, particularly her father with whom she had always had strong ties.[2]

Through Sophie's comments on social life, politics and religion, we discover that she was an educated young lady, sophisticated, yet simple and sensitive. Her education included travelling with her father to Europe, where she enjoyed theatre, concerts, and art galleries. She translated into French and German for her father, played the piano, and enjoyed entertaining the visitors to Eldon House with her concerts.

Her comments provide material that affords a different perspective on Amelia Harris, as well as providing insights into her own personality and life-style.[3] She was, in many ways, a woman ahead of her time, and certainly one who challenged the mores of her day. She looks with favour upon Lady Franklin

[1]Sophie's diary is handwritten on lined, blue paper which has been bound into an album with an attached lock.

[2]Sophie's father, Egerton Ryerson, also kept a diary. For more on Sophie's relationship with her father see C.B. Sissons, *My Dearest Sophie: Letters from Egerton Ryerson to his Daughter*, Toronto: Ryerson Press, 1955.

[3]Sophie's diary supplements that of Amelia Harris, and fills the gap between 8 February and 2 June 1861.

who, despite her age, "seems to get on admirably without a gentleman"[4] and when Sophie travelled alone by train on a visit to her family in Toronto, she too "got on admirably alone."[5]

One of Sophie's entries suggests that the novelty of marriage was beginning to pale in the face of the repetitive domestic routine: "reading, music & reading."[6] She does not say it, but we feel that delivering lunch to Edward's office every day, going to church on Sundays, and playing a game or the piano in the evening had become monotonous. Moreover, her enjoyment of other people, her active social life, and in particular her relationship with male friends, though innocent, were resented by her husband, and criticized by Amelia Harris.[7] These matters aggravated her husband, Edward, and affected the marriage to the point that it ended in a temporary legal separation.[8] Eventually reconciled with Edward, Sophie returned to Eldon House where she became the chatelaine during Amelia Harris' declining years.

Unfortunately, Sophie stopped her diary too soon, and we are thus prevented from learning more about this remarkable woman's views on her life and the society in which she lived.

[4]Sophie's diary, 27 September 1860.

[5]Sophie's diary, 13 December 1860.

[6]Sophia's diary, 24 October 1860.

[7]Amelia's diary comments on Sophia's male friendships, her separation from her husband, and their reconciliation.

[8]Sophia's separation seems to be the reason she concluded her diary, or it may have been that she destroyed entries made after 1861 to erase the record of unhappy days.

Sophia

Oaklands

Saturday 26th

Yesterday I had such a kind letter from Papa he gives me that pretty phaeton which he bought when I was in Toronto as a Xmas present he is so good to me that I shall never be able to repay his generosity – Today I had another letter from him wishing me to enclose his letter as if Edward had agreed to buy the phaeton & to enclose a cheque for £55 – otherwise Mamma wd. never forgive or forget Papa's having given me so handsome a present – kind as she is to me in many ways she cannot bear Papa giving anything away even to his own daughter – At Mrs. [illegible] request I called & refused the Sunday dining at Elmsley tomorrow with Sir John Robinson & afterwards called at the Office for Edward. In the evening we both walked down to the Office as Edward had a good deal of work to attend to before going to Sarnia wh. he intends doing in the morning –

Sophia comments on her father and husband

Sophia Ryerson Harris' Diary

1860

Sep 1 Edward went to the office . . . for a long day's work – the two hours spent at the farm[9] on the previous day had to be made up – so great is the pressure of business that every moment counts. Glad as I am that affairs are in so promising a condition, I cannot avoid feeling uneasy at times lest my dear husband should fall into bad health from over-exertion & little or no rest. It is eight weeks today since I left my Father's house for a new home & a happy one it is. Edward's mother (now mine) is all goodness & kindness & a worthy example for those around her. Teresa & Mr Scott[10] are both happy in their married life. Ours cannot be less so. No two people can thoroughly know & understand each other before marriage & the change must either be for the better or for worse. As each day passes I feel more & more thankful for the happiness that has fallen my lot.

To be a good wife is my greatest desire & I pray to God that he may open my eyes to faults & help me to please Him as far as in me lies. After luncheon Teresa & I arranged the books brought from Teviot Bank[11] – many good works – the greater number of them sermons. Edward received a nice kind letter from Sarah[12] which [s]he sent up by Mr Scott – she alluded to me in a way that could not fail to give me pleasure, more than any other letter from England has yet done. Mr Griffin[13] came in while we were in the hall with books on every side – he was quite contented to grumble to us from the foot of the stairs – apparently not in the best of humors. Perhaps a little disappointed at not hearing from Amelia. . . . Capt & Mrs Taylor are both young people. I should not imagine they had seen much of good or in fact, any society at home but I dare say we may like them after a longer acquaintance. I was late in going for Edward & met [him] half-

[9]In July Edward had purchased a farm at Lobo, ten miles west of London.

[10]Teresa had married William John Scott on 18 August 1859.

[11]Scott's family home, fifty miles south-east of Edinburgh.

[12]Sarah Dalzell, aged 39, who had married Colonel Robert Dalzell in 1846. He had retired from the Army in 1858. They had four children, Robert, Arthur, Mary and Maud.

[13]Gilbert Griffin, the London Post Office Inspector, who had married Amelia Andrina Harris in 1855. They had no children at this time but he had two sons, George and Charles, by a previous marriage. His wife, Amelia, was currently visiting relatives in England.

way looking tired & full of business. But office was forgotten around the dinner table.

Sep 2 Generally speaking people make Sunday a day of rest in the fullest sense of the word & commence by getting up late. We are not an exception to this rule at Eldon which I am sorry to say very often interferes with our being in church at the proper time. Edward & I were late, the Scotts having gone before us. Mr McLean[14] preached an excellent sermon after which we all remained for the Sacrament. Looking back on the past I felt most truly thankful for what had happened & my unworthiness of the many blessings I had received, but prayed to Our Heavenly Father that he would make us both better Christians. At half past 4 o'clock Edward & George[15] started for the farm with "Meg" [horse] – in the meantime I wrote Sarah a long letter thanking her for her congratulations to us both, & alluded to her kindness in thinking of sending us a soup ladle, but hoped she would not hurry about it as we did not think of house-keeping for the present. Mr Griffin came to tea. Afterwards Edward wrote to Mr Portman.[16]

Sep 3 Edward's walk had evidently done him good & if he did not sleep later than usual, he would be all the better able to do another week's work. I wrote to Papa a long letter as kind as I could but did not mention Mele's name as we think so differently on the subject it had better be dropped at once. Also wrote to Miss [?] about poor John[17] & glad I was to be able to say something encouraging. I told her that Dr. Budd[18] thought much might be done tho' the case was serious & that Carlsbad was not approved of at this stage but Scarborough was recommended for a few weeks.[19] Eliza, Mary[20] & Sarah all think John does not look as ill as they were led to believe – so far satisfactory as it gives us hope that John may be all the better for the sea voyage. Received letters from Mamma urging me to go down [to Toronto] & see the grand doings during the Prince's visit.[21] I answered that it made me unhappy to think of leaving Edward for

[14]Reverend John McLean (1828–86), curate at St. Paul's and later Bishop of Saskatchewan.

[15]Edward's younger brother, George Becher Harris, aged 24.

[16]Maurice Portman, Edward's brother-in-law, Helen's husband.

[17]In June 1860, eight months after his marriage, John, aged 30, and his wife Elizabeth (Loring) had gone to England in search of a cure for his medical problems.

[18]A British physician.

[19]Carlsbad, Germany and Scarborough, England were favoured spas at this time.

[20]Eliza Crutchley and Mary Peard, Edward's twin sisters, aged 27, were both living with their respective families in England.

[21]For more on the tour of the Prince of Wales, see Amelia's diary, 5–21 September 1860.

three or four days but if they would feel hurt at not seeing me I should try to overcome my feelings.

Sep 4 One less at breakfast this morning, Mr Scott having a sick headache was unable to make his appearance. After Edward went to the office I underwent the unpleasant operation of head-cleaning, looking very much like a lunatic for two or three hours afterwards. Spent the morning in Mamma's room. Teresa gave us her company the greater part of the time. Commenced *The Woman in White*[22] & found it exciting from the first page. Edward was not ready to leave the office at five, so I amused myself reading the *Globe* for a while. Even George Brown thinks the Toronto ball will in every respect equal the magnificent one given the Prince of Wales in Montreal. The city is busy with preparations & what is better, the roads & pavements are being put in good condition – about the only immediate benefit Toronto will derive from the honor to be conferrred on the town. Edward & I shopped on our way home & most successfully. Edward & Mamma had a two hours' talk after dinner while my attention was divided between music & *The Woman in White*.

Sep 5 When Edward went to the office I found *The Woman in White* capital company & should have been contented till dinner with no other. However, Teresa wanted to make a cake so off we went. . . . Was rather late in going to the office & missed Edward. George walked back with me & Edward met us at the corner. At dinner there was a discussion about the Prince of Wales having refused to enter Kingston until the Orangemen consented to give up their badges & decorations which the latter refused to do. The consequence was all preparations to receive the Royal visitor were made in vain. He only partook of their hospitality so far as eating the dinner which was brought on board the steamer. This decision outraged the Orangemen who chartered a vessel & with all their insignia determined to follow the Prince wherever he went. After dinner Edward & George attended a meeting at Charlie Stevens' to decide about an arch to be erected in front of our windows. . . . George & his boy friends were busily engaged next door trying to make lamps (not exactly Chinese) to illuminate the trees for the Prince of Wales' arrival. This place is thought the best, Eldon is so shaded by the trees that any great display in the windows in the shape of colored lights would be quite lost. . . . Teresa thinks of getting a Prince of Wales' plume for the porch & surprise George who is interested in these proceedings more than anybody & does all he can. . . .

[22]A novel by Wilkie Collins published in England in 1860.

Sep 6 . . . In the afternoon Mr Scott brought me a letter from Mary [Peard] enclosing a short note to Edward. Mary thought John had improved in appearance a few days after his arrival but . . . Mamma heard from Eliza who was in good spirits at having Amelia with her & hinted that it would be for Amelia's enjoyment if we could manage to show Mr Griffin a little more civility, otherwise he might insist upon Amelia's returning at once. Amelia was to go to Mary's & remain until the end of the month. . . . Before we had finished this letter Gilbert brought me one from Amelia. We were all so glad to find that she had met with so much kindness & seemed so thoroughly to enjoy herself. . . . Went for Edward about five, he had received a letter from Mr Portman on business but in it there were some very discouraging allusions to poor John, so much so that we dare not let Mamma know . . . Edward went to the "Arch" meeting again & a plan was decided upon for the arch.[23] After tea Mamma went to bed & Teresa came in our room to hear Edward read Mr Portman's letter. He thought we should never see poor John again, for it was dear John's wish to die in England, & for the sole reason that it would spare Mamma much pain, mental & physical were she not to witness his distress & suffering at the last. This all seems so sad, too sad to realize & we can't help hoping that these heavy trials may not come so soon again to prostrate our dear Mother.[24]

Sep 7 After breakfast Edward & I ran down the hill in search of plums but only found apples. The piano tuner was busy at work when we came in. The Scotts received their plate chest at last & busied themselves nearly all the morning packing & unpacking the valuables for inspection. Telegrams were received from Toronto that the Orangemen intended to maintain their ground which would prevent the Prince from going there & as London intended to side with Toronto there was an immense excitement in the town. Bennett had newly furnished the Tecumseh [Hotel] & said he would be ruined. All the trades-people had taken stock in view of an additional number of purchasers, in fact, the town would be left in a state of bankruptcy were the Prince to pass London. However, the *Globe* took a more favorable view of the matter & made us feel more sanguine of Toronto & London coming to a wiser decision in this unfortunate affair than Kingston or Belleville had done. After dinner George went out to make flowers for our arch. I made some in the afternoon . . .

[23]Processional arches were constructed in all of the towns visited by the Prince.

[24]An allusion to the trials and tribulations undergone by Amelia Harris at the time of the death of Helen Portman earlier in 1860.

Sep 8 Very dark & gloomy, every appearance of the rain continuing all day. At last all had been amicably arranged at Toronto where the Prince arrived about dusk instead of five o'clock as was expected. However, illuminating was carried on rapidly. From all accounts the town looked beautiful, every house having more or less light, the arches in every direction & of various designs were beautifully decorated & lighted up. Many of the public buildings ornamented regardless of expense presented a magnificent appearance. . . . We were all pleased to find that the Prince of Wales opened the Cobourg ball with Louisa.[25] . . . [Edward] brought home the bad news that there was a disturbance in Toronto originating with the Orangemen & no one could tell what the results would be. This made everyone feel down again.

Sep 9 Edward & I alone went to church . . . The Bishop of Rupert's Land preached a very good & short extempore sermon from Hebrews IV: "Let us therefore come boldly unto the throne of grace that we may obtain mercy & find grace to help in time of need." There was something very nice in his voice & manner which I could not help liking. Mr Griffin & the children dined here. . . . After dinner Mr Griffin, Edward & I walked to the W[illiam] Lawrason's. . . . we saw the flowers, the object of my visit. The scaffolding of several arches was up & one was covered with cedar. Of course no one can tell how they will look when finished. Edward wrote Mr Portman . . . about John, I one to Mamma. . . . I sincerely hope dear Mamma is not annoyed with me.

Sep 10 . . . received a letter from Papa who had arranged with the Duke of Newcastle to have the Prince visit the Normal School[26] & was anxious that we should go down in time to be present at half past three o'clock Tuesday. I read my letter to Mamma & she thought Edward ought not to miss such an opportunity. I immediately went to the office to consult Edward & we decided to leave early next day . . .

Sep 11 We reached the station before six in good time & went to the Tecumseh for coffee. As we approached Toronto crowds were making for the Esplanade to witness the regatta, the Prince however being the principal spectator.

Sep 12 . . . Papa drove with me in a cab. Louisa & Edward followed in our carriage. The station was not as crowded as we expected. . . .

[25]Louisa Beatty, a first cousin of Sophia.

[26]The Duke of Newcastle was the member of the Prince's party who was in charge of all arrangements. A Normal School for the training of teachers for the Common Schools had been established at Toronto by Ryerson in 1847.

Our departure was delayed until the Prince had half an hour's start of us. . . . Fortunately we reached London before the Prince. George met us & secured the flags for our arch. No cabs here to be had so Edward & I walked home quickly & everybody set to work & adorned the arch.

Sep 13 After breakfast Mr Scott, Teresa, Edward & I went to the Tecumseh to see the ball room. . . . The decorations were no comparison prettier than at the citizens' ball in Toronto. Mr Griffin in particular deserved great credit for the taste displayed in the whole arrangement of the room. Mr McInnes[27] returned with us to Eldon where he took up his quarters for the night. Mr Scott, Edward, George & Mr McInnes were presented to His Royal Highness at the levée. The crowd around the City Hall was so dense that they [the royal party] left the carriage & wound their way more successfully on foot. . . . [In the evening] Edward & Mr Scott walked to the Tecumseh . . . & saw some ladies en route for the ball room in gorgeous array.

Sep 14 Mamma called Mr McInnes in to see her when he came home from the ball about *five.* It appeared there was much ill-feeling against Mr Becher who managed everything his own way, bringing friends from a distance the Gzowskis, Miss Prince & Miss Bell to dance with the Prince in lieu of townspeople. . . . After leaving Edward at the office, came home & found Mr Griffin anxious for a walk so off we started for Mrs Bill [Lawrason]'s & heard her story. Like everybody else she was charmed at having danced with the Prince who seems to make himself very popular with the ladies. . . .

Sep 15 Edward started for Hamilton at six. My cold . . . made me feel miserable. I read & sewed all the morning but after lunch was obliged to lie down. Mamma did not think Edward could return before night so I slept the less reluctantly & was disturbed in my slumbers by Teresa & Mr Scott who had almost made me believe that dear Edward could not get home before Monday when he walked in & made me happy again. I don't like to think of the first parting for although everybody at Eldon is most kind I feel so lonely when Edward is anywhere but at the office & almost count the hours for his return. No one can fill the place of a kind and affectionate husband. . . .

Sep 16 Not a very bright looking day & no one felt very chirpy. . . . Edward had to go eighteen miles in the country not having done so Saturday as he expected instead of the Hamilton journey. I should have enjoyed the drive very much had I been well. However, Mr Griffin agreed to accompany him much to my satisfaction as I never feel quite

[27]See Amelia's diary, 1 October 1857.

comfortable when he drives any distance alone. We were surprised to see them home before six, two horses go faster than one. . . . Before tea George told us Duncan Askin's melancholy fate. A few days ago he was severely beaten by someone. This was followed by epileptic fits . . . which carried him off this afternoon about five. How awful to think of a man coming to such an end at five & twenty! Wrote to Amelia then went to bed.

Sep 17 . . . We found our way to Mrs Gill's who gave us the particulars. All Saturday [15th] Mr Duncan was delirious to that extent that it required five men to hold him. On Sunday he became quiet & in the afternoon insensible & passed away so quietly that they scarcely knew the moment when he breathed his last. Called for Edward at five, we talked & thought a great deal about Duncan Askin. Practiced [piano] a little after dinner.

Sep 18 It seems the Prince of Wales has managed to see the Falls with less molestation than was expected by going where he was not looked for. H.R.H. the Duke of Newcastle, Sir Edmund [Head] & General Bruce took possession of Mrs Zimmerman's house, the suite were accommodated in the cottages. The Illuminations were said to be very fine, making the great waterfall appear all colored & I can fancy the grandness of the spectacle beyond description. The Prince, Sir Edmund & General Bruce witnessed the scene unnoticed & also got out of the cab at Table Rock, left their names in the visitor's book, much to the gratification of [the] landlady of [the] House. Edward & George went to Duncan Askin's funeral which was a very large one. . . . [Mr Griffin said that] if Blanche doesn't dance with the Prince this time it won't be their fault. Read one of Hans Anderson's pretty stories. . . .

Sep 19 . . . Teresa & I made ourselves very busy trying to make jelly which turned out to be very like syrup owing to an exceedingly stupid mistake. However, we rectified it by adding to the stock. I made an Italian cream. Our preparations were for Sir Edmund Head in case he should accept Mamma's invitation & remain Thursday night at Eldon. Mamma & Teresa both heard from Mr Portman. . . . The weather was not fine or inviting for a walk. I met Edward at the gate coming home rather earlier than usual & with a letter from Mamma enclosed . . . Papa left for Hamilton, indeed everyone but Mamma. After dinner I wrote to Mr Portman while Edward read *Saturday Review* . . . George & Teresa heard from John, he is better but seems rather homesick.

Sep 20 Raining & disagreeable but Teresa had a strong inclination to go out in spite of the weather, so a cab was ordered & off we started first to Mrs D. Askin's. . . . Our excursion was not altogether a pleasant one as our vehicle turned out to be anything but water-proof.

Mamma had a telegram from Sir Edmund Head regretting he could not remain one night in London. . . . My umbrella was left to have the name engraved. Teresa invested in oysters. Our evenings always pass pleasantly. Everybody gets on so well with everybody, Edward is so kind & affectionate to me that I ought to anticipate his wants more than I do. Annoyances that continuously occur in business never affect his uniform kindness to me.

Sep 21 Teresa, Mr Scott & I went to town. . . . Called at the office. Edward's cold was worse . . . Mr Griffin came in the afternoon & gave us an account of the Hamilton ball which appears to have been most successful. The Prince had nothing to do with lists but selected his own partners. Blanche was among the number much to the delight of the whole Widder faction. Miss Powell had her fourth dance with the Prince. Miss MacNab was the most stylish and best dressed lady in the room. Mr McInnes considered her the belle! Edward left for Juston's farm at three with a man who wished to lease it for three years & purchase at the end of that time. Edward did not return till ten. . . .

Sep 22 I had horrid face ache. First of all tried brandy & cayenne pepper, then vinegar as hot as I could bear it, with no effect. I felt most stupid & miserable all day. Music was my only satisfactory diversion. Mr Becher called evidently elated with his trip to Windsor in company with the Prince who as he said "was very sorry to part with us." Mr Becher was decidedly anxious that we should be aware of his importance. Miss Powell seems after all to have secured the Prince's admiration for the time being at all events. Mr Van Koughnet[28] asked the Duke of Newcastle if Miss Powell might go in the steamer from Niagara to Port Dalhousie & was answered in the negative. However, Miss Powell (with a bouquet) & H.R.H. were surprised in a tête-à-tête in the engine room. . . .

Sep 23 My face ache was so severe that I found it impossible to sleep before daylight. . . . However, Edward did nurse famously and brought me such a nice breakfast in the bedroom. . . . Mamma & the Scotts went to church & Edward & George drove to the farm with the black horses. . . . The weather was lovely. I only wished I was able to enjoy it, . . . everybody was so kind & attentive to me. Teresa & Edward spent a great part of the afternoon roasting figs for my benefit. Mr Griffin came over & gave Mamma a little basket of peaches. . . .

[28]Philip Van Koughnet (1790–1873) was a member of the Family Compact, elected to the Assembly of Upper Canada. The last position he held before his death was of Chairman of the Canadian Board of Government Arbitrators. See Bruce W. Hodgins, "Philip Van Koughnet," *Dic. Can. Biog.* X, pp. 693–694.

Sep 24 Practised & ran about the house all the morning with Teresa doing our best to make the spare bedroom look nice & comfortable for Mr Des Voeux[29] who was expected in the afternoon. Edward came home to lunch. At half past four there were no tidings of our guest & we almost gave up all hope of seeing him before night. At five, however, he made his appearance. The train was an hour late. Five years have made a good deal of difference in Mr Des Voeux's appearance, so much so that I should hardly have recognized him elsewhere. He seemed to have remembered me at once. Everybody liked him at Eldon from the first. After dinner we all found ourselves in the library (the pet room) & the expense of living in this country in comparison with England was thoroughly discussed as also the striking features of Canada. Teresa disappeared suddenly & early but nobody else thought of moving until after eleven.

Sep 25 Rather dull in the morning as for weather. Mr Scott took Mr Des Voeux to the Post Office & about the town. Edward came home to lunch and afterwards he & Mr Des Voeux drove some miles in the country & only returned in time for dinner. Our friend seemed very much pleased with what he saw. Our dinner circle was more en famille & Mr Des Voeux I think felt himself at home. We tried to persuade him to prolong his visit which he probably might have done were he not a little depending on Mr Baring (who was waiting at Chicago) for a companion to the Prairies & he had named a day of meeting at Chicago. I played a good deal in the evening. Edward wandered from room to room evidently much engaged in business matters. Mamma appeared tired having exerted herself & done the agreeable to Mr Des Voeux nearly all day & her place nobody can fill.

Sep 26 Edward went to the office before all had finished breakfast, feeling anxious to make up for lost time. This month being a particularly busy one it required Edward's & George's constant attention to keep things in order. Mr Scott & Mr Des Voeux went in the town but all were home for lunch, & afterwards went to the station with Mr Des Voeux. . . . Young Mr King is slightly obstreperous which seemed rather to amuse his Mamma than call forth a reproof. . . . I amused myself [with] a sketch of Sir Robert Peel's life in *Blackwoods*. . . .

Sep 27 Read & worked all the morning. Mr Scott took Chatham [horse] & the dogs to the farm to try his luck shooting. George came home for a moment but had not time to remain to lunch. The *Free*

[29]Des Voeux, a Toronto family.

Press had announced the arrival of Lady Franklin[30] at the Tecumseh. Teresa & I were anxious to make her acquaintance so we called on her but she had just taken her departure for Chicago thence to St Louis & to winter in California & not return to England until spring. Tho' an elderly woman she has but a niece & a maid travelling with her & seems to get on admirably without a gentleman. We saw Mrs Bennet who is rather a sensible woman. Mr MacLean[31] called at Eldon after we returned. He is certainly a most energetic, good man & attends to his flock as well as it is possible for any man to do. Edward went to the office again this evening.

Sep 28 A very cold, raw day but it made me feel more active. George was determined not to lose a moment from the office & work to the very last. He seemed so pleased at the idea of going to the Prairies for a week[32] that everybody felt anxious to have him go & Edward willingly consented to do his best alone in the office. George & I packed the trunk together. All were home for lunch & fared so well that we agreed to have no more dinner. Teresa naturally felt low at parting with Mr Scott for the first time since their marriage. She & Edward saw the "voyageurs" off. Mamma heard from Eliza, Sarah and Amelia & John. The latter spoke of himself as really better & all the others confirmed it. Amelia was at the Packingtons when she wrote & enjoyed herself exceedingly. Mr Griffin is continually worrying about her coming home which is selfish to a degree. He came over expecting to dine but only got a heavy tea. He was not in good tune. We thought Amelia's letter might have vexed him. He would not read it all to us. Edward office again in the evening.

Sep 29 It was almost like a winter morning, we felt the cold quite as much & had such a strong inclination to put up a stove at once. Practising is a good way of making oneself warm but we all found the library fire so comfortable that it did not seem possible to be luncheon time when it was announced. The circle was visibly smaller when Teresa, Mamma & I sat down alone around the long table. Teresa & I were very industrious all the afternoon mending & sewing. Capt & Mrs Taylor called but we could not think of being "at home." Edward came home tired from the office & had a headache in addition. Next week I hope he will be able to take some exercise. . . . Dear Edward looks better & I am sure a short ride every morning would soon give

[30]Lady Franklin, the widow of Sir John, the Arctic explorer (1786–1847).
[31]The curate at St. Paul's.
[32]He and Mr. Scott were planning a shooting expedition.

him a good color. Teresa seems rather dull without Mr Scott. I should certainly feel so were Edward away.

Sep 30 . . . Teresa started for church . . . Edward & I followed late as usual . . . I said a good deal against driving on Sunday unless it were absolutely necessary for it seemed to be so wrong that I could not believe any good would come of it. Perhaps it was unkind of me to speak so strongly when Sunday is the only day Edward can count upon for recreation of any kind but I did it conscientiously for I love Edward so well not to try to prevent him from doing what I really think would be displeasing in the eyes of God. . . .

Oct 1 Edward got up before seven intending to take his first morning ride. I had some milk boiled & when Edward was all ready we discovered that it was raining. We consoled ourselves by finishing the bowl of bread & milk comfortably in bed & were of course late for breakfast again. Mr Wilson dropped in during the morning & for the first time in two months. There was a Becher talk but not much good could be said of him. He had been dishonorable enough to offer Mr Wilson five per cent if he (Mr Wilson) would induce Mr Goodhue to purchase the Ridout place. Mr Wilson laughed at Mamma's only just now having her eyes opened for Mr Becher's character. . . . I went to the office with luncheon & did some shopping on the way home. . . . Played & worked after dinner besides laughing a great deal at Edward's expense.

Oct 2 This morning Edward managed to have a short ride but the rain brought him home in forty minutes. It was quite an unusual thing for me to be dressed & reading the *Free Press* while Edward was in his tub! Mr Griffin brought Mamma a nice present of game; two ducks, four snipe & four quail, & two quail were sent us from the farm so we had quite a supply for one day. . . . We called at the office, gave Edward his lunch, went a second time before going home to get some papers for Mamma but they were not forthcoming. Met Edward Blake. . . . He called at Eldon later in the day & paid a good long visit. Teresa & I felt sure he was going to stay for dinner which happened not to be as good as usual but we determined to make up in fine glass & china. Edward came home late. Played in the evening but did not feel very well.

Oct 3 The day was so mild & pleasant that I was determined to take advantage of it & pay visits after lunch. I set off first to the office with Edward's lunch. He gave me a letter from dear Papa who seems to be dull & in low spirits & I think misses me a good deal. Charlie does not get on with his studies as well as Papa would wish or as he might if a little more encouragement were given him at home but

Mamma's fondness for Charlie disposes her to spare him labor of any kind which in years to come will be a source of regret to all. Called on Mrs Stone. She was not at home. I saw Mrs Flock also Miss Evans. To our surprise Mr Taylor turned up again. He had called at the office. Edward was very busy & told him we
should be glad to see him at Eldon. . . . Mr Griffin had a polite note from me "requesting the pleasure of his company" on which account he came but remained only a few moments as Mr Jackson[33] was left alone at his house. . . . Edward went to the office almost at once after dinner to do some work that must be finished before he leaves for Toronto in the morning. I shall be glad when George returns for the business cannot possibly be done with only one head, . . . He [Edward] certainly allows himself no rest. Fortunately he was able to have nearly an hour's ride before breakfast. . . .
Oct 4 Fortunately I woke at five & it was as much as Edward could do to be ready to leave for Toronto at six. It had rained during the night & the morning was very dark. None of the servants were up so Edward went to the Tecumseh [House] where he could get a comfortable breakfast without any danger of being late for the train. I did not much like seeing Edward go away for it was the first time he had to say goodbye. . . . Made Edward a necktie. Mr Griffin came with the acceptable news that he had induced Mr Taylor to go & see Toronto on which account we should be deprived of his company at lunch. In the afternoon Teresa & I drove in the buggy to the Whiteheads. . . . We preferred walking through the King's. All the way out & particularly in front of Mr King's house the "autumn tints" were most brilliant. The bright green & half-tint of some of the leaves mingled with the almost dazzling scarlet had a lovely appearance. Mrs King was at home & of course had the baby in her arms. It is a very fine & pretty child. . . . We walked thro' the Howel's place as the nearest way of reaching the Whitehead's in "Irish Tandem,"[34] a rather steep & crooked pathway leading thro' three small gates brought us to our destination. The youngest daughter opened the door. Mrs & Miss Whitehead were busy stowing away apples & did not make their appearance for a few moments. Called at the post on our way home & got English letters from John, Mr Portman, Mary & Charles Knight. John is at Scarboro' & still continues to improve. . . . After tea a

[33]Mr. Jackson, a friend of Gilbert Griffin and Maurice Portman, was later to be an active worker in Portman's political campaign.

[34]Walking in single file.

telegram came from Edward, the car had broken down & he would not return before tomorrow. . . . To lose so much time was rather a serious matter for him & George being from home too. Still I could not but feel thankful that no accident had occurred & at the same time I felt very lonely without Edward. Taking all my valuables to Teresa's room I slept with her & as Mamma says "helped her to be afraid." Very soon after the light was put out we both heard a loud noise downstairs & immediately thought of Mr Scott's plate-chest in the pantry which would be well worth anybody's trouble to steal if they could only get it moved. In answer to an impatient ring of Teresa's bell her maid appeared quite as frightened as Teresa & was dispatched with orders to send Burns [man-servant] all over the house. However, the supposed intruder was nowhere visible so we went to sleep without any further alarm. While we were visiting [during the day] Mamma went to the cemetery, it did not make her low for we saw no change until bedtime when she told us.

Oct 5 It seemed like old times to find myself beside Teresa instead of Edward when I awoke. Going to our room it looked solitary enough without my dear husband & how long a day appeared to await his return. Teresa & I went to town & shopped. My part only went as far as paying Dewey's for the gold slip rings. Mamma read an extremely interesting account of Garibaldi's movements. He certainly is a most wonderful man & made more of than any sovereign of the present day. Nothing could exceed the enthusiastic delight with [which] he has been received on his march through the south of Italy.[35] Mr Griffin came in with rather an abusive account of the Prince's reception at Ottawa, Kingston, Belleville from the *Times* correspondent. Tho' his language was strong against the Orangemen one can make some allowance for the disgust an Englishman would naturally feel at the disloyalty shown to the heir of the British throne. Edward returned about ten & looking tired. I was so glad to have him home again.

Oct 6 At breakfast Teresa had a telegram from Mr Scott to say that they would be home at noon. Teresa went to the station & Edward too. Mr Scott & George both looked well burned from constant exposure in the Prairies where the wind had full play. The result of four days' shooting was eighteen birds, but they went too late for the birds were old & wild & rarely came within gunshot. George appeared rather disappointed with his expedition & not anxious to repeat it soon again. Not having eaten anything since two o'clock the day before, they felt

[35]Giuseppe Garibaldi (1807–82), the charismatic military leader active at this time in Italy's fight for unification and national independence.

ravenous & lunch was hurried on. The Scotts went to town in the afternoon. Edward dropped in just in time to have tea. I went to Dewey's, left Edward's ring to be made smaller, then to the office & got a letter from Mamma [Ryerson]. She had been obliged to change her cook & could not leave home with a strange woman in the house. . . .

Oct 7 Mamma, Edward & I went to church. The Bishop preached. Afterwards (it being Sacrament Sunday) we remained for the communion. This day three months we were married & we both thanked God from our inmost hearts for the happiness he had given us & prayed that we might, through divine help, prove ourselves worthy of it all. . . . Edward & George walked to the farm & did not return until nearly eight. The roads were so muddy & tedious. . . .

Oct 8 Edward & George both went to the office earlier than usual. I wrote to Sarah. Mamma read a most interesting sketch of George III from *Harper's* by Thackeray. After lunch Mr Scott, Teresa & I went visiting, first to the Bishop's to see Mrs Edward Blake. She looked extremely well. Her eldest child was in the room & the perfect image of her father. . . . It was so cold & windy that we were glad to find Mrs W. Lawrason at home. . . . We paid quite a long visit & had all the gossip over again about the Prince. . . . Who should we see . . . but Mr Taylor. The Scotts did the civil & asked him to tea while I went to the office. Edward had gone. Both Edward & George were obliged to go to the office again after dinner. Mr Taylor did not come as he promised.

Oct 9 . . . Mr Scott, Teresa & I called for Edward to go to the fair. . . . The show of cattle did not appear to be anything wonderful altho' there were some fine sheep & cows. We came in for a pig fight & monstrous creatures they were. . . .

Oct 10 Mamma made pumpkin pies in the morning. Teresa & I assisted immensely by way of learning. I took a small pie to Edward for lunch, . . . Mr Scott & Edward rode to the farm. They could not have had a more delightful day. Edward came home a little after six looking as if the exercise had done him all the good in the world. Mr Becher called but gave us no news except that the Prince was to send him his portrait. We had Mr Griffin at dinner, he seemed happy enough but left us early & in the same unceremonious way that he has adopted lately. . . .

Oct 11 It was a rainy, cold & disagreeable day. Miss Steers[36] was expected from Woodstock. . . . She is so clever & amusing besides

[36]Miss Steers, the American governess of the Harrises, became a good friend of Mrs. Harris and returns to Eldon House to visit in the 1860s and 1870s.

being so kind that one cannot help liking her. Mr & Mrs Sullivan (her niece) called in the afternoon & Miss Steers went in the town with them. Mr Becher called. I went for Edward. . . . Everybody was gay at dinner. I did not feel very well afterwards & went to my room to lie down. Edward soon followed. His presence did more good than anything & I went to the library again looking as if nothing had been the matter.

Oct 12 Mamma, Miss Steers, Teresa & I spent nearly the whole morning in the library. Miss Steers brought up reminiscences of the past which I very much enjoyed listening to. Mamma seemed quite herself again & had lots of stories to tell too. Edward had his ride before breakfast. News came of the arrival of the *Great Britain* & all felt much relieved, it would have ruined the Canadian line had another steamer been lost. Mr Scott & Teresa drove to the farm in search of autumn tints which are pretty & abundant in those woods. . . . Mr Wilson made a most powerful speech at Brantford & gained his case . . . We could not persuade Miss Steers to sing so I played after dinner. . . .

Oct 13 Edward had his (now) usual ride in the morning. . . . Miss Steers paid Mrs Becher a visit but did not find her overpowering in civility. Fanny, however, was very amiable. . . . Mr Scott took her [Miss Steers] to the station. We were all disappointed at not receiving English letters, probably owing to some delay caused by the Prince of Wales' visit to New York. The English mail would arrive late at night. . . .

Oct 14 Mr Scott & Teresa went to church & Edward rode to the farm. It was a lovely day. . . . He really look[s] better now that he perseveres in getting some exercise every day & I no longer feel anxious, on the contrary I am happy without a care. . . . At the church door some man asked us if we would sit in his pew which we found to be in a swell part of the church & after service he gave Edward a general invitation to sit there. Mr Bredin preached from Deuteronomy XXIX, 29: "The secret things belong unto the Lord our God; but those things which are revealed belong unto us & our children forever." Mr Griffin attempted to sing in the Methodist style when we were at tea. I could not avoid being annoyed.

Oct 15 . . . At one o'clock we had letters from Mary, Eliza & John, the latter still at Scarboro' & improving. . . . All at home feel most indignant at Mr Griffin's ordering Amelia to sail on the 4th of October & are determined if possible to keep her some months longer to improve her health as well as to give her an opportunity of paying a visit to each of her sisters. It is but a small favor for Mr Griffin (under the circumstances) to allow her to remain until spring, when he is not at the smallest expense in any way. Nothing can be more selfish than his conduct. . . .

Oct 18 . . . After dinner I played Trovatore from beginning to end. One really enjoys playing the old airs, it seems to bring before one the whole opera again. . . .

Oct 23 Another miserable day. As nobody was likely to call in such weather I had my head washed & had more time than usual to read & practice. About the only interruption we had was a visit from Mr Griffin . . . anxious to show us that he was not in the least offended. . . . he left Eldon in the usual unceremonious way. . . . What a kind & good woman my dear Edward's mother is, & with all her troubles & anxieties still so *young*, so agreeable & so amusing. One can't help learning a great deal from her conversation. . . .

Oct 24 . . . One evening is pretty much like another at Eldon, reading, music & reading.

Nov 6 [Two ladies] called for subscriptions to the Benevolent Society. Teresa gave five dollars, Mamma two & I one. I afterward thought my donation was too small but Mamma consoled me by saying "If you give less at one time you can give more another." Lining my jacket kept me pretty well employed all day & Mamma of course did all the talking & told us a good [deal] about her early life & the extraordinary circumstance of her aunt having the power of second sight & which made her life miserable. . . .

Nov 9 . . . I heard from my Mother. She had quite expected to see us & invited Auntie & Uncle Duggan to meet us at dinner & of course was disappointed at our not going down. . . .

Nov 10 Another gloomy, miserable day. . . . I saw that Edward was fretted about something. . . . I easily understood how impossible it would be for us to go to Toronto Monday morning.

Nov 11 . . . George came limping in to breakfast with a sore knee, . . . [Dr Wooddruff] said there [was] inflammation under the knee-cap & left a prescription. . . . The Dr put on six leeches & afterwards a hop poultice to draw out the blood. . . . I wrote to Papa & told him that our visit must again be deferred.

Nov 12 . . . Dr Wooddruff told Edward that George must not walk for fourteen or fifteen [days], any inflammation in the knee joint was a most dangerous thing.

Nov 13 . . . [George] is of course not equal to amusing himself reading for any length of time but Mamma's room is now the sitting-room where everybody goes as a matter of course. I brought home some grapes for George. . . . Dr Woodruff came while we were reading the

English letters in Mamma's room, Edward and I seated on the floor for want of chairs. After he [Dr Wooddruff] had gone George told Mamma that we women folk had remained in the room all the time & he had not an opportunity of telling the Dr *everything* & wanted Mr Scott to take a message to him. . . . The Dr came up himself shortly after & again took tea with us & talked some time in the library. We all liked him.

Nov 16 The Doctor seemed to think George rather better . . . at the same time he advised leeching again. The old leeches would not bite so he went in search of others. George became restless & uneasy at his not coming until the afternoon. . . .

Nov 17 Mrs Stone & Flock called rather to my surprise. It seems so short a time since I returned their first visit. Edward thinks they are trying to get into society & fancy they may manage it thro' me. . . .

Nov 19 Edward wrote another letter to Mr Portman & I one to John, . . . Mr Jackson called. . . . He was in very low spirits & told Mr Scott that everything seems to be against him. When he first paid Lucy [Wilson] attention she seemed flattered & certainly gave him every encouragement. For six months he was at the Wilson's daily & his engagement to Lucy was the only gleam of sunshine in his life. . . . Altho' she told him at last that she preferred Bill Bayley, he did not say one world against her. . . .

Nov 20 . . . An article appeared in the *Free Press* on George Brown's good fortune in having gone [into] partnership with a man who has discovered a new process of making paper out of straw, said to be so economical that in the *Globe* office alone it would save them $30,000 a year. The *Times* has offered £10,000 for a reward for the discovery. Making paper from straw is not a new discovery but it was found to be much more expensive, too much so for use. . . .

Nov 21 . . . George much better & determined to get up. We waylaid Dr Wooddruff & . . . he told George that he must not think of such a thing or the consequences might be serious. . . . Mr Scott understood that Wm. Lawrason & his father both intend to support Mr Portman instead of Mr Becher at the coming election . . .

Nov 22 George better but not sufficiently improved to get up as he expected. . . . A ball comes off at the Goodhue's tonight but Mr Jackson has declined & intends going out to the Whitehead's instead, probably not wishing to put himself in the way of being snubbed by Lucy Wilson. . . . After dinner Mamma, Edward & I played dominoes with George. . . . Mamma & Edward had a long talk about business à propos of George's carelessness in accounts. . . .

Nov 23 . . . I received a letter from Mamma [Ryerson] who is very anxious to see us but has given up expecting so often have we changed our plans & unavoidably too, . . . We had dominoes again in Mamma's room.

Nov 24 . . . Colonel Crutchley & Elizabeth wrote to Mamma, Mary & Eliza to me, Col Crutchley & Capt Peard to Edward. They all think John wonderfully [improved]. . . . [Col. Crutchley] thinks it will be a long time before John can attend to business *if at all.* On his judgment we place implicit reliance. . . .

Nov 26 . . . Mr Portman said a good deal about election matters & now that the excitement is over would give a good deal to be free from the whole business & hopes something may turn up to enable him to retire honorably. He cannot understand how he was fool enough to be drawn into the affair at all. We shall all be very sorry if he must stand & is elected. Parliament is a bad place for an idle man (with the present Ministry) & above all for a man of means who spends his money freely. . . .

Nov 28 Teresa & I went with baby to Egan's to have his picture taken. He was very good but we did not like him to sit more than three times, the room was so cold. . . . Hulme Wilson died this morning. . . . After luncheon Mamma took a cab & went over to see Mrs Wilson, she was in bed & said a good deal more about Lucy's grief than her own. She said no one could be more attached & devoted to the child than Lucy had always been to Hulme, but she could not understand her going to the Goodhue's ball when he was not expected to live. . . .

Nov 29 . . . I read a long article on geographical researches . . . to George & Mamma which interested us all very much. . . . I called at the Watson's . . . I was surprised to hear that Mr Leponitière had left his family & gone to England with Mrs Sargeant who was in Toronto for some time & colored photographs beautifully. He brought her out which, of course, caused much scandal & before leaving this last time he obtained leave of absence but took good care not to write to his wife or anybody else. The Wilsons met him walking arm & arm with Mrs Sergeant in London. He told them he was anxious to get something to do in England & if he succeeded would send for his wife & family. This was merely an excuse. Poor Mrs Leponitière with all those children are depending on the eldest son. They have left their comfortable house for a small one. . . .

Dec 2 . . . Mr McLean preached a good & impressive sermon from Revelations I, 4: "Blessed is he that readeth & they that hear the words of this prophecy & keep those things which are written therein for the time is at hand." . . . I wrote to Papa & was sorry not to be able to name a day for our going down but we hope to manage it next week. . . . Edward wrote a business letter to Mr Portman & I wrote an effusion to Mary. Edward's oysters seem to be appreciated & we amused ourselves cooking them.

Dec 3 . . . I received a letter from Papa. . . . If dear Papa would take more care of himself it would make me feel so much happier about him. . . .

Dec 4 George did not leave his room as early as usual & I think felt rather unwell. I took my work & sat with him nearly all the morning. Mr McLean called & was very pleasant. We were talking, among other things, of some of the celebrated divines of our own day. He is a most enthusiastic admirer of Mr Melville and read passages of the one volume of his sermons I happened to have by me. He spoke of the wonderful talent Mr Melville possessed. . . . Dr Cumming he thought rather too "flowery" which was my feeling. . . .

Dec 5 . . . Mrs Cronyn, Mrs Edward Blake & Mrs Versy called, the latter evidently in a fair way to *add* to the Cronyn faction. . . . Edward came home late & went to the office again for two hours after dinner. . . .

Dec 6 Thanksgiving day & a very snowy one too. . . .

Dec 7 . . . Dr Landor came to see Teresa, she is to take no end of medicine, syrup, pills & cod liver oil & what to her is almost equal to medicine, porter & port wine. . . .

Dec 8 . . . A number of English papers were on the breakfast table when we went in but no letter, which surprised us. However, Edward found one at the office for Mamma from Mr Portman & brought it up. He did not give an encouraging account of John, said that Dr Budd found John's liver "much reduced but the spleen was still a hard immoveable mass." The letter was evidently written in low spirits. We could hardly think John worse when Amelia pronounced him better in her letter to Mr Griffin. However, Mamma took the gloomy side & made herself very unhappy fretting. . . .

Dec 10 . . . Mamma had letters from John and Elizabeth which cheered her a good deal. They are staying with Mary. John feels better & hopes to see Eldon again in better health. God grant that he may. Dr Budd wishes John to try acid baths for which purpose he remains in London. . . .

Dec 12 Very busy all day finishing work to go to Toronto tomorrow. Dr Brown came to see baby & paid the usual long visit, abusing all the other doctors in town to a great extent. . . .

Dec 13 Started for Toronto at noon. It was hard to leave my darling. . . . The cars were heated to such an extent with a stove that I was almost in a state of suffocation with my cloak off. Fortunately there was no change & the conductor was very civil. I got on admirably alone. Papa & Charlie [Sophia's brother] met me at the station. Mamma & all were very glad to see me. . . .

Dec 14 . . . Mamma & I went out shopping & called at Auntie Duggan's *en route*. . . . I was so glad to hear from dear Edward, it seems so strange to be away from him. Last night I could not sleep for a long time & pleased as I am to see Papa, Mamma & all I don't like to think of remaining here five days without Edward. . . .

Dec 15 . . . I had a letter from dear Edward, my only enjoyment.

Dec 19 Louisa [Beatty] went with me to French [a dentist] & much to my surprise, he filled an enormous cavity without my feeling the least pain. . . . Edward arrived a little after eight with a box of apples from Mrs Harris. . . .

Dec 20 Auntie Duggan came up early to see if we would lunch with her but it was out of the question so we made her promise to take an early dinner with us instead. Edward & I walked to town & Mamma picked me up & we hurried from one shop to another & finished the commissions in good time. Poor Papa does not seem happy. He told me his troubles but I could only sympathize. Mamma refused to spend Xmas at Eldon but Papa & Charlie will come up on Monday. . . . It was nearly ten o'clock when we reached Eldon & everything seemed so quiet about the place. . . .

Dec 21 Edward & I went up to see Nancy [Cameron] & were horrified to see the change that had taken place in a week. Now death was stamped on her face, she seemed very weak but spoke to us quite sensibly. . . .

Dec 23 . . . George appears rather to avoid Louisa & when we left him alone with her in the library he called to Edward to come out for a walk & evidently was ill at ease. . . .

Dec 24 Teresa & Louisa were wonderfully busy upstairs all the morning & took good care not to let me see what they were doing, but I had a strange suspicion that Teresa intended to give Edward a doll baby as a Xmas box & told Louisa so. . . . I could not think of anything better to give Louisa than a collar which at all events may be useful. I went in the town for it & brought Edward home. Not having heard to the contrary, we expected Papa to arrive in the evening. Edward went to the station to meet him & to our surprise Mamma & Charlie came as well. I was very glad of it. Supper was got ready at once. Louisa shared Mrs Harris' room, giving hers to the newcomers.

Dec 26 . . . Poor old Nancy was taken away. Her uncle and several other relatives came in for her. How much we shall miss her, but we must feel thankful that her sufferings are at an end & that having been a good & faithful servant, she now reaps her reward.[37] Papa seemed much pleased to find us all living so happily together at Eldon. He hopes to be free from debt by Spring & wishes to assist us as far as he can in furnishing our house when the time comes. . . . Charlie is enjoying himself extremely & spends all his time with the Griffins skating or sliding downhill.

Dec 29 My birthday, & may the next find me as happy as the present. In one year two have been taken from Eldon to a brighter & happier home, we trust. Dear, dear Helen & poor, old Nancy. Perhaps we may be numbered with them in another twelve months. How thankful we should be for all the happiness we now enjoy . . . [Mr Jackson] I hear he was very much distressed at Lucy Wilson cutting him on Xmas day. . . .

Dec 30 . . . Edward & I went to the Methodist church. . . .

Dec 31 Teresa & Mr Scott went for their drive & found it exceedingly cold. . . . We made the most of the last day of the old year & sat up till after twelve, marking when the New Year came, kissed all round.

1861

Jan 1 Mamma, Louisa & I received, neither Mrs Harris or Teresa cared to see any one. I fully expected to see all the people who called on me when I was married, the Flocks, Stones, Glass[es] etc. but they had the good sense not to come. . . . Mr Barrow is certainly very much improved since I saw him last, he is now stationed at Kingston and finds it exceedingly dull & stupid there. Mr Wilson & son, Mr Hamilton, the Bishop, Mr Bettridge, Mr Mills . . . were about all our visitors. . . .

Jan 2 Mamma & Charlie left at noon for Hamilton. . . . Dear Papa has been quite alone for a week, but I don't suppose he will mind it when he has his books. . . .

Jan 4 I did not feel wonderfully well and remained at home all day working & copying the "Surrogate Court."[38] . . . Mamma had letter from Sarah. . . . Schooling in England is ruinous for people of merely a comfortable independence. . . .

Jan 6 . . . The Bishop [Benjamin Cronyn] preached but gave us a lecture instead of a sermon. It was the old story about the heavy debts of the church without much prospect of their decreasing. The income

[37]She had died on 25 December.

[38]Documents related to Edward's legal work.

of the church could do little more than defray the necessary expenses. We were told that it was our duty to give more liberally. . . . Edward wrote to Col Dalzell &. . . . I wrote to Papa. . . . I also wrote a long letter to John. Something like a dozen letters were sent from Eldon.
Jan 7 . . . Mamma entertained us ever so long telling *true* stories. One can't help getting fond of her besides admiring her. She is so superior in every way, one in a thousand. She & George played chess. . . . Louisa & I *played music*. . . .
Jan 12 I was busy translating French all the morning. . . . Elizabeth wrote to Edward that John had felt depressed & ill in London. . . .
Jan 14 . . . [Louisa] is such a good, amiable girl. George does not take to her & is scrupulously careful to avoid paying her more than necessary attention. . . .
Jan 16 . . . I wrote to Mr Portman but had little to tell him for we are at present very destitute of news.
Jan 22 . . . In the evening I played a little [piano], corrected French & Teresa & I read together. She translates much more easily than I fancied.
Jan 30 . . . [Edward] & Mamma had a talk & I was very sorry to hear Teresa had told her that I much preferred keeping house to living at Eldon. When Edward went to the office in the evening & the Scotts were upstairs I explained it all. The subject had never been mentioned until Sunday last when Edward & I were passing Haggart's house which Edward said was to let & if Eldon were too full in the spring he would rent it. This was repeated to the Scotts & Teresa asked me if I would like housekeeping. I said "yes, very well" but nothing more for I do not think it would be advisable for us to leave Eldon as long as Mamma wishes us to remain & we feel happy & contented.
Feb 1 Mamma & I made crullers.[39] . . . We all felt uneasy about Mamma in the evening. She was playing chess with George & suddenly leaned back in her chair feeling extremely faint & ill. We got her some cold water & wine which restored her at once but for the moment she fancied she was going to die & still believes that something is wrong with her heart. We sent for Dr Brown but he was not at home, however, Mamma was able to finish her game & felt much better after she got in bed.
Feb 2 . . . Edward & I are quite ready to go in a house of our own at any time & will do so the moment we see it is best. But Mamma seems averse to it now that the family has become so much smaller, & wishes us to remain here as long as we are happy & contented. At

[39]A kind of cake cut from a soft, sweet dough and fried until crisp.

all events we can see how things are when Mr Portman comes out. Teresa asked Mamma how she would do if Mr Portman did not remain & took a house & they went home which they intend to do in 1862. Mamma told her she never made plans but always let things take their course & they would come out all right. . . .

Feb 9 . . . Mamma still ailing. She never seems well in the mornings. She certainly sits in the house too much. I hope Edward may succeed in getting a nice horse that will go well in the harness & be useful to Mamma as well as him. . . .

Feb 11 What a long anxious day it has been to us all. Poor dear Mamma how little we thought when she poured our tea at breakfast that in a few hours her life would hang by a thread. She felt the same strange feeling in the night that she has complained of several times. About 1 o'clock she awoke feeling very dizzy but managed to get up & light the gas & put a bell by her bedside. Dr Brown was sent for. . . . He examined her heart & told Teresa it was affected & that she must have champagne twice a day & should get fresh air every day. She should if possible spend the month of March away from Eldon where there is so much to remind her of dear Helen, but he thought going home to England would really benefit her more than anything. Teresa & I were looking over Elizabeth's things to pack her trunk to send home & Mamma came in the garret & identified John's & Elizabeth's trunks. Shortly afterwards she slid down & as Teresa was holding a glass of champagne to her mouth she fainted. We sent for Dr Landor at once & administered hot brandy & water until she was sufficiently rallied to be examined. He said there was no doubt about it, her heart was affected, & for two or three hours I don't think he felt sure she would rally. Dear Mamma spoke to us all as if her end were near & seemed so composed & resigned to die trusting in the merits of that Saviour who willingly gave his life for us miserable sinners. But oh, what misery to think of losing our dear, dear Mother. How wretched the thought made us. . . . George had been sent by Dr Landor for Dr Brown as he had been attending her & was called in first. Mamma wished to see all her children & Edward was sent for. When he came in I saw the same pale despairing face he had made at the time of Helen's death & knew what he felt. After four o'clock Mamma seemed to improve a little. Dr Brown came about six & remained a long time talking about everything. Teresa & George sat up till twelve, then I took their placc & remained by her bedside till morning. At first she only dozed five minutes at a time but as morning approached she would sleep three quarters of an hour at a time.

Feb 12 Burns [manservant] was most thoughtful & considerate. He never went to bed all night & when I went downstairs a little after six there was a splendid fire & a kettle boiling all ready for me to make tea for Mamma, Edward having in the meantime taken my place in the sickroom. I washed Mamma & combed her hair which refreshed her & she seemed very much better after her breakfast. I washed & dressed dear little baby [Helen's son]. He was so good but rather wondered at seeing me instead of Mam Mam as he calls her. Since his birth she has only missed dressing him twice. Dr Landor breakfasted with us. We sent for him early as Mamma felt a little faint before she had breakfast. Dr Brown also came. Mrs Askin heard of Mamma's illness & made an effort to come & see her. . . . Mrs Wilson was also here & Mrs Cronyn, the latter quite surprised to find Mamma in bed & sick. I felt so tired after luncheon that I was obliged to lie down & slept soundly until dinner time. In the evening Mr Wilson came & reproached himself for not having come more frequently of late.

Feb 13 I sat up with Mamma again until 5 o'clock when I called Mitzie [servant] to take my place. It was such a relief to see Mamma sleep soundly & well. Such an improvement on last night, & in the morning she looked & felt more herself. Dr Landor & Dr Brown both came at the same time, . . . [Dr Landor] approved of her going to Toronto in March where she should go into society & be diverted. Papa would only be too glad to do all in his power to restore her health. . . . I wrote to him of all that had happened, also to John, Edward to Mr Portman, Teresa to Sarah & Mr Scott to Capt Peard. . . .

Feb 14 Mamma slept very well & seemed much better until about eight o'clock when there was a return of faintness. . . . Dr Landor at once accounted for this weak feeling the fast being so much longer than during the day & he said we must give her something just before she goes to sleep for the night & to have a sandwich or beef tea ready to give her when she wakes during the night, then about 6 o'clock in the morning she must take a glass of hot milk & brandy. She must have meat three times a day with port wine or porter & hot wine & water & brandy between times. . . .

Feb 16 . . . No one came to see her in the morning & Teresa thought it better to send for somebody so I wrote a note to Mrs Cronyn for she always cheers Mamma, & in the afternoon she came & really did Mamma good. [Mr Griffin] was too excited & restless[40] to do anything so we made him useful & sent him to look for a spirit lamp. He succeeded in finding an admirable one. . . .

[40]Amelia was expected to return from England momentarily.

Feb 18 . . . We can hardly believe that she [Amelia] is coming home tomorrow. . . .
Feb 19 . . . The Scotts, Edward & George were all at the station soon after twelve hoping Amelia might manage to get here by that train. However, as she did not, Mr Griffin went as far as Paris & met her there, bringing her here by half past five. . . .
Feb 20 . . . We all so much liked listening to Amelia's stories about everybody at home[41] & she can tell them so well. . . . John sent one of his own pictures to Mamma & Eliza such a pretty violet stand, three vases grouped together in imitation of the old Dresden china. . . . The Griffins dined with us. . . . Amelia had been so exasperated with Mr Griffin's conduct to her that she has evidently come to a determination to take her own part & not make a slave of herself. If she continues firm her life will be less miserable for Mr Griffin is a coward at heart. . . .
Feb 23 . . . We were all annoyed with Amelia for we know that this constant talking about Mr Portman & the children makes Mamma think & fret about Helen. Teresa spoke to Amelia again but she seemed vexed & said "she had the Doctor's instructions & knew what to do." Amelia feels so very much older than any of us that it is not easy to say much without making her angry.
Feb 28 Remained in bed till afternoon, not being so well & Dr Landor thought I had better be quiet. How glad one is to see her [Amelia Harris] moving about again – she went downstairs for a short time. . . .
Mar 3 . . . Mamma had come down to dinner & remained until after 8 o'clock – after she left Dr Landor told us a good deal about his Australian life & he would now be worth $100,000 had not Lord John Russell[42] increased the price of land & reduced the price of sheep. . . .
Mar 4 Mamma well again & downstairs all day. Amelia came over with English letters, . . . one from Mary, Mr Portman, John & Elizabeth, but we dare not show to her [Mamma] for poor Mary lost her baby. . . .
Mar 13 . . . Mamma did not chirp up at all & had several faint turns, at five o'clock she seemed so much worse that we sent for Dr Landor – he was concerned about her & wished us to send for Dr Brown, & they consulted together. The worst symptom Dr Landor says is that all

[41]The family in England.
[42]Lord John Russell (1792–1878), Prime Minister of England (1846–52).

the strengthening food she takes has little effect – she seems utterly prostrate, everything has been done for her & she does not rally. The doctors say she may get better but they apprehend the worst. Mamma wished to see the Bishop. . . . We remained downstairs while the Bishop and Mrs Cronyn talked to Mamma. Teresa, Amelia & I were in the room while the Bishop prayed. Dr Landor remained until one o'clock. . . .

Mar 14 Mamma was pronounced a good deal better by the doctors. . . . Dr Landor wrote an account of Mamma which was sent home.[43] He says she has dilitation of the heart & hardening of the cerebral vessels which prevent her food from nourishing properly. This the doctors consider the most alarming symptom about her. . . .

Mar 16 Edward's birthday – I can hardly believe he is nine & twenty. . . . Mr Scott had champagne to drink Edward's health at dinner.

Mar 22 Found a letter from Papa on the breakfast table telling me of poor Charlie's accident. When he was walking with two or three other boys on the pavement to the . . . light procession Wednesday evening one of the men in the procession threw his torch frame on the side walk and it hit Charlie cutting his nose quite thro' the nostril. Two policemen immediately took him in a tavern & rubbed the back of his neck with snow to stop the bleeding. Charlie managed to get home & must have frightened both Papa & Mamma very much coming in with his face covered with blood. Papa at once went for a Doctor & the wound was sewn up. . . . I fear the wound will leave a deep scar. . . .

Mar 25 . . . Dr Landor thought it advisable for Mamma to take advantage of it – as she seemed so well. He & Amelia drove with her in a cab for an hour. The fresh air certainly did her good. . . .

Mar 26 . . . two letters from Papa on the breakfast table, one for me & one for Mrs Harris, both written on his 58th birthday. It was so good of dear Papa to write to me when I should have remembered the day of the month without being reminded & it was such a nice, kind letter. . . . Dr Landor sent me to bed & I amused myself reading *Harper's* all the afternoon and evening. Edward came home soon after six.

Mar 27 Now that I have taken to my room for a few days Jane's [servant] services are necessary to dress me & do everything. . . .

Mar 28 Dr Landor was as usual my first visitor & I don't seem to get any better. He will change my medicine tomorrow, but absolute quiet is necessary, I cannot even walk about the room but have to be waited on like a little child. Mamma keeps much better than we anticipated.

[43]The account was sent home to the daughters and son in England.

. . . I was so glad to see dear Edward at six for the day seems long now. . . . I was so glad to see dear Edward at six.[44]

Apr 1 About twelve AM Dr Landor came to tell me I might get up which was an immense relief for I felt heartily tired of being in the loose box with my shoes off as Mr Scott says. . . . In the evening I devoted myself to music. Mr Scott bought a horse. . . .

Apr 7 We have been married nine months today & have much to feel thankful for. . . .

Apr 8 . . . I went to town with Amelia & paid a visit at the Goodhue's . . . then called to see if the Griers had arrived . . . Sarah was not there. I found Edward at home on my return with the same old headache . . . one does not like to ask questions when he is out of sorts. . . .

Apr 10 . . . Mr Scott drove Mrs Harris, Teresa & me in his new carriage which is a very nice little one but too heavy for Chatham [horse]. . . . Mrs Harris was not in the least tired after an hour's drive & seemed to enjoy it very much. . . .

Apr 15 Fort Sumpter [sic] taken! The great news of the day. It appears the Fort was completely destroyed by fire.[45] . . .

Apr 18 . . . I heard from Papa that the Attorney General hoped to arrange Edward's appointment. . . .

Apr 19 . . . Yesterday Edward heard from Eliza & Mary & the accounts of John are as bad as they can be. He has had another attack & rallied much to the Dr's surprise. He suffers great pain & has been under the influence of chloroform a good deal but now that is changed for opiates. . . . One night he was suffering very much & the doctor left a draught which he did not wish John to take if it could possibly be avoided, . . . He may perhaps live weeks but Eliza does not think he can last many days. . . . The Dr says his case is hopeless & we may perhaps hear of his death next week. He is prepared to die & his only sorrow seems to be for his Mother. He constantly says "my poor Mother." . . .

Apr 20 . . . Dr Landor was here to see Baby & it was decided that the little fellow should be weaned. . . .

Apr 21 . . . Dr Landor came to tea & there was an historical discussion on Henry VIII, Dr Landor mantaining he was a wiser & better king than he is generally supposed. . . .

[44]There is no indication of what Sophie's illness was.

[45]Fort Sumter, a Union strongpoint in Charleston harbour, was attacked by Confederate forces on 12 April 1861 and it surrendered two days later. The incident marked the outbreak of the Civil War.

Apr 24 . . . Edward received the appointment of "Issuer of Marriage Licenses." . . . She [Mrs Harris] does not know how near death John is, poor fellow. . . .
Apr 25 Dr Landor came to see me as he fancied I would be ready for professional visits. He remained nearly an hour & we talked about the War in America, Buonaparte [sic], & the present Emperor & Empress, Prince Napoleon & Princess Mathilde, besides a good many other things. One quite looks forward to his visits. Edward came up to luncheon & brought a letter from Papa. He is now at home having done all his business for this [parliamentary] session. It is indeed fortunate that Papa was able to be in Quebec & look after Edward's appointment himself, otherwise the office would have been given to some of Mr Carling's supporters who had already applied for it. . . .
Apr 26 . . . Capt Peard has arranged to have John buried at East Hampstead beside his child, thinking the expense of bringing him out would be too great. Mr Scott thinks it would cost more than £200. . . .
May 4 . . . Amelia had a letter from Eliza & Edward from Shuldham. The letters had been mailed two days earlier than the last we received so we had no further accounts of poor John. . . .
May 5 The Scotts went to church & Edward & I remained at home in the morning. I took care of Baby & let nurse go too. . . . Edward thought of riding to the farm & asked his Mother if she thought there was any harm in his going. She said no but as he left the room she followed him, put on her cloak & hood & taking him by the arm led him out on the hill. The first words she said were "Is John dead?" Edward of course answered "No" & then she said for the last ten days she had suspected John's illness from Mr Portman's letters & from not having had a line from John for five mails & as letters were not shown her she knew there must be something wrong & of which it was thought best she should not be informed, but for the last two days she found the suspense was more than she could bear so she decided to ask . . . & know[s] everything. It was quite impossible for Edward to disguise facts any longer. . . . He told her of poor John's sad [state] in a manner to distress her as little as possible & she appeared to take the bad news more calmly than Edward expected, . . . when Amelia came over she was in a great state of excitement . . . & said nothing in the world would have induced her to run the risk of telling her Mother of John's dying state until it was absolutely necessary, tho' at the same time she admitted "Edward might be right." He had acted to the best of his judgment & in fact did what was unavoidable. Dr Landor came to tea. Mrs Harris was not well & told him the cause of her trouble. . . .

May 8 . . . Edward drove out to the farm with Mr Glass. They wandered about in search of oil[46] & did not return until nearly eight o'clock. . . .
May 10 . . . Mr Scott, Edward, & George went to the station to meet Mr Portman . . . & the rest of the family met him at Eldon. He is looking extremely well but a little less handsome from having shaved off his moustache. There is something so taking about Mr Portman that everybody who knows him must like him, . . . Mrs Harris seemed wild with joy & could hardly keep from crying all the time. . . . Mr Portman intends going home in July or August & takes Baby with him. He has engaged a nurse & she will be out in a fortnight. Mrs Harris has no idea that Baby is to leave her so soon & I am afraid she will feel very unhappy without the little fellow. As long as Mr Portman remains at Eldon she will not feel poor John's death so much. . . . What surprises one is that Eliza & Mary so strongly advised Mr Portman not to leave Baby in this country as it would be so much better for the children all to grow up together & be with their Father. That is all very well & natural enough but on the other hand Mrs Harris' life is very uncertain . . . unless everything is done to divert her & drown grief she will not be long amongst us. Baby is to her a part of Helen & her affections seem to be centred in the child now. . . .
May 13 It is astonishing to see how well Mrs Harris is since Mr Portman's arrival. She now moves about the house quite as she used to do but at the same time does not like us to think her too well. Mr Portman has quite decided not to run for the county unless he is the only man on the Conservative side, & as Mr Becher, Mr Johnson[47] & Cornish[48] intend to be candidates, he thinks he may get out of it honorably. At all events, he will not spend money for nothing. When he told Mr Labatt his intentions he thought Mr Portman was perfectly right.

Poor John is perfectly resigned to die. . . . Mr Portman says Elizabeth is very odd. . . . When John wished to be buried at East Hampstead Col Crutchley made inquiry in a quiet way about taking him down there. Eliz[abeth] at the same time was bargaining with a man who agreed to take the body across the country cheaper & she told Col C that a man she knew would do it for so much & she talked about it

[46]The first reference to oil in any of the diaries.

[47]Johnson was defeated by Maurice Portman in 1861.

[48]Francis Evans Cornish (1831–78) settled in London in 1819 and was elected mayor of London in 1861. See Amelia Harris' comments on him in her diary on 7 January 1861.

quite openly to John as if it in no way concerned him. The idea of a wife making arrangements of this kind before the husband is dead is indeed repugnant to one's feelings & one's sense of delicacy. . . .
May 14 . . . Mr Portman saw a great many of his friends (political) & they seem determined that he shall stand. . . .
May 17 Got the English letters at last. . . . How glad we all were to hear that John is so much better. His liver has shrunk marvellously & is now only a very little too large. His spleen is smaller too & he is now able to be in his chair again. Dr Budd was so much surprised at the improvement that he says that there is hope even now. . . . Sarah said in her letter "how will Mamma bear parting with the baby" which at once told [of] Mr Portman's intention & Mrs Harris asked him if he intended to bring Baby home? Mr Portman tried to make an evasive answer & said he had not settled his plans yet & hardly knew what he would do. Mrs Harris was quite upset at the thought of losing Baby.
May 18 . . . Edward & Mr Portman drove out to the farm & walked over the place. Mr Portman seemed pleased to see so much improvement. After they returned Mrs Harris came in our room & talked about Amelia. She said she had thought a good deal about her troubles latterly & had decided to have a talk with Mr Griffin & if he promised to do better we had better all forget the past & be civil to him. Amelia must live with him. He has done nothing to justify her leaving him & we should try to make her life as happy as possible under the circumstances. She had talked it all over with Amelia & she will do everything in her power to prevent Mr Griffin's being able to complain if we will all stand by her & overlook as far as possible what is not in our power to remedy. Amelia also talked to Edward. We had rather a dull evening as Mr Portman said, everybody was holding "secret sessions." He did not appear happy. I think he sees the change in the house every day.
May 24 Early in the morning the firing of cannons & ringing of bells announced the Queen's birthday but there were no other demonstrations except a small gathering of the Militia on the barrack common for a short time in the morning. . . .
Jun 20 . . . Edward came home several times during the day & seemed so well that it made me feel happy to look at him. . . . Amelia dined here but was very silent – she generally is when Mr Portman is away. . . .
Jun 25 . . . Poor Edward suffers extremely with rheumatism. I feel quite unhappy about him, he has had it badly for a length of time & Dr Woodruff does not seem able to relieve him at all. . . .
Jun 28 . . . Mr Griffin sent two English letters to Amelia. Teresa

called her aside to read them alone. They found from Mary's letter John was still the same & gave it to Mamma to read, while Amelia went in my room (fearing there might be bad news) to read in Sarah's & it told the sad tale. Poor dear John had died on the 14th. He had been very ill for several days, extremely restless at times altho' he suffered no pain except from extreme debility. Dropsy had set in & his hands & stomach were much swollen. He had not been able to move his hands for some time. Indeed life seemed a burden to him & he longed for death. Three days before he died he said "Will nothing kill me." On the 12th he had been very much worse & Eliza did not leave him till one in the morning & returned early the next day. He was uneasy all day until 5 PM when there was a change for the better. In the evening the clergyman came & prayed which seemed to comfort poor John & Elizabeth very much & when Eliza left Norwood at eleven PM the Doctor said they need not feel alarmed as John would in all probability have a quiet night & they might go to bed without apprehension. Elizabeth undressed & laid down beside John & Miss Smith[49] sat up. At one o'clock she observed a change come over John's face. He became restless, talked a good deal but about nothing in particular. She at once called Elizabeth & at 5 dear John died calmly & quietly without a struggle. Poor John, one can't believe that he is to come back to us no more. It seems as if the Eldon circle were but a name now. Mamma suspected there was something wrong from not seeing Amelia & she went to my room at once & saw from Amelia's face how it was. Her grief was intense & we felt much alarmed but in the evening she became more calm. May God support her through this heavy trial.

Jun 30 Edward had a long letter from Eliza with the same sad news over again. She also sent a memorandum of poor dear John's last request. Mamma was well enough to come down to breakfast & seemed so much more composed than we had any idea she would be, that it was thought advisable to let her see Eliza's letter. She cannot avoid thinking of this new grief all the time & it does her less harm to speak of it openly than not to allude to it at all. . . . Mr Portman was obliged to go in the country electioneering. . . . Edward today decided to go home [England] with Mr Portman on the 14th August. I wish him to go & know that it would be unwise to wait another year when it might be possible for me to accompany him, but at the same time the separation will be a great trial, & even now it makes me so unhappy to think of it that I hardly know how I shall bear it.

[49]An aunt of Elizabeth, who was staying with her at their home, Mortimer House.

Jul 4 . . . Poor John was buried at East Hampstead on the 20th. . . . Col Crutchley, Shuldham & Baby Dalzell only were at the funeral. Col Dalzell went down expressly for it but it rained & they thought he had better not run the risk of cold by going. Elizabeth is to spend ten days at the Smith's & then goes to Mary's. . . .
Jul 5 . . . Mrs Greer [Sophia's cousin] & I went to hear Mrs Guiness at seven AM in the basement of the Methodist church.[50] She gave us a most excellent sermon on faith quite extempore & she did not evince the slightest hesitation or nervousness. Her illustrations were striking & simple & she certainly has a thorough knowledge of scripture. . . .
Jul 7 The first anniversary of our wedding day & how much we have to be thankful for. It has been a happy year to us. God grant that we may live & be a comfort to each other for many, many years. . . . Elizabeth enclosed a few lines that poor, dear John tried to write to his Mother when he had not strength to form a letter, & no one can read a word of it. How sad it made us feel to see this last, sad souvenir of dear John. Mary sent a "translation" as dear John called it. . . .
Jul 8 Everybody was up bright & early to go to the polls. . . . Mr Portman was so excited that he could not sleep & never closed his eyes all night. Mr Scott drove the Bishop, Mr Carling, Edward & George out at 8 o'clock to give their votes first. . . . now that Mr Portman has a majority of 142, his return is certain. . . .
Jul 9 . . . the first report we had from the Polls was a majority of 266 in Mr Portman's favor, but he came home for some luncheon & said he was 213 ahead, he went out again to Montgomery's also Mr Scott & George & we heard nothing more until 6 o'clock when the Post Office messenger brought us the last telegram at the close of the Polls, Portman's majority 306. How delighted we were. Amelia & I went down to the Post Office in spite of the rain to see Mr Portman's reception & hear his speech, they drove him all around the town the band taking the lead in the procession then came Mr P followed by about a hundred teams. There was a great cheering as he passed thro' the streets & when he reached the Committee room [there was] a tremendous enthusiasm & cheering & cries for Portman. He appeared at the window to speak & was received with cheers over & over again. He made a good speech & was followed by Carling, Elliot, & an allusion was made to the slanderous placards. . . .

[50]The Reverend H.G. Guiness and his wife were evangelical preachers who visited London for five weeks. He gave a series of evening lectures and his wife conducted religious services.

Jul 12 Mrs Harris, Edward & I had a long talk about the arrangements for next summer. Now that Mr Portman is returned for East Middlesex he will bring out his children but not before next August. The Scotts talk of going to England in the spring. But if they do not & Mr Portman & the children are at Eldon, Edward & I will take a house. . . .

Jul 14 . . . Mr Portman has decided to sail with Edward on the 7th. I shall go with them to the Falls on the 3rd & we spend our last Sunday together. I feel very miserable at parting with Edward but must try to bear up. I wrote to Papa about the changes in our arrangements & that I should be in Toronto on the 5th.

Jul 18 . . . Dr Brown frightened us about burglars in town. They were in our street a few nights ago & have committed several daring thefts and may take the opportunity of our being alone & pay us a visit. I did not feel courageous enough to sleep alone so I had the cook sleep on the sofa, she being the largest & strongest of the womankind in the house.

Jul 30 A very hot day. The Griffins dined at Eldon. Just before dinner all were sitting in the porch, Mrs Harris became suddenly faint & alarmed us tremendously. Teresa gave her some brandy instantly & sent for Dr Landor. . . . Dr Landor said he did not think there was any cause for alarm. . . .

Aug 1 Mr Portman asked me after breakfast how long I was going to remain at the Falls & seemed very much surprised when I said I shall leave half an hour after you & Edward. Mrs Harris & all evidently expected I should spend a week at the Clifton House but I said without hesitation I could not afford it & the more so as when it was first arranged that I should go down & remain one day at the Falls with Edward Mrs Harris remarked that it would be wiser for me not to go to the Falls but spend that day at Eldon & save our money. . . . [Mrs Harris] evidently felt hurt that I had refused to remain a week with her at the Falls, not wishing to leave the house quite alone or take care of servants, she had counted upon my staying with her, whereas I never for a moment supposed the Scotts were not to accompany her. . . .

Aug 2 Edward failed in his attempt to explain away the impression on his Mother's mind that I did not wish to go with her & wouldn't go. . . . I felt so distressed, for next to my Father, Edward's Mother is dearest to me & anything I can do for her is but a small return for all her kindness to me. . . .

Aug 5 . . . After dinner Edward & I walked under Table Rock as far as we could go & sat down on those seats above the Horseshoe. We both felt miserable knowing how soon the ocean will roll between us. . . . When tea was over we went to pass the last hour in our room. Oh how wretched & heartbroken I felt, it seemed as if I could not part with my darling, we cried together & felt more and more wretched as the time of separation drew near. I had never known grief equal to this. Mr Portman came & bid me good-bye & "God bless you" & in ten minutes my darling must leave me. The parting was over & as Edward closed the door I threw myself on the bed & thought my heart would break. I prayed & prayed to God to comfort me & protect my darling. His arm is strong and mighty, may he throw a shield around my dearest one, my all in earth. . . .

Aug 6 . . . all my trunks were packed & sent by the omnibus to the station & I went with Helen, Lottie & Pussy to the cottage & said goodbye to Mrs Gzowski & looked in the Robertson's cottage & gave them goodbye. Lottie walked to the station with Mr Gzowski, Pussy & me. I was very glad to have an escort home. . . . The lake was very calm & our journey pleasant enough. Papa was at the wharf waiting for me & seemed to feel very happy at having me home again. . . . Mamma was at the door when we reached Victoria St looking very ill. . . .

Aug 7 We have been married thirteen months today & now my dear husband is on the broad Atlantic. . . . Papa suddenly remembered that he had a telegram for me from Edward, "Sailed early all well no time to write." Even these few words were the greatest possible relief to me. I think of my darling all day long. . . .

Aug 8 . . . altho' it did not rain it was exceedingly dull & gloomy. I wrote to Mrs Harris enclosing a letter from Papa asking her to come over to Toronto after she had paid her visit at the Fall [sic]. I said all I could to persuade her to come & I hope she may.

Aug 9 It rained in the morning & continued so dull all day that I was unable to have my photo taken. . . .

Aug 11 Papa, Mamma & I went to morning service in the Methodist church. . . . Papa & I talked a good deal about Charlie, he does not feel satisfied with his improvement or progress in his studies & thinks he will never do very much until he is sent away. Being the only child at home Mamma indulges him in every whim & fancy. . . .

Aug 17 Very miserable. . . . I was very ill in the night. . . .

Aug 20 . . . I had a visit from Mrs Loring.[51] . . . [She is] almost broken hearted with solitude & worry about her affairs which she says are in a most deplorable state. . . .

Aug 22 Wrote to my dear husband. . . .

[51]Elizabeth's mother.

Aug 24 Grandpapa made his appearance before breakfast & remained until evening when he took the cars for Whitby. . . .
Aug 27 The Ryersons have decided to take lodgings at Mrs Ellah's. I drove Auntie & Uncle down there to see the rooms. Auntie Duggan came with me to pay some visits in Yorkville. . . . Judge Draper is always so agreeable, I felt very glad to have seen him. . . . Papa read a most interesting account of the hardships & miseries endured by one of the U.E. Loyalist families beginning as early as 1785 at the very commencement of the American War.
Aug 31 . . . Edward wrote to his Mother & she sent the letter on to me, it was written on board the *Arabia*. . . .
Sep 4 I am truly thankful I was to get Edward's letter shortly after breakfast this morning. . . .
Sep 9 Mamma & I went in the town in the morning . . . & ordered some clothes for Charlie & selected a frame for Papa's picture. . . . I went out boating with Fred before dinner. Mamma & Charlie went to the concert & Papa & I talked French with Milly.
Sep 12 Received two letters from my dear husband & one from Mary. . . . He seems to have enjoyed his visit at the Dalzell's very much. . . . I thought Edward would take to Sarah. She certainly succeeded in making Papa & me like her extremely when we saw her five years ago at Tunbridge Wells, & Col Dalzell too was very kind. They both go to Malta this month which is to be their residence for the present on account of Col Dalzell's health. From Sarah's he went with Elizabeth to Mortimer House. . . . [Edward] went to the church to see poor John's grave. . . .
Sep 18 . . . [Mary] went with Edward to Bognor[52] after their having shewn him the camp at Aldershot, where he & Shuldham lunched with Col Radcliffe, the Colonel of Shuldham's old regiment.[53] Eliza was so anxious to see Edward at Bognor that he put off going to Boulogne for two days. . . . Mary decided to go with Edward to Bognor. Eliza was standing at the window waiting for them. Edward knew her at once altho' she was not as stout as he expected to find her. He does not think Col C in the least altered & the nephews & nieces are all such nice children.
Sep 24 . . . Papa left for Hamilton & London this evening. I was so sorry to see him go. . . .
Sep 30 Went in the town with Mamma . . . we were out nearly all day. Papa gave me $20 dollars besides the $14 dollars I got from him the

[52]Bognor Regis.
[53]Radcliffe is referred to in Charlotte's diary.

other day. . . . He wishes to pay my expenses while I am with him. He is so kind & considerate to me in every way. . . .

Oct 1 . . . I left Toronto at 4:20 PM. . . . Papa & Charlie came to the station to see me off. . . . Teresa & Mr Scott met me at the station [in London]. . . . Mrs Harris seemed very glad to see me. She is looking much better.

Oct 9 In the morning I had a telegram from Edward written at Hamilton saying he would be home at 2 o'clock. . . . Amelia & I walked down to the station early. I felt too restless & excited to remain in the house. The Scotts & George followed. How delighted we all were to see dear Edward again. He looks so well & strong & has such a happy face that [it] is a pleasure to look at him. Miss Meredith[54] has decidely improved in manner & Edward says is very pretty & very sharp. They had a long but a pleasant voyage. . . . Edward has brought me such a lovely ring, the present of all others I prize most. . . . Amelia dined here & of course nobody thought of doing anything but talk for the rest of the day.

Oct 15 . . . The Scotts, Edward & I went to hear the band play. Edward did not seem to care about [it]. It was such a bore speaking to everybody. He introduced me to Miss Meredith. She is a very pretty girl but very Irish & will soon fall to the level of her family & the set they move in. . . .

Oct 22 . . . George & I went to the band in spite of the weather, . . . We met Capt Hibbert & Mr Armstrong[55] going to town. They told us there were very few people at the band. . . . Fanny Becher & Miss Meredith were the only young ladies I saw. Benny Cronyn devoted himself to Miss Isabella Meredith again. . . .

Oct 26 Yesterday I had such a kind letter from Papa. He gives me that pretty phaeton which he bought when I was in Toronto as a Xmas present. He is so good to me that I shall never be able to repay his generosity. Today I had another letter from him wishing me to answer his letter as if Edward had agreed to buy the phaeton & to enclose a cheque for £55, otherwise Mamma would never forgive or forget Papa's having given me so handsome a present. Kind as she is to me in many ways she cannot bear Papa's giving anything away, even to his own daughter. . . .

Oct 28 . . . [a letter] from Eliza. . . . Mr Portman does not think he will bring the children out next year. . . . Mary would gladly take care

[54]Isabella Meredith, the twenty year old daughter of J.W.C.R. Meredith, was returning from a visit to England under Edward's escort.

[55]An officer in the Royal Canadian Regiment.

of them again, but Eliza told Mr Portman if he left them with her he should share their expenses which were necessarily much increased by the addition of two children & two nurses. . . .

Nov 3 . . . I have not yet recovered from my fright. About two o'clock this morning I heard a noise & tapping at the street window of our room & being suddenly awoke by it. I called out what is the matter, do you want to come in (thinking it must be George) & a gruff voice answered "come, let me in. It is very cold waiting out here." This brought me to my senses. Edward went to the window & tried to see who the man was, but could not manage it. I got up & ran into George's room, & as I did so I heard one man say to the other "she is coming," but when Edward & George reached the gate, they had both vanished dispelling the idea of their being drunk.

Nov 4 . . . I had a letter from my dear Father making me a present of the ponies & harness as well as the phaeton, Mamma having consented to part with them feeling persuaded that Papa is desirous of saving for her benefit should he die first, & now that the street railway is so near Victoria Street he will not feel the want of horses very much, especially as she seldom visits. My dear Father has my welfare always at heart & only seeks ways & means to indulge me in every luxury & would willingly deny himself for my gratification & how little I deserve all this kindness. We played euchre in the evening.

Nov 6 . . . I wrote to Mamma enclosing a cheque for the phaeton. I then wrote a private letter to Papa as did Edward thanking him for his magnificent Xmas box. We mailed the letters ourselves after dinner. Edward met Miss Meredith & he walked with her a short distance. . . .

Nov 9 . . . I asked Miss Meredith to come in the evening . . . we all played vingt-et-un till twelve o'clock. As nobody came for Miss Meredith, Edward, George & Mr Clark walked home with her. I had not felt well during the evening & was not at all sorry to see them go. . . .

Nov 14 . . . Mr Scott & Edward attended Mr Becher's political meeting. Mr Portman's friends true to their word came out strong. Mr Becher said in so many words that at this critical time when war with the States might not be far distant they want a great man to represent them & he being the greatest of [the] great should claim their support.

Nov 16 Elizabeth & I read French & German all morning. . . .

Nov 22 Mr Wandesforde[56] made his appearance this morning tho' not at breakfast as we expected, he having gone to the Becher's last night.

[56]J.B. Wandesforde, whose watercolour portraits adorn the Eldon House Drawing Room and this book. See Amelia Harris' diary 27 September 1858 and 1 March 1859 for other visits.

. . . Edward has arranged with Mr Wandesforde to paint three pictures, a full length one of his Mother & a smaller size of each of us. We are to have our photos taken in the morning. . . .
Nov 23 Mrs Harris, Elizabeth & George had their photos taken, Edward & I did not sit as upon consideration Edward came to the conclusion that he could not afford to have ours painted. . . .
Nov 25 The Scotts & I spent the whole morning having photos taken for Wandesforde to paint. Edward had his taken too but our pictures are not to be painted until Edward feels that he can afford it. But Mr Wandesforde thought we had better have the negatives while he was here. . . . Edward has been full of making a water closet off the kitchen for the last two days. He had Rogers [contractor] up this afternoon to tell him the probable cost & when he found it would be well on to $200 he abandoned the idea & wisely too, for it is not right to run in debt without seeing one's way clear. . . . The new dining room carpet has arrived & it is a beautiful Turkey carpet but it ought to be for it cost $200. . . .
Nov 27 . . . Elizabeth went down to the office & rather startled Edward with the large account she brought against Harris Bros. It seemed so enormous that Edward demanded the items. She gave him a memorandum putting down her wedding dress among other things. One can hardly conceive of any woman making such a demand of her brother-in-law & I can't conceive how she could have the face to ask Edward to pay for her wedding dress which amount to the small sum of $360 dollars. She was very cross when she came home & I suppose very disappointed at Edward's reducing the amount she demanded from $1,900 to $1,400 by showing her in the books where different sums had been paid.
Dec 2 . . . The R[oyal] C[anadian] Rifles expect to be ordered to St Catharines any day & to be replaced by the 60th Rifles which will be a decided change for the better as far as we are concerned. . . . [Mamma] says Papa will leave for London Friday morning at seven o'clock in order to take care of the ponies & will be ten instead of five hours on the road which we could not bear to think of in this cold weather. Edward wrote to Papa at once to tell him he must not think of doing anything of the kind as in addition to the long journey we don't wish him to take the part of groom. Edward would of course willingly defray the expenses of some man who could look after the ponies. . . .
Dec 6 . . . A letter from Papa he & the ponies will be here tomorrow.
Dec 7 . . . Elizabeth went down to the office at 12 o'clock & remained there till four talking business with Edward. She fought for every item in her account. She was two hours arguing about the $307 for her

wedding dress, then the $30 dollars given to her by her Mother & her doctor's bill before she was married. The two last items she at last scratched out but the $24 dollars she had given Amelia as a present Edward paid her. . . . [she said] the only happy time of her life was the few months she spent in her own house & she did not think they would deny her those things. . . . He told her that Mrs Harris particularly wished to keep the chairs & sofas, the latter John had given to her & the chairs belonged to Eldon before John thought of marrying. . . .
Dec 8 . . . Elizabeth, Edward & I went to the Methodist church to hear Papa preach. . . .
Dec 10 Papa did not feel at all well. He went to bed so excited he could not sleep for many hours. He sat in the room writing & thinking over his address on the "University Question" all day. I was with him a good deal of [the] time. We were all very much alarmed at Mrs Harris' having another faint turn. . . . Edward wrote a letter to Elizabeth proposing she should name a third person to settle all these matters with him as their feelings were naturally strong on the subject & hers generally mastered her better judgment. Eliz. wrote an answer while Edward was at the lecture with Papa & handed it to me to give Edward. She has changed most wonderfully since Saturday & now offers to give up everything & only take what Edward is inclined to give her. She expressed a strong wish to have the sofa & two armchairs but as Mrs Harris so disliked parting with them she would abide by Edward's promise which was that in case of Mrs Harris' death she was to have them. She spoke very affectionately of Edward, indeed her letter was very nice. The only thing one regrets is that she should have done away with the good impression she made at first by her conduct of Saturday. . . .
Dec 11 Papa left this morning. . . .
Dec 12 I drove out in the phaeton, the roads being tolerably good. As soon as we got out of the town I took the reins in my own hands & got on capitally. . . .
Dec 16 Mrs Harris, Baby & I took our morning drive & returned in time to say good-bye to Elizabeth. I think everybody in the house felt it the greatest possible relief when she had gone. . . . The townspeople are all excitement in anticipation of war & people who have hitherto been looked upon as candidates for any peace Society or congregation of Quakers have undertaken to form & command Rifle companies & are to be manufactured into soldiers as fast as fear of the Yankees, love of their country, & the drill sergeant can make them. Becher thinks should there be war that we will be overrun by the "tallow faces" within a very short space of time. Probably we might be had the

Yankees no one else to attend to besides ourselves, but the South would not be short sighted enough to let them withdraw troops to whip us & then having done it to take them back better drilled & disciplined than ever to finish the work down south. I hope the English will come to some definite understanding with the States & make them fight or be civil for the future, but to endeavour to be fair & courteous & generous to a dishonest & disreputable Govt is as it has turned out absurd. Mr Scott is going to get up a Volunteer Company.[57] . . .
Dec 18 Another telegram was received today & affairs look a little less warlike. . . . [Mr Becher] surprised us by saying that he was to lecture in St Thomas this evening on International Law. . . .
Dec 20 . . . Mr Wilson read aloud the telegram he had received from Government, "That in every Battalion of Militia there should be a Volunteer company ready for active service on the shortest notice."
Dec 21 . . . Mr Portman's letter to Mr Scott received this morning is as wild as it can be about the war. He wants Mr Scott to get up a company for him & to buy all the shot & powder available. He will come out as soon as he can. He will walk from Halifax if he can't get here any other way, & intends to bring out rifles, revolvers, & I don't know what, for at the same time he tells Mr Scott he is not in the least excited. Mr Scott went in the town to see about getting up another company (as his own is nearly complete) & met Mr Mahon who had also received a letter from Mr Portman saying he wants to command a company & was willing to spend $400 dollars on the war. Mr Jackson immediately flew about the town recruiting for Mr Portman & had the bills struck off "Portman's Volunteer Company" but Mr Scott dissuaded him from having them posted about the town. Mr Jackson was too excited. . . . One suggestion which he made in his letter to Mr Mahon has been suppressed, that is that one company should be composed of men British born & those alone, & another of Canadians. Mrs Harris felt very much put out at Mr Portman's saying such a thing in the face of his wife having been a Canadian & his children all having been born in Canada. . . . A telegram arrived this evening with news . . . warlike preparations are going on in England. Troops under orders for Canada but news has reached us that in consideration of the rebellion in the South, Slidell & Mason are to be given up!!!
Dec 22 Mr Scott wrote Mr Jackson a note advising him to take no active measures toward getting up a company for Mr Portman as he would in all probability be out very shortly. At all events, he strongly recommended Mr Jackson to refrain from spending money as he felt

[57]See also Amelia's diary, 16 December 1861 for her commentary on the crisis.

convinced that the way money had been wasted during the election would deter Mr Portman from incurring any further expense now, & he wished Mr Jackson to understand that if any money was expended it must be done on his own responsibility as he (Mr Scott) would not sanction it. . . .

Dec 23 . . . Mr Jackson was very indignant with Mr Scott & told him "he thought any communication that passed between them should be in writing." However, he cooled down in the afternoon & it was amicably arranged that a company should be got up & offered to Mr Portman & bills were struck off forthwith announcing that "volunteers were wanted for a company to be offered to the Honble Mr Portman on his return from England & applications to be received by Mr Jackson & Mr Hutchinson." So Mr Scott is out of the whole business. . . .

Dec 25 It seems hardly possible that a year has gone by since Papa & Mamma & Charlie were here together & poor old Nancy died. Yet how much has happened in that year. Mrs Harris has been very near death but God has spared her to us a little longer. God grant that she may fill her place at Eldon for many years yet! Poor John has gone to his long Home. Who will be the next to follow? God alone can tell. Teresa gave me a nice bag for boots & shoes as a Xmas box & a very pretty silk dressing gown or morning dress to her Mother. The Scotts, Edward & I went to church & remained for the Sacrament. There was a collection for Mr McLean & we contributed $2 dollars. The Griffins came . . . to help us prepare for our dinner party. Amelia presented Teresa & me with such a pretty bouquet each. It was kind of her. Mr Griffin arranged a wreath of autumn leaves & red berries. . . . The Scotts had all their silver out & with our handsome china & Mr Portman's glass the dinner table looked exceedingly well. The dinner was sumptuous. Amelia's Mary [servant] came & helped to cook so everything was done as it should be. Burns & a Mess waiter (Col Bradford's own servant) waited with the assistance of some maid servants & the dinner went off capitally. Our guests were Col Bradford, who took Mrs Harris in to dinner, Capt & Mrs Taylor, the former took Amelia & Mr Scott being last on this occasion took charge of Mrs Taylor but Edward who sat next her did the agreeable. Carving was quite enough for Mr Scott. Capt Howson was allotted to Teresa & I fell to Mr Harkness. We got on capitally. He is very chatty but I should not say there was much in him. He thinks a great deal of the Widders. I said a good word for Blanche. . . . After dinner I played one or two pieces & then we had whist. I played with Col Bradford at one table while Teresa & Mr Harkness being odd ones played écarte. Our friends did not leave till nearly one o'clock. . . .

Dec 31 Mrs Harris, Baby & I took our drive. . . . We met Mr Griffin & Edward Blake & talked to them some time. I bought a handsome prayer book for Charlie & on my way to the office I met all the R.C. Rifles, band & all. Col Bradford asked Edward to dine at Mess. He did not get home till 1 AM, won $6 at whist. I sat up sewing till 2 o'clock 1862.

The Diary of Mary Elizabeth Lucy Ronalds Harris (1845–1901)

Lucy began her diary on the first day of 1868,[1] aged twenty-three and continued writing for twenty-seven years until 1895.[2] A gift from her brother-in-law, Edward, she entitled it a "Daily Journal" and, apart from a regular series of diary entries, it includes pages for monthly accounts which she used to record domestic expenses. Lucy had many qualities, but writing was not one of them. Her prose style was prosaic, her interests pragmatic, and she recorded what she had in her mind faithfully and objectively.

Lucy's diary is the chronicle of the development of a young wife into a mother with four children. Initially, as a young bride her main concern was her husband, a man largely absorbed in his fascination for hunting, curling, and other sports. Gradually she began to focus her attention on her children, and fret over their education. Another major concern was their health at a time when epidemics of scarlet fever and typhoid were frequent. In fact, this diary is the autobiography of an inexperienced young housewife required to take on the role of a dedicated wife to a husband, mother to her children, and nurse to one that was an epileptic. We learn about her handling of all of these responsibilities, as well as problems with servants and an elderly mother-in-law. Despite her busy life, she found time and energy to take French lessons, to attend church services regularly, and to travel abroad.

Unlike Sophie, Lucy was not enamoured of dinner parties as "They cost so much, are troublesome and entertain so very few persons."[3] But she did enjoy socializing with lady friends at tea

[1]Lucy Ronalds had married George Becher Harris on 5 September 1867.

[2]Lucy's first diary was a New Year's day present when she was sixteen years old. Despite its brevity, it tells us about life on her father's farm on the outskirts of Chatham, Canada West. She also gives her impressions of a young girl crossing the Atlantic to England, first with her parents, and then alone. Her father, Henry Ronalds, also kept a diary in 1853. He had been sent to Canada in 1843 to manage the properties which constituted the Ronalds estate, lands acquired initially by William Robertson, the Detroit based fur trader, whose daughter, Elizabeth, had married Henry Ronald's father. There are two other Ronalds diaries: one kept by Henry's grandfather, Hugh, in 1823; and one by a great aunt in 1833. These survive in the Harris Papers and are of interest.

[3]Lucy's diary, 8 January 1880.

parties. In this and other matters, the contrast between Lucy and Sophie is quite evident. Lucy was preoccupied with motherhood and the problems and responsibilities that attended it; Sophie, childless and more sociable, enjoyed a life free of such cares. What they did have in common, however, was a sensitivity that transcends their different experiences as women in the nineteenth century. Indeed, they became good friends for many years until tensions over Edward's handling of family financial affairs caused a rift.

As time passed, Lucy's responsibilities increased and she developed into a mature woman, but the same did not happen with her husband for whom her love was gradually replaced by affection. It was her close relationship with her mother that helped her to maintain her emotional balance. After the death of Mrs Ronalds, however, her diary became her main comfort. Once she wrote " . . . when Mama was taken I lost what I needed most."[4] Later Lucy became close to her mother-in-law, Amelia Harris, who was very fond of her. Indeed, Amelia recorded in her own diary, "I do not think there is a kinder hearted, better woman in the world than Lucy is."[5] Lucy's comments on the Harrises are consistently candid. Of all the diarists, she is the most frank about the developing problem of the Harris finances that was to climax in the 1880s.

[4]Lucy's diary, 23/24 May 1873.
[5]Amelia's diary, 23 August 1879.

Lucy

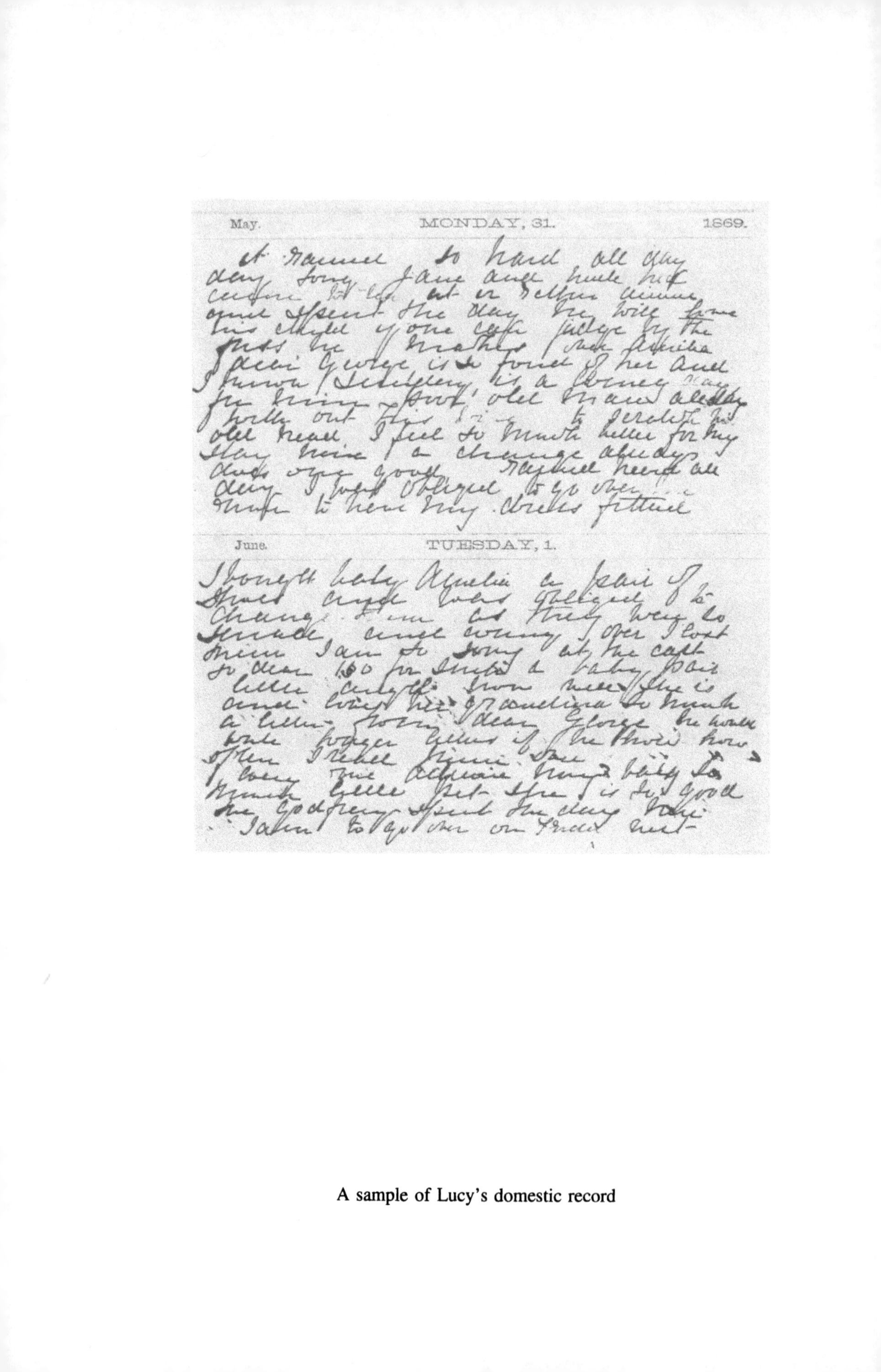

May. MONDAY, 31. 1869.

June. TUESDAY, 1.

A sample of Lucy's domestic record

Lucy Ronalds Harris' Diary

1868

Jan 1 George went to Simcoe with his brother on Friday [to attend] a ball there . . . the first time since I was married he has been away. I missed him far more than I should have thought possible. Slept with Mrs Edward [Sophia]. Only seven calls in the evening. . . . No sleighing. . . . If the roads had been better more people would have turned out. Wore my brown silk. The sulphur springs were opened and a grand lunch given.
Jan 2 Wrote to George and Mama short letters. Mama[6] sent me some whitefish, gave one to Mrs Griffin. The little [Griffin] twins came and spent the evening, in the afternoon Mrs Edward went to a band [concert]. She would rather I had gone but as George was away I did not like going without him for the first time. . . . The [53rd] give a dance. . . . Col Askin[7] called also during the afternoon. . . . A bright clear cold day.
Jan 3 . . . Went for a walk with Mrs Edward before dinner. Had a letter from Mama. . . . Uncle Edward Skae [in Detroit] has lost his situation in the Insurance. Poor Jane [his wife], her troubles are only beginning I fear.
Jan 4 Horrid wet day. Captain [James] Collins [60th] came to afternoon tea and Mr G. Griffin who sent me a telegraph. I was to receive [it] from George who comes tonight. Commenced a . . . petticoat. No letters. Finished my footstool and will send it down to have it made up in Toronto. George came home at six very cold and tired. The ball was splendid – music good and young ladies all one could wish. The long drive was the only drawback and I am rather afraid he has taken cold. I am so happy.
Jan 6 Went to Church in the morning with Mrs Edward. In the afternoon for a walk with George. Saw the Grant's [53rd] house. . . . Captain[s] Collins, and Northey[8] came to spend the evening. . . . Went over to the Askins and came home so tired. . . . A letter from Mama.
Jan 7 Called on Mrs Thompson.[9] . . . Went for a walk and later re-

[6]Mrs. Henry Ronalds in Windsor.
[7]Colonel J.B. Askin, a cousin of Lucy Ronalds' mother.
[8]Officers in the 60th Regiment.
[9]Wife of an officer in the 53rd Regiment.

ceived Mrs Hutchinson. George went to curl and did not get home before six. Uncle Ned Skae came also. . . . An invitation to the 68th Ball for Tuesday next and one for Wednesday in Windsor. The former we shall go to – my first ball since my marriage. . . .

Jan 8 Mrs Read, Mrs Brown, Captain and Mrs Grant.[10] Later Captain Truell 53rd Regt, Captains Northey and Collins called. Finished my apron and now begin my chair. Uncle Ned Skae had tea. He told us the Windsor news as far as he knew. An invitation to the Assembly at Windsor. Wrote a tiresome letter to James Montgomery[11] about the present mismanagement of lands belonging to the Ronalds Estate. Hope something may come of it. . . .

Jan 9 Mr & Mrs Edward went to Toronto in the morning. Wrote to Mama and Aunt Ellen. Thought to make calls but it was too cold. Went to the 53rd Band [concert] with Mrs Griffin and George for a little while in the afternoon. My dress came from Mama also the material to make a cloak and frilling for underclothes. George dined with the 60th. Captain Collins, did not go home until 2 in the morning. I was so lonely. A letter from [Uncle] John [Ronalds].

Jan 10 [Up] early to make some visits. Went to the Bechers, Thomas', Bill Lawrasons and Hamiltons. Mrs Griffin, Mr Becher and Judge [John] Wilson lunched with us. Captains Northey and Collins came for a game of cards in the afternoon. They did not go away until half past six. George dined with Capt Bruce [53rd]. He was home at 12 o'clock and looked so very well. The weather is very cold.

Jan 11 Made my cloak. Sent Betsy [servant] to get me some wool and the tassel for it. Mrs Edward and her husband came from Toronto for the Ball. On Tuesday she goes over on Saturday or rather Wednesday for a fortnight. On her return I shall go and see Mama and get my

[10]All officers or wives of officers in the 53rd Regiment.

[11]James Montgomery, a cousin of Lucy's who lived in London England, was one of the four trustees of the Ronalds Estate, which consisted of substantial land holdings in southwestern Ontario acquired in the 1790s by William Robertson (c1760–1806). On his death in 1806, he left the entire estate to his daughter, Elizabeth Lucy (1798–1892). In 1820 she married Dr. Henry Ronalds of Brentford, a London suburb, and had seven children. The oldest, also named Henry Ronalds, was sent to Canada in the 1840s to manage the Ronalds' property. He bought a farm near Chatham, married Mary Frances Archange Askin of Windsor, and had one daughter, Lucy, who married George Becher Harris. By Elizabeth Lucy Robertson's will, her estate was left in equal parts to her sons, and if none survived, in equal parts to her grandchildren. In 1849 she was declared to be of unsound mind and spent the rest of her life in a series of asylums in the south of England. She died in one of these in November 1892 predeceased by her four sons and by sixteen of the seventeen grandchildren. In due course Lucy inherited the whole estate.

things ready. Miss Leonard, Mrs Becher and the Gzowskis called. Mrs Griffin and her stepson came in the afternoon for a time. No letters from home.

Jan 12/13 Sunday. Went to Church in the morning with George. Later he drew some plans for our house which are I dare say only the beginning. Some time will pass before we are fairly settled in it. Captain Collins came and of course Captain Northey to tea after Church. Captain [R.H.] Truell [53rd] in the afternoon came for a time. I like him so much. Monday: Mr & Mrs Wm Street,[12] Mrs Beddome called. An invitation for a small dance Tuesday next. Finished a quantity of small things.

Jan 14 I wrote a letter . . . to dear Mama – for a few days I have not heard from home and not feeling well rather think I have been cross and altogether out of temper. I feel so ill and tired I wish I could go home for a time. Perhaps when I came back I would be more patient. Others have felt just as bad as I do.[13] Went to the 53rd Ball. Danced with Mr Kirkwood, Capt Thompson, Mr Fife, Capt Collins and as I thought I had better not dance any but the slow dances. I could not say I enjoyed myself as much as I should [have] a year ago.

Jan 15 Going to make a number of calls. Got a horse and sleigh. Went first to Mrs Baileys[14] and found her in. More toys than would fill a country toy shop on the drawing room floor. From there to Mrs Harrene.[15] She was out. Then the Goodhues and saw Miss Minnie. [She] looked quite pretty. . . . Then to the Reads, Major Evans and Bechers. Saw the twins, they are very pretty and seemed very agreeable. . . . Mrs Edward has gone to Toronto and comes back the last Saturday of the month, when I shall go to Windsor.

Jan 16 Went to town to inquire the price of a set of Ashcan[16] for Mrs Chase.[17] Found them dear and not very good I thought. George went to the 60th Barracks to see Captain Northey who is quite ill. Found him improving very slowly and it will be some time before he is well enough to go out. In the evening. We went to a small party at the Lawrasons. They did all they could to make it pleasant and everything was very nice and the floor better than you often see. Came

[12]Son of W.W. Street.

[13]A reference to her pregnancy.

[14]John Wilson's daughter, Lucy married William Bailey. See Amelia's diary, 29 May 1859.

[15]Wife of the Colonel of the 53rd Regiment.

[16]Probably a reference to asghand carpets from the Khorasan district of Persia (Iran).

[17]A socially prominent lady from Detroit and Lucy's close friend.

home at half past one. George looked so nice and outshone every person in the room.

Jan 19/20 Went to church and came home by the Griffins, saw the twins. . . . Mr Becher and Miss Connie came for tea. . . . Made the following calls. The Merediths, Streets, and Lawrasons. At the latter place found Mrs Hutchinson. Mrs Macphie, Mrs Dean & Mrs Hugueson all called and so many more places to go to . . . A letter from Mama. She say[s] the William Casgrains have lost both their children.

Jan 21 . . . The house where the William Merediths live is for rent; we may take it if we cannot get the Holman cottage. I fear we have so small a chance that we may call it one and that is all. . . . Went for a walk with my husband.

Jan 22 Felt lazy and really did nothing all day. I find so little tires me out and by night I am unfit for everything except bed. George is being kind to me in every thing and my married life has been all I could have ever thought or hoped. I fear sometimes it will not continue. Col Askin, Capt Northey and Captain Tufnell called. A letter from Mama. She is very lonely I feel sure.

Jan 23 No news of any sort. Edward went to Toronto by the afternoon train which was two hours late as a freight train west of this place was off the line. . . . George and I went for a walk about five and saw the Meredith's house. The outside will require repairs, also the sheds and out buildings. No calls except Mr Starr the new curate of St Paul's who said the Dean was ill. Mrs Harrene has a son.

Jan 24 Friday. Busy in the house all day. I have many things to do and they all take time. Went for a walk with George. He very kindly comes for me every day he can spare time from the office. Edward Harris came back from Toronto. The ball was the best given in Canada in a private house. Capt Northey went down and will tell us all the news on his return. Scottie Griffin is ill, poor little darling.

Jan 25 . . . A letter from Mama. I will soon see her, find each day longer and longer.

Jan 27 Went to church with Edward as George wanted to go for a bath [Sulphur Springs] which I am rather afraid he over did as he has a bad headache. A letter from Mama asking me to go to the ball in Detroit. I do not care for balls so much and George did not care to come. . . .

Jan 28 Went to the rink with Mr Griffin in the afternoon. Called on Mrs Beddome. Poor little Scottie is very ill with his teeth. A letter from dear Mama she is very lonely and will be delighted to have me with her. Went to Mrs Grant's to see the house they are in. George thinks of taking it. I found it much more convenient than I had heard it was. They only have very little to sell and very few things we will buy.

Jan 29 Went for a drive and enjoyed it very much. Called at Mrs Hugueson's, Mrs Macbeth, Mrs Haughtain, Mrs Menzies', Mrs Adams'. Came home with the delightful idea I had finished my visits when I found more cards waiting, people have all been so very kind in calling on me and I feel it very kind of them as in a place of this size nearly every person has a large enough circle of acquaintances without calling on strangers when they come.

Jan 30 The Band of the 53rd Regt plays . . . every Thursday. Mrs Griffin and I went and a fair number of people. Bessie Dewar was the prettiest girl in London. She has no friends to tell her how to behave, and is to be pitied very much. Captains Truell, Prince and Thompson all came and spoke to me. George came to take me home. He is kind in all things and does far more for me than I deserve. I am often ill and I fear impatient which I seem to be unable to help.

Jan 31 Poor George has a cold . . . He will not take care of himself as he should, I hate to see him looking so ill and wretched. He is so thoughtful and considerate to others when they are not well. I went for a walk by myself. How I dislike walking alone. . . .

Feb 1 Mr and Mrs [John] Walker have come home from their wedding trip. She is really ugly . . . Captain and Mrs Hamilton, Captains Truell and Elmhurst dined [here] tonight. Mrs H. was certainly dressed in the latest fashions her hair fairly on the top of her head, no hoops, few skirts altogether she did not look pretty. . . .

Feb 3 Came down to Windsor by the train that arrives here at five. . . . Mr Leith [conductor] was most kind to me. . . . Uncle Ned was waiting for me at the station. They were both very glad to see me. The Skaes dined with us. I wonder if George will kiss me.

Feb 4 Staid in the house all morning and talked to dear Mama, in the afternoon Uncle Ned came to take me down to Grandmama's. I found them all looking very happy on my return. . . . Mrs John Dougall came in later. I would like to see him [George] if only for a few minutes. Mrs Casgrain and Mrs Chase called.

Feb 5 In the morning made arrangements to go to Detroit as soon after breakfast as possible. Miss Whipple, Mrs Casgrain, Mrs Chase came in and staid for such a time that it was nearly twelve before we started. The crossing on the American side being so bad that we nearly made up our minds to come home again without landing which we did by getting on the plank and walking a distance on the ice. I found things very reasonable as regards prices over there. . . .

Feb 6 A clear cold day. A letter from George. He sent me a sewing machine, one of the small kind, I am to change it for a larger [one] when I like. He is so very good and considerate in every [way] I hope I shall be able to make him a good wife. I do try. Many people come each day to see me. . . .

Feb 8 In the morning we went to Windsor and did some shopping. I bought myself a wrapper and asked Miss Gale to make it for me. She will alter my water proof dress at the same time. We called at . . . Mrs Small, she gives me the blues with her everlasting moans, one would fancy she has the hardest fate a human being could endure. She looks so very helpless one must pity her. I am sorry to hear her husband is not kind, away from her friends she has only him to look to for comfort and help.

Feb 10 We spent the evening on Friday at Mrs Dougall and Saturday with dear old Grandma. I forgot to enter them. . . . Did not go to church as it snowed so hard. Mama advised me to remain indoors, perhaps it was as well. . . . Invited to go to a sleighdrive tomorrow evening. Afterwards Mrs Charles Baby came and asked me to a small party tomorrow night. We went to the Theatricals. They were very good. . . .

Feb 11 . . . My husband did not write me yesterday. I felt quite lonely for a letter. . . .

Feb 12 . . . I wish dear Mama would . . . say she would live with us.

Feb 13 . . . Mama is very kind to me and has given me many things for my house. Dear George also wrote me a very affectionate letter. I trust I may always be able to make him happy, I sometimes fear I will not. He is always so gentle and tender. I try to make him a good wife . . . Grandma spent the day with us, she is growing old.

Feb 14 Wrote to George in the morning and posted it on my way to Detroit. . . . George sent me 40 dollars some of which I spent. Bought cotton and some things I [needed]. Money goes so fast and I try to be careful, . . .

Feb 15 A very kind letter from George, also one from Mrs Harris. She always writes such nice affectionate letters. I wish I did the same. Mrs Casgrain is very ill. . . .

Feb 16/17 Did not go to church as George's train came in at half past eleven . . . I do not think I shall make many visits without him as I had no idea how I missed being with him. Went down to Grandmama's and bid them good bye. On Monday the Skaes drove us up to Windsor. We went over the river. I am very glad we had a chance of going as for the past few days the river has been so frozen that no one could cross. . . .

Feb 18 I came home with George, felt very sorry to leave poor dear

Mama as I know she will be very lonely and dull [and] miss her little girl more this time than before. I nearly fainted in the train, the car was so hot. When I got here found Mr Griffin, [he] came down and wanted us to dine. I did not feel like going but Mrs Harris thought we had better. I went but came home as soon as dinner was over. They sent for a cab and I went to bed. . . . I felt so vexed I had to come home. . . .

Feb 19 Quite ill and miserable all day. This is Mrs Harris' 70th birthday. She is to have some of her old friends. Col & Mrs Askin and Teresa, the Griffins, Judge Wilson, Mr Becher. I was so ill that I did not enjoy the dinner altho every one else did. It is so miserable feeling so ill and pale that . . . George felt nearly as bad as I did.

Feb 20 Still ill, and as it is nothing very serious, one hates to have a Dr at least I know I do. A letter from Mama enclosing my half year's allowance, I returned George forty dollars he sent me. I intend to buy all I shall require for July[18] with my own money and then I shall begin to save. . . .

Feb 21 Captain[s] Gore and Lynnes came from Toronto to the Ball. . . . Miss Meredith of Port Hope is staying with her cousins. She came in the afternoon to call on Mrs Harris. Miss Bella [Meredith] is far the prettiest and most pleasing I think. Captain Lynnes has had a very desperate flirtation with Annie [Meredith]. How it will end I cannot say. I do not think he has behaved very well toward her if it ends as people all seem to think it will. My day for balls is over for at least the present. It will be better for me to remain at home. . . .

Feb 27 Went to Mrs Grant's. Saw her baby things, they are very pretty and dear. . . . I bought one dress for [$]7.50 . . . still one has to have nice things . . . dear Mama wants me to go home. . . .

Feb 28 Passed a horrid night. I barely slept 2 hours . . . I half fear that July will be the end for me at times. I think I shall not recover. George has promised me that if my baby wants its Mother, Mama shall take care of it. Poor Mama, she feels very dull and I know she misses me. . . .

Feb 29 Fancy George only came home at two this morning. He enjoyed his dinner . . . the Thomas' did not rise from the table till eleven to one. . . .

Mar 4 . . . wrote to Mama in answer to her letter received this morning. I am to go home soon for a week. . . .

Mar 6 . . . A letter from Mama containing my dear Father's will. I am

[18]A reference to the expected birth of her child.

to make mine tomorrow as Mama has all for her life time. I will leave all to George to do as he is better [at] it.
Mar 7/8 The snow nearly all gone. More rain than ever. The streets are small rivers going to town. . . .
Mar 9 . . . Bella Meredith is a strange mixture so no good will ever come to her. . . . The river is very high and will do some damage, I fear.
Mar 10 Left London to come to Windsor by train, . . . George came to the train to see me off. He seemed to half wish I was not going. If dear Mama would not have been disappointed, I would not have left. . . . He gave me fifteen dollars, I am . . . getting things for July.
Mar 13 Gave Mrs Thomas 6 nightgowns and 5 petticoats to make at 25 cents a piece. . . .
Mar 15/16 Went to church . . . went to Grandmama . . . I wonder if George misses me as I do him . . . he has shown me he really loves me. . . .
Mar 17 . . . Went down to Sandwich to see Aunt Mellina. Her poor baby lives, it is so sad to see one so young suffer. . . .
Mar 18 Came back to London. Poor Mama was so sorry to see me [leave] . . . Edward met me as George did not get back from Toronto till half past nine. I was so glad to see him and believe it will be the last time I shall go away without him.
Mar 19 . . . [went to] our new house . . . [which] is being papered.
Mar 24 Teresa Askin came early in the afternoon . . . I walked up to our house with her. . . .
Mar 25 Finished my blinds . . . our house looks very much improved and I hope we will be happy in it. . . .
Mar 26 . . . our furniture has come and I am very pleased with it all. . . .
Mar 27 . . . The house finished today and it will look very much better when the carpets are all laid down. . . .
Mar 31 . . . I am pleased to think [that] in a short time we shall be in our own home. Mrs Thomas has a daughter.
Apr 1 Spent the day at our new house arranging things. Tomorrow we go there to sleep. . . .
Apr 2 Came up last evening with George after tea and feel very strange in our new house. May I be able to make it a pleasant one for my husband and be always able to do my duty. . . .
Apr 3 Very much to do. Our cook has come, she is rather above her place. . . .
Apr 5 Went to church with George in the morning. A sermon on charity. . . . The Bishop of Huron is married to Miss Collins. . . . He

has been a director 16 months and had been married 48 years to his late wife. . . .
Apr 23 Mary McNeal came as housemaid, terms 5 dollars a month. . . . Cook came 2 April terms 7 dollars.
Apr 27 I have been ill in the last fortnight and cannot attempt to write up my journal for that time. All were very kind to me while I was ill. This I fear is only the beginning and so little time [left]. . . .
Apr 29 Tomorrow some friends dine with us. Lately I have been so cross to George. I hate to think of it. I am so ill that the least thing upsets me . . .
Apr 30 Our first dinner party is over and no great misfortune. Everything was good and the table looked pretty our friends were good enough to say . . . Mr & Mrs Plumb, Mr & Mrs Griffin dine here, [also] Mrs Edward, Miss Griffin, Captain Lyons R.A., Captain Collins 60th. . . .
May 1 . . . Mrs Chase, an old friend of mine, sent me a pretty little baby jacket white and blue. My baby will be well provided for every[thing] . . . Captain Northey came to bid me goodbye. . . .
May 3/4 Went to church and staid to Sacrament . . . in two months my troubles will be over and I shall be all right, I hope . . .
May 5 Went to market, . . . Got flowers and seeds for [the] garden. . . . had a cab and went to see a nurse . . . as the one I had has disappointed me. . . . A letter from Mama. . . .
May 8 Got up at five. George had to leave for Chatham and will not be home before eleven tonight. I feel so lonely when I think he is not coming to dinner. . . .
May 12 A letter from Mama. Mrs Harris came and spent the day with me. She seemed pleased with our home. About five she went over to Mrs Griffin and I went over to the Askins. . . . 69th Regt came from Brandfield this afternoon. The rest of the 60th left today.
May 20 . . . George played cricket. The 53rd won.
May 22 . . . I have nearly finished all my baby clothes . . .
May 23 Mrs Glass called. A letter from Maggie . . . also from Mama. . . .
May 24/25 Sunday. Queen's birthday is to be kept tomorrow. Went for a long lovely walk today with George. Also down to the House [Eldon].
May 26 I laid in the house all day and went for a walk after tea down to Mrs Harris . . . had a game of bezique. . . .
May 27 Went to Eldon in the morning and commenced a cap for Mrs Harris who showed me how to put in a patch. I sew and stitch so much day after day and no rest. . . . Hardly slept 2 hours all night,

when will it all end. Sometimes I find myself wishing it [pregnancy] were over.

Jun 1/2 George went to church. Heard the Dean preach. . . . Had dinner. Went to see Mrs Harris in the afternoon. Staid to tea. Bella Meredith was there looking so pretty. We came home early after which I wrote Mrs Edward and Mama. . . .

Jun 5 Rain all day in heavy showers. Mrs Edward gave me such a pretty basket. . . . She is so kind. Mama likes the house, made her six caps.

Jun 6 Rained all day very hard. No visitors or others, so did a quantity of sewing. Mrs Harris, Mrs Edward . . . Grand[ma] [and] Mr Ryerson will dine with us tomorrow. Am invited to the 53rd ball on Tuesday next.

Jun 10 Mrs Cleghorn, Mrs Menzies, Miss Fisher called. Mrs Hamilton, Mrs Askin, Teresa and two Miss Hamiltons went for a walk after tea with Mama. . . . The ball was a good one and they enjoyed it. . . .

Jun 12 The Thomas' give a picnic today. I have urged George to go with Mrs Edward but he will not I fear. It is hard that he should miss all pleasure because I cannot join him. Kind my husband is at all times . . . went to Mrs Harris in the evening.

Jun 13 Major Dalzell called to bid us good bye. The 53rd go on Monday to Quebec. . . . No other news of any sort. . . .

Jun 15 A dear little baby girl God gave me.[19] May we teach her to live that when her life ends he will take her to himself. I hope I will be able to do my duty to her. . . . After her birth till now I could not do much.[20]

Jul 29 George's birthday. Our Baby baptized today by Dean Hellmuth. Amelia Archange after her Grandmother. God grant she may be as true a human and good a christian as either of them. Mrs Harris, Mrs Edward and her husband were her Godmothers. I am nearly well.

Sep 5 One year ago I was married. The time seems far longer to both George and I. Mama left me when our little Amelia was 2 months old. I have been so happy. My husband so kind and good he has never said one word to me or found fault with me in any thing I have said or done. . . .

Sep 8 George left for Milton. He will only be home tomorrow. I so dislike being alone altho the baby is company.

Sep 14/15 Left London at 12 o'clock for Windsor. Signed my will first. James Magee and my brother in law also [as witnesses] . . . The

[19]The birth of Amelia Archange.
[20]Probably written on 29 July.

baby did not sleep at all. Mrs Casgrain, Mrs Chase, Mama, Uncle John, Annie all met me. My baby was nearly kissed to pieces.

Sep 19 Our money came from England. A long letter from Archie [Montgomery]. George is to have the appointment.[21] I am glad altho he will have trouble with it. . . .

Sep 26 Came home. They were all so sorry to part with the baby. . . . Both the girls [servants] did so well when I was gone. The house looks very clean and bright.

Sep 27 Went to Mrs Harris in the afternoon, also Mrs Griffin. Saw the twins. They are looking so well. . . .

Oct 9 Very miserable. The hall stove smokes and is unmanageable. I broke the hall window in trying to open it this morning. Afterwards, went to town and got McBride's man . . . [to] see [if] the stove would work. At last the thing works well. . . . George will be home tomorrow afternoon. I am delighted.

Oct 17 The little twins came to see me today. They seem so fond of Amelia and look at her as a wonder of some sort. . . .

Oct 18 Did not go to church as George thought it more prudent for me to stay at home as the church is rather drafty as all churches are I think. In the afternoon did not go to the House [Eldon] not feeling well enough. Went for a walk in to town with Jane and George to look at a stove for our bedroom. . . .

Oct 24 Uncle Ned came . . . he brought . . . some partridges from dear Mama. In the evening a telegraph from George saying he would only be home . . . on Monday. I was so disappointed particularly as Uncle Ned was here. It happened so badly . . . of all the days to be away from home.

Oct 29 Went to hear Vanderhoff[22] read. I enjoyed it so much being the first evening I had spent out since I live in London.

Nov 15 . . . A husband is a dear friend and we miss him more than any other, and mine is the best in the world, so kind and thoughtful. . . .

Nov 17 My birthday, 23 years of pleasure and happiness has been my lot so far. When reverses come may I be able to bear them as a christian woman. Favours I have had, kind parents, a tender loving husband, a baby girl that [is] all love, dear little angel. May her fate be as happy.

Nov 22 Went to church. Found George on my return looking at his papers. The Estate gives him so much more to do. . . .

[21]George was appointed land agent for the Ronalds Estate.
[22]Vanderhoff was a visiting lecturer.

Dec 15 Baby six months old today. I am so happy in having a child who is so good tempered. Little darling I have never been awake one night with her yet. May God spare her to me for many years and strengthen her to make her all she should be. . . .
Dec 22 Staid at home to take care of our baby. She is not well and her little cousins [the twins] have the scarlet fever. I trust our baby will not get it or if she does will have it slightly. . . .
Dec 25 Baby is not well enough for me to have her, so Mama [Mrs Harris] and George will [stay] at Eldon without me. A lovely fine day just as Xmas should be. Mama is not very well. . . .
Dec 29 Made the jelly and charlotte[23] for George's whist party tomorrow night. Ten gentlemen. I hope it will be all right and they will enjoy themselves. I have a cold and feel very ill. No news. They had an afternoon party at Eldon. I was not well enough to go.

1869

Jan 9 Raining hard. Ice in the river all gone, quite a pretty sight to see it going & Glass' fence gone too. . . .
Jan 12 . . . Another fine day to send Baby for a walk. Went to her grandma. . . . Found Mrs Harris not looking well. The baby amused her altho she would not go to her. . . .
Jan 13 Mr and Mrs Edward came to see the baby. Scottie Griffin is better[24] as is Mrs Harris. Had a dreadful dream, thought my baby was dead, could not get to sleep, it seemed so vivid. May God spare our baby to us. . . .
Jan 16 Went to visit Mrs Goodhue and Mrs Ben Cronyn, the former is delighted with her home and [in] fact with her husband and [with] herself. . . .
Jan 20 . . . dark day. Nothing going on in town, except the ball. . . .
Jan 22 Called on Mrs Barker [and] Mrs Street, also went to the House and saw my Mother-in-law who is quite ill with a cold. She complained George does not go and see her often enough.
Jan 24 Went to see Mrs Harris before church, found her better. . . .
Jan 28 Teresa Askin and Mrs Nelson spent the day [here] so George left at five. I am lonely without him and dislike his being away on Sunday so much. . . .

[23]A "charlotte," a baked delicacy in the form of a light pudding.

[24]The child was suffering from the scarlet fever that was affecting the city at this time.

Jan 29 Wet and miserable out. Went to the House [Eldon] and staid for a little while with Mrs Harris while Sophia was at the Sewing Society. Baby so well and happy. . . . No visits from anyone. . . .
Jan 30 . . . a letter from George.
Jan 31/Feb 1 George in Chatham. I went to the House after dinner and [saw] Mrs Harris [who is] much better. . . . No news. Sunday seems so dull without George. I wrote to him this morning . . . I hope God will spare our child. Sometimes I feel as if I loved her too much. . . .
Feb 2 I spent the day at Col Askins. Mary took Amelia in her carriage. She seeme[d] to like it. . . . Mr & Mrs Innis called.
Feb 5 . . . George will be home on Saturday . . . I am so glad. . . .
Feb 9 Will the day never end. So [much] snow. I am alone. Went for a walk . . . I felt so dull. Baby is to be vaccinated tomorrow. . . .
Feb 10 George only came home at $2^1/_2$ this morning. . . .
Feb 11 Mrs Edward, Miss Woodhouse and Selina . . . all came in just as I was going to town . . .
Feb 18 Went up to see Mrs Ben Cronyn . . . [and other calls].
Feb 20 Went to market with Sophia and Miss Warren, the latter staid to dinner. In the afternoon we went to the House [Eldon]. . . .
Feb 25 Went to see Amelia Griffin, she is not well. Poor thing.
Feb 26 Mr & Mrs Walker, Mr & Mrs Hallie, Mr & Mrs Honeywell, Miss Warren, Miss Fitzgerald, Mr Wayright, Simpson and Duffield, all spent the evening with us. They appeared to enjoy it. The supper so very nice and it turned all out well. . . .
Mar 2 . . . All well in Windsor. George left in the late train for Chatham.
Mar 3 . . . I do so dislike being left alone and would give anything if this were to be the last. Mrs Walker and MacHattie called. Miss Lightfoot and Teresa Askin spent the day. . . .
Mar 7 Went to church and staid to the communion . . . [met] George at the Griffins. . . .
Mar 11 . . . George leaves at six for Windsor. I never feel quite so happy when he is away. . . .
Mar 12 Went down early to see how Amelia was. . . . I hope the child will be a girl as I am sure they both wish for one. Went again at 12 . . . and went down a[t] four. She was very bad, . . . she will come soon, I know. I went to Mrs Harris and called at Mrs Griffin's at half past five. A dear little girl. They are so glad it is over. Amelia is pretty well.
Mar 13 George only came at three o'clock. . . .
Mar 18 Mr & Mrs Glass dined here, [also] Sophia and her husband. A good dinner. . . .

Mar 19 Dined at the Walkers. The Thomas', Sweatmans, Ed[ward] Harris were there. A nice dinner and well served. A pleasant evening. I wear my wedding dress and flowers. . . .
Mar 23 If it were not for my dear little baby, I am sure [it] could be so very dull. . . . she is such company for me.
Mar 24 Spent last evening with my Mother-in-law. She gets low when Sophia and Edward are away. . . . Why is it I wonder they so often talk of my money as if it were a great thing? I feel sure it will never come to do me good. If my little Amelia has it, I shall rest in my grave content. Once I fancied being well off made people happy but ease and happiness are quite different things. Each day I am changing more and more.
Mar 25 I often wonder why it is I feel so old in all things and have no heart for everything. I fancy George being away so much makes me low. I know dear Mama is not happy for us. Baby is such a comfort to me. . . .
Mar 27 George will be home at 2. . . . I am so lonely for him, all contentment for me is gone. . . .
Mar 28/29 Easter Sunday. . . . Mama will not come as she promised to. I am lonely alone and dull. George went for a walk. I did not feel well enough to go. Amelia and her baby are doing well. . . .
Mar 31 Another month gone. . . . How time flies. . . .
Apr 2 . . . Finished baby's dress, she looks so pretty in blue. . . .
Apr 5 Mrs Meredith called with Bella. . . . Mrs R. Robertson has a son.
Apr 8 Went to a musical party at Eldon and rather enjoyed it. . . . George came home from Toronto at half past ten. He is away so much, . . . Amelia is growing . . . [she] is a comfort to me.
Apr 9 Went to see Mrs Griffin. Her little one improves so much, it is a fine large child and quite bright looking for one so young . . . we are to dine at the Thomas' on Tuesday. . . . Baby went down to her Grandma Harris in the morning.
Apr 13 Sophia and George went to the Griffin reading this afternoon. Edward came up and sat with me while he was alone. . . . Mrs Askin is very ill, went to see her.
Apr 14 . . . Glass, our new neighbour, came in to have a game of whist. . . . The man must be a donkey to talk as he does.
Apr 15 Wore my gray silk . . . [to] Mrs Thomas'. . . . The dinner was very good. . . . George looked so well. We got home at eleven.
Apr 16 Wore my white and scarlet dress at the ball. I enjoyed it so much. . . . danced with Major Simpson, Captain Bruyere, . . . and enjoyed myself. . . .

Apr 25 Mama [Mrs Ronalds] has her eye inflamed so much that I sent for Dr Woodruff.[25] . . .

Apr 27 George goes to Chatham. . . . Mama is so slightly better that I did not like to leave her. . . .

Apr 28 Not [a] dull day. Judge John Wilson is improving fast they say he may live for months. . . .

Apr 29 Mama's eye is better so we went to the House [Eldon] in the morning. . . .

Apr 30 We dined at Eldon House today. . . . Teresa Askin and Miss Morse called on Mama. No other news.

May 1 Cold, wet and disagreeable. Went to market, brought it all alone as I did not wish Mama to go . . . I find my money does not hold out as it should.

May 2 Went to church with George. We were so late [that] I felt quite ashamed. . . .

May 4 Mrs Wilson called with her baby, a pretty child and beautifully dressed. I like her so much and if I could would have invited her to dinner. I have made up my mind never to ask people if I can help it till I have a home of my own. George is kind to me in all other things and if he had the means, [he] would give me a home tomorrow. I know since I feel that there is a great difference between Sophia and I.

May 5 I have much to be thankful for . . . such a good husband and child, dear Mama is with me. . . .

May 6 A headache and very low. . . . How I wish I could have a better life and I am sure no person tries more than I do. . . . Wish I were different and try and commanded my temper more. Mrs William Meredith called with Bella. Mama goes on Saturday morning. . . .

May 7 Called on Rebecca, Skae and Miss Beddome. I could not ask them to tea as Mrs Harris wanted both my servants for a dinner party. I should have thought one would have [been] enough at a time. I was very sorry it so happened. Mama and I went for a long walk. . . . She goes tomorrow. I shall be so lonely for her. George dined at the House [Eldon].

May 8 The Skaes went with Mama. I felt almost sorry they had to go so soon as I wished so much to be civil to them, still I could not prevent it. . . .

May 16/17 Commenced a dress for my darling little Amelia. She walks so well. . . .

May 18 Went to the Green House for a bath. . . .

[25]No reference to Mrs. Ronalds' arrival.

Jun 13/14 . . . My black dress came on Saturday, . . . such a handsome one and beautifully made – a present from Mama.
Jun 15 Little Amelia's birthday. Dear little child that she may be spared for many years to come. I do so hope and trust she may grow up all we hope for. Now she is a very bright little darling and has many pleasing ways, even at her age calls with her hands and claps them when please[d] she only says Papa and Mama, feels so well and runs all over, little angel.
Jun 21 Did not go out of the house all day. I hope tomorrow it will break. I sleep so little. . . . dear Mama, if she was here, I would like it so much and yet I cannot ask her to come. . . .
Jun 28 Charlotte Adelaide Harris[26] born at Raleigh House.
Sep 13 Went to church . . . George is in Chatham seeing to the lands before the rent comes due next time. He will only be home by the end of the week. I am lonely for him at night, my baby is not well. . . .
Sep 14 [a list of ladies] had been here, a letter from George.[27] . . .

1870

Jan 10 . . . Called at Mrs Meredith, [I am] envious of her lovely carpet – such a nice home.
Jan 11 Mr Goodhue died at ten this evening. . . . Had Amelia's picture taken. Hope it will be good. . . .
Jan 15 Amelia a year and seven months, does not speak yet. . . .
Jan 18 Went over to bid the Askin's goodbye. They go to Chatham on a visit. I fear [they] are in bad way for money from all I can hear about the affairs. Mrs William Meredith called. . . .
Jan 20 I have so much trouble with my cook, she is not willing and is so slow. . . .
Jan 21 George went to Toronto. . . .
Jan 30 Went to church, nearly fainted . . . I hope soon to be better.
May 9/10/11 I have been too ill to write for a long time and am today a little better. In five weeks I expect to be confined. How glad [I shall be] when it will be over. I had to take off my wedding ring as my hands are so swollen. My feet also. I had an idea that perhaps I might never put it on again. If this should be the case I would wish Amelia my little girl to have it when she is old enough to know about her Mother.

[26]Lucy's second child.
[27]There are no more entries for 1869.

Also if I should die as I have not made a will[28] and wish what I have to be shared between what children I have, Amelia is to have the dressing case Uncle John [Ronalds] gave me. My pearls, engagement ring, the diamond ring Papa gave me and what ornaments were given as wedding presents including the bracelet George's sisters gave, and if the other child is a boy he is to give Amelia all the rest of my jewelry except Papa's watch chain, seals and ring. Amelia is to have the watch & chain Aunt Mary left me. The silver from Mrs Lyon, the coffee pot and tea pot Mama gave me. Also what silver came from the Ronalds, forks, spoons and things of that kind. I give to my other child the Byass tea set, in any case should it be son or daughter also a ring set with diamonds and topaz and would wish Mama to look after my children as long as possible.[29]

1871

Jan 14 . . . Egerton Ryerson called. Sophia has not been here for a long time. . . .
Jan 17 Baby is not well, little darling. I hope it will be nothing more than a cold. Mrs Chapman called and came in. I told her about the fear, but she is not afraid. Sophia and Amelia would rarely come in sight of the house.[30]
Jan 21 . . . Mama missed her first train so she went [home] at 12 today. . . . Amelia was so sorry for Mama leaving, she could hardly speak of anything else.
Jan 24 Amelia is so loving. After George left today she came and put [her] little arms around my neck and kissed me so long [and said] . . . "Papa gone in the train." May our children be spared to us and God grant that they may follow in the way of happiness and peace [and] give me patience to do my duty. I am lonely for Mama – letter from her today. How still the house is without George.
Jan 26 The children both the same. Went down [to Eldon] and dressed Miss [Kate] Campbell for the ball. She wore white with flowers in her hair and several ornaments. She is like Teresa Scott . . . only better looking. . . .
Jan 28 George came home late last night and brought me a handsome

[28]It would seem that Lucy's good intentions on 6 March 1868 did not produce a will. It would appear, however, that she made a succession of wills, see 6/7 April and 8 May 1873.

[29]There are no more entries for 1870.

[30]They were afraid of scarlet fever.

pair of carvings and a broach from Detroit, the first handsome present since I was married. Went to market and called on Mrs Harris. . . .
Jan 29/30 . . . Mr Thomas, Edward, George and Walker went to the Asylum for a drive. . . . A parcel from Mama . . . fish and cocoa . . .
Feb 2 . . . I wonder why [I] had bad dreams all night.
Feb 3 George went to Chatham. . . . I sometimes think perhaps I spend too much and forget a husband and lover are quite different people. George [is] so kind and never find[s] fault with what I do. . . . I try my best to save . . . [it] seems to George that I spend too much. . . .
Feb 8 . . . I am sorry that George and Edward do not get on so well. There is chance of my husband leaving the office. . . . I am so sorry. I have had nothing to do with it I am glad to say.[31]
Feb 9 A miserable night. Neither George or I slept. This makes all the difference to us. . . . How Edward could say he [George] was ungrateful . . . for Edward did nothing for George that I know of. . . .
Feb 11 Milly has a cold.[32] . . .

1872

Jan 16 . . . a long letter from Archie Montgomery, who is one of the trustees under my marriage settlement. They are about to increase my allowance. . . .
Jan 22 Miss Warren had dinner with us. . . . George went down to Windsor. . . .
Feb 1 . . . We went to the Asylum to a dance and concert. Both were good and I enjoyed a letter from Mrs Chase. . . .
Feb 2 Went to see Mrs Harris twice today. . . . Mrs Carling called. . . .
Feb 11/12 Did not go to church . . . I had a cold. Later walked to Mrs Harris. Advertised for a cook in the *Herald*, *Free Press* and *Advertiser* on Saturday. . . . No answer. . . . George went to Chatham . . . I have felt so low all day. Ellen [maid] does seem satisfied to stay and girls are hard to get. My accounts all in a mess. God grant that I may become more patient.
Feb 19 . . . I had a letter from James Montgomery today in which he says my allowance will be increased to 200 [pounds] per year and does not feel sure if that includes the 66 pounds or not. . . .

[31]George Harris did withdraw from the Harris and Brothers law firm in July 1871 and established a land agency office.
[32]Lucy's entries for the rest of the year consist of a few brief notes.

Feb 22 . . . [Dinner] at the Evans'. Col Taylor and wife, Dr Landor & wife, Mr Walker, Mr Becher . . . Mr Plumb, Mr Tippy, the Bishop and ourselves. The dinner was good and passed off very well indeed.
Feb 26 Saw Mrs Harris. . . . Mrs Becher called. Frank Cronyn spent the evening with us. We are asked to the Merediths tomorrow evening and to the Beddomes on Thursday.
Mar 10/11 Went to church. . . . Mrs Warren sat in our pew. Later went for a long walk with Mama. . . . George went to Sarnia to sell some land. . . .
Mar 12 Children party at the Griffins. Mrs Walker came and spent the afternoon. . . .
Mar 25 Sat up with Chassie from twelve till 7. . . .
Mar 31 Went to church in the morning being Easter Sunday and later to tea with Mrs Harris. Mama was not well enough to go out.
May 4 Went to the circus with George and Amelia [Griffin] Milly liked it so much. I saw the Carlings, Cleghorns, Bechers, Furnesses. In fact half London. . . .
Jul 29 We go to Sarnia. I take Mary as nurse and leave Sarah to Mama. . . . [Charlotte's] life has been one of pain. Only God in his mercy will do . . . his best for my dear child.
Aug 10 Got home at 11 today. George and Amelia met me at the station. The Dr at Sarnia gives no hope of Baby [Charlotte]. . . . Dear Mama came for me last night. How kind she was to come.
Aug 13 Mama ill. Sent for Dr Cathmole.
Aug 16 At 9 o'clock today Dr Woodruff came. He said dear Mama could not live many hours, that mortification had set in. . . . She said, "dear Lucy, I am not ill enough to die. I do not think if I am called, I am ready." She received extreme unction. Mr Bruyere[33] was very kind. Uncle John came at 5 o'clock. My dear Mother was conscious all the day and knew us all. She died a good Christian as she held [my] hand. Mama died at 20 minutes to 10 PM in my arms. May my end be like hers and [I] pray to God from my heart to give me strength to do my duty in this trial.
Aug 18 Mama buried in the Sandwich church yard at 4 o'clock today – Sunday – beside Fanchette Skae. Now only two graves in different places contained what in life I loved most, my kind Father who died on the 11 of June 1863 after a long illness in his 42nd year. May God in his mercy prepare me as they were prepared to go to Him. Make my deathbed as hers so resigned to her heavenly Father's will.
Sep 13 [A list of ladies called].

[33]A Roman Catholic Priest.

Nov 7 Dr Young came to see me. I have been ailing since the 5 of September.
Nov 8 Mary McLean came on a visit.

1873

Jan 3 . . . Saw Mrs Harris in the afternoon for an hour. Sophie and Edward are in Toronto at a ball. . . .
Jan 4 . . . Went to Mrs Harris' to tea at six o'clock. . . .
Jan 6 . . . George defeated as Alderman, having 230 votes being 30 below the others. I am a little disappointed altho' I know it is far better for him. . . .
Jan 9 . . . Elizabeth [maid] had the day to go out.
Jan 20 Went down to Mrs Harris' in the afternoon, got home late. We are to go to luncheon tomorrow there. Sophia is not well. . . . Mrs Beddome called today. Mrs Hutchinson has a daughter, the 4th child. . . .
Jan 25 Went to town in the morning with Amelia [Griffin] and saw Mrs Harris and Sophia for an hour. Mrs Glass and Mrs William Meredith called with Mr Griffin. . . .
Jan 31 Went to see Mrs Harris this morning. She is well, she gave me a jug of cream for dinner. . . .
Feb 1 Spent the day at the Walkers. . . . Mrs Campbell and Mrs Griffin called.
Feb 14 Up with Charlotte till 2 this morning. . . .
Feb 15 Sent for Dr Woodruff today. Charlotte worse. . . .
Feb 17 Amelia cried . . . all night. Charlotte so ill. I am nearly worn out.
Mar 18 Annie Fraser as cook, 7 dollars a month.
Apr 6/7 The river very high rising fast . . . Amelia [Milly] is at her Grandma's. She is so fond of going there to sleep. We went down to [Eldon House] after tea to see if she wanted to come home. Wrote to Aunt Ellen . . . George left for Chatham. . . . He will not be home till Saturday next. Before he left he made his will as I have just made mine to encourage him. . . .
Apr 13 Easter Sunday fine and clear. A sad day to me. The memories of other Easters when my Father and Mother were living 14 years ago today. All who then seemed much to me were with us, when poor Uncle William was buried. Papa, Mama, Mr McLean, Dr Askin, . . . poor Ellen and how I am so far from that home or even the years of our dear ones. What another year may bring we know not . . .
Apr 15 . . . paid Esther her wages yesterday and increased it 50 cents

as she sleeps with Charlotte. Mrs Ford called to collect for the church today. Young Hellmuth came to ask us to dinner, accepted for George and declined for myself. . . .

Apr 20/21 Stayed in bed all morning. In the evening Sophia and Edward came to see me. . . . The paperhanger began today.

Apr 22 Mr & Mrs Griffin came to see me today. Charly Baby also. George dined at Eldon House. . . .

Apr 23 No visitors. How glad I shall feel when the alterations are finished.

May 8 Raining all day. No visitors except Mcgee who came in the evening to make my will. I have entailed 400 acres to each child I may have and in case of my childrens' death before they have attained the age of 21 years, one half of all the property to George and the balance be divided between my relations on my Mother's side [and] 10,000 dollars to an English Church.

May 14 . . . [Archie] Montgomery [and wife] . . . came at ½ past 9 tonight.[34] . . .

May 15 George aske[d] Archie, . . . Edward and Jessie Campbell to dinner tonight. . . . I hope all will go off well.

May 18/19 Archie Montgomery and his wife went to church . . . with George. They had tea at Mrs Harris. I am not well at all. They went to croquet at the Merediths and enjoyed it very much.

May 22 . . . I can hardly move about at all and feel very weak and to add to all the nurse I engaged in February has written to say she cannot come to me. Latterly I have had so many vexations that I am feeling worn out. . . .

May 23/24 . . . No one knows what I suffer and sometimes I almost wish I could forget all the ties I have and I feel that I was prepared enough to die. For the children, I know it would be hard, and my married life has been a happy one, George being kind and all his family are so considerate to me. Still I feel that when Mama was taken I lost what I needed most. It would have been easy to leave this world knowing she still could take charge of my children. . . .

Jun 15 George Henry Ronalds Harris[35] born at Raleigh House.

Jul 29 Dean Boomer baptized the little boy today. George's birthday. Our other children were baptized on the same day. Milly five and Charlotte three years ago. Dear Mama was here with us. It is nearly one year since she died on the 16th of this month. The babe is called

[34]The Montgomerys are from Brentford, England. Archie was the trustee of the Ronalds Estate.

[35]Lucy's third child.

George Henry Ronalds after Papa and my husband. Ronald we shall call him. Edward Harris, Major Walker were his Godfathers and Mrs Harris his Godmother. I pray God we may bring him up carefully and that he may become a good and just man. Dean and Mrs Boomer, Mr and Mrs Griffin, Edward & his wife, Mrs Harris & Aunt Ellen made the party.
Aug 7 Drove to the Asylum and college today with Mrs Cosgrain. I felt so ill . . . they left at a quarter to six for Sandwich. George going as far as Chatham with them. . . .
Aug 28 Called on Mrs Tilly, Mrs Cronyn [and other ladies].
Aug 30 George came home. Aunt Ellen left for Chatham.[36]

1874

Feb 26 The Archie Montgomerys come on the 10 of March and will spend 2 weeks with us. George is low and despondent.
Apr 2 The Montgomerys left today, they are going to sail on the 25th. . . . She I fear will not live long. Archie spoke very fairly and said he would do all he could for me as a trustee.
Apr 18 George told me that either the house or farm would be mortgaged to pay off the sum we borrowed when Uncle John Ronalds died.
Jun 3 . . . 2 children in our neighbourhood have scarlet fever. God grant it does not come to ours.
Jun 4 Went with George to Eldon House. They now always talk of my Grandmother's death. It has the effect of hardening one to hear people only talk of money and think of nothing else. One thing I am glad in my heart [is] that a settlement was made at my marriage. Dear Mama, if she had lived till now would have been grieved. Not that George or the others are unkind, only they are thoughtless.
Jun 5 One of the children died today of the fever. I do not let Amelia or Charlotte out of the gate at all and hope they may escape. . . .
Jul 1 . . . No news. Nothing going on in town. Sometimes I fear we will become very poor. George does not exert himself enough. I am afraid [he] takes life too easy.
Jul 2 . . . Wrote to Aunt Ellen and Uncle John about the dividing of the farm for in my opinion the girls [her aunts] would get nothing. . . .
Jul 8 . . . passed so many people on my way to have a sulphur bath.
Jul 9 . . . a nice letter from Aunt Ellen, one also from Aunt Teresa. . . .

[36]There are no more entries for 1873.

Jul 16 . . . No visitors all day except Mrs Furness with Alex, Mrs Becher and Connie. . . . On this day in 1844, my Father and Mother were married. Papa has been dead 11 years and Mama nearly 2.
Jul 18 . . . Dinner at the Harris' tonight. Such a good dinner beautifully cooked and very pretty flowers. Amelia and Mr Griffin, Mr Becher and Connie the Scotts and Sophie & Edward, Mrs Harris and ourselves.
Jul 28 . . . [will have] the Eldon House people to dinner tomorrow as it is George's birthday. . . .
Jul 30 . . . Montgomery has not sent my money this time. I never waited so long or wanted it so much. We dined at Eldon House.
Jul 31 . . . George does not seem happy. I find times hard and cannot manage on so little as is given me. . . . I am going to Chatham soon and will perhaps sell my farm.
Aug 6 Took Kate and Baby at six. We arrived quite early at the McLeans [in Chatham]. Went to see my farm . . . am going to sell it as soon as possible.
Aug 7 . . . Returned at ½ past one. Charlotte and Milly so glad to see me again. . . .
Aug 18 Went to the House [Eldon] and did some shopping for them in town. We go to Toronto tomorrow for one day. . . .
Aug 31 Left at 12:50 for Windsor with Kate and the children. George going as far as Chatham with us. Uncle John, Aunt Ellen, Mrs Dougall met me at the station. Found them all looking so well. . . .
Sep 1 . . . Had so many visitors. . . . Everyone seemed so glad to see me. . . .
Sep 2/3 Went to Detroit. Took Kate and the children with me. . . . Saw many pretty things. . . . Bought Grandma some peaches, am trying to be careful of my money . . . I see so many things Grandmama wants badly . . . John does not seem as thoughtful as one would like to see him. Asked Mrs Casgrain to tea [and] enjoyed it very much indeed. They gave Milly such a pretty set of dolls' brushes. . . . I am going to enjoy myself pretty much. Wrote to George and Sophia.
Sep 4 Let Kate go to Detroit to stay with her cousin . . . the children were as usual very cross indeed when she was gone. Eliza drove me over in the morning to shop.
Sep 5 . . . Kate came back. . . . I took some flowers to my dear Mother's grave today. . . .
Sep 6 Went to Detroit in the street car and went to Christ church . . . came back with Mrs Dougall [a cousin] and Mrs Street of Hamilton. Met George. . . . Dined with Wallace and Eliza. . . .
Sep 10/11 Grandma is so much better today. I am going to get her to come to Detroit with me and see her sisters. She has not been there for

5 years. The visit is now over and Grandma enjoyed it so much. Her brother is there, she had not met him for 9 years. Took Aunt Teresa and drove to Grosse Point. Mrs Brush [cousin] was so kind and Ada so polite. I am glad I went down to see them and I asked them to come to us. . . . Took Aunt Ellen and Teresa in the *Dove* to Amherstburg, Grosse Isle, Gibraltar. . . . We remained on the boat all the time and enjoyed the trip. . . .
Sep 12 Left Windsor after a painful parting with Grandma. She always feels my leaving so much. I gave her ten dollars and each of the girls 2 as I left. Jane came to see me off . . . I met George in Chatham so we came home together. The servants had done so well and everything looked so nice.
Sep 13 . . . Went to tea at Eldon House. . . .
Sep 24 . . . Insured my life today for 4,000 dollars.
Oct 9 Went to the House [Eldon] in the afternoon and Mrs Walker invited Milly to a tea party on Saturday. She has been asked out three times this week. . . .
Oct 28 Wrote to Mrs Montgomery . . . signed the deed to Thomas Irwin for 100 acres of my farm. It is too difficult to get good servants . . . I am going to sell 200 acres to pay what I borrowed. . . .
Oct 29 George left at six for Chatham. . . . Thanksgiving day.
Nov 1/2 Went to church and remained for Sacrament. George did not go. All went to Mrs Harris . . . Sophie came and sat with me. The baby is not well. The Griffins came home on Friday last. Went for a short walk with George.
Nov 9 . . . The baby [Charlotte] has cost us so dear already . . .
Nov 10 . . . Called on Amelia Griffin. How changed she is poor woman.[37] It is very hard indeed to have one love taken from us. . . .
Nov 17 Sophie went to Toronto today for a few days. Their cook has left . . . I had many gifts for my birthday. . . .
Nov 26 Mrs Patterson & Miss Glass called. Milly enjoyed her party. She only came home at nine o'clock. They had a magic lantern. Heard today that John B[?] had scarlet fever. They have 7 small children. . . .
Nov 29/30 Went to church . . . D[?] [has] typhoid fever, one child died on Saturday night and another is very ill indeed. Poor people they have nine young children. Another child died at the Bank. Both the little ones are buried today at nine o'clock.
Dec 4 Went to town and let the children out. It is such a fine clear day. Called at Mrs Harris. . . .
Dec 11 . . . Up all night with Ronald.

[37]She had lost a child to scarlet fever.

Dec 12 Children not well at all today. . . .
Dec 14 Baby worse. Went out for an hour, the children have the Griffin's rocking horse. . . . Another little D[?] died today. This is the fourth. . . . Amelia [Milly] is so ill. . . .
Dec 15 Baby is not well. Sent for Dr Woodruff to see the children. Both Milly and her [brother] are ailing. Dr Woodruff says it is scarlet fever. I am in hopes it will be mild and they may be spared. . . .
Dec 17 Ill all night myself just tired out and so anxious. Little M[?] Brown, a child 8 years old died this morning of scarlet fever. She was ill only 40 hours. Dr Woodruff attended her. Amelia Griffin came and sat with us. She is low and never will recover from her sad loss. . . .
Dec 18 . . . How easy the children are having it.[38] I do not sleep at all well, have such bad dreams. Charlotte and Kate [nurse] are pretty well at Eldon House. Kate wants to come home.
Dec 20/21 The children are well. . . . The Dr says that he will not come again unless sent for and told me the symptoms of dropsy and to feed the children pretty well. . . .
Dec 22 I had a dream of the Brushes and that has so often been the form of deaths in our family. God grant that I may bear all that comes as a good follower of our dear Lord.
Dec 23 Children are doing well. . . . Sent Grandma her Xmas dinner, turkey . . . salmon steak, plum pudding, and a plum cake. I also sent cash to my aunts 5 dollars, Grandma ten. . . .
Dec 24 . . . Gave the servants cash. . . .
Dec 25 A fine clear day for Xmas. The children are doing pretty well and we have reason to thank God that our little flock [is] spared and that our home is not a lonely one. Edward came to see us. . . .
Dec 27 Charlotte came home. . . . My poor child. How hard it will be for her who cannot speak at all to tell what she wants.
Dec 31 . . . Sarah [maid] came and asked to go home for 3 days. . . . Paid her in full as she asked for her money. The last day of the year. I am thankful it has gone without bring[ing] us sad memories as it has so many. May I be better prepared at the end of the coming year if God in his mercy spares me. . . .

1875

Jan 1 Fine clear cold day. . . . Went for a short walk . . . left the children with Mary [maid] as Kate went to her aunts. . . . Mr Jeffery, Edward and Mr Griffin came in. . . .

[38]A reference to the outbreak of scarlet fever and typhoid.

Jan 6 Baby and Charlotte both so ill. Kate and I were up with them nearly all night. I had dreadful pains in my bones. So much nursing has used me up altogether. . . .

Jan 7 . . . George and I are going to New York when my money comes. . . . Scarlet fever is a dangerous thing to mind our little ones. . . .

Jan 8 . . . The Masonic Ball was very good I hear. . . . 2 funerals went to the Kensington cemetery today and one on Thursday. So many people are dying.

Jan 17/18 Had a bad night and felt very miserable . . . George did not get up, I carried his breakfast on a tray, he was so vexed, and all day has scarcely spoken. My life is what one might say a pretty lonely one, with looking after the children and sewing. If no change comes, I cannot stand it much longer. . . . I sometimes think how nice it must be to have a sister to talk to. Since my Mother died I have felt sometimes as if I wanted some one to comfort me as she did if only for a few hours. . . .

Jan 19 Carling Meredith elected yesterday for the City conservative. Durrand lost the election. . . .

Jan 25/26 . . . Mrs Harris looks so well and seems very happy. . . . Cook and nurse maid gave notice to leave and I must look out for others. They are always quarelling and I cannot be perpetually making peace.

Feb 2 Went out in the morning, saw Sophie . . . she goes to Toronto for 2 weeks. No visitors. . . .

Feb 5 . . . Went to see Amelia Griffin, found him [Gilbert] in bed looking miserable and old. Archie Campbell has scarlet fever. . . . They say his wife was in Toronto when he was taken ill. His Mother came to see him at once. . . .

Feb 9 Sat with Mrs Harris for a long time and called at the Griffins. . . .

Feb 10 . . . The housemaid I engaged could not come for some days. I decided not to take her, will advertise for another. Letter from Aunt Teresa. . . .

Feb 19 . . . got a present for Mrs Harris as it is her birthday. . . . Kate and baby both ill.

Mar 9 Went to the Falls and saw the Ice Bridge, never had been there in winter so I was delighted. Stayed at [a] Hotel near the Suspended Bridge. . . .

Mar 13 Went to market and called on Mrs Harris. Amelia [Griffin] was there. She is asked to go to England and spend the summer with the Crutchleys. . . .

Mar 22 Miss Warren died at the asylum today. . . . Went to enquire about a cook. . . . Called on Mrs Gibson, Becher and took the children to see Mrs Harris. . . .
Mar 26 Went to market. Bought a dress for Baby. . . . Made pastry and cakes. No letters for me.
Mar 29 Went to church. Easter Sunday. Mrs Harris wanted us to tea in the evening. . . .
Apr 6 . . . Sophia and Edward go to England on the 2 of May.
Apr 8 Went to dinner at Mrs Harris' and met the Bishop and Mrs Hellmuth, Judge G[?], the Campbells. Everything was so nice. . . .
Apr 14 . . . My back is so bad and I am out of sorts and miserable altogether. . . .
Apr 16 Mrs Harris wants us to go there.[39] . . . and we must be ready.
Apr 22/23 In bed, too ill to move. Dr Woodruff says it is irritation of the spine. I am to last for a week in bed.
May 1 I have been in bed since the last time I wrote. . . .
May 14 Dress from England. George did not like the idea of my getting a dress at all and does not like it now it has come. Paid £8 on it. . . .
Jun 11 Mrs Harris is far from well. . . . Ronald is 2 years old today.
Jun 15 Amelia seven years old, a bright happy child. A telegram from Edward [in England] to know if George would like all the Canadian property for £40,000 pounds sterling. . . . God in his mercy grant that it may be for the best. I sometimes think I am wrong to trouble as I do about things but George will someday understand me better than he now does. . . .
Jun 18 Went and did some things at the House [Eldon] today. Made 4 caps, 2 for Mrs Harris, 2 for Mrs Chase . . . I hope they will all fit. . . .
Jun 22 Mrs Landor came [to] spend the day with Mrs Harris. . . .
Jun 27/28 . . . Left for Windsor at one o'clock. Charlotte was delighted.
Jun 30 Went to Detroit with Eliza. . . . Poor Grandma, I fear she will not live very long. . . .
Jul 1 Left home at half past eight and got to Windsor . . . George met me in the station [in London]. . . .
Jul 7 Mrs Landor and Miss Annie, Mrs Wellins and Bella [Meredith], Mrs Glass, Mrs Worthing . . . all called and had afternoon tea. . . .
Jul 10 Telegram from Edward. The whole of the Canadian property

[39]Sophia and Edward are in England.

can be had for 38 thousand pounds sterling. . . .
Jul 15 A letter today from Edward to say that poor Mr Scott is dead. He died on the 16 of June . . . of typhoid fever . . . [Teresa] has about 3,000 sterling for life, a handsome house to live in and 10,000 pounds . . . to do as she chooses with.
Jul 22 My money has come. I am so glad to get it. . . .
Jul 27 A letter from Eliza and Sophia. One for George. The land is sold and the money goes onto the funds. . . .
Aug 2 Engaged Mrs M[?] cook at 9 dollars a month. . . . A housemaid came. . . .
Aug 4 A letter from Sophia. Edward sails on the 5th and she one month later with some Toronto people she knows. . . . her brother was married today to his . . . cousin Lillie. . . .
Aug 7 Thirteen years ago Papa and I sailed from Liverpool to come home. Now it is 12 years since he died. . . .
Aug 16 Today three years ago died my darling Mother. Oh how I have missed her. . . .
Aug 30 Mrs Harris went to Long Point to see her brothers. . . . George went with her. . . .
Sep 1 Mrs Harris got back all safe and looking so well and happy. . . .
Sep 9 Went to the House [Eldon] and worked in the morning . . . Amelia [Milly] and Charlotte went to a party at Cronyns'. The first Chassie has been to. . . .
Sep 18 Went to market for Mrs Harris. . . .
Sep 22 . . . The last day has come. I feel sorry to leave Mrs Harris. It is hard at her time of life to put up with so much from servants. . . .
Sep 23 I am going to try and say nothing about household . . . to George for he dislikes it so much. I do hope I can be patient with them. . . .
Sep 28 . . . Edward and Sophia came at 9 o'clock. . . . Both are looking so well. Edward thinner a good deal.
Sep 30 Kate goes out for the day.
Oct 12 Milly was asked to spend the day with Laura Walker. She brought Milly a pair of doll's gloves from Paris. . . .
Oct 28 Thanksgiving day for a good harvest. Miss Lightfoot called to see the children no other friends. . . .
Nov 2 We went to the other house and found them both well. Mrs Harris has been rather low since Teresa's letter saying she would not have the Griffins. . . .
Nov 11 . . . ill and low spirited all day. Sometimes I feel as if all things were going wrong. George takes life too easy. . . .
Nov 16 George and I think so differently on many subjects that it is

difficult to avoid rocks in doing anything. The marriage settlement is one source of trouble. I am convinced that it is a good thing for the children, he thinks not.

Nov 17 George stayed over to dinner at [Eldon] House tonight as at 3 in the morning [he] goes to Detroit. Am 30 years old today and feel every day of it. Sometimes I feel rather as if the past three years had been a mistake for somehow things are changed to me. . . . I am not so strong as I was is one thing. Judge Moss, Dr and Mrs Landor, the Bishops . . . formed the party. It was a very good dinner indeed.

Dec 6 Went to the other House [Eldon]. I am suffering from my back again so much. . . . I would [like to] see some good Dr about it and also about Charlotte who does not improve in her speaking nearly as much as I could wish. . . .

Dec 13/14 . . . [The cook] gave me warning that she would leave when her month was up if I would not get a washwoman . . . George says let her go . . . I am sorry for cooks are not easy had. . . .

Dec 23 Packed Grandma's box. Sent [aunts] 5 dollars [each] and 10 to Grandma. Sent them a good dinner, a basket to Eliza and a pair of shoes to Annie's baby, an umbrella to Mrs Casgrain. Made 2 caps to Mrs McLean and Mrs Harris, Sophia some mats. . . .

Dec 25 The children enjoyed Xmas. . . . Went to Eldon to dinner and came home late. Milly went to the Christmas tree at the Walkers. Such a lovely day. . . .

Dec 30 . . . George and I had a dispute about mor[t]gaging the farm and house to make payments on the Byass shares. George and Edward had a talk about the same things. Edward has a bitter tongue when he lets it loose. Went to the Masonic Ball. . . . Wore pink and gray silk. . . .

Dec 31 Called on. . . . Poor George is out of sorts and ailing. Had to mor[t]gage the house, I am so sorry to have it done. The last day of the old year. What sorrow or joy another may bring? . . .

1876

Jan 1 Fine warm day . . . Mr Jeffery and son, Mr Walker, Mr Becher, Griffin, 2 Harris [George and Edward] and [list follows] called at Mrs Harris. She is not well, also at the Griffins. . . .

Jan 5 Holmes lost 5 children from scarlet fever.

Jan 6 Had the 2 young Morrisons to spend [the day] as their Mother was confined . . . Captain and Miss West called.

Jan 9 Dr Woodruff came to see me. I am not at all well . . . I do hope I shall soon be better. . . . Had 2 apply for cook's place. . . .

Jan 12 Engaged Mrs Lea as cook at 10 dollars a month and she is to do the washing. . . . No letters.
Jan 13 Did not go out of the house all day. Baby so cross and ill. . . . Edward came up. George in Chatham. . . . Wrote to Aunt Ellen, she sent 4 dollars to me.
Jan 14 Went down in the evening to see Mrs Harris. They told me my cook . . . drank so hard, they had to turn her out. . . .
Jan 15 Went all over to get a cook . . . found one. . . .
Jan 17 . . . No cook yet at all. Baby had an earache all day and cried so hard. . . . Poor little fellow.
Jan 18 Bad wet day. No letters. Wrote to Aunt Jane. . . . Baby better . . . I have a bad cold myself, am miserable with it. No sign of a cook. Got Annie's sister Mary L[?] as cook till someone else . . . shows up.
Jan 21 . . . The Walkers engaged a cook who worked at Mrs Simpson Smith's for 8 years. I hope she will turn out well. I am so . . . disappointed with all which goes wrong. It really is very hard to manage and know what to do.
Jan 24 . . . Eliza came as cook and let Kate go to her aunt's for the night. . . .
Jan 25 Kate came home early and the boy [Ronald] was delighted to see her. Called on Mrs Glass, Miss Habeden . . . and went to the Reeds. George did not come much to my disgust for he had promised me to go. . . .
Jan 27 Went to the House and talked over the party.[40] It was very pleasant. People said I looked well for which I was thankful.
Jan 28/29 . . . Uncle John came in and looked so old and poor. I am afraid things are not going on well with him. . . . Went to the Bachelor's Ball. It was a very good one and everyone said the best Ball for years given in the town. So many pretty girls and such handsome dresses one rarely sees so much in town. I am asked to the Thompsons for the 1st of next month. George says he will go, I am glad.
Feb 9 . . . Milly had her first dancing lesson . . .
Feb 11 Went to see my Grandmother and found her looking so ill. Aunt Hunt is very ill almost dying I fear. Poor old Grandma. She looks very old and very poor. . . .
Feb 14 . . . Sophia and Edward go to England on the 19th. . . .
Feb 15 . . . am feeling most miserable and ill. George has to work hard. . . . My allowance will be about 6 or 7 hundred a year sterling. If I only live long enough to see myself out of debt, I will be very glad.

[40]Sophia's party at Eldon.

Feb 17 Edward [and Sophia] came to say goodbye. George went as far as Paris [Ontario] to see them off. . . .
Feb 19 Mrs Harris' birthday. I am unable to dine with them.
Feb 29 Mr Becher, Mr Walker and Griffin came to see us [Lucy was ill]. Milly went to her dancing lesson.
Mar 7 Mrs Harris . . . ailing and feeble. Amelia [Griffin] came to see her Mother. . . .
Mar 8 Went to see Amelia, found her in bed and feeling very low and miserable. . . .
Mar 24 Letter from Sophia to me, one to George from Edward, also a telegram . . . "all will be settled on Monday next."[41] How much I hope "all well" be for one advantage. I have tried my best to do what is right. . . .
Mar 29 Wrote to my Aunt Ellen. Grandma very ill indeed. How I wish I could go to see them. . . .
Mar 30 . . . A letter from Sophia. She is going to stay in England and enjoy herself as much as possible. The letter in some ways give Mrs Harris more pain than joy. . . .
Mar 31 . . . I am very anxious about Grandma. . . .
Apr 5 A terrible thought that I was obliged to mor[t]gage all my property and . . . if George died tomorrow with a house mortgaged and 600 hundred a year, all the rest would be Edward's and I never would get one copper for the Harris likes his own [way] and I am too plain spoken to get on with him. I feel sometimes as if I were bitter to everyone. It is very hard to see George so indifferent as he is. . . .
Apr 6 Took all the children to have their pictures taken. . . .
Apr 14 . . . A letter from Teresa. Grandma not well. . . .
Apr 20 . . . Mrs Hutchinson came to see me about a Mrs Bright as governess, the terms are only 10 dollars a quarter, the governess does not seem very refined. She may be a good teacher. . . . George and [I] left at 6 PM for Chatham. . . .
Apr 21 Went to see Mrs McLean and gave her ten dollars. She is very poor. She seemed very grateful and told me about her plans for the future. . . . Poor woman she does not know how much it costs to do things. Saw Minnie . . . she is dying. . . .
Apr 25 . . . Edward got home looking well and seems to be quite pleased with his visit. I am glad. Sophia sent the children books. . . .
May 2 George went off at six to Toronto. . . . Went to see [Mrs] Harris for a couple of hours. Mrs Ben Cronyn and Mrs Mallmond called. . . .

[41]A reference to the management of the Ronalds' Estate.

May 3 . . . George gave me a hundred dollars to keep house on, spent 8 and gave him 4 dollars. . . .
May 6 Went to market, took Baby and bought him shoes . . . a noise all afternoon. Poor Miss Meredith died today. Got a telegram from Aunt Ellen. Amelia and Mr Griffin, . . . Becher, . . . came to call. George is to be at home at 11 tonight. Am very tired.
May 9 . . . Grandma will not live very long. . . .
May 12 . . . Poor dear Ada died. . . . She was unconscious for the last two days. Her brother is very ill with typhoid fever and will die soon. . . . it was a sad sight to see. They left the little girl to see her Mother's coffin in the grave. Poor little Lillie. She seemed so frightened. It is the first funeral I ever saw. The pale was covered with flowers, the grave with evergreens and lillys on her birthday. . . . I saw my Grandmother who looked ill and very poor.[42] . . .
May 21 . . . Church with George and Amelia [Milly] . . . Percy Crutchley died on the 6 of [May]. Eliza [George's sister] . . . income . . . [will be of] 11,000 or 12,000 a year.
Jun 6 Chasse so ill. Sent for Dr Woodruff. . . .
Jun 15 Amelia's 8th birthday. Had a small party. . . . All the children were so good. . . .
Jun 28 . . . My back is again so troublesome . . . Charlotte is six years old today. How will she alter in another year I wonder. . . .
Jul 4 . . . Letters from Mrs Dougall, Mary, Mrs McLean, Aunt Alice and Aunt Ellen. Called on Mrs Becher and the Landors, also on Mrs John Taylor and Mrs Furness. . . .
Jul 11 . . . market and can[ned] my strawberries. . . .
Jul 13 . . . Made my currant jelly and ras[p]berries jam. . . .
Jul 18 Went to market and sent ras[p]berries to Mrs Casgrain, Eliza and Grandma. . . .
Aug 24 . . . Sophia and Edward came after tea . . .
Aug 25 I am very tired . . . I am so ill and sorry for myself. . . .
Sep 5 The 9th anniversary of our wedding. Took Baby to market and paid some bills. . . . Walked to the other House [Eldon] with George. Mrs Harris asked me if I was going to increase the number of her grandchildren. I said I thought so. George has been most considerate since our return.[43] I am going to make a fresh will. . . .
Sep 12 . . . Got off at 1:45. George will not come with me. Baby so good all the way. Askin met me in Windsor. Got off at the upper station. Grandma and all looking so well. . . .

[42]Lucy is in Sandwich.
[43]The family had been in the U.S.A.

Sep 16 Went to Windsor and ordered a carriage to take Grandma to see her sister in Detroit and give her a drive. . . . [saw] Mrs Casgrain. Called on Mrs Dougall and enjoyed myself very much. . . .
Sep 19 Left Grandma's at 9 AM. Came to Chatham alone. Baby was very good.[44] . . .
Nov 1 A telegram saying M[?] was dead. I am not well enough to go to the funeral and George said he could not go . . . such a favourite of my poor Father and Mothers . . . George is very indifferent where death is concerned and I feel that when I am gone he would hardly put a stone to mark the spot. . . .
Nov 17 My birthday today. I was born in 1845. Today came a letter saying that my allowance would be 750 sterling in future. I am sorry for Edward led me to suppose it would be 600 a year in addition to the 250 I have at present. I feel as if this would be my last birthday and perhaps it is as well for me to know what my children will have when I am gone. . . .
Dec 5 George gave me 200 to pay bills. I am far from well. . . .
Dec 8 Am quite ill. George got Dr Moore to come and see me. I shall like him very much. Mcgee also made the needful changes in my will. . . .
Dec 21 Aunt Teresa has taken such good care of the children. She is very kind indeed. Packed a basket for my Grandma . . .
Dec 24/25 Xmas day. Santa Claus came much to Ronald's delight. . . .
Dec 31 Amelia [Milly] went to church with Sophia. . . . George has a bad cold. Dr Woodruff came to see him. . . . Mary cannot manage the kitchen very well. Wrote to Aunt Teresa [and to others]. . . .

1877

Jan 1 George suffered much from his foot all night, hardly getting any sleep. A pure clear cold day. . . . Sent Edward and Mr Walker a wild turkey for New Year. The children went down to see their grandma. Kate [nurse] not well and Lizzie my cook so cross. Am very tired today. I trust, I may be more patient this year than last.
Jan 2 George better today a good deal. Dr Woodruff says he must be careful for some time to come, advice George will not follow I am pretty sure. . . . Dr Landor is dying at his home. It is sad – four children not educated yet and very small means. . . .
Jan 3 Mrs Walker & Laura came for Amelia to spend the day there.

[44]She spent eight days visiting her family.

George would go for a drive today. It was so cold that I fear he was not wise. Still he will have his way. He would like to go and curl at Hamilton tomorrow.

Jan 4 Mrs Ben Cronyn has a son. She was married in May 1868 and this is the 6th child. George went to the great curling match at Hamilton. . . . I do not think he was very wise to do such a thing but he wanted to go and it is not worthwhile to contradict people.

Jan 6 Dr Landor died at 9 AM today. His family are very badly off. . . . News came today that Teresa Scott has engaged herself to Mr Littledale who came home from India with them.[45] He is 12 years younger than she is. Walked to the House [Eldon] to see Mrs Harris. Dr Landor's death and Teresa's marriage have made her ill . . .

Jan 10 . . . Mrs Harris is quite unwell yet Sophia and Edward went to Toronto. They dine at the Governor['s] House. . . .

Jan 11 Sat with Mrs Harris a couple of hours. . . .

Jan 18 George very ill. Up the best part of the night with him. Hope he will soon be better. George had 5 leeches on his arm . . . poultice. . . . Mrs Harris sent up some soup for him and some rusks.

Jan 22 More leeches. His arm is better but the foot is again very painful and swollen. . . .

Jan 24 Mrs Becher came to see how George was. Mr Jeffery, Glass and [also] Edward came . . .

Jan 25 June day. Amelia getting on well with her skating. She goes to the rink every day. . . .

Jan 27 George better a good deal.

Jan 31 Mrs William Meredith had a son this morning. . . . She sat with me all yesterday afternoon. . . .

Feb 8 Am not well. Had to get [a servant] to carry up the meat to the garret. Lizzie and Thomas are about as poor servants as one can get. George does not feel the slightest interest in any thing. Some times I feel as if it was no use for me to try to see after things and I am so helpless . . .

Feb 12 Sent Kate to ask how Mrs Meredith's baby was. Came back and said it was dead. Poor little thing it took cold and congestion of the lungs. . . . Sent her a white cross of lovely flowers. . . .

Feb 18/19 . . . Mrs Harris' birthday. Sent her some flowers.

Feb 21 Am not well. Think that tomorrow morning I will be over my trouble. God grant all may be well. . . . Mrs Hutchinson has a son.

Feb 22 Amelia Griffin came up in the morning. Sophia in the after-

[45] See Amelia's diary, 5 January 1877.

noon. She was telling me about Teresa and the Crutchleys. Am not well today. How I wish the baby was born and all was over. Sometimes I feel wonderfully depressed. Wrote to Aunt Teresa.
Mar 11/12/13 . . . I am so lonely without a baby in bed.[46] . . . God only claims his own and I must in future life bear in mind how little divides this world from the next and how nearby our lives we can make heaven seem. Our own time may be nearer than we think . . . Monday early morning we saw that he was to be called from a world that . . . is a place of pain. At six on Monday evening he passed away and now that chapter in my life is closed. May I so live that when I am called away I may join him. . . .
Mar 17 . . . No one has more kind friends than I have. . . .
Mar 20 . . . George went to curl and in the evening went to the Masonic Lodge, he is a Mason.
Mar 24 I think we will go to England in May; to take or not take the children is the question. George wants a change of some sort at once. . . .
Mar 28 A fine clear cold day. Read my French for an hour. . . .
Mar 30 . . . Today George went to curl. Edward came and sat for a time. . . . I walked downstairs the first time in five weeks. Today is Good Friday. How often I have gone to church with my Mother. This day always recalls our old life at the farm. . . . A fine spring day, the river is rising pretty fast.
Mar 31 Charlotte went out of the nursery this morning and found a pair of scissors, she cut off her hair in front and has made herself such an object. . . . One of Charlotte's bad days. . . .
Apr 6 . . . George is very kind and attentive to me. Some of the happy days of my life are, I think, over. I never feel as if I would be so happy again. . . . I got a cab and drove to Mrs Harris. She looked so frail that I do not think she will live very long. She seemed glad to see me. . . .
Apr 10 A very fine day, walked in the garden for half an hour. . . .
Apr 20 Went to the cemetery to choose a lot to lay our baby in. . . .
Apr 27 Amelia had the worst sore eyes I ever saw. When she awakened this morning it was a quarter of an hour before I could open her eyes. Sent for the doctor. He said that her eyes were very bad indeed. . . . I hope that my children will keep well while we are away.[47] . . .

[46]Her third son, George Edward, was born on 25 February and died on 27 February.
[47]On 1 May, Amelia and some of the Eldon staff moved to Raleigh House and stayed until 13 June while renovations were taking place at Eldon. See Amelia's diary, 1 May – 13 June 1877.

May 8 . . . Got to New York by half past 8. Saw Dr Herrick. He examined George carefully, he says that George has no real disease, change of air is what he requires. If he should not feel quite himself when we are in England, he says that the baths at Karlsbad[48] will be good for him. The trouble in his feet is gout.
May 10 . . . Our vessel is very full, 385 cabin passengers. . . .
May 15 Sea very rough indeed. The *Scythian* rolls very much.
May 21 . . . We will stay [in London] at Stantons Hotel for a fortnight and then go and see our friends. In the morning George and I took a walk together, not where many people go and where we met only the poor. The women are the most degraded looking objects. The children are what must strike everyone with sorrow – filthy, pale and ragged. The language one heard was dreadful. "I hope I may see your neck broken" said one little child of seven to another no older. In the afternoon we took a walk to Berkenhead [sic] which we much enjoyed. The view from the hill by the cemetery was lovely. I only wish I had had my little Amelia with me. I pray that our little ones may be well. By the end of the week we will surely hear from them. . . . George I think will be much better for this trip. . . . Found our hotel very comfortable indeed and after a good dinner . . . went to the Strand Theatre. . . .
May 23 . . . Mrs Montgomery came, . . . she is most kind to me. . . . A letter from Edward and one from my own little Milly, my darling. How lonely I am for her. I wish I had brought her. . . .
May 24 Went out with George, we walked about for hours, went to the Cooperatives at Victoria St and Westminster. George got a good many things he wanted. Called on Mrs Tom Leith near Hyde Park. We are asked to luncheon tomorrow there. A very kind letter from Mrs Montgomery asking us to go there on 7 June. . . .
May 25 Charley Crutchley called. . . . Mary Peard . . . and Mrs Dalzell[49] called. . . . Mrs Crutchley came up with Carry, all of them were very glad to see George looking so well.
May 28 . . . we met Helen Peard[50] – she is a nice girl and seems very amiable. . . .
May 30 George went late last night to stay at Archie [Montgomery's] to be ready for the Derby.
May 31 . . . We met Maud Dalzell,[51] Mary Leith and Robert.

[48]The spa in Germany.
[49]George's sister.
[50]Helen Peard is the daughter of Mary and Shuldham.
[51]Sarah's daughter.

Jun 5 . . . letters from the Crutchleys asking us to go there on Sunday.[52] . . . In the afternoon we went to Hurlingham to see polo played.

Jun 6 George went to see Dr Weber. He told him word for word what had been said by Dr Herrick in New York. We are to go to Hamburg and drink the waters. I am so thankful it is nothing more serious. My back is so bad. All the packing does not improve it for me and George leaves me the greater part to do.

Jun 7 We go to Ascot Station at 5 in the afternoon, . . . Julia was there to meet us. A lovely drive through the Park brought us to a very comfortable house. . . . Our bedroom was a very pretty one with dressing room. All the family were very kind. The General I like. Julia has been spoiled. . . . I am glad I saw them all. They asked us to go there on our return from Germany.

Jun 8 The drive from Southall station is very winding and curious. The Montgomery's house much better than the Crutchley's. The taste displayed in the gardens and whole house is wonderful. . . . Archie & his wife came over in the afternoon to stay and dine. My husband played lawn tennis. . . .

Jun 11 Went off to London about my dress. In four days they will collect it to fit me but I doubt its being a good job. Letters from home, all well. . . . We leave on Friday next for Hamburg.

Jun 12 George went to Ascot today. They kindly drove him to Southhall station and in the afternoon Mrs Montgomery drove over to Woodend Green where my Father's Mother is in an Asylum. It was a pitiful sight. She does not speak so that one can understand her in the least. Mrs Montgomery she knew and recognized at once but could not understand who I was at all. To be left alone is very hard. I pray that before old age makes me childish I shall not be left to be a burden to my children.

Jun 13 . . . We called to see Uncle Robert Ronalds, all looks so dark and a dingy since I was there before 15 years ago. We also saw the Brentford church and dined at Archie's – a good dinner. . . .

Jun 15 Got up early to pack. Mr Montgomery was so ill. . . . Mrs M was kindness itself and so was Laura. I fear Mr M will not live many years. He has been a kind friend to all our family.

Jun 16 . . . Left London at 3 PM for Dover on our way to the German Baths. George is better but he will not like work again I fear. . . .

Jun 18 Left Dover at 9 for Ostend. Had a fair passage. I hate the sea and would not cross if I could help it. . . . went on to Bruges and

[52]Sunninghill Park.

remained there. It is such a quiet old town. . . . We saw the old church of Jerusalem and had a drive about the town. All looks so old and queer. . . . In the afternoon we left for Brussels. . . .
Jun 19 . . . Went to the Cathedral and saw again the famous wooden pulpit. . . . Bought a lace handkerchief and small shawl, also gloves for myself and my aunts. . . . Brussels is a small Paris. All is outdoor life. And the poor work very hard beginning when they would be at school. . . . Children not more than 8 years old working till 9 at night. I am anxious about my children. It is long since I have heard from them. We left Brussels at 5 PM. Wrote to Mrs Harris. George wrote to Edward and Captain Peard.
Jun 20 Got to Cologne at 11 at night. A long and tiresome journey. . . .
Jun 21 We again went to the Cathedral. It is certainly a very fine one. I admired it much when we were here before.[53] . . . Went by rail to Bonn. There we took the steamer for Mayence.[54] No wonder the Germans are fond of the Rhine with its grand old ruins and vine covered hills. At Bingen the terraces run up a thousand feet above the river. All looks so grand and old. Some of the curves in the river are most wonderful. All impresses one with the idea that Germany will be the most powerful nation. The soldiers are such a fine healthy race of men and look as [if] they could hold their own even against England.
Jun 22 . . . left for Hamburg by way of Frankfort. It takes an hour and a half to get here. . . .
Jun 23 Got out about ten. We then got our instructions from Dr Diltz, baths in the morning and afternoon and refrain from raw fruits & vegetables, all fresh fish and butter, no wine or beer. Very tired and between that and unpacking I am done up completely. . . . Went to bed early for here one has to rise so early. . . .
Jun 25 . . . Went to church – a pretty little red sandstone one. . . . Wrote to Mrs Harris. . . . George will not write at all. . . . Went to the spring early and had one glass of water. Later in the day went for one walk and baths.
Jun 26 We went to Frankfort on the Main. Saw the pictures at the Frankfort Gallery . . . also the bridges and the old Cathedral. The Jewish quarter in the town is very pulled down but still many curious old sights to be seen. The town is full of squares where the people buy and sell all day long. . . .

[53]Lucy and George visited the places they had been while on their honeymoon in 1867.
[54]Mainz.

Jun 27 A letter from Sophia. Mrs Harris is not well at all. . . . Each day I am more troubled about George. He has become so uncertain and is growing very selfish. . . . He only thinks how he can avoid doing what I ask him. . . . I am sure I try my best but it is so hard to see him each day grow more indolent. . . . I wrote yesterday while I was vexed and I am ashamed to have been so unjust to my husband. . . .
Jun 29 . . . George has joined the tennis club. . . . It is strange he will not write to any one. . . .
Jul 6 George played tennis all afternoon. We went for a drive . . . very pleasant and did us all good. . . . Dreamed of my Father & Mother. George said he dreamed of his. It is very strange!
Jul 10 Take the waters regularly . . . George is to go and see the Dr tomorrow and then I trust he will take our passage. I am in haste to get home to my children.
Jul 13 . . . George lost his ring . . . and made no real attempt to find it again. The attendant at the Bath said they had it. When he went today they said they only meant they would look for it. . . . I gave [him] that ring when Amelia was born. . . . He has never written Amelia a line. His business letters he neglects the same way. . . .
Jul 19 It rained so hard we saw nothing of Saarbracken. Two hours and a half brought us to Metz, where we took a carriage to see the fortifications, which George enjoyed so much. We also climbed to the top of the Tower and there the view repaid us for all the toil of getting there. How the French gave up Metz is wonderful for it was so strongly fortified.
Jul 20 We left Metz at 1/4 past 9 AM and changed cars at Tourney where we got such a slow train that at Bar La Duc we got off and walked up to see the town which was most interesting and had a very good museum. We spent 3 hours and much enjoyed our stay at the station. We had some refreshments and I asked [for] the celebrated confiture made from red and white currants. At Epernay we got some champagne which we had in the rain and at ten PM reached Paris very tired indeed.
Aug 16 Sailed at 3 PM for Canada in the *Moravian* from Liverpool.
Sep 1 Home at half past five.
Sep 5 Our wedding day. 10 years ago we were married and the last year only have I felt how badly I have failed in making my husband happy. I have tried so hard but we do not understand each other of late.
Sep 12 Went to Windsor. . . . Charlotte was so cross in Detroit that I was worn out with her. . . . It seems to me that she has suffered more than anyone I know.

Sep 22 . . . [George's] hatbox found in Pullman car at Montreal. . . .
Sep 28 Sophia decided not to come here for some reason. She is put out with me. . . .
Oct 26 . . . George got home last night with 60 duck, he had good sport. . . .
Oct 29 . . . Advertised for a governess for the children. . . .
Nov 3 Well, my dinner was a great success. It went off so well. I am delighted as now I have paid my debts which is a great thing and am not obliged to invite again for a long time. . . .
Nov 6 My Father's body is to be brought up from Chatham today and put beside our little boys in the new cemetery, Mount Pleasant. . . .
Nov 7 . . . George & I went to the cemetery to choose a spot to lay my Father & uncle in. We are giving the chancel window in the new North Chatham church. It will cost $300.
Nov 15 . . . Another year of my life nearly done. I have not been careful enough to do well. . . .
Nov 17 Today my birthday. 31 years have I lived in this world and done very little good. Packed a basket for my dear old grandma – she is 81 years old on Monday. . . .
Nov 22 Thanksgiving day for a good harvest. . . .
Dec 26 Gave the servants each [$]2.00 for them. . . .
Dec 29 Sophia had [a party] at home. Went for an hour came home very tired. . . . They had 90 people. Every one seemed to enjoy themselves. The Glasses had one at the same time. They had dancing so it was crowded.

1878

Jan 4 The first good snow storm today. George is curling on the river. . . .
Jan 11 Have had such bad pens that I am ashamed to look at my journal.
Jan 17 . . . Went [to Sandwich] to see Grandma with George. . . .
Feb 16 Packed a basket for Grandma. Aunt Ellen went off at 2 o'clock. . . .
Feb 19 . . . Went down and sat with Mrs Harris. I gave Grandma 100 dollars. . . .
Feb 20 . . . Got my allowance 350 pounds. I wonder if there is any mistake. I thought it would be 375.
Feb 25 One year ago my little baby was born. . . .
Mar 12 . . . Had Dr Woodruff [who] says the children have whooping cough, it certainly is a mild kind. . . .

Mar 28 [George] does not say a word about going away. . . .
Apr 8 . . . Sophie had to come out of church, she felt so ill. . . .
Apr 11 Went and helped Sophia . . . about her party. . . . I am afraid she will be too tired to enjoy herself. . . .
Apr 12 The party . . . was a great success. . . . People were better dressed than I have ever seen them in London. . . .
May 6 . . . George is not well. He is low spirited and I feel that he has become very indifferent to me. Perhaps I deserve it all. I do my duty and if he would only trust me we would be better. . . .
May 7 . . . I hope he [George] will again be like he is when we are happy. . . .
May 24 A lovely day, took the children to see their Grandma. . . .
May 27 George so ill. . . .
Jun 6 George about the same. . . .
Jun 12 Mary Peard came out after being away 25 years. After all our trouble she came without a single telegraph. She came in to Eldon after luncheon and every one was impressed to see her. She is a fine looking woman.
Jun 14 Went to Eldon for an hour and think Mary Peard will on the whole enjoy her visit more than the other members of the family will. She is not in love with Teresa Littledale. . . .
Jun 20 . . . I feel I was right to have the house . . . a good home for my children out of the farms I sold. . . . I feel I have been reasonable in asking for things. . . .
Jul 12 . . . Went to the Hutchinson to see the children, Amelia [Milly] did wonderfully well. I am certain her Papa would have been proud of her. Still her French pronounciation [sic] is far from good. She got 3 prizes and went in the afternoon to show them to her Grandma.
Aug 6 Went to the other house,[55] very busy all morning. . . .
Aug 7 Wrote and ordered carpets from Toronto. . . .
Aug 10 Moved and I am afraid George will be ill.
Aug 11 Up all night with George who is very ill.
Aug 16 My bedroom looks so well. . . .
Aug 20 . . . Went to see Mary Peard. Grandmother has been ill. Mary's visit on the whole a failure as far as the pleasure she has given her Mother goes.
Aug 23 We have decided to go to New York with Mary on Monday at 8 AM to see her off. . . . Grandma and Amelia came to dinner with Mary Peard today. Grandma likes the house so much, it is bright and pretty. . . .

[55]Their new house.

Aug 26 George and I went to New York with Mary Peard. . . . Grandma not in the least felt low. In fact Mary Peard was so cold and indifferent to her Mother that her visit was a failure altogether. . . .
Aug 28 Mary Peard and I went out today [in New York] . . . Mary will paint us pretty black when she gets home and once more at the last it was a relief to all to part.
Sep 19 . . . Mr Carling elected for city, majority 63. Walker is very low indeed. Glass also is out for Middlesex and Mahon was defeated in Chatham by a majority of 575. . . . Went to Eldon, Grandma is to come and spend next week with me.
Sep 24 Grandma came . . . and seems to like our house very much. I am glad to have her. Mr Griffin and Edward came up to see her. . . .
Sep 26 . . . all afternoon we had visitors. . . .
Sep 27 I spent a pleasant afternoon with Grandma. . . .
Sep 30 Grandma went away today. . . . Had hall papered.
Oct 5 Went to Eldon. . . . Had a French lesson. . . .
Oct 21 George, Amelia, Ronald and I went to church. The new curate preached a bad sermon. . . .
Oct 28 . . . Ronald had his first punishment today, sent to bed for disobedience.
Nov 5 A letter saying Col Dalzell died on the 19th of Oct.
Nov 19 Grandma's birthday . . . 82 today. . . .
Nov 21 Grandma Harris came up to spend the afternoon. . . . [list of ladies who visited].
Nov 26 English letters. My Father's sister Mary Grant is dead. She died on the 11 of this month . . . of consumption. . . .
Nov 28 . . . I asked [George] 5 months ago to look over papers for me. He has not done so yet.
Nov 29 I am vexed . . . asking Edward to write me a form. Edward has to be consulted in my affairs. . . .
Dec 20 George got me the draft for 30 dollars for Grandma which I send her every year. George is not very happy. I think he has gone on without looking at my affairs for too long. . . .
Dec 25 A fine Xmas day. I am sure the children will enjoy the day. Amelia got 12, Charlotte 7 and Ronald 9 books. . . .
Dec 26 . . . I have no more joy in Xmas day. George curled at the rink all morning and in the afternoon went to sleep. I never heard him say one word all day. Sometimes I wonder how our house seems to others. To me it is very lonely always now.
Dec 30 . . . Went to the convent to make arrangements as to Chassie going there. . . .
Dec 31 . . . Now George thinks as hard about the settlement while I

am thankful it was made. The year is ended. May the next year free us from much of the sorrow we have had and restore my husband's health to him.

1879

Jan 1 [list of gentlemen including George call on some families]. The most perfect day I ever saw. I am I fear rather hard with the children. Poor little things. . . . I must try to be more patient with all for I am far from perfect myself.
Jan 3/4 . . . Charlotte had a convultion [sic] . . . I ran up put her in a hot bath and wrapped her up in blankets. She then had a second one. The Dr came. He thought it was worms. . . .
Jan 11 . . . Amelia had her second French lesson. She did very well. . . . Sophia is quite ill. She has been in bed for five days and looks so delicate. . . . A long letter from Aunt Teresa.
Jan 13 . . . sat with Sophia all morning. . . .
Jan 23 . . . Dr Woodruff says [Charlotte's fits] are epileptic, so my worst fear is realised. I am so grieved for my poor little girl. . . .
Jan 31 George curling all day. He gets more fun and less work than most people.
Feb 4 . . . My allowance came. £375 and letter from Mr Montgomery. I think it will be increased £300 more . . . I think I will pay all my debts and start fresh.
Feb 8 . . . Charlotte had another fit, . . . they are getting closer to each other. . . .
Apr 8 . . . Amelia got the reading prize [at her school].
Apr 30 Charlotte had another fit . . . she faints so often, 6 times today.
May 9 . . . Mrs and Miss Landor, Mrs & Miss Taylor [and many others] called. Mrs Becher liked our dining room so much indeed. People say they think it better than Eldon House as it looks more like a room to be in. I am glad Grandma has enjoyed her little stay here today. We had a long chat. She finds herself very lonely at Eldon often.
May 16 I took Charlotte out in her new spring dress to Mrs Meredith's and to see Grandma. I am feeling out of sorts. George never speaks to me or takes the least interest in what I say or do.
May 17 . . . I would give five years of my life to have my Mother or some person who really cares for me even for an hour to caress and love me.
May 22 . . . My Grandmother is not at all well, from what they say she will not last long. . . .
May 30 . . . a letter from James Montgomery with £300 in addition to

my allowance. This makes me £1,050. We are now comfortable off indeed. . . . We must try to bring up our children better . . .
Jun 12 Worked hard as usual. Mr Jeffery sent me such nice plants . . . Grandma came up and we had 49 people, I think it is rather a success. . . .
Jul 1 . . . A letter from George, he had good sport, killed 7 salmon in one day.
Jul 10 . . . George [arrived], got the 3 largest [salmon], 30, 30½ and 32½ pounds. He is satisfied. . . . Salmon fishing is a very expensive pleasure. . . .
Jul 21/22 Took Charlotte to Dr Hammond[56] [who] charged $20 for his opinion and told me to treat her as he directed for a year, then to bring her back again. The diet must be carefully looked after and the medicine to be increased 5 drops a month till the end of the year. At that time she will be taking 70 drops three times a day . . . with 10 drops on the first of the month. She is to have a T bone [support] in her neck and wear it for 5 months when it is to be removed and after put in again. He said she was suffering from congestion of the brain and that she might get perfectly well in a year. I felt more satisfied than I was before hearing his opinion for if care can do her good she shall have it.
Aug 1 . . . somehow my husband expects a good deal of me. I often wonder if he ever thinks I have any sense of which is due to women. I watch one of his trustees. All I have to see and do [is] wonder how they would get on.
Aug 29 . . . Sat with Mrs Harris for a few hours. I am not well. . . .
Sep 5/6 . . . 12 years we have been married. I wish I could say I was a better woman now than when I changed my name. . . . Oh, if I had my dear Mother to comfort and help me.
Oct 8 . . . I never felt George was so purely selfish as this time. The truth is he loves himself far better than any one else so I must make him understand that it looks bad if nothing else and that he is careless. . . . It makes me so angry when I think how he . . . [denies] me the slightest pleasure. . . .
Oct 13 . . . Asked the Littledales to dinner on Wednesday.[57] . . .
Oct 16 Our dinner really passed off well. I always think I shall not give any more. . . . My life is not what I thought or hoped it would be though I often try. Wish I had some one to go and talk to. Oh, if my poor Mother had lived it would have been better for George and for me. . . .

[56]Dr. Hammond is in New York.

[57]Teresa, George's sister, and her present husband St. George Littledale live in England and are visiting the Harris family.

Oct 27 . . . Teresa, Mr Littledale and Sophie came up. . . .
Nov 6 Thanksgiving . . . I did not go to church as I had not slept well and feel so weak and out of sorts. . . . Went to Eldon . . . Bella and Ada came and sat quite a while with me. . . .
Nov 19 Went and paid visits today. . . . Teresa sails today. . . .
Nov 26 Had a French lesson. . . .
Dec 2 Rachel sent in a lovely dinner. Everything was very good indeed. . . . My friends have been very good coming to see me every day.
Dec 6 . . . ill all day and so miserable.
Dec 9 . . . Dr Moore says it is a gland enlarged in my throat . . .
Dec 10 So many people have been kind enough to come and see me. . . .
Dec 16 Grandma is failing fast and will hardly see the spring. . . .
Dec 25 Christmas day. Santa Claus and all of the dear children. . . . I often think of the days gone and my own childhood. Father, Mother, Home and all have passed away and I am away from all those first friends. A kind husband and loving children are left me, God in his mercy has lifted the cloud from my heart, respecting dear Chassie, and she now gets on better than I hoped. I ought to be a good woman for I have many blessings and few trials. We are nearly out of debt.
Dec 31 Went into town in the morning, paid my bills . . . and am going to pay for all I get next year at the time.

1880

Jan 1 A lovely day, just a little more snow to make it perfect. Went to see Grandma, took her a plant. . . . Went over to see Mrs Robertson who was ill but found her reading a novel. Made a resolve to try no novels. Amelia not at all well, put her to bed early and went to Eldon for a couple of hours. May next year find us all well and happy.
Jan 2 A very nice day. We went out and called to ask after Mrs Robertson. Amelia and [I] sat with Grandma. She was quite well and so bright. The cook is put out and they are bothered as they have visitors coming on Monday. . . .
Jan 3/4/5 . . . George is very low about our expenses being so great but I feel they would be [otherwise] spent with fishing and shooting but he did not consider what it was costing. I do try to keep expenses down but unless both try it does not answer very well. We must try and be more careful than we are. I shall not buy any novels and do all the children's sewing this year. . . .
Jan 8 I am truly glad my dinner is over for I hate dinner part[ies].

They cost so much, are troublesome and entertain so very few persons. Mrs Walker is ill; went to see her. We dined at the Bishops: Gzowskis, Ed Harris, Griffins, Browns, ourselves and four of the family. The butler was intoxicated to a degree but the party was very pleasant.
Jan 16 . . . Dr Ryerson has aged much in the last year and will not live many years, I fancy. We went to Eldon in the evening.
Jan 17 Took Charlotte to the dentist and all three children to town. Saw them home as far as Meredith's corner, then went to Eldon. Mrs Harris better . . . Sophia and her Mother came up to afternoon tea. We went to Eldon about 8 o'clock.
Jan 27 Up all night with the greatest pains in my kidneys. . . . A telegram saying my dear old Grandma [Askin] died this morning. She was 83 and 2 months. . . . She is now enjoying her reward. Trials she never murmured at and bore all as her rightful portion and surely she is permitted to join her loved ones, her husband and children. My poor Mother who [was] such a good daughter, on her deathbed called me to do for my Grandmother. I have done my best and always given her what I could.
Jan 28/30/31 Oh, today they are reunited in heaven. My own time may be near. God in His mercy permit me to do my duty so that when He calls, I may join them above. Got down to Windsor at 9 AM. . . . Poor Grandma died in her sleep. When Aunt Alice got up, she found her dead, though quite warm. At 2 AM she spoke and said she was quite well and free from pain. It was to my Aunt a great shock to find her dead. She looked so lovely, her face so free from suffering and in her pretty cap, she looked younger than in life. Her funeral was very respectable, though not large. I went and I can say for few have I ever felt so much sorrow, she was so gentle and good. I do not know what will become of my Aunt[s] . . . [I] shall give them ten dollars a month to help keep house. . . . It will be a great help to them. Aunt Teresa is offended at not being mistress of the house. I said Jane was the proper person. . . . Jane and Aunt Teresa are the hardest to get on together. Aunt T would hardly say goodbye to me today. She was so angry as I said Jane ought to be the head. I am sorry for them all and will do all I can for them always on my poor dear Mother's account. Got home at ½ past five. Poor George glad to see me.
Feb 5 . . . George went to Toronto today. I should have gone had I been well enough, but I am feeling so miserable, I can not get about very much. Went to Eldon with Amelia in the evening as Mrs Harris was alone. . . .
Feb 6 Today went out and paid my bills as they were owing and in the afternoon went to Miss Dod's class for cooking. . . . Went to

Eldon after and Ronald came down to tell me there was a telegram from his Papa. George bought a pretty glass for the table for me.
Feb 7 Went to get the children's photo taken this morning and came home by way of Eldon. Sophia and Edward come tonight. She is not very well. We shall go down after tea for an hour. I am so uncomfortable all the time. A letter from Jane. All is going well at Sandwich, she says. Wrote to Miss Wilton [nurse] to see if she would come for 200 [dollars] per year.
Feb 9 . . . went to the afternoon and evening classes for cookery. . . .
Feb 10 . . . Sent Rachel [servant] to the evening school of cookery. . . .
Feb 13 . . . George took Amelia and Scott to hear Mrs Scott Siddens[58] tonight. She reads for the benefit of the poor. A letter from Jane Skae who says they have not found the money Grandma left. It is odd it cannot be found for they need it much.
Feb 19 Grandma Harris' birthday – 82 today. She had many lovely flowers . . . Ronald and Charlotte quite ill with colds.
Feb 27 George went to Chatham today. . . .
Mar 12 Made gold and silver cake in the morning. Did the flowers. . . . George curled at Ingersol all day and only got home at 9 PM. . . .
Mar 15/16 Did not go out until the afternoon, then went to dinner at the other House. I do not like going out on Sunday. No letters. A post card from Jane. Aunt Teresa is a little offended with me. . . . Went to Eldon on Monday. Poor Jessie Campbell died on Sunday. I feel sorry for the Campbells, it is their first trouble. Miss Griffin[59] died on Sunday . . . from cancer after great suffering. Griffin feels it much, but hers was a painful illness and one feels death was a relief and she was prepared to go. How little we can tell who will be the next.
Mar 22 Am going to church for the first time since Feb 16th. Came home so tired. Charlotte not well. I am frightened about her, poor little thing. I hope I shall never be called on to leave her for she wants a Mother's care, my poor little one. I hope my life may be spared and I may be guided to do what is best for her. . . . Sat with Grandma [Harris] an hour.
Mar 24 Pray I must for patience, as sometimes I cannot shut my eyes. When I think of what is before me, I feel afraid. Did my French today. I feel I am drifting away and so alone. Sometimes I feel if at the end of twelve years, my husband can care so little to please me, if we live together twelve years more what will life be. I can only try my best.

[58]An American actress.
[59]Gilbert Griffin's sister.

Mar 28/29 Easter Sunday. Went to church with Amelia. Came home by way of Eldon. . . . Took Charlotte and Ronald for a walk. . . . My box came from England today. The flower stand is lovely and so is the tray. I am pleased, though the duty was very high, 15 dollars on the forty I gave Teresa. It prevents one from buying in England. . . .
Mar 31 Had a French lesson and went for a walk. Wrote to Aunt Ellen and will post it on Friday with 5 dollars for them. . . . Cut some of the roses and vines.
Apr 1 Pruned my roses and was busy in the garden all day. . . .
Apr 6 . . . We go to New York on Thursday. Amelia to stay at her Grandmas.
Apr 7 Packed all morning and went to see Mrs Harris to give her goodbye. I hope all will be well when I am away from the children. I wish we could take Amelia with us. We go at 8:40 tomorrow morning to Washington.
Apr 8 Left all safe at home and started on our trip. We shall be home this day fortnight. I think I will try not to expect too much from George. We walked across the bridge [Niagara Falls] and went by Northern Central From Rochester to Washington, where we will arrive at 9 AM tomorrow.
Apr 9 Got to Washington on time and staid at the National Hotel. We walked to the Capitol and saw the Chamber of Representatives, the House and [heard] one or two addresses [in] it, but Americans talk through their noses too much, they are not pleasant to listen to. The view from the dome of the Capitol is very fine indeed. Went also to the White House and saw the East Room where the President hold[s] his receptions and the museum. . . . Saw the play, *Pirates of Penzance*.
Apr 10 Got up and had breakfast at the National. . . . drove to Georgetown. On our return, went to the Home and Museum. Saw the lovely figures, Napoleon the First dying beautifully done in marble, also . . . slave and a veiled nun, a figure, the Indian chief killed at the battle of the Thames.[60] And in the afternoon we staid at the Smithsonian Museum. The Indian relicts are very fine. I had no idea the Indians made such fine articles in older times. One old Indian was there and looked so sad. He said his people was so tired. . . .
Apr 11/14 We overslept ourselves and it was past eleven when we breakfasted so we only went out for a walk and went in the Roman Catholic Church. Saw old pictures presented by Louis 14 of France. Baltimore is a fine city. We got here at 6 PM. George was tired of Washington though I should have preferred spending Sunday there. I

[60]Tecumseh.

turned over the page and forgot my old Indian who said his people were dying so fast and soon would have passed away. Called on Mrs Reynolds, who formerly was Miss Lightfoot. Saw her Mother and sister as she was ill herself. We saw the Peabody Library and the Museum at Baltimore. Got some shoes and left there at 3 o'clock for Philadelphia, where we arrived at half past 7 PM. We are at the Girard House but it is not very comfortable. Such a noisy room and poor fare. In the morning, we took the cars and went to Fairmont Park and saw some of the sight[s] there and came back by another route. The buildings in Philadelphia are wonderfully fine . . . We went to the Exhibition of Natural Sciences [and I] feel so tired. We came home by the Rittenhouse Square and in the evening, went to the play, *Belle Helene*. I do not like French acting as it borders on the uncouth so much. . . . I am glad I have seen Philadelphia as the buildings are so handsome. A telegram from Edward. All are well at home.
Apr 15 . . . got to New York at half past six and have rooms at 35th Ave as the hotel is so full. We went to the Madison Square Theatre and saw *Hazel Kirke*, such a pretty play. . . . A letter from Amelia and one from Sophia. All are quite well at home, no real news going on. Got Sophia's things for her and some for myself. George went off by himself and tomorrow will call on some of our friends. . . . I am glad I came away.
Apr 17 . . . We went to the theatre and saw a play called *My Partners*. I do not care for plays of low life.
Apr 20 . . . We leave at 8 PM tonight for London. . . .
Apr 21 Found the children quite well. Charlotte had been quite ill on Monday, worse than she had been before. Poor little girl, she looked so altered. . . .
Apr 30/May 1 . . . There is some trouble in the Post Office with Griffin. He has been borrowing money from the bank and the accounts have got behind so an Inspector came up to investigate matters. It is too bad that he should behave as he does and one to look at him would never say he was at fault at all. Poor Amelia, she is happy in believing in her husband, for when she finds him out, how sad it will be. He really is a villain. . . . I went to see her but she did not speak of her trouble so I let it pass. Grandma wants George to go and see her but he is too vexed with Griffin to go now.
May 2/3 . . . Poor Mr Becher, I do not think [he] is better. He looks older and very frail . . . he will not live long, I fear. She [Mrs Becher] is a good wife and has nursed him well. Grandma is very low about the Griffin affair. . . .
May 4 Worked hard in the garden all day. Put in my sweet pea seeds

and looked to the roses. Our man is not as good as he was and more of the goose than the swan, a good deal. So much bother about the sewing machines. . . .

May 8 . . . I wish the Griffin trouble was over and that all was going on well again. Mrs Harris bothers more than one thinks about it and you cannot comfort her either.

May 14 . . . Told Mrs Harris that in September I would be ill [i.e. confined]. She was glad. . . . Charlotte often frightens me. Will she ever be better, I wonder?

May 27/28 . . . Mrs Harris wanted to know how Amelia was so [I] had to go out in the heat. I am too good . . . by far and do too much. Today a death notice of a Mrs George Harris. So many people thought it was me. So George, I doubt, would care more than John McBeth does for his poor wife who is dying of consumption. At my age to find that after doing all I could to please my husband does not care for me is hard. My loved Mother is spared the knowledge and it comforts me. Ronald too has loving ways. Amelia is a Harris. Poor little Charlotte, if she could go with me [from] this world I could leave. In September I shall be confined and feel no desire to make plans for the future.

Jun 1 Wrote to Dr Moore about a nurse. Sometimes I feel so bad and get in a fright about myself. Wrote to my Aunts. Amelia not very well. Mrs Harris will stay Thursday and then comes again in July for a month. . . .

Jun 11 Today the anniversary of my poor Father's death. He died in 1863. . . .

Jun 17 Aunt Alice came . . . all well in Sandwich. I shall send them each five dollars when my allowance comes in July and now give them 10 dollars a month to keep house on. . . . I am feeling so tired all the time. I wish I was over it and the baby all safe and well.

Jun 22 Went down the river in a boat with Aunt Alice, Amelia and Ronald. I am so tired. A telegram from George, he is well. But somehow I feel I have changed myself so much. We shall never be as happy again. Were it not for poor Charlotte, I would not care to live much longer for now I see how I have failed in my life and it is hard to find at my age that you have given up everything and you are not even thanked.

Jun 24 A kind letter from George. He says if I wish, he will come home. I only want to rest. Last evening one of Coller's "the Iceman" sons was drowned at the dam. All night they were searching the river for the Body. At 2 AM they found it. It has made me quite ill. Mrs Harris comes on Tuesday, . . . The Griffins cry poverty and debt with

2500 dollars a year, but I gave up my property to my husband and made a fool of myself so I deserve it all.
Jun 25 . . . Mrs Harris comes on Tuesday. Aunt Alice goes away the same day. I shall be careful not to have any of my relatives to stay when she is here after the remark she made about housemaids. . . .
Jun 26 How lonely my life is now. I try and fail so often. I gave Aunt Alice a nice dress and had it made for her. Poor Aunt, how little they have in this world.
Jun 30 . . . The Griffins came this evening to tea. Griffin felt [ill] but by taking a little brandy over [an] hour, he kept himself up. I shall be glad when he is gone for his wife will then have peace.
Jul 3 . . . Cherries all morning to can. . . . John got such small ones it was wearisome to do them. Grandma helped and Amelia came in with a parcel from Sophia, which she sent as a peace offering; a very handsome piece of cashmere and velvet to make a dress. Old Mrs Harris . . . Mrs Beddome and Kitty have all been in to Amelia to say goodbye.
Jul 5 Sat in my room with Ronald and Charlotte, read to them and let Amelia [Griffin] and her Mother have a quiet talk. Poor Mrs Harris, she feels so much and Amelia has more sorrow than she pretends. I gave Scott a five dollar bill for his birthday, he is 14 years old. The Merediths, Beddomes . . . all came to say goodbye to Amelia. I gave her $10 as a little parting gift. She was so glad to get it, poor woman. It is so hard never to have a cent for yourself. The Merediths, Mrs Beddome came to see Mrs Harris. Edward gave Ronald a dog today, a setter pup. . . . I think I have handled the Griffin business pretty well and held my tongue more than I believed I could.
Jul 8/9 Am so ill . . . George, if he was at home, he could talk to his Mother. Two months more and I shall [have] a rest. . . . If he [George] and Edward can educate Griffin's son, then I can certainly have a little of my own money to spend without being obliged to give it to the House. At times I feel very bitter. Fishing and shooting cost so much and we are now spending more than we should. How it will end, I cannot tell. Mrs Harris went to the Bechers to luncheon.
Jul 10 I had a letter from my husband today. He has rather enjoyed his stay. If I went for a month's pleasure, I wonder what would be said. Sometimes I wonder if George can see or think what people say, my being left in the way I am with Mrs Harris to look after and all the care of the place. I shall not say anything but try and make my arrangements and will so that things are done well for the children. . . .
Jul 15 . . . I shall be glad when he [George] comes, for he can talk and decide if he will pay half of Scott's schooling. Everyone has been

told he will. Sometimes I wonder why Griffin should have so much done for him. Mrs Harris does not think anything too good for them while I am told everything is better than I deserve.

Jul 16 . . . A telegram from George. The steamer did not stop as she had Royal party on board so George will not be home before Monday noon. I shall be glad as he can take his Mother out for a drive and I am tired of nursing. How much more dull than when he is at home. I have done my very best and feel that all I can do amounts to nothing. . . .

Jul 30/31 George is very kind in words and feels I did all I could for his Mother. Mrs Harris went down at 11 AM to open the House and came back to luncheon. She left at 5 PM. Edward returns at 6 alone, Sophia remaining in Toronto, . . . George went to a licence meeting and really it bores him to be ten minutes alone with me . . . I could stand it but I do hate to think [that] other persons make their remarks at my being so much alone. I have my children and if I can have their affection I shall have enough to live for.

Aug 6 The Dr told me when he came that Grandma was ill so I sent for a cab and went down. Found her ill and weak with much fever. Staid until after four. Came home tired out. George went off pigeon shooting. I sat up on the veranda as I was so uncomfortable. Mrs Harris better at 9 PM. Sophia came home at 5 this afternoon. . . .

Aug 24 . . . Sophia and Edward came up. Griffin has written to say he thought it would be a good plan to have Amelia [his wife] spend the winter at Eldon and Scott go to the Dufferin College as a boarder. Edward is indignant to a degree.

Aug 26 . . . George has been very kind to me of late. Sophia and Edward . . . come every day. Miss Purdy begins on Wednesday Sept 1st with the children at 30 dollars for three months . . . from 9 to 1. . . .

Sep 18 A fine little baby born at $^1/_4$ before 9 AM. We will call him Edward after George's brother. May God bless the child and prosper him. I was dreadfully ill, did not go to bed for ten days, I could not lie down. George is pleased it is a son. He can, he hopes, go off by the 1st for his shooting.

Nov 9 My little boy was christened by Dean Brown: Edward Montgomery after my old friend. I pray that he may grow up a good man and that I may not die before Charlotte is my prayer. Mr and Mrs Andrew of Chatham and Edward Harris are his Godfather and Mother.

Dec 13 Edward and Sophia going to England. We pay Edward's expenses and Mrs Harris comes to stay. How all these things will end, I wonder much. Mrs Harris does not seem to mind. I hope all will go

on well with the children. Charlotte, I fear, will give us trouble yet.
Dec 14 Am not well. I gain so little each day.
Dec 16 Today has been a sad one. Amelia grieved us both so much. She was reading when she should have been practicing and I feel anything like deceit so much. May the poor child never suffer as we do for her. I wonder how she can be cured. I am so distressed as my Amelia was my pride.[61] . . .

1881

Jan 1 Mr Jeffery, Mr Glass, Chestor, Col Walker, . . . Meredith, Col Taylor, [and others] all called. Grand[ma] [Mrs Harris][62] not well, wrote to Amelia Griffin [in Kingston]. A few New Year cards. . . . George went out with Mr Jeffery to pay visits. I am thankful that the New Year finds us all well.
Jan 18 Baby Edward weighs 18 lbs. He is 4 months old. . . .
Feb 10 My allowance came today. I believe James Montgomery is one of our best friends. I am glad Percy Crutchley will be a trustee for I hope that the children will benefit from it. . . .
Feb 19 Mrs Harris is 83 today. . . .
Feb 22 Amelia began lessons . . . in drawing today. . . .
Feb 26 . . . Nellie [maid] left, her leg was too painful. . . .
Mar 15 George went off . . . I am left again to put all things in order with Eldon. . . . I often wonder why George should never attempt to show me the slightest consideration. But he never thinks I want any enjoyment or amusement at all. . . . I would give much for a kind word or a little attention. As I have made my bed so I must lie.
Jun 14 George got off [for Toronto]. . . . Now we drift further apart as time goes on and my life seems so hard. Poor Charlotte is growing worse and worse. All the blessings in the way or worldly goods I would give if her life could be made bright and her brain like others. I shall endeavour to do what is right. . . .
Jun 15 I called on Mrs Harry Becher, we had not visited for years. . . . Amelia 13 today. Gave her a little party. She had so many pretty little gifts from her friends.
Jun 16 Miserable all day. I feel so much alone. Children all troublesome.

[61]No further entries for 1880.

[62]Amelia Harris had moved to Raleigh House on 28 December 1880 to stay with George and Lucy while Edward and Sophia were in England, returning to Eldon on 24 March 1881.

Jun 17 Am not well. I feel so depressed.
Aug 1 Grandma came up to say she is far from well.
Aug 5 . . . George and Amelia going to the Falls as Amelia has never seen the Falls. Amelia Griffin came [from Kingston] . . . to spend a fortnight with us.
Aug 16 . . . Today I insisted on a settlement being made. I am sorry George never sees the necessity of having things done as they should be at once.
Dec 25/26 Christmas Day. The happiest I have spent since I was married. The children are all well and happy. Mrs Harris bright and cheerful.[63] I had so many pretty presents and so had the children. Poor Charlotte was as happy as she now ever seems to be. . . . Servants good and happy.

1882

Jan 13 A letter from Sarah [Dalzell]. She wants 200 a year to board Amelia beside the wages for a servant and all her lessons would be extra.
Jan 25 George went off at 8:40 to curl at Paris today for the Caledon medal.
Jan 30 Miss Macdonald came with Sophia to see Grandma [staying at Lucy's]. I take no notice of what she [Sophia] does but in the end it will separate us completely, I fear. Wrote letters all morning. Mrs Labatt came. I fancy we shall take th[eir] children to England. I called Mrs Labatt to read Sarah's letter.
Feb 6 . . . I went to see Mrs John Labatt and Mrs Beddome to tell the latter that little Amelia [Milly] was going to England. How much I wish we could all go and remain for I dread my daily life after Amelia has gone.
Feb 13 . . . Mrs Edward went to her Father today. He is worse. . . .
Feb 15 . . . Had my French lesson today.
Feb 20 Dr Ryerson died at 7 AM yesterday morning. Sophia feels it so much for she was proud of her Father in every way.
Feb 21 Grandma so low. George went off at 6 PM to Dr Ryerson's funeral, which takes place tomorrow afternoon.
Feb 23 Children not well, poor Charlotte has such bad turns. Ill all day today. I cannot feel satisfied to leave them as it now is but I must go with Amelia to England. . . .

[63]Amelia Harris had moved to Raleigh House on 22 December 1881 and stayed there until her death on 24 March 1882.

Feb 27/28 Dr Woodruff says that Mrs Harris is seriously ill and does not hold out much hope of her recovery. Wrote to Amelia Griffin to come and will telegraph in the morning. She is very weak and her pulse so irregular. Sat up with her. Edward very low, so is George. Many kind inquiries and I hope she may be better again very soon. Grandma took the Sacrament from the Rev Mr Brown.[64]
Mar 1 . . . I must give up my journal. . . .
Mar 24 Grandma died tonight at twenty-five minutes past eight, a peaceful and painless end. A life well spent brings its reward. She died with Edward, Sophia, Amelia Griffin, and George and [I] beside her. Sophia and I laid her out.
Mar 27 Grandma was buried today at three o'clock from Eldon. A small but respectable funeral, very bad roads and a bad, cold, windy day.
Mar 28 Amelia Griffin left today for Kingston. I shall write nothing about what passed after dear old Grandma died for we are all mortified that Amelia [Griffin] should have treated us all with no consideration. . . .
Mar 29 Today we decide to sail on the 12th so as to be home early in June. Amelia [Milly] will be better away for the summer. Leaving Charlotte, Ronald and Edward is hard, but I must think of Amelia's future as well.
Mar 30 Mrs Labatt called today and it is arranged, we will go on the 12th. Mr and Mrs Labatt go to New York. I shall have my hands full preparing to get off.
Apr 28 . . . I am glad to leave London, it will be better for Milly. . . .
May 2 . . . [Saw] the Peards, had a nice visit [in England] and am perfectly satisfied that my child should have Mary[65] for her Gardian [sic]. . . .
Jul 3 . . . A nice letter from my girl [Milly]. . . .
Nov 17 My birthday and I am so lonely for my child. I shall never separate my self again from her for I feel it so much. She has been unhappy and I fear Sarah [maid] has failed with the children. . . . All my plans are failures. I am so sorry for the children suffer. . . .
Nov 30 Sarah has been forgetting that strangers will not bear her burdens. Ronald gives me much care. I am sorry that my husband does not take any part in bringing up the children or help me as I need help. I give up my journal on this account. I do not complain to him

[64]Curate at St. Paul's.
[65]George's sister, Mary Peard.

but I feel deeply that he does not see the coming sorrows in store for us and I cannot forgive his not looking to the interests of the children, only his brother must come first and the habit of putting off grows each day stronger.[66]

[66]No more entries until 1 January 1883.

The Diary of Amelia Archange Harris (1868–1959)

Amelia Archange began her diary when she was thirteen years old and continued for seventy-seven years, from 1882 to 1959.[1] The entries selected for this publication cover only the first three months. Milly[2] records her observations of the circumstances surrounding the death of her Grandmother, Amelia Harris, and their conversations. She also gives a vivid description of the corpse, a report of the funeral, and of her first visit to the cemetery.

Milly's activities at the time when she began her diary are those of an average schoolgirl. Two weeks after the funeral, her parents took her to England, where she spent two years with her many aunts, uncles, and cousins, and also attended a boarding school in Somerset. A serious minded young lady, her New Year's resolution for 1882 reads, "This next year I mean to strive to get on better & better and in all respects to improve."[3]

Milly lived a very long life and did not marry. She spent much of her life traveling around the world and her diary was her constant companion. She carried it with her everywhere, and she was still making entries in it when she died at Eldon House at the age of almost ninety-two, in the fall of 1959.

[1]On the front cover of Amelia Archange's diary we read, "London & England 1881–1882." It is written in a small (5″ by 4″) school book of about fifty lined pages, one of which, containing part of the entries of 4, 5 and 6 January, is missing.

[2]Amelia Archange was also known as Milly.

[3]Milly's diary, 31 December 1882.

Milly

Music, school. Madeleine Meredith
& Laura Walker called for me
to go to the rink Ida Macdonough
Lillie Despard, Minnie & Lena
Labatt were there. Ice was beautiful
had splendid fun skated all the
skin off my ancles

Wednesday Jan 17
Music, School, Mamma took my
French lesson & I slided down
Mr Walker's hill with Laura Madeleine
& Lena. two college boys skated on
the river & watched us. did not
care for I did not know them.
It was lovely not too cold. Lost at Bezique

Milly comments on the social life of a young girl

Amelia Archange Harris' Diary

1882

Jan 1 Got up at $^{1}/_{2}$ past seven, wrote a letter to Lillie Thompson, had to tear it up. Went to Church, the bishop preached rather a nice sermon. Went to Sunday School. Miss Macbeth came late, she always does. Had tea with Papa and Mamma. Went to bed at $9^{1}/_{2}$.
Jan 2 A bank holiday. Read all morning. Went for a walk with Lila Laing as far as the toll gate. Mamma received 12 visitors. Played cassenia in the evening. Grandma & I won, the first time for two weeks.
Jan 3 A frost for the last 4 days procured one day's skating: of course I went. Did not have much fun all the same. Nobody was there that I knew, except Florence Laing. She introduced me to Kitty Vosburg who seems rather a nice girl. Played bezique and lost of course.
Jan 5 Went to Mrs Stagmen's [dressmaker] to be fitted. Came home & helped mind the baby while the servants were at dinner. Practised [piano]. Drew a little & read all afternoon. Dressed at six for the party. Wore black velveteen & my blue locket & chain. Met the girls going over. Sent the man back and went with them. . . .
Jan 8 Went back to school. Mrs Beddome was not a bit nice. . . .
Jan 9 Music. School. . . . Went for a walk with Minnie Labatt.
Jan 14 Mamma was not well at all – stayed in bed. I went to Church and Sunday School. *Harriet or School Day Life* was my book. Wrote a letter 4 or 5 times. Went to bed in Mamma's bed. Hard frost.
Jan 17 Music. School. Mamma took my French lesson & I slided down Mr [John] Walker's hill with Laura [Walker], Madelene & Lena. [Labatt]. Two [Hellmuth] College boys skated on the river & watched us. Did not care for I did not know them. It was lovely. Not too cold. Lost at Bezique.
Jan 26 . . . We kicked up our heels at school. Laughed almost all the time. Had my photograph taken – they were very good. Skated at the Westminister Rink. Did not like it at all. Skated with Frank Hutchinson.
Feb 1 Neck almost well. Hot vinegar did it. Went to kitchen and made short-cake and taffy in the morning. Grandma quite well. Doctor Ryerson died today. Poor Aunt Sophia, she feels it dreadfully.
Feb 16 . . . Went to call with Mamma. Skated for three quarters of an hour at the Westminister Rink.

Feb 17 Music. Got out early. Stayed in bed all afternoon with a stiff neck. Darcy MacMahon came to tea. I told Ronald and him ghost stories.
Feb 18 Neck no better. Lay on Grandma's sofa. Put hot vinegar on my neck.
Feb 25 Music. School. Stayed in the house. Read in the afternoon.
Feb 26 Grandma is not a bit well. The doctor came to see her.
Feb 27 . . . Came home early. Grandma is very ill. Drawing as expected.
Feb 28 . . . Got out early. Grandma the same. Telegraphed for Aunt Amelia to come. Aunt Sophie has [already] come.
Mar 8 . . . Grandma has been about the same all day. It is so dull in the evenings without her.
Mar 9 Music. School. Grandma is not well. She did not sleep at night. I sleep with Aunt Amelia [Griffin] now.
Mar 10 . . . I got out early. A horrid composition about Jerusalem. Grandma is not so well.
Mar 15 Did not go to school nor have French. Grandma was so bad.
Mar 16 Grandma has rallied again. Mamma did not think she would live through the night.
Mar 17 Went to school & music. I heard that the Labatts were going to England with us. I hope they won't.
Mar 19 Did not go to either Church or Sunday School. When I said good night to Grandma, she said, God bless you my child. You see how near my grave I am. Always remember that no matter how young you are you may die. Try to be so that when the summons comes you may be ready. Mamma did not think she would live through the night.
Mar 20 Grandma is so much better that I am to go to school. It is wonderful how she rallies.
Mar 21 Music. School. Went to town with Minnie Labatt. The report about their going to England by themselves is false. Grandma the same.
Mar 23 . . . Stayed at home all day. Dear grandma is not quite so well.
Mar 24 . . . When I came back from school, grandma was much worse. I did not see her till about 5:30 when Uncle Edward read prayers. The doctor came about 7 and he said she would not live more than three hours. I took care of the children all evening. After they went to bed I sat by the fire for a little while. When I went upstairs and met Mamma who was crying I was told that dear Grandma was dead.
Mar 25 A most distressing day. I saw Grandma. I was not afraid and

kissed her. Grandma is to be moved to Eldon tonight. She wished to be buried from there. The funeral is on Monday at 3. I went down to Eldon after Grandma was carried there. She looks beautiful, every feature is perfect, all the wrinkles have gone. She is to be buried in a nightgown and widow's cap.

Mar 26 . . . The flowers are lovely. I went down & Aunt Sophie wanted me to stay for lunch but I did not. Then she asked me to dinner. I did not care to very much. I had a long talk to Mamma. Dear Grandma left me a shawl pin & 20 dollars. I am so glad for I have so few things of hers.

Mar 27 The funeral took place at 3 o'clock this afternoon. I went down to Eldon. There was not many people. Grandma looked beautiful.

Mar 28 Aunt Amelia went at 2 o'clock this afternoon. It turned out that nearly all Grandma's things are to be divided between Papa and Uncle Edward. I am so glad. I went to the cemetery.

Mar 29 I went to the cemetery this morning to the vault. All the flowers are so fresh. Went down to Eldon & had tea with Aunt Sophie It was so nice. Papa came for me at nine & there was an awful storm. I got my stockings soaking wet.

Mar 30 We are going to England on the 12 in the *Parthia* Cunard line. It is so soon. The Labatts are going with us.

APPENDIX 1

THE HARRIS FAMILY TREE

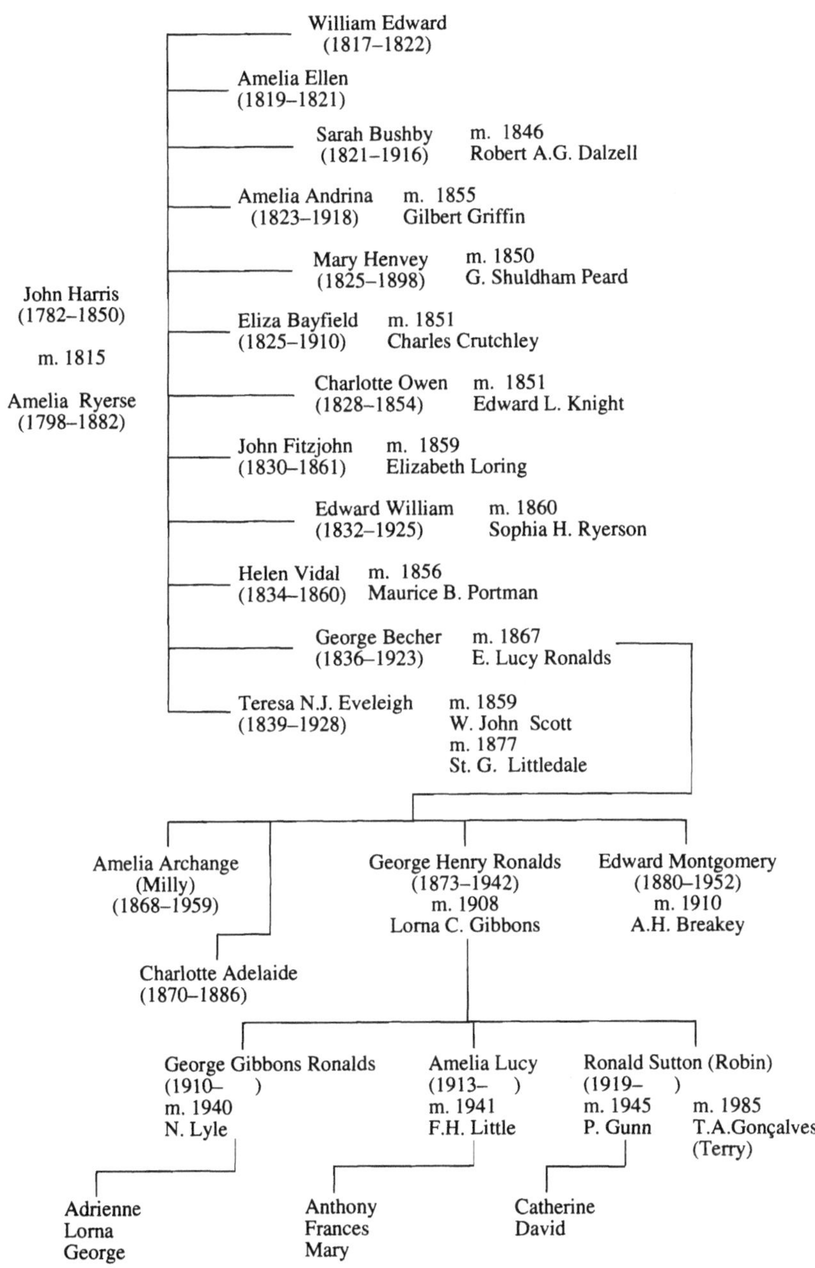

APPENDIX 2

Marriage Certificate No. 37

John Harris
with
Amelia Ryerse

Whereas John Harris of His Majesty's Ship Prince Regent and Amelia Ryerse of Woodhouse were desirous of intermarrying with each other and there being no Parson or Minister of the Church of England being within Eighteen miles of them or either of them, they have applied to me for that purpose. Now these are to certify that in pursuance of the powers granted by an Act of the Legislature of the Province passed in the Thirtythird Year of His Majesty's Reign I Joseph Ryerson one of His Majesty's Justices of Peace having cause thro previous Notice by the Statute required to be given have this day married the said John Harris and Amelia Ryerse together and they are become legally contracted to each other in Marriage. Woodhouse June the Twentyeight 1815.

Witnesses:
(signed) Thos Cummins
(") George J. Ryerse
(") Jon Aldersley (??)
(") Jos Ryerson J.P.
(") John Harris
(") Amelia Harris

Registered this 1st day of July 1815
(Signed Jos R. William Dease Clk.P.)

[On the reverse is a certificate of John Harris Askin, clerk of the peace, London District, dated 29 July 1846, stating that the "within" certificate of marriage was dully registered in the records of District of London in Book A, page 38, number 37 of marriage certificates on 1 July 1815.]

APPENDIX 3

Extracts from Amelia Harris, "Historical Memorandum," 1859, 1879.

1. Samuel Ryerse's arrival at Port Ryerse.

After remaining there [in New Brunswick] several years, his [Samuel Ryerse's] friends entreated him to return to New York, holding out great inducements if he would consent to do so. He accepted the offer of his friends and returned, but he soon discovered that the rancorous, bitter feelings which had arisen during the war were not extinct, and that it was too soon for a British subject to seek a home in the United States. My mother loved her native city, and might not have been induced again to leave it had it not been for domestic affliction. She brought from the healthy climate of New Brunswick four children, all of whom she buried in New York in eight weeks. She gave birth to four more; three of who had also died, and she felt sure if she stayed there she would lose the only remaining one. Therefore she readily consented to my father's proposal to come to Canada, where his old friend General Simcoe, was at that time governor. In the summer of 1794 my father and a friend started for Canada. The journey was then a formidable one, and before commencing it wills were made and farewells given, as if a return was more than doubtful.

On his arrival at Niagara he was warmly greeted by his old friend, General Simcoe, who advised him by all means to settle in Canada, holding out many inducements for him to do so. He promised my father a grant of 3,000 acres of land as a captain in the army, 1,200 as a settler, and that my mother and each of her sons should have a grant of 1,200 and each of her daughters a grant of 600 acres.

It would be much easier for a family to go from Canada to China now, than it was to come from New York to Canada then. He had to purchase a boat large enough to hold his family and goods, with supplies of groceries for two or three years, with farming utensils, tools, pots, boilers, etc., and yet the boat must not be too large to get over the portage from the Hudson to the Mohawk. As there were no waggon roads from Albany to the Niagara frontier, families coming to Canada had to come down the Mohawk to Lake Ontario, and enter Canada in that way. My father found it a weary journey and was months accomplishing it.

On my father's arrival at Niagara, at that time the seat of government, he called on his Excellency Governor Simcoe, who had just returned from a tour through the Province of Canada West, then one vast wilderness. He asked General Simcoe's advice as to where he should choose his resting-place. He recommended the county of Norfolk (better known for many years as Long Point), which had recently been surveyed.

As it was now drawing towards the close of summer, it would require all their time to get up a shanty and prepare for the winter. Consequently, arrangements were made immediately to continuing their journey. The heavy batteau was transported from Queenston to Chippewa, around the Falls, a distance of twelve miles. Supplies were added to those brought from New York, and they once more started on their journey, bidding goodbye to the last vestige of civilization. They were twelve days, making the 100 miles, – not bad travelling taking the current of the river and lake, adverse winds and an unknown coast into consideration.

When my father came within the bay formed by Long Point, he watched the coast for a favourable impression and, after a scrutiny of many miles, the boat ran into a small creek, the high banks sloping gradually on each side.

Directions were given to the men to erect the tent for my mother. My father had not been long on shore before he decided that that should be his home. In wandering about, he came to an eminence which would when the trees were felled, command a view of the harbour. He gazed around there only for a few moments and said, Here I will be buried, and there after fourteen years' toil, he sleeps in peace.

2. The Burning of the Ryerse Farm

. . . In May of 1814 we had several days of heavy fog. On the morning of the 13th, as the fog lifted, we saw seven or eight ships under the American Flag anchored off Ryerse, with a number of small boats floating by the side of each ship. As the fog cleared away they hoisted sail and dropped down three miles below us, opposite Port Dover. Of course an invasion was anticipated. Col Talbot was then in Norfolk, and he ordered all the militia to assemble the next day at Brantford, a distance of forty miles, which they did with great reluctance, as many of both officers and men thought that an effort should be made to prevent the Americans landing, but no resistance was offered. On the 14th the Americans burnt the village and mills of Dover; on the 15th, as my mother and myself were sitting at breakfast, the dogs kept up a very unusual barking. I went to the door to discover the cause; when I looked up, I saw the hillside and fields, as far as the eye could reach, covered with American soldiers. They had marched from Port Dover to Ryerse. Two men stepped from the ranks, selected some large chips, and came into the room where we were standing, and took coals from the hearth without speaking a word. My mother knew instinctively what they were going to do. She went out and asked to see the commanding officer. A gentleman rode up to her and said he was the person she asked for. She entreated him to spare her property, and said she was a widow with a young family. He answered her civilly and respectfully, and expressed his regret that his orders were to burn, but that he would spare the house, which he did, and he said as a sort of justification of his burning, that the buildings were used as a barrack, and the mill furnished flour for British troops. Very soon we saw columns of dark smoke arise from every building, and of what at early morn had been a prosperous homestead, at noon there remained only smouldering ruins. The following day Colonel Talbot and the militia under his command marched to Fort Norfolk (commonly known as Turkey Point), six miles above Ryerse. The Americans were then on their way to their own shores. My father had been dead less than two years. Little remained of all his labours except the orchard and cultivated fields. It would not be easy to describe my mother's feelings as she looked at the desolation around her, and thought upon the past and the present; but there was no longer a wish to return to New York. My father's grave was there, and she looked to it as her resting place. Not many years since a small church was built on a plot of ground which my father had reserved for that purpose, in the graveyard attached are buried two of the early settlers – my father and my mother.

APPENDIX 4

This is the Last Will and Testament of John Harris, of the Township of London in the Province of Upper Canada Esquire.

First I give, devise, and bequeath unto my beloved wife Amelia all the Lands, tenements and hereditaments of which I may die possessed and also all my goods, chattels, money and all my estate of what nature or kind soever the whole to be at her unlimited disposal by sale, gift, devise, or otherwise. And I here by appoint her sole Executrix of this my last will and testament.

And whereas it is my intention in giving her all my estate and appointing her sole Executrix that she should have the means of maintaining, educating and providing for our Children in any way she may think most fit and expedient and whereas it may happen that she may die before me or died after me but without having first made her last will and testament or otherwise disposed of all or any of my estate, real or personal, and in either of these events it is expedient that provision should be made for the maintaining, educating and providing for my Children and for the distribution of my Estate: in case, therefore, my said Wife shall die before me, or die without having first made her last will and testament or having otherwise disposed of all of the Lands and Estate hereafter mentioned: I give, devise and bequeath to my son John the house and premises in which I now dwell with the out houses and appurtenances situated in or near the Town of London which I purchased from the Revd Mr Boswell and one Thomas Oarke to have and to hold the same to him and his heirs for Ever, provided always that he may not be entitled to the property or exclusively to the rents and _____ thereof till he comes of age.

And in case of the Contingencies herein before mentioned next before the devise to my Son John I give, devise and bequeath to my son Edward six hundred acres of Land in the Township of North Dorchester being that part of my military or Naval grant yet undisposed of; also Lot Number Seven in the fifth Concession of the Township of Nissouri to have and to hold the same and his heirs for ever.

And in case of the said Contingencies hereinbefore mentioned and before the devise to my son John I give, devise and bequeath to my son George Lot Number One in the Gore of

Woodhouse containing one hundred and ninety acres more or less – also Lot Number Twenty in the third Concession of Woodhouse which I purchased of one Gaitan Leger containing one hundred acres to have and to hold the same to him and his heirs for ever.

And in case of the said Contingencies hereinbefore mentioned next before the devise to my son John, I give, devise and bequeath to my daughter Sarah Lot Number Eighteen in Concession C and Lot Number Three in the Third Concession of Delaware containing four hundred acres more or less to have and to hold to her and her heirs for ever.

And in case of the said Contingencies hereinbefore mentioned next before the devise to my son John, I give, devise and bequeath to my daughter Amelia Lot Number Eighteen in Concession D in the Township of Delaware, containing two hundred acres and Lot Number Seven in the Sixth Concession of the Township of Dereham containing two hundred acres to have and to hold the same to her and her heirs for ever.

And in case of the said Contingencies hereinbefore mentioned next before the devise to my son John, I give, devise and bequeath to my daughter Mary Lot Number Seven in the Tenth Concession of the Township of Burford containing two hundred acres and Lot Number Nine in the Tenth Concession of South Dorchester containing two hundred acres to have and to hold the same to her and her heirs for ever.

And in case of the said Contingencies hereinbefore mentioned and before the devise to my son John, I give, devise and bequeath to my daughter Eliza Lot Number Seven in the Fifth Concession and Lot Number Eleven in the Sixth Concession of the Township of Dereham containing four hundred acres to have and to hold the same to her and her heirs for ever.

And in case of the said Contingencies hereinbefore mentioned next before the devise to my son John, I give, devise and bequeath to my daughter Charlotte Lot Number Eighteen in the Third Concession of the Township of Dereham, containing two hundred acres and Lot Number Nine in the Sixth Concession of the Township of Westminster containing two hundred acres more or less and to hold the same to her and her heirs for ever.

And in case of the said Contingencies hereinbefore mentioned next before the devise to my son John, I give, devise and bequeath to my daughter Helen Lot Number Twenty Five in the Ninth Concession of the Township of Dereham containing two hundred acres more or less and Lot Number Twenty Two in the Second Concession of the Township of Mosa one hundred and fifty acres and part of Lot Number Eighteen in Concession A in the Township of Dunwich containing sixty acres to have and to hold the same to her and her heirs for ever.

And in the case of the Said Contingencies, hereinbefore mentioned next before the devise to my son John, I give, devise and bequeath to my Executors, Edward P. Ryerse of the Township of Woodhouse in the London District Esquire and John Wilson of the Town of London and District aforesaid Barrister and to the survivor of them hereinafter named, all the residue of my lands, tenements, chattels, Bank and other stock and all the residues of my estate of what kind soever as well as any of the Lands above devised in case any of my Children shall die before me except Lot Number One in the Gore of Woodhouse hereinafter otherwise disposed of in trust, nevertheless, to sell and dispose of all or any part or parts of my said Estate, real or personal, at their discretion, jointly, during the lives of my said Executors or by the survivor of them in case one shall die, for the maintaining educating and providing for my said Children respectively till they become of age or are married. And for their guidance I will and devise that the proceeds of the sale of any of my estate, real or personal, shall be vested in some public stock or in such manner as they or the survivor of them deem best, so as to produce a periodical revenue which may be available for the purposes mentioned.

I also will and devise that as soon as my youngest surviving Child shall come of age that my said Executors or the survivor of them shall make an equal distribution as near as may be of all Estate then in their hands or subject to their control and the more easily to effect such distribution I will and authorize them to sell as they shall see fit all or any of my estate, real or personal, then in their hands or subject to their control or to the control of the survivor of them and divide the proceeds thereof. And whereas it may be attended with inconvenience to keep all the Children out of their shares as a residue of my estate till the youngest becomes of age, I therefore will and devise and hereby empower my said Executors or the survivor of them if they or the survivors of them shall think beneficial or fitting to do, to give to each of my Children as he or she respectively comes of age or gets married Money or property equal to one half of what may be estimated his or her final share of the residue of my estate after the youngest Children are respectively educated and maintained till they become of age, and such allotments or portion so received by either of them respectively shall be at the final distribution accounted as part of his or her final share. Nevertheless, I do not limit or restrain my said executors or the survivor of them from giving any or either of any said Children his or her full share on his or her coming of age or getting married respectively, providing it does not so detract from the Maintenance and Education of the rest as to leave the residue of the family in a worse situation that when the funds appropriate for that purpose were kept together. And I hereby will and bequeath my said Executors or the survivor of them full power and authority to execute assignments and deeds of sale of all or any part or parts of any said Estate, real or personal, hereinbefore devised to them in trust as aforesaid either to actual purchaser or to my Children respectively of such share as may be allotted to them at the final distribution of my estate.

And whereas the Lot Number One in the Gore Woodhouse is next adjoining certain lands which by the entailment of the late Samuel Ryerse will go to my youngest son and it is my intention that the said Lot Number One in the said Gore of Woodhouse shall go to my youngest surviving son who inherits the said entailed land which ever he may be, now in case my said son George shall die before he becomes entitled to the said Lands so entailed by the said Samuel Ryerse, I give, devise and bequeath the said Lot Number One in the said Gore Woodhouse to such of my sons as shall be entitled to the said Land next adjoining the said Lot.

And whereas it may happen that my said Wife Amelia may make her last will and testament and did not dispose of all or any of may said Estate so at her unlimited disposal, I therefore will and declare that all or any of my said Estate, real or personal, not disposed of by her either by sale, gifts, devise, or otherwise shall be subject to the arrangement and distribution hereinbefore made concerning it and shall not lapse exclusively to the heirs any thing hereinbefore contained to the contrary notwithstanding.

And I hereby nominate, constitute and appoint my brother in law Edward P. Ryerse of the Township of Woodhouse in the London District Esquire and John Wilson of the Town of London in the London District Barrister Executors of this my last will and testament and guardians of my said Children.

In witness whereof I the said John Harris to this my last will and testament written on two sheets of paper have the first sheet set my hand and to the last set my hand and seal on the eighth day of May in the year of our Lord one thousand eight hundred and thirty seven.
Signed, sealed, published and declared by the said John Harris as and for his last will and testament in the presence of us, who in his presence at his request and in presence of each other have set our hand as Witness hereto.

Gideon Ackland, Henry C.R. Becher, A.D. McLean

[Attachments:
- Certificates of memorials produced by Amelia Harris as Executrix as recorded in Registry Offices of Counties of Oxford, Middlesex, Norfolk.
- Oaths that Amelia Harris, John Wilson and Edward Ryerse certify the will as that of John Harris and that they will "well and faithfully administer all and singular the Goods, Rights, Credits and Chattels of the deceased, pay his debts and submit" a true, full, and perfect inventory of his Goods, Rights, Credits and Chattels to Court of Probate, Province of Ontario at Toronto.
- Oath by Henry Becher that he witnessed the signing of the will on 14 May 1837.
- Oath of Amelia Harris that John Harris died on or about 25 August 1850.]

APPENDIX 5

TO THE ELECTORS OF THE EAST RIDING OF MIDDLESEX

The London *Free Press* and *Daily Western Advertiser*, 11 June 1861

Gentlemen –

Previous to my leaving Canada for England, last year, I repeatedly pledged myself, at numerous and influential Meetings of the Electors, and, at their oft-repeated requests, to become a Candidate for the Representation of your County at the General Election.

In consequence of the opinion expressed by the Majority of the Meeting held to-day, that the County should choose their own Representative at a Convention, to be held on Saturday next, I consider that now it is due to my many friends and supporters to give you some of my views on the topics of the day and to announce myself as a Candidate for the nomination at the coming Convention, also, to declare my intention to abide by the decision that shall be given by that body.

It is unnecessary for me to dwell upon my feelings and opinions as to the necessity of upholding the connection between Canada and the Mother Country, as I believe loyalty to the British Crown and attachment to that connection, are now the fixed sentiments of every party in the Province.

I should strongly oppose any proposition having for its object the Dissolution of the Union of the Provinces, such a measure would, in my judgement, consign this now rising and prosperous country to a long period of perilous uncertainty as to its future position among nations as well as to a condition of weakness, the consequences of which would indefinitely counterbalance any partial advantages likely to result from it.

In regard to a general Confederation of the North American Provinces as a substitute for the present Union, while personally favourably disposed to the introduction and discussion of a measure of such a nature I am not at the present time in a position to enable me to decide upon so comprehensive and important a question, but this I am prepared to say, that no proposal for so fundamental a change in our Administrative System can ever receive my support which shall not emanate from our Responsible Executive.

I am an advocate for Representation by Population, as I conceive it to be the most legitimate, and, indeed, essential, consequences of a representative Constitution; and while I am disposed to make every fair allowance for the difficulties that beset that question, arising from our peculiar position with the Lower Province, I shall not fail in the event of my being elected to urge upon the Administration the necessity for a prompt and satisfactory settlement.

I am in favour of a Law in reference to Bankruptcy, which would afford relief to the honest but unfortunate Debtor. There is, I am aware, a difference of opinion amongst those who are considered the most competent judges upon the subject, whether such a law should be confined in its operations to Traders, or whether it should be extended to all classes alike. While I incline to the opinion that a Bankruptcy Law should not be limited in its application, I think that the difference between the Mercantile and Farming Communities ought to be consulted by a corresponding difference in the enactments applicable to each.

I shall deem it my special duty to watch over the interests of the Agricultural Body, to advocate and promote every measure calculated for its benefit, and to withstand any movement tending to injure or unduly to burden it. With these objects in view, my endeavours will be more especially directed to procuring a reduction of the present heavy expenses attendant upon necessary litigation to forward the enactment of a moderate and well-considered Homestead Law, and to foster and extend the existing Reciprocity Treaty between Canada and the States of America.

Without undertaking to suggest a definite remedy for the evils of the existing Assessment Law, I cannot help remarking that its present working is not satisfactory and I shall readily support any measure calculated to secure a uniform system of assessment based upon the true value of property, which object although undoubtedly the design of the present law, has not been attained. In connection with this subject I may allude to the Law regulating the sale of land by the sheriff for arrears of taxes, which appears to me to require some alteration and amendment on account of its rash and in some cases, tyrannical operation.

I need scarcely say that I take a deep interest in the Manufacturing Classes and that I shall endeavour on all occasions to advance their interest, which, however depend more upon individual enterprises and industries than upon anything the Legislature can do for their welfare.

I am not disposed to disturb the present arrangement respecting the School Law, as I consider it the best solution attainable at present of a most difficult question.

I think that, looking to the troubled condition of the United States, Canada should offer any inducement to immigrants from there as well as from Europe and use every endeavour to turn our neighbour's quarrels to our advantage. With that end in view I would advocate the giving away of Wild Lands in the newly surveyed townships and in those at present unsurveyed to actual settlers. The benefit that would result from this would, in a few years, infinitely surpass the temporary loss of the trifling sum at present derived from the sale of those lands.

My present opinions and feelings are Conservative, and I am disposed to afford the present Government a frank and cordial support – a support, however, which must not be supposed to extend to any measures running counter to the public sentiment, more especially the momentous question of economy of the Public Finances. I believe that public extravagance leads to public waste, and that the two combined are the sure forerunners of wide-spread monetary and commercial revulsions, such as we have already unfortunately experienced.

In conclusion, then, upon the recommendation of these principles and rules of public conduct, and being, moreover, independent of profession, office or party ties, I trust, without presumption, as a candidate for your suffrage. The shortness of the time between this day and the day named for the Convention makes it impossible for me, on this occasion, to make a personal canvass of the Riding but should I gain the nomination I shall endeavour to see most of the Electors and give them my views on the questions of the day at greater length.

London, June 11, 1861 M.B. Portman

APPENDIX 6

Last Will and Testament of Amelia Harris, 1871, With Codicils Dated 1878 and 1882.

This is the last will and testament of me Amelia Harris of the city of London in the County of Middlesex and Province of Ontario, widow of John Harris late of the same place, Esquire, deceased. I devise the house grounds and premises on which I now live and known as Eldon House, on the west side of Ridout Street in the said city of London and all the land attached thereto belonging to me or which I have the power to devise, to my son Edward William Harris his heirs and assigns for ever. I devise the ninety six acres of lot number One in the Broken Front in the Township of Woodhouse in the County of Norfolk which was willed to me by my father – to my son George Becher Harris his heirs and assigns for ever in fee simple. I devise the unsold portion of the lot known to the Harris Family as the "Twenty five acres" and being the unsold portion of the South-east quarter of Lot number Three on the west side of the Warncliffe [sic] Highway in the Township of London to my daughters who may survive me their heirs and assigns. I wish the children of my daughter Helen Vidal Portman now deceased to inherit a share of the said land so known as the "twenty-five" in the same manner as they would have been entitled to the same had said daughter been living at the execution of this my will and surviving me. All my Plate I wish to be equally divided between my sons, Edward and George, but should either of my said sons die before me I wish the survivor to have the Plate. The Tea Urn I wish to be given to my daughter Sarah – the books I devise in like manner as the Plate. I devise to my sons Edward William Harris and George Becher Harris their heirs and assigns for ever all my wild and other lands not heretofore devised and all other property real and personal not heretofore mentioned and devised and I here make and appoint them my residuary legatees. The Portraits I shall dispose of by gift hereafter with the exception of Amelia's, Mary's, Eliza's, Edward's and Teresa's. I wish them to have their own. And I appoint my sons Edward William Harris and George Becher Harris, Executors of this my will, hereby revoking all other testamentary writings by me at anytime heretofore made.———

In witness whereof I have hereunto set my hand this thirty first day of March in the year of our Lord one thousand eight hundred and seventy one.
Signed by the said testatrix as and for her last will and testament in the presence of us present at the same time who at her request and in the presence of each other have subscribed our names as witnesses.

Signed – James Magee Signed – Amelia Harris
Signed – Geo McNab

This is a Codicil to the last will and testament within written, of me Amelia Harris:

The devise of the "Twenty five acres" being the unsold portion of the Southeast quarter of Lot number Three on the west side of the Wharncliffe [sic] Highway the Township of London as set forth in the within written last will and testament is hereby revoked. I now devise the same to my three daughters Sarah B. Dalzell, Amelia Griffin and Mary H. Peard their heirs and assigns for ever.
Signed by the Testatrix as for a codicil to the within written last will and testament this fifth day of August A.D. 1878 in the presence of us who at her request in her presence and in the presence of each other have hereunto subscribed our names as witnesses hereto

Signed – Wm. J. Clarke
Signed – Geo. C. Evans

This is a further codicil to the last will and testament within written of me, Amelia Harris – The devise of the twenty five acres, being the unsold portion of the southeast quarter of lot number Three, the west side of the Wharncliffe Highway in the Township of London as set forth in the within written last will and testament and the previous codicil thereto is hereby revoked. I now devise the same to my daughter Amelia Griffin [wife of] Gilbert Griffin absolutely. ———
Signed by the Testatrix as and for a codicil to the within written testament this thirteenth day of March A.D. 1882 in the presence of us, who at her request in her presence and in the presence of each other have hereunto subscribed our name as witness hereto

Signed – Kate Carroll Signed – Amelia Harris
Signed – James Magee

Copy of Memorandum left by Mrs Amelia Harris and signed by her 30th March 1880 Eldon House

My dear Amelia –

I leave you a copy of a Memorandum which I leave for Edward and George telling them what I wish done with a few of my personalities – I have not much to leave, but each of my children may like to have a little remembrance of their old home. I pray God to bless you all and that you may live in love and peace with one another.

APPENDIX 7

A Memorandum for my Children when I am gone Written this 22nd Day of November 1881.

I pray God to bless all my children and grant that they may live in peace and love with each other.

The plated ware not particularly mentioned in my will I leave to Edward. Also the dining room clock which I wish him to keep in remembrance of me as I have kept it in remembrance of my parents. The Clock I bought of Mr Scott I give to George and wish him to keep it in remembrance of his old Mother. To Amelia I give the silver plate teapot that Capt Savory gave me and also the small tea set that the Leiths sent me and the ink stand that Teresa gave me and candlesticks that Lucy gave me. I wish Amelia to have the furniture of my room which was given me by Helen namely a dressing table, a large chest of drawers, a sofa and night chair, a little round table and Mother's drawers and my rocking chair. I wish her to have the counterpane, Blankets, Sheets and Pillows that may be in use on my bed when I die. The clock that the Dalzells gave me was for life only after my death it was to go to Amelia. I wish her to have my trunk. Plutarch's Lives I give to Scott [Griffin]. The black silk dress is not made up I give to Sarah and my gold sleeve buttons and spectacles with a gold frame. My gold watch with the chain attached I give to Mary and another small gold chain also black satin for a dress if not made up. To Eliza I give a small drawing of her Uncle Edward's House not for its value otherwise than it was made by dear Chasse and a miniature of myself and Mother's gold sleeve buttons. To Teresa I give a crooked spade Guinea given to me more than fifty years ago by her father. I return her the broach she gave me the gold locket with John's hair in it which he sent me just before his death. The violet vase from Eliza and the Hand from Capt Savory I wish Sophia to have. I wish Lucy to have two small vases that Sarah gave me and my Roman scarf. Edward is to have his choice of the pictures of John's grave and George to have the other. I give George the Picture of John which Mr Wandesforde gave me and also my down spread. I wish Edward to keep the plate of Derbyshire Spar, the pastile burner and envelope case in my room and the Book of Portraits given me by General Crutchley, the bible given me by Capt Williamson and Northey and the Book of Drawings given me by Mr Thomas. The rings given me by Mr Griffin, Sophia, Lucy and Elizabeth [O'Brien] I wish returned to them with my last love. The Photograph Stand that Mr Becher gave me with the photos in it I give to Lucy. My shawl pin given me by Mr Walker I give to my dear granddaughter Amelia Harris. I wish Lucy to have the little bracelet made by Berkeley Portman with Samuel on it and George to have the bracelet he gave me with the head of our Saviour on it. I wish him to look at all books he gave me and take them and also the two small heads that Chasse copied and he had framed for me. Sophia is to have the History of Holland which her Father gave me. Amelia is to have all the photos and odds and ends not given away which are in my room, I give George my books of photos which are in the drawing room and also my Journal. I give the Photo stand with the Crutchley family to Amelia.

As I commence so I end with a prayer that God may bless and keep you all in love and peace.

BIBLIOGRAPHY

CONTEMPORARY MATERIALS

Bremner, Archie. *Illustrated London, Ontario, Canada*, London: London Printing and Lithographing, 1897.

Dent, J.C. *The Story of the Upper Canada Rebellion: Largely Derived from Original Sources and Documents*, 2 vols., Toronto, 1885.

———. *Canadian Portrait Gallery*, 4 vols., Toronto: J.B. Magurn, 1880.

Drew, Andrew and R.S Woods. *The Burning of the Caroline and Other Reminiscences of 1837–38*, Chatham: Banner Printing Co., 1896.

Ermatinger, C.O. *The Talbot Regime or the First Half of the Talbot Settlement*, St. Thomas: Municipal World Review, 1904.

Ermatinger, Edward. *Life of Colonel Talbot and the Talbot Settlement*, St. Thomas: A. McLachlin, 1859.

Head, Francis B. *Narrative*, London: John Murray, 1839.

Horton, William. *Memoir of the Late Thomas Scatcherd, Barrister-at-law, Queen's Counsel and Member of Parliament . . .* , London, Ontario, 1878.

Leonard, The Honourable Elijah. *A Memoir*, London: Advertiser Printing Co., not dated [1876].

Lindsey, Charles. *The Life and Times of William Lyon Mackenzie*, 2 vols., Toronto: P.R. Randall, 1862.

Lysons, Daniel. *Early Reminiscences*, London: John Murray, 1896.

Mockridge, Charles H. *The Bishops of the Church of England in Canada and Newfoundland, Being an Illustrated Sketch of the Account of the Church of England in Canada as Traced Through Her Episcopate*, Toronto: F.N.W. Brown, 1896.

Morgan, Henry James. *The Tour of H.R.H. The Prince of Wales Through British America and the United States by a British Canadian*, Montreal: John Lovell, 1860.

———. *The Canadian Men and Women of the Time: A Handbook of Canadian Biography*, 1st Ed., Toronto: William Briggs, 1898.

———. *Types of Canadian Women, Past and Present and of Women Who Are or Have Been Connected with Canada*, Toronto: William Briggs, 1903.

———. *Canadian Men and Women of the Time: A Handbook of Canadian Biography of Living Characters*, 2nd Ed., Toronto: William Briggs, 1912.

Owen, A.E. *Pioneer Sketches of Long Point Settlement*, Toronto: William Briggs. 1898.

Peard, George Shuldham. *Narrative of a Campaign in the Crimea, Including an Account of the Battles of Alma, Balaclava and Inkerman*, London: Richard Bentley, 1855.

Reed, David B. *The Lives of the Judges of Upper Canada and Ontario from 1791 to the Present Time*, Toronto: Rowsell & Hutchison, 1898.

Ryerson, Egerton. *The Loyalists of America and Their Times from 1620 to 1816*, 2 vols., Toronto: William Briggs, 1880.

———. *The Story of My Life*, Toronto: William Briggs, 1883.

Stead, W.T. *Real Ghost Stories*, Being the Christmas Number of the *Review of Reviews*, 1891.

Tasker, L.H. *The United Empire Loyalist Settlement at Long Point, Lake Erie*, Toronto: William Briggs, 1900.

BOOKS AND THESES

Adams, T.D. *Telling Lies in Modern American Autobiography*, Chapel Hill and London: University of North Carolina Press, 1990.

Aitchinson, J.H. "The Development of Local Government in Upper Canada 1783–1850," Ph.D., University of Toronto, 1953.

Alexander, Sir James. *L'Acadie or Seven Years Exploration in British North America*, 2 vols., London: Henry Colburn, 1949.

Armstrong, Frederick H. *Handbook of Upper Canada and Territorial Legislation*, London, Ontario: University of Western Ontario, 1967.

———. *The Forest City: An Illustrated History of London, Canada*, Northridge, California: Windsor Publications, 1986.

Armstrong, Frederick H. and Daniel J. Brock. *Reflections on London's Past*, London: City of London, 1975.

Bailey, Melville. *The History of Dundurn Castle and Sir Allan MacNab*, Hamilton: Hughes & Wilkins, 1942.

Bannister, J.A. *Early Educational History of Norfolk County*, Toronto: University of Toronto Press, 1926.

Beer, Donald R. *Sir Allan Napier MacNab*, Hamilton: Dictionary of Hamilton Biography, 1984.

Blodgett, Harriet. *Centuries of Female Days: Englishwomen's Private Diaries*, New Brunswick, N.J.: Rutgers University Press, 1988.

Burant, Jim and Judith Saunders. *The Garrison Years: London, Canada West 1793–1853*, Exhibition Catalogue, London: London Regional Art Gallery, 1983.

Burrows, E.H. *Captain Owen of the African Survey: The Hydrographic*

Surveys of Admiral W.F.W. Owen on the Coast of Africa and the Great Lakes of Canada, Rotterdam: A.A. Balkema, 1979.

Buss, Helen M. *Mapping Our Selves: Canadian Women's Autobiography*, Montreal and Kingston: McGill-Queen's University Press, 1993.

Carty, Arthur C. *1826–1926 Milestones, London, Canada*, London: Hayden Press, 1926.

Campbell, Clarence T. *Pioneer Days in London*, London, Ontario: Advertiser, 1921.

Careless, J.M.S. *The Pre-Confederation Premiers: Ontario Government Leaders, 1941–1867*, Toronto: University of Toronto Press, 1980.

Chadwick, Edward Marion. *Ontario Families: Genealogies of United Empire Loyalist and Other Pioneer Families of Upper Canada*, Lambertville, New Jersey: Hunterdon House, 1970.

Cosbie, W.G. *The Toronto General Hospital: A Chronicle*, Toronto: Macmillan, 1975.

Coyne, James H. *The Talbot Papers*, Ottawa: The Royal Society of Canada, 1910.

Craig, G.M. *Upper Canada: The Frontier Years, 1784–1841*, Toronto: McClelland and Stewart, 1963.

———., ed. *Early Travellers in the Canadas, 1791–1867*, Toronto: Macmillan, 1955.

Creighton, Donald. *John A. Macdonald: The Young Politician*, Toronto: Macmillan, 1952.

Creighton, Luella. *The Elegant Canadians*, Toronto: McClelland and Stewart, 1967.

Cronyn, Verschoyle P. *Other Days*, London: private printed, 1976.

de Beauvoir, Simone. *The Second Sex*, New York: Alfred A. Knopf, 1952.

de Pencier, Honor. *Posted to Canada: The Watercolours of George Russell Dartnell 1835–1844*, Toronto: Dundurn Press Limited, 1987.

Dunham, Aileen. *Political Unrest in Upper Canada, 1815–1836*, London: Longmans, Green and Co., 1927.

Fentress, James and Chris Wickham. *Social Memory*, Oxford: Blackwell, 1992.

Fothergill, Robert. *Private Chronicles: A Study of English Diaries*, London: Oxford University Press, 1974.

Freud, Sigmund. *The Interpretation of Dreams*, James Strachey, ed., New York: Avon Books, 1965.

Glazebrook, George P. de T. *Life in Ontario: A Social History*, Toronto: University of Toronto Press, 1971.

Goodspeed, W.A. and C.L. *History of Middlesex County*, Toronto: London Free Press Printing Co., 1989.

Graddol, D. and Joan Swann. *Gender Voices*, Oxford: Basil Blackwell, 1989.

Guillet, E.C. *The Lives and Times of Patriots: An Account of The Rebellion in Canada, 1837–38*, Toronto: T. Nelson, 1938.

Hale, Katherine. *Historic Houses of Canada*, Toronto: Ryerson, 1952.

Halpenny, Francess G., gen. ed. *Dictionary of Canadian Biography V: 1801–1820*, Toronto: University of Toronto Press, 1983.

———. *Dictionary of Canadian Biography VI: 1821–1835*, Toronto: University of Toronto Press, 1987.

———. *Dictionary of Canadian Biography VII: 1836–1850*, Toronto: University of Toronto Press, 1988.

———. *Dictionary of Canadian Biography VIII: 1851–1860*, Toronto: University of Toronto Press, 1985.

———. *Dictionary of Canadian Biography IX: 1861–1870*, Toronto: University of Toronto Press 1976.

———. *Dictionary of Canadian Biography X: 1871–1880*, Toronto: University of Toronto Press, 1972.

———. *Dictionary of Canadian Biography XI: 1881–1890*, Toronto: University of Toronto Press, 1982.

———. *Dictionary of Canadian Biography XII: 1891–1900*, Toronto: University of Toronto Press, 1990.

Hamil, Fred Coyne. *The Valley of the Lower Thames, 1640 to 1850*, Toronto: University of Toronto, 1951.

———. *Lake Erie Baron: The Story of Colonel Thomas Talbot*, Toronto: Macmillan, 1955.

Hampsten, Elizabeth. *Read This Only to Yourself: The Private Writings of Midwestern Women, 1880–1910*, Bloomington: Indiana University Press, 1982.

Harper, J. Russell. *A Century of Colonial Painting*, Ottawa: National Gallery of Canada, 1972.

Harris, Mary J.Y. *Memoirs of Frances Mary Peard*, Torquay: W.H. Smith, 1930.

Henderson, James. "A Study of British Garrisons in London, C.W., 1838–1869," M.A. Thesis, University of Windsor, 1967.

Hill, Alette Olin. *Mother Tongue, Father Time*, Bloomington and Indianapolis: Indiana University Press, 1986.

Hirsch, Marianne. *The Mother/Daughter Plot: Narrative, Psychoanalysis, Feminism*, Bloomington and Indianapolis: Indiana University Press, 1989.

Honey, Terrance W., ed. *London Heritage*, London: London Free Press, 1972.

Hughes, David and T.H. Purdom. *History of the Bar of the County of Middlesex*, London, 1912.

Iacovetta, Franca and Mariana Valverde. *Gender Conflicts: New Essays in Women's History*, Toronto: University of Toronto Press, 1992.

Jenkins, Brian. *Britain and the War for the Union*, Montreal: McGill-Queen's University Press, 1974.

Jung, Carl G. *Man and His Symbols*, London: Aldus Books, 1964.

Kilbourn, William. *The Firebrand: William Lyon Mackenzie and the Rebellion in Upper Canada*, Toronto: Clarke Irwin, 1956.

Kramarae, Cheris. *Women and Men Speaking*, Rowley, Mass.: Newbury House Publishers, 1981.

Lambert, R.S. *Exploring the Supernatural: The Weird in Canadian Folklore*, London: Barker, 1955.

Landon, Fred. *Western Ontario and the American Frontier*, Toronto: Ryerson Press, 1941.

Langton, H.H., ed. *A Gentlewoman in Upper Canada: The Journals of Anne Langton*, Toronto: Clarke Irwin, 1950.

Leveridge, Anne. *Your Loving Anna: Letters from the Ontario Frontier*, Louis Tivy, ed., Toronto: University of Toronto Press, 1972.

Lincoln, Anthony L.J. and R.L. McEwan. *Lord Eldon's Anecdote Book*, London: Stevens and Sons, 1960.

Longley, R.S. *Sir Francis Hincks: A Study of Canadian Politics, Railways and Finance in the Nineteenth Century*, Toronto: University of Toronto Press, 1943.

Lutman, John H. *The Historic Heart of London*, London, Ontario: Corporation of the City of London, 1977.

MacDermot, H.E. *One Hundred Years of Medicine in Canada*, Toronto: McClelland and Stewart, 1967.

Matthews, William. *American Diaries*, Boston: J.S. Canner, 1959.

———. *Canadian Diaries and Autobiographies*, Berkeley: University of California Press, 1950.

———. *British Diaries: An Annotated Bibliography of British Diaries Written Between 1442 and 1942*, Berkeley: University of California Press, 1950.

McKenzie, Ruth, ed. *The St. Lawrence Survey Journals of Captain Henry Wolsey Bayfield, 1829–1853*, 2 vols., Toronto: Champlain Society, 1984; 1986.

McNeil, Mary. *Vere Foster 1819–1900*, Newton Abbot: David and Charles, 1971.

Middleton, Jesse and Fred Landon, eds. *The Province of Ontario: A History*, 4 vols., Toronto: Dominion Publishing Co., 1927.

Miller, Orlo. *A Century of Western Ontario: The Story of London, "The Free Press," and Western Ontario, 1849–1949*, Toronto: Ryerson Press, 1949.

———. *Gargoyles and Gentlemen: A History of St. Paul's Cathedral, London, Ontario, 1834–1964*, Toronto: Ryerson Press, 1966.

———. *This Was London: The First Two Centuries*, Westport, Ontario: Butternut Press, 1989.

Miller, Orlo, with Miriam Wright, Edward Phelps and Glenn C. Phillips. *London 200: An Illustrated History*, London: Chamber of Commerce, 1992.

Newell, Dianne. *Technology on the Frontier: Mining in Old Ontario*, Vancouver: University of British Columbia Press, 1986.

O'Brien, Kate. *English Diaries and Journals*, London: Collins, 1944.

Palmer, Bryan. *Descent into Discourse: The Reification of Language and the Writing of Social History*, Philadelphia: Temple University Press, 1990.

Pease, William H. *Black Utopia: Negro Communal Experiments in America*, Madison: State Historical Society of Wisconsin, 1963.

Penfield, Joyce, ed. *Women and Language in Transition*, Albany, N.Y.: State University of New York Press, 1987.

Poole, Nancy Geddes. *The Art of London: 1830–1980*, London: Blackpool Press, 1984.

Portman, Marjorie. *Bryarston: Portraits of a Family*, Sherborne: Dorset Publishing Company, 1987.

Potter-MacKinnon, Janice. *While the Women Only Wept: Loyalist Refugee Women in Eastern Ontario*, Montreal and Kingston: McGill-Queen's University Press, 1993.

Prentice, Alison and Susan Mann Trofimenkoff, eds. *Essays in Canadian Women's History: The Neglected Majority*, Toronto: McClelland and Stewart, 1985.

Prentice, Alison, et al. *Canadian Women: A History*, Toronto: Harcourt Brace Jovanovich, 1988.

Purdom, Thomas H. *London and its Men of Affairs*, London, Ontario: 1915.

Quaife, Milo M., ed. *The John Askin Papers*, 2 vols., Detroit: Detroit Library Commission, 1928.

Read, Colin and Ronald J. Stagg. *The Rebellion of 1837: A Collection of Documents*, Toronto: Champlain Society, 1985.

Read, Colin. *The Rising in Western Upper Canada 1837–8: The Duncombe Revolt and After*, Toronto: University of Toronto Press, 1982.

Riddell, William R. *The Legal Profession of Upper Canada in its Early Periods*, Toronto: Law Society of Upper Canada, 1918.

Ryerson, George S. *Looking Backward*, Toronto: Ryerson Press, 1914.

Ryerson, Albert W. *The Ryerson Genealogy: Genealogy and History of the Knickerbocker Families of Ryerson, Ryerse, Ryerss*, Alfred L. Holman, ed., Chicago: privately printed, 1916.

Seaborn, Edwin. *The March of Medicine in Western Ontario*, Toronto: Ryerson, 1944.

Smith, Frances K. *John Herbert Caddy: 1801–1887*, Exhibition Catalogue, Kingston: Agnes Etherington Art Centre, 1985.

Schull, Joseph. *Edward Blake*, 2 vols., Toronto: Macmillan, 1975.

Senior, Hereward. *The Last Invasion of Canada: The Fenian Raids, 1866–1879*, Toronto: Dundurn Press, 1991.

Shortt, S.E.D., ed. *Medicine in Canadian Society: Historical Perspectives*, Montreal and Kingston: McGill-Queen's University Press, 1981.

Silverman, Jason H. *Unwelcome Guests: Canada West's Response to American Fugitive Slaves, 1800–1865*, Millwood, New York: Associated Faculty Press, 1985.

Sissons, C.B. *Egerton Ryerson: His Life and Letters*, 2 vols., Toronto: Clarke Irwin, 1947.

———, ed. *My Dearest Sophie: Letters from Egerton Ryerson to His Daughter*, Toronto: Ryerson Press, 1955.

Smith, Philip. *The Trust-Builders: The Remarkable Rise of Canada Trust*, Toronto: Macmillan, 1989.

St-Denis, Guy. *Byron: Pioneer Days in Westminster Township*, Lambeth: Cricklaw Express, 1988.

———, ed. *Simcoe's Choice: Celebrating London's Bicentennial, 1793–1993*, Toronto: Dundurn Press, 1992.

Staton, Frances. *The Rebellion of 1837–38: A Bibliography of the Sources of Information in the Public Reference Library of the City of Toronto*, Toronto: Public Library of Toronto, 1924.

Strong Boag, Veronica and Anita Clair Fellman. *Rethinking Canada: The Promise of Women's History*, Toronto: Copp Clark Pitman, 1986.

Talman, J.J. *Loyalist Narratives of Upper Canada*, Toronto: The Champlain Society, 1937.

Tausky, Nancy Z. and Lynne D. DiStephano. *Victorian Architecture in London and Southwestern Ontario: Symbols of Aspiration*, Toronto: University of Toronto Press, 1986.

Trofimenkoff, Susan Mann and Alison Prentice, eds. *Essays in Canadian Women's History: The Neglected Majority*, Toronto: McClelland and Stewart, 1977.

———. *Essays in Canadian Women's History: The Neglected Majority*, vol. 2, Toronto: McClelland and Stewart, 1985.

Wallace, Elizabeth. *Goldwin Smith, Victorian Liberal*, Toronto: University of Toronto Press, 1957.

Wallace, W. Stewart. *The Macmillan Dictionary of Canadian Biography*, 4th Ed., Toronto: Macmillan, 1978.

Ward, Peter. *Courtship, Love, and Marriage in Nineteenth Century English Canada*, Montreal and Kingston: McGill-Queen's University Press, 1990.

Whitfield, Carol. *British Soldiery in Canada*, Ottawa: Parks Canada, 1979.

Zaslow, Morris, ed. *The Defended Border: Upper Canada and the War of 1812*, Toronto: Macmillan, 1964.

Zeller, Suzanne. *Inventing Canada: Early Victorian Science and the Idea of a Transcontinental Nation*, Toronto: University of Toronto Press, 1987.

ARTICLES

Armstrong, Frederick H. "The Oligarchy of the Western District of Upper Canada, 1788–1841," Toronto: Canadian Historical Association Papers, 1977.

Armstrong, Frederick H. and Daniel J. Brock, "The Rise of London: A Study of Urban Evolution in Nineteenth Century Southwestern Ontario," in F.H. Armstrong, H.A. Stevenson and J.D. Wilson, eds., *Aspects of Nineteenth Century Ontario: Papers Presented to James J. Talman*, Toronto: University of Toronto Press, 1974.

Bunkers, Suzanne L. "Midwestern Diaries and Journals: What Women Were (Not) Saying in the Late 1800s," in James Olney, ed., *Studies in Autobiography*, New York and Oxford: Oxford University Press, 1988, 190–210.

Buss, Helen M. "Anna Jameson's Winter Studies and Summer Rambles in Canada as Epistolary Dijournal," in Marlene Kadar, ed., *Essays on Life-Writing: From Genre to Critical Practice*, Toronto: University of Toronto Press, 1992, 42–60.

———. "Pioneer Women's Memoirs: Preserving the Past/Rescuing the Self," in K.P. Stich, ed., *Reflections: Autobiography and Canadian Literature*, Ottawa: University of Ottawa Press, 1988, 45–60.

Connor, J.T.H. "'A Sort of Felo-de-Se': Eclecticism, Related Medical Sects, and their Decline in Victorian Ontario," *Bull. Hist. Med.* 65, 1991, 503–527.

Cornell, Paul. "William Fitz William Owen, Naval Surveyor," *Collections of the Nova Scotia Historical Society* XXXII, 1959, 61–82.

Cruikshank, E.A. "The Invasion of Navy Island in 1837–38," *Ontario Historical Society, Papers and Records* XXXII, 1937, 7–84.

———. "The Early History of the London District," *Ontario History* XXIV, 1927, 149–150, 164–165, 170.

Franklin, Penelope. "Diaries of Forgotten Women," *Book Forum*, vol. 4, 1979, 467–74.

Garland, M.A. and Orlo Miller, eds. "The Diary of H.C.R. Becher," *Ontario Historical Society, Papers and Records* XXXIII, 1939, 116–143.

Grant, Hugh M. "The 'Mysterious' Jacob L. Englehart and the Early Ontario Petroleum Industry," *Ontario History* LXXXV, 1993, 65–76.

Harris, Robin. "The Beginning of the Hydrographic Survey of the Great Lakes and the St. Lawrence River," *Historic Kingston* 14, 1966, 24–39.

Hitchins, William E. "In Search of the Ghost of Eldon House," *London and Middlesex Historical Society* XVIII, 1991, 42–48.

Hodgins, Bruce W. "John Sandfield Macdonald," in J.M.S. Careless, *The Pre-Confederation Premiers: Ontario Government Leaders, 1841–67*, Toronto: University of Toronto Press, 1980, 264–82.

Island, John S. "Andrew Drew: The Man Who Burned the Caroline," *Ontario History* LIX, 1967, 137–156.

Johnson, J.K. "The Business Man as Hero: The Case of William Warren Street," *Ontario History* LXV, 1973, 125–132.

Johnson, J.K. "The U.C. Club and the Upper Canadian Elite, 1837–1840," *Ontario History* LXIX, 1977, 151–68.

Jones, Howard. "The Caroline Affair," *The Historian* 38, 1976, 485–502.

Kealey, Linda. "Special Issue on Women's History," *Canadian Historical Review* LXXII, 1991, 437–440.

Landon, Fred. "The Common Man in the Era of the Rebellion in Upper Canada," *Canadian Historical Association Annual Report*, 1937, 76–91.

———. "The Duncombe Uprising of 1837 and Some of its Consequences," *Proceedings and Transactions of the Royal Society of Canada* XXV, 1931, 83–98.

———. "London and its Vicinity, 1837–38," *Ontario Historical Society, Papers and Records* XXIV, 1927, 410–38.

———. "London in Early Times" and "London in Later Times," in Jesse E. Middleton and Fred Landon, eds., *The Province of Ontario*, Toronto, 1927.

———. "The Canadian Scene 1880–1890," *Canadian Historical Association Annual Report*, 1942, 5–18.

———. "British Regiments in London," *Western Ontario Historical Notes* XIII, 1955, 5–9.

Miller, Orlo. "The History of the Newspaper Press in London, 1837–1875," *Ontario Historical Society, Papers and Records* XXXIII, 1941, 87–100.

Mitchell, Sally. "Sentiment and Suffering: Women's Recreational Reading in the 1860s," *Victorian Studies* 12, 1977, 29–46.

Parr, Joy. "Nature and Hierarchy: Reflections on Writing the History of Women and Children," *Atlantis* II, 1985, 43.

Phelps, Edward. "Foundations of the Canadian Oil Industry," in Edith G. Firth, ed., *Profiles of a Province: Studies in the History of Ontario*, Toronto: Ontario Historical Society, 1967, 156–55.

Thomas, Clara. "Afterword," in Anna Jameson, *Winter Studies and Summer Rambles in Canada*, Toronto: McClelland and Stewart, 1990, 543–49.

Thurston, John. "Rewriting Roughing It," in John Moss, ed., *Future Indicative: Literary Theory and Canadian Literature*, Ottawa: University of Ottawa Press, 1987, 195–204.

Van Doren, Carl. "Bayard Taylor," in Dumas Malone, ed., *Dictionary of American Biography* XVIII, New York: Charles Scribner's Sons, 1936.

Wise, S.F. "Upper Canada and the Conservative Tradition," in Edith G. Firth, ed., *Profiles of a Province*, Toronto: Ontario Historical Society, 1967, 20–33.

INDEX

Editor's note: Since the principal members of the Harris family appear throughout the diaries they are not indexed except with reference to important events such as births, deaths, marriages, etc..

ADAMS, DR, 196
abortion, 289
Advertiser (London), 342, 436
Agassiz, Louis, 289
Airey, Louisa, 16
Airey, Sir Richard, xciii, 9, 12, 15, 22–24, 27–31, 38, 71, 112, 251
Aldersley, John, xxxiii
Althorpe, Lord, 43, 65
American Civil War, 190, 194, 196, 246–247, 251, 254, 401, 413–414
Anderson, Dr Alexander, lxxxviii–lxxxix, 26–30, 35, 46, 77, 86, 93; and death of Helen Harris Portman, 145–152, 155, 158; illness and death of, 326–327
Anderson, Mrs Alexander, 30, 35, 326, 329
Anglo American Hotel (Hamilton), 114
Ashley, Mr, 78, 83–84, 90
Askin, Cynthia, 21
Askin, Duncan: death of, 381
Askin, Mrs Duncan, 90
Askin, Elisa Van Allen, 49, 219, 222, 227, 236, 257, 271, 273, 276, 282, 292, 297, 304, 306–307, 310–311, 425, 428, 432; death of, 322
Askin, Colonel John B., lxv, 5–6, 21, 56, 63, 87, 218, 227, 257, 271, 276, 419, 422, 425, 431; death of, 297
Askin, Teresa, 264, 428, 430–431, 432; death of, 299
Assize Week, 254
Aurora Borealis, 14, 123
autumn foliage, 386, 389

BACKGAMMON, 14
Bailey, Bill, 111, 188, 391
Bailey, Lucy Wilson, 188; death of, 347
balls (dances), lxvii, 14–15, 23–24, 37, 38, 63–64, 79, 89, 90–92, 94–94, 110, 113, 170, 172, 179, 188, 208, 214, 217, 222, 241–242, 253, 264, 274–275, 284, 296, 321, 341–342, 345, 363, 367, 379–382, 419–420, 422, 425, 444, 447–448
bands, 91, 105, 186, 416, 419–420, 423
Bank of Upper Canada, li, 63, 72, 82
baseball, 350
Bayfield, Captain Henry W., xxxii, xxxix
Beatty, Louisa, 379, 394, 396
Becher, Conny: marriage of, 332
Becher, Fanny, 25, 89, 114, 118, 121, 129, 130, 236, 238–240, 389, 410
Becher, Florry: marriage of, 317
Becher, Harry, 306, 308, 317, 342
Becher, Mrs Harry, 471
Becher, Henry Corry Rowley, xlv, xlvii, xlix, lxiv, lxxvii, lxxxiv, lxxxviii, xcviii, 6, 8, 16–24, 27–28, 30–32, 35–39, 45–46, 49, 54, 56–57, 60, 63, 65, 68, 77, 82–83, 91, 95, 98, 104, 110, 112, 121, 129, 132, 136, 140–143, 159, 163–164 166–167, 170–171, 175, 181–184, 188, 192–195, 210, 223, 226, 233, 240, 243, 245, 251, 256–257, 262, 265, 272–274, 278–279, 282–283, 285, 287, 289, 293, 297–298, 300, 303, 305, 307, 309–310, 315–317, 322, 325–327, 330, 332, 341, 344, 346, 349, 353, 369, 380, 382, 385, 391, 403, 411, 414, 420, 421–422, 425, 437, 441, 447, 449–450, 467
Becher, Mrs Henry, 9, 18–19, 22–24, 37, 39, 52, 100, 118, 121, 130, 180, 239, 389, 437, 441, 450, 452, 467; death of, 251
Beddome, Mrs F.B., 350, 362, 368–371, 421–422, 427, 469, 472, 476
Bell, Captain Edward, 29, 34–35
Benevolent Society, 390
Bervoort House (New York), 356
Biddle House (Detroit), 280
Birrell, John, 28
Bishop of Huron: see under Cronyn and Hellmuth
Blackburn, Josiah, 59–60, 83, 179, 292, 315
Blake, Edward, lxxx, 58–59, 61, 65, 92, 230, 247–249, 294, 316, 326, 336, 385, 388, 416
Blake, Rebecca, 226,
Blake, Samuel Hume, 55, 89
Blake, William Hume, 61
Blondin (Jean François Gravelet), 122
Boomer, Dean, 439–440
body snatchers, lxxxvi, 57
Bohemian, sinking of, 241
Bradford, Colonel, 415–416
Bridges, Mr, 330
Brigham, Bela Brewster, xxxiv
Bright's disease, 290
Brown, George, lxxxii, 49, 79–80, 84, 257, 355, 391; death of, 359

Brown, Dr Vesey A., lxxxviii–xc, 145–147, 152, 155, 160–161, 180, 334, 346, 396–398, 407
Bruce, Captain, 340
Bryanston, 188
Brydges, Charles John, 60, 85, 121
Buchanan, John, xliv
Buchanan, Isaac, 227
Budd, Dr, 393, 404
Burns, Judge Robert E., 48
Burwell, John, xliii, lxv
Bury, Lord, 90
Buss, Helen M., xixn, xxii

CADDY, ANNIE, 30
Caddy, Captain J.H., lxix, 9, 12, 14
Caddy, Mrs, J.H., 6, 11
Caledonia, Province of, 79
Cameron, John Hillyard, lxxxii, 47, 84, 131; death of, 345
Cameron, Malcolm, lxxxii, 49, 72, 223; death of, 343
Cameron, Nancy, lxiii, 93, 124, 173; death of, 176–177, 394
camp meeting, 205
Campbell, Archie, 329, 336, 444
Campbell, Betsy, 49
Campbell, Sir Colin, 71
Campbell, Captain Frank, lxxvii, 3, 15, 31–32, 34–39
Campbell, Louisa, 306–307
Canada First, 336
cancer, xc, 158, 179, 358, 465
card games: playing of, 16, 24, 38, 63, 67–68, 87, 100, 110, 138–139, 272, 367, 415–416, 430, 432, 476; see also cribbage and whist
Carling, John, 54–56, 58, 184, 193, 225–226, 279, 294, 296, 309–310, 314–315, 321–322, 328–329, 351, 353, 362, 402, 406, 437, 460
Carling, Mrs John, 436–437
Carlsbad, Germany, 376, 454
Carnwath, Lord: death of, 324
Caroline, xliv, xlvi
Casgrain, Mrs William, 422–424, 429
Cataract Hotel (Niagara Falls), 122, 234
Cattermole, Dr James, 151, 437
Cavendish, Lord Frederick, 78, 83–84, 90
Central America: sinking of, 44
Chase, Mrs, 421, 423, 427, 429, 445
Chester, Major Henry, 29, 34
chess, playing of: 24, 38–39, 180, 396
childrens' deaths, lxxxix, 276, 290, 323, 334–336, 422, 440, 442–443, 447 453, 468
cholera, 280, 286
Christmas Day, lx–lxi, lxiii, lxiv–lxv, 16, 23, 37, 58, 89, 133, 176, 190, 217, 236, 251, 263, 273, 283, 298, 305, 316, 322, 327, 335, 341, 346, 349, 352, 358, 362, 367, 394, 415, 430, 443, 447, 451–452, 460, 463, 472
Christmas Tree, 447
Christie's Minstrels, lxviii
church attendance, lxxxi
circus, 437; P.T. Barnum's, 326
Clark Hill, 301
Clarke, Mrs, 208
Clear Grits, 184
Clifton House (Niagara Falls), 407
Cockburn, James, 274
Collins, Captain James, 419–421, 427–428
Commission for the Improvement of Inland Navigation, xxxix
Commission on Frontier Fortifications, 194
Confederation, of Canada, 279
conscription, American evasion of, 208, 247
Conservative Party, 182, 225, 336, 351, 403
Cooper, Reverend, 300
Co-operated Society, 343
Cornish, Francis Evans, lxxxiv, 157, 159, 178–179, 182, 222–223, 248, 252, 310, 403
Court of Chancery, 91–92, 239
courtship, lxxi–lxxx
Craik, Robert, 183, 185
Crespigny, Captain, 16–21, 27
cribbage, 101, 110
cricket matches, lxx, 31, 73, 75, 81, 83, 129, 228, 294, 325, 427
Crimea, 72
Cronyn, Ben, 260, 274, 341, 362, 410
Cronyn, Mrs Ben, 430–431, 452
Cronyn, Reverend Benjamin, lxv, lxvii, lxxviii, lxxxi, xcviii, 15, 24, 39, 58, 60, 76, 89, 130–131, 160, 218, 263, 269, 295, 388, 395, 400; became Bishop of Huron, 53; death of, 315; remarriage of, 285–286, 426–427
Cronyn, Mrs Benjamin: death of, 272
Cronyn, Margaret: marriage of, 53, 59, 61
Cronyn, Rebecca, 61
Cronyn, Verschoyle, xcviii, 44, 48, 51, 60–61, 308, 318
croquet, 256, 269, 278–281, 296, 439
Crutchley, Carrie: visit of, 318–319
Crutchley, Charles, 5, 30–31, 35–38, 71, 185, 213, 309, 339, 343, 368
Crutchley, Charley, 242, 366
Crutchley, Eliza Harris, xxxvii; birth of, xxxvi; marriage of, lxxv, 3; visit of, 318–319
Crutchley, Percy, 232, 325; visit of, 364–365
Crysler's Farm, xxxii
Crystal Palace (Toronto), 171
Culley, Margo, xxiii

Cummings, Mr, 85
Cunnyngham, Colonel, 21–23, 26
curling, 362, 368

DALZELL, COLONEL ROBERT, xlvii, 71, 129, 193, 197–198; illness and death of, 283, 351; visit of, 227–228, 231–232, 460
Dalzell, Robert, 19; marriage of, 326
Dalzell, Charlotte (Carrie): birth of, 125
Dalzell, Mary: presentation to the Queen of, 312; marriage of, 332–333; see also under Leith
Dalzell, Maude: engagement of, 366; marriage of, 371
Dalzell, Sarah Harris, xxxvii; birth of, xxxvi; education of, xli; marriage of, xlvii; visit of, 227–228, 231–233
Daniels, James, 73, 178
Davenport, Captain John, xxxiii
Delaron, 21–22
Dent, John Charles, 363
dentist, visit to, 464
Derby, Lord, 68
Des Voeux, Mr, 58, 60–61, 66, 181–182, 383
Detroit, Michigan, 280–281
Dewar, Bessy, 270–271, 423
Diltz, Dr, 456
Dominion Day: celebration of, 279, 294, 312, 351
Donnelly Family, trial for murderers of, 361
Dormans Inn, 18, 32
Dougall, Mrs John, 423–424, 441, 450
Downshire, Lord, 47, 52, 67, 73
Draper, Judge, 409
Dufferin, Lady, 321–322, 345–346
Dufferin, Lord, 321–322, 345–346
Duncombe uprising, xliii
Dundurn Castle, 172, 348
Duggan, Enid, 136, 187, 229
Durrand, James, 321, 335–336, 444

EARTHQUAKE, 50
East Middlesex, lxxxiv, 183, 187, 407
Easter Sunday, 343, 432, 437–438, 445, 466
economic recession: of 1857, 44, 48, 50
Egan, Mr, 94
Eldon House: description of, ix, x, lxii–lxiii; renovations to, 98, 192, 311, 343, 347, 349, 355, 360–361
Elgin, Lord, lxxxii, 19, 22; death of, 236
England's Eleven, lxx, 129
epilepsy, lxxxix, 461
Ercolano: sinking of, xlix, xcv, 74
Ermatinger, Edward, 127–128
Ermatinger, Mrs Edward, 13, 252, 350
erysipelas, 26

Falls City: explosion of, 71
Family Compact, lxv, 382
Ferguson, John, 67, 82–83, 89
Fenians, lv, lxxxiii, 262, 265–268, 275–277, 284–285, 287; invasions of, 267
fires, 17, 90, 195, 252, 255, 276, 295, 345, 353
fishing excursions, 19, 72, 198, 224, 364, 462–463, 469
Fort Sumter, 401
Foster, Vere, 245
Franklin, Lady, 384
Fraser, James H., 337
Fraser River gold rush, 79
fugitive slave settlements, 43
Fuller, Thomas Brock, 337

GALT, THOMAS, 293
Garfield, James (U.S. President): assassination of, 365
Garibaldi, Giuseppe, 387
Garrett, Edward, 44
ghost stories, 311, 478
Glass, David, 321, 328–329, 367, 403, 431, 448, 458, 460
Globe (Toronto), 291, 355, 377–378, 391
gold rush: see Fraser River
Gonçalves, Terry, viii
Good Friday, 18, 27, 222, 453
Goodhue, Fanny, 258
Goodhue, George Jervis, lxv, lxxx, 5–7, 22, 39, 46–48, 57, 74, 90, 160, 179–180, 218, 256, 295, 297, 385, 391–392, 401, 421; death of, 298, 434; estate of, 307, 309
Goodhue, Minnie, 258, 260, 274, 421
Gordon, Major and Mrs, 15, 21, 280
Gourlay, Mrs, 31
gout, 454
Government House, 113, 321, 341, 345–346, 452
Graham, Harry, 33
Grand Trunk Railway, 337
grave robbers: see body snatchers
Great Western Railway, xci, 91, 140, 184, 226, 300, 302, 316, 319, 335
Greer, Mrs A., 222, 233, 401, 406
Greville, Charles Cavendish, 336
Griffin, Amelia Andrina Harris: birth of, xxxvi; education of, xli; marriage of, xlviii; pregnancy of, 228, 266; still born child of, 237–238; miscarriage of, 255; moved to Kingston, 359–360, 469; twins born to, 269
Griffin, Charles, 198, 204, 316
Griffin, Edward Scott: birth of, 269–271; education of, 360, 469–470; illness of, 289, 422, 430; school days of, 338
Griffin, Dr George, 155–157
Griffin, Gilbert, xlvii, li; debts of, 56, 77, 124,

128, 130, 134, 178, 286, 290, 359, 467–468; moved to Kingston, 359–360; poetry of, lxix–lxx
Griffin, Gilbert Jr: engagement of, 312
Griffin, Helen Teresa Amelia: birth of, 269–271; illness and death of, 289–290, 430, 442
Griffin, Sophia: death of, 358, 465
Griffin, Teresa, 331; birth of, 431; illness and death of, 333–334
Grosvenor, Lord Richard, 78, 83–84, 90
Guiness, Reverend H.G., 406
Gzowski, Casimir Stanislaus, lxxx, 44, 65, 67, 165, 229, 257, 296, 341–342, 380, 408, 421, 464

HALLOWELL, CAPTAIN; drawing of, 20
Hamilton, xcii, 53, 54, 102, 114–115, 171, 227, 300, 303, 353, 350, 353, 380
Hamilton, Basil, 111–112, 261
Hamilton, Ellen, 51, 54–55, 58–59, 61, 63–64, 67, 86, 90–91, 99, 202, 224–225, 232, 238, 240, 242, 254, 258–259, 263, 298–299, 304, 306, 308, 314, 341, 344, 349, 363, 367, 371, 428
Hamilton, James, lxv, lxix, xcviii, 6, 52, 56–57, 85, 112, 218, 242, 293, 349, 362, 395, 420
Hamilton, Mrs James, 428
Hamilton, Nicholas: illness and death of, 294
Hamilton, Selina, 299, 304–306, 308–309, 428, 431
Hamilton, Sheriff: death of, 68–69
Hammond, A.C., 45, 93
Hammond, Dr, 462
Hampton, Colonel Wade, 52, 62, 66, 68, 139, 154, 187, 206
Harper, Dr Alfred, 237
Harris, Amelia Andrina: see under Griffin
Harris, Amelia Ryerse: about diary of, 40–42; birth of, xxxiii; death of, lxi, xcviii, 371, 473, 478–479; dreams of, lvi–lvii, 126, 139–140, 191, 200–201, 287–288, 300, 302–303, 306, 358; illness of, 180, 191–192, 200, 202, 222, 246, 254, 265, 298, 300, 305, 317–318, 335, 350, 358, 370–372, 396–400, 449, 453, 471–473, 477–478; opinion of Elizabeth Loring of, 107–108; opinion of Lucy Ronalds of, 275; opinion of William Scott of, 93–94, 97–99, 110–111; and *Recollections of an Early Settler*, 355; views on courtship and marriage of, 93–102, 109–111, 116–117; views on slavery of, 62; will of, lviii–ix, 310–311
Harris, Amelia Archange (Milly), xxiv, xxix, liv, lix, xcv, xcviii, 323, 342, 348, 357, 409, 436, 437–438, 443, 448, 453, 459, 471–473, 477–479; about diary of, 475; birth of, 285–287, 428
Harris, Amelia Ellen: birth and death of, xxxvi; moving grave of, 200
Harris, Charlotte (Chasse): see under Knight
Harris, Charlotte Adelaide: birth of, 434, illness of, 335, 352–353, 369, 437–438, 442, 461, 467–468, 471
Harris, Edward William: birth of, xxxvi, engagement of, 126–127, 130–131; marriage of, 165–166; marriage breakdown of, 198, 201–204, 207, 210–219, 222–223, 226–235, 238–239, 248; political appointment of, 402
Harris, Edward Montgomery: birth of, 361, 470
Harris, Eliza: see under Crutchley
Harris, Elizabeth Loring: courtship of, 109; first reference to, 93; marriage of, lii, 121, 131; remarriage of, 237–238, 244–245; as young widow, 188–190, 193, 196, 209, 213–216, 219, 229; see also under O'Brien
Harris, George, ix
Harris, George Edward: birth and death of, 347, 452–453
Harris, George Becher, ix; defeated as alderman, 323, 438; engagement of, 271, 278; marriage of, liv, 280–281; sporting activities of, 119, 130, 224, 349, 353, 357, 361–363, 365–366, 387, 427, 452–453, 457, 458, 460, 462–463, 465, 469–470; visit to Europe of, 454–457
Harris, George Henry Ronalds: birth of, lix, 324–325, 439–440
Harris, Helen: see under Portman
Harris, John: birth of, xxxi; political career of, xxxix, xlvi, xlviii, lxv, 22; death of, xlv, xlvii, lxxxviii, 3, 35, 46, 93; tombstone for grave of, 319
Harris, John Fitzjohn: birth of xxxvi; death of, liii, lv, lxxxviii, 185, 405–406; marriage of, lii, 115, 121, 123, 131; illness of, 96–97, 136–137, 158–167, 177, 181, 392–393, 396, 402–405
Harris, Lucy: see under Little
Harris, Lucy Ronalds: about diary of, 417–418; birth of children of, 285–287, 347, 361; death of Grandmother Askin of, 464; engagement of, 271, 273, 278; finances of, 447–450, 463–464, 469, 471; pregnancies of, 425, 434, 439, 452–453; marriage of, liv, 280–281; views on married life of, 444, 446, 450, 457, 463, 468–470, 472; visit to Europe of, 454–457; will of, 435, 450
Harris, Mary: see under Peard
Harris, Robin Sutton, ix, xxxin

Harris, Sarah: see under Dalzell
Harris, Sophia Ryerson: about diary of, 373–374; engagement of, 126–127, 130–131; marriage of, 165–166; marriage breakdown of, 198, 201–204, 207, 210–219, 222–223, 226–235, 238–239, 248
Harris, Teresa: see under Scott and Littledale
Harris, Terry Gonçalves, viii
Harris, William Edward: birth and death of, xxxvi, 74, 81; moving grave of, 200; reference to, 365
Harris Family: financial situation of, xlviii–xlix
Harris and Brothers, 119, 125, 130, 183, 195, 224, 249, 252, 262, 304, 313, 412; withdrawal of George Harris from, 436
Harvey, Lord, 43
Hawkins, Sarah, 325
Head, Sir Edmund Walker, li, lxxxii, 64, 75–77, 101, 169, 188, 381–382
Head, Lady, 64, 75–76, 188
Hellmuth, Isaac, lxxxii, 263, 295, 303, 306, 309, 314, 326, 332, 342, 367, 428, 445, 464
Hellmuth, Mrs Isaac, 369, 445, 464
Hellmuth, Isadore, 365
Hellmuth College, 303, 321, 360
Herrick, Dr, 454–455
Hewitt, Captain Edward Osborne, liii, lxxiv, 194–199, 203–204, 207, 211, 213–219, 226, 234
Hincks, Sir Francis, lxxxii, 76, 101–102, 295, 319
Hippesley, Emily: marriage of, 326
Hodder, Dr Edward M., 145–147, 312
Holy Trinity Cathedral, 319
homeopathy, 284
honeymoons, lxxix
Horton, Edward, 70
House of Assembly, 79
household expenses, lxiv–lxv
Howard, Dr Edward, 9–10, 14–18, 20–21
Hungarian: sinking of, 139
hunting excursions: see shooting excursions
Hutchinson, Frank, 476
Hutchinson, Mrs, 420, 438, 459

Illustrated News, 92, 94, 98
Indian Mutiny (Sepoy Rebellion), 43–44, 50, 54, 90

JACKSON, MR, 90, 93, 101, 104, 176, 181, 188, 222, 232, 386, 391, 395
Jameson, Anna Brownell, 179
Jeffery, Joseph, 329, 354, 368, 447, 452, 462, 471
Jones, Thomas: execution of, 289
Josephus, 336

KEKEWICH, EDWARD, 25–26
Killaly, Hamilton Hartley, 136, 221, 260
King, Dr: hanging of, 113
King, Edwin H, 43, 55, 62, 64–65, 67, 93, 99, 121, 134, 139, 143, 147, 181, 188, 221, 254, 386
King, Mrs, 50, 62–63, 73, 88, 99, 188, 254, 386
Kingston, lxi, xcii, 95, 168, 208, 223, 288, 294, 360, 362, 377, 387
Kirkpatrick, George Airey, 95
Knight, Charlotte (Chasse) Harris: birth of, xxxvi; death of, xlix, lv, 4, 74, 86; marriage of, 3; reference to, 299
Knight, Captain Edward Lewis, 3, 5, 8; as prisoner of war, 21, 59, 259

LABATT, JOHN, 183, 220, 403, 473, 479
Labatt, Mrs John, 370, 472–473, 479
Labatt, Minnie, 477–478
lacrosse, 22
Ladies College, 295–296, 303, 308, 316, 321
Landsdowne, Lord, 97
Landor, Dr Henry, xc, 173, 179–181, 184–185, 187–188, 191, 222, 228–231, 237–238, 243, 255, 265–266, 280, 286, 294, 308, 318, 320, 332, 347, 393, 397–401, 407, 437, 450–452
Lawrason, Lawrence, xliii, lxv, xcviii, 6, 23, 46, 49, 60, 69, 70, 74, 241, 391
Lawrason, Mrs L., 87, 160, 241, 254, 306
Lawrason, William, 90, 101, 218, 367, 379, 391, 420, 421–422
Lawrason, Mrs W., 90, 101, 105–106, 147, 254–255, 379–380, 388, 420, 421–422
LeFroy, Sir John Henry, 14
Leith, Mary Dalzell, xcvii; first child of, 344 marriage of, 332–333
Leith, Major Thomas: 343–344; marriage of, 332-333
Leonard, Elijah, 55, 209, 347–348
Leslie, Captain, 211, 228, 236, 245, 254, 264, 269, 276, 280
Leslie, Charley: illness and death of, 250
life insurance, 442
Lightfoot, Miss, 288, 291–292, 431, 446, 467
Lincoln, Abraham (U.S. President): assassination of, 254; reelection of, 250
Literary and Historical Society of Quebec, xxxix–xi
Little, Lucy Harris, ix
Littledale, St. George, lix, xcvi, 339; marriage of, 346–347; visit of, 356–357, 365, 367, 462
Littledale, Teresa Harris: engagement of, 452; visit of, 356–357, 365, 367, 462
London: description of, xci–xcii
London Cricket Club, 81, 83
London Dramatic Association, 242

London Elite, lxv
London Free Press, xlv, lxix, 59, 82, 84, 152, 179, 241, 383–385, 391, 436
Long Point, xcii, 17, 32, 113, 230–231, 234, 241, 243, 245, 303, 349, 357, 361, 366, 446
Long Point Company, 350, 355
Loring, Elizabeth: see under Harris and O'Brien
Lorne, Lord: visit of, 354
lunatic asylum, 187, 286–287, 292, 294, 303, 320, 332, 348
Lysons, Colonel Daniel, 224
Lutyens, Edward, lxvi, 5–6, 14–20; drawing of 20
Lyttleton, Lord, 34

MACAULAY, SIR JAMES, 131
Macaulay, Thomas Babington, 305
Macbeth, George, 24–28
Macbeth, Talbot,
Macdonald, Donald Alexander, 341
Macdonald, John A., lxxxii, lxxxiv–lxxxv, 79–80, 166–167, 174–176, 178, 192, 195, 208–209, 279, 319
Macdonald, John Sandfield, lxxxii, 195, 220, 226, 233, 264, 279, 292, 296, 307, 309, 316; death of, 318–319
Mackenzie, Mrs Alexander, 348
Mackenzie, William Lyon, xliii–xliv, lxvi, 79
MacMahon, Darcy, 478
MacNab, Sir Allan Napier, xliii, lxxxii, 79, 172; death of, 207
MacNab, George, 325
Madison Square Gardens, 467
Magee, James, xcviii, 428, 439, 451
Marks, John Bennett, 89
marriage settlements, lxxvii–lxxviii, 120, 132, 277–278, 326, 332, 366, 436, 447, 460, 469
Mason and Slidell incident, 190, 414
Masonic Lodge, 367, 444, 447, 453
matchmaking, lxxii–lxxiii
Maximilian of Austria, Emperor, 279
McCready, Dr, 155, 158–161, 166
McDonald, Cammy, 342
McGee, Darcy: assassination of, 285, 287
McLean, Reverend John, 147, 150–151, 160, 162–163, 218, 376, 384, 392–393, 415, 438
McFarlane, Maggie: death of, 56–57, 69
McInnes, Donald, lxxx, 46, 53, 62, 68–69, 99, 102, 113–114, 126, 170, 181, 227, 286, 301–302, 319, 349, 352, 354, 380, 382
McInnes, Mary Amelia Robinson, 46; insanity of, 348; death of 353
McKay, Dr, 70–71
measles, 312
Mechanics' Institute, xlvi, lxviii, 22, 143
medical prescriptions and remedies, xc, 382, 390–391, 393, 398, 462, 477–478
Meredith, Edmund, 368
Meredith, Mr J.W.: drowning of, 364
Meredith, Isabella, 171, 188–189, 273, 281–283, 287, 291, 293, 300, 303, 308, 363, 367–371, 410–411, 425–426, 428, 432–433, 463
Meredith, William Ralph, 309, 315, 320–321, 326, 355, 367, 370, 422, 439
Meredith, Mrs W.R., 308, 312, 315, 363, 367–368, 370, 422, 432–434, 439, 452
Methodist Church, 311, 389, 395, 406, 408, 413
Michigan, 267
Michel, Lady, 264
Militia Bill, 193, 195
Monck, Lord, 193–194
Montgomery, Archie, 429, 436, 439–440, 454–455
Montgomery, James, 272, 279, 420, 436, 471
Montgomery's Tavern, xliii, 184
Montserrat, Nicholas, 218, 224–225, 243
Moore, Dr. George, 58, 451, 463
Moore, Mrs: death of, 276
Moravian, sailing of, 457
Morris, James, 106
Morrison, Joseph Curran, 174–175
Mother Shipton's Prophecy, 354, 364
Muncey Indian reservation, 22
music, playing of, 390, 396

NAPIER, GENERAL, 268
Neave, Arundell, lxvi, 5, 7–11, 14–15, 39, 188
Newcastle, Duke of, 168, 170, 172, 379, 381–382
New London, Connecticut: visit to, lx, 356
New Year Cards, 471
New Year's Day, 16, 38, 134, 252, 316, 419, 451, 476; visiting on, lxv, 24, 60, 89, 178, 190–191, 218, 237, 263, 274, 298, 306, 322, 328, 335, 342, 352, 362 , 367, 395, 443, 447, 461, 463, 471
New Zealand, lxxvii, 34–36
Niagara Falls, lxxix, xcii, 79, 122, 187, 206, 229, 233, 245, 269, 281, 407–408, 444, 466, 472
Niagara-on-the-Lake, xxxv, xciv, 300–303
Nind, Mr, 90, 93, 99,
Normal School, 79, 169, 379
Northey, Captain, 278, 284, 419–422, 427
Notman, William, 302, 311

O'BRIEN, ELIZABETH LORING: 285, 323; visits of, 253, 354–355
O'Brien, Esther: death of, 318
O'Brien, William Edward, 230, 237–238, 245, 253

oil speculation, 191, 254–255, 257, 261–262, 264–266, 268–271, 403
Oneidas, 22
Orange Order, 168–169, 175, 182, 269, 332, 339, 351, 377–379, 387
Osborne, Murray, 51, 53–54
Osgoode Hall, xlii, 171
Owen, Captain William Fitz William, xxxii–xxxiii, xxxvi, xxxviii
Owen, Commodore Edward C.R., xxxii–xxxiii
Oxford University, 232

PAGE, MRS: remarriage of, 299–300
paper, making of, 391
Parke, E. Jones, 43
Parke, Thomas, 43
Parliament buildings: burning of (Montreal), 19, Commission of Enquiry into construction of (Ottawa), 197, 199, 209, 221
Palmerston, Lady, 97
Palmerston, Lord, 68, 97
Parr, Joy, xxii
parties, 100–102, 105–106, 273, 292, 448; children's, 442, 446, 450, 476; also see balls
peace society, 413
Peacocke, Colonel, 268, 273, 279
Peard, George: military commission of, 323
Peard, Helen, xxxiv, 454
Peard, Mary Harris, xxxvii; birth of, xxxvi; marriage of, xlvii, lxxv, 35, 39; visit of, 349, 351, 459
Peard, Lieutenant George Shuldham, xlvii, lxvi, 5–19, 22–23, 25, 32, 35, 39, 193, 230, 235
Pequot House (New London, Ct), 356–357
Perry, Mrs, 8
Peters, Samuel, 324, 337
Philadelphia, 467
Phillott, Colonel, 129
picnics, lxix, 17, 74–75, 265, 267, 270, 428
Pioneer dinner, 235
Plumb, Josiah B., xciv, 37–38, 262, 294, 295, 319, 331, 333, 427, 437
Plumb, Mrs Josiah, 242, 246; death of, 289, 427
Plumb, Lizzie: engagement of, 353
Plummer, Ephraim, xcviii
Plummer, John, xcviii, 147
Plummer, Mrs, 66
Police, London Board of, xci
poor relief, 92
Pope, 302
Port Huron, 45
Port Ryerse, xxxi, xxxiv, xl, lvii–lviii, lx, lxxx, xcii–xciii, 18, 101, 105, 229, 243–244, 249, 266, 282–283, 292, 295, 297, 301–304, 313, 324, 361
Port Ryerse Harbour Company, 221
Port Stanley, 20, 279, 295, 355
Port Stanley Railroad, 315–316
Port Talbot, lxv, xciii, 6–7, 16–17, 28, 31, 257, 279
Portman, Berkeley, 140, 167–168, 180, 265, 316
Portman, Edward, 5
Portman, Evelyn, 277–278, 282
Portman, Helen Harris: birth of, xxxvi; marriage of, xlviii–xlix, lxxvii–lxxviii; illness and death of, li, lv, lxxxviii–lxxxix, 143–147; reference to, 326
Portman, Lady, lxxviii, 75, 157, 167–168, 187; death of, 253
Portman, Lord, lxxviii, 43, 68, 90, 157, 167, 187, 221, 230, 277
Portman, Maurice Berkeley, xlviii–xlix; and cotton plantation, l, lxxiv, 62, 65–68, 92, 100, 112–113; Chancery suit of, 52; election of, 186–187; marriage of, lxxviii; political career of, li, lxxxii, lxxxiv–lxxxvi, 139–143, 152–154, 159–160, 162, 164, 171, 175–176, 181–187, 192–195, 199, 205–210, 221, 391–392, 403, 406–407, 411, 415; remarriage of, 282
Portman, Maurice William: 313, 316; birth of, 86
Portman, Maurice Vidal: as baby at Eldon House, 179, 187, 191–192, 207–208, 226, 232, 392, 398, 401–404, 413, 416; birth of, 143
Potter MacKinnon, Janice, xxii
Powell, Miss, 170–172, 382
Price, David Edward, 100, 103
Prince, Captain Robert, 304–305, 309–310
Prince Albert: death of, 190
Prince Arthur: visit of, 296
Prince of Wales: visit of, lv, 168–172, 376–382, 387–389; commemoration of marriage of, 221–222; illness of, 315
Princess Louisa: marriage of, 310; visit of, 354
Prototype, 158, 182
Punch, 92, 94, 98

QUAKERS, 413
Queen Victoria's Birthday, 20, 293, 350, 404, 427
Queen's Hotel (Toronto), 214

RADICAL PARTY, 183, 186, 225, 326
Rainsford, Reverend W.S., 347
Raleigh House, lxi, lxiv, xcvii, 434, 439
Rattallack, Captain, 75–76
reading material, lxviii–lxix, 11, 25, 31–32, 36, 92, 94, 98, 102, 276, 289, 305, 316, 318, 327, 341, 352, 356, 377, 381, 383, 385, 388, 392–393

Rebellion Losses Bill, 19
Reform Party, 351, 355
rheumatism, 265, 404
Ridgeway, battle of, 268
robbery, 325
Robertson, William, 417
Robinson, Christopher, 353
Robinson, Sir John Beverley, 68–70, 188, 207; death of, 220
Robinson, Mary Amelia: see under McInnes
Robinson Hall, 26
Rolleston, Colonel Launcelot: engagement of, 366
Ronalds, Elizabeth Lucy Robertson: liv, 272, 314, 420
Ronalds, John, 435; death of, 314, 440
Ronalds, Lucy: see under Harris
Ronalds, Mrs Henry, 419, 423–424, 432–433; death of, 320, 437
Ronalds, Robert, 455
Ronalds Estate, 420, 429, 439, 449
Ross, Mary: engagement of, 197
Rossin House (Toronto): burning of, 215
Royal Canadian Rifles, 25, 237, 247, 412, 416
Royal Military College (Kingston), 360
Royal Welch Fusiliers, 5, 21, 23, 277
Russell, General Alex, 191, 194
Russell, Lord John, 399
Ryerse, Amelia: see under Harris
Ryerse, Colonel Samuel, xxxi, xxxiii, xxxiv
Ryerse, Edward, xxvi, lx, 17–18, 32–33, 35, 53, 101, 173, 244, 277, 339, 354, 358, 361
Ryerse, George J., xxvi, 18, 33, 64, 124, 173, 244, 260, 340; death of, 342
Ryerse, Patty: death of, 354
Ryerson, Reverend Adolphus Egerton, liv, lx, lxi, lxxxiii, 47, 80, 91, 100, 115–116, 148, 176, 179, 190, 199, 201, 256, 283, 290–291, 296, 306–307, 311, 324, 327, 334–335, 347, 355, 363, 366, 385, 393–394, 395, 400, 402, 410, 428, 435; and charge of using public funds, 72–73, 76, 78–79; death of, xcvii–xcviii, 370, 472, 477; history of Canada of, 100, opinion of Sophia's marriage to Edward of, 127, 130–131, 137, 163, 202, 207, 210, 212, 216–217, 220, 239, 248–249; and university question, 413
Ryerson, Mrs A. Egerton, 302, 329, 334, 345, 352, 395, 408–409
Ryerson, Egerton (Charlie), 176, 313, 385–386, 394–395, 400, 408–410, 416
Ryerson, Dr. George Sterling, 358
Ryerson, Sophia: see under Harris

SALMON, WILLIAM THOMAS, 32–33
Santa Claus, 451, 463
scandals, 88, 219, 315, 392
Scarborough, England, 376
scarlet fever, lxxxix, 275–276, 289–290, 306, 333–336, 430, 440, 442–444, 447
Scatcherd, Thomas, 170
Scott, Miss Beatrice, 118–119
Scott, Teresa Harris: birth of, xl; courtship of, 94–103, 110–111, 114–117, 120; first marriage of, lii, 121; trousseau of, 115–116; remarriage of, 346–347; see also under Littledale
Scott, William John, lii; death of, lix, lxxxvii, 339, 446; first reference to, 87; marriage proposal of, 93–94 reputation of, 97, 99, 107, 117; views on slavery of, 92
Scythia, sailing of, 347, 454
Seeley, Sir John Robert, 305
servants, lxiv–lxv, 49, 72, 78, 90, 95, 106, 124, 135, 163, 240, 243, 294, 300, 303, 308, 313, 315, 324, 326, 330–331, 333, 335 337, 340, 342, 344, 349, 352, 361, 365–366, 388, 397, 400, 415, 420, 426–427, 433, 436, 438, 443–444, 446–448, 451–452, 465, 471–473
shooting excursions, 188, 249, 349, 357, 361, 366–367, 383, 385, 387, 458, 463, 469–470
Sicotte, Louis Victor, 195
Siddons, Mrs Sarah, lxviii, 465
Skae, Edward, 419–420, 423, 429, 433
Skae, Jane, 419, 433, 442, 465
Small, Judge: death of, 293
Smith, Goldwin, 309, 342
Smith, Sir Henry, 67
Smith, Sidney, 174–175
Smithsonian Institute, 466
Southern Railway, 302
St. Louis, Missouri, 91
St. Paul's Church, London, xlii, xlvi, lxv, lxxx–lxxxii, 61, 284, 347, 422
St. Valentine's Day, lxxvi, 92
Stahlschmidt, Mr, 90–91, 93, 104, 106, 108–109
Stanley, Edward, lxvi, 5–12
Stanley, Lord, lxvi, 5
Stantons Hotel (London, England), 454
Steers, Jane, lxiii, 125, 240, 243, 388–389
Stinson, Reverend Joseph, 131
Strand Theatre (London, England), 454
Strathy, James, 30–32
Street, Emily, 54–55, 60
Street, Minnie, 25, 49–50, 80–82
Street, Thomas, lxxx, xciv, 301; death of, 321
Street, William, 421
Street, Mrs William, 421, 430
Street, William Warren, 44–50, 54, 56, 113
Street, Mrs W.W., 49, 113
Stuart, George Okill, 294

soup kitchen, 92
Suez Canal, 339
Sunninghill Estate, 343
Suspension Bridge (Niagara Falls), 233, 444
Swinyard, Mr, 281, 295; boat accident of, 301

TALBOT, MARCUS, lxxxiv, 59; drowning of, 139
Talbot, Colonel Thomas, xlv, xlvii, lxv, xciii, 19, 25–29, 279
Talbotville Royal, 12
Taylor, Bayard, 96–97
teamsters, 187
Tecumseh Club, lxx, 350
Tecumseh House, 91–92, 178, 222, 342, 363, 377–379, 384, 385
Teviot Bank, 113–114, 118
Thanksgiving Day, 176, 315, 327, 442, 446, 458
Thomas, F.W., 274–276, 295, 298–300, 302–303, 306–308, 313
Thomas, Mrs F.W., 426, 432
Thornwood, 32, 114, 118, 318, 351
Toronto Volunteers, 267
Townsend, John Jacob, 30, 335
Townsend trial, 69
Tupper, Sir Charles, 321–322
typhoid, lxxxvii, 339, 442, 446

UNDERHILL, SARAH: death of, xl
United Empire Loyalist, 118, 409
Upper Canada College, xli–xlii, 230
Upper Canada Law Society, xlii

VACATIONS, xciii
vaccinations, 179, 431
Vagabond Club, 83
Vanderhoff, Mr, 429
Van Koughnet, Philip, 47, 172, 174, 382
Vansittart, Henry, 32–33
Vansittart, Mrs Henry, 101
Victoria: sinking of, lxviii, 364
Vidal, Alexander, 156

WALKER, JOHN, 320–323, 326, 328–329, 331, 333, 335–337, 342, 351, 357, 363, 366, 368, 423, 431–432, 437, 447, 449, 451, 471, 477
Walker, Mrs John, 326, 329, 342, 354, 357, 353, 368–370, 423, 431–432, 447, 451, 464
Wandesforde, J.B., 85–86, 94, 121–122, 157, 189, 192, 411–412
War, Franco-Prussian, 302
war, preparations for, 194–196, 246–247, 251–252, 262, 413–414; see also American Civil War
Warren, Miss: death of, 445; replaced as matron of lunatic asylum, 332
Washington, D.C., 466
Weber, Dr, 455
Wells, Rupert Mearse, 61, 331
Westminister Rink, 477
Wetherall, Colonel Edward, 194
Wetherall, Sir George Augustus, 47,
whist, playing of, 16, 24, 38, 67, 367, 415–416, 430, 432
whooping cough, 458
Widder, Blanche, 103–104, 109–110, 132, 134–135, 137, 170, 381–382
Widder, Frederick, 170
Williamson, Captain, 275, 278–279
Wilson, Hughes: death of, 56–57; funeral of, 58
Wilson, Hulme: death of, 392
Wilson, John, xxvi, lxxxiii, 5–6, 16, 19, 23–24, 28, 37, 54, 58, 60, 66, 82, 84, 87–88, 111–112, 121, 124, 134, 147, 149–150, 158, 167, 174, 179, 181–185, 195, 197, 199, 210, 221, 223–229, 235–236, 240, 243, 245, 273 , 274, 290–291, 385, 395, 414, 420, 425, 433; death of, 293
Wilson, Mrs John, 11, 19, 39, 48, 58, 89, 98, 121, 160, 188, 223n, 227, 228–229, 254, 392, 398
Wilson, Lucy, 75, 96, 111, 188, 391–392, 395; death of, 347; see also under Bailey
Wilson, Teresa, 75
Wilson, Thompson; funeral of, 8
Wilson, William, 261; death of, 304
Woodfall, Dr, 288, 290–291
Woodlands Cemetery, xcviii, 360
Woodruff, Dr W., lxxxviii–xc, xcviii, 146, 158, 174, 246, 317, 334, 338, 342–343, 356, 358, 368, 371, 390–391, 404, 433, 445, 450–451, 458, 461
Woodstock and Port Dover Rail Road, 46
Wynniatt, Lieutenant: death of, 311

YOUNG, SIR JOHN, 296
Young, Lady, 296
Young Men's Christian Association, 342

PUBLICATIONS OF THE CHAMPLAIN SOCIETY

Ontario Series

1. *The Valley of the Trent*. Edited with an introduction by Edwin C. Guillet
2. *Royal Fort Frontenac*. Translations by Richard A. Preston, edited with an introduction by Léopold Lamontagne
3. *Kingston before the War of 1812*. Edited with an introduction by Richard A. Preston
4. *The Windsor Border Region*. Edited with an introduction by Ernest J. Lajeunesse, C.S.B.
5. *The Town of York 1793–1815: A Collection of Documents of Early Toronto*. Edited with an introduction by Edith G. Firth
6. *Muskoka and Haliburton 1615–1875: A Collection of Documents*. Edited with an introduction by Florence B. Murray
7. *The Valley of the Six Nations: A Collection of Documents on the Indian Lands of the Grand River*. Edited with an introduction by Charles M. Johnston
8. *The Town of York 1815–1834: A Further Collection of Documents of Early Toronto*. Edited with an introduction by Edith G. Firth
9. *Thunder Bay District 1821–1892: A Collection of Documents*. Edited with an introduction by Elizabeth Arthur
10. *Ontario and the First World War: A Collection of Documents*. Edited with an introduction by Barbara M. Wilson
11. *John Prince, 1796–1870: A Collection of Documents*. Edited with an introduction by R. Alan Douglas
12. *The Rebellion of 1837 in Upper Canada*. Edited with an introduction by Colin Read and Ronald J. Stagg
13. *The Bank of Upper Canada*. Edited with an introduction by Peter Baskerville
14. *The Upper Ottawa Valley to 1855*. Edited with an introduction by Richard Reid
15. *The Eldon House Diaries: Five Women's Views of the 19th Century*. Edited with an introduction by Robin S. Harris and Terry G. Harris

www.ingramcontent.com/pod-product-compliance
Lightning Source LLC
LaVergne TN
LVHW082005060826
844660LV00028B/1239
* 9 7 8 1 4 4 2 6 3 1 4 1 0 *